A LEVEL
ECONOMICS

Ray Powell
Head of Economics
Kingston College

Letts

EDUCATIONAL

First published 1982
Reprinted 1985, 1986, 1987, 1993, 1994
Revised 1984, 1988, 1991, 1993

Letts Educational
Aldine House
Aldine Place
London W12 8AW

Text © Ray Powell, 1993

Typeset by Jordan Publishing Design

Editorial team Rachel Grant, Wayne Davies

Design Watermark Communications Ltd (cover), Jonathan Barnard (text)

Illustrations Barbara Linton, Tek-Art

Design and illustrations © BPP (Letts Educational) Ltd

British Library Cataloguing in Publication Data
A CIP record for this book is available from the British Library

ISBN 1 85758 222 5

Printed and bound in Great Britain by Ashford Colour Press Ltd

Note for readers: Some of the information in this book is liable to change, particularly that which is directly influenced by Government policy. Such information is correct at the time of going to press but the reader should keep in touch with current affairs to ensure an up-to-date knowledge of the subject.

Letts Educational is the trading name of BPP (Letts Educational) Ltd

PREFACE

This book is written for all students taking the Advanced Level and Advanced Supplementary examinations in economics. In recent years, both the style of the examination and the knowledge and skills required of candidates have undergone significant and sometimes fundamental change. As an experienced teacher and Chief Examiner who has worked for two of the larger examining boards, I have written this book to acquaint students with the standards and skills now required by all the examining boards.

The core of the book comprises twenty-seven chapters, which I have chosen after a careful analysis of the syllabus of the examining boards and the subject areas on which questions have been set most frequently in recent years. At the end of each chapter I have discussed a number of representative questions, many of which are selected from recent examination papers.

At all times in writing the book, I have tried to help students to make the most of all the information and skills learned in a taught course but which, sadly, many students fail to reproduce amidst the pressures and stresses of an examination. Answering an examination is not merely a matter of learning and displaying a factual knowledge, important though that can be. Conventional textbooks, excellent as they are, seldom provide guidance on how to develop and make use of the wider range of skills that modern examinations seek to test. It has **not** been designed either **as an examination crammer**, or to provide **a simple means of spotting questions**, nor does it contain model answers to be learned parrot-fashion. The questions at the end of each chapter are there to provide guidance on the different approaches to a particular topic area, and the type of skills required to answer a question satisfactorily. In any case, spotting questions is a dangerous business: Chief Examiners change frequently, and in a discipline such as economics different issues become fashionable and topical.

The following examination boards have given permission to reproduce questions set by them in previous examinations, for which I am most grateful:

AEB: Associated Examining Board for the General Certificate of Education
NEAB: Northern Examinations and Assessment Board
ULEAC: University of London Examinations and Assessment Council
Cambridge: University of Cambridge Local Examinations Syndicate
Oxford: Oxford Delegacy of Local Examinations
O & CSEB: Oxford and Cambridge Schools Examination Board
WJEC: Welsh Joint Education Committee
SEB: Scottish Examination Board

The answers to the questions are my own and none of the above boards can accept any responsibility whatsoever for the accuracy or method of working in the answers given.

I wish to express my special thanks to Keith West who wrote the larger parts of Chapters 15, 16, 25 and 26 and who contributed many ideas to other chapters throughout the book. I am also most grateful to Bill Stevenson who read through the manuscript and suggested many improvements, to Jeremy Lawrence for editing the typescript, to the staff at Letts Educational for their support and patience during the preparation of the book, and to my wife Christine for her encouragement and for all the hard work and long hours spent typing the manuscript in a form fit for the printer. However, any shortcomings the book may possess are entirely my own responsibility.

Ray Powell

CONTENTS

SECTION 1: STARTING POINTS

SECTION 2: A-LEVEL ECONOMICS

SECTION 3: TEST RUN

INDEX   386

STARTING POINTS

In this section:

How to use this book

The structure of this book

Syllabus charts and paper analysis

Examination boards and addresses

Studying and revising Economics

The difference between GCSE and A/AS Level

Study strategy and techniques

Revision techniques

Coursework

The examination

Examination techniques and question styles

HOW TO USE THIS BOOK

This book has been written specifically to prepare candidates for the Advanced and Advanced Supplementary Level examinations in economics set by the various GCE examining boards. It should also prove useful as a preparation for the many business studies and professional examinations in economics of a comparable standard to A-level. The book is organised in a series of chapters chosen both to represent the subject areas with which examination questions deal, and also to prepare candidates for answering questions on 'new' subject areas as yet not well covered in existing textbooks. Thus, while the chapters are conventionally ordered, proceeding from **micro-** to **macroeconomics**, units are included on such topics as the determination of agricultural prices, market 'failures', the implications of budget surpluses and supply-side economics, and areas of controversy between Keynesian and monetarist economists.

Since the book does not attempt to cover every aspect of the Advanced Level syllabuses of the various examining boards, it should not be regarded as a substitute for the many excellent and detailed textbooks that are available, or for sources of up-to-date information such as the *British Economy Survey*, *The Economic Review* and *Treasury Economic Briefing and Bulletin*. It is designed for use throughout a taught economics course, and it should prove especially useful in preparing examination technique in the period immediately before an examination. Make sure that you obtain a copy of your examination syllabus. Each chapter contains two distinct but complementary parts. The first section provides a detailed summary of the underlying concepts used by economists of different schools of thought and points of perspective in approaching the topic, together with a summary of essential, largely factual, information, and a note on how the topic links with the other chapters in the book. The last part contains a selection of representative questions chosen largely from the examination papers set in recent years by the principal examining boards.

The book's aim is to help examination candidates gain the knowledge, techniques and skills, not only to be sure of passing at A-level, but also to realise what is required to achieve the highest possible grades. At all times the book tries to explain in a clear but precise way the new developments taking place in the subject, and to show how these are reflected in recent examination questions and in the answers expected by the examiners.

THE STRUCTURE OF THIS BOOK

The key aim of this book is to guide you in the way you tackle A-level Economics. It should serve as a study guide, work book and revision aid throughout any A-level/AS-level Economics course, no matter what syllabus you are following. It is not intended to be a complete guide to the subject and should be used as a companion to your textbooks, which is designed to complement rather than duplicate.

We have divided the books into three sections. Section One, Starting Points, contains study tips and syllabus information – all the material you need to get you started on your A-level study, together with advice on planning your revision and tips on how to tackle the exam itself.

Section Two, the main body of the text, contains the core of A-level Economics. It has been devised to make study as easy and enjoyable as possible, and has been divided into chapters which cover the themes you will encounter on your syllabus. The chapters are split into units, each covering a topic of study.

A list of objectives at the beginning of each chapter directs you towards the key points of the chapter you are about to read. The chapter roundup at the end gives a summary of the text just covered, brings the topics of the chapter into focus and links them to other themes of study. To reinforce what you have just read and learned, there are worked questions and answers at the end of each chapter. Recent examinations from all the examination boards (including Scottish Higher) provide the question practice. The tutorial notes and suggested answers give you practical guidance on how to answer A-level questions, and provide additional information relevant to that particular topic of study. There is also a Question Bank, with further examples of different types of A-level exam questions for you to attempt.

In Section Three, Test Run, we turn our attention to the examination you will face at the end of your course. First, you can assess your progress using the Test Your Knowledge Quiz and analysis charts. Then, as a final test, you should attempt the mock exam, under timed conditions. This will give you invaluable examination practice and, together with the specimen answers specially written by the author, will help you to judge how close you are to achieving your A-level pass.

A-LEVEL SYLLABUSES

Board	AEB	ULEAC	NEAB	WJEC	Oxford
Syllabus	618	9120		0011	9840
Subject Name	Economics	Economics	Economics	Economics	Economics
Number of Papers	3	3	2	3	3
Paper 1	1¼ hours Multiple Choice 50 compulsory questions (25%)	3 hours Essays 4 questions to be answered from a choice of 12; choosing two from each section of the paper (40%)	*Part 1* 1½ hours Multiple Choice approximately 50 compulsory questions (30%) *Part 2* 1 hour Data Response 1 compulsory questions (20%)	2½ hours Section A: 2 Data Response questions of which one must be answered. Section B Essays (largely Microeconomics) 4 Questions to be answered from 7 microeconomic questions (35%)	3 hours Essays 5 questions from a choice of approximate 14 (40%)
Paper 2	1½ hours Stimulus Paper 2 compulsory questions (25%)	2¼ hours Data Response 3 questions to be answered from a choice of 6; divided into two sections: Section A (numerical data) and Section B (written passages); with at least one question to be chosen from each section (30%)	3 hours Essays 4 questions to be answered from a choice of 12 (50%)	2½ hours As in Paper 1 but largely macroeconomics (35%)	1½ hours Multiple choice • 40 compulsory questi (40%)
Paper 3	3 hours Essays 4 questions to be answered from a choice of 10 (50%)	1¼ hours Multiple Choice 50 compulsory questions (30%)		1½ hours Multiple Choice • 40 compulsory questions (30%)	1½ hours Comprehensive and analysis paper 2 compulsory question one presenting numer data, the other a writt passage (20%)
Paper 4					

Table of topics common to the syllabuses of all the boards

Topic area	Comments
1 The central problem of all economic societies The problem of scarcity, choice, opportunity cost, allocation of resources; the market mechanism; free goods, economic goods, private and public goods; types of economic system.	All boards set questions asking for a comparison of market and comm economies and a discussion of their virtues and disadvantages, together those mixed economies. See Chapter 9, and also Chapters 1 and 8.
2 Demand theory Individual and market demand curves; consumer behaviour; utility theory, movements along and shifts of demand curves; price, income and cross elasticities of demand; substitution and income effects; complementary and competing demand; consumer surplus.	ULEAC and AEB do not require a knowledge of indifference curves, a top which most of the other boards set specific questions. See Chapters 2 and 4 also Chapter 5.
3 Cost and supply theory Firm and industry supply curves; the behaviour of firms; the law of returns and the economic short run; increasing returns to scale and the economic long run; economies and diseconomies of scale; the derivation of marginal total and average cost curves; price elasticity of supply in the market period, short run and long run; movements along and shifts of supply curve.	There is a tendency for all the boards to set questions best answered with knowledge of alternative theories of the firm (managerial and behavic However, the syllabuses only specify the orthodox profit maximising theory firm. Most boards expect a knowledge of the structure of industry in the E economy, the size and growth of firms, the capital market, etc, but there has a movement away from expecting a detailed descriptive knowledge of topics as the various types of business enterprise in the British economy. For th Chapters 3, 4 and 5. For an institutional approach: Chapters and 11.
4 Market equilibrium and the equilibrium firm The concept of equilibrium in economics; the interaction of supply and demand and industry (or market) equilibrium; marginal, total and average revenue; short- and long-run equilibrium. The determination of a firm's equilibrium price and output in different market structures (perfect competition, monopolistic competition, oligopoly, and monopoly).	Questions are being increasingly set on 'market failures' and the circumsto in which goods and services are provided outside the market (public goods, goods, externalities); the revised syllabus of the AEB explicitly recognises this topic area. Also questions increasingly require an evaluation of equilibri different market structures in terms of their desirable and undesirable proper productive and allocative efficiency, etc. For market equilibrium see Chap and 9. For the equilibrium firm: Chapters 6 and 7, and for market failures Ch 8.
5 The theory of distribution Demand for and supply of factors of production; the determination of wages, interest, profits and rent; economic rent, quasi-rent and transfer earnings; wage determination and bargaining in the British economy; the role and effectiveness of trade unions.	See Chapter 13.

Cambridge	Cambridge	Oxford & Cambridge	Oxford & Cambridge	SEB	NISEAC
9070	9072	9633	9635		
Economics	Econ. & Public Affairs	Economics	Econ. & Polit. Studies	Economics	Economics
3	4 (Paper 1 compulsory and one other to be taken)	4 (Papers 1 and 2 compulsory Papers 3 & 4 are options)	4 (Paper 1 compulsory Papers 2, 3 & 4 are options)	3	3
hours iple Choice • compulsory questions %)	3 hours Economics Essay Paper (50%)	1½ hours Multiple Choice • 40 compulsory questions	3 hours Principles of Economics Essays (As an alternative either Paper 3 or Paper 4 of subject 9633 may be taken)	1 hour Multiple Choice 25 compulsory questions (25%)	1½ hours Multiple Choice • Approximately 40 compulsory questions (30%)
hours a-response ompulsory questions sented in graphical or ular or textual form %)	3 hours Structure and working of British Government Essay Paper (50%)	1½ hours Essays 2 questions from a choice of 6 covering 'Principles of Economics'	3 hours Political Thought Essays	1¾ hour Interpretation (Data Response) 2 compulsory questions which normally include macroeconomic and microeconomic material requiring interpretation of both prose and data (30%)	3 hours Essay Paper 4 questions to be answered with 2 from a choice of 5 from each of 2 sections. Section 1: Microeconomics and Methodology Section 2: Macroeconomics (40%)
ours ys uestions to be wered from a choice pproximately 13 %)	3 hours World Affairs since c. 1960 Essay Paper (50%)	3 hours Applied Economics 4 questions must be answered: 2 from each section: Section A: Choice of 9 questions on 'The British and Other Economies'. Section B: Choice of 3 'either/or' questions on 'Documents, Commentaries and Numeracy'.	3 hours Representative Government Essays	2 hours Essay Paper Free choice of 3 from 9 questions covering all parts of the syllabus (45%)	2 hours Data Response Paper 3 compulsory questions using different types of real-world data (30%)
	3 hours English Social and Economic History, 1815–1973 Essay Paper (50%)	3 hours British Economic and Social History since 1780. Essays, Documents, commentaries and statistical questions.	3 hours British Constitutional History since 1830		

• Common shared multiple choice paper

ic area	Comments
he system of National Income Accounts definition and measurement of income expenditure and output; net and gross; onal and domestic; market prices and factor cost; relationship between sures: problems of comparison over time and between countries; the Balance ayments as a part of the National Accounts.	Questions frequently ask for a discussion of the extent to which National Income figures provide a useful measure of economic welfare. Scottish candidates may be required to analyse National Income Accounts in the Interpretation paper. See Chapter 18.
he theory of income and output determination circular flow of income; injections into and withdrawals from the flow; the sumption function; the multiplier; theories of investment; the accelerator; the librium level of income; inflationary and deflationary gaps; the determinants e aggregate levels of employment and prices (inflation theory).	The syllabus content of this topic area reflects the 'Keynesian orthodoxy' of the 1950s and 1960s. Increasingly however, the questions being set require a knowledge of the theoretical issues separating Keynesians and monetarists and their different views of 'how the economy works'. Knowledge of the 'aggregate demand/aggregate supply' model will be very useful, even though the AD/AS model may not be mentioned explicitly in the syllabus. Look mainly at Chapters 20 and 21, but also at Chapters 22, 23 and 24.
Money and banking nature and functions of money and credit; the demand for and supply of ey; the money market; the functions of the Bank of England and commercial ks; reserve ratios and the operation of monetary policy; interest rates, open ket operations and special deposits.	Questions are now set which require knowledge of Keynesian and monetarist views on the role of money, the demand for money, interest rate theory and the role and effectiveness of monetary policy. See Chapters 14, 16, 17 and 24.
international economics theory of specialisation and trade; the gains from trade and the principle of parative advantage; the case against trade; the theory of the Balance of ments and fixed and flexible exchange rates; the terms of trade; the UK ance of Payments; international economic institutions including the Interna-al Monetary Fund, World Bank, General Agreement on Tariffs and Trade and European Economic Community; free trade areas and customs unions.	Questions are frequently set requiring an application of the principle of comparative advantage to a discussion of the regional problem or division of labour and specialisation within a country. Other questions require some knowledge of the operations of macroeconomic policy within an open economy, the effects of the foreign trade multiplier, the Balance of Payments and the money supply, exchange rates and inflation, etc. Use Chapters 25, 26 and 27.
The economic role of the government lic provision and distribution of goods and services; the distinction between ate and social costs; the management of national, regional and local nomies; policy instruments and objectives; fiscal policy; monetary policy; mes policy; direct controls; microeconomic policies; industrial, regional and loyment policies; competition policy; the nationalised industries; the determi-ts of government revenue and spending; the National Debt and the Public tor Borrowing Requirement.	In recent years, questions have increasingly reflected the Keynesian v monetarist debate on the correct role of government in the economy, demand management v 'supply side' policies, fiscal v monetary policy, the implications of taxation, public spending and the Public Sector Borrowing Requirement, etc. Questions on 'the mixed economy' are a key feature of Scottish Higher Grade papers. For microeconomic policy use Chapters 5, 8 and 12. For macroeconomic policy use 15, 16, 17, 20, 22, 23 and 24.

AS LEVEL SYLLABUSES

Board	AEB	ULEAC	NEAB	Oxford	Oxford and Cambridg
Syllabus	984	8120		8740	8430
Subject Name	Economics	Economics	Economics	Economics	Economics
Number of Papers	2	3	2	2	3
Paper 1	2 Hours Written Paper Section A: Between 8 and 12 compulsory short-answer questions. (20%) Section B: 2 compulsory stimulus questions (40%) (60%)	2 Hours Essay Paper 3 questions must be answered, with at least 1 question from Section 1, and 1 question from either Section 2, 3, or 4. Section 1, 2, 3 and 4 correspond to the sections of the syllabus. 3 essay questions will be set in each of the 4 sections (40%)	1¼ Hours Section A: 20 compulsory multiple choice questions covering the whole syllabus (20%) Section B: One compulsory stimulus question drawn from Sections 1 and 2 of the syllabus (20%) (40%)	2 Hours Written Paper Section I: Choice of 8 short answer questions from 16 (20%) Section II: Choice of 2 essay questions from 12. One question must be answered on microeconomics and 1 on macroeconomics (40%) (60%)	1¼ Hours Section A: A mixture of about 10 short answer questions and 10 multi choice questions base on Syllabus Module 1 (20%) Section B: 1 data-response question mus answered and 1 structured question will set on each of the Modules II, II IV* (20% (40%)
Paper 2	1½ Hours Essay Paper Choice of 2 essay questions from 5 (40%)	2 Hours Data Response Paper A range of compulsory data response questions will be set in Section 1 of the paper. One question from section 2, 3 or 4 must also be answered. Two questions will be set in each of these sections which correspond to the sections of the syllabus (40%)	1¾ Hours Section A: Choice of 1 from 4 essay questions drawn from Section II of the syllabus. (20%) Section B: Choice of 2 from 12 essay questions drawn from Section III of the syllabus. Three questions are set on each of 4 policy groups. *Each chosen question must be from different policy groups. (40%) (60%)	1½ Hours Comprehension and Analysis One numerical data response question must be answered from a choice of 2. One prose passage question must be answered from a choice of 2 (40%)	2½ Hours 3 questions must be answered, one from ea of three sections. The questions may involve stimulus material. Section A: 3 essay questions on Module Section B: 2 essay questions will be set or each of the special subjects for each Mod II, III, IV. Section C: 3 essay questions will be set or the content of Modules III, IV* without referenc to the special subject
Paper 3		Coursework 1 investigative study from a choice of topics, based on Sections 2, 3 and 4 of the syllabus. (20%)			

* See summary of syllabuses on pp4–5.

EXAMINATION BOARDS AND ADDRESSES

AEB The Associated Examining Board
Stag Hill House, Guildford, Surrey GU2 5XJ

Cambridge University of Cambridge Local Examinations Syndicate
Syndicate Buildings, 1 Hills Road, Cambridge CB1 2EU

ULEAC University of London Examinations and
Assessment Council
Stewart House, 32 Russell Square, London WC1 5DN

NEAB Northern Examinations and Assessment Board
Devas Street, Manchester M15 6EX

NISEAC Northern Ireland Schools Examinations and
Assessment Council
Beechill House, 42 Beechill Road, Belfast BT8 4RS

Oxford University of Oxford Delegacy of Local Examinations
Ewert House, Ewert Place, Summertown, Oxford OX2 7BZ

Oxford and Cambridge Oxford and Cambridge Schools Examination Board
(a) Purbeck House, Purbeck Road, Cambridge CB2 1PU
(b) Elsfield Way, Oxford OX2 7BZ

SEB Scottish Examinations Board
Ironmills Road, Dalkeith, Midlothian EH22 1LE

WJEC Welsh Joint Education Committee
245 Western Avenue, Cardiff CF5 2YX

STUDYING AND REVISING ECONOMICS

THE DIFFERENCE BETWEEN GCSE AND A/ AS LEVEL

The majority of students who start an A-level course in economics are completely new to the subject; only a minority have studied GCSE economics. For this reason, no mention is made in the individual topic units of the difference between what is required at GCSE and A-level. There is in fact little difference in the range of subjects included in the 'straight' economics syllabuses at GCSE and A-level, though the A-level syllabus tends to be rather wider. However, some examination boards offer 'combined subject' syllabuses at Advanced level, or subjects such as social economics, which is offered as an option by the Southern Examining Group at GCSE. At Advanced level, the Oxford and Cambridge Board allows the combination of economic principles and British economic and social history in a single examination, as an alternative to the 'straight' economic combination of economic principles and applied economics. Similarly, economics can be combined with English social and economic history, or the structure and working of British government, or world affairs since 1945, in the Economic and Public Affairs option offered by the Cambridge Local Examinations Syndicate. Again, this is an alternative to the 'straight' economics Advanced level syllabus available through the Cambridge Board.

The principal differences between GCSE and A-level economics lies not in the syllabus content but in the order of the skills that the examinations try to test. The GCSE examination is largely concerned with testing the **'lower order' skills** of **factual recall** and **description** together with the **understanding** and **application** of simple ideas. In contrast, at Advanced level much more emphasis is placed on the **'higher order' skills** involved in **theoretical analysis** and evaluation. Although the practice of each examining board is slightly different, students should derive useful guidance from the introductions to the syllabuses of the NEAB and the Associated Examining Board; two boards that publish in detail the aims and objectives of their economic syllabuses. By the end of the AEB course, candidates are expected to display the ability to:

❶ recall knowledge of the institutions and main features of the United Kingdom economy and its place within the world economy;

❷ demonstrate knowledge and understanding of the basic concepts and techniques of analysis used by economists;

❸ select and apply appropriate methods and techniques to the interpretation and analysis of economic problems and economic data;

❹ organise and present economic ideas and statements in support of an opinion or conclusion;

❺ evaluate the logical consistency or accuracy of economic statements on the basis of factual evidence and/or theoretical analysis;

❻ synthesise an argument by drawing on different facts or analytical approaches and demonstrate an appreciation of the economic approach.

Most helpfully, the NEAB syllabus specifies six areas of knowledge and skill which the A-level examination is designed to test, providing a guide which should prove very useful to all students of Advanced level economics, irrespective of examination board:

❶ **Knowledge** (30% of total marks)
 • Knowledge of the terminology of economics
 • Knowledge of specific facts relating to economics and economic institutions.
 • Knowledge of general and specific methods of enquiry and of the main

sources of information about economic matters and ways of presenting economic information.
- Knowledge of the main concepts, principles and generalisations employed within the field of economics and of the major economic theories held.

❷ **Comprehension (25%)**
- The ability to understand and interpret economic information presented in verbal, numerical or graphical form and to translate such information from one form to another.
- The ability to explain familiar phenomena in terms of the relevant principles.
- The ability to apply known laws and principles to problems of a routine type.
- The ability to make generalisations about economic knowledge or about given data.

❸ **Application (15%)**
The ability to select and apply known laws and principles to problems which are unfamiliar or presented in a novel manner.

❹ **Analysis and synthesis (15%)**
- The ability to recognise unstated assumptions.
- The ability to distinguish between statements of fact, statements of value and of hypothetical statements.
- The ability to make valid inferences from material presented.
- The ability to examine the implications of a hypothesis.
- The ability to organise ideas into a new unity and to present them in an appropriate manner.
- The ability to make valid generalisations.

❺ **Evaluation (15%)**
- The ability to evaluate the reliability of material
- The ability to detect logical fallacies in arguments
- The ability to check that conclusions drawn are consistent with given information and to discriminate between alternative explanations.
- The ability to appreciate the role of the main concepts and models in the analysis of economic problems.

❻ **Expression**
The ability to organise and present economic ideas and statements in a clear, logical and appropriate form.

The Board notes also that questions frequently overlap these broad objectives, and that although no specific allocation of marks is given to the skill of expression, candidates will inevitably penalise themselves if they fail to express themselves clearly.

STUDY STRATEGIES AND TECHNIQUES

At least 80% of your time as a student will be spent on private study so it is very important for you to acquire those skills which enable you to study effectively. Many hours can be wasted reading books from which you learn very little, or drawing elaborate charts and diagrams which are soon forgotten.

Study will involve you in collecting information, analysing it, clarifying your thinking, assimilating knowledge and expressing yourself clearly. No one is born with these skills, nor are they obtained accidentally: they must be acquired by conscious effort and practice. Here are some suggestions which will help you to develop these skills and make the most of your study time.

Establish targets

Research has shown that a learning period of about 45 minutes produces the best relationship between understanding and remembering. Set yourself study tasks which can be achieved in this period of time and then take a break for 15 minutes or longer before attempting another period of work. Plan reasonable targets which you can achieve in each study session, e.g. to read twenty pages and make notes.

Focus on essentials

There are large numbers of books and articles which deal with topics in the A or AS level syllabuses. Some of this material is inappropriate or duplicates what is written better elsewhere. Try to focus on sections of books, avoid extraneous material and select what you read intelligently.

Select key words and phrases

When you read a section of a book, select words or phrases which will help you to remember what the section is about. These words can be written down for reference and used as personal notes.

Note taking

Far too many students write notes as they write essays, in linear sequences. About 90% of what is written is wasted material and will never be remembered. It is the key words, concepts and phrases which need to be remembered and with practice you can abandon linear notes and learn more effectively by recording only the key words. This skill takes some time to acquire and can best be learned in stages by first writing down long phrases but not sentences and then, after a time, reducing your notes to just the key words and phrases. This form of note taking is suitable for notes made while reading or during a lecture. Remember to record the author and title. Sometimes the page number is also useful for future reference. A fluorescent highlighting pen is useful for identifying key words and phrases. These are not, of course, to be used on text books or journals but on notes you have made or been given.

REVISION TECHNIQUES

You can reduce the need for luck by preparing a revision programme. Since you will have to face a multiple choice paper containing compulsory questions covering the whole of the syllabus, plan a thorough programme and begin it several weeks before the examination, time-tabling periods of each day when you know you can work for up to two or three hours completely free of distraction. It is a good idea, however, to allow yourself a brief relaxation period every half hour or so to facilitate the absorption of the knowledge, ideas, and concepts intensively revised in the previous period. Although you must cover the whole syllabus, concentrate on key concepts and on essential economic theory rather than on detailed historical and descriptive fact.

There are various methods of revising, and not all may suit every candidate. Generally it is not a good idea to read through sheaves of notes or chapters from a textbook, and certainly it is not good practice to 'rote-learn' pages of notes. Nevertheless, you must learn key definitions, though it is even more important to learn how and when to use them. Remember that, as a properly prepared candidate, you will only be able to use a small fraction of your total economic knowledge in a single essay or data response paper. Provided that you have revised in a reasonably structured way in the weeks before the examination, it is certainly not a good idea to work late into the night on the day preceding the examination. Answering an examination paper is a tiring task, especially if you are to display the type of skill the paper is testing; you need to arrive in the examination room as refreshed as possible and capable of thinking clearly not just for a few minutes, but for up to three hours.

If you decide to arrange your revision programme around the use of this book, we suggest that you select one or at most two topic areas for coverage at each revision session. Quickly read the first half of a chapter, making a mental note of key definitions or concepts. Then try to write your own answer plans to two or more questions at the end of the chapter. Check your completed answer plan against the one included in the book and read through the notes on understanding the question. Go back over the chapter to make sure you understand the most important definitions and concepts, which you should now write out in a revision list. Several hours later or on the next day, write in your own words the meaning of the concepts and key definitions. Check what you have written against the explanations given in the chapter. Repeat this exercise frequently throughout your revision period until you feel confident that you thoroughly understand all the concepts and definitions. You might also attempt on later dates to write answer plans to the questions omitted when you first revised the chapter.

COURSEWORK

Currently, ULEAC is the only board to include coursework as part of its AS-level economics syllabus. (None of the boards include coursework at A-level). However, given the strong likelihood that compulsory coursework will be required at both A and AS level (following the major syllabus revision due to take place in the mid 1990s), students and teachers might like to study the requirements and assessment criteria, together with the assessment objectives, outlined by ULEAC for the 'investigative study' which has formed part of the AS level requirements. Why not write off for your copy!

THE EXAMINATION

EXAMINATION TECHNIQUES AND QUESTION STYLES

In order to test a range of skills such as those illustrated in the extract from the NEAB syllabus, most examining boards have recently introduced new examination papers and new types of question. A typical A-level economics examination now includes

❶ an essay paper

❷ a multiple choice (or objective test) paper and

❸ a data response (or stimulus paper).

However, there are variations from board to board which you are advised to check, particularly concerning the type of data response material the board includes in its examination.

Essay questions

There is little doubt that A-level economics has become a more difficult and testing examination over the many years since the day when, with fear and trepidation, the author faced the NEAB examination in the subject. In those days it was common practice for the examining boards to set just two essay papers which allowed candidates a fair degree of scope in choosing the parts of the syllabus to revise, and which included a number of questions testing factual recall and description.

Since the introduction of multiple choice and data response questions, the essay paper has become rather more specialised. Questions answerable simply by factual recall may allow candidates to do well simply by 'rote-learning' pages of notes. Such questions have fallen out of favour with examiners because they fail to discriminate between 'good' and 'bad' candidates on the basis of the ability of a good candidate to practise the higher order skills we have listed. Some, but not all, examining boards have shifted the testing of factual knowledge to the multiple choice paper, leaving the essay paper free to test analytic evaluation and similar skills.

Most boards which have not as yet introduced a separate data response paper have kept two essay papers supplemented by a multiple choice paper. Where two essay papers are set, it is usual for the first paper to cover **microeconomics** and for the second paper to test the **macroeconomic** topics in the syllabus, though the papers of the Oxford and Cambridge Board divide between **economic principles** and **applied economics**. Among the boards which have only one essay paper, the NEAB, ULEAC and the AEB place strong emphasis on applied questions (questions related to current economic problems and government policy). Most boards allow a candidate the 'free choice' of selecting questions (usually five) from any part of the essay paper. The ULEAC paper is the most restrictive, including twelve questions (compared with as many as sixteen set by some other boards), divided into two sections corresponding roughly to the division between micro- and macroeconomics. Candidates are required to answer four questions, choosing at least two from each section.

Because of these differences in both the structure of the essay paper and the 'house style' of the questions set by each board, it is vital for a candidate to study the precise regulations of the examination for which he or she is sitting, and also to analyse a selection of recent papers or specimen papers set by the board. When important changes are made in the syllabus, or when the method of examination is changed, it is usual for the examining board to publish a specimen paper or papers. Each year your teacher should get an Examiner's Report which discusses the insight into the Chief Examiner's approach and demands. Increasingly, via the publications of the Economics Association and schools conferences, the chief examiners are becoming better known and more accessible. If the chief examiner gives a lecture in your area, go and listen! If your teacher does not know who the Chief Examiner is, get him or her to find out and study any textbook he may have written recently.

Essay technique

Most examination boards require a candidate to answer four questions in a three-hour essay paper, allowing about forty-five minutes for each question. It is vital to arrange your time so as to answer all four questions, since all carry equal marks and no allowance is made for answering too few. Spend at least a couple of minutes at the beginning of the examination in carefully reading the paper, paying close attention to the wording of each question. Carefully select four and read each through again; subconsciously you will be thinking about the other questions while working on your first answer! Choose the easiest question to answer first, but remember again to divide your time equally. When a question contains more than one section it is also important to divide your time between each part, assuming, unless the question specifies otherwise, that each carries equal marks. Examiners frequently complain that the second section of a question is either ignored or treated in cursory fashion, with the answer being little more than a footnote.

Nevertheless, if you find that you have allocated your time badly, you must take action to remedy the situation. It may be a good idea to answer one or both of the last two questions with an elongated, though carefully written, essay plan. In general, marks are awarded for relevant points made. It follows that you should make as many relevant points as possible and avoid dwelling on any single point. Of course in a properly developed essay you should have time to elaborate appropriately the points you make, but even so it is easy to spend too much time on a single argument – a variation of the 'law of diminishing returns' applies to economics essays written under examination conditions! The marking scheme may allocate perhaps two, three, or four marks for a particularly relevant argument, and a brief mention of the argument can earn you at least half and possibly all the allocated marks if it is properly related to the question. Candidates frequently waste valuable time by unnecessarily elaborating one argument, while failing even to mention a range of others. It is surprising how often an answer written as a series of points by a candidate pressed for time at the end of an examination earns more marks than the answer the candidate attempted first! Examiners *always* prefer short, well-structured and concise answers to long, rambling and repetitive essays.

Whether your essay is long or short, it must always be addressed to the set question. You will earn no marks at all for writing a 'model answer' to a question not on the examination paper! Long introductory and concluding paragraphs are generally inadvisable since they seldom pick up many marks. Nevertheless, it is good practice to use the first paragraph both to define precisely the terms mentioned in the question and also to state any assumptions you are making in interpreting the meaning of the question. If you think the question is open to more than one interpretation, then tell the examiner and explain why you are favouring a particular interpretation. Many questions are capable of different interpretations and there may be no assumptions and economic theories necessary for a proper development of the answer.

While diagrams and particularly graphs are often appropriate, they should complement rather than simply repeat the information you are providing in written form. Diagrams are often included which fail to earn any extra marks yet which waste valuable examination time. If you cannot correctly remember a particular graph or diagram, then leave it out. A wrongly drawn graph will serve no purpose other than to signal to the examiner in the clearest possible way that a candidate has not understood the essential theory required for answering a question! Draw your graphs large rather than small, and pay careful attention to how you label the axes and all curves.

Every essay question includes at least one key instruction, e.g. calling for a *discussion, evaluation, comparison* or *contrast*. Very few questions can be answered simply by factual description or by an uncritical historical account. Most examination questions test whether you can introduce basic economic theory in a simple but clear way in order to cast light on the specified problem. We include difficult or more advanced theories in this book where relevant to specific examination questions, though as a general rule simple theories used well are always preferable to the latest, most advanced theories obviously misunderstood by the candidate.

Questions asking for comparisons or contrasts should not be answered with two separate accounts. Strictly, a 'comparison' notes points of similarity whereas a 'contrast' notes points of difference, though in practice examiners are unlikely to be pedantic about this distinction. However, it is important to avoid confusing questions asking for a discussion of **causes** with those concerned with the **economic effects** resulting from a particular government policy or change in the economy. When discussing causes and effects it is as well to remember the central importance in economics of the **price mechanism** and the concept of the **margin**. Most economic changes occur at the margin in response to movements in relative price or income, when an economic agent decides it is no longer worthwhile to engage in its earlier pattern of economic behaviour.

Small adjustments rather than **massive structural changes** are the rule; even the 1973 oil crisis, an event regarded as cataclysmic at the time, produced rather slow adjustments that are still taking place. Changes usually take a time to work through; a **trigger event, event A** (such as the 1973 oil crisis or a change in government policy), may directly cause **event B**, which in turn causes **event C** and so on. In general the immediate direct effects of A on B are easier to predict than the later indirect effects further down the 'causal chain'. The chain of direct and indirect effects may be either **dampened** or **explosive**; in the former case event B is smaller than event A, and C is smaller than B, and so on. In contrast a causal chain is explosive if each succeeding event is more powerful than the previous one. Because most economic changes are eventually 'absorbed' through relative price changes and minor adjustments at the margin, economic chains may often be dampened.

Nevertheless, a further complication may be caused by the existence of **feed-backs**, when for example event B feeds back to change the variable associated with the original event A. In terms of essay technique, you should at all times avoid being dogmatic when discussing economic cause and effect, and remember than in economics it is often the case that 'everything depends upon everything else'.

Multiple choice questions

Almost all the examining boards now either set a separate multiple choice paper or include multiple choice questions in a separate section of one of their other papers. Candidates are usually required to answer about fifty compulsory questions within an hour and a quarter or an hour and a half. (The length of the examination depends upon the number of questions in the paper and the 'house style' of the questions – the questions in the common paper set by the Cambridge Local, Oxford Local, Welsh, and Oxford and Cambridge Boards involve more calculation than is usual in the papers set by the other boards, so more time is allowed.)

The multiple choice paper tests the whole range of the syllabus and it can also test certain types of numerical and logical skills that essay questions cannot adequately do. The AEB and ULEAC use their multiple choice papers to test descriptive knowledge, but this is not a noticeable feature of the NEAB paper or of the common paper shared by the other boards.

The structure of the multiple choice paper also varies between boards. Two main types of question are used: single completion and multiple completion. Most single completion questions contain a stem (the question itself) and five possible answers (a single correct answer and four incorrect distractors), though the AEB now sets questions with only four possible answers. Multiple completion questions are similar, but one or more of the possible answers may be correct. (The NEAB also sets two other types of multiple choice question: 'assertion/reason' and 'matching pairs'. Assertion/reason questions are perhaps the most difficult type of question. The candidate must first decide whether the two statements in the question are correct when considered as separate statements. If both are correct, he must then decide whether the second statement provides an explanation of the first. A matching pairs question requires the candidate to select items from one list to match up with items from a second list provided in the question.)

Some multiple choice papers include only single completion questions, whereas others are divided into separate sections with each section devoted to a different type of question. (The common paper shared by many of the boards is of the first type, whereas ULEAC, AEB and NEAB favour the latter approach.) Subject areas listed at the beginning of the board's published syllabus topics. (If the paper is divided into different types of question, it is usual for each section to cover the syllabus in this manner; the largest section of the paper contains single completion questions which thoroughly cover the syllabus, but the coverage of the other sections may be rather sketchy.) Some of the examining boards publish details of the number of questions they intend to set on each broad division of the syllabus, together with the skills the questions are designed to test.

Multiple choice technique

A multiple choice paper allows candidates to spend only a minute or two on each question. Some questions can usually be answered in a few seconds, but others which involve calculation or deep thought may require several minutes. It is important to avoid being delayed by such questions occurring early in the paper, in which case you may never reach some 'easier' questions in the later sections. Try to go through the paper three times in all. On the first occasion, quickly move on from any question proving difficult or involving a calculation, making sure to draw a heavy pencil line around all the questions you do not attempt. Similarly, place a question mark against any question you do attempt, but which gives you serious cause for doubt. If one and a quarter hours are allowed for the paper, try to complete your first run-through in about fifty minutes. On the second run, return to the questions you have placed a mark against, and be prepared to spend several minutes on each. If time allows, scan through the paper a third time, checking whether you have correctly interpreted the wording of each question. If you have second thoughts about any of your answers, take great care to erase completely your initial mark on the answer sheet. Indeed, make sure that all your marks are in the correct positions on the answer sheet since the computer which checks the sheet cannot award credit for any slips on your part.

Finally, allow at least half a minute to guess the answers to any questions still unanswered. Your aim is to maximise your marks, so do not leave any questions unattempted. There is always at least a twenty per cent chance that your guess will turn out to be correct!

Data response questions

Most of the examining boards have now introduced a new data response or stimulus paper, or have incorporated questions of this type into one or other of their existing papers. Data response or statistical questions have been introduced in response to a growing dissatisfaction felt by many teachers, universities and employers that economics students have lacked the ability and confidence to handle empirical data, whether in written, numerical or graphical form. However, there are considerable differences in both the stimulus material that the boards include in their questions, and in the skills which the questions are designed to test.

The Cambridge Board sets statistical questions which require a considerable amount of calculation to work out a correct answer. NEAB sets a single, hour-long compulsory question containing perhaps two or three detailed sources of data which may be in either numerical or written form. Both NEAB and AEB appear to favour the 'incline of difficulty' approach to the setting of data response questions: the question is structured into separate parts, each succeeding part becoming more difficult, in order to test the 'higher order' skills. Thus the first part of a NEAB or AEB data response question may require the candidate to describe some aspect of the data, while later parts require an explanation of the data in terms of economic theory and an evaluation. Properly constructed questions of this type discriminate well between good and bad candidates. ULEAC, which previously set very general questions not noticeably different from essay questions, changed its data response paper in 1986 to include more structured questions which resemble closely the questions set by the AEB and NEAB. These boards set questions requiring interpretation and analysis of the data rather than a set of calculations yielding unique correct answers, arguing that the skill of calculation can be tested more appropriately on the objective test paper.

We have noted only some of the differences between the styles of question set by the examining boards. It is vitally important that a candidate should be familiar with the 'house style' of a board's data response questions. Some boards set a compulsory data response question or questions; with other boards there is free choice. The Oxford and Cambridge Board offers perhaps the most interesting range of choice; data response questions form an optional section within the board's applied economics paper, a paper which also includes a Documents and Commentaries option. This option, which is the only one of its type offered by any of the examining boards, contains questions which resemble data response questions, the principal difference being that questions are set on government publications and other documents which are similar to 'set books'. The Oxford and

Cambridge Board notifies schools and colleges some time before the examination about the publications that candidates are expected to read.

Data response technique

Many of the examination techniques relevant to essay questions are also applicable to the data response paper. It is perhaps even more important to read through the questions to make sure that you thoroughly understand both the data content and the questions. Where a choice is allowed, the rubric at the beginning of the paper will usually advise you to spend at least fifteen minutes reading through the paper; take this instruction seriously and carefully read through each question before you make your final choice.

We have already noted how stimulus questions frequently start by asking for the extraction of simple facts from the data. Avoid the temptation to elaborate your answer to this part of the question since it is unlikely that more than a couple of marks will be allocated for simple description. Conversely, you must not simply describe or paraphrase the data when tackling the parts of a question that require the 'higher order' skill of interpreting or evaluating. Search for the conclusions that can reasonably be inferred from the data, and the more tentative conclusions that really require stronger supporting evidence. Sometimes a question will explicitly ask for a statement of the assumptions upon which the arguments in the data are based or upon which you are making your inferences. It may also ask for a discussion of other sources of information or data that might allow you to draw stronger inferences and conclusions.

Very often the limited amount of data included in a stimulus question is consistent with more than one interpretation, not by itself either proving or refuting a particular economic theory or hypothesis. Nevertheless, the examiner is hoping that candidates will be able to handle basic economic method by stating the assumptions being made in interpreting the data and by discussing how far the data appear consistent with at least one economic theory. So even if a question does not formally ask for a statement of basic assumptions or for a discussion of the limitations of the data, a good answer will show that a candidate is thinking about these issues. You should clearly show the examiner when you are drawing conclusions based solely on the data, and when you are bringing in 'outside knowledge', either in the form of economic theory or descriptive fact, to help in its interpretation.

Numerical questions may be based upon various forms of data, including tabulated schedules, charts and different types of graph. They may also involve either data extracted from real-world sources or simulated data made up specially for the question. Whereas data from real-world sources may contain various inaccuracies, being an estimate of what has happened in the real world, simulated data are completely fictitious. Simulated data on such topic areas as supply and demand, the theory of the firm, the multiplier and comparative advantage may be included to test whether candidates can use basic economic theory to perform simple calculations. Most examining boards now allow the use of electronic calculators in the data response paper (and also now in the multiple choice paper). Nevertheless it is vital to show all your workings, and you should explain to the examiner what you are trying to do at each stage in the manipulation of the data. Stimulus questions try to test economic knowledge rather than arithmetical skills, though there will usually be a single correct answer to a question or part of a question involving a calculation. However, an arithmetic slip should not be heavily penalised, providing that you have clearly shown that you are using the correct economic method to answer the question.

When answering questions based on real-world data sources, it is useful to know the difference between time-series and cross-sectional data, and to be aware of the uses and limitations of data expressed in such forms as index numbers and percentages. Time-series data observe how economic variables change over time, from year to year, quarter to quarter, or month to month. For example, British national income figures for 1990, 1991, and 1992 would form a short time-series. Whereas time-series data are often highly aggregated, cross-sectional data divide up or disaggregate the data into its various components. (The division of annual national income data into wages, profits and rent provides a simple example. Cross-sectional and time-series data can of course be combined together, in which case they are known as pooled data).

Time-series data measuring changes in economic variables such as national income, output and expenditure usually fluctuate both seasonally and also with the upswings and downswings of the business cycle. Seasonal fluctuations cannot of course be detected unless the data are presented in quarterly or monthly form, in which case they may be presented in either seasonally adjusted or unadjusted form. Adjusted data pick up the long-term trend from year to year whereas unadjusted data show the fluctuations occurring from season to season.

If the data contain observations for only two or three years, great care must be taken in interpretation. It is very easy to confuse the long-term trend of the data with relatively short-term fluctuations associated with the business cycle. As a general rule, a time-series must extend over at least five or six years to allow a long-term trend to be detected, and even then there is a danger that structural changes taking place in the economy may have altered the trend. Where it is possible to detect a long-term trend in the data, it may also be possible to extrapolate the trend in order to predict the future. Beware, however, of basing a forecast upon data subject to violent fluctuations, and always be prepared for the possibility that a structural change or 'outside shock' occurring in the future may upset the forecast.

Many economic variables measured in money units are affected by inflation, which can seriously distort time-series data. Check whether data are unadjusted for inflation, in the current prices of each year, or whether the data have either been converted to the constant prices of a particular year, or been expressed in index numbers. Index numbers, which are usually based on 100, can sometimes be confused with data expressed in percentages which must, of course, add up to 100. Cross-sectional data are often expressed in percentages, sometimes in the form of a chart or pie graph. Great care must be taken in interpreting both index numbers and percentages, particularly if absolute totals are not included in the data. A 1% change is seldom exactly equivalent to a one-point movement in an index, and the percentage share of, for example, income tax in total government revenue can fall, yet the absolute total of income tax revenue may still be rising.

As a final word of warning, be especially wary of reading economic interpretations into the apparent steepness or flatness of curves when data are presented in graphical form. By altering the scales on the vertical and horizontal axes it is possible to show changes in an economic variable either by a steep or a flat curve (providing that the variable is rising or falling). So look carefully at the chosen scales whenever a question requires graphical interpretation.

GUIDANCE FOR SCOTTISH HIGHER STUDENTS

The Scottish Examination Board offers two certificates in Economics for the post sixteen-year-old age group:

① The certificate of Sixth Year Studies which is based largely on an in-depth study of one selected topic and is only open to students with previous examination success in Economics;

② The Higher Grade which is normally a one year post-Ordinary Grade course intended for seventeen year olds, although often taken by older or Further Education candidates, for which this book is more suited. The course covers the same range of economic theory and analysis as most A-level courses, but, because of its shorter duration, the questions set may require less depth or development in order to reach a pass standard. A and

B passes are required for university entrance. There are few differences between this course and a typical A-level course in the field of Economic analysis covered by the syllabus. However, here there is not the same emphasis on factual knowledge recall nor on the memorising of traditional theory. More time is spent on the acquisition of numerate and interpretive skills and the application of key concepts and principles to real-world problems (similar to NEAB).

The syllabus aims to develop in candidates:

1 An understanding of the basic concepts and principles of economics;
2 The capacity to apply this understanding to the analysis of economic problems;
3 An understanding of the nature and extent of economic interdependence;
4 An appreciation of the economic dimension of life and of the changing economic framework of the United Kingdom;
5 Economic literacy and numeracy;
6 An appreciation of the applicability and limitations of economic theory in contemporary society.

The examination has three papers. A multiple choice objective test consisting of thirty items of the four-response type and worth thirty per cent of the total marks. These items do not specifically test the knowledge of economic facts and figures but concentrate on the understanding and application of concepts and principles. Paper two is a one hour interpretation paper similar to the data-response type. Here skills tested are mainly those of number and interpretation. The higher skills of evaluation and synthesis are tested along with the others in a two and a half-hour essay paper which breaks down to two analysis questions and two questions of applied economics from a total of twelve. Contemporary and, where possible, Scottish examples are used, and study is normally confined to the decade prior to the examination. Comparative and development economics are largely excluded at this level, but the effects of EC membership on the British economy are studied.

The Scottish Board has several key marking principles which stress the positive and tolerant approach to candidate's work. In general the aim is to give credit to what is correct and relevant and to ignore all else, that is, wrong statements carry no weight and marks are not deducted. The whole emphasis of the examination is on the testing of economic understanding rather than on strict factual accuracy from the candidates.

ADVANCED SUPPLEMENTARY LEVEL

Traditionally, most students in sixth forms and on equivalent courses in colleges have studied three A-level subjects, knowing that three good pass grades are usually required by universities for entry to a degree course in higher education. However, following the introduction of the Advanced Supplementary (AS) examination in 1989, pass grades in two subjects at AS-level are now regarded by universities and polytechnics as equivalent to a pass in one subject at A-level.

The objective of the new AS examination is to give greater choice and flexibility, enabling you to study more of the subjects you enjoy up to A-level standard, and helping to keep your higher education and careers options open. Universities, other higher education institutions and employers recognise the value of more broadly based sixth-form studies. While it is theoretically possible to study six subjects at AS-level instead of three subjects at A-level, a more usual combination is likely to be two subjects at A-level and two at AS-level.

Schools and colleges were expected to offer AS-level primarily on two-year courses. Some schools have decided to enter their students for AS-level at the end of one year, half-way through a two-year course leading to A-level.

Other schools and colleges enter their 'weaker' students for AS-level rather than A-level, believing that it represents an 'easy option'. However, because AS-level requires the same standard of work as A-level, with AS-level passes being graded

A to E in the same way as A-levels, it must not be regarded as easier than A-levels. In each subject, the AS syllabus has been designed to contain approximately half the syllabus content of A-level, but will be examined to test skills of exactly the same degree of difficulty. Indeed, it often appears that rather more than half the equivalent A-level syllabus is included in the new AS syllabuses, meaning that ½ +½ does not equal 1, in terms of the amount of work you are expected to do! Nevertheless, while the same general calibre of work is expected at AS-level as at A-level, the syllabuses aim to take account of the shorter teaching and studying time available.

Not all the GCE examining boards offer economics as an AS-level subject. Oxford, AEB, NEAB, ULEAC and the Oxford and Cambridge Schools Examinations Council have all prepared syllabuses in economics at AS-level. This leaves the NJEC, NISEAC and SEB as the only examining boards which do not offer economics as an AS-level subject.

SUMMARY OF THE AS SYLLABUSES SET BY THE EXAMINATION BOARDS

In contrast to A-level, for which all the examining boards set syllabuses in Economics based on the same common core, there are significant differences in syllabus content at AS-level. The differences arise from the fact that each board has had to select approximately half the A-level syllabus, and the boards have used rather different criteria for making this choice. All the boards offering economics at AS-level, with the exception of AEB and NEAB, have decided to divide their syllabus content into a compulsory section and two or more optional sections from which a choice can be made. The nature of the choice and the content of the options vary considerably from board to board, so we have summarised separately the main details of syllabus content, structure and choice for each board.

AEB

No choice is available, all the syllabus must be covered. The syllabus is divided into four subject areas:
❶ the market mechanism and resource allocation;
❷ money and exchange;
❸ the creation and distribution of income; and
❹ the economic role of government.

The syllabus broadly covers the range of the A-level syllabus; major exceptions are the omission of most aspects of the theory of the firm, the derivation of supply and demand curves, a detailed knowledge of financial institutions and measures of the money supply, the theory of the demand for money and rate of interest determination, international economic institutions, the national income accounts, the structure and theory of taxation, local government, growth theory, competition and region policies.

ULEAC

The syllabus is divided into four sections:
Section 1 A compulsory core covering basic principles: the economic problem, demand, supply, the price mechanism and the allocation of resources, the circular flow of income, the determinants of the level of national income, government expenditure and revenue, money and banking and international trade and exchange.

Additionally, a candidate must select one of three options covering economic issues and policy. The options are:
Section 2 The price mechanism, market failure and government intervention.
Section 3 Unemployment, inflation and macroeconomic policies.
Section 4 The international economy.

NEAB

The syllabus specifically focuses on economic policy and the role of government. There are three subject areas:

❶ The nature of economics and economic systems
    (a) Economies and their problems
    (b) The role of government in a mixed economy
    (c) The methods and techniques of economic analysis

❷ Macroeconomic problems and policies
    (a) Unemployment
    (b) Inflation
    (c) Economic growth
    (d) International economic relations

❸ Microeconomic problems and policies. Candidates must be familiar with *two* of the following:
    (a) Industrial policy
    (b) Urban and regional policy
    (c) Social policy
    (d) Distribution policy

Oxford

The syllabus is divided into 3 sections:
Section A A compulsory section covering the whole syllabus, but not in detail.
❶ Demand
❷ Supply
❸ Price and output determination
❹ Factor markets
❺ The central problems of economic societies
❻ The theory of income determination
❼ Money and prices
❽ International economics
❾ The role of government

Section B Candidates choose from Part I or Part II, in which the microeconomic part of the syllabus is examined in more depth.
Part I   Firms and markets
Part II   Individuals and markets
Section C Candidates choose from Part I or Part II, in which the macroeconomic part of the syllabus is examined in more depth.
Part I   Money and inflation
Part II   The international economy

Oxford and Cambridge

Candidates must study Module I and one other Module, II, III, or IV. For each of the optional modules a special subject is set. Centres will be notified by the board if there is a change of special subject from time to time.

Module I (compulsory): Resource allocation and economic systems
❶ Resources
❷ The economic problem
❸ Allocative mechanisms
❹ The model of circular flow of national income
❺ Specialisation, trade and exchange

Module II (optional): Industrial economics
❶ Production
❷ Motivation
❸ Market structures
❹ Labour market
❺ Government and industry
   Special subject: Privatisation

Module III (optional): The macroeconomic system
❶ National income
❷ Money and prices
❸ Policy objectives
❹ Policy instruments
   Special subject: Deindustrialisation

Module IV (optional): International economics
❶ International trade
❷ International capital markets
❸ Trade and protection
❹ Economic development
   Special subject: The Economics of the European Community

Section 2

A - LEVEL ECONOMICS

Each chapter features:

- *Units in this chapter*: a list of the main topic heads to follow.

- *Chapter objectives*: a brief comment on how the topics relate to what has gone before, and to the syllabus. Key ideas and skills which are covered in the chapter are introduced.

- *The main text:* is divided into numbered topic units for ease of reference.

- *Chapter roundup*: a brief summary of the chapter.

- *2 worked questions*: a typical essay and/or data question, with tutorial notes and our suggested answers.

- *Question bank*: a selection of further examples of essay and data questions.

PRICE DETERMINATION

Units in this chapter

Chapter objectives

According to Professor Lionel Robbins's well-known and long-established definition, economics is 'the science which studies human behaviour as a relationship between ends and scarce means which have alternative uses'. Although by no means all economists agree that this is the best definition of the subject, it does emphasise the importance (except perhaps in Marxist economics) of **resource allocation** as the central problem to be studied. Economics is literally the study of economising, with consumption as the ultimate end to which economic activity is directed.

Production converts the primary resources of the earth's surface into **economic goods**, which are then consumed to satisfy human wants or needs. Some goods, such as air, are known as **free goods** because no scarcity exists and nobody can charge a price for them. Most goods and all services, however, are economic goods. Scarce resources are used up and costs are incurred in the production of economic goods. The cost involved is an **opportunity cost**, which to economists means rather more than just a money cost. Resources which are allocated to one particular end-use cannot simultaneously be used elsewhere; the opportunity cost of using resources in a particular way is the value of the alternative uses foregone. For example, the opportunity cost of a visit to the theatre might be the sacrificed opportunity to spend the same time and money at a football match. In all forms of society or economic system, some mechanism must exist to allocate or ration economic goods (and the resources contained in them) between competing uses. In a market economy, the **price mechanism** operating in a system of interrelated markets acts as the rationing device, determining what is produced, how it is produced and for whom it is produced.

Examination candidates at A Level are often rather better at discussing the relative advantages and disadvantages of economic systems – market economies, mixed economies and planned economies – than they are at showing a detailed understanding of how a simple market operates. In particular, **market plans** and **market action** are almost always confused. The objective of this first topic is to explain, from basic principles, how market price is determined in a single market – leaving the 'market versus planned economy' issue for considering rather later in the book, after other important aspects of market behaviour have been introduced in the intervening chapters.

1.1 UNDERLYING CONCEPTS

The nature of a market

A market is a meeting of buyers and sellers in which goods or services are exchanged for other goods or services. The exchange is usually indirect, by means of money; in modern economies, goods are seldom bartered for each other. Instead, one good is exchanged for money which is then traded a second time for other goods, usually after a time delay. The exchange must be voluntary; a forced transaction is not a market transaction.

A market need not exist in a single geographical location, although transport costs and lack of information may create barriers which separate markets. Markets are decentralised and usually unorganised in the sense that there is no central authority, such as the government, to decide how much is going to be traded and how much each buyer and seller in the market must trade. Price is the only information which needs to be known by each trader in the market.

The functions of price

If the price mechanism is to work efficiently in a market economy, it must simultaneously fulfil three functions:

❶ **The signalling function** Prices must convey sufficient information to all traders in the market for their economic activities and plans to be coordinated. Markets will function inefficiently if prices signal wrong or misleading information, leading in extreme cases to complete market failure or breakdown (see Chapter 8).

❷ **The incentive function** Markets will only operate in an orderly and efficient manner if the buyers and sellers in the market respond to the incentives provided by the price mechanism. If demand rises relative to supply, the price will tend to rise. This provides the incentive for firms to shift resources into producing goods and services whose relative price has risen, and to demand more resources such as specialised labour in order to increase production. This may bid up wages and other input prices, causing households to switch their supply of labour into industries where relative wages are rising.

❸ **The rationing function** When consumers and firms respond to the information and incentives provided by prices, scarce resources are rationed between competing uses. Prices are functioning as an **allocative mechanism**. As we shall see in Chapter 9, the **planning mechanism** or **command mechanism** is the principal alternative allocative mechanism to the price mechanism, but a pure market economy would contain only the price mechanism.

The 'goods market' and the 'factor market'

You will have noticed from the preceding section that both households and firms are simultaneously operating within two sets of markets. On the one hand, consuming households face business enterprises in the retail or goods market, where households are the source of demand. For this demand to be an **effective demand** (demand backed up by money), the households must sell their labour services in the labour market, where it is now the firms who exercise demand. Although a market economy will usually be made up of a vast number of different and often specialised markets, for many purposes we can generalise and consider just a **'goods' market** and a **'factor' market** (one where households sell the services of the labour and capital they own) – the two markets being linked together through the decisions of both households and firms.

1.2 ESSENTIAL INFORMATION

Demand and supply curves

For the rest of the chapter we shall ignore the factor market and restrict ourselves to exploring in greater detail the process of price determination within a single market in the goods market. Fig. 1 illustrates the essential features of such a market.

A **demand curve** D_1 represents household or consumer behaviour in the market, while the **supply curve** S_1 maps out the supply decisions of firms. You will notice that the downward-sloping demand curve shows that consumers demand more of a good at low prices than at high prices. Be very careful of how you interpret this. It is insufficient to say that a demand curve slopes downwards because more is demanded at low prices than at high prices; we need to go further than this and to 'get behind' the demand curve by developing a theory of consumer behaviour to explain demand. This is done in Chapter 2. In a similar way, Chapter 3 develops a theory of the behaviour of firms to 'get behind' the supply curve and explain supply. For the time being, however, we shall accept that normal demand curves slope downwards and normal supply curves slope upwards.

Market plans and market action

The distinction between **market plans** and **market action** is of crucial importance to a proper understanding of the way a market works, yet it is a distinction which appears unknown to a significant proportion of candidates at A Level. A demand curve, such as D_1 in Fig. 1, shows how much of a good all the consumers in the market intend to demand at the various possible prices. **Intended demand** is also known as **planned demand** or **ex ante demand**. Similarly, the supply curve S_1 shows intended supply (planned supply or ex ante supply). It is easy to show that, at almost all prices, it is impossible for both the firms and the consumers to fulfil their plans simultaneously. Suppose that for some reason the price in the market is P_1, as represented in Fig. 1b. Firms would like to supply quantity Q_2 at this price, but households are only willing to purchase Q_1: intended supply is greater than intended demand and **excess supply** results.

You should now ask yourself what will be the quantity actually traded if the price remains at P_1. The answer is quantity Q_1. The amount bought is Q_1, and the amount sold is Q_1; the two are the same, as indeed they must be. Now the amount bought is just another name for **realised demand** (actual demand or ex post demand), and the amount sold is another name for **realised supply** (**actual supply** or **ex post supply**). It follows that realised demand will always equal realised supply whatever the price. This represents an **identity**.

The equilibrium price

The concept of equilibrium is of the utmost importance in economic theory and analysis. Equilibrium is a **state of rest**, when there is no reason for anything to change unless disturbed by an outside shock. Households and firms will be in equilibrium if they can both fulfil their market plans. In Fig. 1b, the price P_1 is not an equilibrium price because the firms are unable to fulfil their plans at this price. Realised demand, of course, equals realised supply at Q_1, but this is largely irrelevant: the crucial point is that intended supply is greater than intended demand at this price.

We now introduce a very important assumption about economic behaviour, which will recur throughout the book: **if any economic agent (such as a household or firm) is unable to fulfil its market plans, a reason exists for**

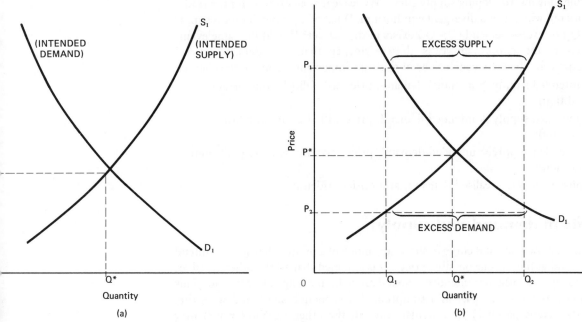

Fig. 1 The determination of equilibrium price in a single market: (a) equilibrium requires intended demand to equal intended supply; (b) the price mechanism ensures convergence towards equilibrium

it to change its market behaviour. At the price of P_1 in Fig. 1b, the firms are unable to fulfil their market plans. If firms react to their unsold stocks (or excess supply) by reducing the price that they are prepared to accept, then the market will **converge** towards the equilibrium price.

Similarly, if the initial price is P_2 in Fig.1b, it may be supposed that the households, who are unable to fulfil their market plans at this price, will bid up the price to eliminate the excess demand in the market.

The equilibrium price, P^*, is the only price which is consistent with the market plans of both households and firms, who consequently have no reason to change their plans. At the equilibrium price, intended demand = intended supply. This is often known as the **equilibrium condition** to clear the market; it must not be confused with the identity: realised demand ≡ realised supply.

In Fig.1b, the market mechanism ensures a convergence towards the equilib-rium price of P^*. Consider, however, Fig. 1c, which includes a (theoretically

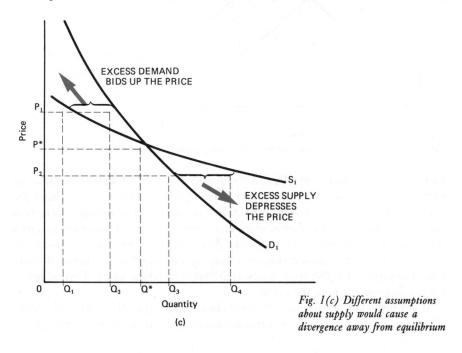

(c)

Fig. 1(c) Different assumptions about supply would cause a divergence away from equilibrium

possible) downward-sloping supply curve. We leave it as an exercise for the reader to work out why this is a divergent equilibrium. What will happen if excess supply (Q_4-Q_3) or excess demand (Q_2-Q_1) exists in the market? Would the same events happen if the supply curve is drawn steeper than the demand curve? To summarise the main conclusions of this very important section of the chapter:

❶ if intended supply > intended demand, price will fall (disequilibrium condition);

❷ if intended supply < intended demand, price will rise (disequilibrium condition);

❸ if intended supply = intended demand, price stays the same (equilibrium condition);

❹ realised supply ≡ realised demand, at all prices (identity).

Shifts in demand and supply

When we draw a demand curve to show how much of a product households intend to demand at the various possible prices, it is assumed that all the other variables which may also influence intended demand are held unchanged or constant. This is known as the *ceteris paribus* assumption. (In economic shorthand we write: $Q=f(P)$, ceteris paribus.) In a similar way, all the other variables which may influence supply are held constant when a supply curve is drawn. Common sense suggests that household income and fashion will influence demand, and costs of production will affect supply decisions, but you should refer to Chapters 2 and 3 for a more detailed explanation. In this section, we shall restrict the analysis to a brief investigation of a change in the **conditions of demand**, when one of the variables which influences demand is assumed to change. The reader should have little difficulty in extending the analysis to a change in the conditions of supply.

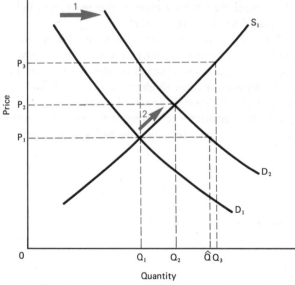

Fig. 2 The effect of a shift in the demand curve within a single market

In Fig. 2, the demand curve D_1 and the supply curve S_1 are drawn to show the initial condition of supply and demand. The equilibrium price which clears the market is at P_1, where quantity Q_1 is traded. A successful advertising campaign persuades households to demand more at all prices and the demand curve shifts upwards (or rightwards) to D_2 (arrow 1). At the existing price of P_1, households now demand $\hat{Q}$. But because conditions of supply have not changed, firms still only intend to supply Q_1 at this price, which is therefore no longer an equilibrium price. Excess demand exists in the market.

It is worthwhile at this point to take a closer look at how the price mechanism eliminates excess demand. If the firms are unable to increase supply immediately, the supply curve will be temporarily vertical and the price will be bid up to P_3. (Chapter 4 explains how supply is completely **inelastic** in the momentary time period.) In the short run, however, firms will respond to the incentive provided by P_3 and increase supply as soon as they can. An adjustment in supply, in response to price, takes place along the supply curve (arrow 2). If the price remained at P_3, the firms would be prepared to supply Q_3. If this amount is released onto the market the price will fall, as the consumers will only take Q_1 at this price. The price falls to the new market-clearing equilibrium at P_2.

Chapter roundup

The next nine chapters develop important aspects of the basic single-market supply and demand model which has been described in this chapter. In particular, Chapters 2 and 3 explain demand and supply curves, and Chapter 4 introduces the concept of elasticity. The other chapters investigate how markets may function when different assumptions are made about market circumstances – time-lags in the supply of agricultural products, producer power, barriers to entry, perfect and imperfect information, etc. Finally, Chapter 10 draws the threads together and assesses the advantages and disadvantages of the market economy as an economic system.

Illustrative questions and answers

1   Essay Question
(a) Explain why, in principle, the price mechanism performs both a 'rationing' and a 'signalling' function. (10)
(b) Explain why each of the following phenomena may be explained by the absence of, or restrictions on, the operation of the price mechanism:
(i) Waiting lists for certain operations in the National Health Service. (5)
(ii) Surplus stocks of farm commodities subject to the EC Common Agricultural Policy. (5)
(iii) Traffic congestion at peak times on city centre roads. (5)
(WJEC, June 1990)

Tutorial note

(a) Draw a supply and demand diagram to show a market in disequilibrium, with the price set below the equilibrium or market-clearing price. Explain the resulting excess demand at this price, and how in a free market situation the price will rise to eliminate the excess demand and restore equilibrium. This illustrates the rationing function of the price mechanism. The signalling function of the price mechanism is best explained by introducing more than one market into your analysis. You could assume, for example, that a successful advertising campaign or a change in fashion has recently made a good – say training shoes – more popular, thus shifting the demand curve rightwards. The price would then rise, signalling to firms in other markets and industries that high profits might be made by producing trainers. In response to this incentive signalled by the high price, firms would shift resources into the production of training shoes. This would cause the supply curve also to shift rightwards, which in turn would bring down the price of trainers. At this point you could return to the rationing function of the price mechanism, since the process you have described illustrates how the price mechanism allocates and rations society's scarce resources between different types of production, and ultimately consumption.

(b) (i) As we explain in Chapter 8, the government may decide to provide certain types of goods, known as **'merit' goods**, free for the consumer. Health care is an example. By providing many health care services at zero price, the government has decided to by-pass the price mechanism as a method of allocating resources, but it has not abolished scarcity. **Quantity rationing** (e.g. via queues, waiting lists and assessment of 'degree of need') have replaced prices as the mechanism for rationing scarce resources between competing uses.

(ii) European Community butter and grain 'mountains' and wine 'lakes', etc. illustrate one of the problems facing governments when they try to stabilise agricultural prices. The EC offers a guaranteed price for certain agricultural products, which is sufficient to earn the farmer **'supernormal' profits** (see Chapter 6). Guaranteed prices and supernormal profits create signals and incentives for farmers to increase production, knowing that the EC will buy all they produce. As a result the rationing function of the price mechanism does not perform properly; continuing overproduction results, which must be destroyed, stored, or converted to an alternative use, e.g. famine relief. See Chapter 5 for further details.

(iii) Traffic congestion at peak times on city roads represents another case of a **market failure** which we explain in Chapter 8. Congestion is an example of what economists call a **negative externality** or **external cost**. In the absence of a system of road pricing such as tolls, motorists who cause congestion fail to pay a price for motoring which reflects the true cost of their use of the road. While they pay for petrol and for the wear and tear of their own vehicles, they do not pay a price for the congestion they cause other road users to suffer. As a result, motoring in congested areas is underpriced; the price of motoring is sending out the wrong signals, encouraging too many cars to use the roads, thus causing congestion.

'Overconsumption' by motorists also means that the rationing function of the price mechanism is not working properly; too many scarce resources are being used by motorists at the expense of their use in other markets and industries.

2   Data Question

ANOTHER PLUNGE IN THE PRICE OF COCOA

We are eating more chocolate every year, but the price of cocoa plunges ever lower. On the London market yesterday, beans could be bought for May delivery at £6.13 per tonne, the lowest market price in real terms for more than 14 years. World consumption, about 2.2 million tonnes a year, keeps hitting new records; yet production is growing even faster. The result has been surpluses for the past six seasons. Oversupply of cocoa is good news for big chocolate eaters such as the British and the Swiss. Countries in Eastern Europe and the Soviet Union have a per capita cocoa consumption which is a third of Britain's and there is the possibility of expanding markets outside the chocolate industry, for instance in pharmaceuticals and cosmetics. Chocolate prices generally have not been cut and are unlikely to be, say industry sources. This is because cocoa accounts for perhaps no more than 10 per cent of the cost of a bar of chocolate, the rest being sugar, powdered milk, labour and other costs. Years of glut have helped chocolate makers to keep their prices remarkably stable worldwide, so boosting purchases. However, the impact of low cocoa prices has been devastating for the economies of the big producers such as the heavily indebted Ivory Coast and Ghana, which rely on bean exports as the main source of revenue.

(Source: *The Guardian*, February 1990)

1 What does the writer mean by the phrase 'the lowest market price in real terms'? (line 3) (2)
2 Explain and illustrate, using demand and supply analysis, why the market price of cocoa has been falling. (4)
3 Discuss the factors which are likely to influence the price manufacturers of chocolate charge for their products. (8)
4 What actions could the major cocoa producers take to protect their economies from the situation described in the passage? (6)

(AEB Wessex A-level Syllabus, June 1991)

Tutorial note

1 Economists distinguish between **nominal prices** and **real prices**. Nominal prices (which are also known as **money prices**) are simply the prices you pay for a good, for example in a shop. By contrast, a real price is measured by taking inflation into account. Suppose, for example, that the UK market price of cocoa (which is a nominal price) rose by 3% between 1990 and 1991, but that inflation was 7%. Then in real terms the price would have fallen by 4%!

2 The information in the passage certainly indicates that the world supply curve of cocoa has shifted rightwards. The demand curve (exercised by chocolate manufacturers) has probably also shifted rightwards, but not to the same extent. The net effect is thus for the market price to fall.

3 Discuss both cost factors and the market power (on the demand side) of the chocolate manufacturers. The passage indicates that chocolate prices have remained stable (which given the rate of inflation, means that in real terms chocolate prices have fallen, but not by as much as cocoa prices). Falling cocoa prices, amounting to about 10% of total production costs, may have been balanced by increases in other costs of production, e.g. labour. Another possibility is that the chocolate manufacturers have sufficient market power to maintain the price of chocolate, thereby benefiting from bigger profit margins as a result of reduced raw material costs. Finally, you could bring in the concept of **price elasticity of demand** (see Chapter 4). Consumers may not be very sensitive to the price of chocolate (i.e. demand may be inelastic), and particularly for luxury brands, they may sometimes regard a high price as a sign of quality and exclusivity.

4 Cocoa growers might form a worldwide producers' organisation which would attempt to restrict output, for example by assigning a quota or production limit to each country. Governments rather than individual farmers would have to organise the scheme. The success of such a producers' 'cartel' would be aided by the fact that there is no substitute for cocoa (as, for example, synthetic rubber is a substitute for natural rubber), but there might be great difficulty in getting the participation (without cheating) of all the cocoa producers in the world. The cocoa-producing countries might also try to diversify their economies in order to become less dependent on cocoa exports (see also Chapter 5).

Question bank

1 What are the functions of prices in a market economy? Why may the price mechanism function imperfectly in the cases of:
(a) the supply of oil;
(b) the control of pollution (8,6,6 marks)

(Oxford, June 1990)

2   Explain the concept of opportunity cost and discuss, with examples, its importance.   (ULEAC, January 1988)

3

(a) Describe the determinants of demand and supply in a market. (8)

(b) Use supply and demand analysis to predict how the prices charged for TV satellite dishes and package holidays abroad may change over the next few years. (12)   (AEB, AS Level, June 1990)

CHAPTER 2

DEMAND

Units in this chapter

Chapter objectives

In this chapter we 'go behind' the market demand curve in order to demonstrate how its shape and essential characteristics are derived from basic economic principles, and from a set of initial assumptions about how consumers behave. Different assumptions about consumer behaviour lead to differently shaped demand curves, so that although conventional downward-sloping demand curves are normally to be expected, it is best to avoid describing this characteristic as a 'law' of demand (which suggests a misleading inevitability about the existence of downward-sloping demand curves).

MARKET DEMAND AND INDIVIDUAL DEMAND

Students often confuse the **market** (or industry) demand curve, which shows how much of a commodity all the consumers in the market intend to buy at all possible prices, and the **individual demand** curve of a single consumer or household in the market. The relationship between the two is very simple: the market demand curve is obtained by adding up all the individual demand curves for every consumer in the market. Henceforth in this chapter, 'demand' will mean individual demand rather than market demand. It will also mean **effective demand** – a demand backed by purchasing power or money.

THE UTILITY APPROACH AND THE INDIFFERENCE CURVE APPROACH

Two different methods can be used to derive demand curves from a set of initial assumptions – the **utility approach** and the **indifference curve approach**. While both approaches lead to the same conclusions, the indifference curve method is preferred at a university level because it is more rigorous and the technique can be extended to other aspects of advanced economic theory. However, at the school or college level, our experience is that students are far better advised to learn simple theories well rather than risk fouling up a more complicated, if academically respectable, theory. For this reason, only the utility approach is explained in this chapter.

2.1 UNDERLYING CONCEPTS

UTILITY MAXIMISATION

The assumption which underlies demand theory is that consumers always seek in the market place to maximise the total **utility** they obtain from the set of goods they buy. Utility cannot be seen, touched, or even properly measured. It is sometimes defined as the pleasure which a consumer obtains from using a good or service. However, it really means rather more than this. Some goods, such as medicine for example, are consumed because they **fulfil a need** rather than because they give the consumer direct pleasure. The assumption of **utility maximisation** also implies that consumers act **rationally**, which in the sense used here means that people act in their own self-interest.

THE EXISTENCE OF CONSTRAINTS

If consumers had unlimited income, or if all goods were free, a consumer would maximise utility by obtaining those goods which gave him utility up to the point of **satiation**. However, all but a few lucky and very wealthy consumers face a number of constraints which limit their freedom of action in the market place. The principal constraints are:

- **Limited income.** Consumers do not possess unlimited means with which to purchase all the goods which would give them utility. The **opportunity cost** to a consumer of choosing one good is the lost opportunity to choose the next best alternative. (Note that the assumption of rationality implies that the 'best' alternative will always be chosen!) A limited income constrains a consumer's freedom of choice, and so, together with the given set of prices the consumer faces, it imposes a **budget constraint** on his market action.

- **The consumer faces a given set of prices.** A single consumer is unable to influence the market prices of any of the goods he might wish to buy: he is a **'price-taker'** rather than a **'price-maker'**.

- **Tastes and preferences are fixed.** A consumer who prefers Good A to Good B today will also prefer Good A tomorrow: the consumer is said to behave *consistently* if his preferences are stable over time.

MAXIMISING V MINIMISING BEHAVIOUR

Demand theory is thus concerned with the way in which a consumer with a limited income and fixed tastes behaves in the face of changing prices. The consumer attempts to maximise a desired objective (utility), subject to a set of constraints. The assumption of maximising or minimising behaviour (on the part of consumers, firms, workers and even perhaps the government) is central to orthodox microeconomic theory. You should note that a **maximising objective** can always be rewritten in minimising terms. Thus, we can rewrite the consumer's assumed objective 'to maximise the utility obtained from a purchased bundle of goods' as: 'to minimise the outlay, expenditure or cost of obtaining the same set of goods'. They are different sides of the same coin.

Whether we set up an assumed objective in maximising or minimising terms depends upon our convenience; we can do either. The reader will find further examples of 'maximising and minimising behaviour' in later chapters, for example in distribution theory and in the theory of the firm.

2.2 ESSENTIAL INFORMATION

DIMINISHING MARGINAL UTILITY

The principle of diminishing marginal utility states that although the total utility derived from a good increases with the amount consumed, it does so at a decreasing rate. It is quite possible that a person may experience increasing marginal utility when more of a good is consumed, at least for the first few units of that good. This is why we refer to diminishing marginal utility as a **principle** rather than as a **law**. The principle is illustrated in Fig. 3. The upward (or positive) slope of the total utility curve in Fig. 3a indicates that **total utility** rises with consumption. The last unit purchased is always the **marginal unit,** so the utility derived from it is the **marginal utility**. (Formally, the marginal utility derived from the n'th unit = the total utility of n units minus the total utility of (n–1) units. If 20 units are consumed, n = 20.) You will notice that the principle of diminishing marginal utility is shown by the **diminishing rate of increase** of the slope of the total utility curve in Fig. 3a. The marginal utility derived from each unit of consumption is plotted separately in Fig. 3b. The principle of diminishing marginal utility is represented by the negative or downward slope of the curve in this diagram.

Fig. 3 illustrates an important lack of rigour in the utility approach to demand analysis. The vertical axes are measured in degrees of utility, 'utils' or 'subjective units of pleasure', which are not really measurable because a 'unit of pleasure' will vary from person to person.

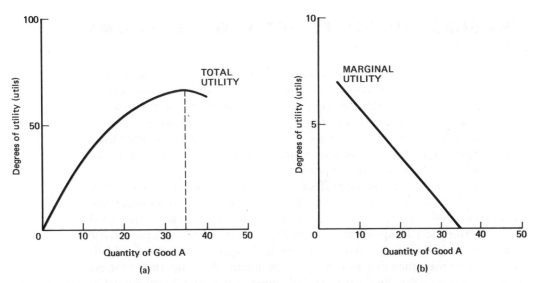

Fig. 3 Utility curves (a) total utility rises at a diminishing rate as an individual's consumption of Good A increases (b) this can also be shown by a marginal utility curve – note that at the peak of the total utility curve, marginal utility drops to zero

CONSUMER EQUILIBRIUM AND THE DERIVATION OF THE DEMAND CURVE

A consumer, constrained by limited income, fixed tastes and the prices which he faces in the market place, will continue to buy units of a commodity until the marginal utility which he gains is the same as that he could have obtained by spending a similar amount of money on another commodity. The equilibrium condition with respect to a single commodity is, therefore, where Marginal Utility = Price. It is an easy matter to extend the analysis to the case where a consumer buys many commodities. Successive units will be bought of each commodity to the point where its marginal utility equals its price. The multi-commodity equilibrium condition is:

$$\frac{\text{Marginal Utility of Good A}}{\text{Price of A}} = \frac{\text{Marginal Utility of Good B}}{\text{Price of B}} = \frac{\text{Marginal Utility of any Good}}{\text{Price of any Good}}$$

Suppose that a consumer can only choose between Good A and Good B and he starts off from a position of consumer equilibrium. At existing prices he is satisfied with the combination of Goods A and B that he buys. The price of Good A now falls, and the situation can now be represented by:

$$\frac{\text{M.U. of Good A}}{\text{Price of A}} > \frac{\text{M.U. of Good B}}{\text{Price of B}}$$

The consumer is no longer in equilibrium: he would be better off substituting more of the good whose relative price has fallen for a good whose relative price is now higher. He is not now maximising utility, and so he has a motive for changing his market behaviour.

When he consumes more of Good A, he moves 'down' the marginal utility curve for Good A, and 'back up' the marginal utility curve for Good B. As he substitutes more of Good A for less of Good B, the marginal utilities adjust until he is once again in equilibrium, when no alternative reallocation will increase his total utility. The equilibrium is achieved at a point of equi-marginal utility, where the marginal utility derived from each good as a ratio of its price is the same for all goods. The essential point is that more is demanded of the good whose relative price has fallen. The **substitution** effect, whereby consumers substitute more of a good whose relative price has fallen for goods whose relative price has risen, helps to explain the downward-sloping demand curve.

THE SUBSTITUTION EFFECT AND THE INCOME EFFECT

If consumer behaviour was determined only by the substitution effect of a price change, demand curves would only slope downwards. This is provided that customers are utility maximisers who experience diminishing marginal utility, and assuming also that they are uninfluenced by future uncertainty or by status. However, if consumers expect even higher prices in the future, they may demand more at high prices for speculative reasons. Similarly, if a high price indicates status, 'status maximisers' may be expected to demand more of a good at higher prices.

When we introduce the **income effect** of a price change, matters become rather more complicated. If the price of one good falls, a consumer's **real income** rises. The nature of this income effect depends upon whether the good is a normal good or an **inferior good**. If expenditure on a good rises when a consumer's real income rises, then the good is a normal one. Conversely, if expenditure on the good falls when income rises, then that good is classed as inferior. It is important to stress that the same good can, for a particular individual, switch from being normal to inferior as his income rises. Suppose that the Income-Expenditure graph in Fig. 4a represents an individual's expenditure on bus travel at different levels of real income. When the person is poor, his expenditure on bus travel rises as his income rises: bus travel is a normal good. But beyond the level of income Y_1, bus travel becomes an inferior good, presumably because the person can now afford to travel by car.

For normal goods, the substitution effect of a price change is reinforced by the income effect, and the two effects together explain the downward-sloping demand curve. But in the case of inferior goods, the income effect works in the opposite direction to the substitution effect. The income effect is, however, likely to be much smaller than the substitution effect, because expenditure on a single good

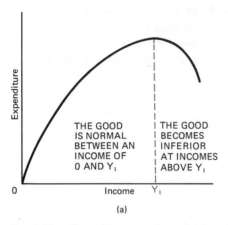
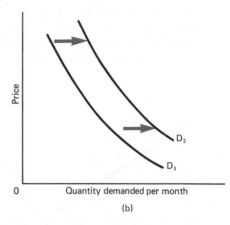

Fig. 4 The effects of income on demand (a) an income expenditure curve for a good which is inferior at high levels of income (b) a shift in the price demand curve for a normal good following an increase in income

is probably only a tiny proportion of a consumer's total spending; real income hardly alters at all if the price of a single good changes. Nevertheless, a theoretical possibility exists that the income effect of a price change will not only be in the opposite direction to the substitution effect but that it will also be stronger. This is the special case of an inferior good known as a **Giffen good** – less of a Giffen good is demanded as the price falls, hence the demand curve slopes upward.

SHIFTS OF DEMAND

In the previous section, the analysis explains how a change in real income, resulting from a change in the price of a good, influences the shape of the demand curve. It is important to separate this effect from the effects of a change in real income which is independent of a change in the good's own price. If a person's real disposable income rises as a result of a wage increase or a cut in income tax, then the demand curve of each of the goods that the person buys may shift. If the good is a normal one, the demand curve will shift to the right (or upwards) and more will be demanded at every price. This is illustrated in Fig. 4b. In the case of an inferior good, however, a rise in real income causes the demand curve to shift to the left (or downwards).

A change in real disposable income is only one of the possible causes of a shift in the demand curve. In general, a change in any of the constraints facing the consumer (sometimes known as the **conditions of demand**) will shift the demand curve. The good's own price is not listed as one of the conditions of demand because the demand curve is itself a 'map' showing how demand responds to price changes. However, changes in the price of a **complementary** or **substitute good** will normally shift a demand curve. Most people in Britain regard bread and butter as complementary goods. If the price of bread rises, the demand curve for butter will probably shift to the left and less butter will be demanded at all prices. Conversely, a rise in the price of a substitute for butter, such as margarine, will normally cause the demand curve for butter to shift rightwards.

The time-period under consideration will also influence demand. Strictly speaking, the horizontal axis of a demand graph should specify the time-period for which demand is being measured. If the time-period is changed, for example from monthly to yearly demand, the ability of consumers to respond to a change in price will also alter. This aspect of demand theory will be investigated in Chapter 4.

CONSUMER SURPLUS

The concept of consumer surplus is illustrated in Fig. 5, which shows the market demand curve of all the consumers in the market.

In Fig. 5, the equilibrium price of 10 pence is the price which every consumer in the market pays for the good in question. It is also the price which the marginal consumer is only just prepared to pay in order to obtain the good. If the price rose above 10 pence, the marginal consumer would either drop out of the market or

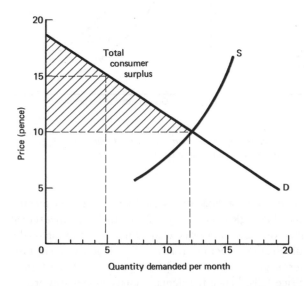

Fig. 5 *Consumer surplus: the shaded area shows total consumer surplus when the market price is 10 pence*

reduce his demand. However, some consumers, who value the good more highly, would be prepared to pay 15 pence for it. They gain a consumer surplus (or surplus utility) equal to the difference between what they would be prepared to pay and what they actually need to pay. The total consumer surplus, the utility which consumers enjoy but do not pay for, is shown by the shaded area of the graph.

Chapter roundup

Although the determination of the shape of the demand curve has been the central theme of this chapter, we have largely ignored a very important aspect of the shape and slope of demand curves: the concept of elasticity of demand. Chapter 4 should be regarded as a very useful follow-up to this chapter.

In this chapter we have dealt only with the microeconomic theory of consumer behaviour – how consumers choose between alternative goods and services. The macroeconomic theory of consumption (covered in Chapter 19) explains how consumers divide their limited income between aggregate consumption on all goods and saving. Although economists agree that a sound macroeconomic theory should be based firmly on microeconomic foundations, students are often confused by the parallel existence of micro- and macro-consumption theory. Think carefully about the context of the question, when you decide how to structure and plan your answer to a question on consumer behaviour.

Illustrative questions and answers

1   Essay Question
    What is the purpose of economic theory? Is it necessary for consumers, firms and governments to have an economic theory in order to make rational decisions?

(NEAB, June 1990)

Tutorial note

Economic theory has two main purposes. Firstly, it provides a 'tool kit' enabling economists to explain the working of both the whole economy (at the macro-level), and of the markets, industries, firms and individuals that undertake economic activity at the micro-level. Secondly, economic theory provides a framework which aids governments, firms and individuals in economic policy and decision making, in pursuit of the objectives of improving people's economic welfare and standards of living.

Most economic theories are **positive** theories: they attempt to explain how the economy works and to predict what will happen in the future if certain actions are taken now. However some economic theories are **normative** theories about what ought to happen: a theory of optimal government policy is a normative theory because it is concerned with how a government should make value judgements when choosing between different policy options. The theory of demand (or consumer behaviour) is a positive theory: the problem or puzzle to be explained is how consumers make decisions when faced with the choice of how to spend their incomes. (The theory does not say how they *ought* to spend their incomes.) Restricting ourselves to positive theories, the usefulness of a theory may be judged by three criteria: (a) **relevance**; (b) **realism of assumptions**; and (c) the **ability to survive empirical tests**.

(a) **How relevant is a theory?** If a 'good' theory explains a trivial problem of no interest to anybody, then it is hardly a useful theory. This, for instance, is the basic Marxist criticism of orthodox economics. Marxists argue that orthodox economics is dominated by the study of the 'uninteresting' problem of individual behaviour in a 'timeless' economy, thereby sidestepping the interesting problems (to a Marxist) of how a capitalist economy comes into existence and changes over time, and the economic relations between *classes* (as distinct from relations between *individuals*).

(b) **How realistic are the theory's assumptions?** All economic theories involve a set of *simplifying assumptions* about economic relationships or how people behave. Thus, in demand theory, economists assume that consumers have the single aim of utility maximisation. This is obviously a simplifying assumption as sometimes people will have other aims, but it may still be a useful way of simplifying.

(c) **Can a theory survive empirical tests?** The *predictions* (or *implications*) of a theory follow logically from its initial assumptions. Thus demand theory predicts a downward-sloping demand curve, but if the initial assumption in the construction of the theory had been that people are status maximisers and that status is indicated by a high price, then the theory would predict an upward-sloping demand curve, showing people demanding more of a good as the price rises. Such a theory would be unlikely to survive an empirical test, except perhaps as a 'special case'. *Empirical testing* means that the predictions of a theory are tested against observed behaviour in the real world. Useful theories survive the process of empirical testing, whereas theories whose predictions are plainly at odds with observed behaviour are discarded.

As we have seen in this chapter, to succeed in maximising utility, a household must consume a good up to the point at which $MU = P$. However, a consumer does not need direct knowledge of this 'marginalist rule', or to have studied an economics course for the theory and the assumption to have relevance. The theory provides an explanation of how people behave, but it not a blueprint that the people themselves must possess to guide rational decision making. However, possession of at least some theoretical understanding can often aid rational decision making. Suppose, for example, that snow and ice are forecast for the next month. A consumer who realises that adverse weather is likely to reduce the supply of fresh vegetables and cause their prices to rise, may well decide to stock up now when vegetables are readily available and prices are low. Consumers who do not understand this basic relationship between supply, demand and prices will fare less well.

Suggested answer

- Explain the purpose of economic theory which we have described.
- Illustrate with a selection of economic theories. Indicate that not all theories are necessarily correct or useful. An incorrect theory may do more harm than good if used as a guide for decision making.
- Explain that economic agents can act rationally, i.e. in pursuit of self-interest, without explicit knowledge of economic theory. Nevertheless some theoretical knowledge might improve the decision-making process. Give examples.

2 Data Question

Table 1: *Average weekly household income in the United Kingdom*

	1970	1975	1980	1983
Gross weekly income	£35.40	£72.87	£147.18	£187.86
Weekly disposable income	£29.54	£58.16	£121.50	£152.50

(Source: Family Expenditure Survey)

Table 2: *The Retail Price Index (1975 = 100)*

	1970	1975	1980	1983
	54.2	100.0	195.6	248.6

(Source: Economic Trends)

Table 3: *Selected commodities or services as a percentage of total household expenditure in the United Kingdom*

	1970	1975	1980	1983
Housing	12.6	13.1	15.0	16.8
Fuel, light and power	6.3	5.5	5.6	6.4
Food	25.7	24.8	22.7	20.8
Alcoholic drink	4.5	5.1	4.8	4.8
Tobacco	4.8	3.6	3.0	2.9
Clothing and footwear	9.2	8.7	8.1	7.0
Durable household goods	6.5	7.4	7.0	7.2
Transport and vehicles	13.7	13.8	14.6	14.7
Services	9.0.	9.9	10.8	11.3

(Source: Family Expenditure Survey)

(a) Explain the terms 'gross weekly income' and 'disposable income'. (2)

(b) Discuss whether the average household in the United Kingdom became better or worse off over the period shown by the data. (6)

(c) (i) Summarise the significant features of the data in Table 3. (4)

(ii) Suggest possible reasons which might explain the changes or the lack of change in the pattern of household expenditure shown by the data. (8)

(AEB, June 1986)

Tutorial note

(a) Gross weekly income is the income from all sources before deductions (such as income tax and national insurance contributions): weekly disposable income is residual income available to spend after these deductions.

(b) You must calculate whether the real weekly disposable income of the average household rose or fell over the period shown by the data. Divide the nominal figure for each year by the Retail Price Index (RPI) for the year and multiply by 100. This converts the data into the constant prices of 1975, the base year for the RPI. This calculation (correctly performed), together with a conclusion, is quite sufficient to earn all 6 marks, but you might also mention that your conclusion also depends on certain assumptions, such as no significant change in factors contributing towards feelings of being 'better' or 'worse' off; leisure time; intangibles such as 'quality of life'; and services provided by the state.

(c) (i) It is important to give an 'overview', highlighting the key changes, rather than to adopt a 'shopping list' approach going through each of the items, but without showing any real understanding of the data. For example, try to group the items into necessities and luxuries and see if there are any changes common to the necessities which separate them from the luxuries.

(ii) A good answer might concentrate on price effects and income effects and show an awareness that proportionate expenditure did not change by very much on many of the items. Your answer to part (b) will tell you whether real income rose or fell over the period. If real income rose and expenditure rose, you could conclude that the good is normal. But if expenditure fell, the good would be inferior. (But be careful! The data show proportional changes in household expenditure rather than absolute rises or falls in expenditure on particular items. Also, the changes in the pattern of expenditure may be caused by relative price changes rather than by changes in income.)

Question bank

1 Explain how an individual reallocates expenditure of goods when the price of one good changes. (O & CSEB, June 1987)

2 Why do households need to exercise choice? Explain how maximising principles influence household choice in the goods market and the factor market. (AEB, June 1988)

3 If bus services are inferior goods, what effects will the following changes have on consumers' total expenditure on bus journeys:
(a) a rise in incomes;
(b) a rise in bus-drivers' wages;
(c) an increase in the annual licence fee payable on private cars? (7,7,6 marks) (Oxford, June 1990)

4
(a) Explain the difference between a 'normal' good and an 'inferior' good. (10)
(b) 'A Giffen good is an inferior good, but an inferior good is not necessarily a Giffen good'. Discuss.   (15)   (WJEC, June 1992)

5
(a) (i) Explain why consumers demand less of a commodity as its price rises.
(7)
(ii) Suggest reasons why, in some cases, consumers may demand more of a commodity as its price rises.   (6)
(In parts (i) and (ii) assume 'ceteris paribus' – factors affecting demand other than price remain unchanged.)
(b) Describe factors other than its own price which may influence demand for a commodity, and explain the effects these other factors may have. (12)
(Scottish Higher, June 1989)

COST AND SUPPLY

Units on this chapter

Chapter objectives

In much the same way that the characteristics of demand curves depend upon the typical behaviour of consumers, so the properties of supply curves depend upon the behaviour of producers or firms. The market supply curve, which shows how much all the firms in an industry intend to supply at various possible prices, is obtained by adding up the separate supply curves for individual firms. For the rest of this chapter, we shall assume that there are a large number of firms within a well-defined industry and that each firm is a passive price-taker, unable to influence the market price by its own decisions on how much to supply. We are really constructing the theory of supply within a perfectly competitive industry, though a more comprehensive treatment of perfect competition is delayed until Chapter 6.

3.1 UNDERLYING CONCEPTS

THE FIRM

A firm is a **productive unit** or business enterprise which sells its output at a price, within the market economy. In the **private sector** of the economy, firms may range from a one-man window-cleaning business (a **sole trader** or **individual proprietor**) to huge 'multinational' **public joint-stock companies**, such as ICI, with branches and plants in many countries. Most **public corporations** or **nationalised industries** in the public sector of the economy are also considered as firms because they sell their output within the market economy. It is not usual, however, to regard **public services**, such as the National Health Service, as firms or business enterprises. Although the NHS is a major customer or market for firms which supply it from within the market economy, most of its own activities take place outside the market economy.

PROFIT-MAXIMISING BEHAVIOUR

In constructing a theory of supply we are not especially interested in the organisational complexities of firms, such as the different forms of ownership and control and the existence of multi-product and multi-plant enterprises. These are aspects of the **internal** structure of firms, which is the subject matter of Chapter 10. In this chapter we abstract from the internal organisation of firms and concentrate instead upon the **external** behaviour of firms when they make decisions on the production and sale of a good or goods within the market. In the context of this chapter, it does not matter who makes the decisions within the firm, as long as the decisions are consistent with a desired goal or objective which is assumed to exist for all firms. In the traditional theory of the firm it is assumed that all firms, whatever their internal structure and whatever the form of market in which they exist, share the common goal of **profit maximisation**.

FACTORS OF PRODUCTION

Economists conventionally divide all the inputs necessary for production to take place into four categories, or **factors of production**. These are land, labour, capital and enterprise (or the entrepreneurial factor). For the rest of this chapter we shall simplify and assume that just two inputs, labour and capital, are all that is needed for production to take place.

THE SHORT RUN AND THE LONG RUN

In economic theory the **short run** is defined as a period of time in which at least one factor of production is fixed. Thus, in the short run a firm can only increase output or supply by adding more of a variable factor, in this case labour, and combining it with the fixed input, capital. In the **long run** it is assumed that all factors of production are variable. The **scale** of the fixed factors can only be altered in the economic long run. From a firm's point of view, the short run is thus a time-period in which its ability to increase supply is constrained by the size of its fixed capital. We must distinguish between a firm's **short-run** or **constrained supply curve**, and its **long-run supply curve**, which is unconstrained except by factors such as the available technology and the prices it must pay to obtain the services of labour and capital.

3.2 ESSENTIAL INFORMATION

THE PRINCIPLE OF DIMINISHING RETURNS

If a firm attempts to increase output or supply in the economic short run by adding a variable input, such as labour, to a given amount of fixed capital, then eventually **diminishing marginal returns** to labour will set in: an extra worker will add less to total output than the previous worker. (Diminishing marginal output and diminishing marginal product are alternative expressions of the same principle.) You should note that the principle of diminishing marginal returns refers to the physical productivity of labour and not to either the money cost of employing labour (the wage) or to the money value of the output which labour produces. The principle of diminishing returns is sometimes known as a 'law', but it must be stressed that when the first units of labour are added to fixed capital increasing marginal returns are likely to be experienced. This is because the employment of an extra worker allows greater **specialisation** and **division of labour** to take place, with the result that total output increases more than proportionately as workers are added to the labour force.

There are two useful ways of illustrating the principle of diminishing returns in a diagram. In Fig. 6, a production possibility curve has been drawn to show how many cars or bicycles a labour force of 100 men can produce if combined with

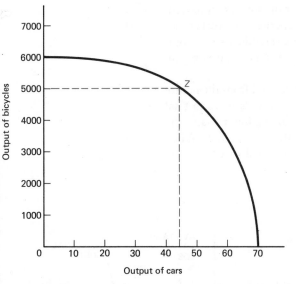

Fig. 6 A production possibility curve

fixed amounts of capital in either the car or the bicycle industry. If all the men are employed in the bicycle industry, the maximum output is 6000 bicycles and no cars. Similarly, 70 cars and no bicycles can be produced if all the men are switched to the car industry. The production possibility curve, drawn between these two extremes, represents all the combinations of bicycles and cars which are possible if some of the men are employed in one industry and some in the other. The point Z on the production possibility curve shows that the total possible output is 5000 bicycles and 45 cars if 50 men are employed in each industry.

Now ask yourself what will happen if workers move out of the car industry into the bicycle industry (or vice versa). Whereas the first 50 workers in the bicycle industry produce a total of 5000 bicycles, the addition of a second 50 workers only increases output by an extra 1000 bicycles. The slope of the production possibility curve, which is concave to origin, is evidence of **diminishing marginal returns** in both industries.

Fig. 7a again illustrates the principle of diminishing returns to labour, but in this example within a single industry. You will notice that the diagram distinguishes between **diminishing marginal returns** to labour and **diminishing average returns** – a source of confusion to many students. The concept of marginal returns refers to the addition to output attributable to the last worker added to the labour force. (Formally, the marginal returns of the n'th worker = total returns of n workers minus total returns of (n−1) workers.) The average return per worker is simply the total output divided by the number of workers employed (total returns/n). The mathematical relationship between any marginal variable and the average to which it is related is:
- if the marginal > the average, the average will rise;
- if the marginal < the average, the average will fall;
- if the marginal = the average, the average will neither rise nor fall.

This is a universal mathematical relationship with a host of economic applications. It is essential for students to understand what it means and to avoid the very common error of misrepresenting the relationship. It does *not* state that an average will rise when a marginal is rising, or that an average will fall when the marginal is falling. Fig. 7a clearly shows that the marginal returns curve begins to fall as soon as the point of diminishing marginal returns is reached. Nevertheless, the average returns curve continues to rise as long as the marginal output of an extra worker is greater than the existing average output – thereby, 'pulling up' the average curve. The point of diminishing average returns is reached only when the output of an extra worker falls below the existing average.

SHORT-RUN COST CURVES

The total cost of producing a particular output is made up of the cost of employing both the variable and the fixed factors of production. This can be expressed as the identity:

$$TC \equiv TVC + TFC$$

Likewise, average total cost can be written as:

$$ATC \equiv AVC + AFC$$

In Fig. 7b, the average variable cost (AVC) curve is illustrated alongside (in Fig. 7a) the average returns curve from which it is derived. Variable costs are the wage costs of employing the variable factor, labour. If all workers are paid the same wage, total wage costs will rise proportionately with the number of workers employed. However, while increasing average returns are being experienced, workers on average are becoming more efficient. It follows that average variable costs per unit of output will fall as output rises, but once diminishing average returns set in, average variable costs will rise with output.

In a very similar way, the marginal cost (MC) curve is derived from the nature of marginal returns to the variable inputs. If an extra worker adds more to total output than the previous worker, yet the wage cost of employing him remains the same, then the MC of producing an extra unit of output must fall. When diminishing marginal returns set in, however, the MC curve will rise.

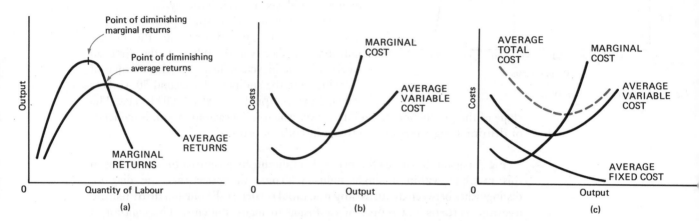

Fig. 7 The derivation of the firm's short-run cost curves (a) diminishing marginal returns and diminishing average returns to labour set in (b) these can be translated into money costs as the marginal cost curve and the average variable cost curve (c) the average total cost curve is obtained by including average fixed costs in the diagram

While the nature of average and marginal returns to the variable factors of production determines the shapes of the AVC and MC curves, a separate, but very simple, explanation is needed for the average fixed cost (AFC) curve. Because total fixed costs do not vary with output in the economic short run, AFC per unit of output will fall as the fixed costs or 'overheads' are spread over larger and larger outputs. A falling AFC curve is drawn in Fig. 7c, which also includes the average total cost curve obtained by adding up the AVC and AFC curves. The short-run ATC curve is typically U-shaped, showing that average total costs first fall and later rise as output is increased. You should note that the MC curve cuts both the AVC and the ATC curves at their lowest points. Check back to the preceding section to make quite sure that you know why this must be so. However, the point where the MC curve cuts the AFC curve is of no significance because the MC curve is derived only from variable costs and not from fixed costs.

THE FIRM'S SHORT-RUN SUPPLY CURVE

We are now in a position to show how the short-run supply curve of a firm in a perfectly competitive industry is derived from its marginal cost curve. (The characteristics of perfect competition as a market form are examined in Chapter 6.) A perfectly competitive firm, being a price-taker, will sell its output at the same market-determined price or average revenue, whatever the output it decides to supply to the market. This means that **total revenue** will always rise by the amount of price or **average revenue** when the firm decides to release an extra unit of output on the market. Now, **marginal revenue** is defined as the addition to total revenue resulting from the sale of an extra unit of output. It follows that marginal revenue equals average revenue for a perfectly competitive firm and is represented by a horizontal price-line such as P_1 in Fig. 8.

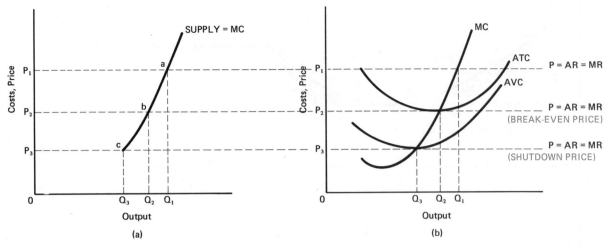

Fig. 8 (a) The derivation of the firm's short-run supply curve from its MC curve (b) only the part of the MC curve above AVC is the firm's supply curve

It can easily be shown that any profit-maximising firm, whatever the market form or structure, will produce the output where MR = MC. (We are now using MR as the economic shorthand for marginal revenue and not marginal returns!)

- If MR > MC, the firm is sacrificing the profit it could make from an extra unit of output. Therefore, it should increase output.
- If MR < MC, the firm is making a loss on at least the final unit of output produced. Therefore, it should decrease output.
- If MR = MC, there is no incentive to increase or decrease output. This is the equilibrium condition for a profit-maximising firm.

Returning to Fig. 8, let us suppose that the market-determined price is P_1. Using the equilibrium condition, the firm will choose to supply Q_1 onto the market, but if the price falls to P_2, supply will be reduced to Q_2. This is the **break-even price**, since the firm will start to make a loss if the price falls below the ATC curve. Nevertheless, if the price falls below P_2 it may still be consistent with profit-maximising behaviour for the firm to continue to supply an output, in the short run at least, even though it is making a loss. As long as the price covers AVC, the size of the loss will be less than the fixed costs the firm will incur if it produced zero output. The **shut-down price** is P_3, at which the firm just covers its variable costs.

Our conclusion is that the firm's MC curve, above AVC, is its short-run supply curve. The curve maps out how much the firm is prepared to supply to the market at each price. We have shown that the MC curve slopes upwards because of diminishing marginal returns to the variable factors of production. It is extremely useful to remember that the slope of the supply curve is derived from the principle of diminishing marginal returns and the assumption of profit-maximising behaviour by firms. You should note the parallel between this analysis and the derivation, in Chapter 2, of the demand curve from the principle of diminishing marginal utility and the assumption of utility-maximising behaviour by households.

SHIFTS IN SUPPLY

In the preceding analysis, the productivity of labour reflected in the principle of diminishing returns, and the wage or money costs of hiring labour determined the position of the firm's MC curve or short-run supply curve. A change in any of the **conditions of supply** will shift the supply curve. If labour becomes more productive, if wage costs fall, or if taxes on the firm are cut, then the supply curve will shift rightwards (or downwards), showing that the firm is prepared to supply more at existing prices.

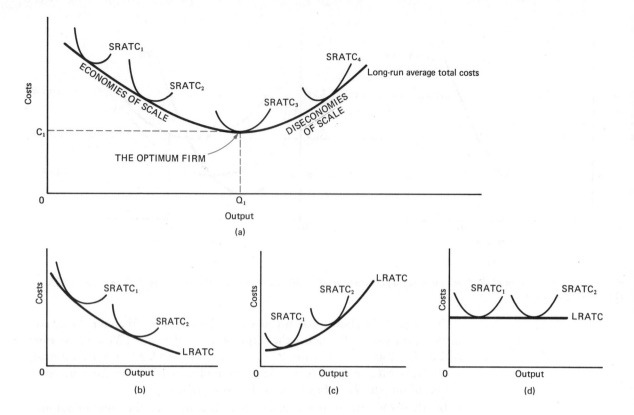

Fig. 9 Long-run average total cost curves (a) economies of scale followed by diseconomies of scale (b) an industry with economies of large scale production (c) an industry with diseconomies of large scale production (d) an industry without economies or diseconomies of scale

LONG-RUN COSTS AND SUPPLY

In the long run, a firm can change the **scale** of the fixed factors of production and move to a new size of productive unit (or a new short-run situation). The long-run average cost curve, which is illustrated in Fig. 9, is a mathematical line drawn as a tangent to a 'family' or set of short-run cost curves, each representing a feasible size of productive unit. A firm can thus move in the long run from one short-run supply curve to another, which is associated with a different scale of fixed capacity. (It is useful to remember that firms can also enter or leave the industry in the long run. This means that the **industry short-run supply curve**, obtained by adding the individual supply curves of each firm, can shift its position in the long run when firms enter or leave the industry.)

The shape of the long-run ATC curve depends upon whether **economies** or **diseconomies of scale** are experienced. Long-run average costs may be falling, rising, or constant. If an increase in all the inputs or factors of production results in falling long-run average total cost, economies of scale exist. Eventually diseconomies of scale may set in when the long-run ATC curve begins to rise. The textbook example of a U-shaped long-run ATC curve is drawn in Fig. 9a. There is no reason, however, why the curve must be U-shaped. An industry, such as the automobile industry, with **economies of large-scale production** is represented in Fig. 9b, while Fig. 9c illustrates **the economies of small-scale production** which might be more typical of agriculture. (Further explanation of industries with economies of large- and small-scale production and a description of the main economies and diseconomies of scale are included in Chapter 10.) Statistical studies have suggested an absence of significant economies and diseconomies of scale in many industries, in which case the correct long-run ATC curve would be the horizontal line in Fig. 9d. If the firm's long-run marginal cost curve is also its long-run supply curve, this would imply a horizontal (or perfectly elastic) long-run supply curve in industries with constant long-run average costs. Firms of many different sizes could coexist without significant differences in costs.

RETURNS TO SCALE

Many textbooks confuse **economies of scale** with the closely related concept of **increasing returns to scale**. Economies of scale refer to long-run money costs of production, whereas long-run returns to scale relate only to the physical output of the factors of production or inputs. If physical output increases more than proportionately as the scale of all the inputs is changed, increasing returns to scale occur. (Decreasing returns to scale and constant returns to scale are other possibilities.) Increasing returns to scale contribute to economies of scale (in the form of technical economies), but some economies of scale are not explained by increasing returns to scale – for example, bulk-buying economies, when a firm uses its market power to buy inputs at low prices.

While it is useful to understand the difference between economies of scale and increasing returns to scale, it is much more important for the student at A level to be absolutely clear about the difference between short-run returns, explained earlier in the chapter, and the long-run returns to scale described in this section. It is the impact of diminishing marginal returns on the costs and profits of a firm in the economic short run that encourages the firm to change the scale of its operations in the long run.

Chapter roundup

In this chapter it has been assumed that a firm exists within a perfectly competitive industry. Further aspects of the supply and output decisions of firms in conditions of perfect competition and monopoly are developed in Chapter 6, while Chapter 7 extends the analysis to imperfect competition. Elasticity of supply is explained in Chapter 4, which is followed in Chapter 5 by a survey of the special problems of agricultural supply.

Illustrative questions and answers

1   Essay Question
    'In the short run, average costs eventually must rise. What happens to average costs in the long run is uncertain.' Discuss.
                                                                (Oxford, June 1990)

Tutorial note

This is a relatively straightforward question testing your understanding of the most significant difference between short-run and long-run costs. Because of the way we define the short run – at least one factor of production being held fixed – the law of diminishing returns affects the way output increases in the short run, causing first marginal costs and then average costs to rise. But in the long run, all factors of production are variable and the law of diminishing returns is no longer relevant. Instead, returns to scale operate in the long run with three possibilities: increasing, constant, or decreasing returns to scale. Increasing returns to scale cause long-run average costs to fall (assuming constant factor prices, i.e. wage rates and the prices of capital goods), whereas long-run average costs are constant with constant returns to scale, and rising with decreasing returns to scale. Hence, whether long-run average costs fall, remain constant or rise is indeed uncertain, since the outcome depends on the nature of the returns to scale experienced by the firm as it expands the scale of its productive capacity.

Suggested answer

- Distinguish between the short run and the long run.
- Explain the law of diminishing returns and how the operation of the law causes short-run average costs to rise. Illustrate on diagrams.
- Explain increasing, constant, and decreasing returns to scale, and how each affects long-run average costs. Illustrate each on a diagram.
- Conclude by agreeing with the assertion in the question.

2 Data Question

A profitable airline is considering the introduction of a new transatlantic flight and is faced with the following costs per flight:

	£
Fuel charges	10 000
Depreciation	700
Insurance	300
Landing charges	500
Interest	500
Labour	5000
Other fixed costs	5000

(a) From the above table distinguish between fixed and variable costs. Give reasons for your choice. (4)

(b) (i) Given a maximum seating capacity of 300 persons per aircraft, what is the minimum price per seat that the airline must charge on this flight to avoid making a loss? (5)
(ii) If the above costs were representative of all flights, what price must the airline charge to remain in business in the long run? (5)

(c) Discuss the factors that are likely to determine the actual price charged. (6)

(ULEAC, January 1987)

Tutorial note

Numerical or statistical data-response questions are of two types: those based on a real-world data source and those containing fictional data. Most of the examination boards only set questions containing real-world data, arguing that the other type is not really a true data-response question and that the skills being tested can be tested just as adequately on the multiple choice paper. Before spending time studying any simulated data questions in this book, check past papers of your own examining board to see what the board's policy is.

This is a deceptively difficult question. Usually with questions of this type, it is possible to calculate a correct answer. However, the answers to questions (b) (i) and (ii) depend upon demand at each price and no data is provided on the matter on demand. To avoid a loss, total revenue per flight must at least equal total costs per flight. Total costs per flight are £22 000 so, providing all 300 seats are sold, the airline must charge £73.34 per passenger. However, it would have to charge a higher price to avoid a loss if less than 300 passengers wished to fly at a price of £73.34. If, at all prices, only one passenger wished to fly, the airline would have to charge £22 000 to avoid a loss! The answer to part (b)(ii) depends upon similar assumptions about demand. We might also add that an amount for 'normal profits' (see Chapter 6) would have to be added to the costs shown in the table for an economist to conclude that it is worthwhile for a firm to stay in business in the long run.

Amongst the factors that you might discuss in your answer to part (c) are: the airline's assumed objectives; the extent to which it is a 'price taker' or 'price maker'; the existence of cartel-style agreements with other airlines; product differentiation and price discrimination; the influence of government regulation or price adminis-tration; and the economics of offering cheap stand-by flights to fill seats when immediately before departure the marginal cost of accepting an extra passenger is very low.

Question bank

1 Explain the distinction between diminishing returns to a variable factor and diseconomies of scale. (60)
With reference to examples, explain how diseconomies of scale might result. (40) (ULEAC, June 1989)

2 Compare and contrast the factors that may determine the supply in (a) the short run, and (b) the long run of (i) tomatoes; (ii) cars; (iii) public transport. (Oxford, June 1991)

3 Carefully explain how diminishing marginal returns and decreasing returns to scale affect a firm's production costs. (AEB, June 1991)

4
(a) Explain the fundamental principles of economics which are conveyed by the notion of a 'production possibility frontier'.
Why are production possibility frontiers typically drawn as curves concave to the origin of the relevant diagram? (10)
(b) Explain how the concept of 'economic efficiency' can be illustrated by a production possibility frontier diagram. (5)
(c) For what reasons can production possibility frontiers shift from one time period to another? (5) (WJEC, June 1992)

5
(a) Why do economists assume that a firm's total cost curve is U-shaped in the short run? (8)
(b) Discuss the various internal economies and diseconomies of scale that a firm may experience, and how these influence the shape of its long-run average cost curve. (10)
(c) Explain what is meant by external economies and diseconomies of scale and why it may be difficult for a firm to estimate their importance when contemplating an expansion of output. (7) (NISEC, June 1991)

6 'In the short run, average costs must eventually rise. What happens to average costs in the long run is uncertain.' Discuss. (Oxford, June 1990)

7
(a) Giving examples, distinguish between fixed costs and variable costs. (8)
(b) Why is it possible for competition between firms to force prices down to ruinous levels in an industry in which production is capital intensive? (17) (Cambridge, June 1990)

8
(a) Explain why and how production on a large scale can lead to greater efficiency in some industries. (18)
(b) How may consumers suffer in a market consisting of a few large firms? (Scottish Higher, June 1990)

9
(a) Describe and explain the behaviour of a firm's average fixed cost and average variable cost as its output increases in the short run. (15)
(b) Explain how a firm may use knowledge of (i) its marginal cost; and (ii) its average variable cost in making decisions about its level of output in the short run. (5 marks each) (Scottish Higher, June 1989)

10

(a) Explain the distinction used in cost theory between the 'short run' and the 'long run'.   (5)

(b) Explain why a given increase in output for a firm might involve increasing marginal and average costs in the short run, but constant marginal and average costs in the long run.   (15)

(c) For what reasons has it been asserted that after some point the long-run average costs of a firm must eventually increase?   (5) (WJEC, June 1992)

ELASTICITY

Units in this chapter

Chapter objectives

Consider the demand curves which are drawn in Fig. 10 and which show the demand for a product such as electronic calculators in two separated markets, the London area market and a market for the rest of the United Kingdom. Demand curve D_2 is quite clearly flatter than D_1. Students are often tempted to use the flatness or steepness of a demand or supply curve to describe its elasticity – the responsiveness of demand or supply to a change in price. However, a careful inspection of Fig. 10 reveals that the slope of the curves is misleading and that flatness or steepness is not a proper indicator of elasticity. In each market a 20% reduction in price from £20 to £16 results in a doubling of the quantity which households intend to buy: despite their different slopes, the demand curves display identical elasticities whenever the price changes. In this example we could calculate the **average elasticity** when the price changes from £20 to £16. Strictly, however, elasticity is a measure of the response of demand to a price change at a **specific point** on a curve, and the concept should not be used to describe quite large changes in price.

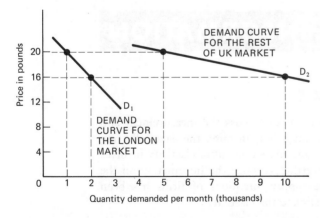

Fig. 10 Demand curves with the same elasticities but different slopes

Whenever one variable responds to another variable, an elasticity can be estimated. Elasticity is an especially useful descriptive statistic of the relationship between any two variables because it is independent of the units, such as quantity and price units, in which the variables are measured. A knowledge of supply and demand elasticities is particularly useful to decision makers both in firms and in government. If we are told, for example, that the demand elasticity of Scotch whisky is 2, then this single statistic contains the information that a 1% price-rise causes a 2% fall in quantity demanded. (Strictly, the elasticity is –2 as the price-rise causes a fall in quantity demanded, but the minus sign is frequently omitted.) The size of the elasticity will indicate the extent to which sales may drop when a tax is imposed upon Scotch whisky: the more elastic the demand (and supply) curves, the greater will be the fall in sales. Since the government's tax-revenue equals the amount of the tax multiplied by the after-tax quantity of sales, the government will experience the least loss in tax-revenue when it imposes a tax on goods with low demand and supply elasticities.

4.1 UNDERLYING CONCEPTS

THE ESTIMATION OF ELASTICITY

Suppose a businessman wishes to estimate how his customers will respond when the price of his product is increased. If he possesses perfect market information, as in perfect competition, there will be no problem: he simply reads off, from a chart or graph displayed on his office wall, the quantities that would be demanded at all possible prices. Unfortunately, many students at A level seem to think that all business decisions are made in this way! Businessmen, however, seldom, if ever, possess perfect information and this means that they cannot be sure how their customers will react to price changes. One method of estimating the elasticity of demand for a good is to collect data on the quantities actually bought at different prices in previous years – but the elasticity statistic which is obtained from such an exercise must be treated with caution. It will have been calculated on **ex post** rather than **ex ante** data: the amount actually bought may not have been the same as the quantity that households had planned or intended to buy. Also, conditions of demand and the general price-level may have changed over the years. To overcome these problems, a businessman could hire a market research team to go into the street with questionnaires, to ask people how much they would buy at various prices.

4.2 ESSENTIAL INFORMATION

ELASTICITY FORMULAE

When an examination question requires you to discuss the measurement and interpretation of elasticity statistics, you must bear in mind the data-collecting problems described in the preceding section: measurement of elasticity involves more than just a textbook formula. Nevertheless, once the information on the planned demand of households or the supply intentions of firms has been collected, a simple formula is used to estimate the elasticity:

- Price elasticity of demand $= \dfrac{\text{Proportionate change in quantity demand}}{\text{Proportionate change in price}}$

- Price elasticity of supply $= \dfrac{\text{Proportionate change in quantity supplied}}{\text{Proportionate change in price}}$

- Income elasticity of demand $= \dfrac{\text{Proportionate change in quantity demanded}}{\text{Proportionate change in income}}$

• Cross-elasticity of demand for Good A with respect to Good B $= \dfrac{\text{Proportionate change in quantity of A demanded}}{\text{Proportionate change in price of B}}$

For example, if the price rises by a third and consumers respond by reducing the quantity demanded by two-thirds, the price elasticity of demand is 2 (strictly –2).

PRICE ELASTICITY OF DEMAND

If a price change results in a more than proportionate change in demand, demand is said to be **elastic**. The elasticity statistic, calculated from the formula, will be greater than 1. Similarly, if the change in demand is less than proportionate, demand is **inelastic**, and the elasticity statistic will be less than 1. It is usually misleading, however, to refer to the whole of a demand curve as elastic or inelastic since the elasticity will generally vary from point to point along the curve.

Before we show how the elasticity varies along the curve, it is useful to introduce an alternative way of describing demand elasticity in terms of price changes:

• If total consumer expenditure **increases** in response to a **price fall**, demand is relatively **elastic**.

• If total consumer expenditure **decreases** in response to a **price fall**, demand is relatively **inelastic**.

• If total consumer expenditure remains **constant** in response to a **price fall elasticity of demand = unity**.

Fig. 11a illustrates some possible changes in consumer expenditure which might follow a reduction in price. When the price falls from P_1 to P_2 in Fig. 11a, total consumer expenditure increases by the shaded area k, but decreases by the area h. The area k, which represents the proportionate increase in the quantity demanded, is clearly larger than area h, which represents the proportionate change in price. Demand is thus elastic at all points on the demand curve between a and b on curve D_1. However, if the price falls from P_3 to P_4 on the same demand curve, the shaded area k' is smaller than the area h'. Total consumer expenditure falls, and demand is inelastic at all points between c and d on the demand curve.

We are now in a position to explain the misleading generalisation that a 'flat' demand curve is elastic and a 'steep' curve is inelastic. Moving along all linear (straight-line) demand curves that slope down from left to right, elasticity of demand falls from point to point along the curve. The 'flat' demand curve illustrated in Fig. 11b is really only the upper part of a curve which, if extended far enough rightwards or downwards, would eventually become inelastic in its lower reaches. Similarly, the 'steep' inelastic demand curve in Fig. 11c is the lower part of a curve which would become elastic in its upper reaches if these could be included in the diagram.

Intuition suggests that if elasticity varies from point to point along a downward-sloping **linear** curve, then we require a **non-linear** curve to show a constant elasticity at all points. The **rectangular hyperbola** illustrated in Fig. 11d is the special case of a non-linear demand curve which shows a **unit elasticity** at all points on the curve.

INFINITE ELASTICITY AND ZERO ELASTICITY

Infinitely elastic (or perfectly elastic) demand or supply can be represented by a horizontal curve, such as those drawn in Fig. 12a. The diagram illustrates a trap awaiting the unwary student. In the case of the perfectly elastic demand curve, consumers demand an infinite amount at a price of P_2 or below; if the price rises above P_2, demand falls to zero as consumers switch to the perfect substitutes which are assumed to be available. In the case of the perfectly elastic supply curve, however, firms are prepared to supply an infinite amount at a price of P_1 or above. If the price falls below P_1, the firms refuse to supply any output onto the market!

Fig. 12b illustrates a completely inelastic supply curve: whatever the price, the same amount is supplied onto the market. Similarly, completely inelastic demand would be shown by a vertical demand curve.

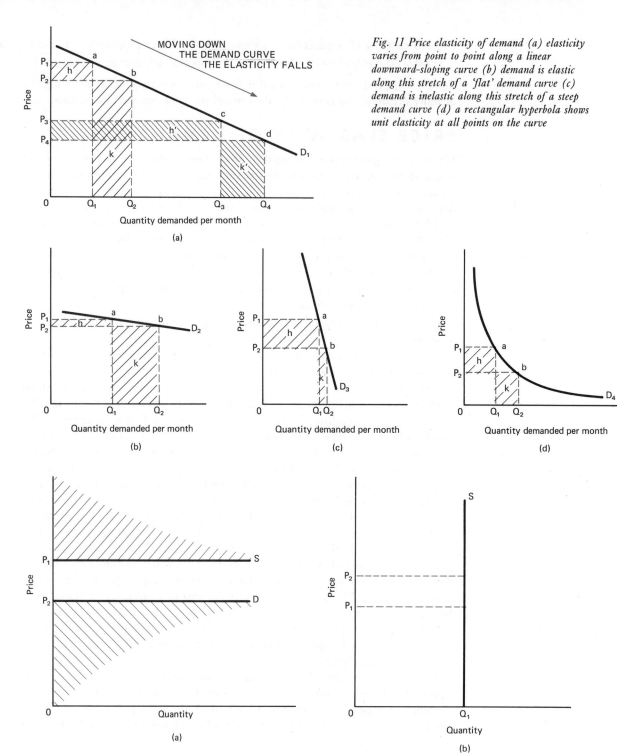

Fig. 11 Price elasticity of demand (a) elasticity varies from point to point along a linear downward-sloping curve (b) demand is elastic along this stretch of a 'flat' demand curve (c) demand is inelastic along this stretch of a steep demand curve (d) a rectangular hyperbola shows unit elasticity at all points on the curve

Fig. 12   (a) Infinitely elastic supply and demand (b) zero elasticity of supply

THE DETERMINANTS OF DEMAND ELASTICITY

- **Substitutability**. When a perfect substitute for a product exists, consumers can respond to a price rise by switching their expenditure to the substitute product. Commodities – for example, British cars – which have close substitutes available tend to be in more elastic demand than those that do not.
- **Percentage of income**. Items on which many people spend a large proportion of their income, such as summer holidays, tend to be in more elastic demand than goods such as matches, on which only a fraction of income is spent.

- **Necessities v luxuries**. Necessities tend to be in inelastic demand, luxuries in elastic demand. Salt is often cited as a commodity with a very inelastic demand: it is a necessity, with no close substitutes, and expenditure on it is only a small part of most households' total spending.
- **The width of the definition**. The wider the definition of a commodity, the lower the elasticity. Thus, the demand for a particular brand of a commodity will be more elastic than the demand for the commodity as a whole. In a similar way, the elasticity of demand for bread will be greater than that for food as a whole.
- **Time**. The longer the time-period involved, the greater the elasticity of demand is likely to be. This is because it takes time to adjust to a change in price. If the price of gas rises, people may be unable to switch immediately to alternative household heating systems because they are 'locked in' to their existing investments in gas-fired appliances. However, the opposite may be true in certain circumstances: some consumers might react to a sudden increase in the price of cigarettes by giving up smoking altogether, and then gradually drift back to their old habits.

PRICE ELASTICITY OF SUPPLY

Supply curves normally slope upwards from left to right, and the mathematical properties of upward-sloping (or positive) curves are different from those of downward-sloping (or negative) curves. The key points to note are:

❶ Any **straight-line (linear) supply curve** drawn from the origin (point O) will display **unit elasticity of supply** at all points along the curve. This is illustrated in Fig. 13a, where a doubling of the price causes an exact doubling of the quantity supplied.

❷ The **'flat' supply curve** drawn in Fig. 13b is **elastic** at all points along the curve, since any price-change would result in a more than proportionate change in supply. But the elasticity falls towards unity, moving from point to point up the curve to the right.

❸ Similarly, the **'steep' curve** in Fig. 13c is **inelastic** at all points, since any price-change results in a less than proportionate change in supply. But in this case the elasticity rises towards unity, moving from point to point up the curve.

❹ However, as in the case of demand curves, the 'flatness' or 'steepness' of a supply curve is a misleading guide to its elasticity. The key point is not the flatness or steepness of the curve, but **whether the supply curve intersects the price axis or the quantity axis.**

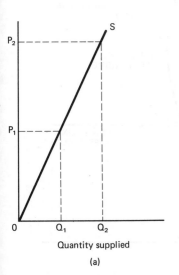

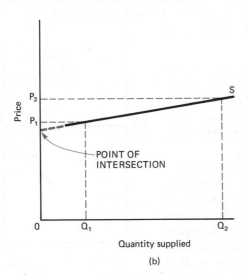

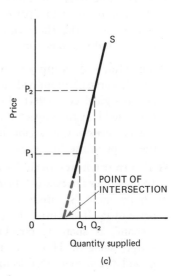

Fig. 13   Price elasticity of supply (a) unit elasticity of supply (b) elastic supply (c) inelastic supply

The rule is:

- If a linear supply curve intersects the **price axis**, the curve is **elastic** at all points.

- If a linear supply curve intersects the **quantity axis**, the curve is **inelastic** at all points.

- If a linear supply curve intersects the **origin**, the elasticity is **unity** at all points along the curve.

In the case of non-linear supply curves, it is possible to use the rule to check the elasticity at a particular point on the supply curve by drawing a **tangent** to the point, and by noting the axis which the tangent intersects. We leave it as an exercise for the reader to do this, and also to draw a 'steep' supply curve intersecting the price axis. You will find that the curve is elastic at all points, showing that a 'steep' curve can be elastic!

THE DETERMINANTS OF SUPPLY ELASTICITY

Suppose the demand for a good such as a car component suddenly doubles at all prices. The factors which may determine whether supply is able to respond include:

- **The number of firms in the industry.** Generally, the greater the number of firms in an industry, the more elastic is the industry supply.

- **The length of the production period.** If production converts inputs into outputs in the space of a few hours, supply will be more elastic than when several months are involved, as in agriculture.

- **The existence of spare capacity.** If spare capacity exists and if variable inputs such as labour and raw materials are available, it should be possible to increase production quickly in the short run.

- **The ease of accumulating stocks.** If it is easy to store unsold stocks at low cost, firms are able to meet a sudden increase in demand by running down stocks. They can respond to a sudden fall in demand and price by taking supply off the market and diverting production into stock-accumulation.

- **The ease of factor substitution.** Many firms produce a range of products and are able to switch machines and labour from one production type to another. If factors of production can be switched in this way, then the supply of one particular product will tend to be elastic.

Fig. 14 The elasticity of the supply curve varies with the time period

- **Time.** The longer the time-period under consideration, the greater the ability of firms to adjust to a price-change. It is useful to distinguish three separate time-periods, the short run, the momentary period, and the long run.

❶ **The short-run supply curve** The short-run supply curve of an individual firm is its short-run marginal cost curve. In Chapter 3 it is explained how the impact of diminishing marginal returns to the variable inputs determines the shape of the MC curve.

❷ **The momentary period supply curve** Fig. 14 illustrates the case of a firm on its short-run supply curve, S_2, producing an output Q_1 at price of P_1. If the price doubles, the firm will respond as soon as possible by increasing supply along S_2. However, in the momentary period the firm is unable to adjust at all. A

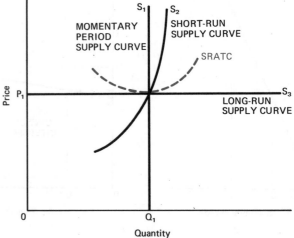

vertical supply curve S_1, drawn through the existing output Q_1, represents the completely inelastic momentary supply curve.

❸ **The long-run supply curve** The perfectly elastic long-run supply curve, S_3, drawn in Fig. 14 represents the special case of a firm in an industry with constant long-run average costs. In the special circumstances of Fig. 14, a firm can increase output beyond Q_1 either by moving in the short run up S_2, or by moving in the long run along S_3 to a new size or scale of fixed capacity. The precise shape of the long-run supply curve will depend upon whether economies or diseconomies of scale are experienced, but in general we may expect long-run supply to be more elastic than short-run supply.

INCOME ELASTICITY OF DEMAND

The income elasticity of demand – which measures how demand responds to a change in income – is always **positive** for a **normal good** and **negative** for an **inferior good**. The quantity demanded of an inferior good falls as income rises. Normal goods are sometimes further subdivided into luxuries or superior goods, for which the income elasticity of demand is greater than unity, and essential or basic goods with an elasticity of less than one. Although the quantity demanded of normal goods always rises as income rises, it rises more than proportionately with income for superior goods (such as dishwashers). Conversely, demand for a basic good such as soap rises at a slower rate than income.

CROSS-ELASTICITY OF DEMAND

This is a statistic which describes the **complementary** or **substitute relationship** between two commodities. A cross-elasticity of demand of –0.1 for bread with respect to the price of butter indicates that a 10% rise in the price of butter is associated with a 1% fall in the demand for bread. In contrast, a cross-elasticity of +0.8 for margarine with respect to the price of butter shows that a 10% rise in the price of butter will result in an 8% increase in the demand for margarine. Whereas the **mathematical sign of a cross-elasticity statistic** depends on the nature of the relationship between the two commodities, the **absolute size of the statistic** indicates the strength of the relationship. Cross-elasticities are negative for complementary goods, and positive for substitutes. A cross-elasticity statistic very close to zero is likely when there is no complementary or close substitute relationship between two goods.

Chapter roundup

There are three important applications of the elasticity concept in public finance, exchange-rate policy, and agriculture. The possible effects of the elasticity of supply and demand on government tax revenue are explained in Chapter 15. Elasticity of demand for exports and imports has an important effect upon exchange-rate policy, which is the subject of Chapter 27. Meanwhile, Chapter 5 develops the theme of how the inelastic supply and demand for agricultural products results in very unstable prices and incomes for primary producers.

Illustrative questions and answers

1   Essay Question
A bus operator understands that the elasticities of demand for coach travel are as follows:
(i)   income elasticity of demand is –0.4;
(ii) price elasticity of demand is –1.2;
(iii) cross elasticity of demand in respect of rail fares is +2.1
The bus operator is unsure whether to continue running a particular service between two towns because it is not currently profitable.

(a) Discuss how the above information might be expected to influence the bus operator in determining whether to continue with the service. (70)

(b) What other factors might also be relevant to this decision? (30)

(ULEAC, June 1992)

Tutorial note

(a) The demand for coach travel is price elastic. This means that the coach operator can increase sales revenue – and possibly move into profit – by reducing prices and attracting more customers. By contrast, sales revenue would fall if prices were raised. The minus sign of the income elasticity tells us that coach travel is an inferior good. This means that if real incomes are rising and people are becoming better-off, demand for bus travel will fall. In these circumstances the coach service is likely to become even less profitable. But if real incomes fall – as in a recession – then demand for coach travel will increase, with the possibility that the service between the two towns can become profitable. Finally the plus sign of the cross-elasticity of demand for coach travel with respect to the price of rail fares indicates that the two methods of travel are substitutes (higher rail fares lead to an increase in the demand for coach travel as people switch to the cheaper method of travel). A cross-elasticity of +2.1 is in fact quite high: it implies that a 10% rise in rail fares relative to coach fares will lead to a 21% increase in coach passengers, i.e. passengers are highly responsive to changes in the relative prices of the different forms of transport. In these circumstances, the coach operator would clearly need to form a view on how rail fares are likely to change relative to the prices he can charge, because this is likely to have a substantial effect on demand, sales revenue and profitability.

(b) There are a large number of possibly relevant factors that you could bring into your answer to this part of the question. You should try to avoid writing a lengthy 'shopping list' of, say, ten or twelve points, without any elaboration or substantiation of any of the factors you list. It is better to introduce just two or three factors and then devote a paragraph to each – bearing in mind that less than a third of the total marks are available for this part of the question. One obvious point to make concerns operating costs. We have already noted that (with demand elastic) sales revenue will rise if the bus operator reduces prices, but will total costs rise faster than revenue? This will have a crucial bearing on profitability. If in the initial situation, the coach always runs two-thirds empty between the two towns, a reduction in fares would probably lead to revenue rising faster than costs as the vacant seats are filled up, at least until the coach is full. But if the service is unprofitable even when the coach is full, fare-cutting is not going to provide a solution. Another factor you could introduce into your answer is the topical issue of regulation and deregulation of bus services. Under the regulated system which existed in the UK until the late 1980s and which still exists in London, bus operators were granted a monopoly. There was no competition and rival companies could not operate the same routes. But in return for protection from competition, bus and coach operators were required to provide loss-making services on routes with relatively few passengers, using revenues from their profitable routes to 'cross-subsidise' the loss-making routes.

With bus deregulation, however, there is no obligation for an operator to continue to provide an unprofitable service. Nevertheless under some circumstances it might be considered worthwhile. It could be a 'feeder' route for the already profitable routes the bus company operates, or the bus company might be trying to force rival operators out of business, hoping the route will become profitable after the competitors have been defeated and forced to withdraw.

2   Data Question
In 1977 a severe frost seriously depleted the annual coffee harvest in Brazil, the world's largest coffee-producing country, and resulted in a decrease in world coffee production of approximately 20%. The repercussions in the coffee market in the USA, the world's largest consuming nation, are shown in the table below:

	1976	1977
Price ($/1b)	2.01	3.20
Quantity (1bs)	12.8	9.4

Prices are in 1976 dollars (i.e. adjusted for general inflation between 1976 and 1977). Quantities are in pounds of coffee per head per year consumed in the USA.

(Source: Begg, Dornbusch and Fisher, *Economics*, British Edition (McGraw Hill).)

(a) Explain why the increase in the price of coffee in the USA in 1977 can plausibly be seen as a consequence of the frost damage to the Brazilian coffee harvest. (6)

(b) Assuming that changes in the incomes and tastes of consumers in the USA can be ignored, what do the data suggest about the price elasticity of demand for coffee in the USA ? (6)

(c) What effect on the incomes of world coffee producers, in 1977, is suggested by the data ? (6)

(d) What means of permanently raising the incomes of world coffee producers is suggested by the 1977 experience ? Why would such means be difficult to implement in practice ? (7)

(WJEC, June 1989)

Tutorial note

(a) The USA is the world's largest coffee-consuming country and the world price of coffee is effectively determined in the US market. Draw a supply and demand diagram to show the US coffee market. Explain how the collapse of the Brazilian coffee harvest caused the world supply curve of coffee to shift leftwards and an adjustment to a new equilibrium (at a higher price and a lower equilibrium quantity) along the world demand curve for coffee.

(b) The data indicate (assuming that income, tastes and other influences upon demand were unchanged) that a 59% price increase caused demand for coffee to fall by 26.5%. Therefore, when calculated with respect to a price fall, the price elasticity of demand for coffee was approximately −0.45 i.e. demand was inelastic.

(c) The data suggest that the income of the world's coffee producers actually increased. When demand is inelastic a price rise causes total consumer expenditure (and hence also total sales revenue received by producers) also to rise. But although the total income of all the world's growers increased, not all producers benefited. Any coffee grower whose crop was completely destroyed by frost would receive no income at all, unless stocks from a previous year could be sold. Incomes increased most for coffee growers in other countries, e.g. in Kenya. Non-Brazilian coffee growers benefited from the price rise without suffering a loss of production since they were not affected by the frosts.

(d) This part of the question relates to the possibility of introducing a support-buying system to stabilise sales revenues or farm incomes. Such schemes, based on the 'buffer stock' principle are explained in detail in Chapter 5, together with a number of problems that result from intervening in the free market, e.g. financing the support-buying operation and making sure that all the participating countries obey the rules.

Question bank

1 The table below shows some estimates of elasticities of demand for apples and oranges using data from the 1989 National Food Survey conducted by the Ministry of Agriculture Fisheries and Food.

Fruit	Elasticity with respect to		
	Price of apples	Price of oranges	Income
APPLES	-0.29	-0.07	+0.32
ORANGES	-0.16	-1.33	+0.14

(a) Explain the meaning of each of the six estimates given in the table; commenting on
   (i) whether demand is elastic or inelastic,
   (ii) whether the goods are normal or inferior, and
   (iii) whether they are complements or substitutes. (12)
(b) Discuss the possible uses of these estimates to producers, sellers and the government. (13)

(NISEAC, June 1991)

2
a) Examine the significance of income elasticity of demand to:
   (i) car telephone producers and (ii) potato farmers. (50)
b) Discuss the cross-elasticity of demand to the Post Office when considering higher postal rates. (50)   (ULEAC, June 1990)

3 Use demand elasticity concepts to analyse the effects on the revenue earned by hotel keepers in the United Kingdom of
a) a rise in real incomes in the United Kingdom (13)
b) a fall in the price of international air travel.

(Cambridge, June 1990)

4
a) Explain why the supply of a commodity tends to increase with a rise in its price. (15)
b) Explain what you understand by price elasticity of supply, and discuss those factors which affect it. (10)

(Scottish Higher, June 1990)

5
a) Explain price elasticity of demand, income elasticity of demand and cross elasticity of demand. (12)
b) If you had the task of promoting a holiday resort with its various attractions how far could these concepts help you? (13)

(Cambridge, June 1992)

AGRICULTURAL PRICES

Units in this chapter

5.1 *Underlying concepts*
5.2 *Essential information*

Chapter objectives

Agriculture is an industry in which there are thousands of producers, few of whom can influence the market price by individual decisions to supply or not to supply. At the same time many agricultural products, for example soft wheat, are relatively uniform or **homogeneous** commodities for which the world price is a ruling market price. In other words, it would seem that agriculture approximates to the economist's abstraction of **perfect competition** as a market form. Yet, if we look more closely, we also see that agriculture is the industry in which governments of a variety of political persuasions have consistently intervened in order to support farm prices and agricultural incomes. In this chapter we examine the causes of fluctuating prices and incomes, and compare some of the ways in which governments can intervene to create greater stability.

5.1 UNDERLYING CONCEPTS

Throughout history, agriculture has experienced two closely related problems.

❶ There has been a **long-run downward trend** in agricultural prices relative to the prices of manufactures and services.

❷ Agricultural prices and incomes have been **unstable from year to year**.

The long-run trend is largely explained by shifts in agricultural supply and demand curves through time, while the short-run instability results from the inelastic nature of agricultural supply and demand, and the effects of good and bad harvests on the position of the short-run supply curve from one year to another.

THE LONG-RUN DOWNWARD TREND IN RELATIVE PRICES

In Fig. 15, the equilibrium price and output of food in an earlier historical period is shown at point E_1. Over time, both the supply and the demand for foodstuffs have increased, but the supply curve has shifted further to the right. Thus the new long-run equilibrium at E_2 represents a larger output at a lower price. The shift in the demand curve for food is explained mainly by an increase in the population and higher incomes. However, food is a necessity with a low income elasticity demand: when real income doubles, food consumption also increases, but by a smaller proportionate amount. Meanwhile, improvements in agricultural technology,

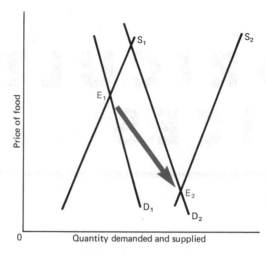

Fig. 15 The long-run fall in agricultural prices

such as the introduction of machinery and fertilisers, have rapidly increased farm yields, thereby causing the much greater long-run shift in supply.

SHORT-RUN CAUSES OF PRICE INSTABILITY

The year-to-year instability in farm prices is caused by **low short-run elasticities of supply and demand** combined with **random fluctuations** in the harvest. Because of the length of the production period between planting and harvesting a crop, it is often appropriate to depict the short-run supply curve as a vertical or completely inelastic line. We are assuming that once the crop is harvested, it will be sold for whatever it will bring. The supply curve S_1, drawn in Fig. 16a, represents supply in a 'normal' year. However, weather conditions and other factors outside the farmers' control will shift the position of the supply curve from year to year. The size of the resulting price fluctuations will depend upon the price elasticity of demand. Demand for foodstuffs in general is inelastic because food is a necessity, so significant fluctuations in price occur as the vertical supply curve shifts up or down the relatively inelastic demand curve.

FLUCTUATIONS IN AGRICULTURAL INCOMES

From a farmer's point of view, fluctuations in his income are more serious than fluctuations in price. If demand is elastic, a fall in price causes a rise in farm income, but when demand is inelastic the opposite is true: income falls when price falls. Following a bad harvest, the supply curve in Fig. 16a shifts to S_3 and agricultural incomes are represented by the rectangle OP_2BQ_2. In the event of a good harvest, the diagram shows that farm incomes decline to the area OP_1AQ_1. Paradoxically, therefore, a farmer may benefit more from a bad harvest than from a good one, when demand is inelastic.

5.2 ESSENTIAL INFORMATION

GOVERNMENT POLICY TO STABILISE PRICE

Suppose a government wishes to stabilise the price of food at the 'normal' year price, P^*. Following a good harvest, the government buys up the amount $Q_1 - Q^*$ to prevent the market price falling below P^* to P_1. If in the next year a bad harvest occurs, the government will supplement supply by releasing food onto the market

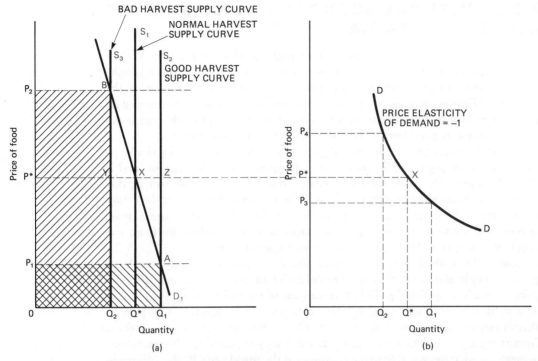

Fig. 16   Short-run price instability of agricultural products (a) without government intervention, both prices and farm incomes fluctuate (b) target prices to stabilise farm incomes

from its stocks; this will prevent the price from rising above P* to P$_2$. Provided that agricultural products can be stored, that the government is prepared to meet the cost of storage, and that good and bad harvests are roughly evenly divided, then the price can be stabilised at P*. If the government wished to make the policy self-financing, it could buy at a lower price and sell at a higher price. Price would now be stabilised within a range, and the costs of storage could be met from the difference between the two **intervention** or **stabilisation** prices, as in the Common Agricultural Policy of the European Common Market (i.e. the European Community).

GOVERNMENT POLICY TO STABILISE AGRICULTURAL INCOMES

The policy described in the previous section is an example of a **buffer stock policy**. Although such a policy may successfully stabilise price, it does not necessarily stabilise agricultural incomes. In the event of a good harvest, farmers' income will be the rectangle OP*ZQ$_1$ if the price is stabilised at P*. Incomes will decline to the area OP*YQ$_2$ following a bad harvest. Farm incomes thus vary directly with the size of production, the exact opposite of the situation in which prices are left free to fluctuate in conditions of inelastic demand.

How then can a government use a buffer stock policy to stabilise incomes rather than prices? The answer is provided by Fig. 16b. The curve DD, with a unit elasticity, is drawn through X, the point which determines farm incomes in a normal year. DD shows the complete range of prices at which the government must operate its buffer stock policy if it is to stabilise incomes. Following a good harvest in which output Q$_1$ comes onto the market, the government must buy at the price P$_3$: farm incomes will then be exactly the same as in the normal year. Symmetrically, the government must release part of its buffer stocks onto the market at the price of P$_4$ in order to stabilise incomes when output falls to Q$_2$ in a bad year.

AGRICULTURAL SUPPORT POLICIES IN THE UNITED KINGDOM

A fundamental change in British agricultural policy took place when the United Kingdom joined the European Community. British farmers are relatively high-cost producers when compared with their counterparts in areas such as the American Midwest, although they are efficient within the constraints imposed by farm size and the British climate. In most agricultural sectors, British farmers are relatively low-cost producers when compared with European farmers.

In Fig. 17, the high British costs of production are represented by the long-run domestic supply curve S_1. On the same diagram, the world price of food is shown by a perfectly elastic supply curve drawn at a lower level of costs P_1; this perfectly elastic supply curve represents an infinite supply of imports at the ruling world price. The diagram implies (perhaps unrealistically) that, without some system of protection or support, British farmers would produce no food: the supply curve S_1 cuts the price axis at a price higher than P_1.

Before the United Kingdom joined the EC, **deficiency payments** or **producer subsidies** were the main form of agricultural support. Essentially, the policy was a 'cheap food' policy, financed out of general taxation: the price of food in Britain was determined by the world price and subsidies were paid to British farmers to keep them in business. This is illustrated in Fig. 17a. British farmers were guaranteed a price of P_2 at which they supplied Q_2. Nevertheless, domestic production was sold to the consumer at the world price P_1, the difference in the two prices being the deficiency payment to the farmers provided by the government. Under this system, the total demand Q_1 was determined at A. Quantity Q_2 was domestically produced and the remainder was imported.

In contrast, the Common Agricultural Policy (CAP) of the EC has dealt with the problem of cheap imports by imposing an **external tariff or levy** which brings the price of imports up to the level of cost, plus normal profits, of European farmers. Suppose the tariff is fixed at P_2 in Fig. 17b. The total amount demanded will be reduced to Q_3 as compared to Q_1 in the deficiency payment scheme. Quantity Q_2 will still be domestically produced and the rest imported.

The external tariff on food imports is only one part of the CAP. As earlier indicated, the Community also operates a buffer stock policy with upper and lower stabilisation prices. The problem has been that for many products the lower of these two intervention prices has been set too high, at a level such as P_3 in Fig. 17b. An excess supply of XY is encouraged and the price can only be sustained if the Community continuously intervenes to purchase the overproduction. This

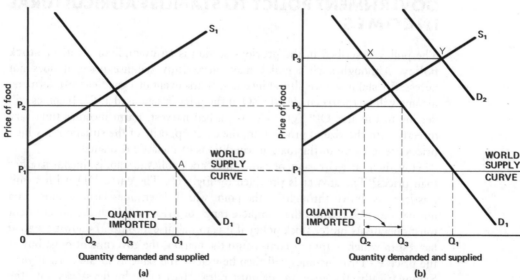

Fig. 17 Farm price support systems (a) a deficiency payment system (b) A buffer stock system plus an external tariff

is represented by the shift in the demand curve to D_2. The effects of bad harvests in causing temporary leftward shifts in the short-run supply curve have been insufficient to reverse the accumulation of the butter 'mountains' and wine 'lakes' which have resulted from the policy.

Recently, the EC has tried to reduce excess production by lowering the prices guaranteed to EC farmers and by paying farmers to take land out of production in a 'set-aside' scheme. For obvious reasons, 'set aside' is much more popular with farmers than lower guaranteed prices; indeed, the strength of the farmers' pressure group has made it extremely difficult for the EC to agree on price reductions.

DYNAMIC CAUSES OF PRICE INSTABILITY

Because of the length of the production period, there may be a supply lag between the decision to produce and the actual supply coming onto the market. We can assume that this year's price has no effect on this year's supply but instead determines next year's supply. Year-long supply lags can be typical of crops such as wheat, though the original cobweb model – described below – was based on the market for hogs in the USA.

Fig. 18 illustrates how the adjustment mechanism from one year to the next may be unstable, being associated with ever-increasing fluctuations in price and output. Suppose that equilibrium is at E where long-run supply and demand intersect. An outbreak of pig disease now disturbs the system and reduces the number of hogs coming onto the market to Q_2. Within the current year, an inelastic short-run supply curve can be depicted by a vertical line drawn through Q_2. A new price P_2, determined at point A on this vertical line, encourages farmers to supply Q_3 onto the market in the next year. A vertical line can be drawn through Q_3 to represent the inelastic short-run supply curve next year. When the supply Q_3 comes onto the market, the price drops to P_3. Price and output then continue to oscillate around the equilibrium in a series of increasing fluctuations. Although in the above example the cobweb model is associated with increasing instability, this is not inevitable. Try drawing a cobweb diagram in which the long-run supply curve is steeper than the long-run demand curve. Following a disturbance, price and output will again fluctuate, but the adjustment mechanism will now be stable, converging towards the long-run equilibrium at E.

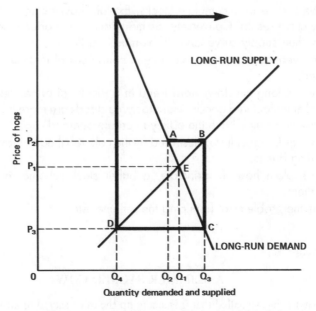

Fig. 18 Dynamic causes of price instability: the cobweb theory

Chapter roundup

In recent years it has become fashionable to talk of 'supply–side economics', which covers government microeconomic policy. This aims to improve the structure of the economy and the performance of industry. Government policy to support agricultural incomes and prices can be considered as a part of this wider microeconomic policy, other aspects of which are developed in Chapter 12 and Chapter 23. Subsidies to the agricultural sector form part of public spending (Chapter 15), whilst external tariffs influence trade (Chapter 25) and the Balance of Payments (Chapter 26).

Illustrative questions and answers

1   Essay Question
(a) Why are primary products prone to fluctuations in price? (50)
(b) What problems arise with schemes that attempt to reduce fluctuations in prices? (50)

(ULEAC, June 1991)

Tutorial note

This question provides a good test of your ability to apply the theoretical analysis explained in this chapter. You will be expected to include the key analysis on how inelastic short-run supply and demand and random fluctuations in supply cause year-to-year fluctuations in agricultural prices and output. You could then go on to explain the long-run downward trend in agricultural prices and, if you have the time, the cobweb theory.

Suggested answer

- Agriculture is dominated by a large number of small producers who are 'price-takers'. In contrast, industrial firms are more likely to be monopolists or 'price-makers', with the market power to stabilise prices if they wish.
- The agricultural production period is usually longer and individual farmers may be unable to accumulate stocks. Explain how an inelastic short-run supply curve results. Conversely, as manufacturers produce more durable goods, their supply curve tends to be more elastic.
- Analyse year-to-year price instability in conditions of inelastic supply and demand.
- Explain the long-run downward trend in agricultural prices relative to the price of manufactured goods. Manufactured goods are more income-elastic and producers may have the ability to create demand.
- Supply lags in agriculture, illustrated by the cobweb theory, may also cause fluctuating prices.
- Briefly explain how, in principle, a buffer stock scheme reduces price fluctuations.
- Outline the problems of financing the scheme, etc.

2   Data Question

A SLIMMER SACRED COW

Brussels has signalled that it is sizing up the most sacred of all European Community (EC) cows, the Common Agricultural Policy (CAP) farm subsidies regime, not to slaughter it, certainly, but to slim it down substantially.

Mr Ray MacSharry, the EC's Agriculture Commissioner, is calling for severe cuts in Community subsidies to farmers and smaller production quotas to stop them producing far more than the EC consumes.

He foresaw EC farm spending rising this year by about 7 billion European Currency Units (ECUs), or 25%, to over 32 billion ECUs, nearly 60% of the Community budget. In 1992 it would rise further by 12.5%. By the end of this month, EC-held beef stocks will have increased to 930 000 tonnes, comfortably over 1987's high of 800 000 tonnes: butter, skimmed milk and cereals are on the same mountain path.

It is the growing cost of a system which concentrates upon price support and rewards ever-greater output whatever the market demands, which is at the root of the reform drive.

The intervention price for cereals would drop from ECU 169 to ECU 90 a tonne, a 47% cut. The subsidised price for beef would fall by 15 per cent and for milk by 10%, with the milk quota for the EC as a whole being cut by 5%.

The CAP, beyond its post-war aim of food self-sufficiency – long since achieved – was always part of social policy to help smaller farmers stay in business. It merely operated in an anti-social way: 60% of cereals output is produced by 6% of cereals farmers, who take 60% of the subsidy even though they are highly competitive. In milk and beef the same sort of ratios occur.

(Source: *Financial Times,* January 24 1991 (adapted))

Answer **each** of the following questions, explaining your reasoning in **each** case.
(a) Explain the basic purposes of the Common Agricultural Policy (CAP).   (6)
(b) Explain why the Common Agricultural Policy (CAP) led to the EC holding ever-larger stocks of beef, butter and other agricultural products?   (6)
(c) Why might Common Agricultural Policy (CAP) subsidies be regarded as an inefficient use of European Community (EC) revenues?   (6)
(d) What are the likely effects of reducing the intervention prices and production quotas?   (7)

(WJEC, June 1992)

Tutorial note

(a) As we have explained in this chapter, agricultural prices are much more unstable from year to year than the prices of most manufactured goods, unless they are supported by some form of administration or regulation. The Common Agricultural Policy (CAP) came into being as a result of the decision to include agriculture in the common market established under the 1957 Treaty of Rome which created the European Community. The CAP's aims are to modernise agriculture, to ensure supplies to the consumer and to give an adequate return to the farmer.

(b) Beef, butter and grain 'mountains' and wine 'lakes' have accumulated because the guaranteed prices offered to farmers for supported products under the CAP were set too high. In effect, high CAP prices guaranteed farmers risk-free 'super-normal' profits. Under these circumstances, as Chapter 6 explains, the 'super-normal' profits created an incentive for farmers who were already producing the supported crops and meats to increase output, and for other farmers to switch their land into agricultural activities supported by the CAP guaranteed pricing system. And once the CAP prices were set, the political power of EC farmers has usually been sufficient to prevent any significant reduction in their levels.

(c) An economic policy can be regarded as efficient if it achieves its desired objective with minimum undesired side-effects or distortions. But as the passage indicates, the CAP's aims of self-sufficiency and an adequate return for farmers could be achieved with a lower level of subsidy. This in turn means that the EC funds 'wasted' on unnecessary farm subsidies could be better spent elsewhere. Large farmers or 'agribusiness' interests enjoy most of the subsidies, even though they were intended to help the small farmers. Finally, butter and grain 'mountains' that become unfit for human consumption and have to be destroyed, themselves represent a grossly inefficient use of resources in a world in which most of the planet's population is underfed.

(d) EC revenues might be put to alternative (and possibly better) use; contributions to the EC budget from member states might be reduced; farmers might be forced in a more competitive environment to adapt, diversify and reduce costs; rural living standards would probably fall; 'marginal' farmers would be likely to go out of business; land would be diverted into non-agricultural uses, e.g. leisure activities such as golf courses; overproduction would be reduced or eliminated; food prices might fall for the consumer. Three or four of these points explained in a little depth would be sufficient to earn the 7 available marks.

Question bank

1   Explain why the prices of primary products such as agricultural produce, raw materials and energy are often unstable.   (AEB, November 1992)

2   With reference to diagrams, show the effects of
(a) a guaranteed price to wheat farmers and
(b) the imposition of maximum price control on milk. Explain the likely outcomes of these two forms of government intervention.   (ULEAC, January 1991)

3
(a) Why do manufactured goods typically exhibit greater price stability than is the case with agricultural commodities?   (50)
(b) What problems arise with attempts to stabilise the prices of agricultural commodities?   (ULEAC, January 1992)

4
(a) Why do the world prices of agricultural goods fluctuate more than those of manufactured goods?   (10)
(b) What measures might the producers of agricultural goods take to stabilise prices and what problems are they likely to encounter in doing so?   (10)
                                                          (AEB, AS-Level, June 1991)

5   With reference to diagrams, show the effects of
(a) a guaranteed price to wheat farmers and
(b) the imposition of maximum price control on milk. Explain the likely outcomes of these two forms of government intervention.   (ULEAC, January 1991)

6
(a) Explain why the European Community needs a policy for agriculture.   (10)
(b) Discuss the economic reasons why reform of the Common Agricultural Policy (CAP) has been advocated.   (10)
                                                          (O&C SEB, AS-Level, June 1992)

PERFECT COMPETITION AND MONOPOLY

Units in this chapter

6.1   *Underlying concepts*
6.2   *Essential information*

Chapter objectives

Perfect competition and **monopoly** are examples of **market structures** or **market forms**. They are opposite or polar extremes which separate a spectrum of market structures known as **imperfect competition**. Fig. 19 illustrates the main types of market structure, including **monopolistic competition** and **oligopoly** which we shall examine in Chapter 7. Monopoly itself can be considered to be the most extreme form of imperfect competition, since there is no competition at all within an industry if a single firm produces the whole of an industry output. Nevertheless, monopoly is usually a relative rather than an absolute concept. This is because a firm will almost always experience some competition from substitute products produced by firms in other industries, even when it has an absolute monopoly in the production of a particular good or service.

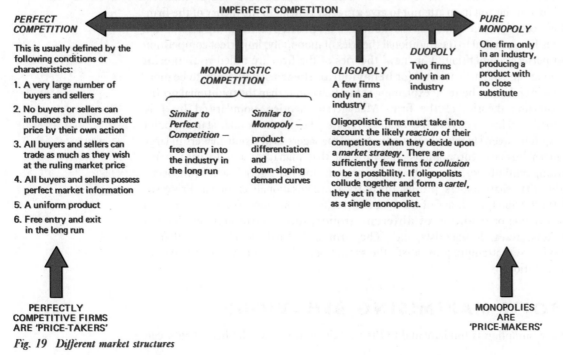

IMPERFECT COMPETITION

PERFECT COMPETITION

This is usually defined by the following conditions or characteristics:

1. A very large number of buyers and sellers

2. No buyers or sellers can influence the ruling market price by their own action

3. All buyers and sellers can trade as much as they wish at the ruling market price

4. All buyers and sellers possess perfect market information

5. A uniform product

6. Free entry and exit in the long run

MONOPOLISTIC COMPETITION

Similar to Perfect Competition —

free entry into the industry in the long run

Similar to Monopoly —

product differentiation and down-sloping demand curves

OLIGOPOLY

A few firms only in an industry

Oligopolistic firms must take into account the likely *reaction* of their competitors when they decide upon a *market strategy*. There are sufficiently few firms for *collusion* to be a possibility. If oligopolists collude together and form a *cartel*, they act in the market as a single monopolist.

DUOPOLY

Two firms only in an industry

PURE MONOPOLY

One firm only in an industry, producing a product with no close substitute

PERFECTLY COMPETITIVE FIRMS ARE 'PRICE-TAKERS'

MONOPOLIES ARE 'PRICE-MAKERS'

Fig. 19 Different market structures

Although the analysis in this chapter is restricted to perfect competition and pure monopoly, you must avoid the temptation to consider either of these two market structures as typical or representative of the real world. **Pure monopoly** is exceedingly rare; the **public monopolies** or **nationalised industries**, such as the Post Office, provide perhaps the best examples. Perfect competition is actually non-existent – it is a **theoretical abstraction** or **model**, defined by the conditions which are listed in Fig. 19. Some economists argue that the emphasis given to perfect competition encourages students to adopt a false perspective in the belief that a perfect market is an attainable 'ideal'. This view will be explored in rather greater depth in Chapter 9.

6.1 UNDERLYING CONCEPTS

THE TRADITIONAL THEORY OF THE FIRM

For many years the theory of the firm was principally concerned with the nature of perfectly competitive markets. The development of this theory owes much to the great nineteenth-century British economist, Alfred Marshall. During Marshall's lifetime the British economy was still dominated by a large number of small firms, for many of which a single owner/decision-maker, or entrepreneur, could be identified. Thus, perfect competition may have been a reasonable approximation to what the economy was like in the late nineteenth century.

ALTERNATIVE THEORIES OF THE FIRM

During the first half of the twentieth century, many economists became dissatisfied with perfect competition as *the* theory of the firm. Their dissatisfaction was a response to the growth in the size of firms and the increasing domination of markets by a small number of large business enterprises. Theoretical models of monopoly and imperfect competition were developed by Edward Chamberlin and Joan Robinson in an attempt to give a greater realism to the theory of the firm. More recently, some economists have attacked the **profit-maximising** assumption that is fundamental to the traditional theories of monopoly, imperfect competition and perfect competition. The 'new' theories of the firm are called **managerial theories** and **organisational (or behavioural) theories**: both claim to be more realistic and hence better at explaining actual behaviour than the traditional profit-maximising theories of the firm. Managerial theories, popularised by J K Galbraith in his book *The New Industrial State* (1967), take as their starting point the split between shareholders as owners and managers as decision-makers in large modern business corporations. It is argued that managers aim to **maximise managerial objectives**, such as sales, growth, and managerial career prospects, rather than shareholders' profits. In contrast, organisationalists such as Professor Herbert Simon, a winner of the Nobel Prize for Economics, see the firm as an organisation or **coalition of different groups**, such as managers, production workers, research scientists, etc. The firm is a **'satisficer'** rather than a **maximiser**, attempting to satisfy the aspirations of the groups which make up the coalition.

PROFIT-MAXIMISING BEHAVIOUR

This assumption is fundamental to the traditional theory of the firm. Profit can be represented by a simple identity:

$$\text{Total Profits} \equiv \text{Total Revenue} - \text{Total Cost}.$$

The firm aims to produce the level of output at which TR–TC is maximised. This is one way of stating the **equilibrium condition of the firm**, for if profits are being maximised, there is no reason or incentive for the firm to change its level of output. Nevertheless, it is usually more convenient for analytical purposes to state the equilibrium condition in alternative form:

$$MC = MR$$

This means that profits are maximised when the addition to total costs that results from the production of the last unit of output (**marginal cost**) is exactly equal to the addition to total revenue resulting from the sale of the last unit (**marginal revenue**). Imagine, for example, a horticulturalist who is unable to influence the price of lettuces in the local market, in which case average revenue equals marginal revenue. Suppose the price of lettuces is 30p each, and that when the horticulturalist markets 98 lettuces each day, the cost to him of producing and marketing the 98th lettuce is 29p. If he decides not to market the lettuce he will clearly sacrifice lp of profits. Let us now suppose that his total costs rise by 30p and 31p respectively when a 99th lettuce and 100th lettuce are marketed. The marketing of the 100th lettuce causes total profits to fall by lp, but the 99th lettuce neither adds to nor subtracts from total profits: it represents the level of output at which profits are exactly maximised. To sum up:

❶ If MC < MR, it pays to increase output (disequilibrium condition)

❷ If MC > MR, it pays to decrease output (disequilibrium condition)

❸ If MC = MR, it pays to keep output unchanged (equilibrium condition) provided that the MC curve cuts the MR curve from below.

THE CONCEPT OF NORMAL PROFIT

The concepts of **normal** and **abnormal** (or **supernormal**) profit are completely abstract concepts, which have nothing to do with how an accountant will measure a company's profits. **Normal profit** is defined as the minimum level of profit required to keep existing firms in production, yet being insufficient to attract new firms into the industry. As such, normal profit is regarded as a necessary cost of production, which is included in the average cost curve. **Abnormal profit** is defined as any extra profit over and above normal profit. We shall now examine what happens to abnormal profits in conditions of perfect competition and monopoly.

6.2 ESSENTIAL INFORMATION

SHORT-RUN EQUILIBRIUM IN CONDITIONS OF PERFECT COMPETITION

Perfect competition can be defined in terms of the conditions of perfect competition, which are listed in Fig. 19. While you must learn the conditions of perfect competition, it is seldom relevant to an examination question merely to repeat the list. Instead, you must learn to use the conditions to analyse the essential properties of a perfectly competitive firm and industry in equilibrium, compared with those of a monopoly in equilibrium. For example, the assumptions that a perfectly competitive firm can sell as much as it wishes at the ruling market price, and that it cannot influence the ruling market price by its own actions, allow us to say that the firm is a **price-taker**. The perfectly competitive firm faces an infinitely elastic demand curve, determined by the ruling market price in the industry as a whole. This **horizontal demand curve** or **price line** is also the perfectly competitive firm's **average revenue** and **marginal revenue curve**.

To show the equilibrium output of a perfectly competitive firm in the short run, we superimpose this horizontal average and marginal revenue curve upon the average and marginal cost curves which were derived in Chapter 3. Using the equilibrium condition MC = MR, the resulting equilibrium output is illustrated at Q_1 in Fig. 20a. Total abnormal profits at this output are represented by the shaded area obtained by subtracting the total cost area (OC_1xQ_1) from the total revenue area (OP_1yQ_1).

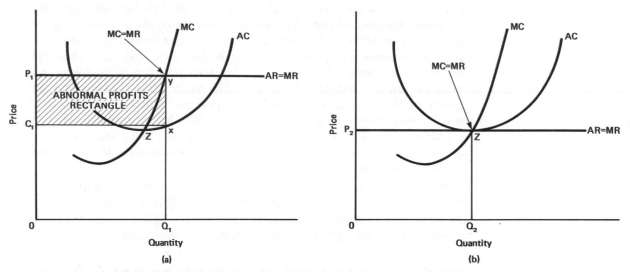

Fig. 20 *Perfect competition equilibrium (a) short-run equilibrium (b) long-run equilibrium*

LONG-RUN EQUILIBRIUM IN CONDITIONS OF PERFECT COMPETITION

In order to distinguish between **short-run** and **long-run equilibrium** in perfect competition, we assume complete freedom of entry and exit by firms in and out of the industry in the economic long run. The market price signals to firms whether abnormal profits, normal profits or losses can be made. The existence of abnormal profits will provide the incentive for new firms to enter the industry, and, in a similar way, existing losses will create the incentive for firms to leave. As illustrated in Fig. 21, the entry of new firms causes the industry supply curve to shift rightwards and the ruling market price falls. Symmetrically, the departure

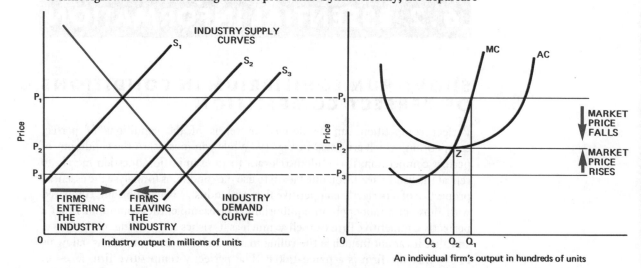

Fig. 21 *Perfect competition long-run equilibrium: the entry and exit of firms produces a long-run equilibrium for an individual firm output Q_2 and price P_2*

of firms causes the industry supply curve to shift leftwards and the price line rises. Long-run equilibrium will occur when there is no incentive for firms to enter or leave the industry: this is represented by the output Q_2 at the price of P_2 in Fig. 21 and 20b. The total revenue area now equals the total cost area, illustrating the fact that abnormal profits have been competed away. It must be stressed at all times that it is **impersonal market forces and individual self-interest,** operating in conditions of freedom of entry and exit, which bring about this long-run equilibrium outcome.

THE CAUSES OF MONOPOLY

An effective monopoly must be able to exclude competitors from the market through barriers to entry. However, the closer the substitutes that competitors can produce, and the more elastic the demand curve facing the firm, the weaker the monopoly position. A monopoly is strongest when it produces an essential good for which there are no substitutes. Monopoly is likely to exist under the following circumstances:

- **Economies of scale** Many industries, for example the aircraft-building industry, are 'decreasing cost' industries with scope for perhaps unlimited economies of scale. In most circumstances, however, the market size will limit the number of firms that can exist in an industry and simultaneously benefit from full economies of scale. Where there is room in the market for only one firm benefiting from full economies of scale, the industry is known as a **natural monopoly.** The existence of economies of scale is a major cause of the growth of large firms and monopoly in manufacturing industry. It may also explain how a large supermarket can monopolise the grocery trade in the limited market of a small town or suburb as a result of driving small grocery stores out of the business.

- **Public utility industries are a special type of 'natural monopoly'** Utility industries such as the electricity, gas, water and telephone industries experience a particular marketing problem. They produce a service which is delivered through a distribution grid or network of pipes or cables into millions of separate homes and businesses. Competition can often be wasteful since it requires the duplication of expensive distribution grids. Given the likelihood of monopoly in these industries, a public policy choice exists between the option of **private monopoly subject to public regulation** and the **public ownership of monopoly,** usually as a **nationalised industry.**

- **Other government-created monopolies** Not all nationalised industries have been either utility industries or monopolies. Nevertheless, industries such as the coal and rail industries were nationalised in order to create state-owned monopolies. The rather complex reasons for such nationalisations are explored in Chapter 14 on nationalised industries. In other instances, the government may deliberately create a private monopoly, for example by granting a **franchise** to a TV company which operates without competition within a particular geographical area. As another example, the **patent law** creates an exclusive right for an inventor to exploit his invention for a number of years.

- **Control of raw materials and market outlets** Firms may try to establish exclusive control over the source of raw materials for their products in order to deny access to competitors. In a rather similar way, British breweries have been known to buy up public houses in order to establish exclusive market outlets for the beer they produce.

- **Advertising as a barrier to entry** It is sometimes argued that small firms are prevented from entering an industry because they cannot afford the minimum level of advertising which is necessary to persuade retailers to stock the goods they produce. Their products are 'crowded out' of the market by the mass advertising, brand-imaging, and other marketing strategies of much larger established firms.

MONOPOLY EQUILIBRIUM

Despite the likelihood of economies of scale in conditions of monopoly, for the time being we shall assume that we are investigating an industry with no economies or diseconomies of scale. It follows from this assumption that the lowest long-run average costs which a firm can achieve will be the same in conditions of perfect competition and monopoly. Nevertheless, the revenue curves will be different in the two market forms. Since the monopoly is the industry, the **monopolist's demand curve** and the **industry demand curve** are identical. There are two

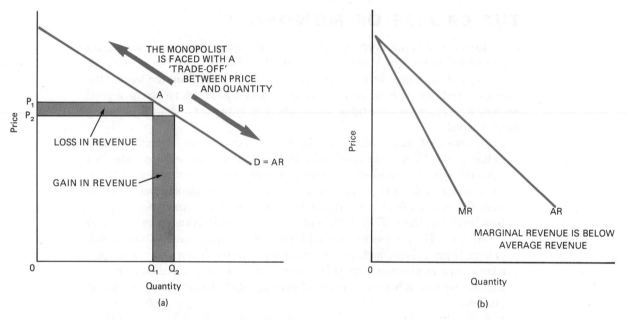

Fig. 22 *The relationship between average revenue and marginal revenue in monopoly.*
(a) MR equals the gain in revenue minus the loss in revenue (b) the MR curve is always below the AR curve

ways of looking at this. If we regard the monopolist as a price-maker, then when he sets the price he must be a **quantity-taker**. Alternatively, if the monopolist acts as a quantity-setter, the demand curve determines the maximum price the monopolist can charge in order successfully to sell the chosen quantity. This is an example of a **trade-off**, an important economic concept which is closely related to opportunity cost. A problem of choice exists because the monopolist does not possess the freedom to set both price and quantity: if he acts as a price-maker, the demand curve determines the maximum output he can sell and vice versa.

Since the **demand curve** shows the price the monopolist charges for each level of output, it is also the monopolist's **average revenue curve**. The demand curve is not the marginal revenue curve, which must be below the average revenue curve. We can use Fig. 22 to explore the relationship between the AR and MR curves in conditions of monopoly. If the monopolist decides to produce output Q_1 in Fig. 22a, the area OQ_1AP_1 will represent total revenue. When output is increased by one unit to Q_2, total revenue changes to the area OQ_2BP_2. Two shaded areas are drawn on the diagram. The area marked as the 'gain in revenue' represents the extra unit sold multiplied by the new price – or the average revenue per unit at the new level of output. The other shaded area shows the 'loss in revenue' which results from the fact that all the units of output comprising the previous level of output Q_1, must now be sold at the price of P_2 rather than P_1. The marginal revenue associated with Q_2 is obtained by subtracting the loss in revenue from the gain in revenue (or average revenue). The resulting MR curve which is drawn in Fig. 22b is twice as steep as the AR curve. This will always be the case provided that the monopolist's demand or AR curve is linear (a straight line), though this mathematical property will not apply if the AR curve is non-linear.

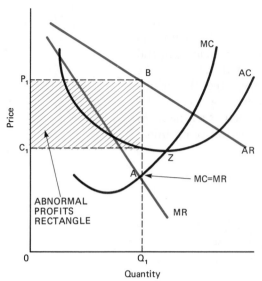

Fig. 23 Monopoly equlilibrium

The equilibrium output in conditions of monopoly is illustrated in Fig. 23. Equilibrium is determined at point A, where MC = MR. It is worth repeating that the equilibrium condition MC = MR applies to any firm, whatever the market structure, as long as the firm is a profit-maximiser. You must avoid the temptation to read off the equilibrium price at point A: point B on the AR curve locates the monopolist's equilibrium price.

As in the case of short-run equilibrium under perfect competition, the monopolist makes abnormal profits, represented by the shaded area of Fig. 23. However, the existence of barriers to entry allows the abnormal profits to persist into the long run, whereas in perfect competition abnormal profits are essentially temporary.

THE MEANING OF ECONOMIC EFFICIENCY

Before we attempt a comparison of the desirable or undesirable properties of perfect competition and monopoly, it is necessary to explain some of the meanings which economists attach to the word **efficiency**:

- **Productive efficiency** This is often called technical efficiency, although in fact the two concepts are slightly different. Production is technically efficient when output is maximised from a given set of inputs (or when the inputs needed to produce a given level of output are minimised). To achieve productive efficiency, or cost efficiency, a firm must use the techniques which are available at the lowest possible cost. Productive efficiency is measured by the lowest point on a firm's average cost curve.

- **Allocative efficiency** This rather abstract concept is of crucial importance to the understanding of economic efficiency. Allocative efficiency occurs when marginal cost is equated to price in all the industries in the economy. If all industries are perfectly competitive and if equilibrium prices prevail, allocative efficiency will automatically occur (provided that we ignore the existence of externalities discussed in Chapter 8). If you check back to Figs. 20 and 21, you will see that P = MC in conditions of perfect competition. Let us look more closely at this. The price, P, indicates the value in consumption placed by buyers on an extra unit of output. At the same time, MC measures the value in production of the resources needed to produce the extra unit of output. Suppose P > MC, as is the case in monopoly: households will pay for an extra unit an amount greater than the cost of producing it. At this price the good will be **underconsumed**. If in contrast P < MC, the value (P) placed on the last unit of the good by consumers will be less than the cost (MC) of the resources used to produce the extra unit. At this price the good will be **overconsumed**.

  Whenever P > MC or P < MC, allocative inefficiency will occur. For any given employment of resources, total consumer utility or welfare can be increased if resources are shifted out of industries where P < MC and into those where P > MC, until a state of allocative efficiency (P = MC) exists in all industries.

EVALUATING PERFECT COMPETITION AND MONOPOLY

If you refer back to Figs. 20b and 21, you will see that a perfectly competitive firm achieves both **productive** and **allocative efficiency** in long-run equilibrium. (The productively efficient output is the lowest cost output, shown at point Z in Figs. 22 and 23 – it is often called the **optimum output** of the firm.) Strictly

75

speaking, however, the firm will be allocatively efficient only if all other industries are perfectly competitive and if there are no externalities present. In contrast, in conditions of monopoly, average cost is above the minimum possible level, and price is not equated to marginal cost. In Fig. 24, the analysis is extended to compare monopoly with the whole of a perfectly competitive industry, rather than with a single firm within the industry. The curve S_1 represents the supply curve of a perfectly competitive industry or the MC curve of a monopoly if all the firms aggregate together to form a monopoly. In conditions of perfect competition,

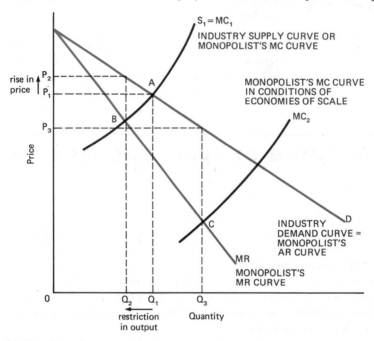

Fig. 24 The effects of economies of scale on price and output in monopoly

industry price P_1 and output Q_1 are located at point A. In contrast, monopoly price P_2 and output Q_2 are determined at point B where MR = MC. The diagram neatly illustrates the standard case against monopoly: that it restricts output and raises the price. Furthermore, this restriction of output is at a point above minimum average cost, resulting in productive inefficiency.

Consider, however, the possibility that a monopoly, but not a perfectly competitive firm, can benefit from **economies of scale**. The curve MC_1 is no longer relevant to the analysis of monopoly price and output, which is now determined at point C. The monopoly price P_3 is now lower and output Q_3 is higher than those achieved in perfect competition. It is possible that the benefits which result from economies of scale may exceed the productive and allocative efficiency losses which occur in monopoly. In these circumstances, monopoly may be viewed as being preferable to perfect competition.

Chapter roundup

Various other aspects of the behaviour or conduct of monopolies, such as price discrimination towards different groups of customers, are examined in Chapter 7. Because the market price conveys misleading information in conditions of monopoly, the existence of monopoly provides a very important form of market failure, the subject of Chapter 8. Some descriptive aspects of the growth of monopoly are introduced in the context of the size and growth of firms (Chapter 10), while Chapter 12 examines government policy towards monopoly and some possible justifications for the existence of monopoly, additional to the economies of scale argument introduced in this chapter.

Illustrative questions and answers

1 Essay Question
   What is an economic model? Describe briefly the model of perfect competition and discuss whether it is realistic and useful.

                                                                    (AEB, June 1988)

Tutorial note

Model building is a technique used by economists firstly to understand the working of the economy and secondly to predict what might happen. Models are small-scale replica of real world phenomena. An economic model, however, is better thought of as a simplification of the real world in which the essential features of an economic problem are explained using diagrams, words, or even algebra. The basic model we have described in earlier chapters is the 'supply and demand model' of a single market within the wider model of a market economy. Within the 'supply and demand model', we construct 'sub-models' both of consumer behaviour to explain demand curves, and of firms' behaviour to explain the nature of supply.

This is where the model of perfect competition fits in. Briefly describe the assumptions of the model, i.e. the conditions of perfect competition, together with the profit maximisation assumption common to all 'traditional' theories of the firm. The model predicts that, in the long run, the 'invisible hand' of market forces 'competes' away abnormal profits and brings about an outcome that is efficient (subject to possible qualification) both productively and allocatively.

You can then argue that the model is unrealistic, but that many economists regard it as useful both as a benchmark against which the competitiveness and efficiency of real-world firms and markets can be measured and as an 'ideal' towards which to try to shift the economy.

Suggested answer

- Explain the meaning of an economic model as a simplification of the real world.
- Give examples of economic models other than the model of perfect competition.
- Explain the assumptions of perfect competition.
- Describe the predictions of the model.
- Argue that the assumptions of the model are unrealistic.
- Explain how many economists nevertheless regard the model as useful.

2 Data Question

   An important part of the case for big business rests on the claim that across a wide range of industries, modern technology requires plants of a very large absolute size and this means that they can supply a relatively large fraction of the domestic market. Anything less would mean that unit
5 production costs are higher than they need to be and are therefore certainly above those of foreign competitors.

   But an efficient allocation of a given set of resources is one which yields both a maximum and 'correct' (in the sense of best meeting consumers' demands) output. The central result from monopoly theory is that resource
10 allocation will be distorted by the ability of monopolists to restrict output below a level that would best accord with consumer demand (that is, price would be greater than marginal cost). Hence, from a given bundle of resources, economic welfare is likely to be lower in the presence of monopoly. To the extent, therefore, that large size is correlated with

15 monopoly (itself a subject of some dispute) allocative inefficiency will result.

However, this may still strike an uncommitted bystander as not getting · to the heart of the matter. Increasingly high on the list of problems associated with very large firms is their alleged effect on the environment.

20 What is the point of these firms ensuring, for example, that they are both technically and economically efficient in a private sense if, in their achievement, the are simultaneously generating very high social costs which do not enter their accounts but which nevertheless impose enormous burdens on the community?

(Source: Michael Utton, *The Political Economy of Big Business*, Blackwell)

(a) Explain in your own words the economic argument lying behind the first paragraph.   (5)
(b) Why, under monopoly, is price normally greater than marginal cost?   (6)
(c) Why might the correlation of a large size with monopoly be 'a subject of some dispute' (line 15)?   (7)
(d) Discuss the implications for the community of large firms 'generating very high social costs which do not enter their accounts' (line 22–23)   (7)

(Oxford, June 1988)

Tutorial note

(a) There are two rather difficult skills you must learn in order to answer data-response questions which are based on passages from newspapers, journals or extracts from books. These are the skills of 'putting things into your own words' and legitimately quoting from the passage without resorting to a word-for-word copying of everything that is on the printed page before you. These skills do not come easily; the best advice we can give you is to have a go at questions like this and gain plenty of practice! With this question you might write: 'Many industries exhibit substantial economies of scale. To produce output at a low average cost, large factories or plants are required, each of which can produce a significant proportion of the total industry market. Smaller factories would incur higher average costs and would not be competitive in world markets.'

(b) Be careful with this question! Students are often tempted to say that the explanation relates to monopoly profits (or super-normal profits), but if you look at Fig. 26, you will see that price can be greater than marginal cost even when no super-normal profits are being made. The correct explanation relates to monopoly profits (or super-normal profits), but if you look at Fig. 26, you will see that price can be greater than marginal cost even when no super-normal profits are being made. The correct explanation lies in the fact that in all imperfectly competitive markets (including monopoly), firms face downward-sloping demand or AR curves. As we have explained in this chapter, the AR curve lies above the MR curve whenever the AR curve slopes downward. We know that for profit maximisation, MR = MC; hence in a monopoly, equilibrium price (or AR) must be above MC.

(c) When the market is very large, e.g. a world market, individual firms can be very large in relation to the typical firm size in particular countries like the UK, but still relatively small and without monopoly power in relation to the total market of which they are members. At the other extreme, a sole proprietor of a grocery store may possess substantial monopoly power in an isolated community such as a Scottish island.

(d) This part of the question relates to 'market failures' which are explained in Chapter 8. Michael Utton is referring to 'negative externalities' or 'external costs' such as pollution, which firms discharge as a by-product or 'spin-off' of their normal production activities. However, the question is asking you to discuss the implications of the externalities rather than to devote space to describing them. You can introduce implications for the wider community (e.g. suffering illness and loss of welfare from pollution unwillingly consumed); implications for the government in terms of the public policy choices to be made to deal with the problem; and the implications for the firms themselves resulting from the regulations and 'pollution taxes' which the government may impose.

Question bank

1
(a) Outline the characteristics and behaviour of firms in perfect competition. (10)
(b) Why has the perfectly competitive model retained some usefulness for economists in the century and a half since it was first formulated?
(Oxford, AS Level, June 1990)

2
(a) Under what conditions would a market be perfectly competitive? Do you think such conditions are likely to exist in the real world? (7)
(b) Derive the short-run supply curve of a perfectly competitive firm. (9)
(c) Under what conditions is a perfectly competitive industry in long-run equilibrium? Does such a position represent an efficient use of scarce resources? (9) (NISEAC, June 1990)

3 Compare and contrast the possible long-run effects of an increase in demand for the products of a) a perfectly competitive industry; b) a monopoly. (Oxford, June 1989)

4
(a) Discuss the factors which give rise to a firm being dominant in a market. (50)
(b) Explain how such a firm might be expected to behave if it wishes to preserve its market domination. (50) (ULEAC, June 1992)

5
(a) Explain what is meant by **monopoly profits**. (15)
(b) What reasons are there for believing that a monopoly agreement between a number of firms may be more harmful than a single firm monopoly, from society's point of view? (5)
(c) Why does the state grant monopoly rights in the form of patents to particular firms? (5) (WJEC, June 1989)

6
(a) What is meant by economic efficiency? (10)
(b) Can monopolies ever be efficient? (15) (AEB, June 1992)

7 Analyse and comment upon the pricing and output decisions of the firm and the industry in perfect competition and monopoly. (Cambridge, June 1992)

8
(a) Analyse the conditions for profit maximisation for a firm operating under conditions of absolute monopoly. (8)
(b) On what basis is the control of monopoly thought to be desirable?
(O&CSEB AS Level, June 1992)

IMPERFECT COMPETITION

Units in this chapter

Chapter objectives

Imperfect competition is the label attached to the wide variety of market structures between the extremes of perfect competition and pure monopoly. A great many theoretical models of imperfect competition have been devised, each model pertaining to a precisely defined market structure and a set of assumptions about how the member firms behave. In this chapter we shall examine just three of the possible market structures:

❶ **monopolistic competition**, in which it is assumed that firms act independently of each other.

❷ **competitive oligopoly**, an example of a market structure in which interdependent firms must take account of the reactions of one another when forming a market strategy.

❸ **collusive oligopoly**, which occurs when firms attempt to overcome the uncertainty associated with guessing how competitors will react by colluding together and forming a cartel.

7.1 UNDERLYING CONCEPTS

As in the theories of perfect competition and monopoly, the **profit-maximising assumption** is fundamental to the models of imperfect competition considered in this chapter. If you refer back to the introduction to Chapter 6, you will see how **managerial** and **behavioural theories of the firm** attack the assumption of profit-maximizing behaviour as being an unrealistic objective for large modern business corporations.

Even if imperfectly competitive and monopolistic firms aim to maximise profits, they may simply not possess the accurate information about their market situation needed to equate marginal cost and marginal revenue. For this reason, imperfectly competitive firms are often modelled as **price-searchers**, seeking by trial and error the price which will maximise profits. In some circumstances, firms may produce a wide variety of differentiated products and services, for which the marginal cost of producing each particular good or service is different. In these conditions, imperfectly competitive firms commonly resort to 'rule of thumb' pricing, without ever consciously setting MC equal to MR. Businessmen may ask their accountants to estimate the cost of one unit of output when producing at near to full capacity. This estimate is called a **standard cost** and is used for price setting. On the basis of this standard cost, firms may adopt **'cost-plus'** or **'mark-up' pricing**, by adding a profit margin to the standard cost. The choice of the profit margin may itself be based on rule of thumb, or historical experience, or what a firm thinks it can charge without falling foul of a government monopoly investigation.

Nevertheless, many economists argue that the gap between the MC=MR rule and actual business pricing behaviour can be bridged. When cost-plus pricing gets businessmen too far out of line with what they would achieve with profit-maximising pricing, they will modify their pricing. Firms which stray too far from the profit-maximising path will experience low profits and falling share prices. While such firms are unlikely to be competed out of business in a highly imperfect market, they may become vulnerable to 'discipline by the capital market'. This means that firms which perform badly are vulnerable to takeover by managers who believe that they can manage the firms' assets more successfully.

7.2 ESSENTIAL INFORMATION

The theory of monopolistic competition

The theory of monopolistic competition was introduced by Edward Chamberlin in 1933 as an early attempt to model the characteristics of imperfect competition. As the name implies, monopolistic competition resembles both perfect competition and monopoly in some respects. Each firm's product is assumed to be a little different from those of its competitors; if it raises its price slightly, it will not lose all its customers. Thus a firm faces a downward-sloping demand curve, rather than the horizontal or infinitely elastic demand curve of perfect competition. Nevertheless, the absence of barriers to entry allows market forces, through the entry of new firms, to shift the demand curve and to compete away abnormal profits in the long run.

The **short-run equilibrium** in monopolistic competition is little different from the monopoly equilibrium illustrated in Fig. 22, except that the demand or average revenue curve is likely to be rather more elastic. Fig. 25 shows the long-run equilibrium, achieved after the entry of new firms has eliminated abnormal profits. As in the case of monopoly, monopolistic competition involves both **productive inefficiency** (the lowest-cost output is not produced) and **allocative inefficiency** (P > MC). However, the consumer is

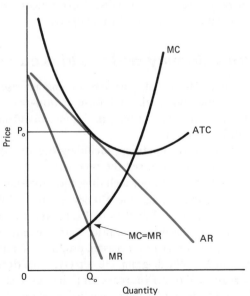

Fig. 25   Long-run equilibrium of a firm in monopolistic competition

presented with a considerable choice between differentiated goods. There may be circumstances in which consumers prefer a wider choice at the expense of an improvement in productive efficiency.

Nevertheless, it is also possible that firms are using advertising and brand-imaging to present the consumer with a false choice between essentially similar goods, in which case advertising is an unnecessary cost and a waste of resources. Advertising may manipulate consumer 'wants' by persuading people to buy products through the association of the product with other desirable properties such as social success. Many economists distinguish between **informative advertising**, which helps the consumer to make a more rational choice between products, and **persuasive advertising**, which distorts the choice.

Competitive oligopoly

Monopolistic competition shares with perfect competition and monopoly the characteristic that member-firms choose their market strategy in a way which is completely independent of the likely reactions of other firms. However, this may not be very realistic, particularly when there are only a few large firms competing within an industry. An **oligopoly** is sometimes defined in terms of an industrial concentration ratio: for example, a four-firm concentration ratio of 70% means that the four largest firms account for 70% of sales. Alternatively, an oligopoly can be defined in relation to the behaviour or market strategy of the member-firms. **Oligopolists are mutually interdependent** since each firm is concerned about the reactions of its competitors. There are a great many separate theories of oligopoly, each modelling a different set of assumptions about how the rivals react. Many of these theories are examples of **games theories**, in which each oligopolist is regarded as a player in a game, choosing a best strategy subject to retaliations.

Reasons for the existence of oligopoly

In many industries there are **economies of large-scale production**, but **diseconomies of scale** begin to set in while output is still well below the total market size. The result is a **natural oligopoly** in which a few firms can produce the total industry output and simultaneously benefit from full economies of scale. In other circumstances, countervailing power may explain the existence of an oligopoly: large **duopolists** such as Unilever and Proctor & Gamble may each possess sufficient market power in the detergent industry to prevent the other emerging as a sole monopolist. Government monopoly legislation may also deter the creation of an outright monopoly.

Price stability and the kinked demand curve

Although oligopolistic markets are characterised by competitive behaviour, the competition often takes the form of **non-price competition** such as:
❶ advertising competition, packaging, brand-imaging and product differentiation;
❷ marketing competition, including the attempt to obtain 'exclusive outlets' through which to sell the product;
❸ quality competition, including the provision of after-sales servicing.

Fig. 26 illustrates the **theory of the kinked demand curve**, a theory originally proposed in 1939 by Paul Sweezy as an explanation of supposed price rigidity and the absence of price wars in conditions of oligopoly. Suppose that an oligopolist, for whatever reason, produces an output Q_0 at a price P_0, determined at point X on the diagram. He perceives that **demand will be relatively elastic in response to an increase in price**, because he expects his rivals to react to the price rise by keeping their prices stable, thereby gaining customers at his expense. Conversely, he expects his rivals to react to a decrease in price by cutting their prices by an equivalent amount; he therefore expects **demand to be relatively inelastic in response to a price fall**, since he cannot hope to lure many customers away from his rivals. In other words, the oligopolist's initial position is at the junction of two demand curves of different relative elasticity, each reflecting a different assumption about how the rivals are expected to react to a change in price. Indeed, if demand is inelastic (and marginal revenue neative) when the oligopolist reduces his price, the best policy may be to leave the price unchanged.

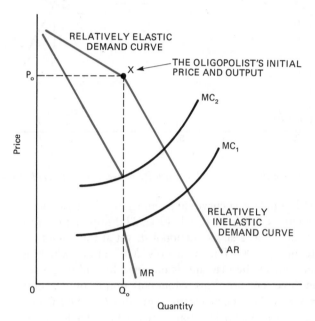

Fig. 26   The 'kinked' oligopoly theory

A second explanation of price rigidity is also suggested by Fig. 26. In mathematical terms, a discontinuity exists along a vertical line above output Q0, between the marginal revenue curves associated with the relatively elastic and inelastic demand (or average revenue) curves. Costs can rise or fall within a certain range without causing a profit-maximising oligopolist to change either price or output. At output Q_0 and price P_0, MC = MR as long as the MC curve is between an upper limit of MC_2 and a lower limit of MC_1. Although the kinked demand curve theory provides a neat and perhaps plausible explanation of price rigidity, it has been subject to many attacks. It is an **incomplete theory** because it does not explain how and why an oligopolist chooses to be at point X in the first place. Empirical evidence casts great doubt on whether oligopolists respond to price changes in the manner assumed. Oligopolistic markets often display evidence of **price leadership**, which provides an alternative explanation of orderly price behaviour. Firms come to the conclusion that price-cutting is self-defeating and decide that it may be advantageous to follow the firm which takes the first step in raising the price. If all firms follow, the price rise will be sustained to the benefit of all the firms.

Collusive oligopoly

The theory of the kinked demand curve illustrates an important characteristic of competitive oligopoly: the existence of uncertainty. An oligopolist can never be sure how his rivals will respond, yet he must take their expected reactions into account when determining his own market strategy. An incentive may exist for oligopolists to collude together in order to reduce uncertainty. Also, by acting collectively the firms may achieve an outcome which is better for all of them than if they had remained a competitive oligopoly. This can be shown by the **principle of joint profit maximisation**, which is illustrated in Fig. 27. We shall assume

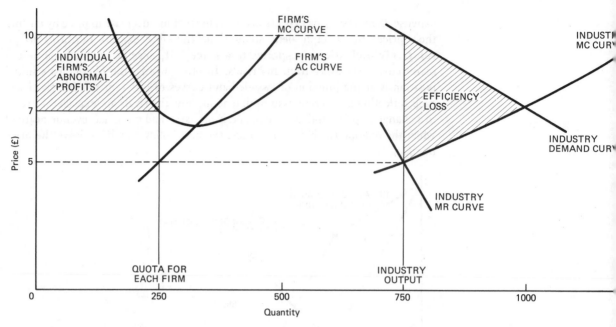

Fig. 27 Joint profit maximisation by a three-firm cartel in which the market is shared equally by the three firms

that there are three firms with similar cost curves in an industry. The cost curves of one of the firms are drawn in the left-hand panel of Fig. 27. Suppose the firms now decide to get together and act as a single monopolist, yet at the same time maintaining their separate indentities. The monopoly MC curve, which is illustrated in the right-hand part of the diagram, is obtained by adding up the identical MC curves of the three separate firms. Monopoly output of 750 units is determined where MC = MR, and each firm charges a price of £10. You should notice that the monopoly output is well below 1000 units, which would be the output if the industry was perfectly competitive. The shaded area in the right-hand panel represents the efficiency loss which is caused by the cartel raising the price to £10 and restricting the industry output to 750 units.

If the firms decide to split the output of 750 units equally between themselves, each firm will be allocated a quota of 250 units to produce. In this situation, the shaded area in the left-hand part of the diagram shows the abnormal profits made by an individual firm. Other forms of market-sharing, based for example on geography or historical tradition, are of course possible.

It is important to stress that the formation of a cartel does not completely eliminate uncertainty. Each member of the cartel has an **incentive to cheat** on the other members: this is because the marginal cost of producing the 250th unit is only £5, yet the marginal revenue received, which equals the price, is £10. A firm can increase its total profit at the expense of the other members of the cartel by secretly selling an output over and above its quota at a price which is less than £10 but greater than the marginal cost incurred. This is an example of a **divergency between collective and individual interest**. The firms' collective interest is to maintain the cartel so as to keep sales down and the price up. Nevertheless, an individual firm can benefit if, while the other members maintain the cartel, it secretly undercuts the agreement by selling more than its allotted market share.

The possibility of price discrimination

Monopolies, and other firms in highly imperfect markets, regularly charge a number of different prices to different groups of customers. Sometimes more than one product is involved, as in the case of first- and second-class rail travel; in other instances the prices may reflect the different transport and handling costs which are incurred in delivering the good or service to the customer. You must not confuse these examples of differentiated prices with the concept of monopoly or oligopoly price discrimination. **Price discrimination** occurs when a firm is able to charge **different prices** for an **identical product**. The costs of production must be the same, irrespective of the type of customer to whom the product is sold. Price discrimination will benefit a firm if it increases the firm's total profits. The necessary conditions for successful price discrimination are:

❶ It must be possible to **identify different groups of customers** or markets for the product.

❷ There must be a **different elasticity of demand** in each market.

❸ Total profits will be increased by **selling at a higher price in the market where demand is less elastic**. (Demand will never be inelastic, since this would imply that marginal revenue is negative.) The markets must be separated to prevent **seepage**, which occurs when customers buy at the lower price in one market in order to resell in the other market at a price which undercuts the monopolist.

Fig. 28 illustrates the simplest case of price discrimination, when a firm's MC curve is assumed to be constant. Profits are maximised by equating MR to the constant MC curve in each market. Output Q_1 is sold at a price of P_1 in the industrial market, while household customers buy Q_2 at price P_2. Marginal revenue is the same in each market at these outputs. If this was not the case, the firm would be able to increase profits by reallocating its output between the markets.

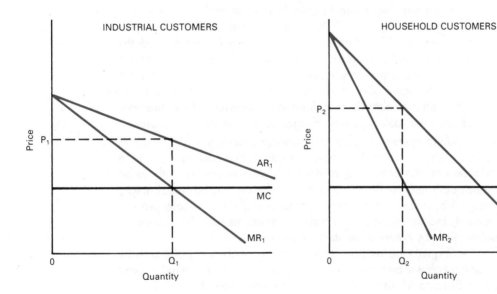

Fig. 28 Price discrimination

Although price discrimination can benefit the producer in terms of higher profits, there may be circumstances in which it is also in the interest of consumers. The classic case concerns the demand for the services of a doctor in an isolated small town. If all the townspeople are charged the same price for health care, the town's doctor is unable to make a sufficient income to cover his opportunity cost: it is in his interest to move to a larger city, thus leaving the townspeople without any medical care. If, however, the doctor is permitted to charge a higher price to the few rich citizens who can afford to pay, he may be able to earn sufficient income to make it worth his while to treat the poorer people at a lower price. Everybody ends up by getting some benefit from the introduction of price discrimination – though, as the next chapter explains, collective provision of a **merit good** such as health care outside the market may be judged more desirable than private provision through the market.

Chapter roundup

This chapter has followed on from Chapter 6 in extending the coverage of market structures to include the main forms of imperfect competition. Certain aspects of the behaviour or conduct of large firms which have been examined in some depth in this chapter are equally applicable to the case of pure monopoly. Likewise, the descriptive aspects of the growth of firms covered in Chapter 10, and the policy-making implications of industrial concentration (Chapter 12), relate to the highly imperfect market structures introduced in this chapter as well as to conditions of pure monopoly.

Illustrative questions and answers

1 Essay Question
(a) Why may firms wish to reduce competition by colluding with each other: for example, by forming a cartel? (12)
(b) Is such a collusion in the public interest and what might be the economic effects of prohibiting collusion? (13)

(AEB, June 1990)

Tutorial note

(a) Begin by arguing that the desire to collude is most likely to occur in a competitive oligopoly. Firms wish to collude to reduce the uncertainty resulting from their interdependence. You can also argue, perhaps with the aid of the theory of joint profit maximisation, that collusion can result in a better outcome for all the firms in terms of increased profits. However, avoid circular statements such as that firms wish to collude to avoid competition, since this information is already contained in the wording of the question. Also, avoid confusing collusion with merger activity, a common mistake.

(b) Define the public interest. Explain that collusive activity which reduces output, raises the price and generally exploits the consumer through manipulation and the promotion of producer sovereignty, is likely to be against the public interest. But some forms of collusion may be more benign, even though they reduce competition. Examples might include joint product development, industry-wide labour training initiatives and the sharing of distribution grids by competitive utility companies.

When dealing with the last part of the question, an obvious point to make is that competition will be promoted! Output may rise and price fall. Covert collusive activity could also replace overt cartel agreements.

2 Data Question

In the typical industrial market – that of a few firms or oligopoly – prices in the neoclassical model are held to be set so as to reflect the maximum return to producers as a group. This, subject to some imperfection in the tacit communication between oligopolists, is the same price that would
5 be charged by a monopolist. No point is better accepted by the neoclassical model than that the monopoly price is higher and the output smaller than is socially ideal. The public is the victim. Because of such exploitation, oligopoly is wicked.

Yet exploitation by modern oligopoly leads to no serious public
10 outcry that production is too small or prices too high. The automobile industry, rubber industry, oil industry, soap industry, processed food industry, tobacco industry and intoxicants industry all fit precisely the

pattern of oligopoly. All are held by neoclassical theory to maximise profits as would a monopoly. In all (these industries), comparative

15 overdevelopment – as compared, for example, with housing, health care, urban transit – is regularly cited in complaint and the effects of their growth on air, water, countryside and health are held against them. Never – literally – is it suggested that their output is too small. Nor are their prices a major object of complaint.

20 We now see the reason – and we begin to see one of the major dividends from a clear view of economic reality. The firms in these industries control prices in response to protective need – in response to heavy capital investment, long-time horizons, extensive specialisation and organisation and, in consequence, the high proportion of overhead costs.

25 The same technology and organisation allows for increasing productivity and falling costs. Of these the public approves. These firms set prices with a view to expanding sales – to growth. Of this, the antithesis of monopoly pricing, the public also approves.

(Source: J K Galbraith, *Economics and The Public Purpose* (1974); reproduced with the permission of Andre Deutsch Ltd.)

(a) Explain briefly the statement that 'the monopoly price is higher and the output smaller than is socially ideal' (lines 6–7). (6)

(b) Why might it, in practice, be difficult for oligopolists to set prices 'so as to reflect the maximum return to the producers as a group' (lines 2–3)? (8)

(c) Why does Galbraith say that firms in oligopoly 'control prices in response to protective need' (line 22)? (6)

(d) How would you expect 'the high proportion of overhead costs' (line 24) to affect the elasticity of supply of the firms discussed? (5)

(Oxford, June 1990)

Tutorial note

(a) With the aid of diagrams similar to those in Chapter 6, compare monopoly and perfect competition equilibrium – in the latter case for a whole market rather than for just one firm within the market. Explain that compared to perfect competition, monopoly produces a smaller output at a higher price. Assuming economies of scale are not possible, and externalities are not produced (see next chapter), the 'social ideal' is the perfectly competitive price and output.

(b) Galbraith is assuming that the oligopolists behave according to the theory of 'joint profit maximisation' which we have explained in this chapter. But this requires collusion by the oligopolists. Even if the government permits the necessary collusion, individual oligopolists may be tempted to cheat on the agreement in order to win more sales and larger profits at the expense of their rivals.

(c) Galbraith might be implying that oligopolists use prices as a barrier to entry, so as to protect their market shares. This may involve setting prices deliberately low in order to deter new entrants to the market. At first sight, such a pricing policy seems to imply that the oligopolists are deliberately sacrificing profits and therefore not behaving as 'profit maximisers'. Behaving in this way, the oligopolists would certainly be sacrificing *short-term profits*, but by successfully protecting the market, it can be argued that they would be maximising *long-term profits*. Such a pricing policy is often called **limit pricing** (i.e. using deliberately low prices to limit entry to the market) or **predatory pricing**, if prices are reduced below costs and force competitors out of business.

(d) The answer to this question depends on whether we are considering short-run or long-run supply. In the short run, supply might be quite elastic – provided that initially the firms have plenty of spare capacity and assuming that the spare capacity can easily be brought into production. Supply would become inelastic as full capacity was approached. Once full capacity was reached, the firms could only step up supply by investing in extra capacity, and since they have 'a high proportion of overhead costs', this implies that a large investment would be required. This could take months, if not years, so in these circumstances long-run supply would be inelastic.

Question bank

1 Examine the main differences in the determination of price and output in conditions of monopoly and oligopoly.　　　(ULEAC, January 1988)

2

(a) Explain why firms in a certain industry may wish to collude with each other in setting prices in a cartel arrangement. (10)

(b) Why might collusion between firms be held to be against the 'public interest'?

(c) For what reasons has it been asserted that collusive agreements often tend to break down in the long run? (5)

3

(a) Explain why petrol filling stations do not operate in conditions of perfect competition.　(10)

(b) Analyse the effects of an increase in demand for petrol on the profits of filling stations.　(15)　　　(Cambridge, June 1990)

4

(a) What features relating to firms' costs curves might explain the emergence of 'oligopoly'?　(7)

(b) Why is it difficult to predict equilibrium price and output which will emerge in an oligopolistic industry in the absence of collusion between firms?(8)

(c) What theory suggests that once a certain price has been maintained for some time in an oligopolistic industry, firms may not always adjust their price in response to changes in their marginal cost curves?

　　　(WJEC, June 1991)

5

(a) Why is it argued that managers of large joint-stock companies do not necessarily pursue policies which maximise the profits of the owners? (20)

(b) What factors might limit the powers of managers in this respect?　(5)

　　　(WJEC, June 1990)

6

(a) Explain how firms in oligopolistic markets are affected by interdependence and uncertainty.

(b) What action might firms in oligopolistic markets take to reduce uncertainty? (10)　　　(AEB, June 1991)

MARKET FAILURES

Units in this chapter

Chapter objectives

In previous chapters we have assumed that the price mechanism generally works efficiently to improve economic welfare and human happiness, provided only that markets are sufficiently competitive. In this chapter we introduce the term **market failure** to describe all the circumstances in which market forces fail to achieve an economically efficient equilibrium. The main examples of market failure we shall identify are:

*   **Failure associated with market structure** Monopolistic and imperfectly competitive market structures provide the best-known examples of market failure. The 'wrong' quantity is produced and sold at the 'wrong' price. In comparison with perfect competition, too little is produced at too high a price, and the market outcome is neither allocatively efficient nor productively efficient. Nevertheless, the market can still function in conditions of imperfect competition, producing at least some of the good or service.

*   **Failure associated with the market mechanism** Even when most of the conditions of perfect competition are met, informational problems may prevent the market mechanism from working properly. A certain minimum level of organisation of a market is required to allow information about market prices to be transmitted to all the participants. A lack of sufficient information about prices in other parts of the market may cause a market to degenerate into bilateral bargaining, where a buyer and seller enter into an exchange in a state of ignorance about prices in other parts of the market.

    In other instances, the adjustment process towards equilibrium may be too slow or unstable, and equilibrium may never be reached. As a result, trading may always take place at disequilibrium prices.

*   **Market failure and the 'new' microeconomics** In this chapter, attention is concentrated upon some examples of market failure which have been largely ignored, at least until fairly recent times, in the more traditional textbooks designed for A-level students. In particular we shall investigate public goods (and 'bads'), merit goods and externalities. Traditionally, microeconomics has been concerned with the manner in which markets function smoothly, relegating the coverage of market breakdown to something of a footnote, if indeed the subject was mentioned at all. In contrast, a modern microeconomic approach is to acknowledge that markets may function inadequately, perhaps more often than they function smoothly, and that in certain situations the market may completely fail to provide any quantity at all of a desired good

or service. In response to this change of emphasis, questions on market failure are regularly appearing in the A-level papers of all the examining boards.

8.1 UNDERLYING CONCEPTS

Market failure v market inadequacy

A market fails completely when there is no incentive for firms to produce a good or service, even though utility would be gained from its consumption. We shall show why markets fail to provide **pure public goods** such as national defence, which by its nature has to be consumed collectively rather than individually. Markets also fail to regulate the production and consumption of **externalities**, with the result that too much of an external 'bad' such as pollution and too little of an external good such as a beautiful landscape may be produced.

In other circumstances, markets will provide some of the good or service, but an inadequate quantity: monopoly and imperfect competition have already been mentioned in this respect. The market mechanism may provide too little of a **merit good**, such as education or health care, and too much of a 'good' such as narcotic drug or alcoholic drink – goods which are sometimes classed as **demerit goods**.

The problem of self-interest

Merit goods, demerit goods, and externalities all illustrate the existence of **divergencies, and possible conflicts, between private and social costs and benefits**. A central proposition of economic theory is that an economic agent in a market situation only considers the private costs and benefits to the agent itself of its market actions, i.e. it always seeks to maximise its self-interest. However, if in maximising its private benefit or interest, it imposes costs on other economic agents or the wider community, private benefit maximisation will not coincide with social benefit maximisation. In an unregulated market, the 'wrong' quantity of the good will be produced and consumed – the 'correct' quantity being that which maximises the social benefit rather than merely the private benefit of individuals.

8.2 ESSENTIAL INFORMATION

Pure public goods and quasi-public goods

A pure public good such as national defence is defined by the properties of **non-exclusion and non-diminishability**. A person can benefit from national defence without having to pay for it. Furthermore, if an extra person benefits from defence, this in no way diminishes the benefits available to others. Most public goods, for example roads, street lighting and broadcasting, are **quasi-public goods** or **non-pure public goods**. Markets could, in principle provide the goods, but for various reasons they do not. Instead, the goods or services are usually collectively provided by the state, often at zero price, and financed out of general taxation.

The essential properties of a public good can be explained with the use of the well-known example of a lighthouse. This is illustrated in Fig. 29. The lighthouse provides a service (a beam of light) for which there is a need; if the service is not provided more ships will be wrecked and transport costs will rise. Lighthouses could be provided through the market if entrepreneurs were able successfully to

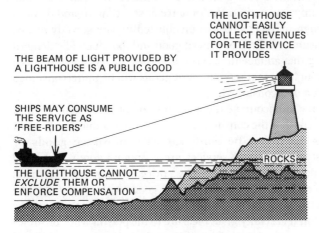

THE LIGHTHOUSE CANNOT EASILY COLLECT REVENUES FOR THE SERVICE IT PROVIDES

THE BEAM OF LIGHT PROVIDED BY A LIGHTHOUSE IS A PUBLIC GOOD

SHIPS MAY CONSUME THE SERVICE AS 'FREE-RIDERS'

ROCKS

THE LIGHTHOUSE CANNOT *EXCLUDE* THEM OR ENFORCE COMPENSATION

Fig. 29   The essential features of a public good

charge a price to passing ships. Now, most goods are called **private goods** because an entrepreneur who provides them can **enforce private property rights** and exclude people who do not wish to pay for consuming the goods. In the case of quasi-public goods, it is theoretically possible to exercise private property rights and to exclude **free riders** – people who consume without paying. A motor toll-road provides an example. However, in many cases the difficulty and cost of collecting revenue may prove prohibitive. A lighthouse company might try moral persuasion in order to collect revenue from passing ships, relying on the fact that it is in the interest of all ship-owners for the service to be provided; an incentive nevertheless exists for any individual ship-owner to become a free-rider, providing that the other ship-owners still pay up. In these circumstances, most ship-owners may be expected to become free-riders, thereby destroying the incentive for the private provision of the lighthouse. While **non-excludability** explains how private provisioning of a public good through a market may break down, the property of **non-diminishability** (or **non-rivalry**) suggests why the good should be provided at zero price or 'free'. Whenever an extra person consumes a public good such as defence or a lighthouse beam, no additional resources are used up. Thus the consumption can be met without transferring resources out of other industries. The marginal cost of meeting the extra consumption is zero. Consumer welfare will be maximised if the greatest possible consumption is achieved – and this will only happen if the price is zero.

Public goods and government goods

A public good is sometimes defined as any good or service provided by the public sector. This is not a very satisfactory definition. A good such as coal produced by a nationalised industry should be regarded as a private good provided through the market. Other goods and services such as education and health care are merit goods rather than public goods, though they share with public goods the characteristic of being collectively provided at zero price, and being financed out of taxation. It is useful to note that public collective provision is not inevitable in the case of public goods: in some instances, private collective provision is possible. A co-operative of ship-owners could provide lighthouses, though it might be necessary to make membership legally compulsory. Modified market provision is another alternative. For example, the difficulty of charging a price to consumers of commercial TV and radio programmes is circumvented by charging advertisers for access to the public good!

Merit and demerit goods

A merit good such as health care or education is a good or service from which the **social benefits** of consumption to the community as a whole **exceed the private benefits** to the consumer. In the case of a demerit good such as tobacco or alcohol, the **social costs** of consumption **exceed the private costs**. If merit and demerit goods are provided through markets at prices unadjusted by any subsidy or tax, people will choose to consume too little of a merit good and too much of a demerit good. It is worth stressing that an incentive certainly exists for merit and demerit goods to be provided through the market, but merit goods will be underconsumed and demerit goods will be overconsumed.

The government can try to encourage the consumption of merit goods and to discourage and sometimes outlaw the consumption of harmful products or demerit goods. **Demerit goods must not be confused with nuisance goods or economic 'bads'.** Most products and services are economic goods that yield utility in consumption – people are prepared to pay a price in order to obtain them, unless of course they can consume the goods as public goods without paying. The consumption of a demerit good, such as a narcotic drug, may not be in the consumer's best interest but it certainly gives pleasure to the person who consumes it, as it fulfils a need. In contrast a 'product' such as garbage is an economic 'bad' because it yields only unpleasantness or disutility: people are prepared to pay a price in order to have an economic bad taken away.

Merit goods and the informational problem

Uncertainty of information may partially explain why people choose to consume too little of a merit good such as health care if it is privately provided at market prices. For example, a person does not know in advance when, if ever, he is going to need the services of a specialist surgeon: sudden illness may lead to a situation in which he is unable to afford the surgeon's services. One market-orientated solution is for a **private insurance market** to come into being, in which case health care would be collectively provided through the market. However, this may still fail to provide a service for the chronically ill or the very poor. **Public collective provision** through a compulsory state insurance scheme is therefore another solution. It is interesting to note that both private and public collective schemes are a response to the fact that the demand or need for medical care is much more predictable for a large group of people than for an individual – an application of the 'law' of large numbers.

Externalities

An externality is a **special type of public good or 'bad'**, its crucial characteristic

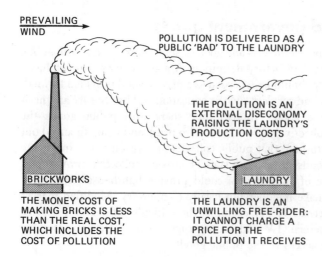

PREVAILING WIND →

POLLUTION IS DELIVERED AS A PUBLIC 'BAD' TO THE LAUNDRY

THE POLLUTION IS AN EXTERNAL DISECONOMY RAISING THE LAUNDRY'S PRODUCTION COSTS

BRICKWORKS

LAUNDRY

THE MONEY COST OF MAKING BRICKS IS LESS THAN THE REAL COST, WHICH INCLUDES THE COST OF POLLUTION

THE LAUNDRY IS AN UNWILLING FREE-RIDER: IT CANNOT CHARGE A PRICE FOR THE POLLUTION IT RECEIVES

Fig. 30 Case study of an externality: Pollution

being that it is generated and received outside the market. This can be demonstrated by considering the well-known example of pollution as an external cost. Fig. 30 illustrates the generation of pollution by a brickworks. The nearby laundry is an unwilling free rider receiving the pollution as a nuisance good or economic 'bad'.

External costs such as pollution, which increase the production costs of the firms that receive them, are examples of **external diseconomies**. Symmetrically, a firm may generate **external benefits** which are **external economies** if they lower the production costs of other firms. The laundry is unable to charge a price through the market to the brickworks for the pollution it unwillingly consumes. In a similar way, a power station discharging warm water into a lake cannot charge a price to fishermen for the external benefit they receive in the form of larger catches of fish. The **market thus fails to provide an incentive** for the brickworks to generate less pollution and for the power station to discharge more warm water. Without such an incentive, too much of an external cost and too little of an external benefit are likely to be generated. Thus governments may become involved in adjusting markets via taxes and subsidies in order to discourage economic bads and to encourage external benefits.

The different types of externality

	External costs	External benefits
Generated in production and received in production	Pollution discharged by a brickworks and received by a nearby laundry. (External diseconomies)	Warm water discharged by a power station and received in the form of bigger fish catches by nearby commercial fishermen. (External economies)
Generated in production and received in consumption	Pollution discharged by a brickworks and received by nearby households	Warm water discharged by a power station and received in the form of bigger fish catches by private anglers
Generated in consumption and received in production	Congestion caused by private motorists increasing production costs for firms. (This is another type of external production diseconomy)	Commercial bee-keepers benefiting from the private gardens of nearby households. (This is another type of external production economy)
Generated in consumption and received in consumption	Congestion caused by private motorists causing a utility loss to other private motorists, pedestrians and households	Passers-by enjoying the view of nearby private gardens

Externalities are essentially **spin-offs** which are generated by one economic agent in the pursuit of its private self-interest and received outside the market by other agents. Divergencies are likely to arise between the private cost and benefit of the generator of the externality and the social cost and benefit to all who receive them. An external cost such as pollution can be regarded as part of the production cost of bricks which is evaded by the brickworks by being 'dumped' on others. The **real cost** of bricks is greater than the **money cost** at market prices because the real cost includes the cost of pollution; bricks are therefore underpriced at market prices, price being less than the true marginal cost. Too many bricks are produced, causing a misallocation of resources (allocative inefficiency).

In this example, pollution is an externality which is both generated and received in production, thereby increasing the production cost of the firms receiving the pollution. Externalities may also be generated and received in consumption. This, and the other possibilities, are summarised in the table above.

Public policy and market failure

Public goods are usually provided 'free' by the state since otherwise they would not be provided at all. This is an example of **public provision** replacing the market. In the case of merit and demerit goods, the government can either **replace** or **modify** the market. A demerit good such as heroin may be judged so harmful that its consumption and sale are made illegal. A **complete ban** on a good is the ultimate **quantity control** which a government can use to regulate sale or consumption. Nevertheless a market may still exist in the form of an illegal black market. Black markets emerge when free markets are severely regulated or suppressed. In other circumstances, a government may decide that less severe quantity controls are more appropriate, such as the creation of no-smoking areas and restrictions on the sale of tobacco and alcohol. The symmetrical equivalent to a complete ban on heroin is to make the consumption of a merit good such as education or vaccination compulsory.

At the same time, **price controls** provide another form of regulation which can be used to modify the market. Minimum price legislation can discourage the consumption of demerit goods, whereas maximum price legislation increases the demand for merit goods – though problems of excess supply and demand are likely to result. For this reason governments may prefer to influence demand by taxing demerit goods and by subsidising merit goods. If a 100% subsidy is given to the private producers of a merit good, it becomes effectively 'free', in the sense that it is available at zero price. An example occurs when free places in private schools are financed by the state. Alternatively, the state can provide the merit good itself at zero or token price, similarly financed out of general taxation.

The problem of externalities can be tackled in a rather similar way with a combination of quantity controls or regulations, and taxes and subsidies to influence price. Discharge of pollution may be made illegal or restricted to certain times of the day or year. Maximum emission limits can be imposed. Since the central problem is the failure of the market to provide incentives to generate fewer external costs and more external benefits, taxes and subsidies can be used to provide the desired incentives. The government could, in principle, calculate the money cost of pollution and impose this as a pollution tax upon the polluter. The imposition of such a tax internalises the externality! More controversially, subsidies can be paid to encourage external benefits, for example those which result from the planting of trees.

In recent years, a more market-oriented solution has been introduced in the United States: the creation of a market in 'pollution permits'. The government grants licences or pollution permits to firms. Those firms which succeed in reducing the pollution they emit can then sell their 'spare' pollution permits to other firms. The firms buying the permits are those that find it more difficult to comply with the **maximum limits** or **ceilings** on pollution which are imposed at the same time as the pollution permits are granted.

Chapter roundup

In this chapter we have investigated in some depth the circumstances in which the signalling and incentive functions of prices (described in Chapter 1) may break down, resulting in the failure of markets to function smoothly. In some situations, markets may fail to function at all. The relative merits of the market economy and the planning mechanism (the subject of Chapter 9) link directly to the question whether individual markets function smoothly or badly. Chapters 8 and 9 are thus very closely related. If a case exists for the public

> provision of public goods and some merit goods, then this will influence the level and pattern of both government spending and government revenue. These examples of market failure are reintroduced in Chapter 15 on taxation and public spending.

Illustrative question and answer

1   Essay Question
    What is cost-benefit analysis? (25)
    With reference to examples, discuss its application to public sector investment. (75)

                                                                (ULEAC, January 1989)

Tutorial note

Cost-benefit analysis (CBA) is a technique for evaluating all the costs and benefits of any economic action or decision, i.e. the social costs and benefits to the whole community and not just the private costs and benefits accruing to the economic agent undertaking the action. CBA is most often used by governments to help decide whether to invest in a major public project such as a motorway, a Channel tunnel or a third London airport, or a major investment by a nationalised industry. However, there is no reason in principle why a private sector investment, or indeed any action by a private economic agent or by the government, cannot be examined by CBA.

CBA is really just an extension of the **Discounted Cash Flow technique of investment appraisal** explained in Chapter 21. Using DCF, a firm attempts to calculate all the private costs and benefits occurring in the future as a result of an investment undertaken now. The central problem is guessing and putting money values to an unknown and uncertain future. CBA is even more difficult because many of the social costs and benefits resulting in the future from an action undertaken now take the form of externalities that are difficult to quantify. How does one put a monetary value to the saving of a human life resulting from fewer accidents on a proposed motorway? What is the social cost of the destruction of a beautiful view? It is extremely difficult to decide on all the likely costs and benefits, 'to draw the line' on which to include or exclude, to put monetary values to the chosen costs and benefits, and to make a suitable comparison between costs and benefits accruing immediately with those that will only be received in the distant future.

Critics of CBA argue that it is 'pseudo-scientific' – value judgements and arbitrary decisions disguised as objectivity. CBA is also criticised as being a costly waste of time and money, a method whereby politicians distance themselves from, and induce delay in, unpopular decisions, deflecting the wrath of local communities away from themselves and onto the 'impartial experts' undertaking the CBA. Nevertheless, the supporters of CBA argue that for all its defects it remains the best method of appraising public investment decisions because all the likely costs and benefits are exposed to public discussion.

Suggested answer

- Explain that CBA is a technique of appraisal, similar to DCF in discounting a future stream of costs and benefits, but including all the costs and benefits, social rather than merely private.
- Explain that CBA is applicable, in principle, to public sector investment

because, in pursuit of the aim of social welfare maximisation, all the costs and benefits generated by the project should be assessed, not just the private costs and benefits.

- Give examples of public sector investment projects that might generate significant externalities that affect social welfare, e.g. a motorway, airport or nuclear power station.

2   Data Question

SINGAPORE'S TRAFFIC PROBLEMS

Singapore is a small, densely populated island of 2.6 million people. In 1987 there were almost half a million motor vehicles competing for space on a limited congested road network.

In order to combat this problem, the government introduced policies to control the use of motor vehicles through differential taxation and a system of road pricing. This involves the payment of a City Area Licence charge for vehicles travelling into central Singapore with fewer than four passengers from 7.30 a.m. to 10.15 a.m., Monday to Friday.

(Source: Singapore: Annual Vehicle Licensing Costs and Purchase Price 1987)

	Type of vehicle			
	Replacement family car	Additional company car	Goods vehicle	
Cost to motorist ($)	1600 cc	1600 cc	2.5 tonnes	1.5 tonnes
Approx purchase price of a new vehicle	40000	40 000	30000	60000
First registration fee (tax)	35000	70000	1500	3000
Annual registration fee (tax)	1000	5000	7000	15
City area licence annual charge	1200	2400	–	–
Road tax	1200	2400	1000	2600

(a) (i)   How does the total 'on the road' payment for an additional company car differ from that for a replacement family car? (2)
   (ii)   Suggest two economic reasons why companies purchase cars for certain employees. (2)

(b)   The annual City Area Licence charge is payable as a tax.
   (i)   Explain the likely purpose of such a tax. (2)
   (ii)   Suggest why goods vehicles are excluded. (2)

(c) (i)   What do economists mean by the term 'externalities'? (4)
   (ii)   What evidence is there in the table to suggest that the Government of Singapore wishes to reduce negative externalities? (4)
   (iii)   If this policy is successful, what are its implications for economic welfare? (4)

(Total: 20 marks)

(Cambridge, June 1990)

Tutorial note

(a) (i)   This part of the question is testing simple arithmetic: just add up the data in the first two columns and compare the totals! You might note that the annual City Area Licence Charge could be optional for a motorist who did not wish to use his vehicle in central Singapore during office hours with less than four passengers.

    (ii) Businesses allow employees the use of company cars because: a car may be necessary for the worker to do his job; to give the employee status; as a hidden pay rise and method of tax avoidance; and to achieve greater employee loyalty.

(b) (i) The City Area Licence charge aims to relieve the negative externality of congestion by discouraging marginal road users from driving in central Singapore at the most congested times, and by encouraging efficient use of vehicles through car sharing.

    (ii) Many goods vehicles have to load and deliver during office hours. Presumably the Singapore authorities took the view that the financial costs incurred by the island's economy would exceed any benefits in the form of reduced congestion.

(c) (i) Give a concise definition of an externality as an economic 'good' or 'bad' produced and received 'outside the market'. Clearly make the distinction between negative and positive externalities (external costs and benefits), and give an example of each.

    (ii) The data shows that the effective tax rate on family cars is nearly 100% and on additional company cars nearly 200%. While these tax rates could be viewed simply as 'revenue raisers', it is much more likely, particularly given the fact that Singapore is a small, completely urbanised island, that the high levels of taxation are designed to reduce the negative externalities of congestion, and also vehicle pollution.

    (iii) Economic welfare will have increased, provided the reduction in external costs (the costs of the negative externalities) exceeds the increase in private motoring costs incurred by vehicle owners and users.

Question bank

1 In what senses could the market system 'fail'? To what extent could your arguments be used to justify the production and distribution of goods and services by the public sector? (Oxford, June 1989)

2
(a) Explain why the emission of pollution by a firm into the atmosphere or into a river may be economically inefficient. (13)
(b) Evaluate two ways of reducing any economic inefficiency caused by pollution. (12) (AEB, June 1990)

3 Explain what you understand by the term 'externalities' and how they might arise in production and consumption. To what extent might 'global warming' be considered an externality and, as such, be solved by economic measures? (JMB, AS-Level, June 1990)

4 Under what circumstances might it be desirable for a government to supply a good or service free of charge?

5 A factory discharges a waste product into a river which has the effect of reducing the quantity of fish caught by fishermen downstream.
(a) Explain why the output of the factory might be considered in excess of its 'socially efficient' level. (9)
(b) Suggest two alternative policy approaches a government might pursue to remove such inefficiency. (9)
(c) Explain why government legislation prohibiting any discharge of waste products might not be desirable on economic grounds. (7)

6

(a) 'If a government supplies genuine public goods to individuals, there is no problem of rationing. If, however, a government supplies private goods then often there is a rationing problem involved.' Explain these statements.   (15)
(b) Consider how rationing problems are solved:
    (i)   In the allocation of student places on certain university degree courses. (5)
    (ii) In the allocation of NHS hospital services.   (5)   (WJEC, June 1991)

7

(a) Why are shortages and gluts sometimes a feature of markets free from government intervention? (12)
(b) Explain why the government may wish to intervene in the market for alcoholic drinks and tobacco products. What forms may this intervention take?   (13)
    (NISEAC, June 1991)

8

(a) Using examples, compare and contrast public goods with merit goods.   (10)
(b) Discuss how public goods and merit goods should be provided and paid for.   (15)   (Cambridge, June 1992)

9

(a) What is meant by the term 'externality'?
(b) Examine alternative policies to resolve the externality problem in the case of lead pollution from cars. (80)   (ULEAC, January 1991)

10

(a) Define external costs and benefits in economics. Give examples to illustrate your definitions.   (30)
(b) Examine the problems that might be experienced in estimating the value of externalities.   (70)   (ULEAC, AS-Level, June 1991)

11

(a) Distinguish between **private** and **social** costs and benefits.   (4)
(b) Explain how an increase in the number of cars on the roads in the UK might lead to a misallocation of resources.   (6)
(c) Indicate what policies the Government might use to remedy this misallocation.   (10)   (AEB, AS-Level, June 1991)

CHAPTER 9

MARKET AND PLANNED ECONOMIES

Units in this chapter

Chapter objectives

In the first eight chapters we have examined how the price mechanism is assumed to work, both in the 'ideal' circumstances of a perfect market, and in the more realistic conditions of monopoly, market imperfection and market failure. We are now in a position to draw together themes and strands of reasoning from earlier chapters, in order to make a comparison of market economies and planned economies as economic systems.

OWNERSHIP AND ECONOMIC SYSTEMS

One way to define an economic system is in terms of ownership of the means of production, distribution and exchange. This approach is favoured by Marxist economists, who analyse the conflict between the employed class and the class which owns the means of production. Marxists are particularly interested in the dynamic change over time of society (and economic systems), in response to the apparent conflict between economic classes. Most Marxist economic analysis has centred on **capitalism** as an economic system. Capitalism is usually defined as a system in which the means of production are owned by private individuals who employ labour in order to produce output for private profit. Marxists believe that the supposed conflicts and contradictions of capitalism will eventually culminate in a final crisis out of which will develop socialism. In socialism the community as a whole, usually through the state, owns the means of production, distribution and exchange. Of course, it is not nearly as simple as this, and to many economists capitalism and socialism may have a number of different meanings.

ALLOCATIVE MECHANISMS AND ECONOMIC SYSTEMS

Market economies and planned economies (command or collective economies) are defined in terms of the allocative mechanism which is assumed to exist in the economic system. In a **pure market economy** all resources, goods and services other than free goods would be allocated through the market, whereas in a **centrally planned economy** a central authority would make all the allocative decisions. Both these extreme situations are obviously unrealistic. Where a very large proportion of economic activity takes place through the market, as for example in the Swiss economy, it is usual to refer to it as a market economy. Where, however, the bulk of economic activity determined by a central planning authority, as occurred in the Soviet Union before its break up, it is customary to refer to it as a planned or command economy even though some activities such as market gardening have been outside the system.

OTHER POSSIBILITIES

It is often wrongly stated that **private ownership (or free enterprise)** is a necessary condition for the existence of a market economy. While it is certainly usual for capitalism to exist within a largely market economy, it is by no means inevitable. **Nationalised industries** in Britain have provided an example of socially owned enterprises operating in the market sector of an economy. Indeed, most of the economies of the advanced industrial nations in Western Europe are referred to as mixed economies and many of the former Eastern bloc countries have begun the process of transforming from command economies to Western-style mixed economies. The mixed economy is a very broad label that covers a variety of possible systems. A **mixed economy** is sometimes defined in terms of **ownership,** as an economy containing **large private** and **public sectors.** It is equally possible to define a mixed economy in terms of **allocative mechanisms;** in this case, the coexistence of **market** and **non-market sectors** defines a mixed economy, each sector usually providing different categories of goods and services. However, some services such as health and education may be provided by both sectors.

Until recently there was a wide measure of agreement in the United Kingdom on the virtues of a mixed economy, the main discussion and controversy being on where to draw the line, within fairly narrow limits, between private and public ownership and between market and non-market provision. This consensus has now been attacked by the advocates of a social market economy, which is much closer in concept to a pure market economy. In a **social market economy,** as much as possible would be privately provided through the market, the state restricting its economic role to that of 'nightwatchman': maintaining orderly conditions in which markets can operate, providing some public goods, and using taxation and transfers to provide a minimum state 'safety net' to protect the victims of a largely unregulated market economy. Advocates of a social market economy are usually monetarist in their approach to macroeconomics.

9.1 UNDERLYING CONCEPTS

The problem of scarcity revisited

The problem of what, how and for whom to produce in a situation where scarce resources have alternative uses was briefly mentioned in the introduction to Chapter 1. Since a major part of the evaluation of market and planned economies must be in terms of how well they perform these allocative tasks, we shall restate the scarcity problem with the use of a production possibility diagram.

The production possibility frontier drawn in Fig. 31a shows what can be produced with the existing quantity of labour, capital, and land at a country's disposal, for a given level of technology or 'technical progress'. Although resources and capacity are limited, a choice of which type of good to produce exists. If we assume just two classes of goods, **capital** and **consumer goods**, the production possibility frontier represents the technological choice available to society between the two groups of goods. A point such as X on the frontier is associated with the output K_1 of capital goods and C_1 of consumer goods. The production possibility diagram also illustrates the following points of interest:

- If society is on its production possibility frontier, at a point such as X, more

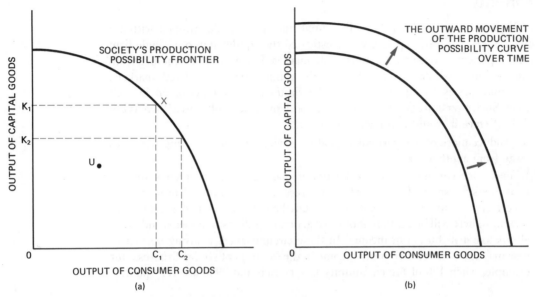

Fig. 31 (a) *The economic problem and society's production possibility curve*
    (b) *Economic growth causes the frontier to move outwards over time*

of one good can only be produced at the expense of some of the output of the other good. For instance, if the output of consumer goods is increased to C_2, the output of capital goods must fall by K_1–K_2. The opportunity cost of the extra output of consumer goods is K_1–K_2, the alternative output of capital goods which is given up.
- If you refer back to Chapter 3, you will see that the shape of the production possibility curve reflects the **nature of returns** to the resources as they are switched between the capital and consumer goods industries. Fig. 31 shows **diminishing returns** in both industries: as more and more resources are transferred into the consumer goods industries, output rises by a smaller extra quantity for each unit of resource transferred.
- All points on the production possibility frontier represent **full employment** of society's resources. A point such as U inside the frontier is associated with **unemployment**. Here it is no longer true that the opportunity cost of increasing the output of consumer goods is the sacrifice of some production of capital goods – production of both capital and consumer goods can be stepped up by utilising unemployed resources.
- An increase in the resources available to the society, or **technical progress** which improves the efficiency with which resources are used, can shift the production possibility curve outwards. This is illustrated in Fig. 31b. Of course, the choice as to which original quantities of capital and consumer goods to produce may influence the outward movement of the frontier. **Capital goods** are goods which are used to produce other goods and services, whilst consumer goods represent the final goods and services purchased by households. The output of capital goods has two purposes. Firstly it replaces the capital that is worn out in producing the current flow of capital and consumer goods (**depreciation investment** which maintains the society's capital stock). Secondly it may also add to the capital stock (**net investment**), thereby enabling a larger output to be produced in the future. In conditions of full

employment it may be possible to increase the standard of living by producing more consumer goods at the expense of capital goods. However, in the long run the standard of living can best be increased by producing more capital goods now, thereby creating the growth in the economy's productive capacity which shifts the production possibility frontier outwards.

General equilibrium in a perfectly competitive market economy

In Chapter 1 we considered how the equilibrium price is determined within a single market, and in Chapter 6 we investigated the equilibrium of a single firm within a perfectly competitive industry or market. For a general equilibrium to occur within a whole system of perfectly competitive interrelated markets, equilibrium prices and quantities must be simultaneously determined in each market. Such a general equilibrium would be both **productively** and **allocatively efficient** since it would be impossible either:

* to produce more of one particular good or service without diverting resources away from another, or
* to make one consumer better off without making some other consumer or consumers worse off. It is important to stress that these optimal properties of a perfectly competitive general equilibrium hold for a given distribution of income. There will be a different optimal general equilibrium for each and every alternative distribution of income! In these circumstances a strong normative case may exist for redistributing income in the interests of **social fairness**, for example, when 1% of the community is very rich and 99% are very poor.

9.2 ESSENTIAL INFORMATION

The advantages of a market economy

Subject to some very strong assumptions about the **absence of externalities** and **economies of scale**, a perfectly competitive market economy in general equilibrium would possess the following advantages:

❶ **Economic efficiency** (productive and allocative) would be achieved.
❷ **Consumer sovereignty** The goods and services produced would be determined by price signals which reflect consumer wants.
❸ **Decentralised decision-making** The optimal production and allocation of resources would be achieved without the need for an expensive bureaucracy. In a market economy the price system acts as a social control mechanism. This is often referred to as the invisible hand principle, describing the proposition that economic order rather than chaos results from the pursuit of individual self-interest in a market economy.

The disadvantages of a market economy

❶ **Economic inefficiency** Productive and allocative efficiency will only be achieved if every market in the system is perfectly competitive and if trading takes place always at equilibrium prices in every market. Unless these almost impossible conditions are met, we cannot be sure that a perfectly competitive market system would be economically efficient.

Of course, the market economies of the real world are in no sense perfectly competitive. In a perfectly competitive system, price (and wage) flexibility would bring about full employment of all available resources in equilibrium. A criticism of the market economies in the actual world is the

persistence of unemployment and the **tendency for business cycles** in the pattern of economic behaviour. Both these phenomena are indicators of inefficient utilisation of resources.

❷ **Producer sovereignty** The existence of increasing returns to scale and economies of scale helps to explain why actual market economies are only distant approximations to the perfectly competitive 'ideal'. If markets are dominated by monopoly and imperfect competition, firms may decide what to produce, perhaps manipulating consumer wants through advertising. In any case, price now functions as a misleading signal, contributing to re-source misallocation.

The case for replacing the market

Supporters of the principle of a market economy argue that, however imperfectly the price mechanism works, it still results in **sufficient efficiency and consumer sovereignty** to justify the system. Nevertheless, many advocates of a mixed economy claim that in a number of specific instances the government planning mechanism should either modify or replace the market:

❶ **The problem of income distribution** The best that can be claimed for perfectly competitive market system is that it may be economically efficient for a given initial income distribution. It is completely 'value neutral' on the desirability or otherwise of the initial pattern of incomes. It is a function of government to use tax and public spending policies to achieve a 'satisfactory' distribution of income.

❷ **Goods which the market fails to provide** We examined in Chapter 8 the nature of public goods, merit goods and externalities. In each case, the market either completely fails to provide the goods in question, or provides the 'wrong' quantities. Governments usually plan the public collective provision of public goods such as national defence, and of merit goods such as education. Governments may also modify the market through regulation, taxation and subsidies, in order to encourage the consumption of market-provided merit goods, or to reduce the divergency between private and social cost and benefit in the case of externalities. You should refer back to Chapter 8 for a detailed explanation of these examples of market failure.

However, in recent years a body of theory known as a **'public choice'** theory has emerged which argues that attempts to correct **market failure** by government intervention may simply lead instead to a **government failure** in which the costs of intervention exceed the benefits.

Command economies

A command economy, in which markets would be largely replaced by a command or planning mechanism, would of course be very different from the type of mixed economy we have just described. In theory at least, it is possible for a centrally planned command economy to achieve exactly the same distribution of resources as would occur in general equilibrium in a perfectly competitive market economy. As a result, there is no theoretical reason why a market economy must be more economically efficient than a command economy. Consider, however, the implications of the complete abolition of prices as sources of information. It has been calculated that in an economy such as the USA the central authority would have to issue over 200 billion orders in respect of a single commodity, allocating precise amounts of the good to each consumer. The costs of a completely centralised control system governing all production and consumption decisions would be immense! Such a command economy is as abstract and unreal an economic concept as the model of a perfectly competitive market economy.

The command economies of the real world, such as the ex-Soviet economy before the break-up of the USSR, have tended to be command economies with some household choice. The command system concentrated on the production decision of what to produce, rather than on the final allocation of goods and services to consumers. A central plan allocated resources to particular industries and productive units which were required to meet the output targets of the master plan. In some circumstances, factory managers were free to set final prices, though it was more usual for the central planners to decide the prices of important commodities such as bread and meat. Prices which were chosen by a central authority with the object of encouraging individual consumers to behave in a certain way are known as **shadow prices**.

Sometimes, shadow prices were deliberately set so as to ration final goods and services which were scarce in relation to an overwhelming unfulfilled consumer demand. In this respect, shadow prices imitated at least one of the functions of market prices. However, in a market economy the price would provide an incentive for producers to enter the industry. This incentive is lacking in a command economy, unless the planners respond to the signals of scarcity by diverting more resources into the particular industry.

Chapter roundup

We have nearly completed our necessarily brief coverage of microeconomic theory. In Chapters 10 and 11 the emphasis is switched away from economic theory as we look at the way firms have grown in the British economy and how they raise finance. We then see in Chapter 12 how government microeconomic policy attempts to make the British economy more competitive. In these chapters, the theory which we have developed in Chapters 1 to 9 will be used to evaluate the aims and effectiveness of government policies.

Illustrative questions and answers

1   Essay Question
    The centrally planned economies of Eastern Europe have recently been placing more reliance on market forces in directing economic activity. Examine the likely economic benefits and problems arising from this changing situation.

(ULEAC, June 1992)

Tutorial note

Although this question appeared in the 1992 examination, i.e. *after* the more or less complete breakdown of most of the centrally planned economies of Eastern Europe, the wording of the question shows that it had been set rather earlier, probably before the collapse of Communist control and the break up of the Soviet Union which took place in 1991. Nevertheless, the question does indicate how the examining boards are now setting questions relating to the economic changes taking place in the former command and centrally planned economies, and how you must take account of the issues involved in this process of economic evolution as you prepare for your examination.

When answering a question like this you must avoid the temptation to write a 'model answer' of the old 'command versus market economy' type, which simply compares the advantages and disadvantages of the alternative economic systems. Nevertheless much of the 'standard' material on different types of economic systems can, with a bit of care, usefully be adapted to the needs of this question. Likewise, you must avoid drifting into an irrelevant (though interesting!)

discussion of the problems resulting from the political fragmentation and ethnic problems that have emerged in the old 'Soviet Empire'. Following Milton Friedman, you might, however, argue that a market economy has the advantage of being compatible with (though not necessarily promoting) a democratic and 'free' political system, whereas central planning and the command system seem to require a more totalitarian political institutions.

Start your answer by stating that economic change has begun to take place in Eastern Europe because of the breakdown of the old system: i.e. the disadvantages of a centrally planned economy were exceeding the advantages to the extent that governments realised that the people they governed would no longer accept the system. Indicate what the disadvantages were: the inability to produce the consumer goods that people wanted; deteriorating infrastructure, particularly for distributing agricultural goods to the cities; worsening shortages and the growth of 'black' markets; an obviously widening gap between economic performance and standards of living between the centrally planned economies and the western market economies etc. You might also argue that countries such as Hungary, Czechoslovakia and the former East Germany were forced against their will, under the Soviet planning system, to establish their main trading links with the USSR when, left to themselves, their people would have preferred to integrate their economies with Western Europe, and in particular with the EC.

Economic benefits will occur if the adoption of private enterprise capitalism and the market economy leads to a significant reduction in the problems we have just listed. Some countries are faring better than others. The former East Germany – for the obvious reason that it is now part of a united Germany – and countries such as Hungary which had for many years been gradually changing into a quasi-market economy and developing links with the west, are transforming their economies with the least difficulty. But at the other extreme are countries like Albania which have poor resource endowments and which exhibit many of the problems more usually associated with the world's poorest less developed countries (LDCs).

Indeed, it is worth making the point that there are already a large number of poor and inadequately developed countries in Africa, Latin America and Asia in which the market system operates, but with a much less obvious degree of success than that displayed in 'First World' countries in Europe, North America and Japan and also in such 'Newly Industrialising Countries' (NICs) as Hong Kong, Malaysia and Singapore. Thus it is by no means guaranteed that the abandoning of central planning and the adoption of capitalism and a market economy will transform all the Eastern European countries into 'leading light' examples of the advantages of the market system. Some may simply end up added to the list of the less successful market economies, with various forms of 'market failure' replacing the 'government failure' which characterised the centrally planning system in these countries.

Various factors such as a favourable resource endowment and actual or potential trading links with other countries can assist the development of a market economy. Arguably however, an **entrepreneurial culture** is also required, which embodies risk taking, 'deal making', hard work and effort, and the ability to accumulate savings and direct them into productive channels. Alongside this 'entrepreneurial culture', there must also be appropriate governmental, legal, financial and educational institutions. But amongst the problems facing the Eastern European countries is the fact that much of both the required institutional and infrastructural framework and the 'entrepreneurial culture' are missing, the latter deliberately suppressed during the communist era. Neither can be implanted overnight; it may take years for both to be properly established. In the transformation process, one of the government's first tasks is to establish private property rights, i.e. who owns what. This involves **privatisation**, but in a country in which the state previously owned almost everything, privatisation is by no means as simple a task to undertake as in countries like the UK. One of the dangers is that during the intervening period as the government attempts to transform the economy, the emerging market economy performs extremely inefficiently. Legitimate market institutions may be subverted by a **criminalised black market economy** typified by racketeering, speculation and the seizure of property and effective power by Mafia-style gangs more reminiscent of Chicago in the 1920s or the drug economy of Colombia today than of a progressive, successful and politically liberal West European or North American market economy.

Suggested answer

- Briefly set out the historical background: countries such as Poland and Hungary breaking away from Soviet influence and abandoning central planning; the Soviet Union first introducing perestroika (economic change involving some introduction of market forces) in the late 1980s, and then the disintegration of the USSR and the central planning system in 1991.

- Explain that this was a response to the failure of the central planning system. Outline the failures we have listed and the other inefficiencies of the central planning system.

- In principle the move to a market economy can mean that 'state sovereignty' is replaced by 'consumer sovereignty', improved efficiency and growth, and greater consumer choice and welfare.

- But not all the world's market economies are successful. Many are backward and inefficient. There is thus the danger that various forms of 'market failure' will replace 'government failure'. In some Eastern European countries it may prove difficult to develop the institutions and culture necessary for a successful market economy.

- Explain the dangers both of criminalised 'black market' economies and of the countries remaining backward, lacking in development and suffering an exodus of the young working population.

- Assess whether the transformation is likely to be successful and whether, in your view, the benefits will exceed the costs.

2 Data Question
The following passage is adapted from an article in *The Economist* (30 November, 1985) entitled 'Servicing the economy'.

In Britain services account for two out of every three jobs, and more than half of total GDP. During the past 35 years, service employment has jumped from 43% to 65% of the total workforce; the proportion in manufacturing has fallen from 40% to 25%. About a quarter of the 13.5m
5 service workers are in the retail or wholesale trades. Another third are in health, education or public administration; 14% work in financial and business services (banks, insurance, etc.); 10% are in transport and communication; and the rest work in hotels and restaurants or provide various personal services from haircuts to cleaning windows.
10 Some economists argue that the growth in service employment simply reflects the fact that the demand for services is relatively 'income elastic': as economies grow richer, people spend a smaller share of their income on food and durable goods and develop new tastes for services. However, although real personal disposable income in Britain has more than doubled
15 since 1950, the volume of spending on services has fallen slightly as a proportion of consumers' expenditure. The relationship between real income and spending on services seems to have shifted down over time. For any particular level of income, households are now spending proportionately less on services. The reason is simple. Over the past 30

20   years, the price of services has risen by a factor of 12, the price of consumer durables by only half as much. This suggests that productivity growth in services has been much slower than in manufacturing. To the extent that the cost of services has risen faster than costs generally, people have satisfied their demand for services by buying durable goods and producing

25   services themselves at home, rather than paying somebody else to do the job.

Over three-quarters of the service jobs created since 1950 have been in two fields:

HEALTH AND EDUCATION During the 20 years to the mid-1970s, the

30   number of jobs in health and education increased by 110%, more than twice as fast as jobs in private services.

FINANCE AND BUSINESS The number of jobs in financial and business services has risen by 150% during the past 30 years. Britain's evolution from an industrial to a service economy has prompted some economists

35   to warn that services cannot earn enough foreign exchange to satisfy the country's insatiable appetite for imported cars and televisions.

(a) Explain the importance of service employment in the United Kingdom economy.   (4)

(b) (i) To what extent do you consider the demand for services to be 'income elastic' (line 11)?   (5)

   (ii) Give two examples of services being produced 'at home, rather than paying somebody else to do the job' (line 25).   (1)

(c) Suggest reasons for the increase in the levels of employment in:
   (i) health and education;   (3)
   (ii) finance and business.   (3)

(d) Why might a service economy experience deficits on its balance of payments?   (4)

(AEB, AS-Level, June 1989)

Tutorial note

(a) This is a very open-ended question, but since it only carries 4 marks, you must avoid the temptation to write too long an answer. Services grow in importance in all advanced economies, and indeed countries like the UK are sometimes called **post-industrial economies**. The growth of services partly reflects the changing pattern of demand as real incomes rise. It also reflects the fact, as the passage indicates, that there has been less scope for productivity growth in many service industries than in manufacturing. The service industries have been more labour intensive than manufacturing; hence the growth of service employment. (To some extent this is now changing; in the recession in the early 1990s, a drastic fall in profits has caused service industries such as banking to begin the task of slimming down the labour force.)

You can also argue that older industrialised economies such as the UK have probably lost the *comparative advantage* in manufacturing which they once possessed, while developing an advantage in the provision of services. (See Chapter 26 for an explanation of comparative advantage.) In recent decades the comparative advantage in manufacturing has moved away from the European and North American countries to the 'Newly Industrialising Countries' (NICs) of the Far East and 'Pacific Rim'. By contrast with manufacturing, industries such as hairdressing and leisure industries produce services which for the most part are 'non-tradeable' between countries. This means that many UK service industries do not suffer from international competition, even when their costs are very high.

(b) (i) Most services are *normal* goods, meaning that demand for them rises with income. Therefore the income elasticity of demand for most services is positive. Because many services are regarded as luxuries, their income elasticity of demand is greater than unity, i.e. demand for them rises at a faster rate than income. However, as the passage indicates, this is often overwhelmed by the *substitution effect* resulting from the fact that, compared to manufactured goods and foodstuffs, the relative price of services has risen over time.

(ii) List any two 'Do-it-Yourself' services, such as painting the house, the use of domestic washing machines replacing laundries, etc.

(c)   In the UK, health care and education are provided for the most part as 'merit goods', outside the price system. Thus although increased demand (as real incomes and standards of livings have risen) is an important factor in explaining growing employment in these service industries, the political decision to increase public spending in their provision is also significant. In the case of health care, also mention the effects of improvements in medical technology which can provide treatments that did not exist a few years ago, and which can keep people alive longer. The growth in employment in financial services in the 1980s had a rather different explanation. Bring in the comparative advantage argument here, the effects of financial deregulation, e.g. the Stock Exchange 'Big Bang' in 1986 (see Chapter 11), and the fact that the City of London has benefited from the 'globalisation' of financial services and markets.

(d)   Keynesian economists believe that the UK economy has become too dependent on services, not so much because of the success of service industries in growing rapidly, but rather because of the **de-industrialisation process** and the decline of manufacturing. As we have mentioned, many service industries are 'non-tradeable' in an international sense. This means that, unlike almost all manufacturing industries, services cannot generate sufficient foreign exchange through their export earnings to pay for manufactured imports and imports of foodstuffs and raw materials which the economy needs to maintain domestic living standards and investment. Professor Tony Thirlwell of Kent University has recently presented a very clear statement of this Keynesian argument in an article entitled 'The Balance of Payments and Economic Performance' in the May 1992 edition of *The National Westminster Bank Quarterly Review*. In his article, Professor Thirlwell argues that if, as demand expands, an economy gets into balance of payments difficulties before full capacity is reached, then demand must be curtailed, capacity is never fully utilised, investment is discouraged, and technological progress is slowed down. This in turn causes a country's traded goods to become less desirable when compared with foreign goods, so worsening the balance of payments still further, and so on in a **vicious circle** of declining competitiveness, balance of payments problems and lack of growth. By contrast, if a country is able to maintain demand up to the level of existing productive capacity without balance of payments difficulties arising, the pressure of demand upon capacity may well raise the country's growth rate. A **virtuous circle** of **export-led growth** is then initiated, in which growth promotes competitiveness and exports, which in turn lead to further growth and so on. In Professor Thirlwell's view, exports and manufacturing both play a vital role in the growth process. He believes that only by expanding exports, can the growth rate be raised without the balance of payments deteriorating at the same time and eventually constraining growth. Exports as a component of demand are unique in this respect; they are the only component of demand that provides the foreign exchange to pay for the import requirements for growth. The role of manufacturing in the growth process is significant for two reasons. Firstly, manufacturing tends to have growth-inducing characteristics that many service industries do not possess, such as greater potential for increased labour productivity. And secondly, all manufactured goods are potentially exportable, whereas only some 20% of service output in the UK is internationally tradable. Thus as resources are switched from manufacturing to services, the current account worsens.

Question bank

1 Outline, briefly, the main characteristics by which economic systems may be classified. Discuss what influences , if any, the nature of the economic system can exert on the level, rate of increase and distribution of national income.
(JMB, June 1988)

2

(a) How are resources allocated in a mixed economy?   (15)
(b) In the light of the economic changes that have occurred within the United Kingdom economy in recent years, discuss whether it is still correct to describe the United Kingdom economy as a mixed economy.   (10)
(AEB, June 1990)

3 'In recent years there has been a trend towards more free-market enterprise in Western mixed economies'.
(a) What do you understand by 'free-market enterprise'? Explain how resources are allocated in the free market sector of a mixed economy.   (15)
(b) Suggest some advantages and disadvantages which may arise as a result to the introduction of a greater degree of free enterprise.   (10)
(Scottish Higher, June 1989)

4 Using examples explain why in mixed economies governments provide some goods and services and intervene in the market for others.
(O&CSEB, AS-Level, June 1990)

5

(a) 'All societies must decide what to produce, how to produce and for whom to produce.' Explain.   (7)
(b) Outline how these decisions are made in a market economy. (8)
(c) Discuss why a free market economy might not result in the 'best' allocation or a 'fair' distribution.   (10)   (NISEAC, June 1990)

6 Outline the essential differences between free-market and centrally planned economies. Discuss the economic problems which may arise in the transition of the Eastern European economies to the market system.
(JMB, June 1991)

7

(a) What distinguishes a command economy from a free-market economy? (30)
(b) What problems arise in assessing the comparative performance of two such economies?   (70)   (London, January 1991)

8

(a) Different economic systems allocate resources in different ways. Identify the main resource allocation decisions which need to be made in an economy. (8)
(b) Explain how the process of resource allocation varies between different types of economic system.   (12)   (O&CSEB, AS-Level, June 1992)

THE SIZE AND GROWTH OF FIRMS

Units in this chapter

10.1   *Underlying concepts*
10.2   *Essential information*

Chapter objectives

This chapter describes important aspects of the structure of British industry, emphasising in particular the manner in which the size of firms has changed. Together with Chapter 11 on the finance of industry, the chapter provides a link between the microeconomic theory of Chapters 1 to 9, and the evaluation of British microeconomic policy in Chapter 12. In this chapter we shall be concerned with business enterprises in the private sector of the economy; nationalised industries are the subject of Chapter 12.

10.1 UNDERLYING CONCEPTS

In microeconomic theory, understanding is facilitated by considering the behaviour of a **single firm** operating a **single manufacturing plant** to produce a **specific product** within a **well-defined industry**. Reality, however, is much more complicated. Though single-plant/single-product firms certainly exist, particularly in the small business sector of the economy, large firms tend to be much more diverse. J K Galbraith has divided the economy into two parts: the thousands of small and traditional businesses on the one hand, and the few hundred technically dynamic, massively capitalised and highly organised corporations on the other. Large businesses in this **corporate sector** of the economy commonly operate in a variety of different industries, producing many different products from a number of separated plants. The largest business corporations are **multinational companies**, such as BP or ICI, controlling subsidiary enterprises and plants throughout the world. Some companies, such as Shell, are also **transnationals**, with ownership and control located in more than one country.

INDUSTRIAL STRUCTURE IN THE UNITED KINGDOM

Published statistics of the output of different British industries are usually based on the **Standard Industrial Classification**. This was first published in 1948, with revisions in 1958 and 1968. The latest revision, introduced in 1980, follows as closely as possible the classification of economic activities used by the EC. It comprises 10 major industrial divisions, including manufacturing, which are then further divided and subdivided into 60 classes, 222 groups and 334 activity headings. In the new structure, the energy-producing industries have been grouped, together with water supply, in a self-contained division. Other features are that, apart from agriculture, forestry and fishing, the various raw material producing industries are included within the same divisions as the corresponding processing industries, e.g. the slaughtering of animals is now included with food manufacturing, and the production of manmade fibres is a separate class adjacent to the chemical industry rather than a part of the textile industry. The SIC does not, therefore, always correspond to the normal description of 'industries' in economics text books. In service industries, the SIC draws a distinction between principals and agents, e.g. in the distributive trades, dealers, buying or selling on behalf of others, are classified separately from wholesalers who actually take ownership of the goods in which they deal.

In comparison with similar industrial countries, the United Kingdom has a relatively small **agricultural sector**, reflecting the reliance on food imports. In 1991, agriculture accounted for less than 2% of Gross Domestic Product. During the 1980s, mining industries – which include North Sea oil extraction – rose to about 10% of GDP, with the massive growth in the output of North Sea oil and gas more than offsetting a decline in the output of coal. However, the outputs of oil and gas probably peaked in the mid-1980s. The **manufacturing sector** is not particularly large in comparison with the relative share of manufacturing in countries such as Japan and West Germany. The share of manufacturing in GDP has fallen from 37% in 1955 to about 21% by 1991. In part, this reflects the importance of **financial service industries**, largely located in the City of London, to the British economy. It may also reflect the fact that many **services**, and the **utility industries** such as the gas and electricity industries, are in the **sheltered economy**, rather than in the **competitive economy**. By the nature of the service they provide, they are sheltered from import competition. Until the recession of the early 1990s at least, the service sector did not experience the de-industrialisation or structural decline, in response to import penetration and loss of export markets, that occurred in the manufacturing sector in the late 1970s and early 1980s. Some economists, notably R Bacon and W Eltis, have argued that the growth of employment in public sector services financed 'outside the market' was an important cause of the decline of manufacturing, through the 'crowding out' effects of taxation. In the 'boom' years of the late 1980s, it was hoped that de-industrialisation had ended, at least in terms of the absolute rather than the relative decline of manufacturing. By the end of 1987, the output produced by a much reduced or 'slimmed down' manufacturing sector had climbed back to the level previously achieved before the big decline in 1979. However, the process of de-industrialisation set in with a vengeance again in the severe recession which began in 1990, affecting services and the economy of the South East, as well as manufacturing in the more traditional industrial areas.

FIRMS

A **firm** or **enterprise** is a unit of control and ownership. A common method of classifying firms is in terms of the **legal status** of the enterprise. On this basis the main types of business enterprise in the United Kingdom are **sole proprietors** or traders, **partnerships**, and **private** and **public joint stock companies**, though other types of enterprise such as **co-operatives** and **building societies**, may be important in certain specialised areas of the economy. The concepts of small businesses and large businesses are less easy to define, since they do not refer to a precise legal status. Most small businesses are sole proprietors, partnerships and private companies, whereas the overwhelming majority of large businesses are public companies. In the early 1980s there were about 800 000 private companies and 8 000 public companies in the UK, though not all were actively trading. Some private companies such as the Littlewoods retailing group are sufficiently big to be regarded as large businesses, and a significant number of public companies are relatively small. When in 1971 the Bolton Committee reported on the role of small firms in the national economy, it found that there were 820 000 small firms responsible for 14% of GNP and 18% of the net output of the private sector. The inclusion of agriculture and the professions would have increased the 1971 total to 1250 000 enterprises, employing 29% of the working population. More recently it has been estimated that there are upwards of 2 million sole traders or unincorporated businesses alone, without taking account of small companies. The government had recommended to the Bolton Committee that a 'small firm might be defined broadly as one with not more than 200 employees', but the Committee decided that this definition was unsuitable for most industries. It used other criteria such as turnover in distribution, and the number of vehicles in road haulage, to classify small businesses. Generally, the Bolton Committee decided to include three further criteria in addition to the employment criterion recommended by the government in its definition of the small firm. These were:

❶ that it has a relatively small share of its market;
❷ that it is managed by its owners or part-owners in a personalised way;
❸ that it is independent.

PLANTS

A **plant** or **establishment** is an individual productive unit within an enterprise, such as a factory, shop or farm. Many manufacturing processes require the separation of production into specific technical operations conducted in different buildings and **workshops**. The manufacture of most automobiles, for example, involves a large number of **vertically related processes** from the casting of engines and the pressing of car bodies to the final assembly of the completed vehicle. Many of these processes may be **internally integrated** within the various plants owned by an enterprise. Sometimes a firm may own several plants, which are vertically integrated, operating in different geographical locations. In other circumstances the separated tasks may be performed in different workshops within a single plant or large factory. In the case of a **multi-product firm** (a **diversified firm** operating in different industries), it is of course usual for different plants to produce the different products, except when products are jointly supplied from a common raw material and manufacturing process.

10.2 ESSENTIAL INFORMATION

THE GROWING SIZE OF BRITISH FIRMS

1 The aggregate concentration ratio

This ratio measures the share of the 100 largest firms in manufacturing output. For most of the twentieth century, the **aggregate concentration ratio** increased, thus indicating the growing importance of large firms. The 100 largest firms accounted for 16% of manufacturing output in 1909; 22% in 1940; and 38% in 1985. Nevertheless, in a world context, British firms are not very large and, where British companies compete in world markets, they may be substantially smaller than their main competitors. Since 1979, the aggregate concentration ratio has decreased (falling to 38% by 1985), reflecting the decline and bankruptcy of many large manufacturing firms in the recessions of the early 1980s and 1990s. These recessions have reduced the importance of both manufacturing industries and large manufacturing firms within the economy.

Evidence on concentration outside manufacturing industry is less satisfactory, though retailing in general, and grocery retailing in particular, have become increasingly concentrated in a few large firms. In 1972 the 100 largest manufacturing firms supplied two-thirds of the output of the food and motor vehicle industries, and half the output of the chemical industry. The importance of the 100 largest firms was least in timber and furniture, and in leather clothing and footwear, accounting for less than 10% of output.

The evidence also indicates that the growth in aggregate concentration has been much more rapid in Britain than in other countries, despite the relative smallness of even the largest British firms.

2 The market concentration ratio

A common measure of concentration within a particular industry is the five firm **concentration** ratio. This ratio shows that, since 1968, the five largest firms have accounted for over 90% of domestic output in a quarter of manufacturing industries. Again, for many products, market concentration ratios are higher in the UK than in the USA, France and Germany. However, the concentration ratio can be a misleading indicator of monopoly power when there is substantial international trade and import penetration. Some economists believe that manufacturing industries in the United Kingdom are subject to much more competition than the concentration ratio suggests.

The fact that little of the growth in manufacturing concentration in the United Kingdom is explained by increasing plant size is of some significance. Between 1930 and 1968 the share of the 100 largest plants in manufacturing output remained the same at 10.8%. The explanation for increasing concentration must lie in the **increase in the average number of plants owned by the largest firms**. This suggests that an important cause of the increased size of firm is due to **takeovers** and **mergers** between existing firms, rather than a result of **internal growth** and the technical expansion of plants.

ECONOMIES OF SCALE

External economies

There are two sets of circumstances in which external economies occur:
❶ **External economies of scale** These occur when an individual firm within an industry, irrespective of its size or scale, benefits from a change in the scale of the industry as a whole. For example, the expansion of a firm which supplies components, in response to the growth of the whole industry, may allow an individual firm to buy components at a lower average cost. Such economies, which are external to individual firms, are internal to the industry.
❷ **External benefits** External economies of the first type are received through the market. This enables an individual firm to buy its inputs at a lower price than would otherwise be the case. In contrast, an external benefit is an externality received outside the market, for example when a farmer benefits from the drainage installed by his neighbour. You should refer back to Chapter 8 for a more detailed explanation of externalities, including external costs as examples of external diseconomies.

Internal economies of scale

It is useful to distinguish between **plant-level** economies of scale, **firm-level economies of scale**, and learning or experience effects, all of which can result in a larger size of firm having a greater opportunity to achieve lower unit production costs. An **internal economy of scale** occurs whenever an increase in the scale of the inputs, including factors of production which in the short run are fixed, results in a fall in the average cost of producing a unit of output. Internal economies of scale can only occur if the size of either the plant or firm is increased. In contrast, learning effects occur after a new technology has been adopted. A learning effect occurs when managers and workers learn from experience how to operate particular technologies more effectively. Although learning effects will usually be associated with a change in the scale of operations, this is not inevitable. Nevertheless the existence of learning effects suggests that the full benefit of economies of scale will not be experienced until some time after the change in scale has taken place.

❶ **Plant-level economies of scale** The main sources of economies of scale at the plant level are increased possibilities for the division of labour, better integration of technical processes within a particular plant, and better utilisation of indivisible items of plant. Most of these advantages are technical economies of scale, though there may be some scope for managerial economies of scale at the plant level as a result of managerial division of labour. Volume economies are a further type of technical economy: as the volume of a plant such as a blast furnace increases, the input of energy required to produce a unit of output may diminish.

❷ **Firm-level economies of scale** Presumably, firms will try to benefit as much as possible from the available plant-level economies of scale. They will also try to take advantage of economies associated with the growth of the firms which are independent of plant size, for example:

- **risk-bearing economies**: spreading risks over a number of products.
- **capital-raising economies**: large firms can often borrow from banks at a lower interest rate than small firms. The next chapter explains how large firms have access to the capital market.
- **bulk-buying and bulk-marketing economies**: large firms may be able to use their market power to buy supplies at lower prices and to market their products on better terms negotiated with retailers.
- **economies in overheads**: the costs of management and research and development can be distributed over a larger output.

❸ **The importance of economies of scale** Empirical evidence suggests that there are considerable economies of scale at the plant level in bulk chemicals and in assembly operations where mass production methods can be applied, e.g. motor vehicles and refrigerators. However, in some cases, scale economies may be as easy to obtain in a number of closely associated plants, not necessarily owned by the same firm, as in a single plant. In many industries the penalty of operating below Minimum Efficient Plant Size is small. The fact that the increase in concentration in the UK since 1945 has been through an increase in the number of plants owned or controlled by firms, rather than through an increase in plant size, suggests that firms have believed that more scope exists for economies at the firm level than at the plant level. Nevertheless, recent studies have concluded that firms which have grown through merger have performed less well after the merger. This may indicate that diseconomies of scale, resulting at the firm level from merger and acquisition, have exceeded the hoped-for scale economies. One such diseconomy is X-inefficiency, which has been identified in American research into mergers. X-inefficiency occurs when, because of social attitudes or institutional factors, a firm is unable to make proper use of its capital, or the technology at its disposal, or its labour force. A company will be X-inefficient if it is unable to implement new ideas and methods, for example if a group of shop-floor workers or managers successfully resists change. The existence of X-inefficiency means that a firm incurs a level of costs greater than the lowest possible cost of producing any output.

VERTICAL, HORIZONTAL AND CONGLOMERATE INTEGRATION

There are various ways in which the activities of a firm can be integrated. At the plant level there is an obvious **technical internal integration of processes**, which are often carried out in separate workshops. This is an example of vertical **integration**. Vertical integration of processes is also a motive for a firm to grow by internal growth, i.e. to invest in new plant in order to extend its operations into producing its own raw materials, components, or market outlets.

Integration can also take place by **acquisition**. A firm may take over or merge with an existing independent firm in order to integrate the existing capacity of the other firm into its operations.

Vertical integration

A firm can expand through vertical integration forwards or backwards. **Backwards integration** occurs when a firm buys into its sources of supply, for example when a car-assembly firm buys a manufacturer of gearboxes. **Forwards integration** involves the buying up of market outlets. This type of integration would take place if a car-assembly firm acquires a chain of retail showrooms.

Horizontal integration

This results when a firm takes over a similar firm at the same stage of production in the same industry. The merger between British Motor Holdings and Leyland Motors which created British Leyland (later to become the Rover Group, now owned by British Aerospace) in the late 1960s was largely horizontal.

Conglomerate integration

This is also known as lateral or diversifying integration. The defining characteristic of a lateral merger is the acquisition of a firm producing a different product in a separate industry. Large firms which have grown through lateral integration into highly diversified companies are known as conglomerates, for example Trafalgar House, whose interests range from construction to publishing.

Statistics on mergers

Many takeovers or mergers will contain elements of vertical, horizontal and conglomerate integration. The Office of Fair Trading has compiled a classification of mergers in the United Kingdom:

| Type | Percentages | | | | | | | | | | |
| | 1970 | | 1974 | | 1980 | | 1984 | | 1987 | | 1990 | |
	No.	Value	No.	Value	No.	Value	No.	Value	No.	Value	No.	Value
Horizontal	84	70	68	65	65	68	63	79	67	80	75	81
Vertical	1	0	5	2	4	1	4	1	3	1	5	3
Diversified	15	30	27	33	31	31	33	20	30	19	20	16
	100	100	100	100	100	100	100	100	100	100	100	100

The data indicates that most mergers are horizontal but a significant minority are conglomerate, perhaps because the opportunity for further horizontal amalgamation has diminished. Vertical motives for merger have been of no significance.

Motives, advantages and disadvantages

The underlying motive for a merger of any type is a company's belief that it can profitably use the assets of the firm which is being acquired. We have already indicated that this belief may be misguided, since the results of many mergers have been disappointing.

- **Economies of scale** This is an important motive in vertical and horizontal mergers. However, a proper productive integration of the plant of the merged companies must take place if the benefits are to be realised. Otherwise, diseconomies of scale may result and the merged firm may perform less well than the previously separate companies.

- **Financial motives** Economies of scale at a plant level are not an important motive behind conglomerate mergers. Financial motives, including the hope of financial economies of scale, are often significant in lateral mergers.

- **Monopoly power motives** Horizontal and vertical mergers may be planned in order to create a monopoly position in the market. The merged company may intend to use its market power to restrict output and raise price so as to increase its profits.

- **Other motives** Vertical mergers sometimes try to achieve security of supply or access to the market. The spreading of risks and the wish to diversify into growing markets are frequently cited as motives behind conglomerate mergers. Many mergers in the 1960s and 1970s had an asset-stripping motive. Asset-stripping mergers can be horizontal, vertical or conglomerate. The asset-stripper takes over a company in order to close it down, usually sacking the labour force and selling off the company's assets which are redundant to his plans. The asset-stripper believes that he can profitably convert the hidden assets of his 'victim' to an alternative use. In many examples of asset-stripping, the land owned by the takeover victim was the most important hidden asset. Asset-stripping earned a bad reputation because it was often associated with closing down productive firms and converting the premises to property speculation. However, some economists view asset-stripping as merely a part of the process of rationalisation which any economy must experience if it is to adapt to changing technology and demand. In the late 1980s, the asset-stripping motive for mergers resurfaced in the form of 'junk-bond' financed takeover bids. ('Junk bonds' are explained in Chapter 11.)

Chapter roundup

You should refer back to Chapter 3 for a theoretical coverage of economies of scale, and to Chapter 8 for examples of externalities which illustrate external economies and diseconomies. In the next chapter, Chapter 11, we examine the way firms finance growth in the British economy, and then in Chapter 12 we introduce further aspects of economies of scale and merger activity, in the treatment of competition policy.

Illustrative questions and answers

1 Essay Question
  Explain what the economist means by a 'firm' and why organisations as diverse as ICI and a corner shop can be said to possess the same essential characteristics from the economic viewpoint. Consider the possible reasons why approximately 90% of firms in the UK are 'small'.

  (NEAB, June 1987)

Tutorial note

A firm is a business enterprise producing (or dealing in) an output of goods or services for sale in the market. As we have seen, a profit-maximising objective is usually assumed, though other objectives such as attaining a target market share (or even simply survival), can be fitted into the economist's view of the firm and its activities. Nationalised industries can be classified as firms, providing that they predominantly concerned with market activity, but public sector services such as the National Health Service and state education are not normally regarded as firms by economists. Nevertheless, the logical thrust of reforms of these services, introduced by the Conservative Government in the early 1990s, is to make hospitals, doctors' surgeries, schools and universities function much more as if they are firms driven largely by commercial profit and loss criteria. You must explain how such profit and loss criteria affect businesses as diverse as ICI and a small corner shop. Start the last part of your answer by stressing that, although there are many more small than large firms, large firms account for a much greater proportion of total output nevertheless. It would take scores of thousands of corner shops to produce an output equal to ICI, especially when the value of the overseas output of this UK-based multinational is taken into account. Reasons for the existence of and survival of small firms include:

❶ Entrepreneurial choice – the owners of small firms may prefer the intimate surroundings and personal contacts of the business environment.

❷ Limited market size – this applies particularly to the provision of services such as hairdressing in local geographical areas.

❸ The demand for a personal or specialised service – again hairdressing provides a good example.

❹ The existence of diseconomies of scale – in these circumstances, cost advantages will create a competitive advantage for small firms.

❺ The absence of economies of scale – many industries display an absence of noticeable economies or diseconomies of scale, and there is likely to be a wide distribution of different-sized firms competing side by side in such an industry. In other industries there may be 'niches' in the market, or in the supply of specialist services to bigger firms, which can best be filled by small businesses.

❻ 'Sunrise' industries – a 'sunrise' industry is a completely new industry based on a new technology or a new product, such as digital watches. To start with, demand is small (accounting for the fact that firms are small). However, the small firms may grow into large businesses or be taken over by large firms in other industries, as the market expands over time.

❼ 'Sunset' or 'geriatric' firms – small firms sometimes survive for a while in a terminal stage of decline before their eventual demise, having shrunk from a much larger previous size. Such firms may be members of a declining industry or they may simply be badly managed firms or enterprises which have run out of entrepreneurial drive.

Suggested answer

- Define a firm as a business enterprise, producing or dealing in goods or services for sale.
- Show how ICI and a small corner shop fit into the economist's definition of a firm.
- Offer a definition of a 'small' firm, and suggest how small firms compare to large firms in terms of contribution to national output.
- Carefully explain (with examples) a number of reasons why small firms are significant.

2   Data Question

If there was one phrase that outlived its relevance almost before it left the mouths of those who used it, 'small is beautiful' must be it. As a catch-phrase signalling the demise of the corporate giant and the rise of the little man, it was the most overused one in business life in the early 1980s.

5   The past few years have rendered the term meaningless as the biggest companies in a wide range of industries from food and drink manufacturing to domestic appliances gobbled up or elbowed out smaller and weaker companies.

During the past few weeks alone, big acquisitions in elevator
10   manufacturing, pumps, power station equipment and printer machinery have tilted market power towards the bigger and tougher company. The merger process has indeed gathered pace over the past three years. In engineering, clever specialist manufacturers will always survive. But the best of the bigger companies are becoming larger through acquisition and
15   joint ventures. They are seeking control of more markets and broadening product ranges in order to offer the customer complete services and systems.

(Source: Adapted from N. Garnett, 'The relentless drive for size',
The Financial Times, 24 August 1988)

(a) Why might the author suggest that 'in engineering, clever specialist manufacturers will always survive' (line 13)?   (5)

(b) Analyse possible alternative motives in the trend towards acquisition.   (5)

(c) What are the implications for consumers of this trend towards acquisition? (5)

(d) If a government is concerned about mergers, what policies can it pursue in order to preserve and promote competition?   (5)

(ULEAC, June 1991)

Tutorial note

(a) 'Engineering' is a label which covers a vast range of different activities. At one extreme, mass-producing car manufacturers like Ford and Nissan invest millions of pounds 'tooling up' to produce a new car model, knowing that they can spread the cost over a long production run of hundreds of thousands of vehicles, Small producers cannot compete in the markets dominated by such large firms because they lack the required technical economies of scale. But at the other extreme there are thousands of small engineering firms occupying specialist market 'niches', often producing custom-made 'one-off' machine tools to the particular specification of a customer who may very well be one of the larger engineering companies.

(b) Introduce the motives we have listed in the chapter: the pursuit of economies of scale; financial motives; monopoly power motives; the spreading of risk and diversification; the 'asset stripping' motive, etc.

(c) Consumers may benefit from lower prices if mergers lead to more efficient production, but they may also suffer if monopoly is promoted and choice is reduced. Refer to Chapter 12 which covers Merger Policy for further details.

(d) Again, see Chapter 12 for coverage of merger policy. Note that the question is asking you to discuss possible approaches to the problems posed by mergers, rather than to give an historical account of UK merger policy. But by all means illustrate your answer from UK experience.

Question bank

1   Distinguish briefly between internal and external economies of scale. How might economies of scale affect market structure? (AEB, November 1989)

2

(a) How would you measure the size of a firm?   (5)
(b) What cost advantages might a firm gain when it increases its size?   (6)
(c) What revenue advantages might a firm gain when it increases its size?   (6)
(d) Do you believe that the cost or revenue advantages are more important in influencing the size of firms in the UK?   (8)

(Cambridge, June 1991)

3   Analyse and explain the likely sources of internal and external economies of scale for a firm in a manufacturing industry of your choice.

(O&CSEB, AS-Level, June 1992)

4

(a) Explain what is meant by the term 'economies of scale' and consider how they can arise in certain situations.   (20)
(b) Why is the output range over which economies of scale are experienced by firms likely to be a significant determinant of the market structure of particular industries?   (5)

(WJEC, June 1990)

5   If economies of scale are so significant, why are there so many small firms in the economy?   (AEB, November 1992)

6

(a) What are the likely advantages and disadvantages to the economy of the increase in the number and size of large-scale multinational companies in the UK?   (15)
(b) How might governments seek to encourage inward investment and to ensure that the activities of such company benefit the UK economy?   (10)

(Scottish Higher, June 1991)

7

(a) Examine the reasons why large firms may be able to produce at lower cost than small firms in the manufacturing sector.   (40)
(b) To what extent does you explanation also apply to the service sector in the UK economy?   (30)
(c) How can the government affect the creation and growth of small firms? (30)

(ULEAC, January 1993)

THE CAPITAL MARKET

Units in this chapter

11.1   *Underlying concepts*
11.2   *Essential information*

Chapter objectives

In Chapter 10 we explained how firms grow through a process of either
internal or **external growth**, or through a combination of both. We now
examine how a firm might **finance** the process of growth, involving as it
does the **investment in new plant** and productive capacity in the case of
internal growth, and the **acquisition of other firms** by **takeover** or
merger when external growth takes place.

11.1   UNDERLYING CONCEPTS

SAVING AND INVESTMENT

Although saving and investment have a similar meaning in everyday language, the
economist uses each word in a distinct way. **Saving** is defined as income which
is not spent on consumption, including funds that simply lie idle. In contrast,
investment involves the productive use of savings in the purchase of capital
goods, stocks, and raw materials. As a generalisation, households make savings
decisions and firms make investment decisions. Nevertheless, 60–75% of the
investment carried out by British firms is financed by internally generated funds,
when a firm provides its own savings out of revenue from the sale of its output.

Alternatively, firms may be able to obtain savings directly from households,
for example by advertising the **sale of shares**. It is more usual, however, for firms
to gain access to the savings of households via financial intermediaries such as
banks, insurance companies and pension funds, known generally as the financial
institutions.

ALTERNATIVE SOURCES OF FINANCE

It is useful to distinguish between internal and external sources of finance, taking
care not to confuse these terms with the concepts of internal and external growth
which were mentioned earlier.

Internal finance

We have already defined internal finance as the savings which a firm generates internally out of revenue. These funds are sometimes known as **ploughed-back profits**. It is worth repeating that self-finance provides by far the most important source of funds for British industry.

External finance

Some 25–40% of the financial requirements of firms in the private sector of the economy are raised through borrowing, the sale of shares, and government grants or subsidy. The main forms of external finance are:

❶ **Trade credit**. This refers to the practice of delaying the payment of bills for as long as possible while trying to persuade customers to settle their debts as quickly as possible in order to improve cash flow. Trade credit is equivalent to an interest-free loan.

❷ **Borrowing from banks**. Bank loans account for approximately 10–20% of the funds which are available to firms from all sources in the United Kingdom. British banks have often been criticised for failing to provide long-term risk capital to British industry. But traditionally British banks have lent to finance investment in working or circulating capital, such as the building up of stocks, in preference to fixed investment in new plant. We shall examine this criticism later in the chapter, paying particular attention to the financial needs of small firms.

❸ **Provision of finance by the government**. This takes two main forms: firstly, the provision of loans to the private sector, and secondly, government grants and subsidies, for example in the form of regional aid and support policies to agriculture.

❹ **Raising funds on the capital market**. Students commonly confuse the **capital market** and the **Stock Exchange**, and exaggerate the importance of both markets as sources of finance for British industry. The capital market is not a single institution. It comprises all the institutions, including banks, insurance companies and pension funds, which are concerned with either the supply of or demand for long-term funds, or securities which are claims on existing capital. It is thus the market for long-term loanable funds, as distinct from the money market which is the market for short-term funds.

11.2 ESSENTIAL INFORMATION

THE ROLE OF THE STOCK EXCHANGE

'When the capital development of a country becomes a by-product of the activities of a casino, the job is likely to be ill done.'– J M Keynes, in the *General Theory*.

The Stock Exchange is often criticised as being a place of mere speculation, a casino where dealers are interested only in making immediate capital gains through buying securities at one price and selling at another. This criticism stems from the fact that the Stock Exchange is the secondary or 'second-hand' part of the capital market. The Stock Exchange is viewed as a casino by its critics because it has little direct role in the raising of long-term funds or risk capital for industry. Fig. 32 illustrates why this is so. The actual raising of new capital takes place when public companies or the government decide to issue and sell new marketable securities. Companies may sell long-dated securities which guarantee a fixed rate of interest (**debentures** or **corporate bonds**) or they may sell a stake in the ownership of the company (**shares**, including **equity**). New issues of shares can be sold when a company goes public for the first time, or when an existing public company decides to raise extra capital by a new equity issue, usually a rights issue. A **rights issue** gives existing shareholders the right to buy at a favourable price. In the 1980s, a pernicious fashion started in the USA: the finance of 'hostile' take-over bids through the medium of 'junk-bonds'. A **'junk-bond'** is a corporate bond which carries a big element of risk since the company that issues it has few assets to secure the loan. Consequently, 'junk-bonds' earn a high rate of interest to compensate for the risk. The funds raised from the 'junk-bond' sale are used to finance the takeover of the 'victim' company, whose assets are then liquidated to pay the interest on the bonds!

New issues are not sold on the Stock Exchange, though occasionally the new issues of small companies are placed through Stock Exchange firms. Instead, new issues are sold on the **primary part** of the capital market, usually through newspaper advertisements arranged by merchant banks, or through direct contact with existing shareholders when a rights issue is made. It is important to stress that the amount of new capital raised through new issues in any one year is only a small fraction of the total trading taking place in existing securities on the Stock Exchange. It follows that most share sales are second-hand deals in which one member of the general public or a financial institution sells an existing security to another person or institution. The person who buys the security prefers to hold an interest or dividend-earning financial asset instead of money, whereas the seller is switching out of securities in order to store his wealth in the more liquid form of money. Thus the majority of security sales reflect individual decisions, called **portfolio balance decisions**, to adjust the form in which personal wealth is held, rather than a decision to supply risk capital to industry. Nevertheless, it is often argued that the Stock Exchange has important indirect roles in the provision of capital and the promotion of efficiency in British industry:

❶ When a private company decides to 'go public', its principal objective is to raise capital by securing access to the capital market. A Stock Exchange quotation, whereby the company's shares are listed and the market price quoted on the Stock Exchange, is certainly useful, and perhaps essential, if the general public is to be persuaded to buy the shares. New issues of shares would find fewer buyers if it was impossible to resell the securities on the Stock Exchange.

❷ The Stock Exchange Council examines the financial structure and control of all quoted companies. There may be greater public confidence in companies if only the shares of 'reputable' companies are quoted.

❸ The Stock Exchange has an important role in the restructuring of British industry in the face of changing technology and demand. Companies which fail to adapt will perform badly, and low profitability will cause share prices to fall. The quotation of a public company's shares on the Stock Exchange provides both an indicator of performance and a means through which the company can be taken over by new owners who believe they can use the company's assets more profitably. The threat of a future takeover can also provide an incentive for the existing managers to improve their performance.

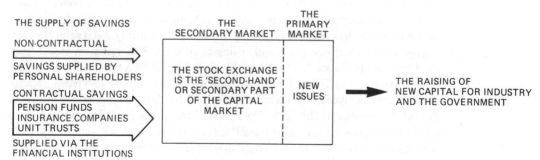

Fig. 32 The stock exchange and the capital market

THE GOVERNMENT AND THE CAPITAL MARKET

Only a small proportion of the securities traded on the capital market and the Stock Exchange represent either new or old capital raised by British industrial companies. A large proportion of securities are overseas securities. Others are British Government Securities, usually called **gilt-edged securities** or simply **gilts**. Gilts are similar to debentures, although the government sells far more gilts than the private sector sells debentures. Thus gilts secure a fixed-term loan to the government, after which the gilts mature and the face value is paid back. In addition, the government guarantees to pay a fixed interest each year during the life of the security. What is not guaranteed is the day-to-day market price at which the security can be resold second-hand on the Stock Exchange, or indeed the price which the government can persuade the general public to pay when it sells the gilt as a new issue.

The total quantity of new gilts which the government sells each year is strongly dependent on the size of the **budget deficit or surplus** and the **Public Sector Borrowing Requirement (PSBR)** or **Public Sector Debt Repayment (PSDR)**. Generally speaking, the higher the level of public spending in relation to tax revenue, the larger the PSBR and the government's need to borrow on the capital market. A large issue of gilts tends to depress their price, thereby converting the guaranteed interest rate or yield into a higher effective or true interest rate. In this way, public spending may 'crowd out' the private sector in the capital market, since the sale of gilts eventually raises interest rates and the cost of borrowing by companies. By contrast, a budget surplus and PSDR allow the government to repay a debt. There is less need to sell new gilts so pressure on interest rates may be relieved.

THE ROLE OF THE FINANCIAL INSTITUTIONS

It is widely believed that a large proportion of the shares in British companies are owned by small shareholders who are ordinary members of the general public. As the following table shows, this is no longer the case.

	1963	1975	1981	1983	1992
Persons and charities	56.0	39.8	30.4	27.0	20.0
Insurance companies	10.1	16.0	20.5	22.0	21.0
Pension funds	6.5	16.8	26.7	29.0	31.0
Investment and unit trusts	12.6	14.6	10.4	10.0	6.0
Overseas holders	6.9	5.6	3.6	4.0	13.0
Others	7.9	12.1	11.7	12.0	9.0
	100.0	100.0	100.0	100.0	100.0

(Source: Stock Exchange Surveys and CSO)

These figures indicate that individuals now directly own well under half of all shares whereas financial institutions, including insurance companies, pension funds, and unit and investment trusts, own the greater proportion. However, one result of the **privatisation** of previously nationalised industries such as British Telecom and British Gas in the 1980s was to increase, at least temporarily, the number of individuals owning shares. This was part of a policy of '**popular capitalism**', i.e. extending share ownership by reserving a proportion of newly issued shares for employees and small shareholders, rather than for the financial institutions. Banks own relatively little equity, though they control a substantial amount through the management and advice given to pension funds and to ordinary shareholding customers of the banks. In fact, the degree of concentration of control over shares in the hands of the financial institutions is greater than the statistics of ownership suggest. The growing power of the financial institutions is an important cause of imperfection in the capital market. Nevertheless, it can be said in defence of the institutions that they represent the growth of the indirect ownership of industry by ordinary workers via their contributions to pension and insurance schemes. Yet while it is undoubtedly true that workers receive the benefit of ownership from the pensions and insurance endowments which are financed through company profits, it is much more debatable whether the growing indirect ownership of shares via the financial institutions gives workers any real control over industry.

THE FINANCING OF SMALL BUSINESSES

Access to the capital market tends to be restricted to **public companies**, especially those with a Stock Exchange quotation. Since most small businesses are sole traders, partnerships or private companies, they must rely on bank borrowing, rather than on the sale of securities on the capital market, as their principal source of external finance. Many owners of small businesses complain that banks treat them much less favourably than large companies when providing loans to finance investment. This view was supported in the report of the **Wilson Committee on The Financing of Small Firms**, published in 1979. Nevertheless, there are several reasons why investments by small firms are riskier than those undertaken by large companies:

- Large firms are likely to engage in a wider range of investments. If one investment fails, the likelihood that at least some of the other projects will succeed reduces the risk of bankruptcy. In any case, large firms usually have greater cash reserves to draw upon in just such a crisis.
- Large public companies are less highly geared. A **high gearing** means that a large proportion of a company's assets are financed by borrowing rather than by shareholders' funds (accumulated profits and shares). Firms must usually pay a fixed rate of interest on their bank loans and debentures, even when no profits are being made. A **high gearing ratio** increases a firm's vulnerability to bankruptcy when business is bad. In contrast, a low-geared public company may survive a recession by suspending the payment of dividends to shareholders. Small businesses are usually highly geared, since they possess little or no equity capital. Banks may simply regard them as less attractive risks in comparison with lower-geared larger companies.

Yet bank overdrafts have always been the principal source of external funds for small businesses, be they unincorporated sales traders or private companies. Outside the banks, the 'venture capital' industries have grown to be a significant supplier of external funds to small- and medium-sized firms.

In the 1980s and 1990s the Conservative Government has actively encouraged the growth of small businesses as a means of reducing unemployment and as an escape from recession. An **Enterprise Allowance Scheme** encouraged the unemployed to start up their own businesses. Applicants to the scheme receive a weekly cash payment to offset loss of unemployment pay while establishing their businesses, also offsetting, it is hoped, the difficulties caused by a lack of start-up capital and the reluctance of banks to lend to the unemployed. The Government also created **Enterprise Zones**, which are inner-city areas exempt from rates and various bureaucratic controls. These may also have attracted new businesses though there is some debate as to whether they have simply caused firms to shift their location, thereby causing areas of 'blight' to emerge in areas insufficiently lucky to have been designated as Enterprise Zones.

The Wilson Committee suggested a number of ways in which the financial position of small businesses could be assisted. The recommendation of a **state-backed guarantee scheme for bank loans** was adopted in 1981. Under the scheme the state rather than a bank takes most of the risk if a business fails and cannot pay back a bank loan. The scheme has encouraged banks to grant term loans to finance long-term growth, thus replacing the more traditional shorter-term overdraft. The Wilson Committee further proposed the creation of **'over-the-counter' markets** throughout the UK in which the shares of small public, but unlisted, companies could be traded. Such **'share-shops'** might encourage a revival of personal share ownership and the local financing of businesses. While 'over-the-counter' markets have yet to emerge in any numbers, the Stock Exchange itself created in 1980 an **unlisted securities market** (USM) as a means for small companies to go public and to tap the capital market, without the expense of a full Stock Exchange listing. Compared to a full Stock Exchange launch, a company could go public on the USM by selling only a very small proportion of its equity. Few of the many companies launched since 1980 on the USM were actually used it to raise new capital; most were simply floated to enable the company's owners to obtain a market valuation of their capital. Indeed, during its short life the USM established a reputation for volatility, largely because the few shares made available in the 'high-flying' companies launched on the USM created conditions for speculation and rapid fluctuations in share price. Before the Stock Exchange crash of 1987, the USM provided a useful route, or half-way stage, for an eventual full Stock Exchange listing and quotation for successful and fast-growing companies (e.g. Amstrad). But after the 1987 Stock Market crash, the USM became moribund. The Stock Exchange changed its rules to make it much easier for smaller companies to go public on the full Stock Exchange without passing through the USM. In 1993 the USM was closed down.

Finally, the Wilson Committee advised the Government to establish a **Small Firms Investment Company (SFIC)** and an **English Development Agency**, intended to be the beginning of a full-scale Small Business Agency. These bodies would function as intermediaries through which small businesses might raise equity capital in the manner of the successful Scottish and Welsh Development Agencies. Although this idea has not yet been taken up, the 1981 Budget announced a **Business Start-up Scheme** to provide tax allowances for investment by individuals in new businesses. Because of its complexity and limited nature, the Business Start-up Scheme had little impact. In 1983 it was replaced by a **Business Expansion Scheme**, a rather simpler and more attractive package of tax advantages. Under the scheme, a number of managed funds have been set up to attract savings from private individuals for investment in growing new firms. However, the BES is due to close at the end of 1993.

Chapter roundup

In this chapter we have considered the financing of businesses in the private sector of the economy. We go on to examine government financial assistance to industry and the financing of investment by nationalised industries in Chapter 12. The financing of public investment in roads, schools and other forms of social capital is discussed in Chapter 15 on public finance.

Illustrative question and answer

1 Essay Question

Why do some economic systems have markets for shares and others do not? Does the behaviour of such markets in general reflect or determine the behaviour of the 'real' economy?

(NEAB, June 1990)

Tutorial note

Start your answer by making the point that Communist or command economies such as the Peoples Republic of China are unlikely to allow a capital market to exist because the political system outlaws or discourages private enterprise. However, this does not explain why perhaps half the countries in the world lack a proper capital market, despite the fact that the majority of them accept and try to promote private enterprise and a market economy. Essentially the role of a capital market is to channel individuals' surplus savings into the finance of investment opportunities undertaken by firms. Many countries have been too poor to generate the flow of surplus savings which is a necessary condition for a capital market to develop. Instead they finance their development by borrowing the excess savings of richer and already developed countries such as Japan, the USA and the UK. This involves either direct investment by 'First World' multinational companies, or the raising of funds on already developed and sophisticated capital markets, for example in New York, Tokyo or London. Often a local capital market lacks the economies of scale of the large established markets which have become increasingly international or globalised. Local capital markets are also less useful for raising funds in the hard currencies necessary to pay for imported capital goods. Nevertheless, many developing countries are trying to promote the growth of their own capital markets, both to make themselves less dependent on foreign multinationals and financial institutions, and also to make efficient use of the indigenous flow of savings that becomes increasingly available as development proceeds.

You might adopt a 'chicken and egg' approach to the second part of the question, arguing that share prices can both reflect and determine events in the real economy. When firms in the 'real' economy are performing well, profits will be high, leading to high share prices. This in turn makes it cheap and attractive to finance additional investment projects by raising further capital through new share or bond issues. The end result may be a 'virtuous growth' cycle in which share prices both reflect the success of, and promote the further development of, the real economy. But in the short term, share prices are also determined by speculation, and speculators try to guess the nature of events which have not yet occurred in the economy. In this situation, share prices act as 'lead indicators', signalling changes that are expected to occur in the real economy in the near future, be they announcements of company profits or trade figures, or changes in government policy. In the extreme, such speculative share price movements can themselves precipitate significant changes in the real economy, perhaps by destabilising it. Thus the collapse of share prices in the 'Stock Market Crash' of October 1987 was caused by a wave of speculative share selling, reflecting the view that share prices had become overvalued. But by destroying confidence and raising the cost of financing investment by new issues of shares, the 'Crash of '87' was one of the factors that brought about the recession in the 'real' economy in 1990, just as the much earlier Stock Exchange crash in 1929 had contributed to the Great Depression in the early 1930s.

Suggested answer

- Describe the role of a share market, and the necessary conditions for its emergence.
- Explain why less-developed economies usually lack a significant capital market. Go on to explain why they are likely to try to establish such a market as a part of the development process.
- Suggest circumstances in which share prices may respond to the 'real' economy, and then give examples of how they may determine events in the 'real' economy.
- Perhaps conclude by arguing that share markets may be too prone to 'short-termism', and that if institutions are not available that can take a more long-

term view, development of the economy's 'real' economy may ultimately suffer from too much reliance on share markets as a source of finance for the country's development.

Question bank

1 How many firms finance growth? Discuss whether shortages in the supply of funds have caused the low rate of investment in manufacturing industry in the United Kingdom. (AEB, November 1988)

2 Discuss the main sources of finance available for business expansion in:
(a) large firms.
(b) small firms. (O&CSEB, AS-Level, June 1990)

3
(a) Identify the main types of financial intermediary to be found in the UK and explain how they facilitate flows of funds between lenders and borrowers. (15)
(b) Discuss the argument that financial intermediation can affect a country's rate of economic growth. (10) (WJEC, June 1991)

4 Distinguish briefly between the money market and the capital market. Evaluate the role of the capital market in the United Kingdom economy. (AEB, November 1989)

INDUSTRIAL POLICY

Units in this chapter

Chapter objectives

In this chapter we examine the meaning of industrial policy and assess the effectiveness of the industrial policy implemented by the UK government in recent years. We shall examine three main elements of industrial policy: **competition policy; private versus public ownership of industry** and **regional policy,** before concluding the chapter with a discussion of the policy mix appropriate for tackling the important industrial problem of **deindustrialisation,** or the decline of manufacturing industry.

12.1 UNDERLYING CONCEPTS

THE MEANING OF INDUSTRIAL POLICY

Industrial policy is part of the government's **microeconomic policy** which aims to improve the economic performance of individual economic agents, firms and industries on the 'supply side' of the economy. Since the 1930s, when industrial policy first began as a response to the Great Depression, all British governments have had some sort of industrial policy. However, significant changes have occurred in the nature of the policy and in the importance attached by different governments to industrial policy when compared to other aspects of economic policy. The most far-reaching changes occurred in the 1980s after the decline of Keynesianism as the prevailing orthodoxy influencing British governments and the ascendancy of **monetarism, supply-side economics** and other elements of the **neoclassical revival.**

INDUSTRIAL POLICY BEFORE 1979

For much of the period from 1945 until 1979, successive British governments pursued an **interventionist** industrial policy, reflecting the Keynesian view that economic problems result from a failure of market forces and that industrial problems can be cured (or at least reduced) by appropriate government intervention. During the Keynesian era, industrial policy (and Keynesian economic policy in general) extended the roles of government and state planning in the economy.

INDUSTRIAL POLICY UNDER THE CONSERVATIVES AFTER 1979

By way of contrast, the industrial policy pursued by Conservative government in the 1980s and early 1990s has been anti-interventionist and based on the belief that the correct role of government is as an **enabling agency**, to encourage rather than reduce the role of market forces and to create the conditions in which market forces can work effectively and efficiently. But although recent Conservative governments have disbanded an interventionist industrial policy in favour of a more free market approach, in some respects the importance attached to industrial policy in the government's overall economic strategy has actually increased. During the Keynesian era, industrial policy and microeconomic policy were generally subordinate and subservient to macroeconomic policy. Keynesian macroeconomic policy was aimed overwhelmingly at the 'demand-side' of the economy, attempting to influence and control output and employment by managing the level of aggregate demand in the economy. But monetarists and other 'free-marketeers' believe that Keynesian demand management policies led to inflation rather than to full employment and economic growth. They also believe that the Keynesian concern with demand management diverted attention away from the 'supply-side' of the economy, where the real problems that must be tackled stand in the way of increased output and employment. It is perhaps not surprising, therefore, that after the monetarist or neoclassical 'counter-revolution' of the 1970s, the 1980s and after, macroeconomic policy has generally been subordinated to a 'supply side' microeconomic policy in which a free market orientated industrial policy has been elevated to a key position.

12.2 ESSENTIAL INFORMATION

COMPETITION POLICY

For over 40 years since its inception in 1948, **competition policy** has formed an important part of the UK government's wider industrial policy. Competition policy is part of industrial policy which covers monopolies, mergers and restrictive trading practices and we shall now look at each of these in turn.

STATUTORY MONOPOLY

Monopoly policy in the UK is seldom concerned with pure monopoly – rather it attempts to regulate highly concentrated industries dominated by a few large firms. **'Oligopoly policy'** might be a better descriptive label. For policy purposes, the UK government defines a statutory monopoly as existing if: either one firm has at least 25% of the market for the supply or acquisition of particular goods and services (a scale monopoly); or a number of firms, which together have a 25% share and so conduct their affairs to restrict competition (a complex monopoly).

THE THEORETICAL BACKGROUND TO MONOPOLY POLICY

In Chapter 6 we have seen how economic efficiency and output are likely to be maximised and consumer sovereignty and welfare promoted, when industries and markets are perfectly competitive. This provides the theoretical basis of the government's policy towards monopoly, mergers and restrictive trading practices. Compared to a perfectly competitive market, monopolies may be expected to reduce output and raise prices and they may have less incentive to innovate. Monopolies may also exploit their producer sovereignty by manipulating consumer wants, restricting choice and discriminating 'unfairly' between different customers. Nevertheless, as we have also seen, the argument that monopolies restrict output and raise prices assumes that monopolies and perfectly competitive firms have similar cost curves. When **economies of scale** are possible, this is unlikely to be the case. Indeed a 'natural' monopoly exists when limited market size makes it impossible for more than one firm to benefit from full economies of scale. It has been argued that splitting up a 'natural' monopoly (such as the gas industry) into a large number of competitive firms would lead to unnecessary duplication of distribution networks. Thus, there is a strong case for these industries to continue to be organized as monopolies. The public policy choice is not so much a choice between competition and monopoly; rather it is a choice between **state monopolies** run as nationalised industries and **private monopoly** subject to severe and effective public regulation. Monopolies are also sometimes justified on the grounds that they promote rather than reduce innovation (since the expectation of monopoly profits allowed by barriers to entry, creates an incentive to develop new products and technologies). They are also justified on the grounds that large domestically based firms might be able to compete in world markets.

CARTELS AND FULLY-UNIFIED MONOPOLIES

Whether innovation is likely to be increased or diminished by monopoly will depend to some extent upon the reason for the creation of the monopoly. It is useful to divide monopolies into:

Cartels

A cartel is usually regarded as the worst form of monopoly, as regards public interest, since it is likely to exhibit most of the disadvantages of monopoly with few (if any) of the benefits. A cartel is a **price ring** which is formed when independent firms make a restrictive agreement to charge the same price, and possibly to restrict output. A cartel acts as a monopoly in the marketing of goods, but the benefits of economies of scale are unlikely to occur because the physical or technical integration of the productive capacity of the cartel's members does not take place. Consumer choice is restricted, and cartels tend to keep inefficient firms in business while the more efficient members make monopoly profits. In these circumstances, it is probable that the incentive to innovate by developing new products and methods of production will be lacking. Cartels are thus **dynamically inefficient**.

Fully unified monopoly

A fully unified or fully integrated monopoly may result by accident rather than design. A dynamic firm grows and benefits from economies of scale, becoming a monopoly as the reward for successful competition! The monopoly position is the result of the firm's success in innovation and reducing costs – all of which indicate that the firm is dynamically efficient. A fully unified monopoly is thus likely to be the 'spin-off' of essentially 'benign' motives for growth. Once the monopoly has been established, the firm may continue to behave well, retaining its innovative habits and using its monopoly profit to finance new developments, though government regulation may be necessary to ensure continued 'good behaviour'.

THE COST-BENEFIT APPROACH OF MONOPOLY POLICY

Because it is recognised that monopoly can be good or bad depending upon circumstances, UK monopoly policy has always taken the pragmatic view that each case of a monopoly or trading practice that restricts competition must be judged on its merits. If the likely costs resulting from the reduction of competition exceed the benefits, the monopoly should be prevented but, if the likely benefits exceed the costs, monopoly should be permitted, provided that it does not abuse its position and exploit the consuming public.

THE MONOPOLIES AND MERGERS COMMISSION AND THE OFFICE OF FAIR TRADING

UK monopoly policy is implemented by the **Office of Fair Trading (OFT)** and the **Monopolies and Mergers Commission (MMC)**, which are responsible to a government ministry, the **Department of Trade and Industry (DTI)**. The OFT uses market structure, conduct and performance indicators to scan or screen systematically the UK economy for evidence of monopoly abuse. Concentration ratios provide evidence of monopolistic market structures, while market conduct indicators allow the OFT to monitor anti-competitive business behaviour. Conduct indicators include:

❶ consumer and trade complaints;
❷ evidence of parallel pricing, price discrimination and price leadership;
❸ evidence of merger activity;
❹ the ratio of advertising expenditure to sales.

The four main performance indicators used to measure business efficiency are:

❶ price movements;
❷ changes in profit margins;
❸ the ratio of capital employed to turnover;
❹ the return on capital employed.

When the OFT discovers evidence of statutory monopoly which, it believes is likely to be against the public interest, it refers the firms to the MMC for further investigation. In most cases, the OFT asks the MMC to decide the relatively narrow issue of whether a particular trading practice is in the public interest, and not to address the wider issue of whether the firm should be split up. The MMC interprets the public interest largely in terms of the effect upon competitiveness of the trading practices it is asked to investigate. The Commission does not possess any powers to implement or enforce its recommendations. Instead, it reports to the DTI, which may either implement some or all of the recommendations, shelve the report and do nothing, or take action completely contrary to the MMC's recommendations. For example, in 1989 the MMC recommended in its report into monopoly in the brewing industry, that the major breweries should be forced to sell off all public houses they owned in excess of 2000. However, the government eventually partially rejected this recommendation. Usually, however, the government complies with the spirit of the MMC's report. The government has quite wide powers to take action (including the ability to make an order requiring that firms split up or sell off assets). But in practice, these order-making powers are seldom, if ever, used. Currently, it is usual for the government to ask the OFT to talk with the firms to persuade them to alter their business behaviour voluntarily. Firms may be asked to abandon any undesirable practices and to give undertakings about their future conduct.

ALTERNATIVE STRATEGIC APPROACHES TO MONOPOLY POLICY

Ever since the establishment of the Monopolies Commission in 1948, UK monopoly policy has been based on a **pragmatic regulatory and investigatory approach,** watching out for monopoly abuse and investigating firms or industries where abuse or inefficiency is suspected. Relatively few firms and takeover bids are actually investigated – the rationale being that the possibility of an MMC investigation creates sufficient incentive for most large firms to behave themselves and resist the temptation to exploit their monopoly power. However, although the 'watchdog' investigatory/regulatory role of the MMC has been central to UK monopoly policy, there are a number of alternative strategic approaches that might be used. These include:

- the compulsory breaking up of all monopolies;
- the use of price controls to restrict monopoly abuse;
- taxing monopoly profits;
- the public ownership of monopoly;
- privatising monopolies;
- removal of barriers to entry.

THE GROWING INFLUENCE OF THE 'THEORY OF CONTESTABLE MARKETS'

It is generally agreed that privatisation alone cannot eliminate the problem of monopoly abuse, since it merely changes the nature of the problem back from public or state monopoly to private monopoly and the commercial exploitation of a monopoly position. The fact that the privatisation of the telecommunication and gas monopolies has been accompanied by the setting up of regulatory bodies such as OFTEL and OFGAS, which provide a source of regulation additional to that available from the MMC and the OFT, is a recognition of this problem.

One method of exposing monopolies – including the newly privatised utility industries – to increased competition, is to remove artificial barriers to entry. The government can remove the protected legal monopoly status enjoyed, for example, by the Post Office for letter deliveries and by bus companies, airline and commercial TV and radio companies. Access to BT's distribution network of landlines can be given to a competitor such as Mercury Communications and private power companies can be allowed to rent the services of the national electricity distribution grid. Import competition can also be encouraged. This can be quite effective in reducing the market power of public and private monopolies producing internationally traded goods and services but it would be less effective in reducing the monopoly power of utility industries, whose products are not generally traded internationally, and consequently are not vulnerable to import competition.

Support for the belief that the most effective (and simplest) way of dealing with the problem of monopoly is to remove any artificial barriers to entry, has been provided by an important 'new' theory known as the **theory of contestable markets.** Before the advent of this theory (and of the wider neoclassical revival of which the theory of 'contestable' markets is a part), monopoly policy and other aspects of industrial policy involved an ever-increasing extension of regulation by government into the activities of private sector firms. Increased intervention was justified by the belief that regulatory powers must be strong enough to countervail the growing power of large business organisations and make monopolies behave in a more competitive fashion. But, one unforeseen result of the spread of government regulation of industry has been that powerful established firms, which the system of regulation was intended to control, have often been able to use the regulatory system to their own advantage. This is called 'regulatory capture'. The beneficiaries of regulation have become the regulated firms themselves, rather than consumers or outside firms attempting to gain entry to the market. This has been because large established firms, already within the market, possess political lobbying power to influence government and the regulators and a monopoly of much technical information relevant to their industry.

Before the advent of the theory of 'contestable' markets, monopoly was normally defined by the number of firms in the market and by the share of the leading firms, measured by a concentration ratio. The basic dilemma facing the policy makers centred on how to reconcile the potential gains in productive efficiency, (that a monopolist's large scale of operation could allow) with the fact that lack of competitive pressure can lead to monopoly abuse and consumer exploitation. But in the theory of 'contestable' markets, monopoly is defined, not by the number of firms in the market nor by concentration ratios, but by the potential ease or difficulty with which new firms may enter the market. Monopoly is not regarded as a problem, even if there is only one established firm in the market; provided that an absence of barriers to entry and exit creates the potential for new firms to enter and contest the market. Actual competition in a market is not essential; the threat of entry by new firms is quite sufficient, according to the 'contestable' market theory, to ensure efficient and non-exploitive behaviour by existing firms within the market.

The theory of 'contestable' markets has had a major impact upon recent UK monopoly policy under the Conservative government, because it implies that a conventional regulatory policy is superfluous, provided there is adequate potential for competition. Instead of interfering with firms' pricing and output policies, the government should restrict the role of its monopoly policy to discovering which industries and markets are potentially contestable and then developing conditions, by policies of **deregulation**, to remove barriers to entry and exit, ensuring that contestability is possible.

Appropriate **deregulation policies** suggested by the theory of 'contestable' markets include:

- the removal of licensing regimes for public transport and TV and radio transmissions;
- removal of controls over ownership, such as exclusive public ownership;
- removal of pricing controls which act as a barrier to entry, such as those practised in the aviation industry.

MERGER POLICY

Recent UK merger policy has also reflected the influence of the theory of 'contestable' markets, since a merger is only referred by the government for investigation by the MMC if the OFT has advised that, on the face of it, the merger might have significant anti-competitive effects. The OFT cannot itself make merger references to the MMC but the office has important screening and advisory roles. The OFT keeps itself informed of all merger situations that might be eligible for a reference to the MMC, by picking up information from the firms themselves and from the financial press. Currently a merger is eligible for reference to the government if the merger creates a combined company with at least 25% of the market, or if the assets of the company being acquired are valued at £30m or more. It is generally assumed by the government that mergers are beneficial; unless it can clearly be shown that the effects are likely to be adverse. In fact, very few eligible mergers are investigated; even fewer are declared against the public interest and prohibited. Critics argue that the policy is applied inconsistently and is much too weak. They believe that the stance of merger policy should be significantly changed to a presumption that mergers have adverse rather than beneficial effects, and that factors such as the 'national interest' should be considered as well as anti-competitive effects, (to prevent UK-owned firms falling into foreign hands).

EC MERGER POLICY

In 1990, a new EC merger policy came into operation to control the growing number of mergers within the European Community. The European Commission has long had powers to control mergers but, before 1990, it did not apply them systematically. Under the new system, the UK and other EC countries will continue to use national policy to deal with smaller mergers, but the European Commission will adjudicate on larger mergers with a 'Community dimension'. As in UK merger policy, nearly all the EC's criteria for judging a merger are competition related. However, although the new EC policy is intended to provide a 'one-stop' regulatory system by clarifying the borderline between EC and national jurisdiction, many commentators fear that the opposite will be the case. They fear that the new system will be an unclear, time-consuming, bureaucratic 'paradise for lawyers', which will cause companies contemplating a merger to register their plans with both national and EC authorities to minimise the chance of falling foul of either.

RESTRICTIVE TRADING PRACTICE POLICY

Restrictive trading practices undertaken by firms in imperfect product markets can be divided into two broad kinds: those **undertaken independently by a single firm**; and **collective restrictive practices** which involve either a written or an implied agreement among two or more firms.

Independently undertaken restrictive practices

In the UK there is no separate legislation dealing with independently undertaken restrictive practices. These might include: the decision taken by a firm to charge discriminatory prices; the refusal to supply a particular resale outlet; and 'full-line forcing' (whereby a supplier forces a distributor who wishes to sell one of his products to stock the full range of his products). Instead, such practices are covered by the monopoly policy we have already described – they are considered as evidence of anti-competitive market conduct or behaviour when the OFT decides on monopoly references. As we have seen, the MMC frequently recommends in its reports that firms drop any trading practices which offend the public interest.

Collective restrictive practices

In contrast to independently undertaken restrictive practices, collective restrictive agreements and practices can be referred by the OFT to a court of law, the Restrictive Practices Court (RPC). The current legal position is that a firm must register any restrictive agreement (such as a cartel agreement) with the OFT. The OFT then automatically notifies the RPC. The restrictive agreement is presumed to be illegal unless the firm can persuade the court that the practice is in the public interest.

THE NEED TO MODERNISE RESTRICTIVE PRACTICE LEGISLATION

Some economists argue that the introduction of restrictive practice legislation, in the 1950s, was a major cause of takeover activity in the next three decades. Firms successfully circumvented the outlawing of collusive practices, such as cartel agreements, by internalising the restrictive practice through merger! However, it is now generally agreed that the current legislative framework is less effective than it ought to be and is in need of revision. The main weaknesses in the current system are:

- Once a collective agreement is registered, it can continue to operate lawfully until the RPC rules whether or not the agreement is in the 'public interest'. But, in practice, it can take several years for an agreement to come to court, unless the OFT pushes for an early decision.

- Companies are able to avoid prosecution by skilfully drafting an agreement to take advantage of the loopholes provided by the eight 'gateways' that allow a 'public interest' defence of an agreement.
- The present laws are ineffective because of concessions granted to many industrial sectors and, in particular, to the professions. These are currently 43 separate exemptions, ranging from agreements concerning the marketing of eggs, to long-established restrictive practices within the professions.
- Although agreements that are not registered are automatically declared illegal if uncovered by the OFT, all too often they remain uncovered. This is because the OFT's powers of investigation are limited. At present, OFT officials can act only when they have firm evidence that a cartel exists (evidence which is usually provided by a disgruntled ex-member of the cartel).
- The maximum fines that the RPC can impose upon guilty firms are much too small to act as an effective deterrent to misbehaviour. The maximum fines bear no relation to the scale of cartel agreements.

To take account of the weaknesses outlined above, the Government published plans in 1989 to reform the law relating to restrictive practice, but has not found parliamentary time as yet in which to introduce the necessary legislation.

PUBLIC OWNERSHIP AND INDUSTRIAL POLICY

The history of nationalisation in the UK extends back to the middle of the 19th century when the Post Office was established as a civil service department. The first public corporation was the Port of London Authority, created in 1908. Other early public corporations were the Central Electricity Board, London Passenger Transport Board and the BBC, set up by Acts of Parliament in the 1920s. Most of the early public corporations represent what has been called 'gas and water' socialism: the regulation, through public ownership, of an essential utility or service regarded as too important to be left to the vagaries of private ownership and market forces. However, the main periods of nationalisation and extension of public ownership in the UK have occurred during the periods since the Second World War when Labour governments have been in office.

In 1929 the British Labour Party adopted the commitment to 'common ownership of the means of production, distribution and exchange'. Although nationalisation has at times been regarded by some Labour Party supporters rather as an end in itself, socialist theoreticians have argued that increased public ownership is necessary to give the government proper control of the key industries (or 'commanding heights' of the economy), deemed vital for the socialist planning of the economy. Socialists have also believed that nationalisation leads to improved industrial relations and to a more equitable distribution of income and wealth amongst the population. In the former case, greater industrial democracy can be promoted as class conflict between capitalists and workers giving way to co-operation between workers and managers to serve the public interest. At the same time, the abolition of private ownership and monopoly profit can allow the payment of higher real wages to the employees of nationalised industries and the charging of lower prices to consumers; both of which should improve distributional equality within society. Nevertheless, it was not originally envisaged by Labour Party politicians that nationalised industries would be subsidised and run at a loss, whether to save the industries from bankruptcy or to provide a subsidised service to the public. Indeed, the Labour Party believed that the key industries, once nationalised, would immediately begin to function more efficiently than under private ownership, thus allowing employers, consumers, taxpayers and the 'wider' public interest all to benefit.

OTHER REASONS FOR NATIONALISATION

Industries have therefore been nationalised in the UK for two main reasons: as an **instrument of socialist planning and control of the economy** and as a method of **regulating the problem of monopoly** – in particular the problem of 'natural' monopoly in the utility industries. There are, however, other possible reasons for nationalisation, some of which have been used by supporters of public ownership as part of an ad hoc justification for keeping industries in the public sector and resisting privatisation. These include:

- to regulate the production of demerit goods, such as alcohol or gambling;
- to regulate the production of merit goods and ensure public health;
- defence and national security;
- to use monopoly profit as a source of state revenue;
- national prestige;
- the rescue of uncompetitive manufacturing industries ('lame ducks' or 'hospital cases').

NATIONALISED INDUSTRY PRICING AND INVESTMENT POLICIES

In terms of pricing policy the nationalisation statutes, which established the major public corporations in the 1940s, were vague, simply requiring that the industries should pay their way 'taking one year with another'. Thus, from the beginning, a potential conflict was created between the commercial objective of being profitable and the public interest duty to provide social, and often uneconomic services, e.g. to citizens living in remote areas. By the 1960s, much more thought was being given to the 'correct' pricing and investment policies nationalised industries should adopt. It was suggested that the pricing policies of nationalised industries should be based on the principle of **marginal cost pricing**, while investment decisions should follow the best practice adopted in the private sector: namely to use the **discounted cash flow techniques** (explained in Chapter 21) to decide whether particular investment projects are worthwhile.

MARGINAL COST PRICING

We have seen that many of the industries taken into public ownership in the UK have been monopolies and that nationalisation can prevent consumer exploitation by the monopoly deliberately restricting output and raising prices. Left to itself, and functioning as private profit maximiser, a nationalised industry would choose a level of output and set a price at which $P > MC$. But as we have explained in Chapter 5, this is **allocatively inefficient**: too little of the good or service would be produced and consumed because the price is too high. To produce the **allocatively efficient level of output**, a nationalised industry should therefore adopt marginal cost pricing, so that $P = MC$. By setting a price equal to marginal cost, the conditions of perfect competition are approximated, while still achieving the productive efficiency or low average costs that economies of scale and the monopoly position of the industry allow.

However, there are a number of difficulties in both the theory and the application of marginal cost pricing.

❶ Marginal cost pricing can be guaranteed to improve allocative efficiency only if all other prices in the economy equal marginal costs. Since many prices charged in the private sector do not equal the relevant marginal costs, it is therefore by no means certain that by instructing a nationalised industry to charge marginal cost prices, allocative efficiency will improve.

❷ In any case, to ensure allocative efficiency throughout the economy, each industry – including the nationalised industries – would have to set price equal to **marginal social cost** ($P = MSC$) rather than just the marginal private production cost incurred by the industry itself. Thus, if the pricing decision of a nationalised industry were to reflect the wider public interest, which is measured by social costs and benefits, the value of all the external costs and benefits generated in the course of production would have to be calculated and included in the price charged by the industry. External costs (or negative externalities) would include the costs of pollution and environmental destruction; while any environmental improvement 'spun off' from production would be an example of an external benefit (or positive externality):

❸ The question of whether price should be set equal to **short-run** or **long-run marginal cost** is significant, since the decision affects a nationalised industry's profitability. Most of the nationalised industries benefit from economies of large scale production and falling 'long-run average total costs' (LRATC). In this situation, long-run marginal costs (LRMC) must be below LRATC. If P = LRMC, the industry inevitably makes a loss and requires a subsidy to finance the resulting deficit. But the use of taxation to finance the deficit of a nationalised industry causes fresh allocative distortions and is likely to reduce industry morale. By contrast, if an industry is instructed to set P = SRMC, profits are made normally, though these are smaller than they would be if the industry were allowed to act 'commercially', as a private profit-maximiser, producing the output at which MR = MC.

❹ Because of 'lumpiness' or **indivisibilities**, it may be difficult or impossible (in practice) to calculate the marginal cost of providing an extra unit of a good to a single consumer.

NATIONALISED INDUSTRY PRICING IN PRACTICE

Partly because of the difficulties we have just listed, the theory of marginal cost pricing has had only a very limited impact upon the actual pricing decisions of nationalised industries in the UK. In practice, the instruction that nationalised industries should set prices equal to marginal cost has been subordinated by successive UK governments who have used nationalised industry pricing as an instrument to achieve other objectives of government policy. In the 1970s, Conservative and Labour governments both used the prices charged by nationalised industry as a **counter-inflation policy instrument**. Prices were kept artificially low and the industries made large losses. More recently, this policy has been reversed. In the 1980s, the Conservative government instructed the industries to act 'commercially', just as if they were private profit maximisers. Since the profits (or trading surpluses) of nationalised industries go to the Exchequer, this represents a form of **'implicit' taxation**, with government revenue from the profits of nationalised industries allowing the level of formal or 'official' taxation to be kept down. Many commentators also believe that the current policy of instructing nationalised industries to set profit-maximising prices, ignoring any wider 'public interest' issues, represents the 'fattening up' of the few remaining industries for eventual privatisation.

PRIVATISATION

Following the major nationalisations of the 1940s, the next 30 years saw little movement on that front. Many of the Acts of Nationalisation, passed by Labour governments, merely reorganised assets already in the public sector. But, equally, there was relatively little denationalisation or privatisation when Conservative governments were in office. The 1950s to the 1970s were the decades of the mixed economy; when the major political parties agreed that the mix of public and private enterprise worked and was 'right for Britain'. But with the election of a radical free-market orientated administration, under Mrs Margaret Thatcher in 1979, this consensus broke down. The Conservative government of the 1980s and early 1990s set about the task of **breaking up the mixed economy** and replacing it with a social market economy.

This has involved an industrial policy based on the interrelated processes of privatisation, marketisation and deregulation which are illustrated in Table 12.1.

Table 12.1 Privatisation and related industrial policies

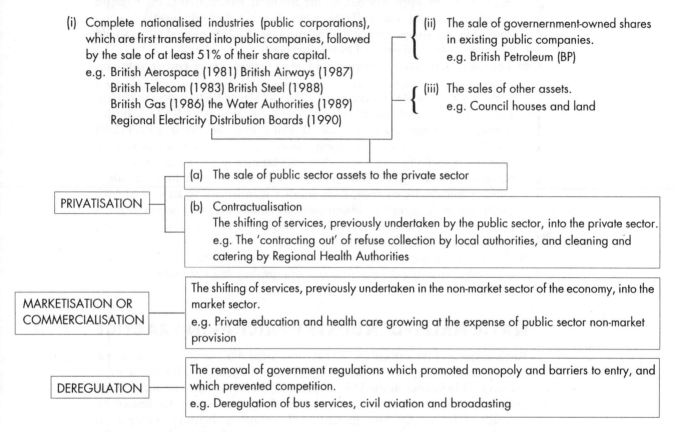

THE CASE FOR PRIVATISATION

The general case for privatisation can only be understood properly when seen as part of the 'revolution' (or 'counter-revolution') in economic thinking known as the **neoclassical revival**.

We have already noted that socialists often seem to regard nationalisation as an end in itself, apparently believing that by 'taking an industry into public ownership', efficiency and equity are automatically improved and the public interest served. In much the same way, many economic 'liberals' (at opposite ends of the political and economic spectrum) seem to believe that private ownership and capitalism are always superior to public ownership, whatever the circumstances; and that the privatisation of state-run industries must inevitably improve economic performance.

Rather more specific arguments that have been used to justify the privatisation programme include:

- **Revenue raising** Privatisation (the sale of state-owned assets) provides the government with a short-term source of revenue which in some years has reached £3–4 billion or more. Clearly an asset cannot be sold twice; eventually privatisation must slow down when there are no more assets left to sell.
- **Reducing public spending and the PSBR** Since 1979, the Conservative government has aimed to reduce both public spending and the Public Sector Borrowing Requirement (PSBR). By classifying the monies received from asset sales as 'negative expenditure' rather than as 'revenue' then, from an accounting point of view, the government has been able to reduce the level of public spending as well as the PSBR. Clearly there are other more concrete reasons why privatisation may cause public spending to fall besides those related to

'creative accounting'. If the state can successfully sell loss-making industries, such as the Rover Group, public spending on subsidies falls. The PSBR can also fall if private ownership returns the industries to profitability, since corporation tax revenue will be boosted.

- **The promotion of competition and efficiency** Most nationalised industries were monopolies. For reasons already explained, Conservative governments believe that nationalised industries are inefficient. Before the beginning of the privatisation programme in the early 1980s, Conservative politicians frequently argued that a major reason for privatisation was to 'promote competition' through the break-up of the state monopolies. However, as we have seen, many of the nationalised industries were 'natural' monopolies, difficult to break up into competitive smaller companies without a significant loss of economies of scale and productive efficiency. There has also been a practical conflict between the aims of promoting competition and raising revenue. To maximise revenue from the sale of a nationalised industry such as BT or British Gas, the government chose to sell the industry whole, without breaking up the monopoly. Therefore, privatisation has tended to switch industries merely from public to private monopoly; with little evidence that either competition or efficiency has been promoted, despite the introduction of some market discipline via the capital market.

- **'Popular capitalism'** Undoubtedly, an important reason for the privatisation programme in the UK has been the motive of extending share ownership to individuals and employees (who previously did not own shares) so as to widen the stake of the electorate in supporting a private enterprise economy. Privatisation has proved generally popular with voters so the Conservative government has seen no point at all in changing a winning programme.

THE CASE AGAINST PRIVATISATION

- **Monopoly abuse** As we have already seen earlier in this chapter (in the context of competition policy), opponents of privatisation argue that, far from promoting competition and efficiency, privatisation increases monopoly abuse by transferring socially owned and accountable public monopolies into weakly regulated, less accountable private monopolies. Evidence of consumer dissatisfaction with the service provided since privatisation by BT and British Gas has been used to support this argument.

- **'Selling the family silver'** Opponents of privatization argue that if a private sector business were to sell its capital assets, simply in order to raise revenue to pay for current expenditure, it would rightly incur the wrath of its shareholders. The same should be true of the government and the sale of state-owned assets: taxpayers ought not to sanction the sale of capital assets, owned on their behalf by the UK government, to raise revenue to finance current spending on items such as wages. In reply, supporters of the privatisation programme argue that, far from 'selling the family silver', privatisation merely 'returns the family's assets to the family', i.e. from the custody of the state to direct ownership by private individuals.

- **The 'free lunch' syndrome** Opponents of privatisation also claim that state-owned assets have been sold too cheaply, encouraging the belief amongst first-time share buyers that there is such a thing as a 'free lunch'. This is because the offer-price of shares in newly-privatised industries has normally been pitched at a level which has guaranteed a risk-free capital gain (or 'one-way bet') at the taxpayer's expense for people buying the government's sell-offs; thereby encouraging the very opposite of an 'enterprise' economy of risk-taking venture capitalism.

REGIONAL POLICY AND THE REGIONAL PROBLEM

Much of the industrial policy implemented by United Kingdom governments since the Great Depression in the 1930s has been specifically regional in character; aiming to improve the overall performance of the UK economy by reducing regional inequalities and by making better use of all the nation's resources, wherever they happen to be located.

For much of the 20th century it has been possible to divide the UK into a 'successful half' (broadly the southern part of Britain including London and the South East, the Midlands and East Anglia) and an 'unsuccessful half' (in the north and west of the UK). The 'successful' south-eastern half of Britain is part of the **'Golden Triangle'** – a 'core' area of post-war growth in Western Europe, stretching between the English Midlands, North Germany and the Paris Basin in France. By contrast, most of the rest of Britain is part of a **European 'periphery' region**, outside the core of the 'Golden Triangle'. The European periphery is sometimes further subdivided into an 'outer' and an 'inner' periphery. In Britain, the 'outer periphery' includes the older area of 18th and 19th century industrialisation, together with the geographically remote, sparsely populated and generally non-industrialised 'highlands and islands' which make up the northern and western fringe of the UK. The 'outer periphery' experienced a much slower rate of growth of output than the rest of the UK during the 1950s and 1960s. By contrast, the 'inner periphery', stretching in a broad belt across central Britain and including parts of the south-west, the Midlands, Lancashire and Yorkshire, achieved neither the prosperity of the 'core' nor the stagnation typical of the outer region. Instead, its experience lay between these extremes.

THE CONVERGENCY APPROACH TO REGIONAL PROBLEMS

In large part, the modern British regional problem is a problem of **mismatching capital and labour**. The northern, 'unsuccessful' half of Britain has combined a surplus of labour with a capital shortage; whereas the southern 'successful' part of Britain has been a region of plentiful capital but relative labour shortage.

In this situation, conventional market theory would predict that wage levels should rise in the south in response to the relative shortage of labour. At the same time, capital should flow northwards and labour southwards; being attracted respectively by the wage differentials emerging between the two halves. Thus, by encouraging capital and labour mobility in this way, the market mechanism should ultimately lead to a process of regional convergence in which differences between regions are equalised, thereby causing the regional problem to disappear.

THE FREE-MARKET APPROACH TO REGIONAL POLICY

The 'free market' approach to regional policy, which broadly argues the case against an interventionist regional policy, is based on the **'convergency theory'** described above. Economists of the 'free market' (or neoclassical) school believe that the market mechanism alone can solve the regional problem and that the proper function of regional policy is simply to create the free market environment in which the price mechanism can operate efficiently. Indeed, according to this view, an interventionist or 'active' regional policy, far from reducing regional differences, actually makes the inequalities worse because it interferes with the efficient working of the market. Free-market economists argue that, over many decades, the policies and legislation of successive British governments created inflexible markets which prevented the price mechanism from functioning properly. They blame planning controls for preventing firms from choosing low-cost locations, and national collective bargaining for preventing the emergence of the regional wage differentials, regarded as necessary for the convergency process to work.

THE 'INTERVENTIONIST' APPROACH TO REGIONAL POLICY

Economists who argue in favour of an 'active' or **interventionist regional policy** reject both the 'convergency theory' and the belief that market forces alone can cure the regional problem. The case for a much more interventionalist regional and industrial policy is based upon two important arguments:

❶ **Regional divergency** Many Keynesian economists believe that market forces actually widen differences between regions rather than reducing, and eventually eliminating, regional disparities in income, employment and standards of living. Although, in principle, low wages should attract firms to regions of high unemployment, by creating depressed regional markets, they can have the opposite effect. Market forces might only be successful in pulling individual firms to depressed regions if the regions possess sufficient external economies, attractive to modern industries. Such external economies are provided, in part, by government investment in infrastructure and social capital; but also by other firms supplying components, specialist services or market outlets, already located in the region. However, the regional problem may exist, in part, precisely because the depressed regions lack a system of established external economies, sufficient to attract inward investment by new firms. Indeed, far from possessing sufficient external economies attractive to modern industry, the disadvantaged regions may contain significant external diseconomies which act as deterrents to incoming firms. Diseconomies result from: remoteness from the European 'core'; derelict buildings; polluted land; unsuitable transport facilities; and a labour force trained in the wrong skills and unused to modern working practices. These may all counter the pull of low wages and a plentiful supply of labour, serving to intensify rather than reduce the regional problem.

❷ **The social cost argument** When making an economic decision in an unregulated market economy, a firm need consider only the private costs incurred by the enterprise itself, together with the private benefits received. Thus, when choosing a suitable location for production, a firm can ignore any **externalities** received by the wider community, which may result from its private choice. But while the firm can ignore externalities, it is the government's duty to take account of external costs and benefits, generated by the private locational decisions of firms, and to formulate public policy that maximises the welfare of the whole community, rather than just the private interests of individual firms. In the absence of externalities, there is no public policy problem; the social (or public) interest coincides with the private interests of firms. In these circumstances, and in the absence of other arguments to justify intervention, the government should refrain from interfering with market forces. But supporters of an active regional policy argue that a case for government intervention exists precisely because the location of industry generates externalities received as social costs by the wider community. These include the costs of under-utilised social capital (for example, schools and housing) in the areas of high unemployment from which workers migrate, and the costs to the community of financing unemployment benefits for the workers who remain. Further social costs, of congestion and over-utilisation of social capital, may be generated in areas such as the South East where industry chooses to locate. By encouraging firms to locate in depressed regions, away from the South East, the savings in social and external costs may exceed any increase in private costs to individual firms, especially if industry is relatively 'footloose' and private costs are much the same throughout the country. In these circumstances, regional policy results in a net welfare gain to the whole community; the actual financial costs to government and taxpayers which are paid to firms as compensation for increased private costs are less than the savings in total social costs.

CAPITAL MOBILITY VERSUS LABOUR MOBILITY

We have already explained how the market disequilibrium of a labour surplus in one half of Britain and a relative shortage of labour in the other half can be cured either by a **greater capital mobility**, or by **greater labour mobility**. Essentially, the former type of policy takes work to the workers; whereas the latter attempts to take workers to the work (assuming that job opportunities exist in the southern 'successful' half of Britain). In principle, regional policy can be based on either approach, or indeed upon both approaches, but under successive British governments, policies to improve capital mobility have been dominant. Governments have generally accepted that a successful improvement in labour mobility, sufficient to reduce regional unemployment, would worsen other aspects of the regional problem. In particular, the social costs of congestion would be increased in the south, with further social costs resulting from a declining population in the north. For this reason, government employment policies have placed most emphasis on improving the **occupational** rather than the **geographical mobility** of labour. Job Centres for labour recruitment and job advertising, training schemes for the young, and retraining schemes for older workers have been established, and in recent years employment legislation has been used to reduce restrictive labour practices which prevented workers from changing occupations.

UK REGIONAL POLICY BEFORE 1984

For the most of the period since the Second World War, British regional policy was based on the active or interventionist approach already described. British regional policy has always involved 'market modification' rather than 'market replacement', i.e. the use of policy instruments to create signals and incentives to encourage firms, voluntarily, to locate in the depressed regions; rather than the enforced location of investment through the command or planning mechanism. In essence, a 'carrot and stick' approach to the regional problem was adopted. **Incentive 'carrots'** were offered to attract firms to the depressed regions, while at various times **planning restrictions** were enforced as a 'stick' (or deterrent) to prevent location in the 'successful' southern half of Britain. The country was divided into **Assisted Areas**, in which the 'carrots' were offered to incoming firms, and the rest of Britain, where planning restrictions were enforced and regional assistance was unavailable. Currently the assisted areas are called **Development Areas** and **Intermediate Areas**. The main form of regional assistance available in the assisted areas has always been financial; namely investment grants, Regional Development Grants (RDGs), and investment tax allowances, together with government investment in social capital or infrastructure.

THE 'CATALYTIC CRACKER SYNDROME'

Pre-1984 regional policy was expensive to the taxpayer in terms of the cost of each new job created. An explanation for this lies in the 'catalytic cracker syndrome'. This refers to the spending of millions of pounds of regional aid on expensive and capital-intensive equipment, such as catalytic crackers in the oil-refining industry, with very few resulting jobs. The 'catalytic cracker syndrome' was encouraged because, prior to 1984, regional aid was channelled largely into the finance of investment by manufacturing firms in new plant and fixed capacity.

THE 'BRANCH FACTORY SYNDROME'

The structure of regional financial assistance available before 1984 also encouraged the 'branch factory syndrome'. Much of the investment in new manufacturing industry in the regions, which took place before 1984, established branch factories owned by large companies with headquarters and main plants outside the assisted areas. Partly because financial assistance was directed at encouraging and rewarding investment, and partly because service industries were largely excluded from receiving aid, pre-1984 regional policy did little to encourage the growth of small businesses indigenous to the regions. Successful growth of such small and often labour-intensive businesses, in service industries as well as in manufacturing, might well have created better-balanced regional economies than in fact resulted from the 'branch factory syndrome'. A greater proportion of service industries could have made the regional economies less vulnerable to the changes in demand that affect heavy capital goods industries, especially severely in times of recession. It is also possible that the growth of businesses, indigenous to the regions, might have produced a situation in which many more owners of businesses actually live within the assisted areas, with profits and higher managerial income circulating within the regional economies. Instead, regional aid largely financed the growth of branch factories owned by British and overseas multinational companies. Typically, such factories were peripheral to the main activities of the parent company, often manufacturing a narrow range of components with which to supply other factories in the multinational's wider sphere of operations. Perhaps more importantly, these branch factories tended to generate only relatively low 'production line' incomes to employees living within the assisted areas. Profits generated by the factories, together with higher managerial incomes, usually leaked out of the regional economy; being transferred to the parent company, or to shareholders and the upper echelons of management living outside the regions. Leakage of income out of a region also contributes to a low regional multiplier. The **regional multiplier** measures the relationship between an injection of government spending into the regional economy and the resulting change in regional income. The smaller the regional multiplier, the less effective the regional financial assistance.

Perhaps the most serious effect of the 'branch factory syndrome' occurred in the severe recessions that affected the whole of British industry in the early 1980s and 1990s. Manufacturing, in general, faced serious difficulties; but it was usually the outlying branch factories, located in the regions, which were the most vulnerable to closure.

RECENT CHANGES IN UK REGIONAL POLICY

In 1984 and 1988 significant changes were made in British regional policy. In part, these were a response to the 'catalytic cracker' and 'branch factory' syndromes we have just described but, at a deeper level, they represented the return to free-market principles by the Conservative government and a rejection of Keynesian and interventionist approaches to economic policy. Before 1984, all manufacturing firms investing in assisted areas (at the time comprising a three-tier structure of Special Development Areas, Development Areas and Intermediate Areas), were automatically entitled to RDGs. Financial aid was not generally available to service industries. The main changes introduced in 1984 by the Conservative government were:

❶ **The map of assisted areas was redrawn** and reduced to a two-tier structure of Development Areas and Intermediate Areas. Approximately 35% of the UK population now lives within the assisted areas.

❷ **The new changes were intended to reduce the cost of regional policy** to the government and to the taxpayer. Besides demoting some areas from assisted area status, the rate at which Regional Development Grants were offered to firms investing in new plant and buildings in Development Areas was reduced from 22% to 15%.

❸ **An element of selectivity (or discretion) was introduced** into regional policy. Before 1984, RDGs were automatically available to manufacturing firms expanding in Development Areas and Intermediate Areas. After 1984, RDGs were available automatically at the reduced rate of 15% in Development Areas, but only on new and not on replacement investment. In Development Areas, any further assistance over and above the 15% RDG was made selective; while Intermediate Areas qualified for selective assistance only. Following the example of other countries in the EC, regional policy was made selective by introducing a cost-per-job limit for the RDG of £10,000, designed to reward investment by labour-intensive firms and to avoid the 'catalytic cracker syndrome'. However the cost-per-job limit was not applied to small firms employing less than 200 employees, in the hope that capital-intensive small firms would be encouraged to grow to a viable size.

❹ **In one significant area, regional policy was extended.** For the first time, service industries, such as advertising and data processing (but not tourism), became eligible for regional financial assistance. A new grant was created which has proved to be especially attractive to labour-intensive service industries. As an alternative to the RDG, which is available only to finance capital investment, labour intensive firms were offered a grant of £3,000 for each new job created; provided that the total turns out to be worth more than 15 per cent of the capital cost of the project.

In 1988, automatic entitlement to RDGs was finally abolished, completing the change to a discretionary regional policy designed to encourage the growth of indigenous small businesses rather than branch factories. The assisted areas and overall cost of regional aid was left unchanged (though at about £400m compared to £700m a few years earlier).

THE EC REGIONAL FUND

In some areas of economic policy, such as agricultural policy, the UK has had to adopt common EC policies replacing, in effect, independent national policy. This is not the case with the regional policy of the European Community, which essentially supplements rather than replaces each country's regional policy. Before 1975, regional assistance from the EC was available from a number of funds such as the **EC Social Fund** which financed the training of young workers. In 1975 a **European Regional Development Fund (ERDF)** was established to create a more unified Community regional policy. Financial assistance from the ERDF is channelled through the British government and is intended to be additional to the government's own regional aid. However, there have been criticisms that the British government has used the receipt of EC funds as an excuse for reducing its own financial assistance to the regions. Development Areas are classified as European Peripheral Regions, which qualify for a higher level of community assistance than other parts of Britain; designated Central Regions. In general, the EC frowns upon continuous subsidies to the regions, preferring investment in regional infrastructure instead. The EC also prefers aid to be selectively available to finance specific projects, rather than automatically available to all firms investing in assisted areas. The changes in British regional policy, introduced in 1984 and 1988, were, in part, a response to the need to bring British policy in line with EC regional policy.

THE EFFECTIVENESS OF REGIONAL POLICY

Studies undertaken into the effectiveness of regional policy have shown that, at best, it has prevented regional disparities from widening; while in years of recession (such as the period 1978–82), regional differences grew worse. However, in 1990, the Confederation of British Industry published an inter-regional comparison showing, for the first time in recent memory, more industrial capacity was employed in northern England than in the south. In part, this probably reflects the effect of high interest rates and bigger mortgages reducing consumer spending much more in the south of England than in the north. But it might also provide support for the 'anti-interventionist' changes in regional policy which we have described. It claimed that a 'new dynamic' was at work in the second half of the 1980s, with the survivors of the recession of 1979–82 doing well and new businesses working to better management standards. Not only was a restructured manufacturing sector performing well in the north in the late 1980s; it was also argued that the regional economy had been boosted by the growth of successful indigenous businesses providing financial and professional services that no longer had to be 'imported' from London and the south-east. However, the regeneration of the northern economy which occurred in the 1980s boom years was brought to a halt by the recession of the early 1990s. And unlike earlier recessions, the economic downturn of the 1990s severely affected service industries in the previously buoyant south-east as well as the more traditional manufacturing regions.

DEINDUSTRIALISATION

In the 1970s and the early 1980s, the UK regional problem became submerged in the wider problem of deindustrialisation. As a result, UK governments switched the emphasis of policy away from regional problems to a more general industrial policy; aimed at halting and reversing the deindustrialization process wherever it was occurring.

Deindustrialisation refers to the structural decline of industrial output in the face of international competition. Some commentators use the term to refer only to the absolute decline of manufactured output which occurred in the severe recession of the early 1980s; but if the term is used in a relative, rather than an absolute sense, deindustrialisation has been occurring for a much longer period (and is still continuing), despite the slow recovery in manufacturing output in the UK after 1981. Indeed, with the onset of recession in the early 1990s, many commentators believe that deindustrialisation will re-emerge as the most significant economic problem affecting the UK economy in future years. Nor should the term be restricted to manufacturing industry; extractive industries such as coalmining and fisheries and possibly also construction and utility industries, have been subject to the deindustrialisation process. Although defined in terms of industrial output, deindustrialisation has been accompanied by an often rapid fall in industrial employment. This has continued despite the recovery in the UK economy, as firms have sought to reduce their loss of competitiveness by 'shaking out' the workforce in order to increase labour productivity.

GOVERNMENT DEINDUSTRIALISATION POLICY BEFORE 1980

During the 1970s, the UK government recognised the problem of deindustrialisation and introduced a set of interventionist policies, aimed at reversing the structural decline of manufacturing. The Labour government believed that deindustrialisation was caused, primarily, by failure of capitalism and the market economy; arguing that private sector firms (especially multinational companies) were becoming unaccountable to the national interest and that markets – including the capital and financial markets – were taking too short-term a view of economic prospects. As a result, industry in general was underinvesting in new capacity, and the financial institutions were failing in their function of providing risk or venture capital to industry on a long-term basis. On this diagnosis, the Labour government introduced an interventionist policy to reverse the deindustrialisation process; based on such measures as nationalisation and the creation of a **state holding agency**, the National Enterprise Board, to take an ownership stake in the private sector in return for providing finance.

DEINDUSTRIALISATION AND THE CONSERVATIVE GOVERNMENT

The policies adopted by the Conservatives, in the 1980s and early 1990s to deal with deindustrialisation, have been different in almost all respects from those of the Labour government in the 1970s. Recent Conservative policy has been based on the assumption that any problems, caused by deindustrialisation, along with the regional problem, result from decades of too much (rather than too little) government intervention. State intervention has prevented the market mechanism from working properly, particularly in the labour market. Firms have been faced with high wage costs which, together with the crippling burden of taxation necessary to finance state intervention, have reduced international competitiveness. According to the 'radical right' philosophy, adopted by the Conservative government, the correct way to deal with the deindustrialisation problem is to 'roll back' state intervention, creating conditions in which private enterprise and entrepreneurial initiative can regenerate the British economy by operating in competitive and efficient markets. The free-market 'supply-side' orientated policies, adopted by the Conservative government to deal with the deindustrialisation problem, have included:

- the encouragement of small business;
- tax cuts;
- abolishing labour restrictive practices and reducing the power of trade unions;
- establishing Enterprise Zones and Urban Development Corporations.

ENTERPRISE ZONES AND URBAN DEVELOPMENT CORPORATIONS

Since the Second World War, population and employment have both declined in large conurbations (built-up areas) throughout the United Kingdom. Population decline has affected large cities (such as London and Birmingham) in the 'successful' south as well as industrial cities in the north. This decline, particularly acute in manufacturing, has reduced employment opportunities for the skilled and semi-skilled manual workers who make up a large part of the working population in industrial cities. Service industries have generally been unable to grow sufficiently to make up for the decline of manufacturing in the large cities. Inner city decline has also contributed to the growth of a high level of public expenditure provided by the local authorities. But increased spending by local authorities, in areas of urban deprivation, has required higher local taxation to finance the spending. By the 1980s, Britain's inner cities were becoming locked into a vicious spiral of decline. Falling employment led to a consequent narrowing of the local tax base, accompanied by growing demands for local public spending from a population increasingly dependent upon welfare benefits. This in turn led to an even faster rate of decline in local employment as firms went out of business or moved out of the inner cities to escape the taxation required to pay for the high levels of local public expenditure.

Before 1979, governments either ignored the growing **'microregional' problem** of the inner cities, concentrating instead on the more conventional problems of 'macroregions'; or they chose to deal with the problem by increasing the level of central government funding for local authorities in the city centres affected. After 1979, the Conservatives adopted a completely different approach; reducing the level of intervention by local and central government alike, and attempting to create an environment attractive to private enterprise.

Enterprise Zones were established, conceived of as areas of reduced 'red tape' and bureaucracy. Firms locating in Enterprise Zones (usually sited on previously derelict urban land in inner cities), benefit from a 10-year 'rates holiday' during which they pay no local taxation and are exempt from the need to obtain planning permission or to make redundancy payments to laid-off workers. By 1986, 28 Enterprise Zones had been established, but a number of studies have cast doubt on their effectiveness in reducing the inner city problem. It is doubtful whether Enterprise Zones have attracted many completely new businesses; indeed, areas of blight have tended to grow up around Enterprise Zones, as businesses have moved into the zones from the surrounding area to benefit from the 'rates holiday'. The Enterprise Zones have tended to attract service industries (such as retail superstores and warehouses) rather than manufacturing, creating employment for low-paid unskilled workers. Their critics argue that Enterprise Zones have failed to make sufficient impact upon the unemployment and social problems of inner cities; and that they are not an appropriate base for the regeneration of areas of urban deprivation.

To supplement the Enterprise Zones, the Conservative government also set up privately sponsored **Urban Development Corporations (UDCs)**. UDCs, such as the London Docklands Development Corporation are, like Enterprise Zones, largely outside the political control of the municipalities in which they are located. Critics argue that far from decentralising power away from the state, the UDCs erode the power of local democracy in the UK and represent a further step towards the centralisation of effective power or decision making in Westminster and Whitehall.

Chapter roundup

Other aspects of United Kingdom industrial structure, and the role of government in industry, are covered in Chapters 10 and 11, while Chapters 6, 7 and 8 explain the causes of market imperfection and failure towards which industrial policy is often addressed. The issue of whether industrial policy should be 'interventionist' or anti-interventionist' is further developed in Chapter 23 on supply-side economies and Chapter 24 on Keynesianism and monetarism.

Illustrative questions and answers

1 Essay Question
   'In recent years, governments have aimed to improve efficiency and growth through policies of privatisation and deregulation.'
(a) Explain what you understand by
   (i) privatisation; and
   (ii) deregulation. (8)
(b) Explain how privatisation and deregulation may lead to improved efficiency and growth in product markets. (9)
(c) Discuss the implications for consumers of such policies. (8)

(Scottish Higher, June 1990)

Tutorial note

(a) With a question like this students often seem to succumb to the temptation to answer a question which has not actually been set, namely to write all they know on the history of privatisation and/or the advantages and disadvantages of privatisation. You must resist this temptation! Define privatisation as the sale or transfer of public sector assets (such as nationalised industries and council flats) to the private sector, perhaps also including 'contractualisation' in your definition, i.e. putting services such as waste disposal previously provided completely by the public sector, out to private sector tender or contract. Deregulation is literally the removal of previously imposed government regulation, particularly those regulations that have promoted barriers to market entry, and restricted competition. Give examples such as the deregulation of the TV and bus industries.

(b) You might not agree that privatisation and deregulation have actually succeeded in promoting efficiency and growth, but you will lose marks heavily if you fail to discuss how they may have these results. Privatisation introduces the profit motive and important sources of 'market discipline' to inefficient firms, via the possibility of bankruptcy or takeover if they continue to perform badly. However, in itself, privatisation may merely transform public monopoly into private monopoly, so deregulation is necessary to supplement privatisation by removing barriers to entry and promoting efficiency through effective competition.

(c) In principle, privatisation and successful deregulation can improve consumer sovereignty by reducing costs, profits and prices and by promoting better services, product development and choice. But it is worth noting that consumer complaints have increased dramatically since privatisation, though this may simply reflect the fact that consumers now believe that the agencies set up to regulate the privatised industries 'possess teeth' and that complaining about the standards of service will now produce results. With this point in mind, you might also note that by setting up external regulatory bodies such as OFTEL, OFGAS, OFWAT, and OFFER, the Conservative government has found it necessary to increase rather than reduce the regulation of the privatised 'utility' industries, telecommunications, gas, water and electricity. This has been called the 'reregulation of the privatised utilities'.

2 Data Question

Region	Economic growth (%)		Unemployment (%)[2]		Diposable income per head (UK = 100)		% change in house prices (1st quarter)		Population growth (%)
	1984–1989[1]	1989	1984	1989	1984	1988	1983–1989	1989–1990	1981–1988
North	3.1	2.0	15.3	9.2	92.8	91.0	62.5	25.2	−1.5
Yorkshire & Humberside	2.9	1.5	11.7	7.2	93.5	93.0	102.8	14.9	−0.1
East Midlands	4.2	3.1	9.8	5.1	96.3	93.9	136.3	−1.2	3.1
East Anglia	4.5	2.5	7.9	3.4	103.4	96.1	182.8	−19.5	7.4
South East	4.0	3.2	7.8	3.6	110.5	114.8	159.1	−13.3	2.0
South West	4.1	2.8	9.0	4.1	103.2	102.9	153.9	−12.1	5.8
West Midlands	4.0	2.8	12.7	6.1	89.8	89.9	139.3	−2.0	0.4
North West	3.5	2.5	13.6	7.9	94.3	93.0	79.4	23.4	−1.5
Wales	3.4	2.6	13.8	6.8	91.6	86.3	103.5	8.0	1.5
Scotland	2.8	2.0	12.9	8.8	99.6	97.3	49.3	16.7	−1.7
Northern Ireland	2.6	2.6	16.1	14.7	89.1	84.3	30.0	−1.1	2.6
UK total	3.3	2.0	10.9	5.9	100.0	100.0	117.8	1.3	1.3

[1] Annual average. [2] Seasonally adjusted

(Sources: *Regional Trends*, 1989 and 1990, CSO; *Economic Trends*, May 1990, CSO; National Westminster Bank, *UK Regional Review*, March 1990 & June 1990)

(a) Making full use of the data, define, explain and account for regional economic imbalance in the United kingdom.   (9)

(b) What data, *not* given in the table, could be used to illustrate regional economic imbalance?   (2)

(c) (i) Using supply and demand analysis, illustrate and explain *two* factors from the table which may have caused house prices to rise sharply in East Anglia between 1983 and 1989   (6)

(ii) To what extent can the fall in house prices in certain regions by 1990 be explained by government policies? (3)

(ULEAC, AS Level, June 1991)

Tutorial note

(a) With a question like this, you must avoid the temptation to write a general essay on the 'regional problem', unrelated to the data presented in the table. Note the three tasks required by the question: *define*; *explain*; and *account for*, and the instruction to *make full use of the data*. Ignore these at your peril! Obviously you should not try to use *all* the data in the table. However the table includes a number of measures of regional disparity which you should draw upon to illustrate the points you are making.

(b) ULEAC frequently sets this type of question, asking you what other data sources or supplementary data would enable you to write a fuller answer. It is not unknown for a candidate to write: 'The data in the Chief Examiner's marking scheme would be extremely useful!' Only two marks are available here, so restrict the answer to just two sensible suggestions e.g. data for the intervening years and for a longer span of years to enable you to assess the long-term trends in each region; data on manufacturing output in each region etc.

(c) (i) Draw a supply and demand diagram to illustrate an initial equilibrium in the East Anglian housing market. Make sure the supply curve is almost vertical to show the inelastic supply of housing in the short run. Draw the demand curve shifting up the vertical supply curve. Offer two possible explanations, e.g. higher incomes; greater availability of mortgage finance; population growth (shown by the data).

(ii) Critics of the Conservative government might argue that the government was completely to blame for the collapse of house prices in the early 1990s. They cite what they say has been the government's irresponsibility, firstly in deregulating financial markets and encouraging an over-heated housing market in the boom of the late 1980s, and then in refusing to take measures to reduce the cost of borrowing and restore confidence to the housing market after the boom burst and house prices began to fall. However you must be very careful with a question like this. Whatever your personal views, avoid too one-sided an answer and don't write answers based on 'conspiracy theories'. Also, don't try to convert the examiner to your own political views. A good working rule is to assume that the examiner marking your script is a bigot with political opinions completely opposed to yours. The last thing you want to do is ruffle your examiner's feathers! So when answering this question, a good strategy might be to suggest that government policies were partly responsible, but that the effect was probably unintentional, and that a number of factors outside the government's direct control, such as the world economy moving into recession, also came into play. A second working rule to remember is; 'stupidity theories' (also known as 'cock-up theories') often offer a more plausible explanation of events than 'conspiracy theories'.

Question bank

1

(a) Why may firms wish to reduce competition by colluding with each other, for example, by forming a cartel?   (12)

(b) Is such collusion in the public interest and what might be the economic effects of prohibiting collusion?   (13)   (AEB, June 1990)

2   'Restrictive practices by firms obviously run counter to the public interest and should be severely punished by the government.' Discuss, illustrating with examples.   (SUJB, June 1987)

3   When, if ever, may the existence of monopoly be justified? Evaluate different ways in which the problems posed by monopoly may be reduced.
                                        (AEB, June 1989)

4   How effective has recent policy been towards monopolies and mergers in the UK?   (10)   (London, S-Level, June 1990)

5

(a) Explain what you understand by privatisation and comment upon the problems of defining it.   (10)

(b) With examples, discuss the economic benefits of privatisation in the UK economy.   (10)   (O&CSEB AS-Level, June 1990)

6   Briefly distinguish between privatisation and deregulation. Discuss the advantages and disadvantages of deregulation for the United Kingdom economy.   (AEB, November 1988)

7

(a) How might privatisation policies be used to increase competition and reduce monopoly?   (12)

(b) Discuss whether the United Kingdom privatisation programme is likely to achieve this result.   (13)   (AEB, June 1991)

8   Argue the case **for** competition between firms generating electricity and **against** competition between firms distributing electricity.
                                        (Cambridge, Special Paper, June 1990)

9   Examine the connection between long-run average costs, product prices and the profits of a firm such as British Telecom (BT).
                                        (Cambridge, Special Paper, June 1991)

10 Why do economies have a public sector? Discuss how and why the composition of the public sector in Britain has changed in recent years.
                                        (JMB, June 1989)

11

(a) In what ways has the regional policy of the UK government changed since 1979?   (13)

(b) Consider the view that present policies are unlikely to have much impact in reducing regional unemployment disparities.   (12)   (WJEC, June 1988)

12

(a) What differences have led some economists to believe that there is a North-South divide in the UK economy?   (5)

(b) What economic factors may have caused these regional differences?   (10)

(c) Discuss the ways in which these regional differences could be reduced.   (10)
                                        (Scottish Higher, June 1989)

THE LABOUR MARKET

Units in this chapter

13.1 *Underlying concepts*
13.2 *Essential information*

Chapter objectives

In earlier chapters we examined the behaviour of firms and how prices are determined when firms sell their output in the goods market or product market. We generally assumed that the prices of the inputs necessary for production, or the **prices of factor services**, were given. We now reverse the assumption, and examine how the prices of factors of production are determined in the factor market, assuming that conditions and prices in the product market are generally given. We shall concentrate on the **labour market** and the **determination of wages**, applying our analysis where necessary to the other factors of production and their prices.

We shall follow the convention of dividing the factors of production into land and labour, which earn rent and wages respectively, and capital, which is further subdivided into loan capital, earning interest, and entrepreneurship, or enterprise, earning profit. This is strictly a theoretical division which conforms neither to official statistics nor to the everyday use of such words as rent and interest. For example, a businessman will think of rent as the payment he makes for the use of a building. However, from a theoretical point of view, part of the payment is the rent of land, but the rest is an interest payment on capital.

Table 13.1

The functional distribution of income Distribution of total income by percentage				The size distribution of Income Distribution of disposable income by percentage			
	1977	1983	1990	Income received by	1977	1983	1988
Income from employment	74	73	77	Top 20% of population	36	38	42
Gross trading profits and surplus of private and public enterprises, minus stock appreciation	19	19	14	Next 21–40% of population	23	23	23
				Middle 20% of population	18	17	16
				Next 20% of population	14	13	11
Other income, including cost and income from self-employment	7	8	9	Bottom 20% of population	10	10	8

The distribution of income between the factors of production is called the **functional distribution of income**. This should not be confused with the **size distribution of income**, which measures, for example, the proportion of total income received by the top ten per cent of income earners, compared with the bottom fifty per cent. Table 13.1 illustrates both distributions of income.

Although the official statistics do not exactly match the theoretical distinctions between the factors of production, they tend to show that the share of wages rose slightly at the expense of profits in the 1970s, but that the reverse was true in the 1980s. There was a sharp recovery in the profitability of industry during the 'boom' years of the mid- and late-1980s, but profits declined rapidly in the recession of the early 1990s. The size distribution also shows a growing inequality in the distribution of income, with the gap increasing between rich and poor.

13.1 UNDERLYING CONCEPTS

Distribution theory introduces no new methods of analysis and only a few new theoretical concepts. It is merely the price theory of the earlier chapters, but viewed from the 'other side'. As we shall see, it can be subjected to the same criticisms as other aspects of conventional price theory. In earlier chapters we examined the interaction of households and firms in the goods market, where households are the source of demand for goods and services supplied by firms. We now view households as the source of supply of factor services, which are demanded by firms in the pursuit of profit.

You should note:

❶ **Wages and other factor prices are assumed to be determined by supply and demand.**

❷ **The assumption of maximising behaviour**. The assumptions of profit-maximising behaviour on the part of firms and utility maximisation by households are as crucial to distribution theory as they are to the rest of price theory. Firms will only demand the services of factors of production if profits can be increased by their employment. Similarly, households will only supply more labour, or hire out the capital or land they may own, if it maximises their net advantage. The concept of **net advantage** covers all the rewards, monetary and non-monetary, which a household gains from the sale of its factor services. For example, if a person enjoys his work, the net advantage obtained from employment will include the pleasure gained from the work itself, as well as the utility of the wage – or more strictly, the utilities obtained from the goods and services bought with the money wage.

❸ **The demand for factor services is a derived demand**. The essential difference between consumer demand in the goods market, and a firm's demand for factor services, is that the latter is a derived demand: the services of labour or land are demanded only because they are necessary in the production of goods and services to sell for profit.

❹ **Entrepreneurial profit, and indeed the entrepreneurial function, is regarded as different from those of the other factors of production**. The entrepreneurial function of risk-taking and the bearing of uncertainty is undertaken by the owners of a business, who bear the financial risks. However, the existence of such a separate entrepreneurial function in modern companies can be questioned. Very often all the important decisions are made by management, who are a part of the labour force. In so far as entrepreneurial profit exists, it is essentially a residual, the difference between the total revenue obtained from the sale of output in the product market, and the other factor rewards which constitute the firm's costs of production.

❺ **Transfer earnings and economic rent.** So far, we have used the term 'rent' in its everyday meaning as the price which must be paid to hire the services of land. To the economist, however, rent or economic rent has a rather different meaning. It is a more general meaning which applies to all the factors of production, yet it is more specific since it refers to only a part of the earnings of each factor. Fig. 33 illustrates the demand and supply for a particular type of labour. L_1 represents a worker who is just prepared to supply labour if the wage is W_1, but who would withdraw from this particular labour market if the wage fell below W_1. We now assume that the firm pays the same wage to all the workers it employs. This is the equilibrium wage W_2, determined where the demand and supply curves intersect at A. Worker L_1 receives the wage of W_2 even though he would be prepared to work for the lower wage of W_1. The part of his wage above the supply curve at point B is economic rent, while the part below is transfer earnings. **Transfer earnings** represent the **factor's opportunity cost**, while economic rent is the difference between what the factor is actually paid and its opportunity cost. If the wage falls below W_1, worker L_1 will transfer out of this particular labour market, or at least decide to supply less labour. Taking all the workers together, their economic rent is shown by the shaded area above the supply curve, while their transfer earnings are shown by the area below. Worker L_2 is the **marginal worker**, who is only just prepared to supply labour at the wage of W_2. All his wage is transfer earnings. The concept of economic rent is sometimes applied to entrepreneurial profit, as well as to the earnings of the other factors of production. In this case, **normal profit** is regarded as a transfer earning, since the entrepreneur will leave the industry if normal profit is not earned. **Abnormal profit** which is earned over and above normal profit becomes the 'economic rent of enterprise'.

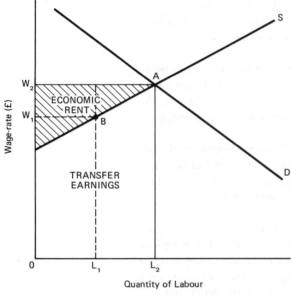

Fig. 33 Economic rent and transfer earnings

13.2 ESSENTIAL INFORMATION

THE SUPPLY OF LABOUR

The **aggregate supply of labour** in the economy is ultimately constrained by the size of the total population. Nevertheless, for a given total population size, the aggregate supply can increase or decrease if, for example, married women decide to enter or leave the working population, which is determined by demographic factors and migration. However, for the purpose of this chapter we are more interested in examining the supply of labour within a single labour market than with investigating the factors which cause the aggregate supply of labour to change.

The **market supply curve of labour** is the sum of the supply curves of each worker in the labour market. A **worker's supply curve of labour** can either **slope upwards**, showing that more labour is supplied as the wage rises; or it can

bend backwards, a case where wage rises cause less labour to be supplied. In both cases, the labour supply reflects the fact that at the margin, a worker must choose between supplying an extra hour of labour and enjoying an extra hour of leisure time. Now both the money wage and leisure time yields utility, but both also respond to the 'law' of diminishing marginal utility. When more labour is supplied at a particular wage rate, the extra income yields less and less extra utility. At the same time, each extra hour of leisure sacrificed results in an increasing utility loss. To maximise utility, labour must be supplied up to the point at which the **MU of the wage = the MU of leisure**; at which point the worker has no incentive to supply more labour at the existing wage rate. A higher wage would be needed to encourage a worker to supply more labour beyond this point; hence the upward-sloping supply curve of labour.

This explanation relates to the **substitution effect** of a wage increase. For example, an hourly wage rate increase from £10 to £12 raises the price of an hour of leisure from £10 to £12. Because leisure has become more expensive, workers decide to supply labour and earn the wage instead.

However, an **income effect** also operates which can result in less labour being supplied. The wage increase raises both the worker's real income and his demand for normal goods. For most people, leisure time is a normal good. Hence, the income effect of the wage increase suggests that less labour will be supplied, since more leisure is being demanded.

The slope of a worker's supply curve of labour will thus depend on the **relative strengths of the substitution and income effects**. If the substitution effect is stronger than the income effect, an upward-sloping supply curve results: but, if the income effect is the more powerful, the supply curve is backward-bending or regressive.

An alternative approach to the backward-bending supply curve is to assume that workers aim to achieve a **target real income**, measured in terms of bought goods and services. A wage increase allows the target to be reached with a lower input of labour, allowing the worker to enjoy more leisure time rather than extra material goods. This is a plausible behavioural assumption when the work itself is unpleasant, (e.g. coal mining).

A backward-bending supply curve has an important implication for tax policy. If the supply curve is upward-sloping, an increase in income tax results in less labour being supplied, because the tax is equivalent to a cut in wages. If, however, the supply curve is backward-bending, the rise in income tax causes people to work longer hours in order to maintain their target incomes.

THE DEMAND CURVE FOR LABOUR

We have already indicated that the demand curve for a factor of production is a derived demand. We assume that a firm will only voluntarily employ an extra worker if this increases total profit. To find out whether profits will indeed increase, a firm must know (a) how much the worker adds to total output, and (b) the money value of the extra output when it is sold in the product market. The amount which is added to a firm's revenue by employing one more worker is called the **marginal revenue product (MRP) of labour.** The two elements which comprise the MRP of labour are represented by the identity:

Marginal Revenue Product ≡ Marginal Physical Product × Marginal Revenue
     (MRP)   (MPP)   (MR)

In Chapter 3 we explained the 'law' or principle of **diminishing marginal returns,** which states that a variable factor such as labour will eventually add less and less to total output as labour itself is added to other factors which are held fixed. In the context of distribution theory it is usual, if rather confusing, to refer to the **marginal physical product (MPP)** of labour. This is exactly the same as the marginal returns of labour. The falling MPP curve which is drawn in Fig. 34a is explained by the principle of diminishing returns!

To find the money value of the MPP of labour, we multiply the MPP by the addition to total revenue resulting from the sale of the physical output in the goods market. In other words, we must multiply MPP by marginal revenue. In Fig.34 it is assumed that conditions of perfect competition exist in the goods market. In a perfectly competitive market, MR is identical to the good's price. Thus the MRP curve is derived by multiplying MPP by a constant price at each level of output. In these conditions, the slope and elasticity of the MRP curve are determined by MPP alone, though a change in the good's price will shift the position of the MRP curve. If the goods market is a monopoly or imperfectly competitive, MR will decrease with output. This causes the MRP curve to be steeper than when the goods market is perfectly competitive.

THE EQUILIBRIUM WAGE

In a competitive labour market, the MRP curve of labour is the **employer's demand curve for labour**. An employer demands labour up to the point where MRP = the marginal cost of employing an extra worker. If the employer goes beyond this point and hires a worker who adds more to total costs than to total revenue, profits must fall. Conversely, if the firm decides to limit the size of the workforce at a point where the MRP of the last worker is greater than the MC

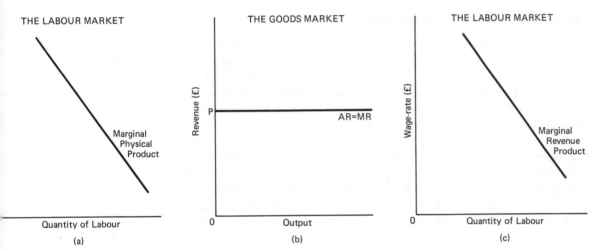

34 How the demand curve for labour (the MRP curve) is derived, assuming a perfectly competitive goods market

of employing him, the firm is sacrificing potential profits. It follows that a profit-maximising firm must demand labour up to the point where MRP = MC. However, the nature of the resulting equilibrium wage depends upon the assumptions made about the competitive state of the labour market. We explore some of the possibilities below.

A perfectly competitive labour market

This is illustrated in Fig. 35a. In these conditions, there are a large number of firms and a large number of workers, all acting independently in the market. An individual firm is a price-taker, in a position to employ as much labour as it wishes at the ruling market wage. The ruling wage is determined at the intersection of the supply and demand curves for labour in the labour market as a whole. The supply of labour for each firm, shown by the horizontal supply curve SS in Fig. 35(a), is perfectly elastic at the ruling market wage. We assume that a firm can employ any quantity of labour it wishes at this wage. In these market conditions, employment is L_1. Each worker receives the equilibrium wage W_1, which is equal to the MRP of labour.

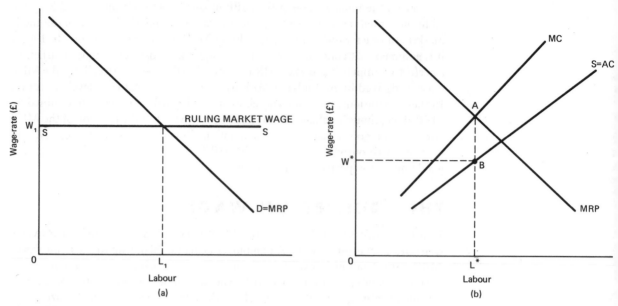

Fig. 35 *The equilibrium wage in different labour markets (a) a perfectly competitive labour market (b) a monopsony buyer of labour*

A monopsony buyer of labour

Fig. 35b illustrates a particular case when the equilibrium wage is not equal to the MRP of labour – though the size of the labour force is still determined where MRP = MC of labour. A single employer is a **monopsony buyer** in the labour market. Assuming an upward-sloping supply curve of labour, the intersection of the supply and MRP curves no longer determines either the equilibrium wage or the size of employment. The supply curve S, or **average cost curve** of labour, shows the wage which must be paid to all workers at each size of employed labour force in order to persuade them to supply labour. However, the supply curve S is not the marginal cost curve of labour! The employer will have to pay a higher wage to attract an extra worker, and the higher wage must be paid to all the other employed workers. Thus the MC of an extra worker includes the total amount by which the wage bill rises. The **MC curve of labour is above the AC or supply curve!**

If the firm wishes to maximise profits, employment will be at L*, immediately below point A on the diagram where MRP = MC. However, the equilibrium wage W* is determined at point B on the supply curve of labour. In this type of labour market, the equilibrium wage is less than the MRP of labour. It is useful to note the similarity between this analysis and that for a monopoly seller within the goods market, which we explained in Chapter 6.

Trade unions and the monopoly supply of labour

We have so far assumed that perfect competition exists in the labour market and that workers always act independently. If the workers join together to form a trade union, they will now act collectively – an **effective trade union being a monopoly supplier of labour.** We shall examine some of the possible effects a trade union might have on wages in the context of one of the questions at the end of the chapter. In some circumstances a union may only be able to raise wages at the expense of employment, whereas at other times it may be able to increase both wages and employment, for example by shifting the demand curve for labour rightwards. This can happen when a union encourages an employer to introduce new technology or methods of working which increase labour productivity, or if a general increase in wages resulting from union activity increases demand in the economy as a whole. Lastly, a union can sometimes exercise sufficient power, through the threat of strikes and the disruption of the continuous flow upon which modern industry is often dependent, to persuade a firm to sacrifice profit-maximisation for the sake of securing at least some profit from uninterrupted production. In this situation, both the wage and the level of employment are determined at a point 'off' the employer's demand curve for labour. The union forces the firm to employ more workers than it would wish to at the wage-rate achieved by the union; hence the firm incurs extra avoidable costs and cannot be maximising profits.

EXPLANATIONS OF DIFFERENT WAGE LEVELS

Many economists argue that the real reason for the existence of different wage levels lies outside the explanation provided by distribution theory. For example, **social and political factors** must surely be highly relevant to any explanation of why female workers are paid less than men in many occupations which require similar skills. Nevertheless, the following reasons are suggested by conventional distribution theory to explain differences in wages.

1 The separation of labour markets

The economy comprises many separated labour markets rather than one large market. In each market, demand and supply conditions are different, resulting in different equilibrium wages. If perfect competition existed throughout the economy, differences in wages would create incentives for labour to move between markets and for entrepreneurs to substitute capital for labour. In this way, market forces would reduce wage variations between different industries and occupations. The continuing persistence of wage differences is explained by the forces which prevent labour mobility and factor substitution:

- It takes time for a worker to acquire the skills required in another occupation. Costs are also involved in acquiring the skill.
- Not all workers will possess the necessary aptitude or ability for a particular type of work.
- There are man-made barriers which prevent a worker from moving between labour markets, for example a union closed shop, or restrictions on entry to medical school.
- Technical considerations can make it impractical for a firm to employ more capital in place of labour.

2 Differences in the elasticities of supply and demand

The elasticities of both the supply of and demand for labour are likely to differ between separated labour markets. If the demand for labour is relatively elastic, a rightward shift of the supply curve will have a greater effect on employment than on the wage level. In a similar way, the effect of a shift in demand will depend on the elasticity of the supply curve. A shift in either curve will have the greatest effect on the wage in a particular market when both the supply and demand curves are relatively inelastic. The time period in question is an important influence on both elasticities, with elasticities being higher in the long run than in the short run. It follows that a sudden change in the conditions of either supply or demand in a particular labour market will cause a larger change in the equilibrium wage in the short run than in the long run. In the long run, market forces serve to reduce wage differentials through the impact of labour mobility and factor substitution.

The supply of unskilled labour is generally more elastic than the supply of a particular type of skilled labour, since the training period of unskilled labour is usually very short. The existence of unemployed labour will also influence the elasticity of supply.

In general, the demand for labour will be relatively inelastic if:
* wages costs are only a small part of total production costs – this is some-times known as the 'importance of being unimportant';
* the demand for the good produced by the firm is inelastic;
* it is difficult to substitute other factors of production for labour, or other types of labour for the particular type in question.

3 The relative importance of monetary and non-monetary rewards

This varies between different occupations. A worker who enjoys his job may be prepared to accept a lower wage than a worker of similar skill and ability employed in an unpleasant occupation. Similarly, the existence of perks and fringe benefits in kind contribute to differences in money wages.

CRITICISMS OF DISTRIBUTION THEORY

❶ The most important propositions of conventional distribution theory are that:
* in competitive markets, the equilibrium wage will equal the value of the marginal product of labour in each market;
* the condition that the wage equals the marginal product of labour in each market is a necessary condition to achieve allocative and productive efficiency throughout the economy;
* the actual combination of labour and other factors of production employed will depend upon their relative prices. In competitive markets, where the price of each factor equals its marginal cost, a firm will employ factors until the

$$\frac{\text{MRP of labour}}{\text{wage}} = \frac{\text{MRP of land}}{\text{rent}} = \frac{\text{MRP of land}}{\text{rate of interest}}$$

The most fundamental criticism of distribution theory is that it does not really explain anything at all. The **theory is circular**. The demand or MRP of a factor depends upon the value of what is produced; this in turn depends upon the effective demand of consumers exercised in the goods market; finally, the consumers' effective demand depends upon the distribution of income. Hence, the distribution of income is dependent upon the distribution of income! To give the theory some sense, an initial distribution of income must be assumed, and this initial distribution cannot of course be explained by the theory.

❷ Even within its own terms, the theory can only explain the distribution of income within a small part of the total economy, assuming that conditions in the rest of the economy are held constant. In these conditions, a fall in the wage may cause an employer to demand more labour. However, if the wage level falls throughout the economy, the resulting decrease in aggregate demand can cause the demand curve for labour in each labour market to shift inwards. Unemployment may follow from the wage cut. This is the Keynesian critique of the microeconomic theory of distribution.

❸ The theory assumes that the marginal productivity of labour can be separated from the marginal productivity of capital. However, in many technical processes capital and labour are complementary rather than substitutes. Output can only be raised by increasing both capital and labour in some fixed ratio. In these circumstances the marginal productivity of labour is impossible to isolate and identify.

❹ The MRP theory of wage determination can only be used to explain the wages of workers employed in the market economy. It is impossible to place a market value on the labour productivity of those members of the British labour force employed in the public services provided by central and local government. The determination of public sector pay provides one example of the importance of differentials, comparability and relativity in wage bargaining. It is by no means always clear, however, whether public sector pay is determined by comparability with the 'rate for the job' for similar employment in the private sector, or vice versa.

❺ Distribution theory is sometimes criticised for unrealistically ignoring the role of collective bargaining and other methods of pay determination in the British economy. In one sense the lack of realism is not very important. The theory states that a firm can only maximise profits if it employs labour up to the point where the MRP of labour equals the MC of labour. If this equality does not hold, the firm cannot be maximising profits! In a perfectly competitive world it would be the forces of competition rather than the deliberate decisions of firms that would bring about the situation where MRP = MC. Firms which strayed away from profit-maximisation would either be competed out of existence, or they would have to mend their ways. However, in a world in which firms may not be profit-maximisers, and in which markets are imperfectly competitive, there is no reason why the predictions of distribution theory should come true.

Nevertheless, distribution theory does tend to encourage the attitude that perfectly competitive markets are normal, that workers are paid what they deserve in terms of the value of what they produce, and that real-world bargaining patterns and institutions such as trade unions are distortions in otherwise perfect markets. While the markets for capital and land may be closer to the conditions of perfect competition, labour markets would probably be highly imperfect even without the existence of trade unions. Indeed, the principal argument used to justify trade unions is that, in their absence, market power would lie in the hands of employers. It is doubtful if labour markets ever existed in which all employers and all workers act as passive price-takers. More typically, market power would lie in the hands of the employers in a labour market in which a small number of employers bargained individually with a large number of workers unrepresented by a trade union. By bargaining collectively through a trade union, workers are seeking to create a market power to equal or exceed that possessed by the employer.

METHODS OF WAGE DETERMINATION IN THE UK

In distribution theory it is generally assumed that wages are determined by individual negotiation between workers and employers and that market forces eventually bring about a ruling market wage. When trade unions are introduced into this analysis, it is assumed that firms decide how much labour to employ at a wage level determined by the union acting as a monopoly supplier of labour. The actual process of wage and salary determination in the UK is both more complicated and more varied.

Collective bargaining

In 1989 there were over 10 million trade union members in the UK, though this represents a significant fall in union membership as compared to a decade earlier. Between 1979 and 1989, union membership fell by nearly 30%. Less than half of the labour force are now trade union members. The pay of most trade union members is determined by collective bargaining. The union represents its members' interests collectively by bargaining with employers to improve pay and other conditions of work. For further discussion of the nature of collective bargaining and its effectiveness, you should refer to the question practice at the end of this chapter.

Individual negotiation

This generally takes place in non-unionised parts of the economy. Highly paid managers, executives and consultants who offer specialist professional services will normally negotiate on an individual basis. At the other extreme, unorganised low-paid workers such as fruit-pickers and other casual workers also negotiate individually. In these circumstances the employer usually has much more bargaining power than the individual worker. Consequently the wage may effectively be determined by the employer on a 'take it or leave it' basis.

State determination

There are various ways in which the state intervenes to influence both market forces and the collective bargaining process:

❶ **Protecting low-paid workers** In low-paid industries such as catering, trade unions are difficult to organise and they tend to be ineffective. **Wages councils** were established to determine minimum rates of pay in these industries, but the Conservative government now intends to abolish wages councils and allow a free-for-all. Wages councils represent a form of **minimum wage legislation**. In some countries, a minimum wage has been established by law, to cover all industries.

❷ **Statutory incomes policies** At various times since the Second World War, British governments have imposed a statutory incomes policy on the process of wage determination. An incomes policy usually lays down an upper limit to wage settlements. During a statutory incomes policy, 'free' collective bargaining is either constrained or perhaps even suspended. Trade unions have often been suspicious of incomes policies which they believe may undermine the bargaining function of a union. The government's main purpose in introducing an incomes policy has usually been to attack the cost-push causes of inflation which result in part from the nature of wage bargaining in the UK. Incomes policies have also been justified as a method of ensuring a fairer distribution of income than that resulting from the collective bargaining process.

❸ **The state as an employer** In most industries where the state or a public authority is the employer, unions are recognised and wages are determined by collective bargaining. However, there are exceptions, such as the armed forces and the police, where normal trade union activity is not allowed. Pay in the armed forces is effectively determined by the state. Also, in recent years the government has suspended collective bargaining for some public sector workers such as teachers. **Pay review boards** have been set up to advise the government on how workers such as teachers and nurses should be paid, usually on the basis of comparability with private sector workers.

❹ **Arbitration and conciliation** In the process of free collective bargaining, a trade union will often demand a pay rise which is greater than the increase the employer is initially prepared to pay. Bargaining is a process in which each side modifies its offer or claim until agreement is reached. The vast majority of agreements are reached without a breakdown in the bargaining process and without dispute. Occasionally, however, agreements cannot be reached and a dispute either occurs or is threatened. Many collective agreements contain negotiating procedures to be followed when the next round of bargaining takes place. The procedural arrangements commonly specify the stage in the breakdown of bargaining at which outside arbitrators or conciliators should be brought in to help both sides reach agreement. In 1975 the Employment Protection Act established the Advisory Conciliation and Arbitration Service (ACAS). If both sides in a dispute agree to it, ACAS may be called in to try to settle a dispute.

Chapter roundup

The process of wage determination, in particular labour markets, is an important part of inflation theories (see Chapter 22). The shape of the supply curve of labour is crucial to the 'supply-side' theory explained in Chapter 23; whilst in Chapter 24, the different views of Keynesians and monetarists are discussed concerning the labour market and the wage determining process.

Illustrative questions and answers

1   Essay Question
    Discuss whether trade unions can increase the real incomes and the level of employment in the industries in which they operate.

(AEB, November 1992)

Tutorial note

In the main body of the chapter we restricted our analysis of trade unions in the context of distribution theory to the rather general statements that

❶   unions can increase both wages and employment for their members if union activity results in the MRP curve shifting rightwards, and

❷   if the main result of union activity is to shift the supply curve of labour leftwards by restricting entry to the labour market, wage rises will normally be at the expense of employment.

Fig. 36a also illustrates a situation in which wages rise at the expense of employment. We assume rather unrealistically that the union can fix any wage-rate it chooses, and that employment is then determined by the amount of labour which employers will hire at this wage. If the wage is fixed at W_2, above the competitive wage determined by supply and demand at W_1, the line W_2AS becomes the supply curve of labour. Employers are faced with a perfectly elastic supply of labour at the union-determined wage, up to a supply of L_3. Beyond this point they will have to offer a higher wage in order to attract more labour. However, they will only willingly employ a labour force of L_2, thereby restricting employment below the competitive level of Ll. At the union-determined wage-rate, there is an excess supply of labour of L_3-L_2. This will create a pressure to undermine the union if unemployed workers are prepared to supply labour at a wage below W_2. Whether W_2 continues as the wage rate will depend upon the union's power to resist wage-cutting. Fig. 36b illustrates a market structure in which the introduction of a union can increase both the wage-rate and employment, without the need to shift the MRP curve rightwards! This is when a monopsony buyer of labour bargains with a trade union which is a monopoly seller of labour. We explained earlier, in the context of Fig. 36b, how in the absence of a trade union the competitive supply of labour would result in an equilibrium wage rate at W^*, and an employment level at L^*. Suppose now that a trade union fixes the wage-rate at W_1. At this wage-rate the supply curve of labour is the line W_1XS, and the marginal cost curve of labour is W_1XZ MC. You should note that the MC of employing another worker is the same as the union-determined wage, as long as the labour force is below L_1. If a labour force above L_1 is to be employed, the wage must rise in order to persuade additional workers to supply their labour. Because all workers must be paid the higher wage, the MC of employing an extra worker is now above the supply curve. Between the horizontal section of the MC curve for levels of employment below L_1, and the 'competitive' section of the curve Z MC, is a vertical line or discontinuity, XZ. The equilibrium level of employment at the wage of W_1 is Ll This is determined where the MRP curve intersects the vertical section of the MC curve between X and Z. The union can increase both the wage-rate and the level of employment as compared with the situation without a union. Providing of course that the union possesses the required power, both the wage-rate and the level of employment can be increased up to an employment level of L_2 determined at point Y. Wages can be increased beyond Y up to a level fixed at A, but only at the expense of some of the extra employment which the union created.

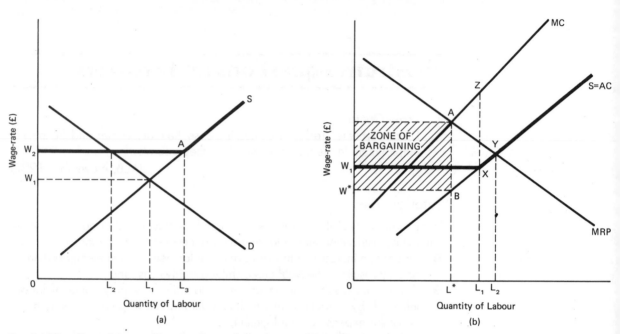

Fig. 36 *The effect of the introduction of a trade union into different labour markets (a) competitive demand for labour (b) monopoly demand for labour*

Suggested answer

- Distinguish between an increase in the money wage and the real wage. If an increase in the money wage causes or is associated with an equal increase in prices, there is no increase in the real wage. In order to increase the real wage of its members, a union must secure a rise in the wage-rate which is greater than the rate of inflation.

- In these circumstances, employment and the real wage may rise if the MRP curve shifts rightwards. Whether such a shift in the demand curve for labour is the result of the union's existence, or would have taken place anyway, is open to debate.

- If the union raises the real wage by restricting entry to the labour market, thereby shifting the supply curve of labour leftwards, employment is likely to fall. However, the unemployed may not be members of the union!

- Introduce and explain other market situations such as those we have explained in these notes.

2   Data Question

(a) To what extent do the data in the opposite tables indicate an improvement in the living standards of *either* male manual *or* female non-manual workers over the period 1981 to 1986?   (6)

(b) Account for the differences in average weekly earnings and average hours of work per week in 1986 between:
   (i) manual and non-manual workers;   (8)
   (ii) male and female workers.   (6)

(ULEAC, AS-Level, June 1990)

Table 1

| | Average weekly earnings and average hours of work per week (Full-time workers) | | | |
| | 1981 | | 1986 | |
	Earnings (£)	Hours	Earnings (£)	Hours
Male				
All	136.50	41.7	203.40	41.8
Manual	118.40	44.2	170.90	44.5
Non-manual	161.20	38.4	243.40	38.6
Female				
All	89.30	37.2	134.70	37.3
Manual	2.10	39.4	104.40	39.5
Non-manual	95.60	36.5	144.30	36.7
All adults	121.60	40.3	181.20	40.4

Table 2

| | Retail Price Index | | | | | | |
	1980	1981	1982	1983	1984	1985	1986
Index	100.0	111.9	121.5	127.1	133.4	141.5	146.3

(Source: *Annual Abstract of Statistics*, CSO, 1988)

Tutorial note

(a) Table 1 shows *nominal* earnings, which you need to convert – with the aid of the Retail Price Index data in Table 2 – into details of *real* earnings, i.e. data which shows the *purchasing power* of the workers' nominal earnings. Proceed in the following way:

(i) for your chosen category of worker (either male manual or female non-manual) divide average earnings in 1981 by the RPI for 1981 (111.9), and then multiply by 100, which is the price index for the base year (1980).

(ii) repeat for 1986, dividing average earnings in 1986 by the RPI for 1986 (146.3) and again multiplying by 100. You now have two figures which show average weekly real earnings for 1981 and 1986 for your chosen category of worker. You are now in a position to assess whether standards of living have risen. However, to make a fuller assessment, divide the figures you have just calculated by average weekly hours worked to calculate whether real *hourly* wage rates increased between 1981 and 1986. And if there is time, you might mention that the data do not indicate whether earnings have become more or less equal *within* the category of male manual or female non-manual workers, and they do not allow you to assess other contributing factors to standards of living such as the value people place on leisure time and 'quality of life' factors.

(b) (i) and (ii) Start your answers by briefly stating what the differences were: non-manual workers, both men and women, earned significantly more than manual workers, but worked fewer hours a week; while males (in aggregate) also earned significantly more than women, but in this case they worked slightly longer hours. Then suggest at least one possible reason for each of the four differences that the question requires you to explain.

163

Question bank

1 'Britain's top-paid City executive earns more than £2.5 million a year... up to 25 times higher than that of an average school teacher... Economics textbooks are packed with rationales for big pay differentials'.

(M. Prowse, 'Why the City Pays Too Much', *Financial Times*, 9 October 1987)

Outline an economic theory of pay differentials and explain whether or not you feel it gives a satisfactory explanation of the example quoted.

(NEAB, June 1988)

2

(a) How does economic theory explain why some groups of workers are paid more than others?

(b) Discuss whether this theory fully explains why women are often paid less than men. (10)   (AEB, November 1991)

3 'Economic rent can be earned by all factors of production. The elasticity of supply of a factor is critical in this respect.' Discuss.

(ULEAC, January 1992)

4 Consider how economic theory might be used to explain the following examples of wage differentials:

(a) The higher-than-average wages earned by a star footballer like Ian Rush. (7)

(b) The tendency for unionised workers to earn on average more than non-unionised workers. (6)

(c) The higher wages of manual workers on North Sea oil rigs compared with manual workers on shore. (6)

(d) The tendency for university graduates to earn on average more than non-graduates. (6)   (WJEC, June 1992)

5

(a) Outline how trade unions may influence the supply of labour. (40)

(b) Examine the extent to which a significant reduction in the power of trade unions would:

(i) make the wage structure more flexible;

(ii) improve long-term living standards. (30+30)   (ULEAC, June 1991)

6 Why do some people earn low wages?   (Cambridge, June 1990)

7 Assess the case for and against replacing national collective bargaining with an alternative system such as regional bargaining or profit-related pay as a method of determining wages.   (AEB, June 1992)

8

(a) 'Wages are the reward to the factor of production 'labour', but the other factors of production also gain rewards which can provide income to finance household expenditure.' Explain. (8)

(b) Concentrating on labour, explain why it is not necessarily certain whether an individual will wish to work longer or shorter hours if they are offered a rise in the hourly wage rate. (10)

(c) Explain why, if there is a set length of the working week, an individual may decide to give up work if either income taxes or state benefits are set too high. (7)   (NISEAC, June 1991)

9 What are the functions of a trade union? Are changes in UK government policy likely to have affected the ability of trade unions to raise the wages of their members?   (NEAB, June 1989)

MONEY

Units in this chapter

Chapter objectives

In earlier chapters we have examined in some detail how the economy functions and the price mechanism operates – yet up until now we have almost completely ignored a key feature of economic life in a modern market economy: namely the role of money in facilitating production and exchange. We begin the chapter by examining briefly the **nature** and **functions of money** in a modern monetary economy. Having surveyed how modern forms of money came into existence, we then go on to explain the **relationship between money and other forms of financial asset** such as 'near monies', and to introduce the main measures of the '**money supply**' such as **M0** and **M4**. The chapter continues with an explanation of how most money now takes the form of **bank deposits which are created by the private enterprise banking system**. We conclude the chapter by covering the '**demand for money**' – or the various motives people have for wanting to hold 'money balances' – and the **determination of the rate of interest**.

MONEY AS A MEDIUM OF EXCHANGE AND UNIT OF ACCOUNT

In a developed market economy, nearly all the exchanges involved in production and distribution require the use of money as a **medium of exchange**. In a very simple economy, exchange could be based on barter, but barter is inefficient and impractical in a more complex economic system. Successful **barter** requires a '**double coincidence of wants**': if someone wishes to buy a typewriter, he must find another person who not only has a typewriter to sell, but who also wants the goods which the purchaser is selling. Time and energy will be wasted in searching the market to establish the double coincidence of wants. The existence of such **transactions** and **search costs** is likely to discourage specialisation and large-scale production in an economy.

Besides functioning as a medium of exchange, money usually acts as a **unit of account**, allowing the prices of all goods to be compared. In modern economics the unit of account is almost always the medium of exchange, but there are exceptions – the prices of antiques or racehorses offered for sale at an auction are sometimes expressed in guineas, even though the guinea has long ceased to be a monetary unit.

MONEY AS A STORE OF VALUE

Monetarists and **Keynesians** hold rather different views on the nature and functions of money. Monetarists have inherited what is sometimes known as the classical tradition, which separates the role in the economy of '**real**' and '**monetary**' **forces**. They believe that the relative prices of goods, which are determined in the real economy by the forces of supply and demand, are independent of money even though they are commonly expressed in monetary units of account. Money merely determines the general price level. For example, if the amount of money in the economy doubles, all prices double, but relative prices and equilibrium outputs in the economy remain the same.

Keynesians argue that this view of the role of money ignores the essential function of money as a **store of value**. For example, a person who sells his labour and receives money in exchange may decide to store the income he received in the form of idle money instead of using it to demand goods and services. This can result in a lack of demand for the output which is currently being produced, resulting in the breakdown of the monetary linkage between the markets of the real economy. Thus, the function of money as a store of value is an important part of the Keynesian argument that unemployment can be caused by a lack of effective aggregate demand in an economy.

THE HISTORICAL DEVELOPMENT OF MONEY

Commodity money

In order to function as money, an asset must be an acceptable medium of exchange and a possible store of value. Early forms of money which replaced barter were commodities, such as beads, shells, cattle and slaves, usually with an intrinsic value of their own. Gradually the precious metals, gold and silver, replaced other forms of commodity money because they possessed to a greater degree the other desirable characteristics necessary for a commodity to function as money: relative **scarcity**, **portability**, **durability**, **divisibility**, and **uniformity**.

Representative money

Nevertheless gold and silver are vulnerable to theft and difficult to store, and it became the custom for precious metals to be deposited with goldsmiths for safekeeping. The goldsmiths developed into banks, and the **gold receipts** which they issued became **bank-notes** or **paper money**. The notes were acceptable as a means of payment since they could be exchanged for gold on demand. Although relatively worthless in itself, the money represented ownership of commodities with an intrinsic value.

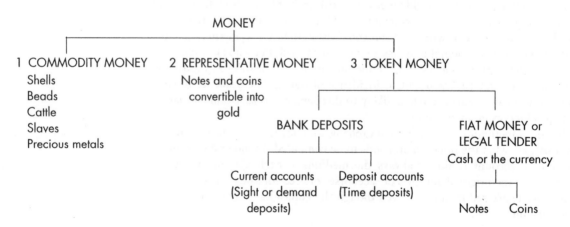

Fig. 37 Historical and present-day forms of money

Token money

Banks discovered that they could increase their profits by issuing notes to a value greatly in excess of the gold deposits which they held. Imprudent banks would over-expand the note issue, and depositors suffered in the crashes which periodically occurred when banks could not meet demands by the public to convert notes into gold. As a direct result of these bank crashes, the 1844 Bank Charter Act largely removed from English and Welsh banks the right to issue their own notes, though some banks continued to issue notes on a limited scale until the last 'country' bank merged in 1921. This change in the law encouraged a new development in banking, the **creation of deposit money**. Instead of issuing its own notes when a customer requested a loan, a bank would make a ledger or book-keeping entry, crediting the customer's account with a loan or bank deposit. Such a bank deposit is obviously a store of value. However, a bank deposit is also a medium of exchange if it is customarily accepted that payment can be made by shifting ownership of the deposit, for example through the medium of a cheque.

Bank deposits are of course **token money**. They are **customary money** rather than **legal tender**, and generally accepted as money because of people's confidence in the banks and the monetary system. Bank deposits make up by far the largest part of modern money, between about two-thirds and 85 per cent of the money supply, depending on how money is defined. In contrast, **cash** (notes and coins, or the currency) is just the 'small change' of the system. Nowadays the state has a monopoly of the issue of cash, in England and Wales at least, and cash has gradually developed to become purely token money, just like a bank deposit. Unlike a bank deposit, however, cash is usually legal tender – 'fiat money' made legal by government decree – which must be accepted as a medium of exchange.

14.1 UNDERLYING CONCEPTS

MONEY, NEAR MONEY, AND MONEY SUBSTITUTES

It is generally agreed that bank **current accounts (sight deposits** or **demand deposits)** function as money. They are both a store of value and a medium of exchange since cheques can be drawn on the deposit and are accepted in payment of a debt. Nowadays many people use credit cards as a medium of exchange. However, a **credit card** is not a store of value, and its use merely delays the settling of a debt through a cash transaction or the shifting of a bank deposit. A credit card is a **money substitute** rather than a form of money in its own right.

Whereas a money substitute is a medium of exchange but not a store of value, the reverse is true of **near money**. Financial assets such as building society deposits were until recently regarded as near monies. A building society deposit is a substitute for a bank current account or a cash holding as a convenient form of storage for wealth or value, but it does not serve directly as medium of exchange unless cheques can be drawn on the deposit.

THE PROBLEM OF DEFINING THE MONEY SUPPLY

Thirty years ago, neither economists nor politicians gave much attention to the precise definition of the money supply, since it was generally accepted that 'money did not matter' in the macroeconomic management of the economy. As we shall see in later chapters, this is no longer the case. According to the **monetarists**, money does matter, and the control of the money supply is an important part of monetarist economic management in general, and monetary policy in particular.

Even if it is accepted that monetarist theory is correct (we shall later see that Keynesians dispute this) practical monetarism may be impossible if the money supply is a 'will-o'-the wisp' which cannot by its nature be controlled. Suppose that the monetary authorities (the Bank of England and the Treasury) decide either to restrict the rate of growth of the money supply or to reduce the absolute size of the money stock. The more successful they appear to be in controlling whatever they define as the money supply, the more likely it is that near monies, outside the existing definition and system of control, will take on the function of money as a medium of exchange. The phenomenon is related to **Goodhart's Law**, which states that as soon as a measure of the money supply (e.g. M4) is adopted as a target for monetary control, any apparently stable, former relationship between it and the price level will break down, rendering the measure useless as a control variable. In this sense, 'money is as money does'! Keynesians sometimes argue that the money supply is impossible to control, since it passively adapts to whatever level is required to finance the transactions which are desired at the existing price level. We shall examine the implications of this argument in the context of monetary policy in Chapter 17 and inflation in Chapter 22.

Whether or not this view on the impossibility of controlling the money supply is completely accepted, it does help to explain why policy makers have commonly used more than one definition of the money supply. The **'narrow definition'** favoured in Britain has been **M1**, comprising cash and bank sight deposits. However, wealthy individuals and companies will normally hold interest-earning deposit accounts or time deposits alongside their current accounts or sight deposits. Should time deposits be defined as money? Unlike a sight deposit, the ownership of a time deposit cannot be shifted by cheque; hence a time deposit is not a medium of exchange. But to compete with the building societies, the banks have allowed deposit accounts to become increasingly more liquid. A customer may keep a very low balance in a current account, upon which cheques can be drawn; when a large payment is due to be made, part of the deposit account is simply shifted into the current account. Bank customers therefore treat their deposit accounts as money, a practice encouraged by the banks in order to attract funds away from building societies and National Savings Certificates. For this reason, time deposits are included in the wider measure of money M3. But because building society deposits have become as liquid as bank deposits, M1 and M3 have

Table 14.1 *The monetary aggregates in the United Kingdom*

M0	Notes and coin in circulation; the banks 'till' money and their 'operational' (or working) deposits with the Bank of England
M1	Notes and coin in circulation; UK private sector sterling bank deposits
M2	Non-interest bearing component of M1; private sector interest-bearing 'retail' sterling bank deposits; private sector holdings of retail building society shares and deposits and National Savings Bank ordinary accounts
M3	M1 plus private sector holdings of sterling bank deposits and sterling bank Certificates of Deposit (CDs)
M3c	M3 plus private sector holdings of foreign currency bank deposits
M4	M3 plus private sector holdings of building society shares and deposits and sterling CDs less building society holdings of bank deposits, bank CDs and notes and coin
M5	M4 plus holdings by the private sector (excluding building societies) of money market instruments (bank bills, Treasury bills, local authority deposits), certificates of tax deposit and National Savings instruments (excluding certificates, SAYE and other long-term deposits)

now given way to **M2** and **M4** (which include building society deposits) as the main measures of '**narrow**' and '**broad**' money respectively.

'Narrow' money (M2) and 'Broad' money (M4)

The definition of **M2** is based upon the distinction between '**retail**' and '**wholesale**' deposits. Retail deposits are liquid – or relatively liquid – deposits held by the general public which are likely to be spent. They include a range of building society deposits, as well as bank sight deposits. By contrast, wholesale deposits are normally owned by banks and financial institutions themselves, and held in other banks and financial institutions. They reflect asset portfolio management decisions of banks and other financial institutions and have relatively little effect upon the retail spending decisions of the general public. Therefore wholesale deposits, and any other deposits which are unlikely to be translated quickly into spending power, should be excluded from measures of the money supply which are designed primarily to monitor 'retail' conditions. This is the logic behind the creation of M2, which includes retail deposits held in all financial institutions – building societies as well as banks – but excludes both wholesale deposits held by banks in other banks, and also long-term deposits. **M4**, which has replaced M3 as the favoured measure of 'broad' money, includes long-term as well as short-term or retail bank and building society deposits, but excludes wholesale deposits (which do however figure in M5, the widest of the 'official measures of money).

'M0' or the 'Cash base'

Although M1 and M2 have conventionally been regarded as '**narrow**' **money**, in 1983 an even narrower measure, **M0**, was created by the United Kingdom monetary authorities. The definition of M0 is limited largely to cash in circulation with the general public. M0 is a measure of the '**cash base**' to the monetary system (sometimes called the '**monetary base**'). Although as we noted earlier, cash is the 'small change' of the monetary system, it is significant as the one part of the money supply over which the authorities – since they alone issue cash – can exercise a monopoly control.

14.2 ESSENTIAL INFORMATION

THE CREATION OF BANK DEPOSITS

Bank deposits form the largest part of both M2 and M4. Bank deposits are the main form of money because banks possess the ability to create new deposits or credit. We shall delay until Chapter 17 an explanation of how this is done in the complex conditions and institutional framework of the British monetary system. In this chapter we restrict the analysis to a very simple model of credit creation in an economy in which there is just one commercial bank which has a monopoly of all bank dealings with the general public. For our purposes a **bank** is defined as an institution which:

❶ accepts deposits which can be transferred by cheque; and

❷ makes advances (which can be either overdrafts or term loans).

We shall further assume that the commercial bank aims to maximise profits, but is required to hold a reserve of 10% cash against its total deposit liabilities. The 10% cash ratio may be a reserve requirement of the central bank, or it may be chosen for prudential reasons by the bank itself.

Suppose that a member of the public now makes a new deposit of £1000 in cash.

From the bank's point of view £1000 is both a liability and an asset, and will be recorded as such in the bank's balance sheet:

Liabilities	Assets
Deposit £1000	Cash £1000

As things stand, all the bank's deposit liabilities are backed with cash. If this remained the position, the 'bank' would simply be a safe-deposit institution. However, the bank can increase profits by crediting £9000 to the account of a customer who has requested a loan.

On the assets side of the balance sheet this will be shown as an **advance** of £9000 – whether the loan is an overdraft or a term loan granted for a definite period or term of years does not matter. Since the bank must honour any cheques which are drawn on the account up to the value of £9000, **deposit liabilities** have increased by exactly the same amount as **interest-earning assets**:

Liabilities	Assets
Deposit £10 000	Cash £1000
	Advances £9000

Both the customer who made the original deposit and the customer in receipt of the advance can draw cheques to a combined value of £10 000 on their deposits. The initial £1000 has expanded deposits, and hence the money supply, to £10 000. As we are assuming a monopoly bank, there is no danger of customers drawing cheques payable to customers of other banks. Nevertheless, there could be a cash drain from the bank, if customers decide always to keep some proportion of their money assets in the form of cash. A cash drain would limit the bank's ability to create deposits to a figure somewhat below that illustrated in our example.

Deposits will be expanded whether the bank expands advances or purchases interest-earning assets such as securities or bonds from the general public. Suppose the bank creates £6000 of advances and purchases £3000 of bonds. The bank pays for the bonds with a cheque for £3000 drawn on itself, thereby increasing total deposit liabilities to £10 000 when the payment is credited to the account of the person who sold the bonds. The spectrum of assets owned by the bank is different from the previous position, but the deposit liabilities, which represent the creation of money, are the same as in our last example:

Liabilities	Assets
Deposits £10 000	Cash £1000
	Bonds £3000
	Advances £6000

Of course, the assumption of a monopoly commercial bank is completely unrealistic, but it does illustrate the central principle of credit creation – that **the banking system as a whole can create an expansion in bank deposits (and thus the money supply) which is a multiple of the liquid reserves held by the banks.** Because, in our example, cash is the only liquid asset or reserve held to back fractionally the bank's deposit liabilities, the ability of the banks to expand deposits is dependent on the cash ratio. The **money multiplier** measures the maximum expansion of deposits (or **'low-powered' money**) which is possible for a given increase in cash (or **'high-powered' money**) deposited in the banking system. Assuming that there is no cash drain, for our model we can write:

$$\text{money multiplier} = \frac{1}{\text{cash ratio}}$$

In Chapter 17 we shall see that British banks have usually kept some form of **liquid assets ratio** or **reserve ratio**, rather than the simple cash ratio of our model. It is useful, therefore, to write the money multiplier more generally as:

$$\text{money multiplier} = \frac{1}{\text{liquid assets ratio}}$$

When we assume a **multi-bank** system, similar to that in the UK, the general conclusions of our model still hold. If the increase of £1000 in cash deposits is spread over all the banks, deposits can expand to £10 000 providing that every bank is prepared to create deposits to the full extent the cash ratio allows. However, if only one bank is willing to expand deposits to the full, it will soon face demands for cash which it cannot meet. Customers will draw cheques on their deposits which will be paid into the accounts of the customers of the banks that have refused to expand credit. When the cheques are cleared, the bank must pay cash to the other banks, equal to the shift in deposits. To avoid this possibility, the bank will restrict the extent to which it is prepared to expand deposits. However, if all banks expand credit to the full, payments to customers of other banks will largely cancel out. The banking system as a whole can expand deposits to £10 000, though some banks may gain business at the expense of others.

THE DEMAND FOR MONEY

So far we have assumed implicitly that banks will create new bank deposits, and hence increase the supply of money, to the fullest extent possible. In our model, the ability of the banks to create new deposits is constrained, firstly by the size of the cash base of the banking system, and secondly by the prudential requirement to maintain a cash ratio – in Chapter 17 we shall extend the analysis to the situation where the monetary authorities decide the reserve ratio and then attempt to influence the reserve assets in the implementation of monetary policy.

However, we have begged the question of whether bank customers actually **demand** and take up all the new deposits or credit which the banks are prepared to create. The actual **money stock** in the economy will be determined by both the demand and the supply of money.

The nature of the demand for money is one of the most important areas of debate between Keynesian and monetarist economists, a debate which is significant both in terms of economic theory and practical policy-making. Unfortunately, in a book of this type we can do no more than scratch the surface of the issues involved. Keynesians and monetarists share common ground in believing that part of the demand for money results from **transactions** and **precautionary motives**.

The transactions demand for money

A certain amount of money is required as a medium of exchange so that people can undertake day-to-day purchases of goods and services. The transactions **demand for money** depends upon:

- **Real income** – people with high incomes are likely to require larger transaction balances to finance their purchases for the simple reason that they usually plan to spend more than poorer people.
- **The price level** – a rise in the price level is likely to increase the transactions demand for money, since more money is needed to finance the same real expenditure.
- **Institutional factors** such as the length of time between pay days – if a worker is paid a salary of £800 once every four weeks instead of £200 weekly, he is likely to keep a larger balance, on average, in his bank deposit or in cash in order to finance the expenditure planned over the month.
- **Financial innovation**, such as the development and availability of near monies and money substitutes may also affect the transactions demand for money.

The precautionary demand for money

A certain amount of money may be held to meet unforeseen emergencies, though it is more usual nowadays to hold such assets in building society deposits and other

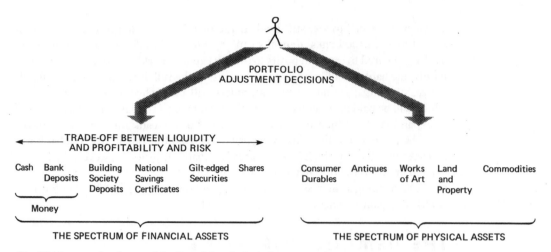

Fig. 38 An example of some of the financial and physical assets in which an individual may decide to store his personal wealth

near monies. For most purposes the **precautionary demand** for money can be merged into the transactions demand, since it is also likely to be determined by real income, the price level and institutional factors.

The speculative demand for money

If money balances were required only for transactions and precautionary purposes, the demand for money function would be inelastic with respect to the rate of interest, resembling the curve labelled L_{t+p} in Fig. 39(a). However, Keynes argued the existence of a third **speculative motive** for holding money balances in which changes, and expected changes, in the rate of interest become the crucial influences over people's demand to hold money. The speculative demand for money is shown as the curve L_s in Fig. 39(b).

The **speculative demand** is sometimes called the demand to hold **passive or idle money balances** as a store of value or wealth – in contrast to the essentially active nature of transactions and precautionary balances which are held as a medium of exchange. Fig. 38 illustrates how money is just one of the assets in which an individual may decide to store his portfolio of wealth. However, for our purposes we can simplify and assume that an individual can store in wealth in just two assets: money and bonds. Money possesses the advantage of instant spending power, or complete liquidity, but it earns little, if any, interest or income. In contrast, bonds earn fixed rates of interest but suffer from being relatively illiquid.

Now, the higher the rate of interest the more attractive it becomes to store wealth in bonds rather than money. Thus the demand for idle money balances is inversely related to the rate of interest. However, speculation about future interest rates explains the particular non–linear slope of the L_s function shown in Fig. 39(b). Although bonds have the advantage of earning an income, we saw in Chapter 11 how the price of bonds varies inversely with the rate of interest. If the rate of interest rises, then bond prices must fall, and owners of bonds must suffer capital losses. Clearly, it is in the interest of bond owners to guess correctly future changes in interest rates. If they expect, or speculate, that interest rates will rise, they should sell bonds and hold their wealth in money since changes in the rate of interest do not involve any change in the value of money. Bond holders will prefer liquidity, to evade capital losses that would result from holding bonds. But if interest rates are expected to fall, people should move out of money and purchase bonds so as to benefit from future capital gains. Finally, there will be a value of the rate of interest which people regard as 'normal'; if the actual rate is below the 'normal' rate, people will expect the actual rate to rise, and if it is above it they expect it to fall. This part of Keynes' theory of the speculative demand for money

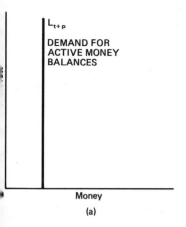

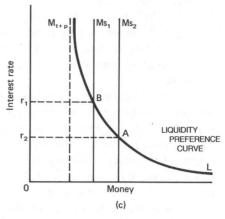

Fig. 39 The demand for money (a) the transactions and precautionary demand (L_{t+p}) (b) the speculative and asset demand (L_s) (c) the demand for money curve (liquidity preference curve) and the determination of the rate of interest

explains the upper (vertical) and the lower (horizontal) sections of the L_s curve. Keynes argues that at some low rate of interest everyone will expect the rate to rise, thus making them unwilling to hold bonds. For any further fall in the interest rate below this level, demand for money will be perfectly elastic. The resulting horizontal section of the L_s function Keynes called the **liquidity trap**. In a similar way, there will be some high rate of interest at which everyone will expect the rate of interest to fall, making them unwilling to hold money as a passive wealth asset. For any further rise in the interest rate above this level there will be no further movement out of money and into bonds; hence the L_s function will be completely interest-inelastic or vertical.

THE DETERMINATION OF THE RATE OF INTEREST

In Fig. 39(c) we bring together the demand for, and the supply of money to illustrate the Keynesian theory of the determination of the rate of interest. The rate of interest can be regarded simply as the price of money, and as in any market, an equilibrium price will be determined where demand equals supply. We obtain the demand for money function, (which is often called the **Liquidity Preference function**), by adding up the transactions, precautionary, and speculative demands for money. The supply of money is shown as a vertical, and completely interest-inelastic, line labelled Ms_1. This is derived from the simplifying, and rather unrealistic, assumption that the money supply is a policy instrument completely controlled by the monetary authorities. If the authorities fix the money supply at Ms_1, the rate of interest is determined at r_1; if they then increase the money supply to Ms_2, the rate of interest falls to r_2. However, in Chapter 17 we shall suggest that the reverse relationship is perhaps more relevant to the conduct of monetary policy – changes in the rate of interest being used to achieve change in the money supply!

SOME IMPLICATIONS FOR MONETARY POLICY

In later chapters we shall explain how Keynesians have often argued that fiscal policy is both more powerful and predictable than monetary policy as a method of influencing the level of output in the economy. The theory developed in the preceding sections can be used to illustrate why Keynesians doubt the effectiveness of monetary policy. In Keynesian theory, the main transmission mechanism through which monetary policy affects output and the 'real economy' is via the effect of the interest rate upon businessmen's investment decisions. But even supposing that investment is highly responsive to changes in the rate of interest – and Keynes' theory of the marginal efficiency of capital which is explained in

Chapter 21 suggests that it is not – monetary policy may have little effect if the Liquidity Preference curve is flat or interest-elastic. In these circumstances, a large change in the money supply is likely to cause little or no change in the rate of interest, and hence investment. Conversely, if the demand for money curve is nearly vertical or interest-inelastic, the effect on the rate of interest may be quite powerful.

It is therefore not surprising that Keynesians and monetarists often disagree on the interest-elasticity of the demand for money, which, as we have seen, depends upon the existence of a speculative motive for holding money. Monetarists usually adopt the old 'classical' view that denies the existence of the speculative demand. Their argument is that the demand for money is interest-inelastic, people holding money balances largely to finance spending or transactions. Any increase in the money stock can cause significant changes in interest rates, but according to monetarists, the main effect will not be on investment and output but on prices as people spend their suddenly increased money holdings.

Chapter roundup

As yet we have hardly touched upon the various controversies between Keynesian and monetarist economists. In particular, we need to discuss further whether the main effects of monetary expansion will be on real income or output or on prices. This issue is discussed in Chapter 22. In this chapter we have introduced a simple model of credit creation and we have discussed in a general way whether the authorities can control the money supply. It is now generally agreed that the government's fiscal and monetary policies should not be treated as if they are independent of each other – public spending and its method of finance have significant effects both on the money supply and the government's freedom of choice in monetary policy. With this in mind, we shall examine the determinants of government revenues, expenditure and the PSBR, before we go on in Chapter 17 to examine the detailed methods by which the authorities attempt to implement monetary policy.

Illustrative question and answer

Essay Question
(a) Why are there several definitions of money in the UK? (30)
(b) What issues arise for the monetary authorities in controlling the supply of money?   (70)

(ULEAC, June, 1992)

Tutorial note

The proliferation of definitions or measures of the money supply reflects the period when 'pure' or 'technical' monetarism became increasingly influential in the UK from about 1970 to around 1985. From 1976 onwards, the government needed a precise measure of money because anti-inflation policy in general, and monetary policy in particular, was based upon the 'automatic policy rule' of announcing a target rate of growth for the money supply, for a medium-term period of about three years ahead, together with a firm commitment to implement monetary policy so as to 'hit' the target. But as we have explained in this chapter, the operation of 'Goodhart's Law' meant that as soon as the 'monetary authorities' (i.e. the Bank of England and the Treasury) used a particular measure of money, say M3, as the operational target for monetary policy, any previously stable relationship between the measure and inflation broke down. For example, other financial assets which were not included in the definition of the targeted measure of money, would begin to function as money. For a few years the monetary authorities responded to this situation by 'inventing', and then targeting, ever-wider measures of money, for example M2 and M4, in response to the fact that the nature of money was changing. We have also explained how the authorities reacted to this situation in the opposite way: designating M0 as the narrowest measure of money, on the basis that the authorities can, in principle, completely control the cash which is the major component of M0.

Around 1985 the UK government abandoned the 'pure' or 'technical' monetarism which we have described, largely because it was not working and because the 'credibility' upon which the policy depended to have any chance of success had evaporated. (To mark this event, the headline 'Monetarism, it's dead; Official!' appeared in *The Times* newspaper.) Thus the need for ever-more measures of the money supply (a proliferation which in its time was nicknamed 'monetary madness') has now diminished – unless of course the UK monetary authorities once again come under the influence of 'strict' monetarists such as Professor Sir Alan Walters.

Suggested answer

- Explain that a 'narrow' measure of money such as M1 or M2 takes account of the 'medium of exchange' function of money, whereas broader measures such as M3 and M4 reflect the 'store of value' function.
- Relate the proliferation of measures of money to the period of relatively 'pure' or 'technical' monetarism, pre-1985, when counter-inflation policy and monetary policy were based on trying to control the growth of the money supply.
- Introduce the implications of 'Goodhart's Law' which suggests that such a policy is unlikely to be successful in controlling both monetary growth and inflation.
- If monetary growth cannot be controlled by acting *directly* on the *supply* of money, one alternative is to aim at *indirect* control by using interest rates to influence the *demand* for money.
- A further alternative (embodied in ERM membership in 1990) is to abandon 'domestic monetary targetry' as the main weapon of counter-inflation policy, and switch instead to using a fixed exchange rate as the main policy instrument to control inflation (see Chapters 22 and 27).

Question bank

1
(a) What is meant by 'money'? (5)
(b) Explain why the use of money in an economy improves the efficiency of production and exchange. (12)
(c) Explain why some economists believe that increases in the quantity of money lead to increases in prices. (8) (Scottish Higher, June 1989)

2
(a) Explain how the banking system creates bank deposits. (15)
(b) How might total bank deposits be affected by:
(i) The government's budget moving from deficit into surplus? (5)

(ii) A large-scale sale of shares to the general public resulting from the privatisation of the electricity industry? (5) (AEB, June 1990)

3

(a) Outline the main functions of money and explain why it is impossible to have just one definition of the money supply.

(b) Why do people demand money? Outline the liquidity preference theory of interest rate determination. (9)

(c) Why may the UK government be reluctant to see interest rates fall to relatively low levels? (6) (NISEAC, June 1991)

4 Discuss the economic effects resulting from the widespread use of credit cards such as Access and Visa. (AEB, November 1991)

5 Explain the meaning of the term 'demand for money'. Compare the Keynesian and Monetarist views of the demand for money and indicate their respective policy implications. (NEAB, AS-Level, June 1989)

6 Explain what is meant by 'money' and discuss the problems which arise in applying this definition in the practice of monetary policy. Outline the basis of the difference between 'broad' (e.g. M4) and 'narrow' (e.g. M0) definitions of money and explain their role in the current monetary policy of the Government. (NEAB, AS-Level, June 1990)

7 What problems are involved in measuring the supply of money in the UK? Explain whether or not you regard the supply of money as an indicator or a determinant of the state of the economy. (NEAB, June 1991)

CHAPTER 15

TAXATION AND PUBLIC SPENDING

Units in this chapter

Chapter objectives

This is the first of two chapters devoted to important aspects of **public finance**. This chapter, which covers the structure of **taxation** and **public expenditure** in the United Kingdom, emphasises the more microeconomic elements of public finance, leaving until Chapter 16 a consideration of what happens in the economy as a whole when government expenditure is different from revenue and a **budget deficit** or **surplus** occurs. The macroeconomic and monetary implications of public finance are further developed in later chapters.

It is worth stressing at the outset that taxation and public spending are 'opposite sides of the fiscal coin'. Thus an argument for (or against) public spending is usually also an argument for (or against) taxation.

A large part of the public sector exists in the non-market economy, which means that the output of goods and services produced is not sold at a market price. There are of course important exceptions, particularly the activities of nationalised industries, which exist largely in the market economy. In some cases the distinction is rather unclear, when for example an art gallery is largely financed out of taxation even though a token price is charged for admission. We shall, however, follow the convention of excluding from our definition of public spending the direct spending by nationalised industries, since the expenditure is largely financed from the revenue raised by selling the industries' output in the market place. In this chapter we restrict our analysis to the direct spending by central and local government and the taxation which largely finances this spending.

15.1 UNDERLYING CONCEPTS

TYPES OF TAXATION

A **tax**, which is a compulsory levy charged by a government or public authority to pay for its expenditure, can be classified in a number of ways:

❶ **According to who levies the tax** Most taxes are levied by central government in the UK, but the council tax (or poll tax) and the uniform business rate are examples of local government taxation.

❷ **According to what is taxed** The major categories here are taxes on income, expenditure and capital, though other categories include pay-roll and poll taxes. Personal income tax is the most important tax on income in the UK, though employees' National Insurance contributions (NIC) and corporation tax (a tax on company income or profits) are other examples. The Inland Revenue is the department of the civil service mainly responsible for collecting taxes on income and capital, whereas the Board of Customs and Excise collects expenditure taxes. Expenditure taxes are usefully divided into *ad valorem* or percentage taxes such as value-added tax (VAT), and specifie taxes (or unit taxes) which include the excise duties on tobacco, alcohol and petrol. A specific tax on, for example, wine is levied on the quantity of wine rather than on its price. Thus a bottle of expensive vintage claret bears the same tax as a bottle of cheap table-wine. Similarly, a user tax such as a television licence or motor vehicle tax is levied irrespective of either the price or the current market value of the TV set or car.

From 1989/1990 until 1993, a poll tax has temporarily replaced the local rates as the main form of local taxation in the UK. Prior to its short life in the early 1990s, a poll tax, which is a tax 'on being a human being', was last levied in the United Kingdom in the 14th century, when it triggered a peasants' revolt that caused its hasty withdrawal! Viewed as a 'community charge', a poll tax was classified as an expenditure tax levied to pay for local government services provided. Taxes on wealth and capital have never been significant in the United Kingdom. The main current capital tax is inheritance tax, a tax on gifts from the dead to the living, which replaced capital transfer tax (CTT). CTT was a short-lived tax levied during the 1970s and early 1980s which had extended the taxation of wealth to cover gifts made during life as well as the inheritance of estates. Finally, amongst a number of miscellaneous taxes, are employers' National Insurance contributions, a form of pay-roll tax in which the amount of tax paid varies with the number of workers employed.

❸ **Direct and Indirect Taxation** These concepts are often used interchangeably with taxes on income and expenditure, though it is not strictly true that a tax on spending must be an indirect tax. Income tax is a direct tax because the income receiver, who benefits from the income, is directly liable in law to pay the tax (even though it is frequently collected through the PAYE scheme from the employer). In contrast, most taxes on spending are indirect taxes since the seller of the good, and not the purchaser who benefits from its consumption, is liable in law to pay the tax. Nevertheless, as we shall see later, the seller usually tries to pass on the incidence of the tax to the purchaser by raising the price of the good by the amount of the tax! There are, however, examples of direct taxes on expenditure, such as the stamp duty paid by the purchaser rather than by the seller of a house.

❹ **Progressive, Regressive and Proportionate Taxation** In a progressive tax system a progressively larger proportion of income is paid in tax as income rises, while in a regressive system a progressively smaller proportion is paid. A tax is proportionate if exactly the same proportion of income is paid in tax at all levels of income. You should note that in these definitions the word progressive is completely 'value neutral', implying nothing about how the revenue raised by the government is spent. Nevertheless, progressive taxation is likely to be used by the government to achieve the social aim of a 'fairer' distribution of income. However, progressive taxation cannot by itself redistribute income – a policy of transfers in the government's public spending programme is required for this. Progressive taxation used on its own will merely reduce post-tax income differentials compared with pre-tax differentials. Progressive, regressive and proportionate taxes can also be defined in terms of the marginal and average tax rates. The marginal tax rate measures the proportion of the last pound paid in tax as income rises, whereas the average tax rate at any level of income is simply the total tax paid as a proportion of total income. In the case of a progressive income tax, the marginal rate of tax is higher than the average rate, except when no tax at all is paid on the first band of a person's income. If income tax is regressive, the marginal rate of tax is less than the average rate, while the two are equal in the case of a proportionate tax.

TYPES OF PUBLIC SPENDING

We have already noted why we are excluding the direct spending by nationalised industries from our definition of public spending. Amongst the various divisions that can usefully be made between types of public spending are those between **central** and **local government spending**, and between **capital** and **current spending**. Capital spending involves public or social investment in a project (or public work) such as a new hospital, school or motorway. Current spending includes items such as the wage costs of staffing and the maintenance costs of running existing capital assets.

Perhaps the most important distinction to be made between types of public spending is between **real** and **transfer expenditure**:

❶ **Real expenditure** Real expenditure occurs when the government directly provides goods and services which add to national output. All capital spending is real expenditure, as is the current expenditure on the wages and salaries of civil servants, local government officers, teachers, police, the armed forces and workers in the National Health Service. In contributing directly to output, real expenditure uses up scarce resources; indeed it is sometimes known as the 'direct command of resources' by the government.

❷ **Transfer expenditure** Conversely, transfer expenditure merely redistributes income between different members of the community. Tax revenues are used to provide income via pensions, welfare benefits, grants and subsidies both to households in the personal sector and to firms within the corporate sector. The various forms of regional and industrial aid and assistance, including the transfers to nationalised industries, are an important part of total transfers. Transfers do not contribute directly to production although their administration uses up scarce resources, and indeed transfers to low-income groups usually encourage consumption since poorer people have high marginal propensities to consume. Massive transfers from central to local government also take place within the public sector. A large part of the spending of local authorities is financed in this way. Interest payments on past government borrowing (which we cover in more detail in the context of the PSBR and the National Debt in Chapter 16) are a form of transfer from taxpayers to those people who have lent to the government. Strictly, however, the term 'transfer payment' (which must not be confused with the transfer earnings of Chapter 13) is restricted to payments which are not made in return for some productive service.

Statistics which show public spending as a percentage of either GDP or GNP are sometimes used to indicate the relative importance of real expenditure by the government. However, great care must be taken in using such statistics; the figures can be very misleading unless both transfers and the spending by nationalised industries have first been excluded.

15.2 ESSENTIAL INFORMATION

THE PRINCIPLES OF TAXATION

Adam Smith's **four principles or canons of taxation** are commonly used as the starting-point for analysing and evaluating the operation of a tax system. Adam Smith suggested that taxation should be **equitable, economical, convenient** and **certain**, and to these we may also add the canons of efficiency and flexibility:

❶ **Equity** A tax should be based on the taxpayer's ability to pay. This principle is sometimes used to justify progressive taxation, since the rich have a greater ability to pay than the poor. A tax system should be fair, but there are likely to be different and possibly conflicting interpretations of what is fair or equitable.

❷ **Economy** Collection of a tax should be easily and cheaply administered so that the yield is maximised relative to the cost of collection.

❸ **Convenience** The method of payment should be convenient to the taxpayer.

❹ **Certainty** The taxpayer should know what, when, where and how to pay, in such a manner that tax evasion is difficult. (Tax evasion is the illegal failure to pay a lawful tax, whereas tax avoidance involves the arrangement of personal or business affairs within the law to minimise tax liability.)

❺ **Efficiency** A tax should achieve its intended aim without side-effects. If, for example, the raising of the top rate of income tax in order to raise revenue results in increased disincentives to work, then the tax is inefficient. Since it is usually impossible to avoid all the undesirable side-effects of a tax, the tax system should attempt to minimise them.

❻ **Flexibility** If the tax system is used as a means of economic management then, in order to meet new circumstances, certain taxes may need to be easily altered.

THE AIMS OF TAXATION

The **aims of taxation** should not be confused with the principles or canons of taxation, although an aim may well be to arrange the tax system as much as possible in accordance with the principles of taxation. It is useful to distinguish between a number of aims or objectives of taxation and to note how the importance attached to some of the objectives has varied according to the changing fashions in economic thought:

❶ **Revenue raising** One of the oldest and most obvious aims of taxation is to raise revenue so as to pay for government expenditure. Before the Keynesian 'revolution' of the 1930s most economists believed that revenue-raising was by far the most important objective of taxation. Indeed, many went further and argued that the levels of both public spending and taxation should be as low as possible, with the government restricting its activities to the provision of goods and services that could not be provided adequately and privately through the market. According to this pre-Keynesian or neoclassical view, recently revived in modern monetarism, a government should engage in the financial orthodoxy or 'sound finance' of balancing its budget.

❷ **The correction of market 'failures'** In the traditional view we have just described, the primary purpose of government intervention in the economy is to correct or to reduce the various market failures which we first introduced in Chapter 8. A government may be justified in using taxation to:

(a) **Tax monopoly profits**, both to deter monopoly and to remove the 'windfall gain' accruing to a monopolist as a result of barriers to entry and inelastic supply.

(b) **Finance the collective provision of public goods and merit goods**. The market might fail to provide public goods such as roads and defence, while education, health care and other merit goods might be underconsumed at market prices.

(c) **Discourage the consumption of demerit goods**. Demerit goods such as tobacco might be overconsumed at market prices. Note that a conflict may arise between the revenue-raising aim of taxation and this aim of reducing the consumption of demerit goods.

(d) **Alter the distribution of income**. The government may decide that the distribution of income resulting from unregulated market forces is undesirable. Taxation and transfers can be used to modify the distribution of income resulting from market forces.

❸ **Keynesian economic management** While Keynesians certainly accept that taxation should be used to achieve such objectives as the provision of public goods, and the switching of expenditure away from demerit goods, they go much further by arguing that taxation should also be used to correct what they regard as arguably the greatest market failure of all: the tendency for unregulated market forces to produce unemployment and unacceptable fluctuations in economic activity. In subsequent chapters we shall explain how Keynesians have advocated the use of taxation, public spending and the budget deficit as policy instruments in a **discretionary fiscal policy** aimed at controlling the level of effective aggregate demand in the economy to achieve the objectives of full employment and stable economic growth, without an excessive inflationary cost. We shall also show how monetarists reject the use of the demand management techniques involved in a discretionary fiscal policy, supporting instead the older view that the government should balance its budget and restrict the role of public finance to the correction of more conventional market failures at the microeconomic level.

THE MEANING OF FISCAL POLICY

Fiscal policy has various meanings. It is sometimes used as a rather general term referring to any aspect of a government's policy towards the level and structure of taxation and public spending. During the Keynesian era, fiscal policy took on the narrower and more specific meaning we introduced in the previous paragraph involving the use of taxation and public expenditure in the macroeconomic management of demand. Such a discretionary fiscal policy can be contrasted with the fiscal stance currently advocated by monetarists based on an **automatic fiscal rule** to balance the budget or to reduce public spending as a percentage of gross domestic product (GDP). Increasingly, attention is also devoted by both Keynesians and monetarists to the microeconomic objectives and effects of fiscal policy on the supply-side of the economy, examining such areas as the role and effectiveness of government grants, subsidies and tax allowances in regional and industrial policy, and the general question whether public spending financed by taxation or borrowing displaces or 'crowds out' private spending.

TAXATION AND THE LEVEL AND PATTERN OF EXPENDITURE

Indirect taxes such as VAT will affect consumer preferences and spending patterns by causing relative price changes. The total level of expenditure can be reduced by levying higher taxes, assuming there is no dis-saving and that the tax revenue is not spent by the government. Some taxes are also considered as **automatic stabilisers** which reduce the amplitude of fluctuations in the business cycle. For instance, when there is full employment, inflationary pressures may be caused by money incomes rising faster than production. A progressive income tax can then drain off some potential consumption into taxation. Conversely, in a recession, transfers such as unemployment pay will tend to boost consumption while the government's tax revenue will fall at a faster rate than national income.

THE INCIDENCE OF TAXATION

The **formal incidence** of a tax refers to which particular taxpayer is directly liable to pay the tax to the government. In the case of indirect taxes upon expenditure such as VAT, the question arises whether the seller of the good who bears the formal incidence can **shift the incidence** or burden of the tax onto the purchaser by raising the price by the full amount of the tax. A firm's ability to shift the incidence of a tax depends upon price elasticity of demand. Fig. 40 illustrates the situation where demand is relatively elastic and only a small proportion of the tax can be successfully shifted.

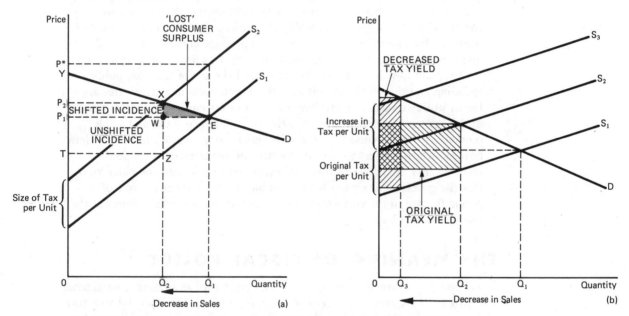

Fig. 40 Elasticity and taxation (a) the ability of a supplier to shift the incidence of an expenditure tax depends upon elasticity of demand (b) an example of a tax increase producing a fall in the government's tax revenue when demand and supply are both relatively elastic

The imposition of a tax raises a supplier's costs; thus at each price the firm is prepared to supply less. If the tax is a specific or unit tax charged at the same rate irrespective of the good's price, the supply curve will shift upwards, from S_1 to S_2, the vertical distance between the two curves showing the tax per unit. If all the tax is to be successfully shifted, the price must rise to P*. This will only happen if demand is completely inelastic. In any other circumstance, some consumers will reduce their purchases as the price rises. However, many consumers will still want the good and so the price is bid up from P_1 to P_2. The size of the government's tax revenue is determined by the amount bought and sold at the new equilibrium (Q_2) multiplied by the tax per unit. This is shown by the rectangle TZXP$_2$. You should now note that the part of the tax rectangle above the initial equilibrium price, P_1, represents the successfully shifted incidence of the tax, whereas the part of the tax rectangle below P_1 cannot be shifted and must be borne by the supplier. When demand is relatively elastic, only the smaller proportion of the tax can successfully be shifted.

We leave as an exercise for the reader the tasks of drawing appropriate diagrams to show what happens when demand is inelastic and to show the converse effects resulting from the imposition of a unit subsidy paid to the supplier.

THE TAX YIELD

If the principal aim of a tax is to raise revenue, the government will wish to maximise the tax's yield. In the case of taxes upon expenditure the government needs to consider the price elasticities of both demand and supply of the goods upon which taxes are levied. When a tax is first introduced, it will produce a positive yield provided that at least some of the good is bought and sold after the imposition of the tax. However, the quantity bought and sold will usually fall after the imposition of a tax, so the government may not receive the revenue it was expecting. If the size of the tax is increased, the absolute size of the government's revenue may rise, fall, or indeed stay the same, depending on the elasticities of supply and demand. Fig. 40b illustrates the effects of an increase in taxation when demand and supply are both relatively elastic. In this case the tax yield falls. Although the government receives a larger tax revenue from each unit bought and sold at the new equilibrium, the loss in revenue resulting from the fall in sales more than offsets the revenue gain. When demand and supply are relatively inelastic, however, government revenue will increase.

Some important public policy implications result from this analysis. If the government wishes to maximise revenue it should tax as many goods and services as possible. Not only will this **widen the tax base**, but it will also reduce the elasticity of demand for the bundle of goods and services being taxed, taken as a whole. If only one good is taxed, demand is likely to be relatively elastic since untaxed goods are likely to contain some fairly close substitutes! Conversely, if the government aims to use taxation to switch expenditure, for example away from a demerit good such as tobacco, it should tax specific types of goods rather than wide categories. On this basis it could introduce different rates of taxation, for example taxing high tar and low tar cigarettes at different rates in order to switch expenditure away from the more harmful good. In a similar way, it can use tariffs or import duties to switch expenditure towards home-produced goods. In this way there may be a significant 'trade-off' between the revenue-raising and the expenditure-switching aims of taxation.

TAXATION AND CONSUMER SURPLUS

In Chapter 2 we introduced the concept of consumer surplus as the utility obtained by consumers from the goods and services they purchase, which is valued over and above the price paid. Essentially, consumer surplus is a **measure of welfare**: the more consumer surplus a person obtains, the greater his personal welfare. At the initial price of P_1 in Fig. 40a, consumer surplus is shown by the triangle P_1EY. The imposition of a tax reduces consumer surplus to the smaller triangle P_2XY. The question now arises as to what happens to the consumer surplus no longer received by the purchasers of the good or service. The answer is that the part shown by the rectangle P_1WXP_2 has been transferred to the government in the form of tax revenue, but the part represented by the small triangle WEX is completely 'lost'. On the basis of this analysis, economists have argued in favour of reducing taxes to as low a level as possible; the lower the rate of taxation, the smaller the loss of consumer surplus.

However, the conclusion is not as clear-cut as is suggested by this analysis. Low-income groups are likely to obtain a greater utility from an extra pound of income (or from the goods and services an extra pound can purchase) than high-income groups. Correspondingly, the welfare loss experienced by a rich person who loses a pound in taxation is likely to be smaller than the welfare gain accruing to a poor person receiving the same pound in the form of a transfer payment. This argument can justify progressive taxation and the redistribution of income through transfer payments. (The effect of taxation upon consumer surplus is very similar to what happens when the formation of a monopoly raises the price of a good. Part of the consumer surplus is transferred to the monopolist as a monopoly profit, but part is 'lost' to everyone.)

OTHER ASPECTS OF TAXES ON INCOME AND EXPENDITURE

❶ **Taxation and incentives** It is often argued that a progressive income tax damages the economy through its effects on personal incentives. After all, the most obvious way legally to avoid an income tax is to work fewer hours, or even to stop working altogether. It is argued that expenditure taxes are preferable to income tax because they have no effect on the choice between work and leisure. Instead, expenditure taxes affect the choice between saving and spending, and they also switch expenditure into the consumption of untaxed goods and services.

Nevertheless, economic theory does not prove that an increase in income tax inevitably must have a disincentive effect upon personal effort. If the **supply curve of labour is upward-sloping**, a disincentive effect will result, since a tax increase is equivalent to a wage cut and less labour is supplied as wages fall. But in circumstances where workers aspire to a 'target' disposable income, when the **supply curve of labour is perverse** or **backward-bending**, a tax rise will mean that people have to work longer to achieve their desired target income. The tax is an incentive to effort!

❷ **Fiscal drag and fiscal boost** Fiscal drag occurs in a progressive income tax structure when the government fails to raise tax thresholds or personal tax allowances at the same rate as inflation. Suppose that prices and all money incomes double. In the absence of taxation real incomes will remain the same. However, real disposable incomes will fall if inflation drags low-paid workers, who previously paid no tax, across the tax threshold to pay tax for the first time. In a similar way, higher-paid workers may be dragged deeper into the tax net, possibly into higher tax bands where they will pay tax at steeper marginal rates. In these circumstances the government's total revenue from income tax will rise faster than the rate of inflation, even though the tax structure has not been changed.

Conversely, in times of inflation fiscal boost is likely to reduce the real value of specific expenditure taxes (but not of *ad valorem* taxes such as VAT). Unless the government adjusts the rate of specific taxes to keep pace with inflation, their nominal value will stay more or less the same, but their real value will decline.

The simultaneous occurrence of fiscal drag and fiscal boost (such as occurred in the period of rapid inflation in the UK in the 1970s) shifts the structure of taxation away from taxes on expenditure and towards taxes on income. This can be avoided either by replacing progressive income tax with a proportionate tax, and specific expenditure duties with ad valorem taxation, or by indexing personal tax allowances, income tax bands, and the rates at which specific duties are levied.

❸ **The poverty trap and the unemployment trap** The vulnerability of the tax structure in the UK to the process of fiscal drag is closely related to the emergence of a phenomenon known as the poverty trap. The poverty trap occurs because the tax threshold at which income tax is paid overlaps with the ceiling at which means-tested welfare benefits cease to be paid. If a low-paid worker is caught within this zone of overlap, he not only pays tax and National Insurance contributions on an extra pound earned, but he also loses part or all of his right to claim benefits. The resulting 'marginal tax rate' may be very high indeed, sometimes over 100 per cent.

The existence of the poverty trap supports the argument that the major disincentives to personal effort resulting from the structure of taxation and welfare benefits in the UK are experienced by low-paid rather than by highly paid workers. Not only is the 'effective marginal tax rate' paid by the lower income groups frequently higher than the top rate of 40 per cent paid by the well-off; poorly paid workers are likely to experience less job satisfaction and to have less scope for perks and fringe benefits. Indeed the low-paid may be tempted to escape from the poverty trap either by avoiding tax through not working at all and living off benefits, thus becoming trapped in unemployment, or by evading tax through working in the untaxed 'hidden economy' or black economy.

The poverty trap is undoubtedly made worse when fiscal drag draws low-paid workers into the tax next. Amongst the policies which could eliminate or reduce the effects of the poverty trap are the raising of tax thresholds and the replacement of **means-tested benefits** either by untaxed or universal benefits granted as of right (such as child benefit) or by benefits subject to tax 'clawback'. In the latter case, the government grants a benefit as of right and without a means test, but 'claws back' a fraction of the benefits through the income tax system from recipients who are above the tax threshold. Alternatively, the introduction of a **negative income tax (NIT)** has been suggested to merge the existing income tax and benefits structures. In a NIT scheme there would be a single tax threshold, above which people would pay (positive) income tax, and below which they would receive payments from the Inland Revenue (negative income tax) in lieu of welfare benefits. Amongst possible disadvantages of a NIT scheme are its tendency to reinforce the means-testing principle (though some may consider this an advantage), and the argument that civil servants in the Inland Revenue Department are not the most appropriate 'experts' to assess welfare needs. Avoid confusing the poverty trap with the **unemployment trap**. Low-waged people in work are caught in the poverty trap whereas the unemployment trap affects some of the unwaged or unemployed people. As we have noted, the low-waged may escape the poverty trap by choosing voluntary unemployment instead, thus entering the unemployment trap. Also avoid confusing the poverty trap with real poverty. Low-income families in the poverty trap are relatively poor but the real poor are not in work.

HOW PROGRESSIVE IS THE BRITISH TAX SYSTEM?

Over the years, the poverty trap and occasional fiscal drag have tended to reduce the advantages to the low-paid accruing from the progressive structure of British taxation. In any case the British income tax structure is probably much less progressive than is commonly supposed. Employees' National Insurance contributions are generally a regressive tax falling most heavily as a proportion of income on low-paid and middle-income groups, while the degree of progression in the upper reaches of the income tax structure is greatly reduced by the possibilities of legal tax avoidance open to the better-off. On the expenditure side, some excise duties such as tobacco duty are probably regressive whereas others, including petrol duty, are progressive. Value-added tax is probably slightly progressive since some necessities are currently excluded from the tax, but this may be countered by the fact that the low-paid spend a larger fraction of their income than the well-off, their savings being correspondingly lower. Moreover, the introduction of VAT in 1972 was a regressive change to the tax structure since VAT replaced purchase tax, which had been a distinctly progressive tax levied on a narrower base composed largely of luxuries. Finally, the poll tax, which existed from 1989/90 to 1993 was an extremely regressive tax; a duke paying the same as a dustman.

THE CONTROL OF PUBLIC EXPENDITURE

Textbooks sometimes portray the level and pattern of public spending as a tractable policy instrument capable of being 'fine-tuned' or easily adjusted in the macroeconomic implementation of fiscal policy and the management of the economy. In practice, however, the control of public expenditure presents a number of formidable difficulties:

❶ Much expenditure is on necessary services such as education, the police and health care which are difficult to cut.

❷ Control of public expenditure is made more difficult in a democracy by the popularity of state spending and the unpopularity of cuts.

❸ As we have already explained, many types of expenditure change autonomously for reasons outside the government's direct control, and sometimes these changes occur automatically in the upswings and downswings of the business cycle.

❹ Central government may have little direct control over local government. To gain greater control, it can attempt to impose limits (and to place external financing limits upon nationalised industries).

THE RELATIVE IMPORTANCE OF THE DIFFERENT TYPES OF TAXATION IN THE UK

The table which follows shows the approximate importance of the major categories of taxation in total tax revenue, including National Insurance contributions which were forecast for 1992/3 in the 1992 Budget.

Table 15.1

Income	%	Capital	%	Expenditure	%	Miscellaneous	%
Income Tax	25.9	Capital Gains Tax	0.5	Value Added Tax	17.4	Rates/Poll Tax	9.6
			0.6	Excise and			
Corporation Tax	7.3	Inheritance Tax		Customs Duties	11.9	Others	8.6
National Insurance Contributions	16.8			Vehicle Excise	1.4		
Total	50.0		1.1		30.7		18.2

Less than 20% of local authority expenditure was financed by the domestic rate and poll tax. Central government transfers accounted for nearly 50% of local government revenue, with the remainder divided between the business rate and income from other sources, such as the sale of assets and services.

CASH LIMITS

Each year before the beginning of the next financial year on April 5th, the government announces its Budget. Traditionally, the Chancellor of the Exchequer has undertaken two main tasks on Budget Day, which before 1994 was usually in March. He prepares the way for the introduction of the government's Finance Bill (later to become the Finance Act which authorises the collection of taxes in the next financial year) and secondly he publishes a Financial Statement or 'Red Book' containing the Treasury's review of the economy. But until recently, the government only announced its tax plans on Budget Day, and not the changes it intended to make in the level or structure of public spending. Instead, public expenditure plans were published nearly six months earlier in the Chancellor's Autumn Financial Statement, which sometimes functioned also as a supplementary 'mini-budget'. However, in 1993 the government brought the public spending and revenue sides of its budget together by abolishing the Autumn Financial Statement, and bringing the date of the Budget forward to November.

Before 1976 the annual survey on public spending contained in the White Paper was conducted in **constant prices**, or in '**volume' terms**. This approach meant that expenditure estimates were based on physical inputs such as people, buildings and equipment needed. This emphasis on the use of real resources reflected the

Keynesian approach to demand management in the economy. However, the pricing of the inputs included in the White Paper was based on out-of-date figures, causing a serious problem in the 1970s when in a period of increasing inflation government expenditure rose rapidly and actual spending exceeded the budgetary projection. If the prices paid by a department rose, more cash was made available to enable the volume of the programme to be maintained. This caused budget deficits and increased the PSBR, as explained in Chapter 16. To prevent this happening, the government introduced cash limits for the first time in 1976. These were grafted onto the volume system of planning, requiring volume plans to be revised each year at the expected prices of the year subject to the cash limit. In 1981 the Government decided to plan all public expenditure from the outset in cash rather than volume terms. By 1981 cash limits were covering about 60% of total public expenditure. If inflation is faster than the government anticipates or allows for, and the volume of spending cannot be maintained within the cash limit, then the volume must now be reduced and factor inputs dispensed with. As a result 'finance now determines spending' rather than spending determining finance.

Until recently, government expenditure (on transfers such as pensions, unemployment pay and welfare benefits) lay outside the system of cash limits. This part of public expenditure is largely 'demand-led'. Thus, an ageing population tends to increase expenditure on pensions whilst spending on unemployment pay and welfare benefits fluctuate with the business cycle, providing further examples of automatic stabilisers. Demand-led growth of expenditure on welfare budgets reduces the ability of the government to control public spending. In an attempt to improve its overall control of welfare expenditure, the Conservative Government extended cash limits by establishing a 'capped' Social Fund in 1988.

Chapter roundup

This chapter is closely linked with Chapter 16 because the levels of taxation and public spending largely determine government's budgeting position and the PSBR. This in turn influences the money supply and monetary policy as explained in Chapter 17. We then go on in Chapters 19, 20, 22, 23 and 24 to develop the roles of taxation and public spending as fiscal policy instruments in the Keynesian theory of aggregate demand management, comparing the discretionary fiscal policy of the Keynesians with the older balanced budget tradition revived by the monetarists.

Illustrative questions and answers

1   Essay Question
    How should the services currently provided by local authorities be financed?
    (AEB, June 1992)

Tutorial note

The reform of local government finance has been extremely topical in recent years and looks likely to remain so through the rest of the 1990s. In 1992 when this question was set, the poll tax or 'community charge' had replaced property 'rating' as the tax levied by local authorities to pay for their spending (though under both systems transfers or grants from central government had grown to be by far the main source of finance for local authority spending). During its short life, the poll tax was unpopular and it became increasingly unworkable. Therefore the poll tax was replaced in 1993 by a 'council tax', which like the old system of local authority rates is based on property values. Houses have been divided into groups according to their estimated market values; local authorities now levy the 'council tax' according to the 'property band' that a household occupies. Because property values were estimated before the worst of the slump in house prices that took place in the early 1990s, the new tax has been criticised for treating the South East of England unfairly. Property values fell by more than a third in the South East in the early 1990s, while holding up much better in the northern parts of Britain. However it must be remembered that house buyers in the South East had fared much better than their northern counterparts during the 1980s boom in house prices, benefiting to a greater extent from untaxed capital gains (because house prices increased most in the South East) and from income tax relief on their mortgages (because their mortgages were larger).

Back in 1981, The Conservative government published a Green Paper inviting discussion on various options for financing local government: a poll tax; a local sales tax; a local income tax, and a property tax in the guise of reformed domestic rates. The Green Paper also briefly considered but rejected other possibilities such as: local duties on petrol, alcohol and tobacco; a local vehicle excise tax; and a local payroll tax. Very much in line with such *canons of taxation* as *economy, efficiency* and *equity*, the Green Paper assessed each potential tax against seven criteria:

(i) Is it practical?

(ii) Is it fair?

(iii) Does it make councillors, who take decisions on local expenditure, accountable to the local tax payers?

(iv) Are the administrative costs acceptable?

(v) Are the implications for the rest of the tax system acceptable?

(vi) Does it encourage proper financial control? and

(vii) Is it suitable for all tiers of local government?

This particular question has been worded so as to allow a variety of possible responses. You could adopt a 'service by service' approach, perhaps arguing that services such as parks and libraries should be financed in a different way from the police. (The distinction between services provided as *public goods* and *merit goods* could be relevant here.) Or you could introduce a long list of possible sources of finance, including some that we have not previously mentioned, for example the sale or 'commercialisation' of local authority services such as admission to leisure centres, with or without the privatisation of the actual provision of the services. At the other extreme you might compare just two sources of finance, say a poll tax and a property tax. We suggest that you select say three or four alternative sources of finance, and then base your assessment against the type of criteria we listed in the previous paragraph. When we compare a poll tax and a property tax for example, a poll tax, (at least in an 'uncapped version') scores quite well in terms of accountability but much less well when measured against the criteria of economy and equity. In the early 1990s, the poll tax proved to be about three times more expensive to collect than the property tax (the local rate) which it had replaced. And although property taxation can be regressive in particular instances (e.g. when a single person and several income earners live next door to each other in identical accommodation), on average the poll tax was much more regressive. The old local rating system promoted various inefficiencies (for example, deterring home improvement), but so has the poll tax. The poll tax has encouraged the inefficient use of housing; retired people continuing to live in large houses after their families have grown up and moved away. It also has promoted widespread evasion and deregistration from electoral roles. For these and other reasons , the 1981 Green Paper came out strongly against a poll tax, but this did not stop the government which commissioned it from introducing such a tax!

Suggested answer

- Briefly set out the historical background to the question.
- Specify a number of alternative methods of finance such as: a revival of the poll tax; a return to the rating system (note: part of the rating system remains, i.e. the business rate levied on commercial property); the 'council tax'; local income and sales taxes. Mention also, that other alternatives might include: an extension of central government funding of local authorities; or an abolition of local government with its activities being taken by central government or non-governmental bodies such as Urban Development Corporations; or 'commercialisation' and possibly also privatisation of local authority services.
- Select, say, three of the alternative sources you have listed.
- State the criteria against which you are going to assess the alternatives: e.g. efficiency; economy; equity; accountability, etc.
- Carefully assess each alternative against these criteria, perhaps making the point that different forms of finance may suit different services. By all means mention the political context, but don't drift into political abuse.
- Reach an argued conclusion.

2   Data Question

LAWSON'S TAX MIRAGE

Nigel Lawson's claims to be a tax-cutting Chancellor seem impressive. The 30 per cent basic rate of income tax he inherited in 1983 was cut to 25 per cent: the top rate chopped down from 60 per cent to 40 per cent.

The image of Lawson as a generous, tax-cutting Chancellor was due to the falling marginal rates of personal income tax. But these play only a minor role in determining the nation's tax liability. The combined changes in tax-free allowances and in taxes such as national insurance contributions, VAT and excise duty, far outweigh any tinkering with marginal tax rates.

The 'reforms' of corporation tax are a case in point. The rate of tax was reduced gradually from 53 to 35 per cent. But at the same time tax-free allowances for investment and inflationary increases in the value of stocks were withdrawn. Between 1978–79 and 1988–89 taxes as a proportion of company income actually rose from 13 per cent to 18 per cent.

Taxes have been reshuffled rather than reduced over the past decade. Offsetting the modest fall in income taxes have been much larger increases in taxes on companies and consumer spending, notably the doubling of VAT in the 1979 Budget. In practical terms, fiscal drag means that when spending and inflation accelerate, tax revenues grow even more rapidly. As a result the consumer boom of the late 1980s increased the Government's tax receipts. Company profits swelled and consumers spent more on VAT-carrying goods and services.

(Source: *Business,* February 1990 (adapted))

Selected taxes as % of Gross Domestic Product (GDP)

	1978–9	1988–89
Income tax	10.8	9.3
National Insurance	7.0	6.9
Corporation taxes	2.3	3.9
VAT	2.2	5.8
Excise duties	3.3	4.0
Other	6.9	7.7
Total taxation	33.1	37.6

(Source: *Lloyds Bank Economic Bulletin,* April 1989)

189

Answer each of the following questions, explaining your reasoning in each case.

(a) What does the data show about the change in the tax burden between 1978–79 and 1988–89?   (4)

(b) Explain how the Government's tax revenue can be affected by changes in
  (i) tax-free allowances   (4)
  (ii) prices   (4)
  (iii) personal incomes   (4)

(c) Between 1978–79 and 1988–89 real GDP rose by 25% and real personal incomes rose by 22%. Discuss the case for and against an increase in tax revenue as a percentage of GDP. (9)

(WJEC, June 1992)

Tutorial note

(a) With a question like this it is important to 'group' the data and to obtain an 'overview', rather than to describe each row of the data in detail, in effect doing nothing more than converting numerical data into sentences. Thus the data shows the overall tax burden growing as a proportion of GDP, and shifting away from the taxation of income (corporation tax is an exception, presumably become company profits were buoyant in 1988) and towards the taxation of expenditure.

(b) (i)   You must describe how the process of 'fiscal drag', explained in the chapter, and the raising of tax allowances affect tax revenue.
   (ii) Illustrate how 'fiscal boost' (also explained in the chapter) erodes the real value of specific excise duties unless they are raised in line with inflation, However, VAT revenues are generally 'inflation proof'.
   (iii) Fiscal drag is also relevant here; relate your answer to the 'progressivity' of income tax. Also discuss the effects upon tax revenue of people's decisions to save rather than spend as income increases.

(c) You could approach this question in a number of ways, but remember to obey the instruction to consider arguments *for* and *against*. The 'case for' could include the 'automatic stabiliser' effects of an increase in taxation to stabilise the business cycle, and the argument that the 'welfare gain' resulting from how the tax revenues are spent can exceed the 'welfare loss' directly suffered by the tax payers. Elaborate with examples of 'justifiable' forms of public spending, such as the relief of poverty and the provision of public goods and merit goods. The 'case against' is usually made most forcibly by supply-side economists and other free-market orientated economists who distrust the role of 'big government'. They argue that even when public spending is well-intended, its favourable effects upon the economy are all too often more than offset by the damaging effect upon incentives and economic growth resulting from the increased burden of taxation needed to finance the expenditure.

Question bank

1 In 1978 the standard rate of income tax in the UK was 33% and the top rate was 83%; in 1990 the standard rate was 25% and the top rate was 40%. Examine the likely economic consequences of these changes.

(ULEAC, June 1992)

2

(a) Explain how the imposition of a selective excise tax on the production of a particular commodity can affect the long run equilibrium price and output of this commodity. (15)

(b) Under what circumstances will the burden of the tax rest entirely on the consumers of the commodity? (5)

(c) Why is it argued that the imposition of such a tax results in a net social loss? (5)   (WJEC, June 1990)

3

(a) Under what circumstances might a government decide to increase taxes? (30)

(b) What criteria are relevant when considering the relative merits of direct and indirect taxes?   (ULEAC, June 1991)

4 'There are two microeconomic criteria by which to assess a tax: efficiency and equity'. With reference to these criteria, examine the effects of

(a) a reduction of the higher income tax rate;

(b) an increase in the duty payable on cigarettes. (NEAB, AS-Level, June 1990)

5 Explain why taxes are necessary and outline the desirable properties of a good tax. Compare the Community Charge with alternative ways of raising revenue to finance local government.   (NEAB, June 1991)

BUDGET DEFICITS AND SURPLUSES

Units in this chapter

16.1 *Underlying concepts*
16.2 *Essential information*

Chapter objectives

In this chapter, we examine the overall financial position both of central government and of the wider public sector. We also consider the implications of the **borrowing requirement**, that results when the government runs a **budget deficit**, and of the **debt repayment** that becomes possible in the event of a **budget surplus**.

KEYNESIAN DEFICIT FINANCING

Until quite recently (1987/88), UK governments almost always ran budget deficits. Budget deficits were largely the result of the dominance of Keynesian views on the role of economic management and fiscal policy. Broadly speaking, the Keynesian view has been that when households save too much and firms invest too little, unemployment will be caused by a lack of effective **aggregate money demand (AMD)** in the economy. In these circumstances, the government should borrow the excess savings of households in order to inject demand back into the economy through public spending. For much of the postwar era, until the late 1970s, such deliberate deficit financing occupied a central place in the **discretionary fiscal policy** used by Keynesians to fine-tune the level of aggregate expenditure in the economy.

MONETARISTS AND THE GOVERNMENT'S BUDGETARY POSITION

Since the 1970s, the use of discretionary fiscal policy and the budget deficit as a policy instrument to manage demand, has been attacked by the monetarists. We shall explain, later in this Chapter (and in Chapters 17 and 22) how monetarists regard the level of public spending, and its method of finance through the **public sector borrowing requirement (PSBR)**, as an underlying cause of inflation (via an excessive rate of growth of the money supply). To finance the budget deficit and PSBR, the authorities borrow from: private individuals, (i.e. the general public); from overseas; or from the banking system. If the funds are borrowed from the general public, monetarists argue that competition for funds takes place which raises interest rates and crowds out private sector consumption and investment. Overseas borrowing eventually leads to a drain of national resources in interest payments while borrowing from the banking system expands the money supply. It is therefore not surprising that, since monetarists believe that each method of financing a budget deficit and PSBR gives rise to undesirable consequences, they argue against the principle of deficit financing and large-scale public sector borrowing.

Monetarist theory first began to influence UK governments in the mid-1970s, becoming a dominant influence upon the Conservative administrations of Mrs Margaret Thatcher, (especially in the early 1980s). In the late 1980s and early 1990s, 'pure' monetarism has arguably been of less significance, certainly as an influence upon practical policy, than other aspects of the 'neoclassical revival', such as 'supply-side' theory. Nevertheless, although Mrs Thatcher's first administration (elected in 1979) was firmly committed to monetarism, the government's aim was to reduce rather than to eliminate the budget deficit and the PSBR. The government was not committed to balancing the budget, let alone to securing a large budget surplus and negative PSBR or **public sector debt repayment (PSDR)**.

In the outcome, Mrs Thatcher's administrations were much more successful than they dared hope (until 1991 at least) with respect to the fiscal policy elements of their central macroeconomic strategy: the MTFS. (This contrasts with the monetary policy elements of the MTFS, which have seldom been 'on target'!) The budget deficit and the PSBR fell rapidly from the early 1980s onwards (both in absolute terms and as proportions of GDP) until, in 1987/8, the budget moved into a significant surplus and the positive PSBR gave way to a PSDR. This gave the government the opportunity to reduce the National Debt by 'retiring' (or redeeming) existing debt without needing to undertake any net new borrowing which, in the era of budget deficits, would have expanded the National Debt.

However, the Conservative government's 'success' in achieving a large budget surplus and PSDR was more the result of autonomous changes taking place 'naturally' in the economy than of deliberate government planning. After the deep recession of 1979/81, the economy entered a period of continuous growth for the rest of the 1980s. During a period of rising incomes (and falling unemployment after 1986), government revenues from progressive taxation rise faster than income, while demand-led public spending on unemployment pay and welfare benefits fall. Thus, the budget deficit tends automatically to fall in the upswing and boom of a business cycle, and to rise when the economy enters a recession. This is the **'automatic stabiliser'** or **'built-in stabiliser'** effect of progressive taxation and government expenditure that we mentioned in Chapter 15. In the years of continuous growth in the late 1980s, the stabilising effect was sufficiently powerful to move the budget into surplus. But the Government has not been able to sustain a continuing surplus and PSDR. With the economy entering recession in 1990, the budget moved into deficit in 1991. The Government now recognises the 'counter-cyclical' nature of the budgeting position and aims for a balanced budget 'over the course of the business cycle' rather than in any particular year, thereby accepting the effect of automatic stabilisers on its finances.

At the time of the Budget in March 1993, the government expected the deficit to be around £35 billion, rising to £50 billion in 1993/4. Most of this rise is due to the recession but the government hopes that economic recovery will reduce the 'cyclical' element of the deficit and PSBR after 1994.

16.1 UNDERLYING CONCEPTS

COMPONENTS OF THE PUBLIC SECTOR

The United Kingdom public sector is made up of three parts: central government;

local government; and public corporations or nationalised industries. Central and local government, considered together, are known as 'general government'. When defining and measuring the budget deficit or surplus, and its related borrowing requirement (or debt repayment position), it is important to make clear whether the whole of the public sector is being discussed or just central government alone. The PSBR is the difference each year between the income and expenditure of the whole of the public sector; a difference which (when expenditure exceeds income) has to be met from borrowing. In the case of a public sector surplus, income exceeds expenditure and the PSBR is negative. As we have already mentioned, a negative PSBR is also known as a PSDR; though this implies that the public sector surplus is actually used for the early 'retirement' (or redemption) of debt or past public sector borrowing. (This need not be the case because, as a part of monetary policy, the government could use its excess revenues to purchase private sector financial assets (such as commercial bills) rather than to redeem its own debt. But, since the public sector budget surplus that emerged in 1987 was used by the government for debt repayment rather than for other purposes, we shall continue to describe a negative PSBR as a PSDR.) In the event of a public sector deficit, the PSBR is made up of the CGBR, the LABR and the PCBR, which are respectively the borrowing requirements of central government, local government, and public corporations. The CGBR and LABR taken together are known as the GGBR (general government borrowing requirement). Expressed as identities, the relationship is:

PSBR $\equiv$ CGBR + LABR + PCBR

and GGBR $\equiv$ CGBR + LABR

Likewise, in the event of a public sector surplus:

PSDR $\equiv$ CGDR + LADR + PCDR

and GGDR $\equiv$ CGDR + LADR

As already indicated, the public sector finances were in deficit for most of the period from 1945 until 1987 (with the PSBR averaging over £10bn, during the earlier years of Mrs Thatcher's administration, from 1979 to 1984). The PSBR was greatly reduced in 1985 and 1986, falling to £2.25bn in 1986, before the budget moved into surplus in 1987, creating a PSDR. The surplus rose to £14.5bn in 1988, or 3% of GDP, but fell to £7bn in 1989/90. In its 1990 budget, the government predicted a further fall in the surplus/PSDR to £3bn in 1991/2, with a balanced budget returning in later years. However, for the 'counter-cyclical' reasons already explained, the public sector's budgetary position deteriorated at a much faster rate than the government predicted, leading to a quite rapid return to budget deficits and a positive PSBR.

THE BUDGETARY POSITION AND THE NATIONAL DEBT

The budget deficit (or surplus) and the related borrowing requirement (or debt repayment) are all examples of **financial flows** (not to be confused with stocks). The budget deficit or surplus is the difference, measured per month, quarter, or year, between the much larger flows of income (mostly from taxation) and expenditure. The PSBR is the flow of new borrowing that must be undertaken to finance a public sector deficit. In each year for which the public sector is in deficit, the flow of net new borrowing undertaken, (the PSBR), adds to the stock of public sector debt. Conversely, the flow of debt repayment (or negative borrowing), allowed by a public sector surplus, causes the stock of accumulated public sector debt to fall.

Just as it is important to distinguish between the budgetary positions of central government and the whole of the public sector, so care must be taken to avoid confusing the **public sector debt** with the **National Debt**. The National Debt is a confusing term since it usually refers to central government alone rather than to the wider public sector. The National Debt is the **stock** of all historically accumulated borrowing which central government has not yet paid back. The total outstanding public sector debt is larger than the National Debt, which only records central government debt. (You should refer to Question 1 at the end of this chapter for further discussion of the economic significance of the National Debt.)

PRIVATISATION AND THE PSBR/PSDR

Although taxation is the main source of government revenue, government income from taxation is boosted by revenue from other sources such as:
- sale of assets;
- sale of services (such as the publications of Her Majesty's Stationery Office);
- profits (trading surpluses) of nationalised industries;
- royalties;
- dividends paid on government owned shareholdings;
- rents;
- interest payments paid to the government.

(Borrowing by the government is not classified as a source of revenue; as we have seen, when expenditure exceeds revenue, borrowing finances the resulting deficit!) As a result of the privatisation programme, income from the sale of assets has been a significant source of government revenue (in most of the years since the early 1980s), contributing several billion pounds each year to the public purse. However, in its financial accounts, the Conservative government has classified the privatisation proceeds as 'negative expenditure' rather than 'revenue'. Thus in 1989/90, privatisation revenues of £4bn, resulting mainly from the sale of the water authorities, succeeded in bringing general government expenditure down from £202bn to £198bn! Privatisation revenues have also contributed significantly to the budget surplus and PSDR in the late 1980s. If we exclude government income from privatisation, the PSDR of £7 billion for 1989/90 reduces to £3 billion.

We should note that privatisation can only continue to earn a substantial income for the government as long as there are significant public sector assets available for sale which the general public also wishes to buy. The longer the privatisation programme continues, the fewer are the remaining assets that the government can sell, with the list including, for example, motorways, prisons and police stations. Thus, in the 1990s, dwindling revenues from the sale of assets are likely to be a further contributory factor (along with the economy being in recession) to the re-emergence of a very large budget deficit and a positive borrowing requirement. (We might also note that some commentators claim that the 'real' value to the taxpayer, of asset sales in the privatisation programme, is much smaller than the nominal value recorded in the government's accounts. To make an industry attractive to buy, the government has often 'written-off' large amounts of debt owed by the industry to the government.)

16.2 ESSENTIAL INFORMATION

FINANCING THE BUDGET DEFICIT AND PSBR

Budget deficit and PSBR financing can be looked at in two ways:
❶ **By the type of liability used to raise funds** The largest part of the PSBR is financed by the sale of **long-term government securities (gilts)**, though if the government is unable to sell new issues of gilts at acceptable prices and interest rates, Treasury bills are sold.

❷ **By the economic sector which provides the funds** The government tries to finance most of its deficit and PSBR by borrowing from the 'non-bank general public'. Part of these funds are provided by households (the personal sector), largely through the purchase of **National Savings securities**. However 'non-bank' financial institutions such as **pension funds** and **insurance companies** account for the bulk of the funds provided by the general public, though indirectly these funds are the contractual savings of households. The institutions are the principal purchasers of long-dated **gilt-edged securities** or **'gilts'**. When the government finances the PSBR by borrowing outside the banking system it is said to be **funding the PSBR**. If all the PSBR is financed in this way, the government is 'fully-funding' the PSBR. As we shall explain in the next chapter, since the mid-1980s the UK government has followed a deliberate policy of 'fully-funding' the PSBR as a part of its monetary policy. This has meant that little or none of the PSBR has been financed through **borrowing from the banking system**, for example through Treasury bill sales. However in the restatement of the MTFS in the March 1993 budget, the Chancellor announced a relaxation of the 'full-fund' rule to allow the sale of debt to the banking system. Finally, besides selling debt to the UK 'non-bank general public' and the banking system, the government can **borrow overseas**. But in most years the overseas sector is a very small contributor to the financing of the PSBR. Its importance varies with the exchange rate and with changes in official reserves.

EFFECTS OF THE PSBR

The traditional Keynesian view of the PSBR

Until the 1970s the Keynesians paid very little attention to the effects of the PSBR on the economy. Instead, the Keynesian emphasis was placed on the direct fiscal effects of the budget deficit and increased government expenditure on aggregate demand, and then on the levels of output and employment in the economy. We shall explain in Chapters 19 and 20 how and why the Keynesians believed that an increased budget deficit could increase or 'crowd in' output and employment via the **national income multiplier**. Keynesians either ignored or played down the importance of the indirect monetary effects which result from the method of financing the deficit. The PSBR itself was viewed as a marginal influence on the 'real' economy. Keynesians believed that the principal monetary effect of a rising PSBR occurs through increased interest rates which result from the increased need of the government to sell securities. But, as we explain in Chapter 21, the Keynesians also believe that interest rate changes have a rather weak effect on private sector investment and the level of economic activity.

Monetarism and the indirect monetary effects of the PSBR

In complete contrast to the Keynesians, monetarists place great emphasis on the indirect monetary effects of the PSBR and dispute the strength of the direct fiscal stimulus to output and employment of a budget deficit. According to the monetarists, the monetary effects of an increase in the PSBR include:

> The **'crowding out' of private sector investment as a result of increased interest rates caused by the growth in the PSBR.** The crowding-out theory helps to explain why monetarists believe that fiscal policy is ineffective in stimulating output and employment; in the extreme case of crowding out, an extra £ of public expenditure simply displaces a £ of private sector spending.

- **An expansion of the money supply**. In some years in the 1970s, movements in the PSBR appeared to be highly correlated with movements in the money supply. This led monetarists to claim that an increase in the PSBR must cause a direct and predictable increase in the money supply. However, in other years the correlation was not nearly so strong, and there is now a more general agreement that the effects of an increase in the PSBR on the money supply depend on how the government borrows.

A budget deficit and positive PSBR can be financed in four ways:

$$\text{PSBR} \equiv \begin{array}{l} \text{New} \\ \text{currency} \\ \text{issue} \end{array} + \begin{array}{l} \text{Borrowing} \\ \text{from the} \\ \text{banks} \end{array} + \begin{array}{l} \text{Borrowing} \\ \text{from the non-bank} \\ \text{private sector} \end{array} + \begin{array}{l} \text{Borrowing} \\ \text{overseas} \end{array}$$

Of these, the financing of the public sector deficit by the issue of currency and by borrowing from the banking system directly increase the money supply, but borrowing from the non-bank private sector and from overseas do not.

❶ **The issue of new currency** The government can finance the PSBR by borrowing directly from the Bank of England. It sells its own securities to the Bank in return for an increase in the note issue which enters into circulation when spent by the government. Eventually, the increased note issue finds its way into the asset structure of the commercial banks, enabling a multiple expansion of the money stock to take place via the deposit creation process.

❷ **Borrowing from the banks** The same effect will take place if the government finances its increased spending by borrowing directly from the banks through the sale of Treasury bills. Money is directly created because the banks purchase the bills by drawing cheques on themselves, thereby creating bank deposits. Less directly, money may also be created through the money multiplier process because Treasury bills are highly liquid assets which, as we shall explain in Chapter 17, form part of the banks' reserve assets.

❸ **Borrowing from the non-bank private sector** If the government sells gilts and National Savings Certificates to the general public (the non-bank private sector) the effect on the money supply is generally neutral. The increase in bank deposits resulting from the injection of government spending into the economy is countered by a fall in bank deposits as a result of the purchase of government securities by the general public.

❹ **Overseas borrowing** If the balance of payments on current account is in deficit, the government can simultaneously finance part of the internal deficit (the budget deficit) and any external deficit (a balance of payments deficit) by selling government securities to the residents of other countries. The effect on the money supply is neutral since the government is essentially borrowing sterling which has flowed into foreign ownership in payment for goods and services imported by British residents. The same result occurs if British residents pay for imports in foreign currencies. In this case, the general public sell sterling to the Bank of England in exchange for foreign currencies. This brings into the public sector sterling which can then be used to finance the borrowing requirement, and the country's foreign exchange reserves fall by an amount exactly equal to this method of financing. Whether the government borrows directly overseas, or whether it runs down foreign currency reserves, there is no effect on the domestic money supply.

The 'New Cambridge School' and the PSBR

In the late 1960s a crisis occurred in Keynesian economics, which continued to develop in the 1970s. A consequence of the failure of traditional Keynesian demand management policies to secure continuing full employment, economic growth and price stability, was the emergence of a breakaway 'new school' of Keynesian economists, the **Cambridge Economic Policy Group (CEPG)**.

Traditionally, Cambridge has been the academic centre of Keynesianism. The older-generation Keynesians at Cambridge University are sometimes known as the 'Old School' Keynesians. There are a number of well-publicised differences which separate the 'Old' and 'New' School Keynesians. Paradoxically, the New School shares with the monetarists a belief in the virtues of medium-term economic policy and a distrust of short-term demand management via the traditional Old School instrument of discretionary fiscal policy. However, unlike the monetarists, the New School retains the essentially Keynesian belief in the need for extended government intervention in the economy, particularly through incomes policy and import controls. An important element of the New School model of 'how the economy works' is the net acquisition of financial assets (NAFA) of each of the three broad sectors in the economy, the private sector, the public sector, and the overseas sector. Any net accumulation of financial assets by one sector must be exactly balanced by an increase in the financial liabilities of one or both of the other sectors. In a two-sector economy comprising just the private and public sectors, the private sector surplus (or net saving) must exactly equal the public sector deficit. The principle holds true with the inclusion of a third sector, the overseas sector, and can be expressed as an identity in which the net acquisition of financial assets by each sector must sum to zero:

$$\text{Private sector NAFA} + \text{Public sector NAFA} + \text{Overseas sector NAFA} \equiv 0$$

Thus a public sector deficit (or PSBR) must mean that the other two sectors are net accumulators of financial assets or claims against the public sector. It also follows that, unless there is an increase in the net saving or surplus of the private sector (households and firms), an increase in the public sector deficit must lead to the overseas sector accumulating financial claims against the UK, i.e. the financial surplus of the overseas sector is the UK's balance of payments deficit. According to the NAFA identity, the main effect of an increase in the PSBR will be to increase the balance of payments deficit, providing that the net saving of the private sector is relatively stable. This was the reasoning suggested by the CEPG to explain the simultaneous increases in the PSBR and the balance of payments deficit which occurred in the early 1970s. However, it should be noted that empirical evidence from more recent years does not support the CEPG's rather mechanical theory that the main effect of PSBR is on the balance of payments, because personal savings have varied substantially.

The PSBR/PSDR and economic policy

The growing importance of the PSBR (or PSDR) as economic policy variables has essentially been a part of the emergence in the 1970s and 1980s of monetarist economic policies. The PSBR first became prominent in official policy when the Labour government signed a 'Letter of Intent' to the International Monetary Fund in 1976. The IMF insisted on the adoption by the UK government of a monetarist economic policy as the condition for the granting of an IMF loan to tide the country over the 1976 sterling crisis. Consequently, the signing of the Letter of Intent, in which for the first time the British government announced a PSBR target, marked the transition from Keynesian short-term demand management to monetarist medium-term policy in the UK. In the monetarist strategy, targets for several years ahead were announced for variables such as the PSBR and the money supply. Monetarists then implemented policies aimed at achieving the targets, at the same time hoping that the announcement of the targets would alter peoples' economic behaviour by influencing expectations. The monetarists argued that people would begin to behave in ways which would make the attainment of the announced targets easier, for example by reducing wage claims, once they believed that the government was both finally committed to its targets and prepared to take whatever action was necessary to achieve the targets.

However, an important problem which strikes at the heart of this monetarist philosophy results from the fact that the key variables for which targets were announced, the PSBR, the money supply, are by their nature highly unpredictable. The 'announcement effect' on expectations may 'backfire' if the government is singularly unsuccessful in achieving its openly declared targets! In general, British governments were more successful in achieving the PSBR target than the money supply target, though the need to finance increasing unemployment caused the PSBR target adopted by the Conservative government in the early 1980s to go off course. Originally, in its **Medium Term Financial Strategy, (MTFS)**, the Government announced a target of reducing the PSBR from 5 % of GDP in 1979 to 1½% in 1983/4. When it became clear that this would not be met, in its 1982 budget the government revised the target for 1983/4 to 2¾%. According to the Conservative government, the MTFS 'plots the path for bringing inflation down through a steady reduction in the rate of growth of the money supply, secured by the necessary fiscal policies'. The level of public spending and the PSBR target (the government's fiscal stance) are essentially determined by and supplementary to the monetary stance: the target rate of growth of the money aggregates such as M4. In recent years, formal money supply and PSBR targets have been abandoned, being regarded now as **policy indicators** rather than **targets**. In summary, the PSBR and PSDR have been variously interpreted as policy instruments, intermediate objectives, and economic indicators in the pursuit of monetarist economic policies. We have described their role as intermediate policy objectives in the preceding paragraphs. Alternatively, the PSBR can be regarded as a policy instrument in its own right, in attaining the money supply objective. In this light the PSBR is the intermediary between fiscal and monetary policy. Finally, some monetarists argue that since the PSBR (and the money supply) are notoriously difficult to forecast and control with any degree of accuracy, they are best used as general economic indicators rather than as either policy instruments or objectives in their own right.

Indeed in recent years, the 'other PSBR' – the **private sector borrowing requirement** – has attracted a growing attention. This is because monetary growth in the 'Lawson boom' of the late 1980s seemed to be much more closely related to the mushrooming growth of private sector borrowing from the banking and financial system, rather than to public sector borrowing, which became negative during the period of budget surplus from 1987/8 until 1990/1.

Chapter roundup

Because of the central importance of the PSBR and PSDR in the economy, many of these links have inevitably been demonstrated in the earlier sections of the chapter. The PSBR is intertwined with fiscal policy (discussed in Chapters 15 and 21) and monetary policy (Chapter 17); it is also central to many of the issues between Keynesians and the monetarists (Chapter 24). The size of the PSBR and its method of financing have direct implications for inflation and unemployment (Chapter 22), and interest rates and investment (Chapter 21).

Illustrative questions and answers

2   Essay Question
    Explain what is meant by the National Debt and describe its main
    components. Examine critically the view that the National Debt is always
    a burden upon the economy.

                                                                    (AEB, June 1987)

Tutorial note

The first part of the question is straightforward and requires simple recall of facts and ideas. The National Debt is the total stock of outstanding borrowing which the central government has not yet paid back. It can be considered in terms of marketability, liquidity and source, i.e. from whom the government has borrowed. Most of the National Debt is marketable, comprising Treasury bills and gilts. Gilts are examples of long-term securities or stock which promise to pay the purchaser a specified rate of interest for a certain length of time, and then repay the original nominal sum. Gilts and Treasury bills can be resold before they mature, on the capital market and money market respectively. However, National Savings Certificates, premium bonds and certain other paper assets are not marketable and can only be redeemed, or cashed in, by the original buyer or his agent selling them back to the government.

The liquidity of the National Debt is also significant, varying from three months for Treasury bills to twenty years or more in the case of gilts. In the past, 'undated' stock, such as Consols and the famous 1939 War Loans, were issued with no redemption date, thus leaving repayment at the option of the government. The government may decide to issue more long-dated stock and fewer 'shorts'. This is known as funding. We shall explain in the next chapter how funding has been used as a technique of monetary control, because fewer shorts, such as Treasury bills, mean fewer liquid assets in the banking system and less potential for the multiple creation of bank deposits.

The National Debt can also be categorised by source. The main holders are internal, public and private financial institutions and individuals. The Bank of England, commercial banks, insurance companies, pension funds, building societies, public companies and trust funds all hold government debt. The external debt is that part of the National Debt which has been sold overseas. External holdings may be either in sterling or in other currencies.

The second part of the question seeks a careful consideration of the economic importance of the National Debt. It needs to be related to other factors, such as Gross Domestic Product (GDP), growth, national resources, inflation and the PSBR (and CGBR).

In the UK, National Debt is a declining percentage of GDP and national income. This could be explained by economic growth, if the economy grows in real terms faster than the National Debt. However, the main explanation lies in inflation. If the rate of inflation is greater than the rate at which the CGBR adds to the National Debt, the money value of the debt as a proportion of money GDP will usually fall. Similarly, if the rate of inflation is greater than the nominal interest rate the government pays to debt-holders, the government gains and debt-holders lose. In these circumstances the real burden of the debt on tax-payers is falling. However, debt-holders may begin to realise that they have been suffering from 'money illusion' in lending to the government at negative real rates of interest. When this happens, the government may experience considerable difficulty in persuading the general public to buy new debt, at least at current interest rates.

The larger the National Debt, the greater the money cost of debt servicing. The cost of servicing depends on the average liquidity of the debt, its total size, and the rate of interest offered when the debt was first issued. This servicing has to be met out of current income and borrowing. The greater the cost of servicing, then the greater the level of taxation and the PSBR. Current income which could be used for other purposes finances debt interest incurred by earlier generations. Effectively, this is a transfer from tax-payers to holders of the debt, rather than a burden on the community as a whole. The National Debt is also classified as, and divided into, the Deadweight Debt and the Reproductive Debt. Suppose that the government sells gilts and uses the revenue to build a hospital or some other capital project. The hospital will deliver a stream of consumer services during the life of the gilts. This type of borrowing is not a burden on future generations. In contrast, if borrowing finances current spending, for example on wars, it can be regarded as a burden on future generations whose taxes will pay the interest on deadweight spending indulged in by the government today. A large part of the National Debt is deadweight debt incurred to pay for past wars. Since the deadweight debt does not cover any real asset, interest payments on the debt are a burden on the country's citizens.

If the holders of the debt are external, however, then interest payments are a drain on national resources. In Britain's case the external burden is small, but a less developed country, without either large domestic savings or a developed banking sector, could be heavily reliant on outside lenders. Much of current income might be needed to pay interest on foreign borrowing, resources would flow out of the economy, and development could be impeded.

Suggested answer

- Define the National Debt.
- Distinguish between the main forms of debt on the basis of marketability, liquidity, and source.
- The importance of the National Debt depends in part upon whether it is regarded as a burden. Discuss the circumstances in which it may and may not be burden. Take care to distinguish between the absolute size and the relative size of the debt, its money value and its real value.

2   Data Question

We have reached an important position as regards fiscal policy. This is also very different from what was believed in the early eighties. It was then thought that a prudent fiscal policy which involved reducing the PSBR to a small percentage of GDP, or perhaps zero, would avoid 'crowding out'
5   of private sector investment and leave sufficient resources in the economy to be devoted to the accumulation of wealth.

We were asked to believe that monetary policy would ensure that there would be no inflationary excess of demand over output and that a prudent fiscal policy would ensure that this demand was properly distributed
10   between consumption and investment. The PSBR is now forecast to be about minus £14.2 billion which is about minus 3 per cent of GDP and roughly similar to last year; but last year many observers were saying that this fiscal policy was too lax! Why such a change?

The reason for this is the behaviour of private sector spending.
15   Keynesian economists (who ran for cover in the early 1980s) have always known that there is no such thing as a 'prudent fiscal policy' in the abstract; fiscal policy can only be said to be prudent in the light of the private sector's decisions. And, in the United Kingdom recently, these have been historically abnormal.
20   The fundamental reason is the behaviour of consumer spending. The personal sector savings ratio, now 5 per cent, was as low as 3 per cent in mid 1988. This compares with 10–15 per cent in the late 1970s. This personal sector savings ratio is not only abnormally below the levels witnessed through much of the last two decades, but it is also worrying that at
25   present the British private sector does not want to save to make resources available for investment. This is why the government needs to run a large surplus.

(Adapted from: David Vines, 'Is the "Thatcher Experiment" still on course?', *The Royal Bank of Scotland Review*, December 1989

(a) (i)   Explain what is meant by the 'PSBR' (lines 3 and 10).   (3)
     (ii) In your own words, explain and comment upon what, according to Vines, was regarded as a 'prudent' fiscal policy in the early eighties (lines 8 and 9).   (6)

(b) (i) Using lines 20–26, explain how the behaviour of the private sector in the late 1980s differed from that of the late 1970s. (3)

   (ii) What would you expect to be the economic consequences of this change in behaviour, and why would they be 'worrying' (line 24)? (3 and 4 marks)

(c) In the light of the changed behaviour discussed in (b), how would Keynesian economists expect a prudent fiscal policy to change (lines 20–26)? (6)

(Oxford, June 1991)

Tutorial note

(a) Provided that economic agents in the private sector (households and firms) are underspending their incomes, there is a case for the public sector to run a budget deficit of more or less the same size (to be financed by public sector borrowing – the PSBR) so as to prevent deficient aggregate demand emerging and depressing economic activity. Any larger public sector deficit and borrowing requirement would be imprudent because it would divert productive resources away from the 'wealth-creating' private sector to the supposedly 'wealth-consuming' public sector (to use the 'monetarist' parlance that was fashionable in the early 1980s). At the time, monetarists also argued that a large PSBR was imprudent for a second reason besides 'crowding out', namely that it leads to excess monetary expansion and inflation. However, this argument is not mentioned in the passage.

(b) (i) During the 'Lawson boom' in the late 1980s, the private sector departed on a spending spree or binge, 'overspending' its income. In these circumstances it could be argued that a prudent fiscal policy involves the public sector running a budget surplus and negative PSBR to take excess demand out of the economy.

   (ii) One consequence of the change in behaviour is mentioned in the passage: investment no longer being financed by domestically generated savings. As a further consequence, UK investment had to be financed by capital inflows from abroad. This brings us to the consequences for the balance of payments: instead of saving, the private sector was spending on imports, leading to a massive deterioration in the current account of the balance of payments, which was financed in the capital account by the capital inflows we have just mentioned. This was 'worrying' because it raised the question of whether the UK could continue to pay its way in the world and/or whether the rest of the world would continue to be willing to supply the capital flows to make good the shortfall of UK-generated savings. The behaviour of the private sector has also proved 'worrying' because arguably, the severe recession of the early 1990s has been a 'debt recession' directly induced by the overspending of the late 1980s. To finance their spending, households and firms borrowed far too much and accumulated too much debt during the 'Lawson boom'. In the early 1990s they reduced spending and increased saving so as to reduce indebtedness as a ratio of income. Thus the 'overshoot' of the late-80s boom triggered an equal overshoot on the downside of the economic cycle, but this time in the direction of a collapse in confidence and a debt-induced recession.

(c) Firstly, a Keynesian would argue that there is a case for the government allowing the public sector finances to move 'naturally' into deficit during the recession, acting as an 'automatic stabiliser' to reduce the fluctuations in the business cycle. (By 1991, the Conservative Government had partially accepted this argument.) Secondly, by 1992, many Keynesians were arguing that the debt-induced recession had become so serious and severe, that 'prudent fiscal policy' would involve a massive but selective increase in public spending directed at industry to restore business confidence. (The Japanese government apparently accepted the logic of this argument, but not the Conservative Government in the UK.)

Question bank

1 Are budget deficits necessarily inflationary? (Oxford, June 1991)

2 Explain how a government's budget deficit or surplus can be affected by whether the economy is in boom or recession. In the light of your explanation, discuss whether a case exists for a discretionary fiscal policy aimed at smoothing and stabilising the business cycle by managing the level of aggregate demand. (AEB, S-Level, June 1992)

3
(a) What determines whether the UK has a public sector borrowing requirement or a public sector debt repayment? (40)
(b) Discuss the likely economic consequences of the UK experiencing either a high public sector borrowing requirement or a high public sector debt repayment. (60) (ULEAC, June 1990)

4 Since 1987, the UK government has moved from a position of having a budget deficit to a budget surplus.
(a) Explain what is meant by this statement. (5)
(b) What may be the effects on an economy of a budget surplus sustained over several years? (20) (AEB, November 1990)

MONETARY POLICY

Units in this chapter

17.1 *Underlying concepts*
17.2 *Essential information*

Chapter objectives

Monetary policy refers to any deliberate attempt by the monetary authorities (the Bank of England and the Treasury) to achieve their economic objectives using monetary instruments, such as changes in interest rates, the money supply and controls over bank lending. The traditional approach to monetary policy adopted by many textbooks is rather artificial; implying that over the years British monetary policy has been largely concerned with controlling the supply of money with a view to controlling the level of aggregate demand in the economy. Textbooks often describe monetary policy in a simple mechanical way, emphasising how the authorities attempt to control the banking system's ability to create new deposits or credit by influencing the size of a reserve or liquid assets ratio. In fact, the objectives and methods of implementation of monetary policy have changed very significantly in recent years, as has its importance relative to other policies such as fiscal and incomes policies. We shall spend some time, therefore, describing the background to monetary policy in the UK before we deal with the more precise detail of how the policy is currently implemented.

17.1 UNDERLYING CONCEPTS

INSTRUMENTS AND OBJECTIVES

At the risk of gross oversimplification, it is useful to conceive of economic policy as a problem of assigning particular **policy instruments** to particular **objectives**. Postwar British governments have faced the same broad range of objectives, namely:

❶ to create and maintain full employment;

❷ to achieve economic growth and improved living standards;

❸ to achieve a fair or acceptable distribution of income, both between regions and different income groups in society;

❹ to control or limit inflation, or to achieve some measure of price stability;

❺ to attain a satisfactory balance of payments, usually defined as the avoidance of an external deficit which might create an exchange rate crisis.

The order in which we have listed these objectives is by no means accidental. There is general agreement that objectives 1 to 3 are the **ultimate objectives** of economic policy – though there is considerable disagreement both on the nature of full employment and social fairness, and on how to attain them. In contrast, objectives 4 and 5 are **intermediate objectives**, or possibly constraints in the sense that an unsatisfactory performance in terms of controlling inflation or the balance of payments can prevent the attainment of one or other of the ultimate policy objectives.

Keynesian monetary policy

For most of the postwar period, until about 1970, British monetary policy under both Conservative and Labour governments could be described as Keynesian. **Keynesian monetary policy** displayed the following characteristics:

❶ Monetary policy was regarded as independent of fiscal policy, which was the principal Keynesian policy instrument used to manage demand in the pursuit of full employment and stable growth. In general, Keynesians have believed that fiscal policy is more effective than monetary policy in influencing the level of aggregate money demand in the economy, while monetarists adopt the reverse view.

❷ Nevertheless, the Keynesians did use monetary policy on occasions as a supplementary policy to 'back up' or reinforce fiscal policy in the task of demand management.

❸ More usually, however, monetary policy was assigned other objectives, particularly National Debt management. Being the largest borrower in the economy, the government stands to benefit from low interest rates. For much of the Keynesian period, the overriding aim of monetary policy was to procure orderly financial markets in which the government could sell new securities (gilts and Treasury bills) at favourable prices, thereby easing the problems of financing the National Debt and the PSBR. Since Keynesians have believed, until recently at least, that the money supply is both impossible and unnecessary to control, they gave little attention to this aspect of monetary policy. (As we explain in Chapter 22, Keynesians do not locate the cause of inflation in an excess supply of money.) Instead, Keynesian monetary policy usually allowed the money supply to adapt passively to whatever level was consistent with the government's interest rate target. However, some attempt was made to influence consumer demand (and thus indirectly the supply of money) in the course of demand management via the structure of interest rates and controls on bank lending.

❹ Occasionally, the interest rate target of Keynesian monetary policy was switched away from the **'normal' objective of low and stable interest rates and National Debt management** to a **'crisis' objective of high interest rates to protect the exchange rate**. During most of the period we are discussing, the British Balance of Payments was in persistent deficit. Capital outflows occurred, which meant that the authorities had to sell reserves and buy pounds in order to maintain the fixed exchange rate. In the resulting sterling crisis, monetary policy and high interest rates were usually used to support the exchange rate and stem the capital outflow. This aspect of monetary policy became much less significant in the 1970s when the authorities allowed the pound to float. Nevertheless, monetary policy was used to support the exchange rate both before and after entry into the ERM of the European Monetary System in 1990. However, monetary policy was freed from the need to support a fixed exchange rate after the £ left the ERM in 1992.

MONETARY POLICY UNDER THE MONETARISTS

The 1970s were a decade of transition in which monetary policy changed in a rather haphazard way from the Keynesian policy we have just described to a policy displaying the following monetarist characteristics:

❶ An important monetarist objective is the control of inflation. As we shall explain in Chapter 22, monetarists believe that inflation is caused by an excess supply of money. The immediate objective of economic policy must therefore be to control the rate of growth of the money supply in order to reduce the rate of inflation. By 1980, under a broadly monetarist Conservative government, attempted control of the rate of growth of the money supply had replaced the other aims of monetary policy.

❷ We have already noted that monetarists believe that monetary policy can have a greater expansionary or contractionary effect on aggregate money demand and the level of money national income than fiscal policy. Sometimes textbooks imply that monetarists wish, therefore, to use monetary policy in place of fiscal policy in order to manage the level of demand in the economy. In Chapter 24 we shall explain why this view of monetarism is essentially misconceived. Under monetarism, monetary policy is a medium-term policy for influencing and stabilising the general economic environment, rather than a tool of short-term or discretionary demand management. The framework of monetary policy in the 1980s has been the **Medium Term Financial Strategy** adopted by the Conservative government in its 1980 budget. The MTFS incorporated the monetarist view that the firm announcement of a money supply target for several years ahead would itself bring down the rate of inflation, through its effect on expectations. Nevertheless, for the reasons we suggested in Chapter 14, the government has found that a money supply target is almost impossible to achieve, and according to the monetarists' own philosophy, a failure to achieve an announced target may influence expectations adversely! Consequently, since 1979 the Conservative government has moved away from the announcement of a single money supply target, such as M3. In some years in the early 1980s, the Conservative government responded to M3's 'misbehaviour' by 'moving the goalposts', i.e. by raising and widening the M3 target band for the next year, while still claiming that the MTFS was necessary for the control of inflation. Finally, the government abandoned the formal announcement of targets for measures of money such as M3. Currently, M4, M0 and other monetary aggregates are used as mere indicators of the 'tightness' or 'looseness' of monetary conditions. These are monitored along with other monetary indicators – the value of money GDP (also known as nominal GDP) and the exchange rate – to assess whether the MTFS is 'on course'.

❸ Monetarists place great emphasis on the interdependence of fiscal and monetary policy, arguing that the ability to control the money supply depends upon the fiscal policy adopted by the government. In general, monetarists believe that increased levels of government spending financed by increased borrowing from the banks are mainly responsible for excessive monetary growth, and hence ultimately for inflation. Accordingly, lower levels of public spending and a smaller PSBR are regarded as a necessary condition for controlling the money supply and reducing the rate of inflation. (If however, the PSBR is financed through the non-bank sector, there is no reason why the money supply should expand.)

THE MONEY SUPPLY AND THE RATE OF INTEREST

We explained in Chapter 14 how the **rate of interest** is the price of money. Simple supply and demand analysis indicates that, if the supply of any commodity is restricted relative to demand at the existing price, then price will rise. This suggests that monetary policy cannot hope to achieve simultaneously the twin objectives of restraining the growth of the money supply and low interest rates. In the next sections we shall describe the very important changes in the implementation of monetary policy which occurred in the 1970s and 1980s. During the 1970s, in the transition from Keynesianism to monetarism, it was often unclear whether the objective of monetary policy was the control of the money supply or the traditional Keynesian target of interest rate stability. However, by the end of the decade the Conservative government, under strong monetarist influence, was committed to the money supply target and the acceptance that interest rates would have to be both higher and more volatile than they had been in the past.

17.2 ESSENTIAL INFORMATION

THE BANKING SYSTEM IN THE UK

In Chapter 14 we defined a bank as an institution which accepts deposits that can be transferred by cheque and which makes loans and advances. Until the 1979 Banking Act there were no legal restrictions to prevent any institution calling itself a 'bank'. Officially, however, the UK banking sector comprised all the listed banks which recognised the uniform reserve ratio, together with the Banking Department of the Bank of England (the central bank) and the discount market institutions. In order to regularise the situation, the 1979 Banking Act introduced restrictions on authorised banks by establishing a two-tier system of 'recognised banks' and 'licensed deposit-taking institutions'. It is now an offence to take deposits unless authorised to do so by the Bank of England. The authorised listed banks are divided into three main groups, the **British banks, overseas banks** and **consortium banks**. In recent years there has been a rapid growth in the operations in the UK of overseas and consortium banks, and also the more specialised British banks. In response to this growth, the controls which formerly applied only to the clearing banks have been extended to all listed banks. A consortium bank is a bank which is owned by a group of other banks, including at least one overseas bank, but no one bank owns more than 50% of the share capital.

For our purposes we shall concentrate attention on the clearing banks, the institutions in the Discount Market, and the Bank of England:

The clearing banks

All the banks which we have mentioned, with the exception of the Bank of England, are commercial banks in the sense that the ultimate objective of their owners is to make a profit. The clearing banks, and in particular the London clearing banks, are by far the most important of the commercial banks, both in terms of the volume of their deposits and in the fact that the current accounts or sight deposits, which they accept and create, function as a most important part of the supply of money. The clearing banks are also known as primary banks and retail banks, since most of their deposit business is with firms and members of the general public.

The banks and the Discount Market

In Chapter 14 we used a simple model of the banking system to explain the principle of credit or deposit creation. We assumed in this simple model that banks possess just three assets: cash, bonds and advances. Before we explain the role of the Discount Market and its important relationships with the clearing banks on the one hand, and the Bank of England on the other, we shall firstly introduce a rather more detailed version of the assets side of the balance-sheet of a clearing bank:

Table 17.1 *The asset structure of a UK clearing bank*

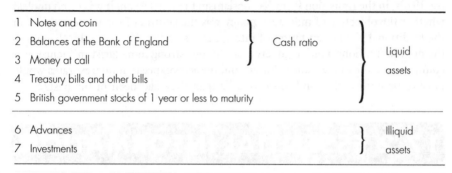

1 Notes and coin	
2 Balances at the Bank of England	} Cash ratio
3 Money at call	} Liquid assets
4 Treasury bills and other bills	
5 British government stocks of 1 year or less to maturity	
6 Advances	} Illiquid assets
7 Investments	

In arranging the structure of its assets, a bank faces a 'trade-off' between liquidity and profitability. Since the illiquid assets in the balance sheet are the most profitable of a bank's assets, it will expand deposits by as much as possible through the purchase of bonds or securities (investments) or through the creation of advances. However, in the event of a loss of deposits to other banks or a cash drain to the general public, the bank must be able to convert some at least of its interest-earning assets into cash. (It is important to note that balances at the Bank of England are equivalent to cash.) Banks come to possess highly liquid interest-earning assets, money at call, Treasury bills and commercial bills as a direct result of their special relationship with discount houses and brokers of the London Discount Market or money market. The money market is a market in short-term money or funds, as distinct from the long-term market, the capital market. Firms in the private sector may decide to raise funds in the money market by the sale of commercial bills (or bills of exchange) for the purpose, for example, of financing trade or a temporary cash-flow problem. In a similar way the government can obtain temporary funds through the sale of Treasury bills, which the Bank of England sells on behalf of the government. A commercial bill becomes a marketable security when it is endorsed or accepted, usually by a merchant bank in its function as an accepting house. Specialised financial institutions known as discount houses then purchase the accepted bills of exchange and Treasury bills. Instead of receiving a formal rate of interest, the discount house earns a discount rate, which is the difference between the discount price paid for the bill on the day of issue and the face value received when the bill matures three months or ninety-one days later.

In practice, many bills are resold by the discount houses to the banks before they mature, thereby accounting for item 4 in Table 17.1. Item 5, government stocks with one year or less to maturity, is essentially similar. From a bank's point of view, short-dated government securities, including Treasury bills, are highly liquid. If the banks are ever in a situation in which they need to restore their cash ratio, the banks can either encash their securities as they mature or sell them to the general public at only a small capital loss. Money at call, which is item 3 on the balance sheet, also results from the relationship between the banks and the discount houses. Each week the discount houses may purchase new issues of bills to the value of many millions of pounds.

Money at call, which comprises overnight and very short loans or advances that the clearing banks can quickly recall from the discount houses, is a very cheap source of finance which enables the discount houses to conduct their discounting business at a profit.

The Bank of England

Although the '**narrow function**' of the money market is as a source of short-term money for the private sector and the government, its **wider function**, with which we are much more interested, is to act as a 'buffer' between the Bank of England and the clearing banks: a buffer through which the Bank of England implements monetary policy. And just as we make a distinction between the narrow and wider functions of the money market, so it is useful to separate the wider function of the Bank of England, the implementation of monetary policy, from the narrower functions which we shall first consider:

❶ **The 'narrow' functions of the Bank of England:**
   The Bank of England is the **country's** central bank. It is organised in two departments, the Issue Department responsible for note issue, and the Banking Department which conducts the banking business which we shall now describe. The Bank of England is:

   • **The government's bank**, keeping the government's principal bank accounts, receiving tax and other revenue, and paying for goods and services bought by the government. The Bank manages the National Debt on behalf of the government, selling new issues and redeeming maturing Treasury bills and gilts. The Bank also manages and holds Britain's gold and foreign currency reserves, implementing the government's exchange rate policy and any exchange control regulations which are in force.

   • **The bankers' bank** The commercial banks hold deposits at the Bank of England (item 2 in Table 17.1), which enable the settlement of debts between the banks.

   • **General banking supervisor** The Bank of England decides who can operate as a bank and the ways in which banks must operate in order to protect depositors. Recent banking legislation has expanded this function.

   • **The 'lender of last resort'** Traditionally, the Bank of England has been prepared to supply cash to the banking system in order to maintain confidence and to prevent bank failures.

   • **Banker to other countries** The Bank acts as banker to other countries that wish to hold their foreign currency reserves in sterling on deposit in London.

❷ **The 'wider' function of the Bank of England:** the implementation of monetary policy. Together with the Treasury, the Bank of England controls the banking system and implements the country's monetary policy. Earlier in the chapter we discussed the changes which have taken place in the broad objectives of monetary policy; we shall now examine the more detailed changes which have occurred in the Bank of England's techniques of monetary control.

THE TECHNIQUES OF MONETARY CONTROL

In this section we explain the various policy instruments or techniques of control, which the monetary authorities can use to try to 'hit' one or other of the targets of monetary policy. We shall examine:
• open market operations;
• funding;
• imposing required reserve ratios upon the banks;
• direct controls upon bank lending; and
• control via interest rates.

It is important to realise that not all these instruments or techniques of control will necessarily be used; some which found favour during the Keynesian era have been rejected as unsuitable under monetarism.

❶ **Open market operations** Traditionally, a main technique of control used in the United Kingdom's monetary policy has been through open market operations (OMO) – a policy of the Bank of England buying or selling gilts on the capital market (and also bills on the Discount Market). In principle, a sale of gilts to the general public should lead, via the money multiplier, to a multiple contraction of credit and bank assets (shown on the right-hand side of a bank's balance sheet) and to an equal fall in total deposits (shown on the left-hand side). Contractionary OMO reduce total bank deposits by proceeding through the following stages:

- The public buy gilts by drawing cheques on their deposits in the clearing banks.
- The cheques are paid into the Bank of England, causing a shift of deposits away from the clearing banks and into the Bank. The balance sheets of the clearing banks will now show an equal fall in customers' deposits on the liabilities side, and balances at the Bank of England on the assets side.
- The cash ratio thus falls, followed (in principle) by a multiple contraction of deposits and credit when the banks reduce their rate of deposit creation in order to restore their cash ratios.

In practice, however, banks can restore the cash ratio by recalling 'money at call'. This passes the cash squeeze initiated by the Bank of England onto the discount houses, who find themselves in the classic exposed position of 'borrowing short and lending long'. At this stage, the discount houses go to the Bank of England (in the Bank's role as lender of last resort), and obtain cash with which to repay the clearing banks. If this were the end of the story, it would appear that the cash squeeze initially started by the Bank of England, would be rendered ineffective by the Bank's subsequent willingness (in order to maintain confidence and liquidity), to re-supply the cash back to the banking system, via the discount houses. But although the clearing banks restore their cash ratios with cash supplied in this way by the Bank of England, they do so by running down their holdings of other liquid assets. And, if the banks were initially operating close to their desired ratio of liquid assets to total deposits, they must now reduce lending and total deposits to restore their liquid assets ratio. Thus in practice, a clearing bank's **liquid assets ratio** (or **reserve assets ratio**) tends to be a more important fulcrum of control in the operation of monetary policy than its **cash ratio**.

The Bank of England can, of course, use open market operations to expand rather than to contract total bank lending and deposits. In this case the central bank buys securities from the general public, paying for the gilts with cheques drawn on itself.

❷ **Funding** The term 'funding' can be applied both to the stock of National Debt and to the flow of the PSBR, but the effects on the money supply are rather different. **Funding the National Debt** has a **contractionary effect** on bank deposits whereas the effect is **neutral** when **funding the PSBR** (strictly 'fully-funding' the PSBR). The government funds the National Debt by selling long-dated debt (mostly gilts) to replace maturing short-dated debt (Treasury bills). The general public thus buy illiquid securities from the government, paying for them with bank deposits which are taken out of circulation. The effect is broadly similar to contractionary open-market operations, supplemented by a further possible contraction resulting from a reduction in the supply of bills to the banking system, as funding alters the composition of the National Debt in favour of long-dated securities.

In the event of a budget deficit, the government **fully-funds the PSBR** by selling just sufficient new long-dated debt to cover its borrowing requirement. Once again, the public buy illiquid securities and pay for them with bank deposits; in this case the bank deposits circulate back to the banking system when spent by the government in its public spending programme. The overall effect on the money supply is thus neutral.

However, 'over-funding' the PSBR would occur if the government sold more long-dated debt than needed to fully-fund its borrowing requirement. The effect on the money supply would again be contractionary – indeed 'over-funding' the PSBR is really just another name for contractionary open-market operations.

❸ **Imposing required reserve ratios upon the banks** Open-market operations and funding the National Debt are examples of techniques of monetary control which seek to influence the credit and deposit-creating abilities of the commercial banks by **acting on the supply of cash and liquid assets** available to them. In principle, both OMO and funding can engineer a multiple contraction of total bank lending and deposits because, as a part of normal banking practice, the commercial banks choose to keep prudent cash and liquid asset ratios. But instead of leaving the clearing banks free to decide their own **prudent ratios**, the monetary authorities have sometimes imposed **required reserve asset ratios** upon the banks. When left to themselves, the banks might, for example, choose to operate on a liquid assets ratio of 20%. But, if the central bank imposes a required ratio of 30%, the commercial banks must undertake a multiple contraction of bank deposits until liquid assets equal the required ratio, unless the banks are able to purchase extra liquid assets from the general public by offering bank deposits in exchange. In order to bring about a further reduction in lending and bank deposits, the central bank could simply raise the required reserve assets ratio. Conversely, the authorities could reduce the ratio if they wished to encourage an expansion in lending and deposits.

For many decades, until 1981, the United Kingdom monetary authorities did indeed impose required cash and liquid assets upon the British clearing banks, though since that date, for reasons we shall shortly explain, required ratios have been largely abandoned. However, the UK authorities have never engaged in a policy of raising or lowering the required ratios from year to year in order to contract or expand total bank lending. Instead, the authorities operated **special deposits policy**, which had an effect similar to the raising or lowering of a required reserve ratio.

As a part of normal banking practice, the UK clearing banks keep **working (or operational) balances at the Bank of England** (item 2 in Table 17.1) which form part of their cash ratios. In the 1960s and 1970s the Bank of England frequently called for special deposits, equal for example, to 2% of the clearing banks' deposit liabilities. Immediately upon the call for special deposits, part of the banks' operational balances at the Bank of England became frozen or completely illiquid, ceasing, therefore, to be a part of the cash ratio. The effect was equivalent to raising a required cash ratio by 2%. Similarly, the release of special deposits was equivalent to reducing the required cash ratio. There have been no calls for special deposits in the UK since about 1980. Required reserve ratios were abandoned by the Bank of England in 1981 and there is little sense in calling for special deposits in the absence of required ratios imposed on the banking system. Indeed, even when required ratios were imposed, calls for special deposits were probably more effective as a 'tax' upon the banking system than as a serious constraint upon the banks' lending and deposit-creating ability. Although the Bank of England usually paid money-market rates of interest on all special deposits, a call for special deposits 'taxed' the banking system because it prevented the banks from using more profitably the funds that became tied up at the Bank of England.

❹ **Direct controls on bank lending** As seen above, the imposition of required reserve asset ratios, and calls for special deposits, are forms of control imposed on the commercial banks which limit the banks' freedom to act commercially, in their self-interest. However, the monetary authorities can, if they wish, impose a form of control that interferes much more severely and directly in the banks' freedom to make their own commercial decisions. Such controls are known as **direct controls**, of which are two types: **quantitative** and **qualitative**.

- **Quantitative controls** These involve imposing maximum limits upon the amount that banks can lend, or upon the rate at which banks can expand total deposits.

- **Qualitative controls** These are '**directional**' **controls** which instruct or 'persuade' banks to lend only to certain types of customers, e.g. business customers requiring credit to finance investment or exports might be given a high priority, with consumer credit relegated to a much lower position. **Selective higher purchase controls** represent another form of directional control.

Direct controls on bank lending were widely used as a technique of monetary control in the United Kingdom in the 1960s and 1970s. However, for reasons which we shall explain shortly, direct controls on lending, together with required ratios, have been abandoned in the 1980s and 1990s, though a future Labour administration might reintroduce them.

❺ **Control via interest rates** All the techniques of monetary control which we have so far described operate on the ability of the clearing banks to supply credit and to create bank deposits though by causing security prices to rise or fall, open market operations and funding affect interest rates also. The final technique of control we shall consider attempts to influence the supply of credit and bank deposits through an indirect route, by acting on the general public's demand for bank loans. Whereas the direct controls on bank lending which we described in the previous section ration the quantity or supply of credit available, **by raising or lowering interest rates, the monetary authorities can seek to ration demand via price.**

As well as using open market operations to raise or lower interest rates, the Bank of England has another instrument at its disposal: the **discount rate** or **lending rate at which it undertakes the lender of last resort function of supplying cash to the banking system through the discount market.** Changes in the Bank of England's lending rate affect interest rates in two ways. In the first place, it usually has an immediate effect on the bill discount rate at which the discount houses conduct business with the clearing banks and, therefore, on other short-term interest rates. The bill discount rate is normally a fraction of a per cent below the Bank of England's lending rate; if it were higher, then the clearing banks might find that there were no bills on offer since the discount houses could obtain a better price by selling their bills to the Bank of England instead! It follows, therefore, that the Bank of England can force the bill-discount rate down by reducing its own lending rate. Secondly, changes in the Bank of England's lending rate tend to act as a psychological signal to financial institutions and markets that the Bank of England wants interest rates to move in a particular direction.

THE ABANDONMENT OF REQUIRED RATIOS AND DIRECT CONTROLS

We have already mentioned how, under monetarism, monetary policy has been used primarily to control the growth of the money supply. Yet, in achieving (or failing to achieve) this control, the monetarists have rejected and largely abandoned the use of required reserve ratios, calls for special deposits and direct controls on bank lending. How do we explain this paradox? The answer is really quite simple. Most monetarists belong to the '**classical**' or '**free-market**' school of economic thought, which regards markets as inherently stable and efficient; and government interventionism as destabilising, distortive and inefficient. Monetarists apply this view of the world to monetary policy as well as to other aspects of economic theory and policy making. Thus, although monetarists wish to achieve control over monetary growth, they reject as unsuitable the more interventionist techniques of monetary control which constrain artificially the commercial freedom of the private enterprise banks to act in their own best interest in the market economy.

DISINTERMEDIATION

Disintermediation is an example of a distortion or inefficiency caused by direct controls on bank lending. In the 1960s, UK monetary policy (which was then basically Keynesian) relied heavily upon the more interventionist forms of control which we have described: required reserve ratio; calls for special deposits; and quite stringent qualitative and quantitative controls on bank lending. These controls discouraged competition amongst the clearing banks. But the controls encouraged other financial institutions to become banks by developing banking business in competition with the high street clearing banks. At that time, the finance houses and the other financial institutions which developed into 'fringe' banks or 'secondary' banks were not subject to the interventionist controls imposed on the 'primary' banks by the Bank of England as a part of monetary policy. This competitive advantage allowed the 'fringe' banks to 'cream' banking business away from the clearers who were subject to restrictive controls. This process is called **disintermediation – when only part of the banking system is controlled, banking business disintermediates away from the banks subject to the restrictions, towards those that are not**. When quantitative and qualitative controls on bank lending were removed in the UK in the 1970s, much banking business 'reintermediated' back to the primary banks. The clearing banks' 'financial economies of scale' enabled them to charge lower interest rates than the secondary banks, and their branch networks allowed easy access.

Disintermediation has also had an international dimension, which has been especially significant for the UK since 1979 when the British Government abolished foreign exchange controls. In the conditions of free movement of funds between countries which have existed since 1979, banking business would simply disintermediate overseas if the Bank of England imposed controls on UK banking operations that limited their commercial freedom and raised their costs. This is perhaps the main reason why the Bank of England has largely abandoned required reserve ratios. The monetary authorities now believe that all banks operating within the UK must be free to choose their own liquidity ratios if they are to compete on an equal footing in what has become a truly international and global market for banking services. Thus, while the Bank of England has tightened up and extended its supervisory role over all banks and financial institutions, domestic and overseas-owned, operating within the UK, at the same time it has largely abandoned direct intervention in commercial banking activities undertaken by the banks.

MONETARY BASE CONTROL

The abolition in 1981 of a required liquid assets ratios imposed upon the banks and the suspension in 1982 of an officially announced **Minimum Lending Rate (MLR)**, were thought at the time to herald a move to switch monetary policy towards a **system of monetary base control**. In the 1970s many 'academic' monetarists such as Professor Milton Friedman, then of the University of Chicago, had argued that once 'monetarist' governments were elected in countries, such as the UK and the USA, they should pursue control of the money supply by adopting a strict policy of monetary base control. The basic principle of monetary base control is quite simple. The state (or the monetary authorities) can, in principle, **exercise monopoly control over the supply of cash or 'high-powered'** money which forms the monetary base. By reducing the supply of cash to the banking system (using techniques such as open market operations and funding), the authorities can engineer a multiple contraction in the part of the money supply which they do not themselves issue, namely bank deposits. Required reserve ratios need not be imposed on the banks. The banks can be left to choose their own liquidity ratios as a part of normal prudent banking practice. But, for monetary base control to have a predictable effect upon the total money supply, the money multiplier must be fairly stable, i.e. it is assumed that the commercial banks will not react to a cash squeeze simply by altering their ratios, leaving total bank deposits unchanged.

To be effective, a system of monetary base control would require the **abandonment by the central bank of its lender of last resort function.** Normally, when the Bank of England squeezes cash through contractionary open market operations or funding, it immediately gives the cash back to the banking system via the discount market, in its role as lender of last resort. In a strict system of monetary base control, this practice would cease. Once cash was squeezed, it would not be re-supplied by the authorities and the banks would have no option but to reduce total deposits in order to restore their ratios.

RECENT MONETARY POLICY

In the early 1980s, the Conservative government claimed to be firmly committed to monetarist theory and policy, including a strict adherence to a 'tight' monetary policy aimed at controlling the growth of the money supply in order to combat inflation. However, during the 1980s, the Conservative government's monetary policy proved to be much more pragmatic or discretionary than originally intended. The band within which the monetary target, Sterling M3, was set in MTFS was first widened, and eventually in 1983 its targeting was dropped. Indeed, monetarist 'purists' have on occasion claimed that the government's monetary policy has not really been 'monetarist' at all, but a form of 'quasi-Keynesianism'. Other commentators argue that the success in reducing inflation (which nevertheless remained high in the 1980s relative to inflation in the economies of the UK's main competitors) had much less to do with monetary policy than with external events such as the falling prices of oil and of other commodities. Indeed, in terms of domestic policy alone, the success of the 'battle against inflation' may have owed more to a 'good old-fashioned deflation of demand', which raised unemployment to over three million, than to any success in 'hitting' monetary targets. The Sterling M3 target was seldom achieved successfully.

In so far as the government attempted in the 1980s and early 1990s to operate monetary policy so as to control the rate of growth of the money supply, we can identify the following main strands of policy:

❶ **The move to a system of monetary base control has not been pursued** We have already noted that the changes in the system of monetary control introduced in 1981 were thought at the time to indicate the possibility that a fully fledged monetary base control system would eventually be introduced. This has not happened, perhaps because there are two potential problems involved in a strict system of monetary base control. These are:

- To have a predictable effect upon the total money supply – which is made up largely of bank deposits – control of cash or the monetary base relies on a stable money multiplier. If the money multiplier varies, changes in the monetary base may simply be 'absorbed' in a change in the money multiplier, without a predictable effect upon the total stock of money.

- Strict monetary base control might produce politically unacceptable fluctuations in interest rates which also conflict with other objectives, such as National Debt management. The effective abandonment of the lender of last resort function might also lead to bank crashes with unacceptable effects on financial confidence.

We can use Fig. 41 to illustrate how the limited system of monetary base control introduced in 1981 contrasts with both the largely Keynesian monetary policy of the previous years and a notional system of strict monetary base control.

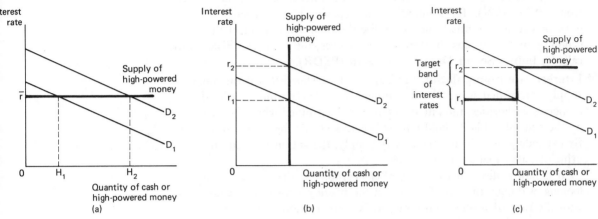

Fig. 41 A summary of different monetary policies (a) the system before 1981 (b) a monetary base control system (c) the modified base control system introduced in 1981

- We have already noted that monetary policy cannot simultaneously reduce both the money supply and interest rates and that a successful reduction of the former will almost inevitably be at the cost of higher rates of interest. During the Keynesian era, monetary policy was aimed principally at an interest rate target, usually chosen to reduce the cost of managing the National Debt. Such an interest rate target is shown as r in Fig. 41(a). Suppose the demand by the general public to hold cash shifts from D_1 to D_2; then the authorities were always willing to supply cash to the banks to enable the interest rate to be attained. This is illustrated by the perfectly elastic supply curve of cash, or high-powered money, with respect to the rate of interest shown in Fig. 41(a).

- In contrast, in a monetary base control system illustrated in Fig. 41(b), the authorities choose a target stock of cash or high-powered money that is completely inelastic with respect to the interest rate. In Fig. 41(b) the supply of high-powered money is shown by a vertical line; if the general public's demand for cash increases from D_1 to D_2, successful control of the monetary base must mean that the rate of interest is allowed to rise from r_1 to r_2.

- Fig. 41(c) summarises how UK monetary policy has usually operated in the 1980s and early 1990s. The authorities have attempted to control the monetary base, but only within a narrow and undisclosed range of interest rate flexibility. Thus the supply of cash or high-powered money is completely inelastic within the range, shown by r_1 and r_2 in Fig. 41(c). But the supply of cash becomes perfectly elastic if interest rates move outside the target range as the authorities increase or reduce the cash supply so as to keep the rate of interest within the target band.

- ❷ **PSBR control** When first elected in 1979, the Conservative government believed that excess monetary growth was caused largely by the growth of public spending and its method of finance via the PSBR. The government therefore put into motion a policy of cutting public expenditure and the PSBR to achieve control over the rate of growth of the money supply. In the early 1980s, the government also overfunded the PSBR; it sold more new gilts than were needed to finance or fund the PSBR. For various technical reasons, overfunding was dropped in 1985. Since then, the authorities have followed a 'Full Fund' rule instead; designed to have a **neutral** rather than a **contractionary** effect on the money supply.

When there is a budget deficit and a positive PSBR, the government puts more money into the economy than it receives from taxation. The 'Full Fund' rule requires that it must take the same amount out again by funding. However, with a budget surplus and a negative PSBR (as existed from 1987 to 1991), 'full funding' means repaying just sufficient government debt to offset and neutralise the money taken out of the economy by the surplus. In these circumstances, the negative PSBR can be called a **Public Sector Debt Repayment (PSDR)**.

❸ **Interest rate manipulation** In Chapter 14 we stated that if the money supply is regarded as a policy instrument, completely controlled by the monetary authorities, the rate of interest is determined when the demand by the general public to hold money balances equals the supply of money. By expanding or reducing the money supply, the authorities can, in principle, alter market interest rates.

It is now realised that this is perhaps completely the wrong way of looking at things. Instead of regarding the **money supply as exogenous**, with the **rate of interest endogenously determined** within the supply and demand framework, it may be more correct to treat the **rate of interest as exogenous**, and the **money supply as endogenous**, i.e. a complete reversal of roles. According to this view, the rate of interest can be used as the policy instrument to achieve a money supply objective, rather than vice versa, Referring back to Fig.41(c) in Chapter 14, let us suppose that the rate of interest is r_2. According to the revised view we have just explained, the general public wishes to hold money balances equal to Ms_2 at this rate of interest. We now assume that the money supply or stock of money passively adapts or accommodates itself to exactly equal the size of money balances the public wish to hold at the current interest rate. The money supply is therefore endogenously determined at Ms_2. If the authorities wish to reduce the money supply to Ms_1, they raise interest rates to r_1, thereby achieving their money supply target by acting on the demand for money, effectively rationing the demand for money via price or the cost of borrowing.

There is no doubt that during the 1980s and early 1990s, the government's monetary policy has often been implemented in the manner we have just described, acting indirectly on the demand for money, rather than directly on its supply. In part this no doubt reflects Goodhart's Law and the difficulties involved in directly controlling the money supply.

Chapter roundup

In this chapter we have developed the simple theory of deposit and credit creation explained in Chapter 14. On several occasions we have referred to the links between monetary policy and fiscal policy and the PSBR (Chapter 16). In the next chapters we largely ignore the roles of money and monetary policy in the economy, as we construct and explain an essentially Keynesian national income/expenditure model of the economy. However, the debate and controversy about the importance and roles of the money and monetary policy are reintroduced in Chapter 22 on inflation and Chapter 24 on the Keynesian/monetarist conflict.

Illustrative questions and answers

1   Essay Question
    The use of the interest rate alone to manage the level of aggregate demand
    has been likened to playing golf with only one club. Explain the mechanism
    by which interest rates may influence the level of aggregate demand and
    evaluate their effectiveness compared to other tools of monetary and fiscal
    policy.

(NEAB, A and AS-Level, June 1990)

Tutorial note

Interest rates can influence aggregate demand in two main ways. Firstly, interest
rates influence consumption spending by households (see Chapter 19), and
secondly they affect investment spending by firms, via the marginal efficiency of
capital which is explained in Chapter 21. The statement in the question implies
that governments can use interest rates to influence the level of aggregate
demand. This was more true of economic management during the Keynesian era
than it has been under the 'monetarist' and 'supply-side' influenced Conservative
governments that have been in office since 1979. Although in recent years the
Conservative government has been urged by some of its own supporters to use
interest rates to manage demand in order to lift the UK economy out of deep
recession, interest rates have generally not been available for this purpose. This
is because interest rates have become tied up in the government's counter-
inflation policy, particularly since the UK entered the Exchange Rate Mechanism
of the European Monetary System in 1990. Before ERM entry, the government
had been prepared to raise or lower interest rates, not so much to manage
demand, but as the main weapon in its attempt to control the growth of the money
supply. As we have explained in this chapter, in the mid-1980s monetary policy
became largely based on a strategy of trying to achieve monetary control by
rationing the general public's demand for money via price, i.e. the rate of
interest. However, in the late 1980s and particularly since ERM entry in 1990,
there has been a major change in the government's monetary policy and counter-
inflation strategy. The Conservative government switched to the belief that a high
fixed exchange rate (rather than domestic 'monetary targetry') can provide the
main source of discipline in the fight against inflation. (See Chapters 22 and 27
for further detail.) Recently therefore, the Conservative government has indeed
relied on interest rates as just about the one and only tool of discretionary
economic policy (hence the 'one club golfer' analogy), but interest rates have
been set to maintain the £'s exchange rate within the ERM. Interest rates in
particular – and monetary policy in general – have therefore been generally
unavailable for other policy purposes, be they demand management or control
of the money supply.

Suggested answer

• Define the interest rate as the price of borrowed funds.
• Explain how, in principle, an increase in interest rates makes saving
  more attractive and therefore reduces consumption. Likewise a decrease
  in interest rates encourages consumption.
• Investment spending by firms is also influenced by the rate of interest,
  though the effect depends on the interest elasticity of the MEC function.
  But firms may be expected to reduce or postpone investment in new fixed
  capital when the cost of borrowing rises.
• If a government wishes to manage aggregate demand, it might be easier
  to do so using interest rates rather than other monetary and fiscal

instruments. It is generally easier to alter short-term interest rates than tax rates and public spending plans (fiscal policy), and interest manipulation lacks the disadvantage of direct controls on bank lending (another monetary policy instrument), of distorting competition in financial markets.

- However, using interest rates to manage demand may be ineffective if people do not respond sufficiently or in the expected way, or if changes in short-term interest rates do not sufficiently affect long-term interest rates.

- Perhaps most significantly, the manipulation of interest rates to achieve purely domestic objectives may simply not be an available policy option when the exchange rate is fixed. Use UK experience since ERM entry in 1990 to illustrate this point. Thus, if a government wished to manage demand while maintaining a fixed exchange rate, it would have to use fiscal policy for this purpose.

2   Data Question

High interest rates are damaging for a number of reasons. First, by adding to industrial costs they make goods and services more expensive and they can push the over-borrowed company into bankruptcy. Secondly, they crush the enterprising spirit: if you can earn so much simply lending your
5   money, why go to the trouble of expanding your business? Thirdly, they suck into Britain large sums from the international money markets and this reinforces support for the pound, which many industrialists think is overvalued. Fourthly, they push up the cost of mortgages and it is this that works through more quickly than anything else in demands for higher
10   wages.

High interest rates, therefore, are inflationary and counter-productive, in that they undermine other economic objectives of the Government. They can, in the short term, actually increase the money supply since borrowers will tend to borrow more to cover their higher loan charges. The
15   need for some more effective control of credit creation is not a matter of economic principle; it is a question of judgement and management. The Government and the banks do need some more effective levers, whether in the form of a monetary base control or some more immediate control on personal borrowing.
20   Such measures by their very nature need not be permanent and could be eased when there are signs of a continuous slowing down in the money supply. There will be many who would say this won't work, but then the present system isn't working at all well. The existing high level of interest rates is putting into jeopardy the economic, social and political objectives
25   of the Government.

(Source: Lord Rippon in a letter to *The Times*, 11 October 1989)

(a) Explain why the author suggests that 'high interest rates are inflationary'. (4)
(b) Why would high interest rates 'suck into Britain large sums from the international money markets' (lines 6 and 7)? Explain carefully why this might be undesirable.   (6)
(c) How might high interest rates 'undermine other economic objectives' (line 12)?   (5)
(d) The author suggests the need 'for some effective control of credit creation', other than interest rates (line 12). Examine the effectiveness of alternative controls available to the authorities.   (5)

(ULEAC, January 1992)

Tutorial note

(a) High interest rates can be both deflationary and inflationary. By reducing consumption and investment demand, high interest rates dampen demand-pull inflationary pressures in the economy; but they also contribute to cost-push inflation. As Lord Rippon indicates, high interest rates add to production costs for firms who have to borrow; they raise import costs via a higher exchange rate brought about by the capital inflows they attract; and they add to the living costs of house owners with mortgages, which can then lead on to inflationary wage demands.

(b) This question develops a point we have already made. As Chapters 26 and 27 explain, owners of 'foot-loose' capital funds (often known as 'hot money'), switch their funds between currencies so as to earn the highest interest rate on offer. Thus if sterling interest rates are higher than those on offer for other currencies, capital funds will be placed in sterling deposits within the UK banking system. In part, this may be undesirable for the reason indicated in the answer to part (a): namely it leads to an overvalued exchange rate which might contribute to cost-push inflation. Even more damaging, however, is the likely contribution of the overvalued exchange rate to de-industrialisation. Finally, 'hot money' flows are extremely unstable; what flows in can just as easily flow out, and a massive capital outflow can trigger a full-blown sterling crisis.

(c) The overall effect of high interest rates is deflationary rather than inflationary; this undermines the domestic economic objectives if pursuing growth and full employment.

(d) As we have explained in the chapter, monetarist and free-market critics of credit controls argue that they are (i) inefficient, reducing the competitiveness of the banking system, and (ii) ineffective – in the absence of foreign exchange controls, credit controls simply do not work as people can borrow abroad. Keynesians reply by arguing that (i) credit controls do work in some other EC countries, and (ii) it is possible to devise new forms of control such as higher required monthly repayments on credit card debt that would be effective in controlling consumer credit.

Question bank

1

(a) In the UK banking sector, what are the main functions of the following institutions:
(i)   the commercial banks;
(ii) the discount houses;
(iii) the Bank of England?   (9)

(b) Explain the part played by the commercial bank in the credit-creation process.   (8)

(c) How can the Bank of England limit the ability of the commercial banks to create credit?
Explain how the discount houses are affected if the Bank of England restricts the growth of the money supply.   (8)   (NISEAC, June 1990)

2 Outline briefly the main differences between Keynesian and monetarist approaches to monetary policy. In 1986 the money supply (Sterling M3) grew by about 18 per cent, whereas price inflation was about 3 per cent. What are the implications of this for government policy to control inflation?
(NEAB, June 1987)

3

(a) What do you understand by monetary policy?(10)

(b) How does membership of the exchange rate mechanism of the European Monetary System affect a government's ability to pursue an independent monetary policy?   (15)   (AEB, June 1992)

4 Why has monetary policy in the United Kingdom in the 1980s moved towards the control of interest rates, whereas monetary theory tends to concentrate on control of the money supply? (Oxford, June 1989)

5

(a) Explain the role of the Bank of England in the United Kingdom economy. (12)

(b) Discuss how the Bank of England might attempt to control total bank lending in the United Kingdom. (AEB, November 1992)

6

(a) Outline the objectives of monetary policy in the UK in recent years. (40)

(b) Discuss the problems that the Bank of England has encountered in operating monetary policy. (60) (ULEAC, January 1991)

7

(a) What problems face the Bank of England in attempting to control the supply of money? (70)

(b) How have the responsibilities of the Bank of England changed as a result of the UK joining the ERM? (30) (ULEAC, January 1993)

8

(a) How does the Bank of England attempt to influence the level of short-term interest rates in the UK? (10)

(b) Explain why the Bank might use short-term interest rates as a means of ultimately influencing:

(i) The stock of broad money in the UK (i.e. an aggregate which includes all commercial bank deposits) (8)

(ii) The sterling exchange rate. (7) (WJEC, June 1991)

CHAPTER 18

NATIONAL INCOME ACCOUNTING

Units in this chapter

Chapter objectives

The macroeconomics which we know today originates in the publication in 1936 of *The General Theory of Employment, Interest and Money* by J M Keynes. In the prewar years, Keynes's predecessors, the **neoclassical school of economists**, who then dominated economic thought in western economies, concentrated their attention on how individual markets function and on how relative prices are determined in those markets. Before Keynes, economics usually meant microeconomics! When attention was turned to the determination of the general level of employment in the economy, it was believed that the economy automatically tended towards a full employment equilibrium, provided only that market forces in the individual markets which made up the economy were allowed to work.

However, in the United Kingdom of the 1920s and '30s it occurred to some economists, and in particular to Keynes, that the economy had settled into an **underemployment equilibrium**, in which mass unemployment could persist from year to year. Keynes formed the opinion that the existing body of economic thought failed to provide an adequate explanation of the persistence of mass unemployment. The growth of modern macroeconomic theory was a direct result of the need felt by Keynes and his followers to construct what they thought was a better and more general theory capable both of explaining the interwar depression and of suggesting how full employment could once again be achieved. In the next three chapters we shall introduce and explain the essential elements of Keynes's theories of income, output, and expenditure, which provide the theoretical framework for understanding the modern macroeconomics with which the name of Keynes is so closely associated.

Keynes was just as interested in practical policy as in abstract theory, and indeed the logic of his theory suggested that governments could achieve and maintain full employment by intervening in the economy and managing the level of demand. Such policies would require accurate information on what was being produced and on the composition and level of income and expenditure. During Keynes's lifetime there was a distinct lack of such information. The growth, in the postwar era, of a system of **National Income Accounts** developed directly out of the need to have comprehensive and up-to-date statistics on national income, output and expenditure if government was to intervene successfully in the economy. The principal function of the National Income Accounts has always been to provide the basic data for economic policy-making, particularly at the macroeconomic level, and for economic forecasting.

18.1 UNDERLYING CONCEPTS

ACCOUNTING IDENTITIES

Many of the problems experienced by students in the understanding of macroeconomic theory stem from an initial failure to recognise and understand the meaning of an **accounting identity**. The most basic of all the identities used in the system of national income accounts is:

$$\text{National Income} \equiv \text{National Product} \equiv \text{National Expenditure}$$

or in economics shorthand (in which it is convenient to use the letter Y for income):

$$\text{(i) } NY \equiv NP \equiv NE$$

We shall keep to the mathematical convention of using the $\equiv$ sign to indicate an identity, in which the left-hand side of the $\equiv$ sign always equals the right-hand side. By definition, the two sides of an identity expression must be equal! It is also useful to note that all the identities used in the system of national accounts are **ex post identities**, measuring what has actually happened in the economy, rather than what people wish or intend to happen.

THE CIRCULAR FLOW OF INCOME

The identity $NY \equiv NP \equiv NE$ tells us that actual incomes received in the economy are equal to both actual expenditure and the actual output produced in the economy. The identity holds because all three are measures of the same thing, the flow of new wealth or income produced in an economy in a specific time period, usually a year. This can most easily be explained by assuming a highly simplified economy in which all income is spent on consumption and where there is no government sector or foreign trade.

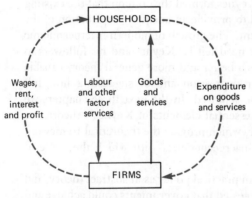

Fig. 42 The circular flow of income

Fig. 42 illustrates the circular flow of income in such a two-sector closed economy comprising households (the **personal sector**) and firms (the **corporate sector**), and two flows, the 'real' flow of goods and services shown by the continuous line, and the money flow of income and expenditure represented by the broken line.

In such an economy it is obvious that if all income is spent on consumption, total expenditure must equal total output, since the value of total output is itself equal to the wages, rent and other factor rewards which go to make up income.

It is less obvious that the identity still holds when we relax the simplifying assumptions, for example by assuming that households now save part of their income in idle money balances. In this situation, consumption expenditure will indeed be less than national output, part of which will accumulate as unsold stocks. However, as a further part of the system of accounting identities, investment is defined not only as **planned** or **intended investment** on new machinery or raw materials but also as **actual** or **ex post investment**, which includes **unsold stocks** or **unintended inventory accumulation!** In these circumstances, national expenditure (actual consumption + actual investment) will still equal national output or product!

CAPITAL, WEALTH AND INCOME

In Fig. 42, national income is represented as **the continuous flow of new wealth** produced from the national capital stock. It is essential to distinguish **capital** and **wealth**, which are **stock concepts**, from **income**, which is a **flow**, measured for a particular period of time. The **national wealth** comprises all those assets which have value, whereas the **national capital stock** is that part of the national wealth which is capable of productive use. It follows that all capital is wealth, but not all wealth is necessarily capital. The national capital stock, which includes social capital such as roads and schools as well as private capital in the form of machines, raw material stocks and factories, is a measure of the physical wealth assets which are capable of producing more wealth. (The value of labour skills possessed by the population is sometimes defined as human capital. While such human capital is

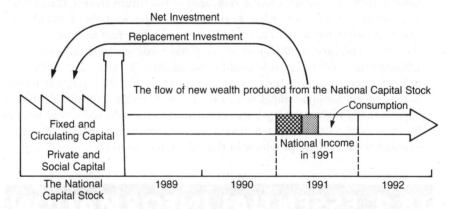

Fig. 43 National income as an economic flow

undoubtedly a national resource, it is not included in the definition of the national capital stock.)

We can use Fig. 43 to illustrate some very important economic relations:

❶ The size of national income or output which can be produced in a particular year is ultimately limited by the size of the national capital stock.

❷ Part of the national capital stock will be worn out in producing this year's national income. Assuming conditions of full employment in which the capital stock is being used to capacity, part of this year's national income must make good the national capital stock if the economy is to be capable of producing the same size of national income next year. Investment which makes good the national capital stock is known as **replacement investment** or **depreciation investment**. **Gross national product** and **gross national income** measure the size of output or income produced before allowing for depreciation, whereas **net national product** and income measure the goods and services available after replacing the national capital stock. As an accounting identity:

$$NNP \equiv GNP - I_{REPLACEMENT}$$

A similar distinction can be made between gross and net national income. However, in the presentation of official national income statistics it is conventional to treat national income as already being net of depreciation or capital consumption. Hence, in the official statistics, the above identity can be rewritten as:

$$NY \equiv GNP \quad I_{REPLACEMENT}$$

Official statistics also measure money national income, which should not be confused with real national income, the flow of real goods and services produced. **Money national income** is simply **real national income** valued at current prices.

❸ If economic growth is to occur, real national income or output must increase over time. Of course, if there is already spare capacity, including unemployed labour, in the economy, some growth in output can take place without the need to increase the size of the national capital stock. But once full capacity is reached, economic growth requires that extra investment, known as net investment be undertaken, over and above the depreciation investment which merely replaces the existing national capital stock. Total investment in the economy may be expressed as:

$$I_{GROSS} \equiv I_{REPLACEMENT} + I_{NET}$$

❹ Finally, we can use Fig. 43 to illustrate the 'trade-off' between current and future consumption and standards of living. The higher the rate of net investment, the smaller is the current output available for consumption purposes. However, the diagram implies that the higher the rate of net investment out of current national income or output, the higher the growth rate and hence the greater the future ability to produce goods and services for consumption. Thus higher living standards in the future require the sacrifice of consumption now! According to this rather simple analysis, it would seem that all a society has to do is to decide how much of current income should be consumed, and how much should be saved and made available for investment. Unfortunately, even if people could agree on this decision, the problem of procuring economic growth is not as simple as this. For example, a reduction in current consumption might make existing investments unprofitable. It may well be that a high rate of private sector investment is linked to the level of business confidence associated with a buoyant consumer market. We shall examine some of these problems in the subsequent chapters.

18.2 ESSENTIAL INFORMATION

THE THREE WAYS OF MEASURING NATIONAL INCOME

The **circular flow of income** depicted in Fig. 42 is a very great simplification of reality. We have already introduced some complications into the circular flow, which represent **injections** and **withdrawals** from the flow of income: households save part of their incomes, and firms retain profits in order to finance investment, and they may also hold stocks of unsold goods. We reserve until Chapter 19 an analysis of how saving and investment, together with other important injections and withdrawals resulting from foreign trade and government intervention in the economy, affect the level of income or output.

Nevertheless, it remains true that even with the introduction of the government and foreign trade sectors into our model, the identity which states that income, output, and expenditure totals are equal, still holds. Any one of these national income aggregates can be used to measure the economy's flow of output.

1 The income method

We have already explained why, conceptually, national income must equal national output, since all payments for goods and services produced are also incomes. Income in this sense is a payment for productive services rendered, whether by labour or the services of land and capital. **Transfer payments**, such as **pensions, welfare benefits** and **unemployment pay**, must be excluded from the estimate of national income, since they are simply transferred from one group of people to another without the recipients adding to production. If such transfers were wrongly included in national income, the error of **double-counting** would occur.

Nevertheless, the national income statistics include arbitrary judgements on what is and is not 'productive work'. Thus an imputed rent is estimated for the values of the services received by owner-occupiers from the houses they live in, equal to the rent which would be paid if they were tenants of the same properties. But the housekeeping allowance paid by a husband to his wife is excluded, implying that housework is unproductive! It follows that if a man marries his house-keeper, or if he decides to paint his own house where previously he employed a decorator, the estimates of national income will fall!

The gap between the GDP total obtained by the income and expenditure methods is often used to approximate the size of the 'black economy' – this refers to unrecorded income where a good or service is provided and the cash payment is not declared officially. Various estimates of the black economy have been made. The Inland Revenue has estimated that activity in the black economy accounts for up to 7.5% of national income, while independent authorities have guessed that the figure might be as high as 15%. Supply-side economists argue that punitive tax rates caused the growth of the black economy, and that tax cuts ought to result in its decline.

An estimate of British national income in 1991, based on the measurement of factor incomes, is shown in Table 18.1, taken from the 1991 National Income and Expenditure 'Blue Book'.

Table 18.1

Factor Incomes 1991	£m
1 Income from employment	329 808
2 Income from self-employment	57 507
3 Gross trading profits of companies	60 674
4 Gross trading surplus of public corporations	3119
5 Gross trading surplus of general government enterprises	119
6 Rent	44 092
7 Imputed charge for consumption of non-traded capital	4490
8 Total domestic income	499 809
9 *less* Stock appreciation	−2825
10 Gross Domestic Product (GDP) – income based	496 984
11 Statistical discrepancy (income adjustment)	17
12 Gross Domestic Product (GDP) at factor cost	497 001
13 Net property income from abroad	328
14 Gross National Product (GNP) at factor cost	497 329
15 *less* Capital consumption	−63 968
16 National Income ≡ Net National Product at factor cost	433 361

Table 18.1 illustrates the important distinction between national and domestic income (and product). Total **domestic income**, which is shown in row 8, is obtained from the addition of the various factor incomes in rows 1–7. Total domestic income is converted into **Gross Domestic Product** in row 10 by subtracting stock appreciation, which results from inflation and is not a reward to a factor of production. A **statistical discrepancy** (which used to be known as a residual error) is then added to make the income-based estimate of GDP equal to the expenditure-based estimate. The decision as to where in the national accounts to include a residual error is essentially arbitrary. Although, conceptually, national income must equal national product and expenditure, the national income statistics are only estimates of what has happened in the economy. Mistakes in data collection inevitably occur, so a 'mistakes item' must be inserted in this table to ensure its equality with the expenditure table. Thus **Gross Domestic Product (GDP)** at factor cost in row 12 is a measure of the incomes received by factors of production through employment in the UK economy. GDP is not the same as **Gross National Product (GNP)** because part of the domestically generated incomes may flow overseas to foreign owners of companies operating in the UK. Similarly, citizens living in the UK may receive incomes in the form of dividends and other profits remitted on assets they own abroad. GDP (in row 12) is converted into GNP (in row 14) by adding the **Net Property Income from Abroad** which results from such dividends flows. You will notice that the estimate for net property income from abroad in 1991 is positive. If this figure is correct (National Income estimates are continuously revised in the months and years following first publication) it shows that dividends and profits flowing into Britain exceed those remitted from the UK. Finally, the estimate for **National Income** (or **Net National Product**) in row 15 is obtained by deducting **capital consumption** or **depreciation** from Gross National Product.

2 The output method

This method of calculating national income involves adding up the money values of all goods and services produced in the economy. As with the income method there is a danger of double-counting. Only the money values of final goods and services sold to consumers must be totalled, or alternatively the 'value added' by each industry, including the producers of raw materials and capital (or intermediate) goods. A distinction must also be made between **Gross National Product** (and **Gross Domestic Product**) **at market prices**, and GNP (and GDP) at **factor cost**. Market prices, or the prices consumers pay for final goods and services, are inflated by the effect of indirect taxes, but deflated by government subsidies paid to firms. National income aggregates at market prices must be converted to factor cost by subtracting indirect taxes and adding subsidies. The distinction between GNP at market prices and at factor cost, and other important national income aggregates, are summarised in Fig. 44.

One of the most significant problems in the estimation of national product results from the fact that a large part of national output is not sold at a market price. In the case of public services, such as education, health care, police and administration, the value of inputs, including wages, is used as the measure for the value of output. In the case of production which takes place in the 'non-monetised' economy, such as 'do-it-yourself' home improvement and housekeeping, either an **inputed value** must be estimated or, as we have seen, a decision is taken not to include such estimates in the measurement of national income. In developed industrial countries this may not be a serious problem; but quite obviously it would be rather absurd to omit an estimate of the non-monetised flow of output in a developing economy with a proportionately large subsistence agricultural sector.

Table 18.2 illustrates the calculation of GDP at factor cost by totalling the value added by groups of industries and services. You will notice that stock appreciation

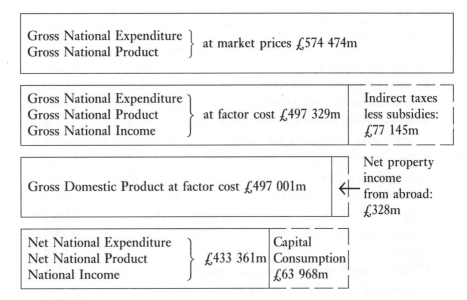

Fig. 44 *The national income aggregates in 1991*

Table 18.2

Gross domestic product by industry, 1991

1	Agriculture, forestry and fishing	8772
2	Energy and water supply	28 273
3	Manufacturing	104 283
4	Construction	33 686
5	Distribution, hotels and catering, repairs	73 024
6	Transport and communication	34 755
7	Banking, finance, insurance, business services and leasing	88 179
8	Ownership and dwellings	34 839
9	Public administration, national defence and compulsory social security	34 786
10	Education and health services	49 643
11	Other services	33 915
12	Total	524 155
13	Adjustment for financial services	− 27 171
14	plus statistical discrepancy	17
15	Gross Domestic Product (GDP) at factor cost (income based)	497 001

has already been deducted from the figures. As before, GDP could be converted into GNP by adding the net property income from abroad.

3 The expenditure method

Table 18.3 shows how GNP (and GDP) at market prices and factor cost are estimated by measuring expenditure on the outputs produced in the economy. The main components of domestic expenditure are shown in rows 1–4, which add up in row 5 to total domestic expenditure at market prices. To convert this figure to Gross Domestic Product at factor cost (row 12), not only must indirect taxes be deducted and subsidies added, but a deduction must be made for domestic expenditure on imports (row 8). Similarly, the value of exports (row 6) must be added, since it represents expenditure on a part of British Domestic output.

Table 18.3

Expenditure 1991	£ m
1 Consumers' expenditure	367 853
2 General government final consumption	121 899
3 Gross domestic fixed capital formation	95 442
4 Value of physical increase in stocks and work in progress	−5303
5 Total domestic expenditure at market prices	579 891
6 Exports of goods and services	135 115
7 Total final expenditure	715 006
8 *less* Imports of goods and services	−140 415
9 Gross Domestic Product at market prices (expenditure based)	574 591
10 *less* Taxes on expenditure	− 83 023
11 Subsidies	5878
12 Gross Domestic Product at factor cost (expenditure based)	497 446
13 Statistical discrepancy (expenditure adjustment)	−445
14 Gross Domestic Product at factor cost	497 001

THE USE AND MISUSE OF NATIONAL INCOME STATISTICS

Since national income statistics are the main source of data on what has happened and is happening in the economy, they are frequently used as indicators of economic growth, economic and social welfare, and for purposes of comparison with other countries. We have already mentioned some of the various problems in the construction and use of national income statistics, particularly the distinction between money and real national income, and the problem of imputing or excluding the value of activity in the non-monetised sector of the economy. We shall now summarise the most important problems which arise in the use of national income statistics.

Comparisons over time

❶ Money national income is a misleading indicator of economic growth. For the growth rate to be calculated, money national income of each year, expressed in current prices of that year, must be deflated to show real income in the constant prices of a single year. An index number, such as the Retail Price Index, used to deflate GNP to constant prices is known as a GNP deflator.

❷ Population usually grows over time, so real GNP per head of population (per capita) is a better indicator of living standards than the aggregate real GNP figure.

❸ The quality of goods and services available is likely to change over time, presenting a particularly difficult problem in the use of GNP statistics.

❹ More generally, the GNP figures cannot measure changes in intangibles, which affect the quality of life and the general level of welfare in society. Externalities, including both external benefits and costs, usually escape measurement in national income statistics, as do such intangibles as the value people place on leisure time and living close to work. When externalities are measured, what is in effect a welfare loss may appear as a welfare gain! For example, if motorists spend more time each day sitting in congested traffic, they will regard this as a welfare loss. However, as far as the national income statistics are concerned it will appear as extra consumption expenditure on the outputs of the vehicle and petroleum industries.

Comparisons between countries

❶ We have already mentioned how comparisons of GNP per head between countries are misleading if the relative importance of the non-monetised economy is greatly different.

❷ Further problems occur in the comparison of real income per head if different commodities are consumed. For example, expenditure on fuel, energy and building materials is likely to be greater in a country with a cold climate than in a warmer climate.

❸ A reliable comparison of real GNP per capita requires the accurate deflation of money GNP figures to constant prices in each country. There are considerable differences in statistical method and sophistication between countries, in the construction of both national income accounts and price indices. In addition, artificially managed exchange rates may distort comparison of internal price levels within countries, and even if exchange rates reflect the prices of goods which are traded internationally, they will not reflect the prices of goods and services which do not enter into international trade.

Chapter roundup

Throughout this chapter we have stressed that the system of national income accounts measures what has actually happened in the economy. We now go on in the next three chapters to introduce an essentially Keynesian national income/expenditure model of an economy, in which we are interested in whether planned or intended expenditure in the economy is consistent with the national output which is actually being produced. In particular, we shall examine what is likely to happen in the economy if planned expenditure either exceeds or falls short of actual output.

Illustrative questions and answers

1   Essay Question
'GNP statistics are useful for comparing the economic welfare of developed countries, but not for comparisons of welfare between developed and less developed countries.' Discuss.

(Oxford, June 1991)

Tutorial note

In the chapter we have briefly surveyed some of the limitations of national income statistics, both with regard to comparisons over time and between different countries. We have indicated how comparisons of GNP per head between countries are misleading if the relative importance of the non-monetised economy is greatly different. Related to this are differences in the degree of statistical sophistication in the collection of data, particularly between developed and developing countries, and a lack of international uniformity in methods of classifying and categorising the national accounts. As we have also indicated, further problems occur when making comparisons because different commodities are consumed in different countries.

A common method of comparing GNP per capita in different countries is to convert the GNP figures for each country into a common currency such as the

US dollar. However, this calculation suffers from the assumption that the exchange rates between local currencies and the $ are correctly valued in the sense that a dollar's worth of output in one country becomes immediately and accurately comparable with a dollar's worth of output in another country. This can never be so. The purchasing power of a currency over domestically produced goods and services which do not enter into international trade or compete domestically with imports, may be completely different from the currency's purchasing power over imported goods. Exchange rate changes only reflect the price changes of internationally traded goods such as automobiles. Thus, in so far that there is a much wider gap in developing countries than in developed countries between price changes of internationally traded and non-traded goods, GNP figures measured in US dollars tend to underestimate real levels of income and output in developing economies. A solution to this problem is to make comparisons of GDP figures between countries using specially constructed exchange rates that take into account differences in the internal price levels of non-traded goods and consumption patterns.

Suggested answer

1   Briefly explain the meaning of GNP and related concepts, and indicate your interpretation of the term 'economic welfare'.
2   Explain why GNP statistics are used as a measure of welfare and standards of living, but describe their limitations.
3   Suggest that these limitations or weaknesses become greater, so even more caution must be used, when making comparisons between countries.
4   Explain the factors which make comparison of GDP statistics of developed and developing economies especially misleading.

2   Data Question
Answer the questions below with reference to the table:

Growth and Use of Resources in the UK at 1980 Market Prices
(Note: All figures are in £ million apart from the index numbers.)

	1979	1980	1981	1982	1983	1984
Consumers' expenditure	137.6	137.0	136.6	137.6	143.1	145.1
General government current expenditure on goods, wages, salaries and other services	48.3	48.9	48.8	49.3	50.2	50.7
Gross domestic fixed capital formation	43.9	41.6	37.7	40.1	41.9	45.4
Increase in stocks and work in progress	2.5	−2.9	−2.6	−1.0	0.7	0.1
Exports	63.1	63.1	62.0	62.8	64.1	68.5
Total final expenditure	295.3	287.7	282.6	288.7	300.1	310.1
Less imports	−59.9	−57.7	−55.8	−58.5	−62.0	−67.8
Gross Domestic Product	235.4	230.0	226.8	230.3	238.1	242.3
Index numbers (1980 = 100)	102	100	99	100	104	105

(Source: *Social Trends*, H.M.S.O., 1986)

(a) Explain the meaning of the phrase 'use of resources at 1980 market prices'.
(4)

(b) With specific reference to the data, what can be inferred about:
(i)   changes in living standards;   (5)
(ii) changes in the state of the economy?   (5)

(c) Explain what further information you would require in order to make a more accurate assessment of changes in living standards and the state of the economy over the period shown. (6)

(ULEAC, June 1988)

Tutorial note

The table shows some of the main components of national expenditure on resources; measured at 1980 prices so as to get rid of the effects of inflation from the data. Consumers' expenditure and imports indicate the 'bought' component of living standards, whilst government spending might reflect, in part, the contribution of state-provided public goods and merit goods. However, the data does not indicate the less tangible elements of living standards, such as those arising from externalities and reductions in the length of the working week. Therefore, further information on these would be useful, together with details of employment and distribution amongst different income groups. The data also indicates the trough and upswing of the business cycle and the state of the balance of payments.

Question bank

1   Consider the uses and limitations of the statistics for 'national income' in gauging changes in a country's standard of living over time.

(WJEC, June 1990)

2   'The deterioration of the environment makes gross national income a defective guide to economic well-being'. Discuss.

(Cambridge, June 1991)

3   Explain the words 'Gross', 'National' and 'Product' in the term 'Gross National Product'. Should GNP exclude activities not bought and sold in markets, such as housework and state provision of education?

(Oxford, June 1991)

4
(a) What is meant by the term 'National Income' and briefly outline the three methods by which it may be estimated. (10)
(b) Show how National Income statistics can be used to estimate the rate of economic growth. (8)
(c) Discuss why the maximisation of the rate of growth may not be a desirable goal of economic policy. (7)

(NISEAC, June 1991)

5   'Calculations of Gross national Product (GNP) especially in poor countries are largely guesswork, and even if they were accurate the GNP itself can be a very poor measure of welfare.' Discuss this view of the problems of measuring and using GNP statistics.

(Cambridge, June 1992)

6   What information is needed in order to estimate Gross National Product from the output, income and expenditure approaches? Why may these estimates differ from one another? (13 and 7 marks)

(Oxford, June 1990)

CHAPTER 19

EQUILIBRIUM NATIONAL INCOME

Units in this chapter

Chapter introduction

In Chapter 18 we briefly mentioned the fundamental difference between the **neoclassical** (or **pre-Keynesian**) view of 'how the economy works', and the view of Keynes himself. According to the older view, the operation of the price mechanism in each of the individual markets which make up the economic system automatically tends towards a situation in which there is full employment of all resources, including labour, in the economy – in other words towards a **full employment equilibrium**. We shall see in Chapter 24 how modern **monetarists** adopt essentially the same view of the stabilizing nature of market forces (and the destabilising effects of government intervention).

In contrast, the Keynesians believe that the price system contains no self-regulating mechanism that automatically produces full employment, and that government intervention can be a stabilising force in the economy. Left to itself, a market economy may tend towards an equilibrium in which there is either mass unemployment resulting from deficient demand, or demand-pull inflation in conditions of 'over-full' employment and excess demand. In this chapter we develop and explain an elementary national income and expenditure model of the economy and illustrate these Keynesian propositions.

19.1 UNDERLYING CONCEPTS

THE INTERRELATIONSHIPS BETWEEN MARKETS

A market economy is, of course, an interrelated system of markets. At the macro-economic level we usually consider such markets in highly aggregated form, dividing the economy into three great markets: the **goods market** (or **product market**) in which output is produced, the **labour market** (which is a part of the wider **factor market**) and the **money markets**. In this chapter we concentrate attention on the interrelationships between the goods market and the labour market – the markets of the 'real' economy. At the outset we must stress, as a word of warning, that more advanced analysis than that considered in this chapter investigates the simultaneous interrelationships between all three sets of markets in which the role of the money markets is particularly important. In this chapter we largely ignore the role of money in the economy, though in Chapter 21 on investment we shall consider the effects of money and the rate of interest on the level of output in the goods market.

EQUILIBRIUM NATIONAL INCOME

In Chapter 1 we introduced the concept of **equilibrium** in the context of a single market within an economy. We defined equilibrium as a state of rest, or a condition in which the plans of all the economic agents in the economic model are fulfilled and consistent with each other. We shall continue to use this concept of equilibrium in examining the conditions necessary to achieve an equilibrium level of national income or output within the goods market of an economy. Nevertheless, equilibrium is a state towards which the economy is heading; the equilibrium will not necessarily be reached. It is more realistic to think of the economy as being in a state of disequilibrium, tending, in the absence of outside disturbances or 'shocks', towards the equilibrium level of national income. Essentially, national income and output will be in equilibrium when the planned or intended aggregate money demand (AMD) of all the economic agents in the economy in the current period equals the output (or income) produced in the previous period.

19.2 ESSENTIAL INFORMATION

A TWO-SECTOR MODEL OF THE ECONOMY

For the time being we shall construct a two-sector model of the goods market in the economy by pretending that there is no foreign trade and no government sector. We are assuming a closed economy in which households (or the personal sector) exercise consumption demand for final goods and services, and firms (or the corporate sector) demand investment goods. In this highly simplified economy, AMD (or planned expenditure) is represented by the identity:

$$\text{(i) } AMD \equiv C+I$$

This identity is essentially different from all the identities introduced in Chapter 18. It is an **ex ante identity** defining planned or intended demand in the economy in terms of the consumption and investment intentions of households and firms. In contrast, the national expenditure identity in the economy is an **ex post identity**, measuring what has actually been spent on consumption and investment:

$$\text{(ii) } E \equiv C+I$$

We must now introduce theories to explain how and why households and firms make consumption and investment decisions. For the sake of simplicity we shall delay the discussion of theories of investment until Chapter 21, for the time being assuming that the level of investment in the economy is given outside our model, at a level $\bar{I}$. We must, however, introduce a theory to explain how consumption decisions are made by households. Such a behavioural theory, which explains how consumption plans are formed, is called a **consumption function**.

THE CONSUMPTION FUNCTION

❶ **The pre-Keynesian consumption function** In Chapter 2 we constructed a microeconomic theory of demand for one particular good or service, where households or consumers choose between a large number of available goods and services. We saw that an important variable influencing the demand for a specific good or service is its price relative to the prices of all other goods and services. The microeconomic theory of demand can be expressed as the functional relationship:

$$Q_d = f(P), \text{ ceteris paribus}$$

When in contrast we construct a macroeconomic consumption function we take the relative prices of goods as given, and concentrate attention instead on how household decisions are made to divide expenditure between consumption on all goods and services, and saving. The choice between consumption and saving is expressed by the identity:

$$\text{(iii)} \quad Y \equiv C + S$$

Ex ante, the identity states that, at each level of income, planned consumption and saving must add up to equal the level of income. By rewriting the identity, we can define planned savings as being simply that part of income which households do not intend to spend on consumption:

$$\text{(iv)} \quad S \equiv Y - C$$

In the pre-Keynesian era, the predominant view was that the rate of interest was the main variable influencing the division of income between C and S. The pre-Keynesian savings and consumption functions can be written as:

$$\text{(v)} \quad S = f(r)$$
$$\text{and (vi)} \quad C = f(r)$$

The lower the rate of interest, the greater the consumption and the lower the saving at each level of income. Saving is a positive function and consumption a negative function of the rate of interest.

❷ **The Keynesian consumption function** Keynes accepted that the rate of interest was a variable which influenced consumption decisions, but he believed that the level of income was a much more important influence. In general terms, we can write the Keynesian consumption function as:

$$\text{(vii)} \quad C = f(Y)$$

and, from identity (iii), the Keynesian saving function is:

$$\text{(viii)} \quad S = f(Y)$$

The essential features of the Keynesian consumption and savings functions are expressed in Keynes's own words in the *General Theory*:

> The fundamental psychological law, upon which we are entitled to depend with great confidence..., is that men are disposed, as a rule and on average, to increase their consumption as their income increases, but not by as much as the increase in their income.

Fig. 45, which illustrates the Keynesian consumption function, also introduces the importance of the '45° line' in national income and expenditure models of the economy. Provided that the axes of the diagram are measuring in the same scale, a line drawn at 45° to origin locates all points at which output or income on the horizontal axis equals expenditure measured on the vertical axis.

Fig. 45 also shows that planned consumption (C) is made of two elements:
- **autonomous consumption** This is the part of consumption which does not vary with the level of income. In Fig. 45, autonomous consumption is equal to the vertical distance (a) at all levels of income.
- **income-induced consumption** Because the consumption function in Fig. 48 is drawn as a straight line (a linear consumption function) it can be expressed as the equation:

$$\text{(ix)} \quad C = a + cY$$

At any level of income, $c\Delta Y$ measures income-induced consumption, since an increase in income of ΔY induces an increase in planned consumption equal to $c\Delta Y$. The greater the value of (c), the steeper will be the slope of the consumption function and the larger the increase in consumption resulting from an increase in income. In fact (c) is the measure of the **marginal propensity to consume**, a concept to which we shall shortly return.

In Fig. 45, the consumption function crosses the 45° line at point Z, indicating that at the level of income $\hat{y}$ households plan to consume all their income. At any level of income below $\hat{y}$, planned consumption is greater than income, from which it follows that planned saving must be negative! Similarly, at any level of income above $\hat{y}$ households plan to consume less than their income, and planned saving is therefore positive. This relationship between consumption and saving is clearly shown in Fig. 46, both in the separately plotted savings function (S) and in the shading between the consumption function (C) and the 45° line.

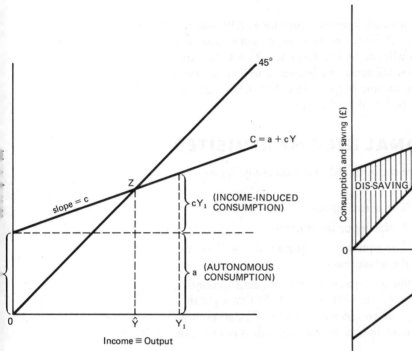

Fig. 45 *The Keynesian consumption function*

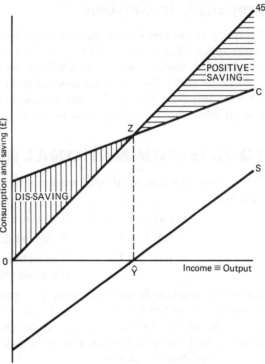

Fig. 46 *Deriving the savings function*

THE PROPENSITIES TO CONSUME AND SAVE

In order properly to understand the Keynesian consumption and saving functions, it is necessary to introduce and define the propensities to consume and save:

The average propensity to consume (APC)

This is the proportion of income which households plan to consume. (Formally, $APC \equiv \dfrac{C}{Y}$.) If income is £10 and households plan to consume £8, the APC is 0.8. When the APC is 0.8, the average propensity to save (APS) must be 0.2, since the APC and APS always add up to unity. In Fig. 45, the APC falls as income rises, though total consumption, of course, rises. APC is greater than unity at all levels of income below $\hat{y}$, equals unity at $\hat{y}$, and falls below unity at levels of income above $\hat{y}$. Conversely, the APS rises from negative to positive values as income rises, equalling zero at $\hat{y}$.

The marginal propensity to consume (MPC)

This is the proportion of the last unit of income which households intend to consume. Formally, $MPC \equiv \dfrac{\Delta C}{\Delta Y}$ and $MPS \equiv \dfrac{\Delta S}{\Delta Y}$

Again, the MPC and the marginal propensity to save (MPS) must total unity. As we have already indicated, the slope (c) of the consumption function in Fig. 45 is the marginal propensity to consume. In this diagram, the MPC is assumed to be constant at all levels of income. Since however, the MPC is likely to decrease as income rises (though remaining between unity and zero), it would be more realistic to draw a consumption function whose slope diminishes at higher levels of income.

The relationship between the average and marginal propensity to consume

Returning to our previous example in which household income is £10, planned consumption £8, and the APC 0.8, we shall now assume that if income increases by £1 to £11, planned consumption will rise by just 60 pence. The MPC is 0.6 and MPC < APC. The APC must now fall as income increases, in this case from 0.8 when income is £10 to 0.78 when income is £11. Since APC falls as income rises, it follows that the MPC must be less than the APC.

EQUILIBRIUM NATIONAL INCOME REVISITED

We can now represent our simple two-sector model of the economy in just three equations:

(ix) $C = a + cY$:   The consumption function

(x) $I = \bar{I}$:   Autonomous investment

(xi) $Y = C + I$:   The equilibrium equation or condition for the whole model

It is vital to avoid confusing the equilibrium equation $Y = C + I$ with accounting identities such as $Y \equiv C + S$, $E \equiv C + I$, and $AMD \equiv C + I$. At first sight they appear very similar, but the meanings are completely different! The accounting identities hold true at all levels of income, but, as we shall see, this is not the case with the equilibrium equation.

We can illustrate the concept of equilibrium national income in one of two ways, using either the upper or the lower panel of Fig. 47. For the time being we shall refer only to the upper panel. The crucial difference between Fig. 47 and our earlier diagrams is the inclusion of autonomous investment, $I = \bar{I}$, in the diagram. (Remember, we are treating investment as a constant, the value of which is determined outside our model.) Using the identity $AMD \equiv C + I$, we simply add autonomous investment $(\bar{I})$ to the consumption function (C) to obtain the AMD function (labelled C+I). This is also called the **planned expenditure function**.

Let us now suppose that the level of income or output actually produced in the economy is Y_1. Making use of the property of the 45° line, we can also show this level of income or output by the vertical line Y_1e. At this level of income or output, planned expenditure, shown by the line Y_1f, is greater than the output available.

Thus, at income Y_1, Y<C+I. This is a **disequilibrium condition**, since the planned expenditure of the households and firms is greater than the output produced.

In a similar way we can show that a level of income such as Y_2 is also a disequilibrium level of income, since at income Y_2, Y>C+I, which again is a disequilibrium condition. At Y_2, actual output Y_2h exceeds planned expenditure Y_2g by the amount gh.

At Y_1, firms can only meet the planned expenditure in the immediate period by **destocking**, whereas at Y_2 they will experience **unintended stock**

accumulation. Because, in each situation, planned expenditure differs from the output firms have actually produced, we now assume that firms react by changing the output they plan to produce in the next period. More precisely, we assume that firms react to destocking by increasing output to meet demand, and they react to unintended stock accumulation by reducing output. (For the time being we are also assuming that spare capacity exists so that firms can increase output, and that prices remain constant.)

    If, when $Y < C+I$, firms increase output

    and, when $Y > C + I$, firms decrease output,

    it follows that only when $Y = C + I$ will output remain unchanged.

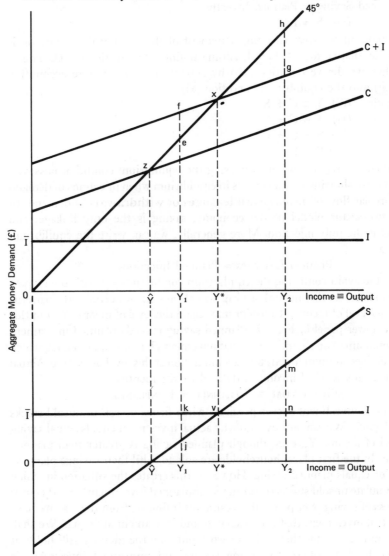

Fig. 47 Equilibrium national income

    In Fig. 47, national income is in equilibrium at Y^*, the only level of income where $Y = C + I$. Only at this level of income are the plans of the households and firms fulfilled and consistent with each other. At any other level of income or output, unintended destocking or stock accumulation creates an incentive for firms to change the level of output.

    Fig. 47 is an example of a **'Keynesian cross' diagram** in which equilibrium is determined at point x where the AMD or aggregate expenditure function crosses the 45° line. In the most simple and unrealistic version of the Keynesian theory we assume that output quickly responds to any change in demand. This means that the 45° line is the **aggregate supply function** in the model. Thus the equilibrium condition can also be stated as:

aggregate expenditure = aggregate supply

Be sure to avoid confusing point x on the AMD function with point z on the consumption function. The equilibrium level of income is determined at x, whereas z merely determines the single level of income at which APC = 1 !

SAVING AND INVESTMENT

The lower panel of Fig. 47 illustrates an alternative way of stating the equilibrium condition of national income. You will notice that the equilibrium level of income Y* is located where the savings function (S) crosses the investment function (I). Thus the equilibrium condition can be written as:

Planned Saving = Planned Investment

or (xii) S = I

It is important to stress that this statement of the equilibrium condition is merely an alternative to Y = C + I, adding nothing new to the model. This is shown when we derive equation (xii) by substituting the ex ante accounting identity (iii) into the equilibrium condition (xi):

substituting (iii) $Y \equiv C + S$

into (xi) $Y = C + I$

we get $C + S = C + I$

or (xii) $S = I$

Nevertheless, this method of expressing the equilibrium condition possesses the advantage of showing that income is in equilibrium when injections of demand into the circular flow of income equal **leakages** or **withdrawals** of demand. In a simple two-sector model of the economy, saving is the only leakage, and investment is the only injection. More generally, we can write the equilibrium condition as:

Planned Leakages = Planned Injections

It is vital to avoid confusing the equilibrium condition S = I with the ex post identity which states that **actual saving** will always equal **actual investment**, whatever the level of income. Consider once again the level of income Y_2, but this time in the lower panel of Fig. 47. Planned saving exceeds planned investment by the amount nm. You should notice that nm equals gh in the upper panel, which we earlier defined as unintended stock accumulation at this level of income. Actual investment at any level of income is defined by the identity:

(xiii) I ACTUAL $\equiv$ I PLANNED $+$ I UNPLANNED

and unplanned investment occurs precisely when firms 'invest' in unsold stocks of finished goods. We can now explain why actual investment equals actual saving at the level of income Y_2, even though planned saving is greater than planned investment. In the first place, households are able to fulfil their savings plans, so actual saving equals planned saving. However, this creates the situation in which firms accumulate unsold stocks (resulting in unplanned investment) exactly equal to the excess of saving over planned investment! It follows from the way we have defined actual investment that actual savings and investment are equal. We shall leave it as an exercise for the reader to work out why the identity still holds at the income level Y_1 where destocking occurs and unplanned investment is negative.

THE EQUILIBRIUM EQUATION IN A FOUR-SECTOR ECONOMY

We shall complete the chapter by extending our model in a very simple way to include **a government sector** and an **overseas or foreign trade sector**. Government spending (G) and overseas demand for the country's exports (X) represent additional injections of demand into the circular flow of income, whereas taxation (T) and import demand (M) are leakages. The AMD identity now becomes:

(xiv) $AMD \equiv C+I+G-T+X-M$

In order to keep the model as simple as possible, we shall treat the values of G, T, X and M as being autonomously determined outside the model, just as we have already treated I in this way. This is a highly artificial assumption since we might expect some at least of these components of planned expenditure to be related to the level of income. However, we shall delay relaxing this assumption until we examine the multiplier theory in Chapter 20. We are also rather artificially assuming that households plan consumption decisions out of pre-tax income and that the level of taxation, T, is not determined by the level of income. In Chapter 20 we see how the model changes when we assume that consumption decisions are made out of post-tax disposable income. Since we are making the assumption that all the components of planned expenditure, with the exception of consumption, are autonomously determined outside the model, the AMD function drawn in Fig. 48a has the slope of the consumption function (the MPC), and its position is determined by adding the values of I, G and X to, and subtracting the values of T and M from, the consumption function. The equilibrium condition for the model now becomes:

$$(xv) \quad Y = C + I + G - T + X - M$$

or alternatively: $(xvi) \underset{\text{(leakages)}}{S + T + M} = \underset{\text{(injections)}}{I + G + X}$

As in the two-sector model of the economy, the equilibrium level of national income is depicted in Figure 48a and b at Y^*, where the AMD function crosses the 45° line.

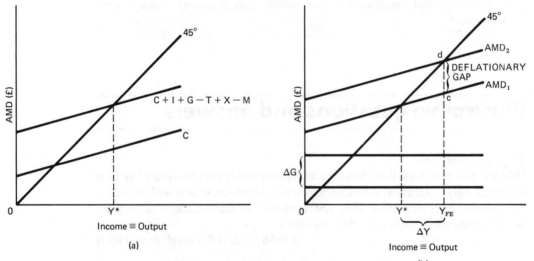

Fig. 48 (a) Equilibrium national income in a four-sector economy
(b) Equilibrium national income and full employment equilibrium

EQUILIBRIUM NATIONAL INCOME AND FULL EMPLOYMENT EQUILIBRIUM

Suppose that the equilibrium level of income Y^* is insufficient to employ fully the available labour force in the economy. We can represent the size of national income or output which will employ all the labour force at Y_{FE} in Fig. 48b. The existing level of planned expenditure represented by AMD_1 brings about an equilibrium level of national income at Y^* rather than at Y_{FE}. In Keynesian terms, unemployment is caused by deficient demand in the economy. If any of the components of planned expenditure such as C, I, G or X autonomously increase, the deflationary gap between AMD_1 and AMD_2 might be closed, bringing about an equilibrium level of income at the full employment level.

Keynes, writing in the depression economy of the interwar years, believed that the deficient demand was either caused in the first place, or certainly reinforced, by a collapse of private sector consumption and investment demand. (The tendency of households to save too much is called the 'paradox of thrift'. According to the Keynesian view, saving, which is an individual virtue, becomes a vice in the economy as a whole if unemployment is caused by too little consumption. We shall examine Keynes's theory of deficient investment demand, the marginal efficiency of capital theory, in Chapter 21.)

If Keynes was correct, it would be unwise to rely on an autonomous recovery in consumption and investment to close the deflationary gap and bring about full employment. Instead, the government could deliberately use the policy instruments at its disposal, government spending (G) and taxation (T), to inject demand into the economy through a budget deficit. Essentially, the government borrows the excess savings of the private sector, which are injected back into the circular flow of income in public spending. This is the theoretical basis of Keynesian demand management or discretionary fiscal policy, used by the Keynesians to control the level of aggregate demand in the economy to a level consistent with achieving equilibrium national income at full employment.

Chapter roundup

In Chapters 20, 21 and 22, we expand on important aspects of the Keynesian income/expenditure model of the economy. Then, in Chapter 23, we introduce the aggregate demand/aggregate supply (AD)/AS) macromodel which, in recent years, has begun to replace the income/expenditure model as the theoretical framework within which macroeconomic issues are investigated.

Illustrative questions and answers

1   Essay Question
What factors determine the ratios of consumption and saving to national income in an economy? Explain why the Chancellor of the Exchequer may wish to reduce consumption and increase saving, and evaluate the relative merits of taxation and interest rates in achieving this objective.

(NEAB, A and AS Level, June 1989)

Tutorial note

For the first part of this question, the consumption and savings functions are relevant. In the chapter we have explained in some detail how both consumption and saving are related to the level of income (in Keynesian theory), and we mentioned that the rate of interest will also influence them. You should carefully explain how, according to the Keynesian theory, the proportions of income which households plan to consume and save vary as income rises, illustrating the theory with a consumption function drawn on a 45° line diagram. However there are other influences upon consumption and saving which you can also bring into your answer. These days economists agree that it is not just *current income* this year, but also *income expected in the future*, that influence decisions to consume and save out of current income. This is the basis of the '**permanent income**' and '**lifecycle' theories of saving and consumption**. With the life-cycle theory, it is useful to divide savings into two kinds: **contractual** and **non-contractual** (or **discretionary**) **savings**. When a person puts some money aside to finance the buying of Christmas presents or a summer holiday, the savings are discretionary. Saving during part of the year is usually followed by dissaving a few weeks or months later, so discretionary saving may net out to close to zero over a medium term period. By contrast, people undertake contractual savings through pension funds and life insurance policies, often saving to finance eventual retirement. Contractual savings are usually positive during the saver's working life, becoming negative after retirement and perhaps netting to zero over the whole lifecycle from birth to death. But unexpected 'windfall' events can sometimes cause dramatic changes in people's contractual savings. For example the house price boom in the late 1980s made house owners feel much wealthier. Many decided that they did not need to save so much out of current income because the appreciation in value of their houses was doing their saving for them; hence savings collapsed and consumption soared, But the house price collapse in the early 1990s has had the opposite effect, particularly in the South East of England. House owners have felt much less wealthy and – if their mortgages are large in relation to the eroded values of their property – burdened by debt. In these circumstances, house owners have frantically increased the proportion of income they save (the 'return of thrift'), to try to restore the real value of their net wealth.

This question was set at the tail-end of the 'Lawson boom' in the late 1980s when – as we have just indicated – too little saving and too much consumption was very much the problem. In such a situation, the Chancellor would wish to increase saving to dampen down demand and close an 'inflationary gap. But taking a more long-term view, he would also like to encourage saving to provide the funds to finance investment in productive capacity, to enable economic growth to take place. Higher interest rate (i.e. monetary policy) will directly reward saving and discourage consumption, though this depends on savers' responsiveness to the rate of interest, and the question of whether savers are more influenced by 'nominal' or 'real' interest rates also complicates things. The Chancellor can also use fiscal policy to encourage savings, for example by exempting savings from income tax and capital gains tax. This can be quite effective, especially in directing funds into types of saving that the government wishes to encourage. The government can also tax consumption by raising expenditure taxes such as VAT. This is probably less effective in encouraging saving, but it does have the advantage (for the Exchequer) of increasing tax revenues, whereas tax relief on savings results in a revenue loss.

Suggested answer

1 Briefly define consumption and saving.
2 Explain how income divides into consumption and saving according to the Keynesian consumption and saving functions.
3 Introduce other determinants of saving and consumption: the rate of interest; wealth, expected future income, etc.
4 Indicate why the Chancellor may wish to encourage saving: to manage demand; to promote investment and growth.
5 Explain briefly how reducing interest rates and altering taxes may encourage saving. Suggest at least one advantage and disadvantage of each.

2   Data Question
Table 19.1 gives data relating to personal income, expenditure and saving in Great Britain.
(a) What is meant by the term 'total personal disposable income'?   (2)
(b) Calculate the average propensity to consume in 1978.   (2)
(c) Calculate the marginal propensity to consume between 1987 and 1988. Comment on your result.   (4)
(d) (i)   What do you understand by the term 'saving ratio'?   (2)
    (ii) Analyse the factors which may have influenced the trends in saving and consumption during the period 1978–88.   (6)

(e) Examine the possible effects of the falling saving ratio on:
    (i)   the rate of inflation;
    (ii) the Balance of Payments.   (4)

(ULEAC, June 1991)

Table 19.1

	Total personal disposable income (£bn)	Consumers' expenditure (£bn)	Saving ratio %
1978	113.1	100.2	11.4
1979	35.7	118.7	12.6
1980	160.0	137.9	13.8
1981	176.1	153.6	12.8
1982	191.3	168.5	11.9
1983	206.1	184.6	10.4
1984	220.9	197.5	10.6
1985	238.8	215.5	9.7
1986	256.9	237.4	7.6
1987	275.7	259.3	5.9
1988	303.4	289.8	4.5

(Source: *An Economic Profile of Britain, 1989,* Lloyds Bank)

Tutorial note

(a) In the UK national income statistics, the distinction is made between *original, gross, disposable* and *final* income. Initially households receive *original income* from various sources, mainly employment, occupational pensions which are really deferred pay, and investments in shares, etc. The addition of cash benefits or *transfers* given by the state, such as the state pension and unemployment pay, gives *gross income.* The subtraction of direct taxes such as income tax and National Insurance contributions, and the poll tax, would yield *disposable income.* 'Total personal disposable income' is therefore the aggregation of the disposable income of all UK residents – but individuals, not companies in the 'corporate sector' of the economy. (In fact we can take the classification two stages further: deducting indirect taxes such as VAT from *disposable income* yields *post-tax income. Final income* is then calculated by adding the imputed value of the benefits people receive from services consumed 'in kind', such as education and health care, provided by the state.)

(b) There is in fact a minor inaccuracy in questions (b) and (c). As we have explained in this chapter, *propensities* to consume and save are '*ex ante*' concepts, i.e. they measure what people *wish* or *plan* to do, before the event. But the data in the table are '*ex post*', i.e. a measurement after the event of how much households *have ended up* consuming (*actual* or *realised consumption*). Nevertheless, since by their nature, the average and marginal propensities cannot be measured directly, '*ex post*' data such as that in the table are often used for their calculation. Thus, the ratio of consumers' expenditure (column 2) to total personal disposable income (column 1), gives an estimate of the APC for each of the years, after the deduction of income tax.

(c) Calculate the MPC in a similar way, except make sure you first deduct the 1987 levels of consumers' expenditure and personal disposable income from their 1988 levels. This gives you the changes between the two years from which you can complete the calculation of the MPC. You will find that, according to the data, the MPC was negative between 1987 and 1988 indicating that consumption was rising by a greater absolute amount than income. See if you can relate this to what we have written about consumption, saving, wealth and house prices during the 'Lawson boom' of the late 1980s, in the guidance notes for the Essay Question.

(d) (i) Unlike the 'ex ante' average propensity to save, the 'saving ratio' is an 'ex post' concept, measuring total realised savings as a ratio of total personal disposable income. But for the reason we have explained (in the context of consumers' expenditure and the APC), the savings ratio is often used as a measure of the APS.

(ii) Refer to the guidance note to the Essay Question; this question covers similar ground.

(e) In the late 1980s, the falling savings ratio boosted consumer demand (as your calculation of a negative MPC in 1988 indicates). This would have added to demand-pull inflationary pressures during the 'Lawson boom', and it also 'sucked' imports into the economy via the marginal propensity to import, contributing to a rapidly deteriorating balance of payments on current account.

Question bank

1

(a) List the main leakages and injections in a model of national income determination for an open economy with a government sector. Why are the leakages often regarded as being 'endogenous' variables, whilst the injections are regarded as being 'exogenous' variables? (10)

(b) 'A simple Keynesian model of income determination shows that the economy can be in equilibrium with either inflation or unemployment or neither.' Explain. (8)

(c) 'Empirical evidence shows that the model is too simple, for in reality both unemployment and inflation co-exist.' Discuss. (7)

(NISEAC, June 1991)

2

(a) What are the main injections and withdrawals in the circular flow of income model? (10)

(b) An open economy experiencing a deflationary gap receives an increase in investment of £100m. Analyse the likely consequences for the economy's national income. (10)

(Cambridge, AS-Level, June 1989)

3 What factors determine the ratios of consumption and saving to national income in an economy? Explain why the Chancellor of the Exchequer may wish to reduce consumption and saving, and evaluate the relative merits of taxation and interest rates in achieving this objective. (NEAB, June 1989)

4 Discuss the economic relationships between consumption, income and investment. (AEB, November 1990)

THE MULTIPLIER

Units in this chapter

20.1 *Underlying concepts*
20.2 *Essential information*

Chapter objectives

In this chapter we develop an important aspect of the Keynesian national income/expenditure model of the economy which we introduced in Chapter 18 and 19. In Chapter 19 we explained that when **aggregate money demand (AMD)** is greater (or less) than the income or output produced in the previous period, national income will rise (or fall) until an equilibrium is reached when AMD equals the available output. We now introduce the multiplier theory and investigate in more detail the process by which income or output changes when an autonomous change occurs in any of the components of planned expenditure.

The concept of the **multiplier** was first developed in 1931 by R F Kahn, who at the time was a colleague and former pupil of Keynes at Cambridge. The early theory was essentially an **employment multiplier**, which modelled how a change in public investment, for example in road-building, might cause a subsequent multiple expansion of employment. Keynes first made use of Kahn's employment multiplier in 1933 when he discussed the effects of an increase in government spending of £500, a sum assumed to be just sufficient to employ one man for one year in the construction of public works. Keynes wrote:

> If the new expenditure is additional and not merely in substitution for other expenditure, the increase of employment does not stop there. The additional wages and other incomes paid out are spent on additional purchases, which in turn lead to further employment ... the newly employed who supply the increased purchases of those employed on the new capital works will, in their turn, spend more, thus adding to the employment of others; and so on.

By the time of the publication in 1936 of Keynes's famous *General Theory*, the multiplier had become a vital part of Keynes's explanation of how an economy can settle into an **underemployment equilibrium**. In the *General Theory*, Keynes focused attention on the **investment multiplier**, explaining how a collapse in investment and business confidence can cause a multiple contraction of output. From this, it was only a short step to suggest how the **government spending multiplier** might be used to reverse the process. Analytically, in terms of the Keynesian expenditure/income model of the goods market in the economy, an increase in public spending which is unaccompanied by an increase in taxation has an identical expansionary effect to an autonomous increase in investment. Indeed, nowadays the concept of the **National Income multiplier** is used as a generic term to include the multiplier effects which result from a change in any of the components of demand. Thus the **autonomous consump-**

tion multiplier, the **investment multiplier**, the **government spending multiplier**, and various forms of **tax and foreign trade multipliers** are all examples of specific National Income multipliers. At a local level, the **regional multiplier**, which we briefly mentioned in Chapter 12, is sometimes identified. A regional multiplier indicates by how much regional income or output will increase when additional demand is injected into the regional economy. However, the **money multiplier** discussed in Chapters 14 and 17 should not be classified amongst the Keynesian or National Income multipliers, though its existence serves to illustrate that multiplier effects occur whenever a change in one variable cause multiple and successive stages of change in another variable. Indeed, if fiscal and monetary policy are interdependent, an increase in government spending can result in simultaneous fiscal and monetary multiplier effects.

20.1 UNDERLYING CONCEPTS

THE DYNAMIC MULTIPLIER

It is often forgotten that the multiplier process is essentially a dynamic process which takes place over a considerable period of time. In order to illustrate this, we shall continue to adopt for the time being the assumptions of Chapter 19: namely that the values of all the components of aggregate expenditure, with the exception of consumption, are determined autonomously. Only the consumption decisions of households are related to level of income through the marginal propensity to consume (MPC). We shall assume that the MPC is 0.8 at all levels of income, which of course means that the marginal propensity to save (MPS) must be 0.2. Saving is the only income-related leakage of demand in the economy. Whenever income increases by £10, consumption spending increases by £8, and £2 is saved. Finally, we shall assume that prices remain constant in the economy and that a margin of spare capacity and unemployed labour exists which the government wishes to reduce.

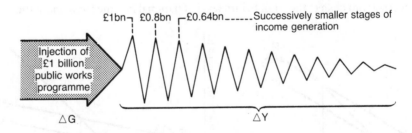

Fig. 49 The multiplier process when the marginal propensity to consume is 0.8

Suppose the government now increases public spending by £1 billion, but keeps taxation at its existing level. The government could, for example, decide to increase transfer incomes such as pensions, welfare benefits and unemployment pay, or even aid to industry. Alternatively, the government might invest in public works or social capital, for example in road construction. Fig. 49 illustrates that the increase in public spending represents an initial increase in incomes for the factors of production who are now employed in the construction scheme. At the second stage, demand for goods and services produced largely by the private sector will increase when the households employed in the public works spend 0.8 of their increase in income on consumption, in total £800 million. Further stages of income generation then occur, with each succeeding stage being smaller than the previous one. In our particular model, each successive stage is exactly 0.8 of the previous stage because the MPC is 0.8 at all levels of income and saving is the only income-induced leakage. Assuming that nothing else changes in the time it takes for the process to work through, the eventual increase in income resulting from the initial injection is the sum of all the stages of income generation.

The value of the government spending multiplier $= \dfrac{\text{change in income}}{\text{change in government spending}}$

$$\text{or } k = \frac{\Delta Y}{\Delta G}$$

where k is the symbol for the government spending multiplier. Provided that saving is the only leakage of demand, the value of k depends upon the marginal propensity to consume. In fact, the formula for the multiplier in this model is

$$k = \frac{1}{1-c} \text{ where c is the MPC}$$

$$\text{or } k = \frac{1}{s} \text{ where s is the MPS}$$

The larger the MPC (and the smaller the MPS), the larger is the value of the multiplier. In our model, the value of the multiplier is 5 (i.e. $\dfrac{1}{1-0.8}$), indicating that the initial increase in public spending will subsequently increase income by £5 billion in total.

We have stressed the dynamic nature of the multiplier process in order to emphasise that the economy is likely to be in a permanent state of disequilbrium. It is wrong and artificial to imply that the multiplier is an instantaneous process, involving a move from one equilibrium level of national income to another. Not only does the process take time; it is also very likely that the economy will experience the 'outside shock' of an autonomous change in one or other of the components of planned expenditure while the multiplier process is working through. It is useful to think of the economy as tending towards an equilibrium as the multiplier process works through, yet unlikely to reach a state of equilibrium because of the renewed impact of 'outside shocks'.

THE COMPARATIVE STATIC MULTIPLIER

Fig. 50 illustrates the multiplier concept in terms of the change in the level of AMD necessary to change the equilibrium level of national income from one static

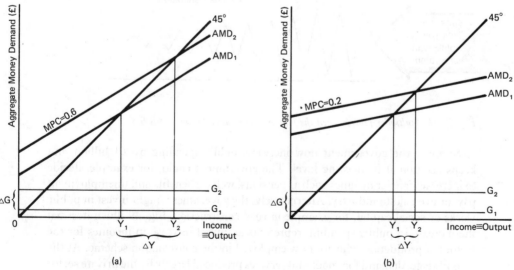

Fig. 50 How the size of the multiplier is determined by the marginal propensity to consume
(a) MPC = 0.6 (b) MPC = 0.2

equilibrium to another. Since saving is the only income-induced leakage of demand from the economy, the slope of the AMD function depends on the value of the MPC. An initial equilibrium level of income, Y_1, is determined by the level of planned expenditure AMD_1. When the MPC is 0.6, as in Fig. 50a, an injection of government spending shown by ΔG increases the equilibrium level of income to Y_2. The change in income from one equilibrium level to another, ΔY, is two and a half times the change in government spending. However, a comparison of the equilibria indicates nothing about the length of the time path from one equilibrium to the other. The slope of the AMD function is less, and the MPC is smaller in Fig. 50b. Thus the multiplier is also smaller, equal to 1.25 when the MPC is 0.2.

20.2 ESSENTIAL INFORMATION

THE SIMPLE MULTIPLIER

Our purpose is to show that there is no unique formulation for the multiplier; as we change the assumptions of our model, treating taxation and import demand as income-related, we shall arrive at different formulas for the relevant multiplier. Firstly, however, we shall restate the elementary multiplier in a model of the economy in which all the components of aggregate demand except consumption are autonomously determined outside the model. Equation (i) is a behavioural equation showing the consumption function, and equations (ii) to (vi) depict the other components of aggregate demand, which are autonomous:

    (i) $C = a + cY$, where c is the MPC

    (ii) $I = \bar{I}$: investment

    (iii) $G = \bar{G}$: government spending

    (iv) $T = \bar{T}$: taxation

    (v) $X = \bar{X}$: exports

    (vi) $M = \bar{M}$: imports

The equilibrium condition for the model is:

    (vii) $Y = C + I + G - T + X - M$ or

    (viii) $Y = a + cY + \bar{I} + \bar{G} - \bar{T} + \bar{X} - \bar{M}$

Since saving is the only income-induced leakage of demand, the simple multiplier in this model is $\dfrac{1}{1-c}$ or $\dfrac{1}{s}$, where s is the marginal propensity to save. If, for example, private investment changes by ΔI, or government spending changes by ΔG, then the resulting change in the level of income, ΔY, is represented by

    (ix) $\Delta Y = \dfrac{1}{1-c}(\Delta I)$ in the case of the change in investment;

and by (x) $\Delta Y = \dfrac{1}{1-c}(\Delta G)$ when government spending changes. The formulas of the investment and government spending multipliers are identical.

THE TAX MULTIPLIER

If we assume that households make consumption decisions out of **post-tax disposable income** rather than out of pre-tax income, a different formula emerges for the tax multiplier. We can now write the equilibrium condition as:

    (xi) $Y = a + c(Y - \bar{T}) + \bar{I} + \bar{G} + \bar{X} - \bar{M}$ or

    (xii) $Y = a + cY - c\bar{T} + \bar{I} + \bar{G} + \bar{X} - \bar{M}$

Following an autonomous change in taxation equal to ΔT, the change in income, ΔY, is represented by:

$$(\text{xiii}) \quad \Delta Y = \frac{1}{1-c} \Delta (-cT) \text{ or}$$

$$(\text{xiv}) \quad \Delta Y = \frac{-c}{1-c} (\Delta T)$$

where $\dfrac{-c}{1-c}$ is the tax multiplier.

This expression tells us two important things about the tax multiplier. In the first place, it is negative, which means than an autonomous increase in taxation results in a fall in the equilibrium level of income, the size of the fall being a multiple of the absolute change in taxation. Secondly, since the value of c (the MPC) is less than unity, the value of the tax multiplier in this model is always less than the value of the government spending multiplier $\dfrac{1}{1-c}$. For example, if the MPC is 0.8 the government spending multiplier $\dfrac{1}{1-c}$ will be 5, and the tax multiplier $\dfrac{-c}{1-c}$ will be 4. As an exercise, you might calculate the size of the two multipliers for other values of the MPC. Whatever the chosen value of the MPC, you will find that the absolute size of the government spending multiplier (forgetting the plus and minus signs) is always equal to the tax multiplier plus one! Thus a given increase in tax revenue has a smaller multiplier effect than a similar change in government spending. The explanation for this lies in the fact that disposable income falls by an amount equal to the size of the tax increase, but since part of disposable income is saved, spending does not fall by the full amount of the increase in taxation. In the initial stage of the multiplier effect, the change in spending is $-c\,\Delta T$ rather than $-\Delta T$. Summing all the successive stages of the multiplier process, the total change in spending and income equals $\dfrac{-c}{1-c}(\Delta T)$ rather than $\dfrac{-1}{1-c}(\Delta T)$.

THE BALANCED BUDGET MULTIPLIER

Now let us suppose that the government decides to increase public spending and taxation by equal amounts, so that $\Delta G = \Delta T$. The combined multiplier effects of ΔG and ΔT are shown by:

$$(\text{xv}) \quad \Delta Y = \frac{1}{1-c} (\Delta G) + \frac{-c}{1-c} (\Delta T)$$

Since $\Delta G = \Delta T$, we can rewrite this as:

$$(\text{xvi}) \quad \Delta Y = \left(\frac{1}{1-c} + \frac{-c}{1-c} \right) \Delta G$$

$$\text{or } (\text{xvii}) \quad \Delta Y = \left(\frac{1-c}{1-c} \right) \Delta G$$

The expression $\dfrac{1-c}{1-c}$ is the **balanced budget multiplier**, which must be 1.

This means that an increase in public spending financed by an equal increase in taxation has an expansionary effect on the level of income exactly equal to the size of the injection of public spending. (If you find the algebra difficult, you can note from the previous section that when, for example, the MPC is 0.8, the government spending multiplier is 5, and the tax multiplier is -4. The balanced budget multiplier is simply the addition of the two multipliers; in this case $5+(-4)=1!$).

TAXATION AND IMPORT LEAKAGES

Up to this point in the analysis we have treated taxation and import demand in a highly artificial way. We have assumed that they are unrelated to the level of income, being determined instead exogenously outside our model. This is unrealistic, since a part at least of both taxation and import demand are likely to be dependent on the level of income. For the sake of simplicity, we shall now assume that all of taxation and import demand are income-induced, being determined endogenously within our model in the following ways:

(xviii) $T = tY$, where t is the **marginal rate of taxation**

and (xix) $M = mY$, where m is the **marginal propensity to import**.

We can write the equilibrium condition for the new version of our model as:

(xx) $Y = a + cY + \bar{I} + \bar{G} - tY + \bar{X} - mY$

In this particular model the multiplier is:

$$k = \frac{1}{1 - c + t + m}$$

or $$k = \frac{1}{s + t + m}$$

The three income-induced leakages of demand in the model all affect the value of the multiplier. The greater the propensity to import, and the higher the rate of taxation, the smaller will be the multiplier effect resulting from a change in any of the autonomous components of demand. There is no such thing as a *unique* formulation of the multiplier, relevant to all the possible models we could specify. In general terms, however, the government spending or investment multiplier will be:

$$k = \frac{1}{\text{marginal change in income-induced leakages}}$$

THE MULTIPLIER AND ECONOMIC POLICY

Keynesian demand management

In earlier chapters we briefly explained how Keynesians have advocated the use of discretionary fiscal policy to control or influence the level of aggregate demand in the economy. The greater the size of the government spending multiplier, the smaller the increase in public spending which is needed to bring about a desired increase in money national income. Similarly, the larger the tax multiplier, the smaller the tax cut which would be necessary. If the multipliers are large, and if most of the increase in money national income is in **real output** rather than in the **price level**, fiscal policy will be an effective way of controlling the economy.

But, as we have explained, the marginal propensity to import and high marginal tax rates reduce the size of the multiplier. The British economy is relatively small, compared for example with the USA, and open to trade. In recent years the propensity to import has noticeably increased. It is very doubtful whether the government spending multiplier is much higher than 1, and indeed, as we shall shortly explain, it may be less than 1.

Monetarism and 'crowding out'

We have also indicated that the multiplier effect resulting from an increase in government spending will be greatest when taxation remains unchanged. According to this logic a government should deliberately increase the size of the budget deficit if it wishes to maximise the expansionary effects of an increase in public spending. However, our analysis has ignored the monetary effects of the widening budget deficit. It is precisely upon these **monetary effects** of fiscal policy that monetarists concentrate attention, arguing:

❶ That increased borrowing to finance the budget deficit causes interest rates to rise. Higher interest rates reduce private investment, thereby countering the expansionary effects of the increase in public spending. The net size of the multiplier may even be zero if the increase in public spending 'crowds out' and displaces an equal amount of private spending. Indeed 'extreme' monetarists have gone further, arguing that fiscal multipliers can be negative in the long run if 'productive' private investment is crowded out by 'unproductive' public spending. It is worth noting that the 'crowding out' view of 'modern' monetarists is by no means new – it is essentially a revival of the old 'Treasury view' against which Keynes personally argued in the early 1930s.

❷ Insofar as a multiplier results from an increase in public spending financed by a budget deficit, the main effect may be on prices rather than on real income or output. Monetarists argue that expansionary fiscal policy will increase the rate of inflation if the budget deficit and PSBR are financed by methods which increase the money supply. Keynesians agree that fiscal stimulation can lead to inflation rather than an expansion of real output if the economy is at or near full capacity and full employment. The area of dispute between Keynesians and monetarists is whether the government spending multiplier will expand real output or prices when there is a considerable margin of spare capacity in the economy.

FISCAL POLICY MULTIPLIERS

We have already noted that the taxation multiplier is likely to be smaller than the government spending multiplier. However, there may also be variations in the nature of the multiplier depending on whether an increase in public spending is channelled into **public works** or **transfer incomes** and on whether changes in taxation involve direct or indirect taxation. In times of mass unemployment and gravely deficient demand, public works may be an effective fiscal policy instrument since:

• they can be directed to regions of especially high local unemployment;
• by providing lasting social capital, they can improve a region's economic infrastructure and create an environment attractive to private investment;
• the government is seen to be 'doing something about unemployment' – public works are likely to employ large numbers of manual workers;
• public works are not 'import intensive'; a large fraction of the initial injection of income is spent on the outputs of domestic industry, thereby increasing the size of the multiplier.

However, public works are not a very suitable policy instrument for the **discretionary management of demand** at or near the full employment level. Public works are slow to start, difficult to stop, and altogether difficult to 'fine-tune'. Discretionary tax changes may be more appropriate for controlling demand, except perhaps in conditions of very high unemployment. The multiplier effect of a tax change occurs through its impact on private sector consumption and investment. However, the size of the effect will be reduced if the propensity to import is high. As an alternative to both public works and tax cuts, a government can expand demand by increasing public spending in the form of transfer incomes paid to lower income groups, or even by redistributing the existing level of public spending through greater transfers. The transfer income multiplier tends to be larger than other fiscal multipliers because the poor have higher propensities to consume and lower propensities to import than the better-off. Nevertheless, it is not usually practicable to raise and lower the level of welfare benefits and unemployment pay as a part of discretionary demand management. Instead, transfer incomes such as income support, which form a state 'safety net' for the poor, act as an **automatic stabiliser** dampening or reducing the multiplier effects which result when 'outside shocks' hit the economy. As incomes fall, the increase in the total volume of transfer incomes paid to the unemployed and the poor reduces the total contraction in income and demand. Similarly, the 'means tested' nature of many transfer incomes and the progressive nature of income tax create an automatic stabiliser which reduces the multiple expansion that follows an injection of demand into the economy. As the economy approaches full employment, fewer people qualify for transfer incomes and the proportion of income paid in taxation increases. The volume of public spending falls while that of taxation rises.

Chapter roundup

The multiplier theory is very closely related to the concept of equilibrium national income examined in Chapter 19. In particular, you should refer to the discussion of deflationary gaps (in Chapter 19) and inflationary gaps (Chapter 22), which illustrate how the size of the multiplier determines the level of government spending needed to achieve equilibrium national income at the full employment level, without inflation. In Chapter 21 we now go on to contrast the accelerator principle with the multiplier, showing how the two concepts can be brought together in dynamic Keynesian models of economic growth and of the business cycle. In Chapter 24 we reintroduce the contrast between the Keynesian and monetarist views on the size and effectiveness of the government spending multiplier.

Illustrative questions and answers

1 Essay Question
a) Distinguish between discretionary and automatic fiscal policy. (30)
b) Examine the impact on the value of the multiplier of a reduction in the marginal rate of income tax. (70)

(ULEAC, AS level, June 1990)

Tutorial note

a) The difference between **discretionary** and **automatic** economic policy can be explained by using the analogy of flying an aeroplane. One possibility is for the pilot to fly the aircraft manually, making discrete decisions from second to second on the plane's height and speed, the best course to fly and on whether to avoid cloud etc. Alternatively he might set the aircraft's automatic pilot for the next three hundred miles, in which case the plane will fly on a set course at a pre-chosen height and speed. Discretionary fiscal policy resembles the first course of action, with tax rates and public spending decisions being the 'levers' or instruments which the government is prepared to change to meet new circumstances whenever deemed appropriate.

Discretionary fiscal policy is usually associated with Keynesian demand management of the economy. By contrast, monetarists and 'supply-side' economists have urged that governments abandon the use of discretionary macroeconomic policy and adopt instead automatic policy rules analogous to the aircraft flying a considerable distance on automatic pilot. In terms of fiscal policy, this has involved the announcement of medium-term targets for public spending and borrowing chosen to be consistent with the medium-term monetary targets upon which monetarists recommend that 'automatic' monetary policy should be based. Once the medium-term targets have been announced, then the theory is that the government should implement fiscal (and monetary) policy 'on automatic pilot' so as to 'hit' the targets. We may also identify a more 'microeconomic' element of such an 'automatic fiscal policy': centring on the announcement of a target rate of income tax (say 20%) which the government announces that it wishes to achieve so as to create 'supply-side' incentives in the economy.

b) A reduction of income tax rates would raise the value of the multiplier. Taking the formula for the multiplier as $\frac{1}{s+t+m}$, with s = 0.1, m = 0.4 and t = 0.4, then the value of multiplier would be $\frac{1}{0.9}$, or approximately 1.1. But if the marginal rate of income tax (t) were to be reduced to 0.2, the value of the multiplier would rise to $\frac{1}{0.7}$, or approximately 1.43. However it would be wrong to conclude that monetarist and supply-side economists believe that income tax rates should be cut in order to increase the size of the multiplier and hence to make discretionary fiscal policy more powerful. Instead as we have noted, they recommend tax cuts – not to boost demand 'Keynesian-style' – but as a part of a free-market orientated supply-side fiscal policy.

2   Data Question
Study the data below, then answer the questions which follow.
The following is data for a hypothetical closed economy which initially is in short-run macroeconomic equilibrium.

(i)   The consumption function is given by the equation
$$C = 100 + 0.8\ Y_D,$$
where C denotes consumption in £ billion and Y_D denotes disposable after-tax income in £ billion.

(ii) All government revenue is raised by a 25%, proportional income tax. Hence
$$Y_D = 0.75Y$$
where Y denotes national income in £ billion.

(iii) Private investment spending £1400 billion.

(iv) Government expenditure on goods and services = £2500 billion.

(v)   National income (Y) = £10 000 billion.

(a) What are the initial values of consumption, savings and government tax revenue?   (5)

(b) What is the relationship between the average propensity to consume and the marginal propensity to consume in this economy? How does the average propensity to consume vary as disposable income increases?   (5)

(c) Suppose that private investment spending subsequently decreases to £1000 billion. What, other things being equal, is the change in national income that is predicted by the Keynesian income-expenditure model?
                                                                                        (5)

(d) If government expenditure and the tax rate remain unchanged, what is the government budget deficit or surplus at the equilibrium level of national income **following** the decrease in private investment?   (5)

(e) Suppose the government wishes to achieve a return to the original national income of £1 000 billion via increasing after-tax disposable incomes by means of non-taxable cash benefits paid to households. If the consumption function is unchanged, by how much must government expenditure on cash benefits increase?   (5)

(WJEC, June 1988)

Tutorial note

We have not explained in the main body of the chapter precisely how the multiplier formula is derived from the equilibrium condition for national income, except to say that

$$k = \frac{1}{\text{marginal change in income-induced leakages}}$$

We shall now take the opportunity provided by this question to show in detail how the multiplier formula is derived in any particular national income model.

Representing the marginal propensity to consume out of disposable income as c, the marginal rate of income tax as t, and autonomous consumption as a, the equilibrium equation for this model is:

(i) $Y = c(Y - tY) + a + \bar{I} + \bar{G}$

or (ii) $Y = cY - ctY + a + \bar{I} + \bar{G}$

If we collect all the Y terms on the left-hand side of the equation, we get:

(iii) $Y - cY + ctY = a + \bar{I} + \bar{G}$

or (iv) $Y(1 - c + ct) = a + \bar{I} + \bar{G}$

Dividing both sides of the equation by the expression, we get:

(v) $Y = \dfrac{1}{1 - c + ct}(a + \bar{I} + \bar{G})$

The expression $\dfrac{1}{1 - c + ct}$ is the multiplier in this particular model.

Since c is the marginal propensity to consume, the multiplier can also be expressed as: $\dfrac{1}{s + ct}$, where s is the marginal propensity to save. This is the multiplier formula for an economy on which decisions to consume and save are made out of post-tax disposable income. If we extend the model by introducing the overseas sector; with the import equation being $M = mY$, the multiplier would become $\dfrac{1}{s + ct + m}$. If, in contrast, consumption and savings decisions were made out of pre-tax income, the multiplier would be $\dfrac{1}{s + t + m}$. (We introduced this multiplier earlier in the unit.) Since the MPC (c) is less than one, the value of ct must be less than the value of t. Hence the multiplier is larger when consumption decisions are made out of post-tax income because the leakages of demand are smaller.

(a) $C = £100$ bn $+ 0.8$ ($£7500$ bn)
   $S = £10\ 000$ bn $- C$
   $T = 0.25$ ($£10\ 000$ bn)

(b)   The marginal propensity to consume is constant at $0.8Y_D$ at all levels of income. APC > MPC at all levels of income. The average propensity to consume falls as income rises, being greater than unity at low levels of income and falling through unity at the level of income at which $C = Y_D$. As income rises, the APC falls towards $0.8Y_D$, but always remains above $0.8Y_D$.

(c)   This part of the question tests the multiplier:

$$\Delta Y = \frac{1}{s + ct}(\Delta \bar{I})$$

(d)   The government's budgetary position is $(\bar{G} - tY)$. Calculate whether the budget is in surplus or deficit at the initial equilibrium level of national income, and at the subsequently lower level of income following the fall in investment.

(e)   Since the formula for the government spending multiplier is the same as for the investment multiplier, an increase of government spending or cash benefits of the same size as the decrease in investment will have the desired effect.

Question bank

1
(a) Briefly explain the meaning of the multiplier.   (20)
(b) Examine the likely multiplier effects in the South East of England resulting from the building of the Channel Tunnel.   (80)

(ULEAC, June 1990)

2   In a closed economy without government sector the multiplier is 5. In the UK it is estimated to be 1.3. Explain the multiplier process and suggest reasons why the two values quoted are so different. (Cambridge AS, June 1992)

3
(a) Examine the factors which influence the size of the national income multiplier.   (40)
(b) Distinguish between the different multiplier effects of:
    (i)   an increase in social security payments;   (30)
    (ii) a cut in the top rate of income tax.   (30)

(ULEAC, January 1992)

4
(a) What do you understand by the term 'recession'?   (20)
(b) Analyse the policies which a government could use to lift the economy out of recession.   (80)

(ULEAC, June 1992)

5   Assume an initial situation where there are unemployed resources and a balanced budget (i.e. government tax revenues are equal to its expenditure).
(a) Explain why, other things being equal, an increase in government expenditure on goods and services of £1 billion might be expected to raise national income by an amount greater than £1 billion.   (15)
(b) Given the present UK tax system, explain why an increase in government expenditure of £1 billion, with no change in tax rates, could increase the budget deficit by less than £1 billion, once the higher income level was achieved.   (5)
(c) Suppose the government increased both its spending and its tax rates to keep its budget balanced. Why could this result in an increase in national income?   (5)

(WJEC, June 1992)

6
(a) Outline the multiplier process.   (8)
(b) In economy A, the size of the multiplier is 4; in economy B it is 2.
    (i)   What factors might explain this difference?   (6)
    (ii) Comment on the policy implications of this difference.   (6)

(Cambridge AS-Level, June 1992)

7
(a) Distinguish between discretionary and automatic fiscal policy.   (30)
(b) Examine the impact on the value of the multiplier of a reduction in the marginal rate of income tax.   (70)

(ULEAC AS-Level, June 1990)

CHAPTER 21

INVESTMENT

Units in this chapter

21.1   *Underlying concepts*
21.2   *Essential information*

Chapter objectives

In developing the simple Keynesian model of Chapters 19 and 20, we assumed that the level of planned or intended investment demand in the economy is autonomous or independent of the level of income or output currently being produced. Since this is obviously a gross oversimplification, we shall devote most of this chapter to an explanation and brief comparison of a number of theories of investment. Economists generally agree that investment decisions are made by businessmen for a variety of different reasons. Consequently there is no 'correct' investment theory; instead, each theory may explain a different and relevant aspect of how investment decisions are made. However, our general conclusion will be that a large part of investment is indeed autonomous of the level of income, being determined by factors such as the cost of borrowing (the rate of interest), **expectations about future profitability**, the **relative prices of capital and labour**, and **the nature of technical progress**. Nevertheless, a certain part of investment may indeed be related to the level of income, and more particularly to the rate of change of income, via the **acceleration principle**.

21.1 UNDERLYING CONCEPTS

THE DIFFERENT TYPES OF INVESTMENT

We have explained in Chapter 11 how economists distinguish between **saving** and **investment**. Investment involves the demand for, and expenditure on, capital goods capable of producing more income and wealth in the future. Domestic investment includes the purchase of new capital equipment and buildings – the **fixed capital formation** of Chapter 18 – and also the accumulation in the form of **stockbuilding** of **increased stocks of raw materials, work-in-progress** and **finished goods**. Whilst the purchase of financial claims such as shares or debentures are not in themselves regarded as a part of domestic investment, the acquisition of paper claims on other countries is an important part of **overseas investment**, additional to the direct purchase of physical assets overseas. To the extent that they are not offset by counter-claims held by foreigners, increased holdings of foreign currencies and foreign customers' trade debts to British exporters represent a net increase in the nation's total assets.

A large part of the investment which adds to the nation's capital stock is public or **social investment** in such assets as roads, hospitals and schools. House-building can also be an important part of investment. If expenditure on new dwellings is included in investment, why not include the purchase of other consumer durables such as televisions and cars? Logically, there is no reason why they should be excluded, since they can be regarded as capital assets yielding a service to their owners. The exclusion of consumer durables is therefore an important omission from the official estimates of investment.

INVESTMENT AND SIMPLE KEYNESIAN MODEL

In the context of our simple Keynesian income/expenditure model of the economy, 'I' represents the ex ante net investment demand of the private sector. It is worth noting that:

❶ Total or **gross investment** is much larger than **net investment** since it includes capital consumption or depreciation. Indeed over half of the gross investment in the UK economy is replacement investment which makes good capital consumption. Net investment adds to the nation's capital stock, thereby enabling economic growth to occur by creating the potential to produce a bigger output in future years.

❷ The investment function I shows the **planned** or **intended** investment decisions at each level of income of all the private sector business enter-prises in the economy. However, ex ante or planned investment will not always equal ex post or realised investment. Chapter 19 explained how unintended stock accumulation (or unplanned investment) occurs when the actual output produced in the economy is greater than intended expendi-ture or AMD. Ex ante investment only equals ex post investment at the equilibrium level of national income or output!

❸ The investment function is usually taken to include only the intended net investment of the private sector. A significant part of total investment, both gross and net, is public investment undertaken by the government and other public authorities such as nationalised industries. However, since 1979, spending cuts, together with the privatization of many of the for-merly nationalised industries have led to a decline in public investment as a proportion of the total. An increase in public investment, for example in public works such as road construction, is usually represented by a change in government spending, G, in the Keynesian model, though investment by nationalised industries can be included along with private investment in the investment function I. However, the statistics indicate that total fixed investment in the economy is strongly influenced by government policy and factors which influence the housing market. The kind of investment decision upon which we shall now concentrate attention – that of a private sector firm considering whether to purchase extra plant or machinery – is not nearly so typical as it is often considered to be.

21.2 ESSENTIAL INFORMATION

THE MICROECONOMIC THEORY OF INVESTMENT

Distribution theory revisited

Just as the **aggregate consumption function** of Chapter 19 is built up from the microeconomic theory of how individual utility-maximising households choose to divide their income between consumption and saving, so the **investment function** is similarly obtained by aggregating all the individual investment decisions of profit-maximising business enterprises. We start from where we left off in Chapter 13 (on distribution theory) by stating that, in perfectly competitive markets, a profit-maximising businessman or decision-maker will employ each factor of production, including capital, up to the point where the value of its marginal product equals the marginal cost of employing the last unit of the factor. According to this theory the demand for capital, and hence the level of investment, depends on the **marginal productivity of capital** and the **rate of interest**. Other things being equal, the lower the rate of interest, the greater both the demand for capital and the level of investment. The declining marginal productivity of capital means that extra capital is not worth employing unless the rate of interest falls. If technology allows a firm to substitute one factor of production for another, then changes in the relative prices of factors of production will influence how a firm produces its desired level of output. For example, a rise in the price of labour relative to the rate of interest will create an incentive for firms to employ more capital-intensive methods of production, thereby increasing the demand for capital and the level of investment.

It is likely, however, that the ability of a firm to switch between the employment of capital and labour is limited, at least in the short run. We may be justified in assuming the existence of a technologically determined **capital output ratio** which indicates the amount of capital needed to increase output by one unit. If, for example, the capital output ratio is 3, then when a firm's existing capital is fully utilised, an investment of £3 is required in order to increase output by £1 in each future year (assuming constant prices).

Discounting the future

Nevertheless, a businessman's demand for capital goods is rather different from his demand for labour. It is insufficient to state that a profit-maximising firm will invest up to the point where the **current** marginal product of capital equals the rate of interest. We must modify the businessman's decision rule to take account of the fact that most of the returns on a new investment are future returns, which are produced over the useful economic life of the investment. In general terms, we can state that a profit-maximising businessman will invest in a new capital asset if:

$$\left. \begin{array}{l} \text{the rate of return per cent} \\ \text{per period he expects over} \\ \text{the life of the capital assets} \end{array} \right\} > \left\{ \begin{array}{l} \text{the rate of interest per cent} \\ \text{per period that must be paid} \\ \text{for borrowed funds to finance} \\ \text{the investment} \end{array} \right.$$

Although our businessman may know the current cost of the investment and the rate of interest, he cannot know with complete certainty either the length of the asset's useful economic life or the details of the net returns or income stream which will be produced in each year of that life. Instead, he must forecast them, knowing that an asset's useful economic life may be much shorter than its technical life. The development of new technology or changes in input prices may render a machine productively inefficient long before it actually wears out. Likewise, an estimate of a machine's future net return or income stream is fraught with uncertainty: not only must the physical product or output of the machine be calculated for each year of its expected life, so also must the prices at which the output is sold, and the amounts and prices of other inputs such as raw materials and labour.

Assuming that estimates have been made of all these variables, and that the net returns have been calculated for each year of the asset's expected life, we can restate the firm's investment decision rule as:

$$\left. \begin{array}{l} \text{invest in all projects for which the} \\ \textbf{discounted present value} \text{ of the} \\ \text{stream of prospective returns} \end{array} \right\} > \left\{ \begin{array}{l} \text{the known cost of} \\ \text{capital asset} \end{array} \right.$$

This is the basis of the **discounted cash flow (DCF)** technique of investment appraisal. If a firm is to maximise the profits resulting from an investment, the year in which the profits or net returns are received is crucial, since £1000 received this year is worth more than the same amount received next year (again assuming constant prices). Income received this year can be reinvested (or lent at the current rate of interest) so as to be worth more by next year. Money received next year must be equal to that received this year plus the rate of interest if the incomes received in each of the two years are to be of equal value. It follows that income received earlier in the life of an investment is worth more than similar income received later.

The DCF method of investment appraisal 'picks up' information about both the shape of a project's expected income stream (or cash flow), and the rate of interest. Estimate of profits in each of the years of the expected life of an investment project are expressed in terms of their value in the year of the investment – known as the **present value (PV)**. The businessman or decision-maker chooses an appropriate rate of discount which reflects the rate of interest that would be paid to borrow the funds which finance the cost of the project. If the PV of the expected future income stream is greater than the cost of the investment, the firm can expect to 'do better' by investing in its own capital project rather than by lending out the equivalent funds to earn the going rate of interest. Quite clearly, the higher the rate of interest, the higher the appropriate test discount rate. An investment project judged as just worthwhile when tested against an 8% discount rate would fail a 10% test.

Regardless of the complexities introduced by the DCF principle and the problems of anticipating the future, the general conclusion reached is the same as that suggested by simple marginal productivity theory: that a firm's demand for investment funds is inversely related to the rate of interest. At higher rates of interest, fewer projects are worthwhile to a profit-maximising firm. However, as we shall shortly see, the introduction of the role of uncertainty about the future into the determination of investment decisions takes on a special significance in the Keynesian macroeconomic theory of investment.

THE LOANABLE FUNDS THEORY

The pre-Keynesian theory of the determination of the aggregate level of investment in the economy is based in part on the marginal productivity theory of individual investment decisions which we described earlier in this chapter. This is represented by the investment function I in Fig. 51, which is drawn as a downward-sloping curve showing that the demand for investment funds (or loanable funds as they were known in this theory) is greater at lower rates of interest. We introduced the other part of the loanable funds theory in Chapter 19 in describing the 'classical' theory of savings as a function of the rate of interest. The curve, S in Fig. 51, shows that the supply of loanable funds or savings is greater at higher rates of interest. Thus, in the loanable funds theory, the aggregate levels of both investment and saving are determined by the rate of interest. As in any market, the market price (the rate of interest) tends to rise or fall to bring about an equilibrium which clears the market. In Fig. 51, planned investment equals planned saving at the equilibrium interest rate, r*. You should note also that the loanable funds theory is a theory of the determination of the rate of interest in the goods market of the economy. This contrasts with the Keynesian theory of

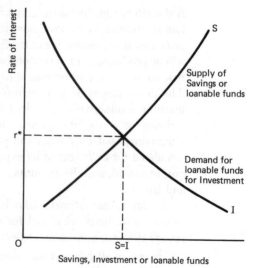

Fig. 51 The 'Classical' loanable funds theory

the rate of interest, which we explained in Chapter 14. In the Keynesian theory, the rate of interest is treated as a purely monetary phenomenon, whose value is determined in the money market.

THE KEYNESIAN MARGINAL EFFICIENCY OF CAPITAL THEORY

The 'classical' loanable funds theory has largely been discredited and replaced by Keynes's own theory of investment, the **marginal efficiency of capital (MEC)** theory (also known as the **marginal efficiency of investment theory**). We saw in Chapter 19 how Keynes rejected the 'classical' view that the aggregate level of savings is largely determined by the rate of interest. (Note, however, that the rate of interest may still be important in directing savings between competing financial intermediaries such as banks and building societies, even though in the Keynesian theory it is the level of income that determines aggregate saving.) The rejection of the 'classical' savings function is insufficient in itself to destroy the loanable funds theory, since it merely leads to the conclusion that the savings function is vertical or 'interest-inelastic'. Of much more significance in our present context is the Keynesian view that the rate of interest is determined in the money market (see Chapter 14), being taken as given or exogenous by businessmen contemplating investment decisions.

It is worth noting, however, that there is one part of the loanable funds theory that Keynes did not completely reject: the investment function which is inversely related to the rate of interest. But while the pre-Keynesian investment function was stated in terms of the **current** marginal productivity of capital, Keynes incorporated into the theory the view we have already explained, that businessmen base investment decisions on their expectations of the **future** income stream resulting from each investment. Since the marginal efficiency of capital, which is the Keynesian investment function, is very closely related to the discounted cash flow technique of investment appraisal, we shall compare the two:

❶ **A second look at DCF** Suppose that a businessman is contemplating investing in a machine costing £1000, with an expected life of three years and no scrap value or disposal costs at the end of this life. Using the DCF method of investment appraisal, he can write the present value of the stream of prospective returns over the three years as:

(i) $PV = \dfrac{Q_1}{1 + r} + \dfrac{Q_2}{(1 + r)^2} + \dfrac{Q_3}{(1 + r)^3}$

where $Q_1 \ldots Q_3$ are the returns expected in each year and r is the *known* rate of interest or discount. As we previously explained, the investment is worthwhile if the PV exceeds the initial cost of the investment.

❷ **MEC** Alternatively, we can rewrite formula (i) so as to calculate directly the rate of return which the businessman expects to obtain by purchasing the asset. We simply replace the unknown PV of formula (i) by the known cost of the asset, £1000. The unknown is now the rate of return which we shall call i:

(ii) $\dfrac{\text{asset's cost}}{(£1000)} = \dfrac{Q_1}{1 + i} + \dfrac{Q_2}{(1 + i)^2} + \dfrac{Q_3}{(1 + i)^3}$

Solving formula (ii) for i, we obtain the rate of return which makes the present value of the expected income stream exactly equal its initial cost. The rate of return, i, is the **marginal efficiency** of the capital asset, also known as the **internal rate of return**.

If the MEC is calculated for each and every possible capital project available to all the business enterprises in the economy, we can rank the projects in descending order. With the rate of interest, r, assumed to be exogenously determined in the money market, the aggregate level of investment in the economy is now itself determined where:

the marginal efficiency of capital = the rate of interest

or   i = r

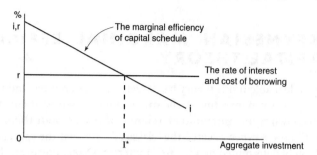

Fig. 52 The Marginal Efficiency of Capital Theory of Investment. The aggregate level of Investment is determined at I* where the marginal efficiency of capital (i) equals the co borrowing or rate of interest (r)

THE MARGINAL EFFICIENCY OF CAPITAL AND MONETARY POLICY

The greater the **interest elasticity** of the investment function (or the MEC curve), then the greater also the effectiveness of monetary policy in influencing the level of aggregate demand. By reducing interest rates, an increase in the money supply can induce businessmen to engage in investment projects they would not consider worthwhile at higher interest rates. Conversely, a decrease in the money supply will reduce investment.

The interest elasticity of the investment function is also important when considering whether the economic system contains the 'self-righting' property automatically to achieve an equilibrium level of national income at the full employment level. According to the 'classical' or pre-Keynesian view, falling interest rates in a depressed economy will create the incentive for businessmen to increase investment, thereby also increasing the level of aggregate demand in the economy. This effect will be greatest if investment is highly interest elastic.

THE IMPORTANCE OF EXPECTATIONS AND UNCERTAINTY

Keynes doubted the interest elasticity of investment and he also believed that there was a lower limit (called the Liquidity Trap) below which the interest rate would not fall even in a depressed economy. However, even if the rate of interest is able to fall to a very low level and investment in its turn is responsive to the rate of interest, the MEC theory provided Keynes with a further very powerful explanation of why investment could collapse in a depressed economy. The position of the MEC curve depends on the state of businessmen's expectations about the future – or their 'animal spirits', in Keynes's colourful language. In a severe depression, business confidence is likely to be very low, causing a collapse of investment. The investment function or MEC curve shifts inwards, resulting in a situation in which little investment takes place even at very low interest rates. Indeed, given Keynes's belief that the consumption function is essentially stable, he needed a theory of an unstable investment function in order to explain how, in conditions of unregulated market forces, a collapse of investment could deepen a depression.

THE ACCELERATION PRINCIPLE

Thus, in the Keynesian view, **expectations** and the state of **business confidence** are more important determinants of investment than the rate of interest, and the level of investment is determined largely autonomously of the current level of income. Nevertheless, a part at least of net investment may be related to the rate of change of income or output, via the **acceleration principle**.

We have already mentioned in an earlier section how two motives exist for firms to invest in more capital equipment: firstly, when wages rise relative to the cost of capital, and secondly, when technology changes in such a way as to require larger quantities of capital than before – resulting in a larger capital output ratio. Assuming now that both the relative prices of capital and labour and the capital output ratio are fixed, a third motive for investment exists when firms believe that aggregate demand is increasing or will soon do so. In order to produce the extra output which they will now be able to sell, firms will need to invest in additional fixed capital, provided of course that an increase in sales is consistent with profit maximisation. This is the basis of the accelerator theory of investment, in which it is assumed that firms try to keep to an optimal relationship between the amount of capital they possess and the volume of output. We can illustrate the acceleration principle by means of a numerical example:

Table 21.1 The acceleration principle

		Yearly sales	Existing capital	Desired capital	Replacement investment	Net investment	Gross investment
1st period							
Steady sales	year 1	£2000	£8000	£8000	£800	0	£800
	year 2	2000	8000	8000	800	0	800
2nd Period							
Rising sales	year 3	2200	8000	8800	800	800	1600
	year 4	2400	8800	9600	800	800	1600
	year 5	2800	9600	11200	800	1600	2400
3rd Period							
Levelling off	year 6	3000	11200	12000	800	800	1600
	year 7	3000	12000	12000	800	0	800
4th Period							
Falling sales	year 8	2800	12000	11200	0	0	0
5th Period							
Levelling off	year 9	2700	11200	10800	400	0	800
	year 10	2700	10800	10800	800	0	800

We shall suppose that a firm initially sells an output of £2000 and that, because demand is unchanged, the output is stable from year to year. We shall further assume:
- a fixed capital output ratio of 4:1, which means that £4 of capital is required to produce £1 of output per year;
- the firm's capital has a life of ten years, after which it needs replacing;
- initially the firm possesses £8000 of capital which is exactly enough to produce its yearly output; and
- the initial capital has been built up evenly over the years, so that 10 per cent of it needs replacing each year.

In the first period of Table 21.1 the demand for the firm's output remains stable. The firm has no need for additional capital so net investment is zero. Gross investment is solely replacement investment or depreciation of £800.

In Period 2, however, demand for the firm's output starts to grow. In year 3 when sales increase by £200, the firm needs additional capital of £800. A 10 per cent increase in demand or sales has had an accelerated effect upon investment: gross investment has increased by 100%! In year 4 when sales increase by the same absolute amount of £200, investment remains constant, but in year 5 there is once again an accelerated effect on investment when the rate of growth of sales again increases.

In the third period the rate of growth of sales slows down in year 6 and levels off completely in year 7. Note that investment declines in year 6 even though sales are still growing. Investment can decline without an actual decline in sales; all that is required is for the growth rate of sales or demand to slow down! In year 7 there is no need for any additional capital so net investment again is zero and gross investment equals replacement investment.

In the fourth period, when the level of sales absolutely declines, the firm will actually need less capital. Consequently, part of the capital which is wearing out need not be replaced and gross investment falls to zero in year 8.

Finally, in Period 5, we see a symmetrical effect to that observed in Period 3: in year 9 when sales continue to fall but the rate of decline in sales slows down, gross investment begins to recover. The firm must replace part at least of the capital which is wearing out if it is to meet demand, while in year 10, when capital is once again just sufficient to meet demand, replacement investment is back at its initial level of £800.

Thus the acceleration principle provides a second explanation (the first being the role of expectations and the state of business confidence) for the observed great instability of investment. In our numerical example, net investment depends upon the change in consumption (and indirectly, via the propensity to consume, upon the change in income), but investment fluctuates by a much greater percentage than consumption. The five periods of our example broadly represent phases in the upswing and downswing of the business cycle. Consumption rises in the upswing of the cycle, but it must grow steadily if investment is to remain constant. However, it may be impossible to sustain a rapid growth of sales, and once the rate of growth declines, investment will begin to fall. In this way, the growth of consumption demand in the upswing of the business cycle creates the conditions for a subsequent collapse in investment and the beginning of the downswing.

CRITICISMS OF THE ACCELERATOR THEORY

❶ It is too mechanical. It assumes that all firms react to increases in demand in the same way. Some firms may wait to see if the higher level of demand is maintained, whilst others may order more machinery and plant than is immediately required.

❷ If firms already possess excess capacity left over from a previous boom in demand, they can simply utilise their spare capacity to increase output without the need to invest in any additional fixed capital.

❸ An increase in demand may occur at a time when the capital goods industries are themselves at full capacity and unable to meet a higher level of investment demand. In these circumstances, a rise in the relative price of capital goods may encourage firms to economise on capital and to employ more labour, and it may also lead to technical innovation which reduces the capital output ratio.

Chapter roundup

Our emphasis in this chapter has been on explaining investment as one of the components of aggregate demand in the simple Keynesian model of the economy (Chapter 19 and 20). Essentially, we have concentrated on investment as expenditure on new goods. However, there is another side to investment in its later effects on the supply of output, and as the engine of economic growth. In Chapter 10 on the size and growth of firms and Chapter 11 on the capital market we examined how firms finance investment, while much of the basic theory of investment stems from the principle of diminishing marginal productivity, which is discussed in Chapter 13.

Illustrative questions and answers

1   Essay Question
Discuss the economic relationship between consumption, income and investment.
(AEB, June 1990)

Tutorial note

This question provides an opportunity to revise some of the most important relationships in the simple Keynesian model of Chapters 19 and 20, and also to indicate briefly how the introduction of the acceleration principle can extend the model:

(i)   **A revision of earlier concepts**

    (a)   We saw in our discussion of the Keynesian consumption function in Unit 19 that we may write the consumption function as

$$C = a + cY$$

    An increase in autonomous consumption (a) will have a **multiplier effect** on the equilibrium level of income.

    (b)   However, a part of consumption is directly related to the level of income via the **marginal propensity to consume** (c). Thus an autonomous increase in consumption results in an increase in income (via the multiplier), which in turn causes an increase in income-related consumption (via the MPC).

    (c)   An autonomous increase in investment will also have a multiplier effect upon income, which again induces a change in consumption.

(ii)   **Multiplier/accelerator interrelationships** In the simple Keynesian model of the economy in Chapters 19 and 20 we **compared static equilibria**, noting the **multiplier effects** in the move from one equilibrium level of income to another. We ignored the possibility of subsequent **accelerator effects** resulting from the changes in income induced by the multiplier. When the acceleration principle is incorporated, the Keynesian model is converted from a simple comparison of equilibrium levels of income into a **dynamic model** of the economy showing how income, expenditure, and output continuously change through time. If k represents the multiplier, and v the capital output ratio (or accelerator), we can portray the dynamic movement of the economy through time as:

$$\underbrace{\Delta I \rightarrow k \rightarrow}_{\substack{\text{multiplier} \\ \text{effect}}} \quad \underbrace{\Delta Y \rightarrow v \rightarrow}_{\substack{\text{accelerator} \\ \text{effect}}} \quad \underbrace{\Delta I \rightarrow k \rightarrow}_{\substack{\text{multiplier} \\ \text{effect}}} \quad \Delta Y \ldots \text{etc}$$

Depending on the values of the multiplier, k, and the accelerator, v, such dynamic Keynesian models of the economy can be used to model **economic growth**, and the cyclical fluctuations around the growth path – the **business cycle**.

Suggested answer

1   Briefly explain the multiplier and show how income changes in response to an autonomous change in either C or I.

2   Show how the level of C will then change via the MPC.

3   Introduce the accelerator effect on I resulting from the changes in Y and C.

4   Suggest that a continuing interaction between the multiplier and the accelerator can take place.

2   Data Question

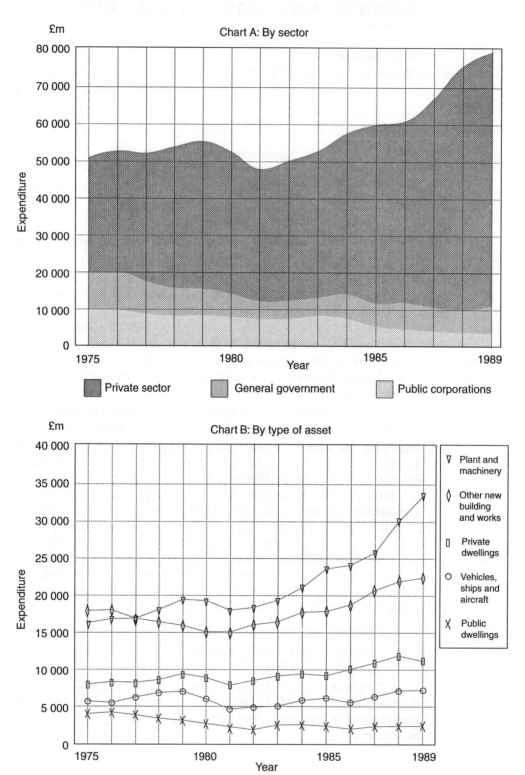

Gross fixed capital formation in the UK (at constant 1985 prices)

The charts show details of gross fixed capital formation in the UK when measured at constant 1985 prices.

(a) What is meant by 'gross fixed capital formation at constant 1985 prices'?

(3)

(b) Why do the figures shown overstate the actual addition to the capital stock?

(2)

(c) How do you account for the changing balance between private and public expenditure shown in Chart A? (4 marks)

(d) Analyse possible reasons for:

    (i) the decline in expenditure on all types of asset between 1979 and 1980:

    (ii) the expansion in expenditure on most types of asset between 1984 and 1989. (6)

(e) Between 1989 and 1991 the UK economy went into recession. Examine the likely economic consequences of the recession on capital expenditure and the Retail Price Index. (5)

(ULEAC, January 1992)

Tutorial note

a) Gross domestic fixed capital formation is the official term or jargon used in the National Income Accounts for total investment undertaken by both the private and the public sectors in the economy, in fixed capital such as plant and machinery, and before allowing for depreciation or 'wear and tear' in the existing capital stock. It has been measured at 'constant prices' so that the figures can be compared for more than one year without being distorted by inflation.

b) As we have just indicated, the 'gross' figures do not allow for depreciation or capital consumption.

c) Private sector investment grew over the period shown by the data, whereas public sector investment fell. This was true during the period 1975 to 1979 when a Labour government was in office as well as from 1979 onwards when the Conservatives had been returned to power, so the trend cannot be explained solely in terms of the 'anti-public sector' policies pursued by Mrs Thatcher's administrations in the 1980s. In effect from 1976 onwards and under pressure from the IMF, the Labour Government had been forced to implement what has been called 'monetarily constrained Keynesian' policies which involved cutting public spending. After 1979, the Conservative Government continued to implement monetarist policies which involved cutting public sector spending. The privatisation policies pursued by the Conservatives, which shifted public corporations such as BT into the private sector as PLCs and contracted out the provision of services to the private sector, also contributed to the continued fall in public sector investment. Note that private sector investment also fell in the deep recession at the beginning of the 1980s, but recovered during the boom years of the rest of the decade. A continuation of the data into the 1990s would show another steep fall in private sector investment when recession returned in 1990.

d) (i) and (ii) Your answer to this part of the question involves developing the point we have just made, namely the relationship between investment and the business cycle. You must also make use of the information in Chart B which shows the change in investment expenditure on different types of asset such as machinery and vehicles. To earn the full 6 marks you need some theoretical explanation, for example in terms of the accelerator theory and the role of business confidence in affecting investment.

e) Use the accelerator principle to explain that a slowing down in the rate of growth of output can induce an absolute fall in investment or the demand for new capital goods. Of course the recession of the early 1990s involved an absolute fall in output rather than a mere slowing down, leading to an even more severe fall in investment as firms cancelled or postponed investment projects, or even went bankrupt. You might also suggest that a collapse of confidence, illustrated for example by gloomy CBI surveys of business intentions, shifted the MEC function leftwards.

Question bank

1

(a) Describe what is meant by the marginal efficiency of capital schedule. (6)

(b) Consider the consequences of shifts in the marginal efficiency of capital schedule. (12)

(c) Why did Keynes assert that such shifts are likely to occur in practice between different periods of time? (7)

(WJEC, June 1988)

2 Define technical progress and outline the forms it can take. Analyse the possible economic effects of rapid technical change upon the British economy. (NEAB, June 1980)

3

(a) Why is it asserted that the behaviour of investment spending in an economy is a critical determinant of the level of unemployment? (13)

(b) What factors are likely to affect the size of the change in income and employment in response to an initial change in investment? (6)

(c) Why might a change in investment spending be caused by a prior change in either the money supply or the demand for money? (6)

(WJEC, June 1991)

4

(a) What do economists mean by the consumption function? What can cause a movement along the function and what can lead to a shift of the function? (8)

(b) Explain what is meant by investment and discuss the main determinants of investment. Carefully distinguish between autonomous investment (which is an exogenous variable in a simple income determination model) and induced investment (which is an endogenous variable). (10)

(c) Outline how an increase in the level of autonomous investment can raise the equilibrium level of national income in a closed economy with no government sector. What is the relevance of the marginal propensity to consume in this analysis? (7)

(NISEAC, June 1990)

5

(a) Distinguish between gross investment, net investment and depreciation. (20)

(b) Explain the factors which affect the level of investment in the private sector of the economy. (80)

(ULEAC, January 1991)

UNEMPLOYMENT
AND INFLATION

Units in this chapter

22.1   *Underlying concepts*
22.2   *Essential information*

Chapter objectives

In this chapter we introduce important theories which attempt to explain the twin economic evils of **unemployment** and **inflation**, and we also examine some suggested policy solutions. Firstly, however, we shall take a general look at the very different approaches adopted by some of the major schools of economic thought to these two problems.

THE NEOCLASSICAL VIEW

The neoclassical economists who preceded Keynes (and whom Keynes rather confusingly labelled as 'classical') regarded the **level of employment** as being determined by the **'real forces' of supply and demand** in one large competitive labour market, whilst the **quantity of money** determined the **price level**. They accepted that there would always be a certain amount of **frictional** and **structural unemployment** – these are terms we shall define later – but believed that, provided real and money wages were flexible, in a competitive economy market forces would always tend to bring a out a long-run equilibrium at a minimum level of unemployment. (We shall later explain how, in recent years, **monetarists** have labelled this the **natural rate of unemployment**.)

The **neoclassical theory of aggregate employment** originates in the **microeconomic theory of the diminishing marginal productivity of labour**. We saw in Chapter 13 how in competitive labour markets a firm's equilibrium employment of labour is determined where the marginal product of labour equals the real wage. In conditions of diminishing marginal returns, firms will only employ additional workers voluntarily if there is a fall in the real wage. If markets are sufficiently competitive, the excess supply of labour will cause the real wage to fall until unemployment is eliminated. The pre-Keynesians explained persistent mass unemployment in terms of uncompetitive forces such as trade unions which prevent wages from falling. In this sense they viewed such unemployment as essentially **voluntary**. The workforce as a whole is to blame for the unemployment of some of its members, not because they are workshy, but because of the refusal of those workers in employment to accept lower real wages.

For the neoclassicals, the determination of the price level was completely separate from the determination of the level of employment. While the 'real forces' of supply and demand determine levels of output and employment and the equilibrium values of relative prices, **monetary forces** determine the **price level** (via the **quantity theory of money** which we shall shortly explain). Thus if the quantity of money doubles, relative prices and levels of output and employment remain the same, but all prices double.

THE KEYNESIAN VIEW

Keynesians reject the older view that 'real' and 'monetary' forces are separate. Money provides a vital link between the markets of the real economy, and when this link breaks down, unemployment can result. Keynesians place great emphasis on the **store of value function of money**, arguing that demand-deficient unemployment can result when money incomes are stored in idle holdings of money rather than spent (Chapter 14). In contrast, the pre-Keynesians had never seriously entertained the possibility of such a lack of aggregate effective demand, accepting instead **Say's Law** that '**supply creates its own demand**'. Keynes actually reversed Say's Law: instead of 'supply creating its own demand', Keynesian theory is based on the idea that '**demand creates its own supply**'.

Keynes also claimed that the neoclassical theory of employment is guilty of the fallacy of composition. What is true for a single firm or market is not necessarily true for the economy taken as a whole. If the money wage paid by one firm falls, it will indeed be prepared to employ more workers, but if all money wages fall by the same proportion it does not follow that, collectively, all employers will employ more labour. Consider two possibilities. In the first place, prices of goods may fall as much as money wages. If all money wages and prices fall by the same proportion, the real wage will remain the same. Secondly, if prices fall by less than the money wage, the real wage will indeed fall, but a general fall in real incomes may reduce aggregate demand. If unemployment is already being caused by too little demand, a wagecut policy may cut demand still further. Keynes argued that, far from curing mass unemployment, a wagecut policy could make matters worse!

Keynes also rejected the quantity theory of money, the cornerstone of the pre-Keynesian (and the monetarist) theory of inflation. We shall explain shortly why the Keynesians reject this theory, and how Keynes adapted his theory of mass unemployment caused by deflation and deficient demand to the conditions of inflation and excess demand in the fully employed economy of World War II.

THE MONETARIST VIEW

In many ways monetarism, or the '**New Classical Macroeconomics**' as some versions of monetarism are now known, is simply a revival of the old pre-Keynesian economics. Keynes had written the *General Theory* in order to construct what he thought was a better and more general explanation than that provided by neoclassical theory of the outstanding problem on the agenda in his day: deflation or mass unemployment. Keynesian economics 'ruled' as long as its policy prescriptions ensured relative full employment, growth and price stability, although monetarist critics of Keynesianism now argue that full employment was *coincidental with*, and not *caused by*, Keynesian economic management. When, from the late 1960s onward, there was a simultaneous failure to achieve these objectives in the British economy, Keynesianism became vulnerable to attack from, amongst others, a revival of the 'old economics'. Monetarism essentially accepts the old 'Classical Dichotomy' that the real and monetary economy are separate; the real forces of supply and demand determine 'real things' – output, employment and relative prices – whilst money, a veil behind which the real economy operates, determines 'money things' – the overall price level. Thus, growing unemployment is explained by monetarists largely in terms of workers voluntarily pricing themselves out of jobs, whilst, via a revival of the old quantity theory of money, irresponsible governments creating too much money are blamed for inflation.

22.1 UNDERLYING CONCEPTS

TYPES OF UNEMPLOYMENT

The most important distinction to be made between types of unemployment is between the concepts of **voluntary** and **involuntary unemployment**. According to both the pre–Keynesians and latter day monetarists, persistent mass unemployment is voluntary, explained by workers choosing higher real wages and fewer jobs. In contrast, Keynesians explain a part at least of mass unemployment in terms of **demand deficiency** outside the control of workers. In this sense, such unemployment is involuntary. Before taking the discussion further, we shall firstly introduce a more detailed classification of specific types of unemployment.

Real-wage or 'classical' unemployment

As we have already noted, the pre–Keynesians believed that unemployment can be caused by real wages being too high. In a competitive labour market, market forces would tend automatically to eliminate this type of unemployment. However, in uncompetitive labour markets, trade unions may resist wage cuts and price the unemployed out of jobs.

Frictional unemployment (transitional unemployment)

This results from the time–lag involved in the move from one job to another – note the assumption that an unfilled vacancy exists elsewhere. Frictional unemployment is directly related to the geographical and occupational immobility of labour. Factors such as the lack of information or the required skill, and the cost of moving, can prevent a worker from filling a job vacancy. Consequently, the number of unfilled vacancies can be used as a measure of frictional unemployment. In recent years, monetarists and other 'free market' economists have argued that much frictional unemployment in the UK is voluntary, caused by welfare benefits being too high and too easily available. They believe that many of the unemployed have chosen to remain idle, living on welfare benefits, in preference to doing a low–paid job.

Casual unemployment

This is a special case of frictional unemployment, which occurs when labour is employed on a short–term basis in trades such as tourism, catering, building and agriculture. When casual unemployment results from regular fluctuations in demand or weather conditions, it can be called **seasonal unemployment**.

Structural unemployment

Structural unemployment arises when a firm or industry suffers a structural decline, having become uncompetitive in the face of either changing costs and technology or changing demand. The growth of international competition is a particularly important cause of structural unemployment. For many years in the 1950s and 1960s, structural unemployment in Britain was regionally concentrated in areas of declining staple industries. Such regional unemployment was more than offset by the growth of employment in other industries and services which took the place of the declining industries. However, in more recent years structural unemployment has afflicted all parts of the UK, spreading right across the manufacturing base. We shall argue that the return of mass unemployment in the 1970s, 1980s and 1990s is explained in large part by the re-emergence of structural unemployment in the **deindustrialisation process**.

Technological unemployment

This is a special case of structural unemployment resulting from the successful growth of new industries using labour-saving technology such as automation. In contrast to **mechanisation**, **automation** involves machines rather than men operating other machines. Whereas the growth of mechanised industry usually involves an absolute increase in the demand for labour, automation of production can lead to the shedding of labour even when industry output is growing.

Demand-deficient unemployment (Keynesian or cyclical unemployment)

This type of unemployment was identified by Keynes as the cause of persistent mass unemployment between the wars. Economists generally agree that some unemployment may be caused by lack of demand in the downswing of the business cycle, but Keynes went further. He argued that the economy could settle into an underemployment equilibrium caused by a continuing lack of effective aggregate demand (see Chapters 19 and 20).

Residual unemployment

This term covers any other cause of unemployment. It includes the workshy (though some of these may be regarded as frictionally unemployed, i.e. choosing to be unemployed rather than at work) and the unemployable. It is now recognised that long-term unemployment in itself may cause a worker to become unemployable, as a result of both the erosion of job skills and work habits, and of the employer's perception that a worker with more recent job experience is a 'better bet'. We should also mention **hidden unemployment**, which strictly is not unemployment at all but a measure of **overmanning**. Hidden unemployment occurs when firms could produce the same output with fewer workers. It can be caused by trade union pressure and restrictive practices, the high costs of making workers redundant, or by the desire of firms to hang on to skilled workers in a recession in the belief that the workers will be needed when demand picks up.

INFLATION, DEFLATION AND REFLATION

Inflation is usually defined as a **persistent or continuing tendency for the price level to rise**. Although **deflation** is strictly the opposite – a persistent tendency for the price level to fall – the term is usually used in a rather looser way to refer to a reduction in the level of activity or output. In this sense, a deflationary policy reduces the level of aggregate demand in the economy. Some economists find the terms **disinflation** and **disinflationary policy** preferable. Likewise, **reflation** refers to an increase in economic activity and output, and a reflationary policy stimulates aggregate demand. In a sense, inflation is reflation 'gone wrong', increasing the price level rather than real output.

TYPES OF INFLATION

Suppressed inflation

Although inflation involves the *tendency* for the price level to rise, it is not inevitable that prices will actually rise. Strong governments may successfully introduce tough price controls which prevent the price level from rising, without at the same time abolishing the underlying inflationary process. The **suppression of rising prices** diverts the inflationary process into quantity shortages, queues, waiting-lists and black markets.

Creeping inflation

The inflation rate experienced by most industrialised countries in the 1950s and early 1960s was fairly stable from year to year, averaging less than 5%. However, throughout the period it gradually crept upwards, developing into a stratoinflation in many countries in the late 1960s and early 1970s. In the early 1990s, the UK government has had to take care lest the low rate of inflation, achieved by deflating the economy, begins to creep upwards once again.

Stratoinflation

Whereas creeping inflations were typical of industrial countries in the postwar period, **stratoinflation** was the experience of developing countries, particularly in Latin America. In a stratoinflation the inflation rate ranges from about 10% to several hundred per cent, and it may be particularly difficult to anticipate.

Hyperinflation

The transition from a creeping inflation to a stratoinflation in the early 1970s raised fears of an acceleration into a **hyperinflation**. The famous German inflation of 1923 was a hyperinflation, and similar but less publicised hyperinflation occurred in other countries in central and eastern Europe at the end of both World Wars and have recently occurred in Eastern Europe, following the break up of the USSR. However, hyperinflations are usually short-lived and they should not be regarded as typical. A hyperinflation usually occurs in a severe political crisis when a government turns to the printing press to create money to pay its debts. Inflation can accelerate to a rate as high as several thousand per cent a year. During hyperinflation, money ceases to be a medium of exchange and a store of value, and normal economic activity may completely break down.

Stagflation (or Slumpflation)

In the 1970s and early 1980s the incidence of both relatively high rates of inflation and increasing unemployment in the developed world led economists to coin the word 'stagflation'. It combines stagnation in the economy (low or negative increases in output) with price inflation. As we shall see, its existence made conventional Keynesian demand management policies seem inappropriate and politically damaging as a means of controlling either unemployment or inflation. In the early 1990s, there is once again a fear of a renewed stagflation affecting the UK economy.

22.2 ESSENTIAL INFORMATION

THE ADVERSE EFFECTS OF INFLATION

The seriousness of the adverse effects of inflation greatly depends on whether the inflation is **anticipated** or **unanticipated**. It was relatively easy to anticipate more or less fully the creeping inflation of the 1950s and 1960s. Indeed in these years it was sometimes argued that a mild amount of inflation was harmless or even perhaps beneficial. This was because creeping inflation accompanied an expanding economy and became associated by businessmen with growing markets and healthy profits. This view may well explain why the control of inflation was regarded as a relatively minor policy objective. In contrast, it is very difficult for people fully to anticipate a stratoinflation as the actual inflation rate varies substantially from year to year. The adverse effects will be much more severe and may completely destabilise the economy. Generally speaking, the main adverse effects of inflation are:

❶ **It can be unfair.** Weaker social groups in society such as old people on fixed pensions lose, while others in stronger bargaining positions gain. This is an example of how inflation affects the distribution of income and wealth. Nevertheless the indexing of pensions has reduced this particular disadvantage of inflation. In the absence of indexation, inflation also raises the average rate of taxation through the process of **fiscal drag** (see Chapter 15).

❷ **A second important distributional effect occurs between borrowers and lenders.** Inflation tends to redistribute wealth from lenders or creditors to borrowers or debtors. In an inflation the rate of interest may well be below the rate of inflation. This means that lenders are really paying a negative real interest rate to borrowers for the doubtful privilege of lending to them! The biggest borrower of all is usually the government. Inflation can be thought of as a hidden tax that redistributes wealth to the government and reduces the real value of the national debt. This suggests that governments may not always be as keen as they pretend to control inflation completely!

❸ **Inflation distorts many types of economic behaviour and imposes costs upon economic agents.** It can distort consumer behaviour by causing people to bring forward their purchases if they expect the rate of inflation to accelerate. This would probably affect sales of consumer durables such as washing machines and it might also lead to the hoarding of goods such as groceries. If this were the case the savings ratio might be expected to fall as people borrowed or used up savings in order to finance consumption. However, an interesting feature of the inflation in the 1970s was the sharp rise in the savings ratio. This suggests that greater uncertainty may have caused people to save more. A large part of savings is intended to finance old age and retirement. If the inflation rate suddenly accelerates, existing planned savings become inadequate to finance retirement and people increase their savings to top up or supplement their existing stock of accumulated savings, in an attempt to restore the real value of accumulated savings. However, in response to a much lower and more stable inflation rate, the savings ratio fell dramatically in 1983, causing a rapid growth in consumer expenditure that fuelled, for a time at least, the growth of output and economic recovery. At the beginning of the 1990s, the savings ratio rose again in a 'return to thrift', causing a reduction in consumption spending, which contributed to the severity of the recession experienced in the UK.

❹ **Similar uncertainties affect the behaviour of firms and impose costs upon them.** Long-term planning becomes very difficult. Firms may be tempted to divert investment funds out of productive investment into commodity hoarding and speculation. Profit margins may be severely squeezed in a cost inflation and firms can attempt to avoid this by making capital gains on property, land and even fine art and antiques rather than by using their funds in normal production.

❺ **'Shoe leather' and 'menu' costs.** In a period of rapid inflation, consumers spend more time and effort shopping around checking on which prices have or have not risen. The extra costs incurred are called 'shoe leather' costs. By contrast, 'menu' costs are incurred by firms or producers as a result of having to adjust printed price costs, vending machines, etc. more quickly.

⑥ **In a severe stratoinflation money becomes less useful as a medium of exchange and a store of value.** More money may be needed to finance the buying of goods at higher prices, but this is countered by the disadvantages of holding money which is falling in value. In a hyper-inflation the use of money may completely break down and be replaced by less efficient barter. This imposes extra costs on most transactions.

THEORIES OF INFLATION
The Quantity Theory of Money

Old theories seldom die; they reappear in a new form to influence a later generation of economists and politicians. This is certainly true of the **quantity theory of money**, which is the oldest theory of inflation. From the 18th century to the 1930s, it was *the* theory of inflation. The quantity theory went out of fashion in the Keynesian era, but modern monetarism has restored the quantity theory to a central place in the current controversy on the causes of inflation.

Early or 'naive' versions of the quantity theory are usually distinguished from the revival of the quantity theory in a more sophisticated form by Milton Friedman in the 1950s. However, all versions of the quantity theory, old and new, form a **special case of demand inflation** in which rising prices are caused by excess demand. The distinguishing characteristic of the quantity theory is the location of the source of excess demand in **monetary** rather than **real forces** – in an excess supply of money created or condoned by the government.

At its simplest, the quantity theory is often stated as 'too much money chasing too few goods'. Indeed to some this is a definition of inflation, though as a definition it rather begs the question of the cause of a rising price level. The theory can also be written as a simple equation:

$$MV = PT$$

This says that the **money supply** times the number of times money changes hands (the **velocity of circulation**) equals the **price level** times the total number of **transactions**. This is the famous **Fisher equation of exchange**, devised by the American economist Irving Fisher. In the Fisher equation, T includes second-hand purchases of goods and services. Strictly these should be omitted from a measure of national income or output, so it is usually better to rewrite the equation of exchange as:

$$MV = Py$$

in which y is a measure of transactions involving currently produced output or real national income. Py is thus money national income. In this form the equation of exchange is known as the **Cambridge equation**.

The equation of exchange illustrates the very important difference between an identity and a behavioural equation. As the equation stands, it is merely an identity or truism implying very little more than that the amount bought always equals the amount sold. To convert the equation into the quantity theory, two strong assumptions have to be made and the theory stands or falls with these assumptions: The price level is determined by the money supply and not vice versa, or:

$$P = f(Ms)$$

where Ms is the money supply, to be distinguished from the demand for money (Md). Keynesians in particular have attacked this assumption. They argue that the money supply passively adapts or accommodates itself to finance the level of transactions taking place at the current price level. To generalise, monetarists believe that the money supply actively determines the price level, whereas Keynesians have argued that the price level determines the money supply. Keynesians agree with what they consider to be the trivial point that an expansion of the money supply is needed if inflation is to occur, but they argue that if the money supply is restricted so that current level of transactions cannot be financed, then a drop in output and employment will occur. Near monies may take on the function of money, thus rendering control of the money supply ineffective. This (extreme?) Keynesian view of **'reverse causation'** can be summarised as:

$$Ms = f(P)$$

Rewriting the Cambridge equation as:

$$Ms = \frac{1}{V}Py$$

and accepting the first assumption, it is easy to see that an increase in the money supply Ms will feed through to an increase in the price level P provided that V and y are relatively constant. Keynesians have attacked the quantity theory by attacking this assumption. They have argued that even if the assumption that the money supply influences the price level is correct, then the influence could be very small if an increase in the supply of money was 'absorbed' in a lower velocity of circulation, V, rather than in an increase in the price level. However, in response to evidence that V has slowed down in recent years, monetarists now argue that the velocity of circulation need only be predictable, and not necessarily constant.

This dispute extends into an argument about the **transmission mechanism** through which an increase in the money supply is supposed to increase the price level. Modern versions of the quantity theory are usually stated in terms of the demand for money:

$$Md = \frac{1}{V}Py$$

Monetarists believe that the demand for money is a stable function of the level of money income, money being required solely for transactions purposes (the transactions demand for money). When the government increases the money supply, people find themselves possessing larger money balances than they wish to hold. They simply spend their excess money holdings, thereby providing the mechanism by which prices are pulled up. Keynesians attack this **cash balance mechanism**, arguing that since people hold money for speculative reasons – the speculative demand for money – it does not automatically follow that an increase in the money supply is spent. If the demand for money is unstable, the effects of an increase in the money supply are unpredictable.

Even if it is agreed that the velocity of circulation is constant and that the demand for money is a stable function of money income, Keynesians have a third line of attack. An expansion of the money supply may increase **real output**, y, rather than the **price level** P, particularly if there is substantial spare capacity in the economy. Thus the Keynesians stress the reflationary potential of monetary policy, though because it is unpredictable it should be used as a supplement or 'back-up' to fiscal policy. Milton Friedman has admitted that monetary expansion can increase real output, but he argues that the effect is short-lived and that the main long-term effect is on the price level.

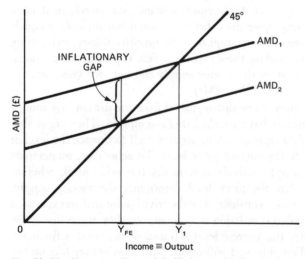

Fig. 53 The Keynesian 'Demand-Pull' theory of inflation

The Keynesian 'demand-pull' theory of inflation

In an influential pamphlet published at the beginning of the Second World War, Keynes adapted his theory of deficient demand in a depressed economy to explain how inflation could be caused by excess demand in a fully employed economy. The theory is illustrated in Fig. 53 in which the maximum level of real output the economy is capable of producing with existing capacity is Y_{FE}. However, the level of aggregate money demand exercised by the various sectors in the economy, shown by AMD_1, is greater than the output that can be produced. Excess demand pulls up prices, resulting in an equilibrium level of money national income at Y_1. A sustained reduction in aggregate demand to AMD_2 is necessary to close the inflationary gap so as to achieve full employment without inflation.

Although the monetarist and the Keynesian theories are both demand theories of inflation, the Keynesian theory locates the engine of inflation firmly in the 'real' economy. Taken together, the combined claims on output of households, firms, the government and the overseas sector are greater than the output that can be produced. Thus inflation is explained by the real forces which determine how people behave. In the British economy of the postwar years in which governments were committed to pursue the objective of full employment, people could behave both as workers and as voters in an inflationary way. As workers, they could bargain for money wage increases in excess of any productivity increase without the fear of unemployment, while in the political arena they could add to the pressure of demand by voting for increased public spending and budget deficits. We have already noted how, in a trivial sense, Keynesians admit that inflation is a monetary phenomenon, since the money stock must expand to accommodate and sustain a rising price level. But Keynesians dispute that inflation is caused by a simple prior increase in the money supply; they believe that the real causes lie much deeper.

Cost theories of inflation

During the postwar years, **creeping inflation** continued, even in years when there was little or no evidence of excess demand in the economy. This prompted many Keynesians to switch their allegiance away from the **demand theory** of inflation to **cost-push** or **structuralist** theories which explain inflation in terms of the structural and institutional conditions which prevail on the supply side of the economy. Such 'Keynesians' are sometimes called **post-Keynesians** or **neo-Keynesians**.

Cost-push theorists argue that growing monopoly power in both labour and goods markets has caused inflation. Strong trade unions are able to bargain for money wage rises in excess of any productivity increase. Monopoly firms are prepared to pay these wage increases partly because of the costs of disrupting modern continuous-flow production processes, and partly because they believe they can pass the increased costs on to the consuming public in higher prices. It is often assumed in the cost-push theory that prices are formed by a simple 'cost-plus' pricing rule. This means that monopoly firms add a standard profit margin to their costs when setting their prices.

The cost-push theory has become a very popular theory with newspapers and the general public. It suggests the simple conclusion that **trade union 'pushfulness'** and perhaps 'big business' are responsible for inflation. However, the question is often begged as to why unions became more militant in the 1960s and 1970s. **Marxist** versions of the cost-push theory locate the reason for increased labour militancy in a defensive struggle by workers to restore their real wages which are being squeezed by capitalists attempting to maintain the rate of profit. Some Marxists regard inflation as the outcome of a distributional struggle within the 'crisis of capitalism'. Other cost-push theorists argue that changed conditions in the labour market in the era of full employment led to aggressive rather than defensive union behaviour. The 'guarantee' of full employment by the state in the postwar years and the provision of a 'safety net' of labour protection legislation are said to have created conditions in which unions could successfully be more militant.

In explaining inflation, cost-push theorists place great emphasis on the roles of **pay relativities** and **different rates of productivity growth** in different industries. Suppose there are two sectors within an economy: one with a fast rate of growth of labour productivity and the other with a zero rate. Firms in the high productivity sector are prepared to pay wage increases equal to the rate of growth of productivity. Cost inflation need not therefore occur in this sector. However, workers with similar skills in the zero growth sector bargain for the same wage increases in order to maintain their comparability or to restore the differential relative to less skilled workers. Cost inflation thus occurs in the sector with zero productivity growth as the firms pass the increased wage costs on to consumers in higher prices.

A **wage-price 'spiral'** is unleashed as each group of workers attempts in a **leap-frogging process** to maintain or improve its real wage and its position in the pay 'league table'. Cost-push theorists essentially view the labour market not as one large competitive market but as a collection of non-competitive and separated markets for different trades and skills. Although workers realise that if all wages rise at the same rate as productivity, then inflation will probably fall, they also realise that what is in the interest of workers *collectively* need not be in the interest of a *single* group acting in isolation. A group that accepts a wage increase lower than the current rate of inflation will probably suffer if other workers do not behave in a similar fashion. Thus a group acts to preserve its relative position in the pay 'pecking order', even if its members know that by fuelling inflation a large money wage increase may be only a small real wage increase or even a decrease.

THE RISE OF THE PHILLIPS CURVE

In the late 1950s and the early 1960s a great deal of energy was spent by economists in debating whether inflation is caused by excess demand or by cost-push forces. After 1958 the debate was conducted with the aid of a recently discovered statistical relationship, the **Phillips curve**, which is illustrated in Fig. 54. The Phillips curve purported to show a stable but non-linear relationship between the rate of change of wages (the rate of wage inflation) and the percentage of the labour

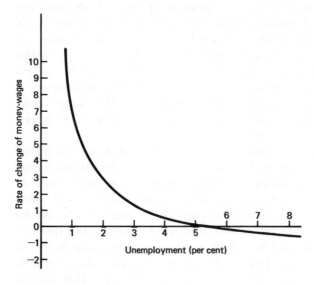

Fig. 54 The Phillips curve

force unemployed. Taking the rate of growth of productivity into account, Phillips estimated that in the UK an unemployment level of about 2.5% was compatible with price stability (or zero inflation), and that an unemployment level of 5.5% would lead to stable money wages. Economists grasped on the supposed stability of the Phillips relationship over a period of nearly one hundred years to argue that it provided statistical support for the existence of a 'trade-off' between inflation and employment. Using the Phillips curve, economists believed that they could advise governments on the **opportunity cost in terms of inflation** of achieving any **employment target**. In offering this advice, the non-linearity of the curve was significant. At low levels of unemployment a further reduction in unemployment would incur a much greater cost in terms of increased inflation than a similar reduction at a higher level of unemployment. Indeed, the Phillips curve appeared to justify the Keynesian view than an unemployment rate of about 1½% should be regarded as full employment; any lower level of unemployment, or 'over-full employment' would be associated with an excessive cost in terms of inflation.

Nevertheless, the Phillips curve was never, in itself, a theory of inflation. In its early years the Phillips curve was most often used by Keynesians of the demand-pull school, including Phillips himself, to illustrate how the rate of inflation varied with the amount of excess demand in the economy. In the **demand-pull interpretation**, the level of unemployment was used as a measure of excess demand which served to pull up money wages in the labour market. However, the Phillips curve was also accommodated in the **cost-push theory**, the level of unemployment being interpreted as a measure of trade union 'pushfulness'. The Phillips curve could illustrate and provide statistical support for both theories of inflation, but it could not decide between the two.

THE FALL OF THE PHILLIPS CURVE

Around 1970 a growing level of unemployment accompanied by a much higher rate of inflation appeared to signal the breakdown of the Phillips relationship. According to the monetarists, this greatly damaged the credibility of both the cost-push theory of inflation and the demand-pull theory, at least in its Keynesian version. It is worth noting, however, that many Keynesians now claim that the Phillips curve was never a 'true' part of Keynesianism, merely excess baggage added on, the rejection of which does not destroy essential Keynesian theory. Nevertheless, neither the demand-pull nor the cost-push theorists had predicted the emergence of the stagflation or slumpflation of the 1970s. Yet a leading monetarist, Milton Friedman, had predicted the breakdown of the Phillips relationship a number of years before it actually happened. It is not surprising, therefore, that the simultaneous appearance of increased unemployment and accelerating inflation greatly boosted monetarism.

There are at least two competing theories of what has happened to the Phillips relationship. In the version favoured by some cost-push theorists, the inverse relationship between inflation and unemployment still exists, but the trade-off is now at much higher rates of inflation and levels of unemployment. The continuing growth of non-competitive forces in the structure and institutions of the economy are blamed for a rightward shift of the Phillips relationship. The cost-push school favours the use of an incomes policy as the only method which can once again achieve both a lower inflation rate and a lower level of unemployment.

In contrast, monetarists argue that even at the height of the Keynesian era there was never a stable relationship allowing a long-term trade-off between inflation and employment. The statistical relationship identified by Phillips is at best short-run and unstable. According to monetarists, the 'true' long-term relationship between unemployment and the rate of inflation lies along a vertical line, on which no trade-offs are possible, running through the **natural rate of unemployment** also known as the **'non-accelerating inflation rate of unemployment'** (NAIRU). This is shown in Fig. 55. To understand this conclusion we need to

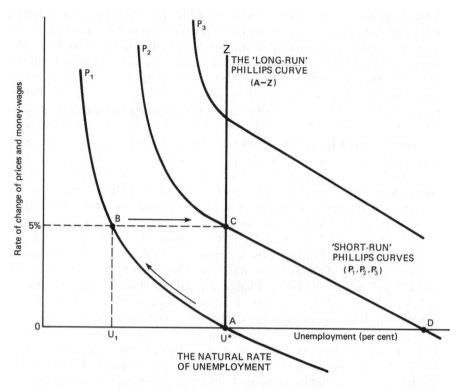

Fig. 55 The expectations-augmented Phillips curve

introduce two theories, one old and one relatively new, to help explain the monetarist view of 'how the economy works'. The old theory, the monetarist theory of aggregate employment, is essentially the pre-Keynesian employment theory discussed earlier in the chapter, whilst the new theory introduces the role of expectations into the inflationary process. According to the monetarist theory of employment, the 'natural' levels of employment and unemployment (U* in Fig. 55) are determined at the equilibrium real wage at which workers voluntarily supply exactly the amount of labour that firms voluntarily employ. Since monetarists do not recognise demand-deficient unemployment it follows that, at the natural rate, unemployment is composed largely of frictional and structural unemployment.

We now introduce the **role of expectations** into the inflationary process. In order to keep the analysis as simple as possible, we shall assume that the rate of productivity increase is zero. Thus, the vertical axis in Fig. 55 measures the rate of increase both of money wages and of prices. Suppose that the economy is initially at point A. Unemployment is at the natural rate U*, and the rates of increase of prices and money wages are zero and stable. In these circumstances, workers may expect the future inflation rate also to be zero. If the government is dissatisfied with the level of unemployment at U* and expands demand, it may believe that it can successfully trade-off along the Phillips curve P₁ to a point such as B. The cost of achieving U₁ appears to be an inflation rate of 5%. But will the new situation be stable? Not so, say the monetarists. Workers are only willing to supply more labour beyond the natural level of employment if the real wage rises, but a rising real wage causes employers to demand less labour! Initially, more workers may enter the labour market in the false belief or illusion that a 5% increase in the money wage is also a real wage increase. We call this **money illusion**. Similarly, if firms falsely believe that revenues are rising faster than labour costs, they will employ more labour. In other words, an increase in employment beyond the natural rate can only be sustained if workers and employers suffer permanent money illusion in equal but opposite directions!

Gradually, both workers and employers will realise that they have confused money quantities with real quantities and that they have suffered from money illusion. Without permanent money illusion, employment can only stay above the natural level if inflation accelerates to keep employees' expectations about the rate of inflation consistently below the actual rate. As workers continuously adjust their expectations of future inflation to the actual rate and bargain for ever-higher money wages, the short-run Phillips curve shifts outward from P_1 to P_2 and so on. Thus a level of unemployment below the natural rate can only be sustained if the government finances and accommodates the accelerating inflation by expanding the money supply. But even in these circumstances the inflation will eventually accelerate into a hyperinflation and into a breakdown of economic activity, causing unemployment to rise above the natural rate. According to this logic, any attempt to reduce unemployment below the natural rate involves the short-run cost of accelerating inflation, whilst eventually having the perverse effect of increasing unemployment above the natural rate to an unnecessarily high level.

The theory just described is sometimes known as the theory of the 'expectations-augmented Phillips curve'. Supporters of this theory, which was originally conceived by Milton Friedman, tend to take the view that the economy must suffer rather a long period of unemployment above the natural rate to rid the economy of the effect of expectations built up while unemployment was below the natural rate.

Suppose, once again, that the government has expanded demand and the money supply, moving the economy to point B in Fig. 55. Unemployment is U_1. It now realises its 'mistake', and refuses to allow the money supply to grow by more than 5% a year. According to the Friedmanite school, the economy now moves to point C as workers and employers gradually realise that the real wage has not changed. Inflation has stabilised at 5%. But if the government wishes to get back to point A, it must get there via point D, which is at a much greater level of unemployment. This journey is necessary in order gradually to reduce expectations of inflation. Just as inflation accelerates whenever unemployment is below the natural rate, so it decelerates when unemployment is above the natural rate. In each case this is explained by economic agents gradually adapting their expectations of inflation to the actual rate. Above the natural rate of unemployment, actual inflation is always below expected inflation.

Accordingly, expectations are continuously revised downwards and the economy can only return to zero inflation and unemployment at the natural rate when the expected inflation rate has fallen to zero.

RATIONAL EXPECTATIONS

The message of the 'expectations-augmented Phillips curve' is gloomy. The economy must experience a lengthy period of deflation and unemployment above the natural rate as the penalty to be paid for an 'irresponsible' reduction in unemployment below the natural rate. However, in recent years many monetarists have tacked on to the Friedmanite concept of the natural rate of unemployment, an alternative theory of how expectations are formed.

According to this theory, it is unrealistic to assume that a rational economic agent acting in its self-interest will form expectations of future inflation only on the basis of past or experienced inflation. If economic agents on average correctly forecast the results of events taking place in the economy now, it is in their self-interest quickly to modify their economic behaviour so that it is in line with their expectations. Thus if workers believe that the government means business in reducing the money supply and the rate of inflation, they will immediately build a lower expected rate of inflation into their wage-bargaining behaviour. In this way, inflation can be reduced relatively painlessly without a lengthy period of unemployment above the natural level.

In recent years an important division has developed between **monetarists of the Friedmanite school** and those of the **rational expectations or 'Neo classical'** school. According to the Friedmanites, governments can reduce unemployment below the natural rate as long as workers and employers suffer illusion. However, according to the rational expectations school, workers and employers instantly realise their mistakes and 'see through' any attempt by an 'irresponsible' government to reflate the economy; thus demand management policies can never succeed in reducing unemployment below the natural rate, even in the short run. Monetarists of both schools usually agree that although the government cannot in the long run reduce unemployment below the natural rate, it can reduce the natural rate itself by policies designed to make the labour market more competitive, hence policies to reduce trade union power and to abolish the closed shop, together with other 'supply-side' policies.

SUMMARY: THE THREE STAGES IN THE DEVELOPMENT OF THE MONETARIST THEORY OF INFLATION

❶ 'Mark I' of the monetarist theory of inflation was the revival by Milton Friedman in the 1950s of the **quantity theory of money**. This explained inflation as a purely monetary phenomenon, caused by the government creating or condoning excess monetary growth.

❷ 'Mark II': the incorporation of the **theory of adaptive expectations** into the inflationary process. The weakness of the 'Mark I' theory is that it fails to explain why a government might be prepared to expand the money supply on a continuing basis to finance an inflation. Milton Friedman's theory of the 'expectations-augmented Phillips curve' provides an explanation and also, we should note, explains inflation in terms of the 'real' economy rather than purely as a monetary phenomenon.

❸ 'Mark III': the 'New Classical' school. Whereas the 'Mark II' explanation of inflation is based on a **theory of adaptive expectations**, the New Classical School has replaced this with the theory of rational expectations. In the adaptive expectations theory, workers and employers slowly change or adapt their expectations of future inflation to the current rate of inflation. By contrast, in the 'New Classical' explanation of inflation, it is rational for economic agents instantly to adapt their expectations of the future to all the up-to-date information that is available.

Chapter roundup

The monetarist theories of inflation, the quantity theory of money, the rational expectations hypothesis, and the concept of the natural rate of unemployment, have had a great influence on British government policy in the 1980s, and in particular on the monetary policy discussed in Chapter 17. In contrast, the authority of the Keynesian demand-pull theory of inflation has greatly diminished, at least in monetarist circles. This theory originates out of the Keynesian income/expenditure model of the economy described in Chapter 19. Yet the other inflation theory favoured by Keynesians – the cost-push theory with all its implications for the effectiveness of incomes policy (Chapter 24) – waits in the wings, ready to re-emerge if and when monetarist and free-market theories suffer a decline.

In this chapter we have omitted any discussion of the international nature of inflation and, in particular, of the role of the exchange rate in the inflationary process. This defect will be remedied in Chapters 24 and 27. Nevertheless, we should not conclude this chapter without mentioning the monetarist argument that cost-push theories suffer the defect of explaining inflation solely in terms of institutional conditions in domestic markets. According to the monetarists, such theories inadequately explain why similar increases in the rate of inflation have occurred in a larger number of countries with widely different domestic conditions and institutions.

Illustrative questions and answers

1   Essay Question
a)   What do economists mean by the 'natural' rate of unemployment?   (10)
b)   How might 'demand-side' and 'supply-side' economic policies affect the
'natural' rate of unemployment?   (15)

(AEB, November 1992)

Tutorial note

As we have explained, the term the 'natural' rate of unemployment was first
introduced by the leading monetarist Milton Friedman, when putting forward the
theory of the 'expectations-augmented' Phillips curve in the late 1960s. However
the 'natural' rate or level of unemployment is really just a revival of the old
neoclassical or pre-Keynesian belief that a competitive market economy automatically self-adjusts to an 'equilibrium' level of unemployment made up of
frictional and possibly structural unemployment. It is the level of unemployment
that exists at the equilibrium real wage which equates the aggregate demand
for labour with the aggregate supply and clears the labour market, i.e. all
'classical' or 'real wage' and 'demand-deficient' unemployment has been
eliminated. Related terms are the 'non-accelerating inflation rate of unemployment' (NAIRU) and the 'full employment rate of unemployment'.

Monetarist and 'supply-side' economists believe that 'demand-side' policies
in the sense of expanding aggregate demand to try to reduce unemployment,
cannot reduce the 'natural' rate of unemployment. Indeed if the government
expands demand to try to reduce unemployment below the economy's 'natural'
rate, or if demand management leads to the neglect of the economy's 'supply
side', such policies may in fact have the long term effect of increasing the
'natural' rate of unemployment. They argue that free-market or 'anti-interventionist' 'supply-side' policies (which we describe in the next chapter) should be used
as the only way of reducing the 'natural' rate of unemployment. By contrast,
Keynesians argue that there is still a role for demand management, and also for
'interventionist' 'supply-side' policies as well as for the more 'free-market'
variety.

Suggested answer plan

1   Explain the 'natural' rate of unemployment, illustrating the concept on a
diagram to show the aggregate demand for, and aggregate supply of ,
labour, or on a Phillips curve diagram.
2   With the aid of a Phillips curve diagram, show the effects of an expansion
of demand which reduces unemployment below its 'natural' rate.
3   Explain the monetarist or 'supply-side' argument that 'free-market' 'supply-
side' policies are needed to reduce the 'natural' rate of unemployment.
4   Summarise the Keynesian counter-view in favour of more interventionist
'supply-side' policies and in support of at least some demand-management.

2   Data Question
It is important to identify the actual economic costs of inflation and to try to
quantify them, so that they can be compared with the costs of the policies aimed
at reducing inflation. These latter costs are usually seen in terms of higher
unemployment, if restrictive monetary and fiscal policies are used to control
inflation, or a misallocation of resources, if prices and incomes policies are used.
Traditionally the costs of inflation were seen in terms of its adverse effect on
income distribution. More recently attention has been focussed upon the

adverse effects of inflation on output and employment.

(Source: Adapted from: A Griffiths and S Wall,
Applied Economics, Longman, 1986)

(a) Examine the impact of inflation on income distribution.   (8)
(b) Outline the economic costs to the nation of higher unemployment resulting from the adoption of restrictive monetary and fiscal policies to control inflation.   (6)
(c) Explain why the use of prices and incomes policies to combat inflation might cause a misallocation of resources.   (6)

(ULEAC, AS-Level, June 1991)

Tutorial note

a)   It is usually argued that people with fixed incomes such as pensioners suffer during periods of rapidly rising prices because inflation erodes the real value of their incomes. However this argument is usually less strong when pensions and other 'fixed incomes' are 'index linked' to a cost of living index such as the RPI. It is also useful to know that in the UK, state pensions, unemployment pay and many other welfare benefits used to be linked to the **index of average earnings** rather than to the RPI. This meant that state transfer incomes received by people who were out of work increased at the same rate as the average earnings of people in work. But since the 'index-linking' of transfer incomes was switched to the RPI in the early 1980s, the gap has widened between the real incomes of people in and out of work. This is because the pay of people in work rises on average at a faster rate than inflation whereas pensions and benefits increase exactly in line with inflation (as measured by the RPI). The linking of transfer incomes to the RPI thus means that the poor who depend on benefits become *relatively worse off* compared to people in jobs, even though their real incomes more or less maintain their value (assuming that the RPI is an accurate measure of inflation as it affects the poor).

b)   In 1991 the Chancellor of the Exchequer, Norman Lamont apparently said that 'unemployment is a price well worth paying for the control of inflation'. But while this is an extremely important and interesting issue, it is not the subject of this question. Restrict your answer to describing and assessing the deflationary costs of restrictive fiscal and monetary policies, and resist the temptation to take issue with the Chancellor and to debate whether the costs are worthwhile!

c)   See Chapter 24 for an explanation of how a prices and incomes policy may distort market forces and resource allocation.

Question bank

1
(a) Distinguish between voluntary and involuntary unemployment.   (20)
(b) Analyse the effects of supply-side policies on both these types of unemployment.   (80)

(ULEAC, June 1990)

2   'Wage increases raise firms' costs and therefore cause inflation.'
'Wage increases raise disposable income and therefore employment rises.'
Critically evaluate each of these statements.

(ULEAC, January 1992)

3 Why might unemployment rates differ among countries in the developed world? To what extent is an increase in aggregate demand likely to solve the problem of unemployment?

(NEAB, June 1991)

4
(a) What is meant by the term 'full employment'? Ignoring for the time being any other considerations, why is it desirable to have full employment in an economy? (7)
(b) Outline the main causes of unemployment in the UK economy at present, and discuss what can be done to reduce its level. (10)
(c) When attempting to reduce the unemployment rate, why might the UK Government face a conflict with some of its other macroeconomic policy goals? Does this imply that the optimal unemployment rate is not zero? (8)

(NISEAC, June 1990)

5
(a) Distinguish between 'Keynesian' or 'demand-deficient' unemployment and other types of unemployment. (10)
(b) Why might economies be prone to periodic demand-deficient unemployment? (15)

(WJEC, June 1992)

6 'The Phillips curve is no longer relevant to economic policy'. Discuss.

(ULEAC, January 1988)

7
(a) What relationships exist between the rate of inflation and the level of unemployment in an economy? (10)
(b) Discuss the policy implications of these relationships with specific reference to the UK. (10)

(O&CSEB, AS-Level, June 1990)

8 Identify and evaluate the causes of inflation in the UK economy at the present time.

(Cambridge, AS-Level, June 1992)

9
(a) Explain what is meant by a change in the 'value of money' and consider how such changes are measured in practice. (10)
(b) Consider whether the stability of the value of money ought to be a central objective of government macro-economic policy. (15)

(WJEC, June 1990)

10 'Inflation is triggered by excess demand but sustained by rising costs.'
(a) Explain this statement. (15)
(b) Discuss its implications for the successful control of inflation. (10)

(AEB, November 1992)

11
(a) Explain how the rate of increase in retail prices in the UK is measured. (30)
(b) Why are there conflicting views as to whether the recorded rate of retail price increases provides an accurate picture of inflation in the UK? (30)
(c) Explain why the rate of increase in the retail price index would be of much less concern than at present if the UK were a closed economy. (40)

(ULEAC, January 1993)

12
(a) What are the causes of unemployment in the UK?   (9)
(b) Explain and evaluate the measures you would advocate to reduce the level
     of unemployment in the UK.   (16)

(Cambridge, June 1991)

13 Explain and comment on the policies which might be used to combat
    inflation caused by excess demand.

(Cambridge, June 1991)

SUPPLY-SIDE ECONOMICS

Units in this chapter

Chapter objectives

Though first coined in 1976, by Professor Herbert Stein of the University of Virginia, the term **'supply-side economics'** came into prominence in 1980, to describe the economic policies which Ronald Reagan promised in his successful campaign for the American presidency. Supply-side economics became a dominant part of **'Reaganomics'**, the nickname given to the American Federal Government's economic programme in the early 1980s. The term was then applied to describe much of the underlying ideology, and dominant thrust of the policies, adopted by other **'free-market' orientated governments**, including the Conservative administrations of Mrs Margaret Thatcher in the UK (for which the nickname **'Thatcherism'** paralleled and indeed outlasted, the 'Reaganomics' of the USA). In terms of basic economic philosophy, supply-side economics is closely linked to the emergence of the **'radical right'** or **'New Right'** out of a more narrow monetarism which we shall describe in Chapter 24.

There are many diverse, and often competing 'schools', of economic and political theory within the 'radical right' revival, including the **'rational expectations'** or **'New Classical'** school. Although the various schools of the 'radical right' disagree over points of both emphasis and detail, they share an extreme distrust (and often dislike), of government intervention in the economy; and a matching belief in the virtues of market forces. Thus, the ascendancy of supply-side economics and of other 'free-market' orientated ideas, in the late 1970s and during the 1980s; and the growing confidence of its academic theoreticians, have been closely related to the decline of Keynesianism in the face of the apparent inability, in the 1970s, of Keynesian policies to deal with stagflation and the breakdown of the Phillips 'trade-off' between full employment and the control of inflation.

23.1 UNDERLYING CONCEPTS

The 'strict' meaning of 'supply-side economics'

In its original meaning, as developed by the 'radical right', supply-side economics describes a particular way at looking at the effects of the government's **fiscal policy** upon the economy. During the Keynesian era, most economists had regarded fiscal policy, and especially the government's use of taxation, as affecting the economy almost solely at the macro level through its effect on aggregate demand. For Keynesians, the size of the government's budget deficit, or surplus, was the key to fiscal policy, regardless of whether a deficit resulted from higher levels of public spending or from tax cuts. The impact of public spending increases or tax changes upon the economy at the micro level was largely ignored.

By contrast, supply-side economics is concerned with the microeconomic effects of taxation and public spending. In many respects, supply-side economics is simply a revival of the old 'classical' public finance theory that disappeared from view during the Keynesian era. Central to supply-side economics is the idea of a tax cut (not to stimulate aggregate demand Keynesian-style) but to create incentives by altering relative prices, particularly those of labour and leisure, in favour of work, saving and investment. **Professor Arthur Laffer**, a prominent American 'supply-sider' (and adviser to President Reagan in the 1980s), has described supply-side economics as

> providing a framework of analysis which relies on personal and private incentives. When incentives change, people's behaviour changes in response. People are attracted towards positive incentives and repelled by the negative. The role of government in such a framework is carried out by the ability of government to alter incentives and thereby affect society's behaviour.

A broader interpretation of 'supply-side economics'

As we have just explained, in its original meaning supply-side economics relates exclusively to fiscal policy and tax cuts, and their effects upon incentives. However, it is useful to conceive of supply-side economics in broader terms than fiscal policy alone. In this looser interpretation, we can define supply-side economic policy as **the set of government policies which aim to change the underlying structure of the economy and improve the economic performance of markets and industries and of individual workers and firms within markets**. Supply-side policies are **microeconomic** rather than **macroeconomic**, since they aim to improve general economic performance by acting on the motivation and efficiency of individual economic agents within the economy. Supply-siders, together with other 'radical-right' economists, believe that while the economy is always close to its 'natural' levels of output and employment, these 'natural' levels can be unnecessarily low because of distortions (often blamed on 'twenty-five years of Keynesian policies') which reduce both an individual's willingness to supply labour and a firm's willingness to employ labour and supply goods. Supply-siders therefore recommend the use of microeconomic policies which they believe will remove these distortions, improve incentives and generally make markets more competitive. In the Keynesian era, microeconomic policy (along with macropolicy) usually extended (rather than reduced) government interventionism in markets, in fields such as **regional policy, competition policy** (or anti-monopoly policy), **labour market policy** and other aspects of **industrial policy**. By contrast supply-side microeconomic policy centres on a 'rolling back' of the functions of the state and a reduction of the level of government intervention in the economy. Along with tax cuts (to create incentives to work, save and invest) and welfare benefit cuts (to reduce the incentive to choose unemployment), supply-side economic policy, in its wider interpretation, includes policies of **privatisation, marketisation** and **deregulation** (described in detail in Chapter 12). Supply-siders – and other schools within the 'free market revival' (be they self-styled monetarists or New Classical economists) wish to create an **'enterprise economy'**, through the promotion of entrepreneurship and **'popular capitalism'**; to replace the **'dependency culture'** and **statism** they see as the legacy of several decades of Keynesianism and a misguided consensus around the supposed virtues of a mixed economy. Indeed, for supply-siders, and other members of the 'radical right', the mixed economy is better described as a 'mixed-up' economy!

23.2 ESSENTIAL INFORMATION

SUPPLY-SIDE ECONOMICS AND THE SUPPLY CURVE OF LABOUR

Supply-side theory depends crucially upon the assumption that the supply curve of labour is 'upward-sloping' and not 'backward-bending', and that increases in income tax create disincentives for the further supply of labour. (Refer back to Chapter 13 at this stage for an explanation of the supply curve of labour.) An 'upward-sloping' supply curve of labour implies that increases in the marginal rates of income tax, being equivalent to cuts in wage rates, have a disincentive effect upon the supply of labour. Workers decide to supply less labour (choosing more leisure time instead) and they may also prefer the untaxed supply of labour in the informal 'black' or 'underground' economy to the more formal supply of 'taxed' labour in the 'overground' economy.

SUPPLY-SIDE ECONOMICS AND UNEMPLOYMENT

'Supply-siders', and other more free-market orientated economists, argue that the growth of **voluntary unemployment** explains much of the high level of unemployment occurring in the UK since the 1970s. Workers do not necessarily voluntarily leave their jobs and choose unemployment, but once unemployed (for whatever reason) they choose to remain unemployed for a much longer period than was previously the case. In part, this may be a 'discouraged worker' effect: repeated job rejections, in conditions of high unemployment, may discourage further attempts to find a job. **'Search theories'** have also been used to explain a growth in voluntary frictional unemployment. Suppose a worker earning £300 a week loses his job and that vacancies exist which pay £150 a week; other conditions of work being similar. The worker may choose to remain unemployed rather than to fill the vacancy because:

- the wage does not meet his aspirations;
- he is uncertain whether better-paid vacancies exist which he does not know about.

Accordingly, unemployment is viewed as a **voluntary search period** during which an unemployed worker scans the job market for a vacancy that meets his aspirations. Voluntary unemployment ends either when the worker finds a vacancy which meets his aspirations or when he reduces his aspirations sufficiently, to accept the vacancy he knew about in the first instance.

Search theorists argue that such voluntary frictional unemployment has increased because, in the Keynesian era, the state created for the unemployed a 'safety net' of welfare benefits such as unemployment pay. A higher real level of welfare benefits could then be used by the unemployed to finance a longer search period, thus delaying the decisions to reduce aspirations and fill a vacancy. Highly relevant here is the **replacement ratio**; the ratio of disposable income when unemployed to disposable income in work. An increase in the replacement ratio, caused perhaps both by higher welfare benefits available to the unemployed, and also by fiscal drag and higher taxation affecting the low-paid, encourages workers with few skills to offer in the job market, to choose unemployment in preference to work. This is the **'unemployment trap'**, to which we referred in Chapter 15.

Since 'supply-side' economists, such as Professor Patrick Minford, have argued that much recent and current unemployment in the UK is 'voluntary frictional', it is not surprising that they recommend free-market orientated 'supply-side' policies as the appropriate remedy. Such policies include cuts both in marginal income tax rates and in welfare benefits, together with a tightening of rules to make benefits more difficult to claim. Supply-siders claim that tax cuts increase the incentive to work, while reducing the real value of benefits decreases the incentive to choose unemployment. Neo-Keynesians reply by arguing that tax and benefits cuts involve an unacceptable and socially divisive increase in inequality. They also believe that only a small part of current unemployment is of the 'voluntary frictional' kind, so free-market orientated supply-side policies will not have much affect on the rump of involuntary structural unemployment resulting from the deindustrialisation process, from the effects of an overvalued exchange rate, decades of under-investment both by the private sector, and by the state in social capital or infrastructure.

THE LAFFER CURVE

The assumption by supply-siders of an upward-sloping supply curve of labour leads on to the supply-side argument that high rates of income tax and the overall burden of income tax upon taxpayers create disincentives which eventually, as taxation increases, diminish national income and cause total tax revenue to decline. This can be illustrated by a 'Laffer curve', which we have drawn in Fig. 56:

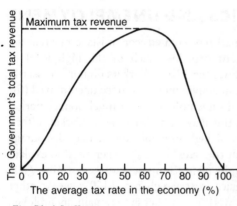

Fig. 56 A Laffer curve

The Laffer curve shows the government's total tax revenue as the average tax rate increases from 0 to 100%. Tax revenue is zero when the tax rate is 0 per cent; and it is assumed also to be zero at an average tax rate of 100% (there being no incentive to produce output other than for subsistence if any extra output is completely taxed away). In between these limiting rates, of 0 and 100%, the Laffer curve shows tax revenue first rising and then falling as the average rate of taxation is increased. Tax revenue reaches its maximum at the highest point on the Laffer curve, after which any further increase in the average tax rate becomes counter-productive as total tax revenue falls.

Supply-siders have argued that the increase in the burden of taxation, that took place in the Keynesian era in the UK and USA, to finance the growing government sector, raised the average tax rate towards or beyond the critical point on the Laffer curve at which tax revenue is maximised. If this was the case, then the policy of tax cuts recommended by the supply-siders would have the paradoxical effect of actually raising tax revenues. A growing national output, stimulated by lower tax rates, would yield higher total revenues despite the reduced tax rates, and the effect would be reinforced by a decline in tax avoidance and evasion as these activities became less worthwhile at less penal rates of taxation.

THE CHOICE BETWEEN CONSUMPTION AND SAVING

As we have already noted, the central idea of supply-side economics is that fiscal policy works by changing relative prices or incentives. So far we have drawn attention to the **labour/leisure choice**, developing the policy implication of the Laffer curve that income tax cuts can stimulate the supply of labour, with the government actually benefiting from higher total tax revenues, despite lower tax rates, at a higher resulting level of national output. However, it is too simplistic to explain supply-side economics solely in terms of the theory that 'across the board' personal income tax reductions are self-financing; and that the prime aim of 'supply-sidism' is to secure more revenues for the government and to improve its budgetary position. Rather, the essence of 'supply-sidism' is the overcoming of the economy's inability to grow without a rapid rise in inflation, together with a reversal of the declining competitive position of industry.

Supply-siders argue that a second choice, facing individual economic agents, is as important as the labour/leisure choice. This is the choice between consumption and saving. The cost, to an individual, of spending a £ of income on consumption is the future income stream given up by not saving and investing the £. The present value of the income stream is in part determined by marginal tax rates. The higher the marginal tax rate on investment income, the lower is the value of the income stream that savings will yield. Thus, high rates of taxation levied on investment income, make current consumption of income cheap in terms of the investment income foregone. As a result, savings and investment decline. Supply-siders argue that the increased public spending and deficit financing of the Keynesian era stimulated aggregate demand; but that the Keynesians completely ignored the adverse effects we have just described of the higher levels of taxation that accompanied the Keynesian expansionism. As a result, expansionary Keynesian fiscal policies, designed to boost output and employment, led only to rising inflation, as the aggregate supply of output failed to respond to the demand stimulation. By contrast, the tax cuts advocated by supply-siders are not designed to stimulate aggregate demand. Instead they are intended to produce price incentives which encourage households to save rather than to consume; and businesses to invest so that the growth of the economy can proceed without the additional demand which results from higher incomes hitting the wall of stagnant national output and dissipating into inflation.

THE KEYNESIAN INCOME/EXPENDITURE MODEL REVISITED

Perhaps the most serious weakness of the **Keynesian income/expenditure model**, examined in Chapters 19 and 20, is the model's lack of a proper 'supply-side'. Within the model, the 45° line illustrated on a 'Keynesian cross' diagram, such as Fig. 48, represents the Keynesian aggregate supply function. Following any increase or decrease of aggregate expenditure, the aggregate supply of output adjusts upwards or downwards to equal the level of aggregate expenditure at a new equilibrium level of national income. However, the model tells us little about a key question of interest: how much of the adjustment to the new equilibrium level of income will be a change in **real output** and how much will be represented by a change in the **price level**? Because of this inadequacy within the basic Keynesian model, another macroeconomic model, known as the **aggregate demand/ aggregate supply model (or AD/AS model)**, has come into prominence in recent years.

THE AGGREGATE DEMAND/AGGREGATE SUPPLY MODEL

The main differences relating to the nature of aggregate supply which separate Keynesians and supply-siders (together with most monetarists and other members of the 'radical right'), can be explained using the AD/AS model illustrated in Fig. 57. In this figure we show aggregate demand for, and aggregate supply of, real output as functions of the price level. For the most part, there is little disagreement between Keynesians and supply-siders about the nature and shape of the aggregate demand curve; it is the **aggregate supply curve** that is the centre of dispute and interest. The AD curve shows demand for real output (in contrast to the AMD or aggregate expenditure curve of the 'Keynesian cross' diagram which shows demand for nominal output). The AD curve is drawn downward-sloping, showing that the aggregate demand exercised in the economy for goods and services increases as the price level falls. There are two main explanations for this. The first is a **real balance effect** or **wealth effect**. Assuming a given nominal stock of money in the economy, a decrease in the price level increases people's stocks of real money balances, i.e. the same amount of money will buy more. Thus people feel wealthier and demand more goods. Secondly, increased real money balances cause the rate of interest to fall, further stimulating consumption and investment spending.

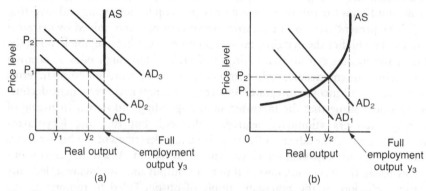

Fig. 57   The AD/AS model (a) with an 'inverted L-shaped' schedule
(b) with an upward-sloping AS schedule

KEYNESIAN AGGREGATE SUPPLY

As we have noted, Keynesians and supply-siders disagree fundamentally over the specification of the aggregate supply schedule, which shows how much real output firms are willing to supply at various price levels. Fig. 57 shows an 'inverted L-shaped' Keynesian aggregate supply function. Following an expansion of aggregate demand, which shifts the aggregate demand function from AD_1 to AD_2, real output increases from y_1 to y_2, but there is no increase in prices. But once full employment is reached, at the level of real output y_3, any further increase in aggregate demand (e.g. to AD_3) causes prices and not output to rise. Fig. 57(a) thus illustrates the 'traditional' and rather simple Keynesian view that an expansion of demand will reflate real output rather than inflate prices, provided the economy is below the full employment level of income.

KEYNES'S AGGREGATE SUPPLY FUNCTION

It is now generally agreed that the 'inverted L-shaped' aggregate supply function is not the one that Keynes himself had in mind in the *General Theory*. We can distinguish between **Keynes's own aggregate supply function** and the **'Keynesian' function** we have just described, i.e. the aggregate supply function implicitly adopted by many followers of Keynes (the 'Keynesians'), but not by Keynes himself.

In contrast to the 'inverted L-shaped' AS curve, **Keynes's AS function**, depicted in Fig. 57(b), is upward-sloping until the full employment level of income is reached. Following an expansion of demand from AD_1 to AD_2, the price level must rise to create the conditions in which firms are willing to supply more output. The difference between the two functions is explained by different assumptions about the marginal productivity of labour. With the 'inverted L-shaped' AS curve, it is assumed that the marginal product of labour is constant as output increases, until full employment is reached. But Keynes accepted the standard neoclassical assumption that firms face a declining marginal productivity of labour as they increase the supply of output in the short run. In this situation, the real wage rate paid by the firms must fall (to match the declining marginal product of labour), in order to persuade profit-maximising firms to demand more labour and to increase the supply of output. Given a constant money wage rate (which is assumed for all short-run AS curves), a rise in price level reduces the real wage rate and produces the conditions in which firms are willing to employ more labour and supply more output. Hence, the upward-sloping AS function, showing that a rise in the price level is necessary to persuade firms to supply more output.

THE SUPPLY-SIDERS' AGGREGATE SUPPLY FUNCTION

It is important to emphasise that both the **Keynesian 'inverted L-shaped' AS function** and **Keynes's own upward-sloping AS function** are short-run functions, derived from assumptions about the short-run marginal productivity of labour and a constant money wage rate. In particular, we must emphasise that there will be a different short-run AS function for each and every money wage rate. The supply-siders' short-run AS function, which is illustrated by the curves AS_1 and AS_2 drawn in Fig. 58(a), is broadly similar to Keynes's upward-sloping AS curve. But, unlike Keynes's upward-sloping curve, the supply-siders' short-run AS curve lacks a vertical section. It remains upward-sloping at all price levels since supply-siders (along with most monetarists and neoclassical economists) assume that firms continue, in the short run, to employ more labour and supply more output, as (at a constant money wage rate) the price level rises and the real cost of employing labour falls.

It is at this point in the analysis that we introduce the really crucial difference between **Keynes's AS function** and the **supply-side (and monetarist) AS function**. As we have just explained, in both Keynes's and the supply-siders' analysis, a rise in the price level must accompany an expansion of aggregate demand from AD_1 to AD_2 to induce firms to increase their supply of output. But, in Keynes's analysis, the money wage rate paid by firms to workers remains unchanged despite the increased price level eroding the real wage rate. There is thus no reason for the AS curve to shift. For supply-siders, and monetarists, this is not the case. For each money wage rate there is a different short-run AS curve, with an increase in the money wage rate shifting the short-run AS curve leftwards. If the government increases aggregate demand from AD_1 to AD_2 and workers then respond to the resulting higher price level by pushing up the money wage rate to maintain their real wages, then the AS curve shifts to the left from AS_1 to AS_2. The net effect is that the 'new' AD and AS schedules once again intersect at the initial level of real output y_n. For supply-siders, monetarists and New Classical economists, Y_n is the 'natural' level of output towards which market forces and a flexible price mechanism eventually adjust (it represents the long-run equilibrium level of output or production potential associated with the 'natural' levels of employment and unemployment of labour which we investigated in Chapter 22). The vertical line drawn in Fig. 58, between the intersections of each pair of short-run AD and AS curves at this 'natural' or equilibrium level of output, is the

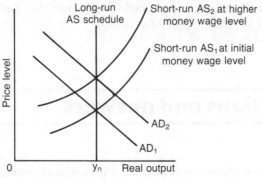

Fig. 58 The 'supply-siders' (monetarists/neoclassical) version of the AD/AS model

supply-siders' long-run AS schedule. It carries the supply-side message, shared by most anti-Keynesians on the 'radical right', that the short-run expansionary effect on output and employment, resulting from the government increasing aggregate demand, is negated in the long run by the way the supply side of the economy responds.

THE GROWING INFLUENCE OF SUPPLY-SIDE ECONOMICS

Today, many economists who would not regard themselves as supply-siders claim that their analysis has always incorporated supply-side effects. However, true believers in supply-sidism would dispute this claim. Be that as it may, few economists or politicians of whatever persuasion or 'ism', now call for large budget deficits as the way to achieve full employment; while almost all voice agreement with the idea that the tax structure should be used to create incentives for work, saving and investment. Arguably, by the 1990s, supply-sidism has become a more significant part of the now-dominant neoclassical revival than monetarism (since for many, monetarism has been discredited by the apparent breakdown in its central postulated relationship between the rate of growth of the money supply and inflation).

The heyday of supply-side economics probably occurred – in the UK at least – in the mid and late 1980s. During these years, government ministers claimed that their free-market supply-side policies had produced a British 'economic miracle', characterised by sustained economic growth and increased industrial competitiveness. Recessions, if they ever occurred again, would be mere 'blips' – short and shallow, over almost before they began. But in the light of the severe and deep recession which hit the UK economy in the early 1990s, the confidence of the supply-siders and other free-market economists has been severely dented. This has been matched by the growing confidence of Neo-Keynesians calling for much more interventionist supply-side policies to aid British industry, in particular the manufacturing sector.

Chapter roundup

As we have emphasised throughout this chapter, supply-side economics developed in the 1970s and 1980s as part of the wider neoclassical revival to replace the previous hegemony of Keynesian economics. The basic Keynesian macroeconomic model, that the AD/AS model of the supply-siders replaced, is covered in Chapters 19 and 20. Monetarists and supply-siders, both being a part of the wider neoclassical revival and resurgence of free-market economics, share many similar views. Some of the major conflicts and controversies separating Keynesians and monetarists, which relate closely to the content of this chapter, are explored in Chapter 24. Also of relevance are Chapter 12 (on industrial policy) and Chapter 13 (on trade unions and wages) in which the supply curve of labour is explained, which provides the microeconomic underpinning of much supply-side theory.

Illustrative questions and answers

1   Essay Question
'There can be no doubt that the transformation of Britain's economic performance in the 1980s ... is above all due to the supply-side policies we have introduced

to allow markets of all kinds to work better.' (Nigel Lawson, Chancellor of the Exchequer, July 1988). Discuss.

(ULEAC, AS-Level, June 1991)

Tutorial note

By the time Nigel Lawson expressed this view in July 1988, the UK economy had benefited from seven years of continuous economic growth, starting from the depths of a severe recession which had lasted from 1979 to 1981. While accepting that growth was to be expected during the 'upswing' of the business cycle, the Conservative Government went further and claimed that its 'supply-side' policies were responsible for significantly improving the economy's long-term growth trend. The Government claimed that the abandonment of Keynesian demand management and interventionism had paved the way for a 'supply-side' led 'British economic miracle'. At the time the UK had moved close to the top of an EC 'league table' measured in terms of the growth in productivity and employment, the fewest days lost in strikes etc.

But by 1991, the picture was much less rosy. 1990 saw the collapse of the 'Lawson boom' and the UK economy entered the longest (if not the deepest) recession since the 1930s. Initially the Conservative Government believed that the recession would be a mere 'blip', interrupting only temporarily the continuation of growth and economic success brought about by its supply-side 'revolution'. However, with the recession fast developing into a more severe 'slump' or 'depression', Keynesian economists have argued that it was the boom years of the mid and late 1980s that constituted the true 'blip', temporarily disrupting the on-going and depressing story of low growth, de-industrialisation and declining competitiveness that have afflicted the UK economy since at least the 1970s. The Keynesians further argue that the 1980s boom, far from being the result of successful supply-side policies, was largely caused by a massive and irresponsible boost to demand, brought about by tax cuts and the removal of controls on bank lending – policies introduced by the Chancellor of the Exchequer Nigel Lawson himself.

Suggested answer plan

1 Briefly describe the state of the UK economy in the late 1980s.
2 Explain how, in principle, supply-side policies could have brought about the economic success experienced at the time.
3 Discuss whether the evidence supports the view that supply-side policies were responsible for this success.
4 Introduce the possibility that demand expansion rather than supply-side policies were responsible for the 1980s boom.
5 Draw an overall conclusion, and indicate that whatever the truth, the economic success did not continue into the early 1990s.

2 Data Question

Table 1 Distribution of the workforce

| | Thousands | | | |
	1979	1983	1986	1989
Employees in employment:				
Manufacturing	7 253	5 252	5 227	5 191
Services	13 580	13 501	14 297	15 427
Other	2 340	2 024	1 863	1 835
Self-employed persons	1 906	2 221	2 627	2 986
Unemployed	1 312	3 127	3 312	1 842

(Source: *Annual Abstract of Statistics* 1990 edition *Social Trends* (20) 1990 edition)

Table 2 *Gross domestic product at current prices*

	1979	1983	1986	1989
		£ million		
Whole economy	172 804	260 399	324 031	394 787
Manufacturing	48 714	61 299	76 485	93 433

(Source: *Annual Abstract of Statistics* 1990 edition)

Table 3 *Output per person employed*

Index numbers 1985 = 100	1979	1983	1986	1989
Whole economy	89.1	96.7	102.9	107.4
Manufacturing	79.9	91.8	103.1	115.7

(Source: *Economic Trends Annual Supplement* 1990 edition)

Table 4 *Visible trade of the United Kingdom*

	1979	1983	1986	1989
Volume index numbers 1985 = 100				
Exports	83.1	87.6	104.0	110.7
Imports	83.5	87.0	107.1	129.5
Value (£ million)				
Visible balance	−3 444	−1 509	−9 364	−20 826

(Source: *Annual Abstract of Statistics* 1990 edition)

(a) (i) Describe the main changes in the distribution of the United Kingdom's workforce between 1979 and 1989, as shown in Table 1.   (4)
   (ii) Examine the possible causes of the changes you have described.   (7)
(b) To what extent do the data support the view that the United Kingdom economy has gone through a period of deindustrialisation?   (5)
(c) Discuss the significance of the changes which have occurred in United Kingdom manufacturing industry for the performance of the economy.   (9)
(AEB, June 1992)

Tutorial note

a) (i) The data shows the growing importance in the tertiary or service sector and the decline of employment in manufacturing and primary industries (the 'others' category). Note also the growth of self-employment.

   (ii) You can argue that the growth of service employment reflects the increased demand for services as income increases; the reduced scope for both productivity increases and labour-shedding in the service sector compared to manufacturing; and the relative protection of many service industries from import competition. The decline of employment in the primary sector was probably concentrated in the decline of the coal mining industry, while the growth of self-employment reflected government encouragement of small businesses and the fact that some of the workers who were laid-off in the recession of the early 1980s started their own small businesses. The decline of employment in manufacturing reflects the de-industrialisation process which we discuss below.

b) You must draw on the information in all four tables for your answer to this question, and not just Table 1. Start your answer by stating what you understand by deindustrialisation (see Chapter 12), and then look for evidence of the process in the data. Beware of Table 2! At first sight, Table 2 implies that manufacturing output rose throughout the period shown by the data, though not as rapidly as total output. However the table shows nominal output (at current prices) before the effects of inflation have been taken into account. Since no data on inflation has been included in the question, you cannot calculate the changes in real manufacturing output.

For the most part, the data covers the upswing in the business cycle and the 'Lawson boom' in the economy in the middle and late 1980s. And while the tables cover the recession which affected the UK economy in the early 1980s, the data ends just before the second very severe recession which hit the UK economy in 1990. In fact this question provides an excellent illustration of an important skill which data response questions can test: namely *your ability to separate the long-term trend in the economy from cyclical variations around the trend*. As we have explained in the guidance notes to Question 4, at the height of the 'Lawson boom' around 1988, the Conservative Government and its supporters were claiming that its 'free-market' 'supply -side' policies had brought about a British 'economic miracle'. Manufacturing output had in fact climbed back from the depths of the earlier recession, rising past its 1979 level, supporting the argument, so the Government claimed, that a *'re-industrialisation'* rather than *'de-industrialisation'* of Britain was taking place. The data on labour productivity in Table 3 and the shedding of labour indicated by Table 1 might support this view. But Keynesians claim that the Government did indeed make the mistake of confusing the cyclical upswing with the long-term trend, and that while the credit-led extended boom of the 1980s masked the de-industrialisation process (though the import penetration implied by the trade figures in Table 4 provide some continuing evidence of deindustrialisation), de-industrialisation returned with a vengeance to scourge the UK economy in the early 1990s.

c) For this part of the question you should develop the points we have just made in the guidance notes to part (b); for example does 'manufacturing matter', and can, and are, service industries taking the place of manufacturing in the UK economy?

Question bank

1 Although many economists agree that the most important problems facing the UK economy lie on the 'supply-side' of the economy, there is much less agreement about the policies appropriate to deal with these problems. What are the 'supply-side' problems facing the economy and why is there disagreement about the appropriate policies?

(AEB, June 1989)

2

a) What do the aggregate demand and aggregate supply curves represent?
(8)

b) Explain what is meant by the term 'supply-side economics' and outline the effect that 'supply-side policies' may have on the aggregate supply curve.
(7)

c) How might policies such as tax reform, privatisation and measures to improve the working of the factor markets, strengthen the supply side of the economy? (10)

(NISEAC, June 1991)

3 'Microeconomic policies to increase aggregate supply, such as those directed towards training, enterprise and productivity, are more effective than expansionary macro-economic policies in reducing unemployment.' Discuss.

(Oxford, June 1988)

4 What factors determine the level of aggregate supply in the economy? Explain how reductions in taxation might be used to increase aggregate supply and discuss how successful such a policy is likely to be.

(JMB, June 1990)

5 Use the concepts of aggregate demand and supply to analyse the effects of an increase in exports on output, employment and inflation.

(Oxford, June 1990)

6
a) What do economists mean by the 'natural' rate of unemployment?   (10)
b) How might 'demand-side' and 'supply-side' economic policies affect the 'natural' rate of unemployment?   (15)

(AEB, November 1992)

7
a) Consider how, in principle, a government could use fiscal policy as an instrument for directly influencing aggregate demand in an economy.   (15)
b) In the UK since 1976 fiscal policy has not generally been used with this intention. What arguments could explain government policy in this regard? (10)

(WJEC, June 1991)

8 'UK Governments in the 1980s were primarily concerned about increasing incentives, generating greater competition and eliminating market imperfections.'
a) Outline the various policies which were implemented to achieve these objectives.   (40)
b) On what criteria could the effectiveness of these policies be evaluated? (60)

(ULEAC, January 1991)

KEYNESIANISM AND MONETARISM

Units in this chapter

24.1 *Underlying concepts*
24.2 *Essential information*

Chapter objectives

In the preceding chapters, frequent mention has been made of **Keynesian** and **monetarist** views and of points of controversy and disagreement which separate economists of the two schools. In this chapter we firstly gather together and summarise some of the themes of the earlier chapters, before extending the discussion to other aspects of the controversy such as the role of incomes policy and the international nature of inflation. Besides emphasising that Keynesianism and monetarism are broad labels which encompass a wide variety of different viewpoints, we shall also note the existence of another school of thought, the self-styled 'radical-left' or neo-Marxian school which rejects both Keynesianism and monetarism.

24.1 UNDERLYING CONCEPTS

Monetarism takes its name from the belief held by all monetarists that inflation is explained by the **quantity theory of money**; according to strict monetarism, all inflation is caused ultimately by a prior expansion of the money supply. In fact, monetarism means rather more than this, extending to encompass a large part of the pre-Keynesian or 'classical' view of how the economy works. As we have explained in Chapter 23, monetarism has formed an important part of the neoclassical revival (or 'radical-right' revival) which has also spawned other free-market orientated 'schools of thought', interrelated with monetarism, including the New Classical and 'supply-side' schools.

KEYNESIANISM

Keynesianism is a label attached to the theories and policies of those economists who claim to have inherited the mantle of the great English economist, J M Keynes. In *The General Theory of Employment, Interest and Money* published in 1936, Keynes created a theory of the working of the whole economy, and from this foundation modern macroeconomics developed. Keynes argued that no automatic tendency exists for unregulated market forces to bring about full employment and that persistent mass unemployment could be caused by deficient demand. Before his death in 1946, Keynes adapted his **theory of deflation and** deficient demand to the **problem of inflation caused by excessive demand**. However, although he did not live to see it, the 'true' Keynesian era dawned in the years after 1945 when, in the United Kingdom in particular, Keynesianism became the new economic and political orthodoxy. Essentially, Keynesianism became associated with an increased level of government intervention in the economy, especially through **budget deficits** and **fiscal policy**, to **'fine-tune' or manage aggregate demand** to a level consistent with achieving relative full employment and economic growth without excessive costs in terms of inflation or Balance of Payments crises.

MONETARISM

Monetarism takes its name from the belief held by all monetarists that inflation is explained by the quantity theory of money; according to strict monetarism all inflation is caused by a prior expansion of the money supply. In fact, monetarism means rather more than this, extending to encompass a large part of the **pre-Keynesian** or **'classical'** view of how the economy works. Indeed, **'the New Classical Macroeconomics'** is probably a better descriptive label than monetarism of the true roots of the views held by many members of the monetarist school.

SOME FUNDAMENTAL ISSUES OF DISPUTE

Later in the chapter we shall examine some of the issues of dispute between Keynesians and monetarists on particular aspects of government policy. First, however, we shall look at some rather more fundamental differences in the views held by the two schools on the nature of the economy:

1 The separation of 'real' and 'monetary' forces

Many monetarists appear to accept the old 'classical' view (known as the **Classical Dichotomy**) that real and monetary forces in the economy are separate. Via the quantity theory of money, an increase in the money supply causes the price level to rise, but it leaves unaffected the equilibrium values of relative prices and levels of output and employment. This view, which is completely rejected by Keynesians, carries the implication that a policy of monetary expansionism will in the long run increase prices but not output and employment, though in the short run (a period of up to five or ten years according to Milton Friedman) some monetarists agree that monetary changes can primarily affect output.

2 The stability of market forces

Monetarists see a market economy as a calm and orderly place in which the market mechanism, working through incentives transmitted by price signals in competitive markets, achieves a better or more optimal outcome than can be attained through government interventionism. In essence, risk-taking businessmen who will gain or lose through the correctness of their decisions in the market-place 'know better' what to produce than civil servants and planners cocooned by risk-free salaries and secured pensions. And provided that markets are sufficiently competitive, what is produced is ultimately determined by the wishes of consumers, who also know better than governments what is good for them. According to this philosophy the correct economic function of government is an **enabling** function rather than a **providing** function, to act as 'nightwatchman' by maintaining law and order, to provide public goods where the market fails, and generally to ensure a suitable environment in which 'wealth-creating' private enterprise can function in competitive markets subject to minimum regulation.

This view of the correct economic role of government leads monetarists generally to **reject discretionary intervention** in the economy as a means of achieving goals such as reduced unemployment. At best, such intervention will be ineffective, at worst it will be destabilising and damaging. To ensure that such intervention does not take place, governments should adopt, if necessary by law, fixed or automatic policy rules. Many monetarists recommend the adoption of a **fiscal** rule to **balance the budget** or **reduce the PSBR** to a fixed percentage of GDP; a monetary rule to expand the money supply in line with the growth of real GDP; and an **exchange rate rule** either to keep to a fixed exchange rate or to allow the exchange rate to float freely. (The debate between Keynesians and monetarists on the respective merits and demerits of discretionary policy and automatic rules is sometimes conducted in terms reminiscent of a motor manual. Thus Milton Friedman argues the advantage of a 'fixed throttle' increase in the money supply, rejecting the 'fine-tuning' of demand advocated by the Keynesians.)

In contrast, Keynesians adopt a rather different view of the functioning of an unregulated market economy. In particular, they stress:

- the **imperfect nature of generally uncompetitive markets**, the growth of monopoly power and producer sovereignty, and the importance of uncertainty about the future and lack of correct market information as potentially destabilising forces;
- the **possible breakdown of money linkages between markets**. In market economies money is used as a means of payment for market transactions, but people receiving money incomes from the sale of labour in the labour market may not necessarily spend their income on the purchase of goods and services in the goods market. Instead they may decide to hold idle money balances. Thus Say's Law that 'supply creates its own demand' breaks down and deficient demand causes involuntary unemployment of labour and other resources.

Thus monetarists emphasise the optimal aspects of a competitive economy in a state of general (and fully employed) equilibrium, and the role in attaining such an equilibrium of private economic agents reacting to price signals in conditions of near-perfect market information. In competitive markets the market mechanism working through **flexible** prices will move the economy towards a full employment equilibrium. In contrast, the Keynesians emphasise the **inflexible** nature of prices and particularly wages. They also see the economy in terms of **disequilibrium** rather than **equilibrium**. The economy is subject to the uncertainty of random 'shocks' or autonomous changes which, by inducing destabilising multiplier effects, hold no guarantee of a smooth and orderly movement to a full employment equilibrium. By managing the level of demand the government can 'know better' than unregulated market forces. It can anticipate and counter the destabilising forces existent in the market economy, achieving a better outcome than is likely in an economy subject to market forces alone.

In summary, therefore, monetarists lay great stress on the essentially stabilising properties of market forces, seeing discretionary government intervention as destabilising and inefficient. Conversely, Keynesians justify discretionary interventionism on the grounds that it stabilises an inherently unstable market economy.

24.2 ESSENTIAL INFORMATION

KEYNESIAN OBJECTIVES AND INSTRUMENTS

In order to explain the principal points of difference between Keynesian and monetarist policies, we shall adopt an **objectives and instruments approach**. First we must identify the objectives, goals or targets which governments or their policy-makers wish to achieve. Once we have specified the objectives, the next stage is to assign a particular policy instrument to a particular objective.

In the earlier part of the Keynesian era, and especially in the 1950s and early 1960s, the Keynesian policy-makers in the United Kingdom relied on one principal policy instrument – the use of discretionary fiscal policy. Fiscal policy was used to achieve three policy objectives: **full employment, a satisfactory balance of payments** (and the protection of a fixed exchange rate), and **control of inflation**. In order to create full employment, tax cuts and increases in public spending resulting in a budget deficit were used to expand demand. However, an increased level of demand also raised imports and pulled up the price level. Eventually, either a balance of payments crisis or an unacceptable rise in the inflation rate, or both, would cause the policy-makers to initiate a reversal of policy in which fiscal policy would be used to deflate demand in order to protect the exchange rate or to reduce inflation. Thus Keynesianism became associated with 'stop-go' management of the economy.

It is worth noting that in this era discretionary **fiscal policy** was used as the principal tool of demand management, partly because the Keynesians believed it to be more effective than discretionary monetary policy, but also because **monetary policy** was in the main assigned to another objective, that of **National Debt management**. Nevertheless, the role of monetary policy was not absolutely clear; it was also used as a supplementary tool of demand management to 'back up' fiscal policy, and as a means of protecting the exchange rate through high interest rates in the recurrent balance of payments crises of the era. In a credit squeeze, demand would be deflated through the use of monetary policy instruments such as open-market operations and the raising of interest rates.

During this first period of Keynesian management of the British economy, successive British governments were committed to preserving a fixed exchange rate. The **exchange rate** was thus a **target** rather than an **instrument** of the policy. But in the latter part of the Keynesian era in the later 1960s and the early 1970s, many Keynesians came to the conclusion that if 'stop-go' was to be avoided a separate policy instrument must be assigned to each of the three principal objectives of policy. Accordingly, the Keynesian assignment rule became:

INSTRUMENT		OBJECTIVE
Fiscal policy	:	Full Employment and Growth
Exchange Rate policy	:	Balance of Payments
Incomes policy	:	Control of Inflation
Monetary policy	:	National Debt Management

KEYNESIANS AND THE EXCHANGE RATE

The Keynesians believed that their ability to achieve sustained full employment and economic growth by means of expansionary demand management policies was severely constrained by the tendency of the balance of payments to go into serious deficit whenever full employment was approached. Increasingly in the early 1960s, Keynesians argued in favour of abandoning the commitment to maintain a fixed exchange rate. **Devaluation** should be used as a policy instrument to 'look after' the balance of payments, leaving fiscal policy free to pursue the objective of full employment. (You should refer to Chapters 26 and 27 for a detailed explanation of the effects of a change in the exchange rate on the balance of payments.) The ideas of '**export-led growth**' and of the existence of a '**virtuous circle**' became fashionable amongst Keynesians in the 1960s. They argued that a devaluation (or downward float) of the exchange rate improves the competitive position of exports and worsens that of imports. The improved balance of payments position then stimulates growth which in turn stimulates productivity. The competitive position of exports then further improves as a result of falling average costs of production. The process continues, with exports stimulating growth, stimulating competitiveness and so on. Conversely, it was believed that an overvalued exchange rate could explain Britain's predicament in the 1960s, trapped in a **vicious circle** of uncompetitive exports, slow growth, and a worsening balance of payments position.

Nevertheless, neither the 1967 devaluation of the £ nor its floating in 1972 succeeded in achieving for Britain the 'miracle' of export-led growth. Against this background, economists of the Keynesian persuasion increasingly turned their attention to **incomes policies**, and even to **import controls**, in the search for additional policy instruments with which to manage the economy successfully.

KEYNESIANS AND INCOMES POLICY

As it became increasingly clear that, on its own, discretionary fiscal policy or demand management was unable to secure both full employment and price stability, Keynesians, or post-Keynesians, of the cost-push school turned their attention to incomes policy as the appropriate instrument to reduce inflation. However, many economists dispute the idea that an incomes policy should be regarded as a well-defined policy instrument. They argue that 'incomes policy' has become a label for a wide variety of statutory and voluntary, short-term and long-term policies for the freezing, restraint or 'planned growth' of wages, incomes, and even prices. Incomes policies can vary from emergency ad hoc measures, usually of short duration in response to a panic or crisis, to the long-term forward planning of the growth of incomes, based on some social consensus.

Other economists take the view that the control of inflation is not necessarily the main objective of an incomes policy. Many Marxists argue that its main function is to squeeze wages so as to alter the distribution of income in favour of profits. A popular view is that incomes policies should be used to pursue a 'social fairness' policy in which job evaluation replaces market forces as the determinant of wages. One result of this proliferation of interpretations as to what is meant by incomes policy is that it is exceedingly difficult to evaluate the effectiveness of incomes policies in controlling inflation. This is because it is almost impossible to compare a 'policy-on' period with a period of 'policy-off' as no one can agree on what exactly constitutes an incomes policy.

Nevertheless, the incomes policies introduced by successive British governments in the 1960s and 1970s went through four identifiable stages in the cycle of their rather short lives:

❶ Incomes policies have almost always been introduced as unthought-out and temporary measures by governments elected to office on an anti-incomes policy platform. Indeed, in the first months in office the government may well have been busy dismantling an earlier policy inherited from its predecessor. The first stage of an incomes policy has usually been a **wage freeze** introduced in response to a crisis – either of inflation or in the balance of payments. Free collective bargaining may be suspended for the duration of the wage freeze.

❷ Traditionally, governments have used the wage freeze as a breathing space for thinking out the detailed strategy of the second or '**planned growth of incomes**' stage. In this critical stage of an incomes policy, the government allows market forces to work but imposes constraints on their operation, particularly in the labour market. A statutory incomes policy imposes legally binding limits on free collective bargaining, and sometimes on prices as well. In contrast, a voluntary incomes policy will rely on exhortation, an appeal to the national interest and national unity, or to some form of social contract between government, employers and unions.

Restraint on the wage-bargaining process may take the form of a maximum limit for wage rises. Usually the government chooses a **wage ceiling** on the basis of the estimated rate of growth of productivity. For example, if productivity grows at 3%, a limit on wage rises of 7% should be consistent with 4% inflation. In practice, however, an upper limit on wage rises becomes interpreted as the norm, or even as a lower limit which every self-respecting union negotiator must attempt to exceed.

❸ The second stage of an incomes policy has usually lasted as long as it is accepted as socially fair by the people upon whom it is imposed. In the third stage, the **incomes policy begins to disintegrate** when this consensus breaks down. Workers begin to resent and fight against the incomes policy when they see other groups in society successfully evading the policy. **Wage-drift** provides one form of evasion. In a period of incomes policy, workers may try to negotiate locally at the plant level rather than through national collective bargaining. It is usually much more difficult for the government to 'police' thousands of local agreements than the much smaller number of national collective agreements. Thus total earnings drift away from basic wage rates which are still usually negotiated nationally, but only certain groups of workers will benefit from the process. Other methods of evasion include job re-gradings and the tendency for higher-paid workers – particularly managers – to take a larger part of their real income in the form of fringe benefits or perks. The feeling of social unfairness will also intensify if certain types of income, such as profits and the income of the self-employed, are outside the bounds of the incomes policy, or if there is no restraint on prices.

In the third stage of incomes policy, workers begin to claim, and the government begins to allow, **special case treatment,** whereby certain groups of workers bypass or exceed the limits on pay rises. Some groups, usually the higher paid, claim special case status on the grounds of a higher-than-average rise in productivity, whereas others, usually the lower paid, argue that they merit special treatment on the basis of 'social fairness'.

❹ Incomes policies in the UK have finally collapsed under one of two sets of circumstances. Either the government, having lost its resolve, has allowed the policy to fade away in a spate of 'special cases', or the election of a new government has defeated the policy at the ballot-box. However, before too long an incoming government has usually found it necessary to reintroduce an incomes policy despite its avowed intentions. Even the monetarist Conservative government elected in 1979 operated an informal incomes policy applied to wages in the public sector where the government is the employer! This incomes policy was a logical consequence of the cash limits and external financing limits imposed respectively upon government departments (and local government) and nationalised industries. Wage increases exceeding these limits would not be compatible with the government's achieving its PSBR and money supply targets.

In much the same way, the Conservative government imposed a 1½% pay rise ceiling on all public-sector workers in 1992, arguing that the deteriorating state of the public sector finances meant that this was the maximum that could be afforded.

Immediately following the final collapse of an incomes policy, there is usually a 'catching up' period in which workers frantically attempt either to make up what they see as lost ground, or to restore differentials. Indeed, the sudden rise in the inflation rate which occurs in the catching-up period creates precisely the conditions in which a 'new' incomes policy is introduced to reduce the rate of inflation. Thus, because of the catching-up period between incomes policies, it is very difficult to assess just how effective incomes policies have been in reducing inflation.

MONETARISTS AND INCOMES POLICIES

Most monetarists completely oppose the use of an incomes policy except as an informal policy to control pay increases in the public sector, where the state is the employer. As we have explained, monetarists accept the neoclassical tradition of the allocative efficiency of market forces and retain a suspicion of the economic power of the state. Incomes policies are undesirable because they interfere with and distort the working of the market mechanism, and extend the economic role of the state. Nevertheless, some economists take up a more eclectic or pragmatic position between the extremes adopted by cost-push Keynesians and monetarists. The eclectics argue that an incomes policy may sometimes have a useful role in reducing inflationary expectations, without at the same time greatly distorting market forces.

MONETARIST INSTRUMENTS AND OBJECTIVES

While the Keynesians have consistently searched for an ever-wider range of policy instruments with which to conduct the management of the economy, the monetarists have argued that the correct role of government is to **minimise its intervention in the economy**. While monetarists usually believe that discretionary monetary policy has a more powerful influence on the level of money national income than fiscal policy, it is wrong to draw the conclusion that monetarists advocate its use in the management of the level of demand. Not only would a discretionary monetary policy be unpredictable in its effects, the main effect of monetary expansion would be a rising price level rather than a growth of real output. Monetarists usually reject the use of discretionary economic management policies of any kind – **fiscal policy, monetary policy, incomes policy** and **exchange rate policies**. Instead, they argue that the economic function of government is to create the conditions in which market forces, working through price signals and private incentives, can properly operate. Nevertheless, it is still useful to analyse monetarist economic policy in terms of instruments and objectives, even though the monetarists prefer the announcement of firm policy rules to a discretionary intervention in the working of the economy:

❶ The **ultimate objective** of monetarist policy is to create conditions in which market forces and private enterprise can ensure full employment and economic growth.

❷ Control of inflation is seen as a necessary condition or **intermediate objective** which must be achieved before market forces can work properly.

❸ Monetarists believe that inflation is caused by an excessive rate of growth of the money supply. Therefore control of the money supply is a necessary **intermediate (or immediate) objective** of policy. Nevertheless, control of the money supply may be difficult to achieve. Some monetarists believe that it should be regarded as a general indicator of whether or not the policy is 'on course', and used in conjunction with other indicators or intermediate targets such as the exchange rate and the rate of growth of Money GDP.

❹ Monetary policy cannot be separated from the **fiscal stance** adopted by the government. At the root of monetarism is the belief that the levels of public spending and the PSBR must be used as a **policy instrument** to achieve control over the rate of growth of the money supply. A tight fiscal stance and the reduction of both public spending and the PSBR as a proportion of GDP will also reduce undesirable '**crowding out**' in the economy by freeing a greater volume of resources for use and employment in the private sector. Some monetarists recommend a '**balanced budget**' **fiscal policy rule**.

❺ Monetarists place considerable emphasis on **supply-side** or **microeconomic policies** which have the general objective of making markets more competitive. Competition policy and industrial relations policy (perhaps a euphemism for anti-trade union policy) are examples, together with cuts in income tax rates to promote supply-side incentives.

MONETARISTS AND THE EXCHANGE RATE

Practical monetarism thus involves the adoption of two automatic policy rules:

❶ A **fiscal rule** to balance the budget or to reduce public spending and the PSBR as proportions of GDP;
and

❷ A **monetary rule** to allow the money supply to grow at some predetermined rate, for example based on the rate of growth of real GDP.

There is much less agreement amongst monetarists on the form of a third rule to be adopted for the exchange rate. Monetarists generally fall into one of two camps, advocating either a **fixed** or a **freely floating** exchange rate. Those monetarists who have studied the inflationary process in a regime of fixed exchange rates such as existed before 1972 are sometimes called **international monetarists** or **global monetarists**. In such a system, the **world inflation rate** is determined by the rate of growth of the **world money supply**. For a country like the UK, the domestic inflation rate must converge with the world inflation rate to maintain the fixed exchange rate. The domestic money supply responds endogenously to 'accommodate', or finance, the rate of inflation 'imported' from the rest of the world. Thus, instead of changes in the domestic money supply causing inflation, with fixed exchange rates, the 'imported' rate of inflation changes the domestic money supply. This is the reverse of the 'traditional' theory of monetarism, developed originally by Milton Friedman as appropriate either for a closed economy or for a system of floating exchange rates. Nevertheless, in a fixed exchange rate system, the rate of world inflation is still caused by world monetary growth.

At the beginning of the 'monetarist experiment' in the early 1980s, many monetarists seemed to prefer a completely **free** or **cleanly floating exchange rate** because this is consistent with their view that market forces and not the government should determine as far as possible the level of activity within the economy. As in the case of other forms of government intervention, many monetarists believe that an attempt by government to manage the exchange rate will create distortions and inefficiencies and is in any case in the long run unable to defy market forces. (The £'s brief experience in the **Exchange Rate Mechanism** of the European Monetary system, from 1990 to 1992, gives considerable support to this view. We develop this theme in Chapter 27.) Additionally, a floating exchange has the advantage, in theory at least, of isolating the economy from international inflationary pressure. As has just been explained, with a fixed exchange rate, a country may 'import' inflation from the rest of the world. Many monetarists, and also many Keynesians, argue that this is what happened in the 1960s when the USA expanded its domestic economy and built up a huge balance of payments deficit against the rest of the world. Because the dollar was the cornerstone of the Bretton Woods system of fixed exchange rates (to be explained in Chapters 26 and 27), the Americans managed to persuade other countries to maintain their fixed exchange rates against the dollar and to accept dollars in payment for US imports from the rest of the world. The resulting outflow of dollars from America into the reserves of the rest of the world greatly swelled international demand and, in the monetarist interpretation, added to the excessive rate of growth of the world money supply. If, instead, other exchange rates had freely floated against the dollar, the rest of the world would not have imported the dollars created by the American authorities. The American balance of payments deficit would simply have resulted in an excess supply of dollars on foreign exchange markets which would then have caused the exchange rate of the dollar to fall until the US deficit had been eliminated.

Nevertheless, the kexperience of floating exchange rates in the 1970s and 1980s has convinced many monetarists – and Keynesians as well – that a floating exchange rate contributes to the inflationary process. They argue that a completely fixed exchange rate provides a source of discipline for workers and business enterprises within the domestic economy. If, for example, workers bargain for wage increases of 10% when the average rate of growth of productivity is only 4%, then the domestic price level is almost sure to rise. But in a regime of freely floating exchange rates, international competitiveness need not be adversely affected. The exchange rate may simply fall to maintain the initial relative price of British goods compared with foreign goods. But the inflation process does not stop here. Workers may respond to the rising money price of imports by demanding even higher money wages in an attempt to increase the real wage. This causes a further rise in prices, followed by a fall in the exchange rate and further wage increases in a vicious inflationary spiral accompanied by a plummeting exchange rate.

The floating of the exchange rate may also remove a source of discipline from the behaviour of governments. Indeed, the acceleration in the rate of inflation experienced simultaneously by many countries in the 1970s has been explained in terms of the breakdown of the Bretton Woods system of fixed exchange rates in 1971 and 1972. Governments apparently felt free to reflate demand, hoping that a floating exchange rate would 'look after' the balance of payments. They also hoped that in a regime of floating exchange rates there would no longer be a need periodically to deflate demand in order to support the exchange rate. As a result, simultaneous reflation by many countries in the early 1970s caused a world-wide increase in demand which world output was incapable of meeting, and inflation resulted.

By the mid-1980s many economists, both monetarist and Keynesian, had swung round to the opinion that a fixed exchange rate was needed to impose the necessary counter-inflationary discipline upon the behaviour of workers and firms in the setting of wages and prices, and upon government in avoiding the temptation to reflate demand 'irresponsibly'. This was perhaps the most significant reason why the £ joined the fixed exchange rate system of the ERM in 1990. But ERM membership at the high parity at which the £ was fixed, provided not so much a source of discipline as a straitjacket. Monetary policy in general – and interest rates in particular – had to be set to attract capital flows into the £ to support the overvalued exchange rate. As a result, the government lost almost all its freedom to pursue an economic policy aimed at protecting the domestic economy from the recession which hit the UK economy in 1990. Opponents of fixed exchange rates and also supporters of the ERM who believed that the £ should have entered the system at a much lower parity, now agree that ERM entry at an overvalued exchange rate in 1990 caused the UK recession in the early 1990s to be much longer and deeper than would have been the case if the £ had stayed out of the ERM.

'NEW SCHOOL' AND 'OLD SCHOOL' KEYNESIANS

We have already mentioned that Keynesians of the cost-push school favour the use of an incomes policy as a means of controlling inflation. One group of neo-Keynesians, or post-Keynesians, whose members subscribe to the cost-push theory of inflation is the **Cambridge Economic Policy Group (CEPG)**. The members of the CEPG are also known as the 'New School' Keynesians, a title which distinguishes them from the more traditional 'Old School' supporters of demand management and discretionary fiscal policy. In common with monetarists, New School Keynesians are doubtful of the virtues of short-term discretionary management of the economy. Instead, they prefer a more **medium-term policy**, aimed at improving the structure or supply side of the economy. Nevertheless, in contrast to monetarists, the New School shares with the older school of Keynesians a belief in the need to increase rather than to reduce government intervention in the market economy. Members of the CEPG argued in the 1970s that a close link exists between the budget deficit and the balance of payments; in short, that a larger budget deficit has an adverse effect on the balance of payments. In consequence, the government's fiscal stance should be used to achieve a desired balance of payments target. This would mean that fiscal policy is unavailable for use as a policy instrument to secure the domestic target of full employment. The New School has at times recommended the use of **import controls**, not so much as a means of protecting the balance of payments, but as a policy instrument to achieve full employment by increasing the volume of domestically produced output.

To complete the picture, both incomes policy and the exchange rate have been recommended by various members of the New School as appropriate policy instruments to control inflation. However, different members of the New School hold different views which have been subject to frequent change and adjustment. In the early 1980s, New School views had a significant influence on the Alternative Economic Strategy adopted as Labour Party economic policy. As with the Old School of Keynesians, the New School attaches a relatively small importance to monetary policy in its assignment of policy instruments to policy objectives.

KEYNESIANS, MONETARISTS AND THE NATURE OF AGGREGATE SUPPLY

An important area of dispute between Keynesians and monetarists centres on assumptions made by each school about the nature of the **aggregate supply of real output** in the economy. 'Extreme' Keynesians believe that an expansion of aggregate demand, along an **'inverted L-shaped' aggregate supply curve**, will reflate output (without inflation) until full employment is reached, when any further demand stimulation will cause prices to rise. For more 'moderate' Keynesians (and probably for Keynes himself), the AS curve is upward-sloping. In these circumstances, an increase in aggregate demand will stimulate both real output and prices until full employment is reached. However, for many monetarists, supply-side economists and other members of the neoclassical/'radical right' revival, the long-run AS curve is vertical, located at the 'natural' or equilibrium level of output in the economy. It carries the message that any demand stimulation will, in the long run, cause prices to rise rather than output. (For a more detailed discussion of these issues, refer back to Chapter 23 on supply-side economics.)

A CRITICISM OF KEYNESIAN AND MONETARIST ECONOMICS

With the decline of traditional or Old School Keynesianism, both monetarism and the New Keynesian School have had an influence upon the conduct of economic policy in the UK. The influence of the monetarist school has of course been considerable and often dominating. Nevertheless, we should not conclude this chapter without mentioning, albeit briefly, the arguments of another school of thought which attacks and rejects both Keynesianism and monetarism. This is the **'radical-left'** or **neo-marxian school**, which experienced something of a revival at the academic level in some British universities in the 1970s and 1980s, but which has had little or no influence upon the conduct of UK policy. Marxists analyse the problems of the British economy in terms of the historical development of **capitalism** as an economic system, and of the particular stage of development in which the British economy finds itself.

According to the Marxist view, Keynes made respectable the extension of the economic role of the state in a non-socialist economy. Government intervention could make the capitalist economy function better, without changing the fundamental nature of capitalism as an economic system. For a time, Keynesian economic management did indeed contain and reduce the inconsistencies and contradictions which Marxists identify within the capitalist system, but it did not eliminate them. Marxists argue that this is demonstrated by the role of the state in capitalist economies such as the UK. On the one hand, the state provides necessary services which allow private capital to be more profitable. These services include the management of demand, the provision of external economies, and the maintenance of social order. But on the other hand, most of the economic functions of the modern state are not directly productive and the growth of the state imposes an increasing burden of taxation upon private capital. Marxists argue that in the short run the state has been able to reduce this burden and to achieve full employment, but only at the expense of pursuing inflationary policies. The modern state now finds itself in an impasse, with capitalism in a state of crisis. A further extension on Keynesian lines of the role of the state to restore full employment will either add to inflationary pressure or, by increasing the burden of taxation, it will erode the vital requirement for capitalist accumulation – the rate of profit.

Yet if the monetarists' alternative is adopted and the state 'rolled back' to become a mere 'nightwatchman' over the economy, the necessary functions of the state for private capital will not be performed. Thus Keynesian economic management will produce runaway inflation and declining profitability, whereas monetarism will result in mass unemployment and social conflict. According to Marxists, neither Keynesian nor monetarist economic management can deal with the true causes of the crisis, which lie within the nature of capitalism itself. The controversy between Keynesians and monetarists is irrelevant; only a change in the system, to socialism, will eliminate the crisis in capitalism. Needless to say, most 'orthodox' Keynesians and monetarists dispute the Marxian analysis, though some would accept that it usefully adds to the discussion about the current problems facing the economy. However, there is a widespread dismissal by Keynesians and monetarists of the Marxist view that the problems would somehow be eliminated or reduced if the capitalist system was replaced with socialism, and recent changes in Eastern Europe and the breakup of the USSR have hardly added to the authority of Marxian economics or the Marxist interpretation of history.

Chapter roundup

In this chapter, which concludes our main section on macroeconomic theory and policy, we have attempted to draw together many of the themes introduced in earlier units from Chapter 14 to Chapter 23. The essentials of the Keynesian national income-expenditure model are covered in Chapters 18 to 22. Chapters 14 to 17 cover areas of monetary and fiscal dispute between Keynesians and monetarists, including the topical issue of the importance of the PSBR and its effects upon the economy. Chapter 22 concentrates on the dispute about the causes of unemployment and inflation, while Chapter 23 surveys the main elements of 'supply-side' economics which, along with monetarism, forms an important part of the neoclassical revival.

We have made some mention in this chapter of the impact that the balance of payments and the exchange rate have on the task of domestic economic management. This theme is developed in more depth in Chapter 26 on the balance of payments and Chapter 27 on the exchange rate.

Illustrative questions and answers

1 Essay Question
Distinguish between monetary and fiscal policy. Discuss the role of fiscal policy in the management of the economy by a 'monetarist' government.
(AEB, June 1989)

Tutorial note

Many of the candidates who answered this question in 1989 wrote as follows: 'monetary policy is control of the money supply; fiscal policy is Keynesian demand management. Since monetarists reject Keynesian demand management, a 'monetarist' government does not have a fiscal policy.'

While there is an element of truth in this approach, it is only an element and the answer is much too narrow. You should define monetary policy more broadly as 'the part of the government's overall economic policy that attempts to achieve its objectives using monetary instruments such as controls on bank lending and the rate of interest'. Likewise, fiscal policy can be defined as 'the part of the government's overall economic policy that attempts to achieve its objectives using the fiscal instruments of taxation and public spending'. It is then useful to distinguish between the 'macro' and 'micro' elements of fiscal policy. At the macro level, a 'monetarist' government might use fiscal policy to reduce the overall size of the public sector to avoid 'crowding out'; and to create the fiscal conditions (via PSBR control) thought necessary for the success of a 'monetarist' monetary policy aimed at controlling monetary growth.

Under monetarism, it is useful to think of fiscal policy (at the macro level) being determined by the needs of monetary policy; while macro policy in general is subordinated to some extent below micro policy in a 'monetarist' government's overall economic strategy. Micro fiscal policy is essentially the 'supply-side' fiscal policy we described in Chapter 23, centering on the role of tax cuts to create incentives to which private economic agents may respond.

Suggested answer plan

1 Define both fiscal policy and monetary policy in the broad terms we have indicated.
2 Explain how a 'monetarist' government is likely to reject the use of fiscal policy as an instrument of short term demand management, adopting instead a much more medium-term strategy.
3 Describe the more macro elements of monetarist fiscal policy, e.g. reducing public spending, balancing the budget, etc.
4 Describe the more micro elements and relate them to 'supply-side' economics, e.g. tax cuts to create incentives.

2   Data Question

The rehabilitation of market forces in the early 1980s was seen at first as an aberration from the postwar consensus, and one that was likely to be short-lived. But I have little doubt that, as a longer perspective develops, history will judge that intervention and planning were the aberration, and that the market economy is the normal, healthy way of life.

Needless to say, belief in the system of free markets does not imply that markets are infallible, any more than examples of irrational market behaviour in any way undermine belief in the market system. What matters is that free markets bring greater benefits and fewer (and more readily corrected) costs than statism.

This is a truth increasingly recognized throughout the world: the lesson that the way to economic success is through the market place.

(Source: N. Lawson, *The State of the Market*, IEA Occasional Paper 80, 1988)

(a) What did Mr Lawson mean in referring to the 'postwar consensus'?   (6)
(b) Critically appraise the statement that 'free markets bring greater benefits and fewer (and more readily corrected) costs than statism'.   (14)
(c) What examples might Mr Lawson have had in mind in support of his case in favour of market forces?   (5)

(ULEAC, S Level, June 1990)

Tutorial note

At the economic level, the '**postwar consensus**' referred to the wide measure of agreement amongst economists (during the three decades after 1945) on the virtues of Keynesianism and the mixed economy. At the political level, this was the '**Butskellite consensus**', named after two centrist politicians, one Conservative (Rab Butler) and the other Labour (Hugh Gaitskell), who were influential in ensuring that every British government, from 1950 until the election of Mrs Margaret Thatcher's Conservative administration in 1979, subscribed to the 'postwar consensus'. The mix of private and public ownership and market and non-market provision of goods and services were regarded as 'about right for Britain'. The election of a Labour government might extend the state sector at the margin, via some extra nationalisation, while conversely a Conservative administration (prior to 1979) might tinker with denationalisation; but there was general agreement on the virtues of Keynesian-inspired management of aggregate demand and of state provision of public and merit goods such as education and the National Health Service.

The second part of the question calls for a discussion of whether the benefits of free (and presumably competitive) markets, in terms of consumer sovereignty and the various types of efficiency we have explained at length earlier in this book, exceed the disadvantages resulting from the many examples of market failure we have also explained. Under '**statism**', market failure is regarded as so serious that state intervention completely replaces the market. Nigel Lawson probably had in mind a much different role for the state: essentially a **minimalist 'enabling' role** to create the competitive conditions in which markets can function efficiently. The examples Nigel Lawson might have had in mind (in 1988), in support of his case in favour of market forces, would include any benefits he believed had resulted from the programmes of privatisation and deregulation pursued in the 1980s. Since 1988 many of the economic changes taking place in Eastern Europe might also be cited; though the move towards the marketisation of formerly Communist and 'statist' economies, has also exposed some of the deficiencies of exclusive reliance on the virtues of the market.

Question bank

1 Are monetarism and supply-side economics inextricably linked?

(Cambridge, June 1988)

2 Assess the arguments for and against attempts to control inflation through prices and incomes policies.

(ULEAC AS-Level, June 1991)

3 Discuss the role of fiscal policy in a modern economy, in both its microeconomic and macroeconomic spheres.   (10 marks each)

(Oxford, June 1990)

4 Are budget deficits necessarily inflationary?

(Oxford, June 1990)

5 Discuss the difference between 'Monetarist' and 'Keynesian' views with regard to the significance of the quantity of money on the macroeconomic behaviour of economies.

(WJEC, June 1991)

6 Both in 1980–82 and 1990–91 in the UK, government policies designed to reduce inflation were associated with increasing unemployment. Discuss why this might have occurred and consider whether an effective 'incomes policy' could have a role to play in reducing inflation without increasing unemployment.

(WJEC, June 1992)

TRADE

Units in this chapter

Chapter objectives

The underlying basis for trade is the same, whether trade takes place between individuals or business enterprises, on a **regional basis** within a country or **internationally** between countries. Although in this chapter we shall concentrate on international trade, the basis for all voluntarily undertaken exchange and trade is the belief that both parties can gain. Trade begins when an individual productive enterprise produces an output that is surplus to its own needs, which it is able to exchange for the surplus of some other individual or productive enterprise, increasing the welfare of both. Before the development of money, the exchange was achieved through barter. Nowadays, a commonly accepted currency serves as the medium of exchange for internal trade within a country, but **payments difficulties** prevent the full development of international trade. Countries may lack a **means of payment** acceptable to other countries, and **risks** and **uncertainties** about exchange rates may reduce trade. Deliberately imposed restrictions on trade, such as **tariffs**, and other forms of **import control**, may create further **barriers to trade**.

World trade is dominated by the advanced industrial nations, whose exports and imports usually exceed 20% of GDP. Because of the size of its huge domestic market the USA is somewhat of an exception, with the value of US exports and imports equalling only about 8% of GDP. The largest proportion of the trade of industrialised countries (the 'North') is with each other, rather than with the less developed countries (LDCs or the 'South'). A considerable growth in 'North/South' trade may be necessary if the **development gap** between the countries of the world is to be reduced.

25.1 UNDERLYING CONCEPTS

The case for specialisation and trade

The general case for specialisation and trade centres on the proposition that countries or regions can attain levels of production, consumption and economic welfare which are beyond the production possibility frontier open to them in a world without trade. Assuming full employment of all factors of production, a country can only increase the production of one good or service by diverting resources away from the production of other goods. Whenever resources are scarce, the opportunity cost of increasing the output of one industry is the alternative output foregone in other industries in the economy. If, however, a country concentrates scarce resources and factors of production into producing the goods in which it is most efficient, total world production can increase. **Gains from specialisation** and trade are possible if countries can agree to exchange that part of the output which they produce that is surplus to their needs. Having stated the general case for trade, we shall now examine some more specific arguments in favour of specialisation and trade.

The benefits of competition

In Chapter 6 we explained how market forces operating in a perfectly competitive market economy can, subject to rather strong assumptions, achieve a state of **economic efficiency**, defined as a combination of **productive** and **allocative efficiency**. Within an isolated and relatively small economy, markets may be too small to be competitive and monopoly may predominate. Exposure to international competition is likely to make markets more competitive and hence more efficient.

The benefits of economies of scale and division of labour

The **benefits of division of labour** were first recognised in the 18th century by the great classical economist Adam Smith. Smith discussed the division of labour in the context of workers **specialising in different productive tasks** within a factory which itself specialised in producing a particular type of product. He then went on to extend the analysis to **specialisation between regions and countries**. Thus, it should be stressed that there are many different levels at which the benefits of the division of labour can be attained: **division of labour within a plant**; **division between plants** within a firm; **division between firms** within an industry; division **between industries** within a country; and finally **division of labour between countries**.

Adam Smith suggested three reasons why division of labour increased production and efficiency:

❶ workers become better at a particular task – '**practice makes perfect**';
❷ **time**, which would be lost when workers move between tasks, is saved;
❸ **more and better capital** can be employed in production.

The latter advantage cited by Smith is particularly important, since it is closely related to the benefits of economies of scale. If a country specialises in producing the goods in which it is already most efficient, a large scale of production may allow it to benefit from **increasing returns to scale** and **economies of scale**. In other words, its industries become even more efficient, when, for example, long production runs allow firms to introduce more advanced forms of machinery and improved technology. In the absence of international trade, the limited extent of the domestic market may prevent a country from benefiting from economies of scale. Thus, by **extending the market**, international trade and specialisation allows the full benefits of the division of labour and economies of scale to be achieved (though we should also note that the possibility of diseconomies of scale and other disadvantages of the division of labour form the basis of a case against trade).

Increasing the range of choice

The international immobility of some factors of production and the unique allocation of natural resources in each country mean that **the production possibilities open to each country are different**. In the extreme, the production of some goods or services may be exclusive to a particular country. A simple example will show in this situation how wider choice can result from trade. If there are just two nations (A and B) and one can only produce bread and the other jam, then if each country's production exceeds its needs, both countries can gain by trading their surplus rather than letting it rot. Thus the welfare of each nation is increased as they both have bread and jam, rather than bread or jam.

25.2 ESSENTIAL INFORMATION

THE PRINCIPLE OF COMPARATIVE ADVANTAGE

Even when there are no economies of scale or increasing returns to scale, the theory of comparative advantage indicates that gains can still be realised from international trade. This is easiest to show when each country in our two-country model has an **absolute advantage** in producing either bread or jam, but is able to produce the other commodity if it wishes.

Absolute advantage

We shall assume:

- Factors of production are perfectly mobile within each country and they can be instantly switched between industries. However, factors are immobile between countries, though final goods and services can be traded.
- There are constant returns to scale and constant average costs of production in both industries in both countries.
- Both commodities, bread and jam, are in demand in both countries.
- The limited resources and factors of production in each country are fully employed.

Suppose now that each country has equal resources and devotes half of its limited resources to bread production and half to jam. The production totals are:

	Bread (units)	Jam (units)
Country A	10	5
Country B	5	10
'World' total	15	15

The relative or **comparative cost** of bread production is lower in country A than in country B, but the position is reversed in the production of jam. Country A has an absolute advantage in bread production, whereas the absolute advantage in jam production lies with country B. If each country specialises in the production of the commodity in which it is most efficient and possesses the absolute advantage, we get:

	Bread (units)	Jam (units)
Country A	20	0
Country B	0	20
'World' total	20	20

The gains from specialisation and trade equal 5 units of bread and 5 units of jam, provided that there are no transport costs.

Comparative advantage

It is less obvious that specialisation and trade are also worthwhile even when a country can produce all goods more efficiently at a lower absolute cost than other countries. This phenomenon is explained by the principle of comparative **advantage**, or a comparison of the **relative** efficiency of production in different countries rather than their **absolute** efficiency.

Suppose that country A becomes more efficient in both bread and jam production. If each country devotes half its resources to each industry, the production totals are:

	Bread (units)	Jam (units)
Country A	30	15
Country B	5	10
'World' total	35	25

Country A possesses an absolute advantage in both industries, but whereas A is six times as efficient in bread production, it is only 50% more efficient in jam production. Nevertheless, if country B produces an extra unit of jam, it need give up only half a unit of bread. In contrast, country A must give up two units of bread in order to increase production of jam by one unit. We say that **a country's comparative advantage lies in the good which it can produce relatively cheaply**, at a **lower opportunity** cost than its trading partner. Country A (which has the absolute advantage in both commodities) possesses a comparative advantage in bread production, whereas country B (with an absolute disadvantage in both) has the comparative advantage in jam production.

If each country specialises completely in the activity in which it possesses a comparative advantage, the production totals are:

	Bread (units)	Jam (units)
Country A	60	0
Country B	0	20
'World' total	60	20

You will notice that compared with the situation without specialisation and trade in which each country devoted half its resources to each industry, there is a gain of 25 units of bread, but a loss of 5 units of jam. Thus, in the case where one country is more efficient in both activities, we cannot say, without some knowledge of demand and the value placed on consumption of bread and jam by the inhabitants of the two countries, whether a welfare gain will result from **complete specialisation**. We can be more sure of a welfare gain if at least as much of one good and more of the other results from specialisation and trade. We can obtain this result by devising a situation in which country A, the country with the absolute advantage in both goods, decides not to specialise completely, but to devote some of its resources to jam production. For example, if country A produces 5 units of jam with one-sixth of its resources and 50 units of bread with the other five-sixths, then the production totals are:

	Bread (units)	Jam (units)
Country A	50	5
Country B	0	20
'World' total	50	25

Compared with the situation without specialisation and trade, there is a gain of 15 units of bread.

THE TERMS OF TRADE

The rate of exchange of bread for jam, or the **terms of trade**, will determine the benefits of trade for these trading partners. The limits to the exchange are set by each country's **opportunity cost ratio**. In the example where country A has an absolute advantage in the production of both goods, country A will be prepared to give up no more than 2 units of bread for 1 unit of jam, whilst country B will require at least ½ a unit of bread for 1 unit of jam if trade is to be worthwhile. Thus the terms of trade must lie between ½ unit of bread and 2 units of bread for 1 unit of jam. The exact rate of exchange, or the relative price of the two commodities, will be determined by the strength of demand.

In the real world where millions of goods and services are traded, a nation's average terms of trade are measured with index numbers. The average prices of exports and imports are calculated using weighted indices and the export index is divided by the import index to give the **terms of trade index**. A rise in the index shows an improvement in a nation's terms of trade, indicating that a given quantity of exports now pays for more imports than previously. We shall examine the causes and effects of changes in the terms of trade in greater detail in Chapters 26 and 27. It is worth noting, however, that a rise in the exchange rate of the £ and a domestic inflation rate higher than that of our trading partners, can both 'improve' the terms of trade, but that the effects of the 'improvement' are not necessarily beneficial in other respects.

THE CASE AGAINST TRADE

The case for specialisation and trade is based on the proposition that all countries taken together will gain in terms of increased production, efficiency and welfare, provided that the terms of trade lie within the opportunity cost ratios. However, there is no guarantee that the gains are distributed equally amongst the trading countries. Although restraints on free trade will probably reduce world welfare, individual countries may feel that it is in their self-interest to restrict the freedom of trade. Not all the arguments put forward to justify restrictions on trade are strictly economic: social and political factors are also involved.

Economic arguments

❶ **The protection of 'infant industries'** This argument is quite strong when there is scope for industries to benefit from economies of scale. A newly established industry, in for example a developing country, may be unable to compete with other countries in which established rivals are already benefiting from economies of scale. Protection may be justified during the early growth of an 'infant industry'.

❷ **To avoid the dangers of overspecialisation** The benefits which result from specialising in accordance with the principle of comparative advantage will not be obtained if the disadvantages of the division of labour outweigh the advantages. **Diseconomies of scale** may be experienced. Agricultural **overspecialisation** can result in monoculture, in which the growing of a single cash crop for export may lead to soil erosion, vulnerability to pests, and falling agricultural yields in the future. Overspecialisation can also cause a country to be particularly **vulnerable to sudden changes in demand** or in the cost and availability of imported raw materials or energy, or to new inventions and changes in technology which eliminate its comparative advantage. The greater the uncertainty about the future, the weaker the case for complete specialisation. If a country is self-sufficient in all important respects, it is effectively neutralised against the danger of importing recession and unemployment from the rest of the world if international demand collapses.

❸ **To cushion home employment** The model of comparative advantage assumes that factors of production are both fully employed and perfectly mobile within countries. If large-scale unemployment exists, there is a case for using factors inefficiently rather than not to employ them at all. Countries may also regard as unacceptable the costs of structural unemployment resulting from complete freedom of trade. Structural unemployment occurs when old industries decline in response to changes in either demand or comparative cost and advantage. There is a **case for selective and temporary import controls** to ease the problems of adjustment to the new conditions, whilst still accepting that in the long run trade should be encouraged and that a country should adapt to produce the goods in which it possesses a comparative advantage. Indeed the New Cambridge School have argued that import controls will boost the economy to such an extent that, although the structure of imports will change, the volume of imports will not actually fall once growth has taken place. This is the **paradox of import controls**, a counter to the free-trade view that 'what keeps imports out, keeps exports in.'

❹ **To prevent dumping** Exports are sometimes sold at a price below their cost of production and below the market price in the country of origin. Dumping may be motivated by the need to obtain foreign currency or a foothold in a foreign market, or by the hope of achieving productive economies of scale.

❺ **To avoid 'unfair' competition** It is sometimes claimed that low-wage countries in the developing world exploit local labour in order to produce cheap goods and that such activity is unfair. However, the developing countries are simply specialising in producing goods in which a plentiful supply of labour gives them a comparative advantage. It is essentially a value judgement whether this is 'fair' or 'unfair'.

❻ **To raise revenue** Tariffs are sometimes justified as a means of raising revenue for the government, but in modern economies this is a comparatively unimportant source of government revenue.

Political and social arguments

❶ **Economic sanctions** Economic sanctions have been used for centuries to buttress political decisions. An **embargo** on trade may weaken a political enemy and it may also encourage cooperation between politically sympathetic countries. Embargoes and other import controls are often imposed on trade in armaments and military goods.

❷ Restrictions are also commonly placed on the **trade in harmful goods (demerit goods)** such as narcotic drugs.

❸ Restrictions may be imposed for **strategic reasons**, to ensure that a country is relatively self-sufficient in time of war.

ARGUMENTS AGAINST PROTECTIONISM AND RESTRICTIONS ON TRADE

We have already covered the principal arguments involved, in our explanation of the case for trade. We have shown that, subject to some rather strong assumptions about the full employment of resources and the nature of demand, welfare losses will result if countries fail to specialise in accordance with the principle of comparative advantage. Countries may use import controls and other restrictions on trade to gain a short-term advantage at the expense of other countries (the 'beggar my neighbour' principle). However, retaliation by other countries is likely to cause a long-term welfare loss which is experienced by all countries, since protection props up inefficient and monopoly producers and redistributes income in favour of the protected.

METHODS OF PROTECTION

The decision to protect is made deliberately by a government. The method chosen may affect demand, supply or price. The demand for goods can be influenced by **tariffs**, **subsidies** and **exchange controls**. Supply can be manipulated by **embargoes, quotas, administrative restrictions** and **voluntary agreement**.

Tariffs

Tariffs, which may be specific or ad valorem, are taxes placed on imported, but not on domestic, goods. The ability of a tariff to reduce imports depends upon its size and upon the elasticity of demand for the imported good. If the country which imposes the tariff produces close substitutes, demand for imports is likely to be price elastic. In these circumstances, a tariff will reduce imports by switching demand towards the domestically produced substitutes. Conversely, if demand for imports is price inelastic, the main effect of the tariff will be on import prices rather than on the quantity of imports. (Refer back at this stage to the analysis in Chapter 15 on the various effects which follow an increase in expenditure taxes. A tariff is simply an example of an expenditure tax.)

Subsidies

These are provided in many, often clandestine, forms to avoid GATT restrictions on subsidies and dumping. The provision of export credit, VAT remission and regional aid may reduce total costs for exporters and thereby distort trade by affecting market prices. Support can be given to exporters by government agencies, such as the Export Credit Guarantee Department. At the same time, subsidies to domestic producers enable them to compete more easily with imported goods.

Exchange Control

Some nations control the amount of currency which can be used for buying imports. Usually foreign currency earnings (from exports) are deposited with the central bank, which authorises the withdrawals for the buying of imports. In this way, selective control of imports can be achieved. In Britain, up to 1979 when **exchange control** was abolished, transfers of cash and overseas investment were limited to protect the Balance of Payments.

Embargoes

As we have already mentioned, some goods are completely banned from entry into a country. This encourages smuggling and the development of black markets.

Quotas

The import of a certain quantity of goods may be allowed, usually via licensing arrangements, for example footwear into the UK. Although acting on supply rather than demand, a **quota** has the same effects as a tariff in that it raises prices and domestic output whilst cutting the volume of imports.

Administrative restrictions

These are used by many nations as a **covert method of protection**. A Japanese trading practice, considered by other countries to be unfair, has been the withholding of information on product specifications from foreigners but warning domestic producers of changes well in advance. Similarly, Britain has refused to admit poultry from countries which use vaccination rather than slaughter as the means of controlling foul pest.

Voluntary agreements

One government may try to persuade another to pressurise its exporters into limiting supplies to certain markets, for example Japanese government restraint over Japanese car exports to the UK and other EC countries. In April 1993, Japan agreed a voluntary cut in car exports to EC countries of 9.4% for 1993 (excluding the production of cars from 'transplant' factories armed by Nissan, Toyota and Honda in the UK). However, as car sales were expected to fall by a greater amount in the recession-hit EC market, European car manufacturers claimed that the agreement is in fact a 'sell-out' that will increase the overall share of Japanese imports in the EC market.

THE GENERAL AGREEMENT ON TARIFFS AND TRADE (GATT)

Towards the end of the Second World War, the American and British governments decided to establish new international institutions which would have the general aim of preventing a breakdown of world trade similar to the collapse which had contributed to the interwar depression. The intention was to create an **International Trade Organisation (ITO)** to liberalise trade, and an **International Monetary Fund** (see Chapters 27 and 28) to supervise the postwar system of payments and exchange rates. Because the charter to establish the ITO was never ratified, **GATT**, which was originally a temporary substitute for the ITO, survived as the most important international forum for expanding world trade and seeking the multilateral reduction of tariffs and other barriers to trade.

The General Agreement which came into operation in 1948 was based on four principles:

❶ **Non-discrimination** The 'most favoured nation' clause binds countries to extend reductions in tariffs to the imports of all GATT members.

❷ **Protection through tariffs** Where protection is justified, it should only be through tariffs and not through import quotas and other quantity controls.

❸ **Consultation** between members.

❹ **Tariff reduction through negotiation** GATT should provide the framework through which successive rounds of tariff reduction are negotiated.

The history of GATT can be divided into two. During the 1950s and the 1960s the economic climate was such that countries were willing to negotiate tariff reductions, culminating in the 'Kennedy Round' of 1967. In more recent years, the main achievement of GATT has been in preventing members from reintroducing protectionist measures rather than in achieving any further notable liberalisation of trade. In recent years, the 'Uraguay round' of tariff-reduction talks have been taking place under the auspices of GATT. These talks have threatened to break down and usher in a new era of trade protectionism, particularly with regard to trade between the EC and the USA. The main advantages of tariff cuts have accrued to the advanced nations. In order to extend the tariff reductions of GATT to developing countries and to help primary producers, the United Nations established the United Nations Conference on Trade and Development (UNCTAD). This started in 1964 and meets every four years. However, because the problems of the developing countries are so diverse, cooperative trade developments have been limited.

REGIONAL ECONOMIC GROUPINGS

Free Trade Areas and Customs Unions

GATT allows the continuation of any system of tariffs in operation when GATT was signed. It also allows the creation of either a **Free Trade Area (FTA)** or a **Customs Union (CU)**, both of which aim to liberalise trade between members, without extending most favoured nation treatment to non-members. Members of a FTA, such as the **Latin American Free Trade Area (LAFTA)**, are free to choose their trading policy with outsiders. Britain was a founder member of the **European Free Trade Area (EFTA)**, but left in 1973 to join the **European Community (EC)**. The EC is a Customs Union, in which a common external tariff restricts members' freedom of action. A Customs Union usually involves a much closer economic integration between members, who adopt common policies additional to the common external tariff.

With the creation of a **Single European Market** on January 1st 1993, the EC has developed into a proper **common market**, perhaps eventually leading to a full **Economic and Monetary Union** and even a **Political Union**. Common economic policies have been established which either considerably replace the freedom of separate policy action in member countries (the **CAP** and the **Common Fishery Policy**) or supplement the policies of individual members (**Regional and Competition Policy**). Most members of the EC are or have been members of the **exchange rate mechanism** of the **European Monetary System** (Chapter 27), which has been interpreted as a step towards full Monetary Union.

The effect on a country of its joining a Customs Union will depend on the size of the common external tariff, on whether the tariff is applied to all traded goods, and on the pattern of the country's trade. If a growing proportion of the country's trade is with the members of the CU, then there may be a strong case for joining, particularly if the common external tariff is high. However, FTAs are more consistent with the philosophy of GATT than are Customs Unions. The latter are more likely to encourage trade between members by diverting trade from non-members. The distortive effects of the common external tariff on trade with the rest of the world can depend on the extent to which the CU is 'inward'- or 'outward'-looking. Customs Unions can be **trade-diverting** or **trade-reducing** rather than **trade-creating**. They do not take comparative advantage to its logical conclusion, favouring instead internal producers against lower-cost external producers. The members of the EC claim to be outward-looking, citing for example the Lome Convention of 1975 (subsequently renewed) which enables sixty less developed countries to export duty free to the EC, and without reciprocity.

Suppliers organisations

Occasionally, producing countries cooperate in order to exploit the world market, for example by forming an **international cartel**. Primary producing countries justify the formation of agreements such as that of the **Organisation of Petroleum Exporting Countries (OPEC)** in order to countervail the market power of industrial countries. For most of the 20th century, the terms of trade have moved against primary producers and in favour of industrial countries.

Indeed, the adverse effects of the terms of trade on developing countries, together with profit remittances to developed countries, may have far exceeded the benefits of any aid. By creating a monopoly in the supply of a primary product, countries hope to reverse the movement in the terms of trade. International producers' cartels are most effective when governments can control supply, when there is unity of purpose and action amongst members, and when the demand of the industrialised countries is greatest.

BRITISH TRADE

Major changes have taken place in the structure of Britain's exports and imports over the last thirty years. As Table 25.1 illustrates, in 1955 over one-third of the United Kingdom's trade was with developing countries, while less than a third was with other European countries. This reflected what was still partly a 'traditional' pattern of trade in which the UK exported manufactured goods, largely to Commonwealth countries and other developing countries, in return for imports of food and raw materials. This pattern is now completely out of date, the current pattern of British trade being dominated by the exchange of both exports and imports with other industrial countries, particularly those in the EC.

Table 25.1 The geographical pattern of Britain's trade

Visible trade by area	1955		1985		1992	
	Imports %	Exports %	Imports %	Exports %	Imports %	Exports %
EC	12.6	15.0	46.0	46.3	52.5	56.4
Other West Europe	13.1	13.9	17.1	12.0	11.6	7.9
North America	19.5	12.0	13.8	17.0	12.6	13.0
Other developed countries	14.2	21.1	7.5	4.8	7.1	3.6
Total developed countries	59.4	62.0	84.3	80.0	83.8	80.9
East Europe and former USSR	2.7	1.7	2.2	2.0	1.3	1.5
Oil-exporting countries	9.2	5.1	3.3	7.6	2.5	5.6
Other developing countries	28.7	31.2	10.0	10.1	12.4	12.0

The United Kingdom is by no means unusual in its pattern of trade. The largest part of the international trade of all industrialised countries is with other industrial countries. However, what Table 25.1 does not show is a major structural change which has turned the UK from being a net exporter to becoming a net importer of manufactured goods. This change is illustrated in Tables 25.2 and 25.3. From the beginning of the Industrial Revolution until about 1983, the UK benefited from a **balance of trade surplus in manufactured goods**. But in recent years, the balance of trade in manufactured goods has moved severely into deficit, reflecting both the declining competitiveness of British manufacturing in international markets and the absolute decline of manufacturing output which occurred in the years of **deindustrialisation** in the early 1980s. The deficit in manufacturing goods cannot be blamed completely on the poor performance of more traditional industries such as shipbuilding and automobiles; the UK has a rather serious deficit in the trade of high-tech 'sunrise' industries in the field of information technology. Although manufacturing output recovered in the 'boom' of the mid- and late 1980s, it declined again seriously in the recession of the early 1990s and the balance of trade in manufactured goods has continued to deteriorate, causing a re-emergence of the UK's 'traditional' current deficit problem, despite North Sea oil's continuing contribution to the payments position. Table 25.3 shows how severe the deficit in the visible balance of trade would be without the contribution of North Sea oil, which most commentators believe reached its peak in 1985.

Table 25.2 The commodity pattern of Britain's trade

Visible trade by commodity	1955		1985		1992	
	Imports %	Exports %	Imports %	Exports %	Imports %	Exports %
Food, beverages, tobacco	36.2	6.5	10.9	6.3	10.7	8.0
Fuel	10.4	4.6	12.4	21.3	5.5	6.4
Industrial materials and semi-manufacturers	47.9	35.3	31.4	28.4	28.1	29.3
Finished manufacturers	5.2	49.1	43.7	41.3	50.1	49.5
Others	0.3	4.5	1.6	2.7	5.6	6.8

Table 25.3 Visible balance of trade

	£m 1975	£m 1985	£m 1989	£m 1992
Food, beverages, tobacco	−2701	−3592	−4875	−4713
Fuel	−3057	+8163	−71	−104
Industrial materials and semi-manufacturers	−915	−2549	−9540	−4779
Finished manufacturers	+3241	−3102	−15 907	−9531
Others	+99	−1031	+3250	+1829
Total	−3333	−2111	−27 143	−17 598

Trade in oil has, in fact, had several effects on the geographical pattern and commodity composition of Britain's exports and imports. Besides contributing directly to exports via sales of oil to the rest of the world, North Sea oil production has resulted in a considerable saving of oil imports. Less directly, via its effect on the Balance of Payments and an over-valued exchange rate, North Sea oil production undoubtedly contributed to the uncompetitiveness of British manufacturing industry, particularly in the early 1980s. (This is the so-called 'Dutch disease' effect, which we explain in Chapter 26, though high interest rates, resulting from a tight monetary policy, have probably been mainly to blame for an overvalued exchange rate.) Finally, a further development has been the growth in importance, since about 1970, of the oil-exporting countries, particularly in the Middle East, as a market for UK manufacturing exports.

Chapter roundup

Although trade gives an international dimension to economics, the theory of trade is essentially based on the concepts of scarcity, production possibilities and opportunity cost, division of labour and economies of scale which we first introduced in Chapters 1 to 6. We now examine some of the complications, distortions and barriers to trade which result from the fact that countries may lack an acceptable means of payment for trade (Chapter 26 on the Balance of Payments), while in Chapter 27 we see how exchange rates can cause further distortions and uncertainties.

Illustrative questions and answers

1   Essay Question
In recent years there have been increased calls in many countries for the reintroduction of import controls.
(a) What forms may import control take?   (10)
(b) Discuss the economic arguments for and against a return to trade protectionism.   (15)

(AEB, June 1990)

Tutorial note

For the first part of the question, list and briefly describe the main forms of import controls; dividing them into physical restrictions, such as embargoes and quotas on the one hand and on the other, tariffs and export subsidies which distort the relative prices of imports and exports. You might also mention how administrative procedures and bureaucracy can deter imports; and explain less direct forms of import control such as foreign exchange controls and the promotion of an undervalued exchange rate.

Structure the second part of your answer around the 'free trade versus import control' arguments, making sure you introduce comparative advantage into your discussion. Import controls may be a 'second best' solution to counter the protectionism already introduced by other countries; you might argue that the 'first best' alternative would be to persuade all countries to abandon import controls.

Suggested answer plan

1 Classify import controls into physical restrictions and policy measures that affect the relative price of imports.
2 List and briefly describe at least four types of import control.
3 Explain that protectionism already affects the pattern of world trade, arguably giving an unfair competitive advantage to those countries enjoying protection.
4 There is therefore, a case for those countries currently at a disadvantage to introduce retaliatory import controls.
5 Briefly explain some of the standard arguments in favour of protectionism: infant industry arguments; ensuring the orderly decline of 'sunset' industries; anti-dumping, etc.
6 Explain, using the principles of comparative advantage, how nevertheless, if all countries introduce protectionism, there will be an output and efficiency loss compared to a situation without protectionism.

2 Data Question

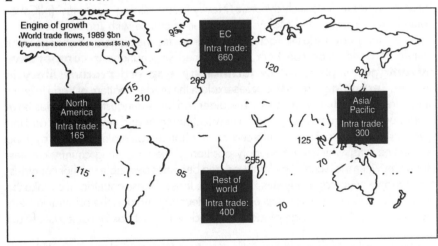

(Note: 'Intra trade' refers to trade between countries within each trading block.)

The world economy shows signs of moving towards a system partitioned in three blocks: the Americas, the European Community and the Asia-Pacific region centred on Japan. The United States has signed a free trade agreement with Canada and has started preliminary talks about similar arrangements with Mexico and Chile. There is the possibility of an American free trade zone spanning the continent. The EC is busily engaged in Project 1992, which will create the world's largest single market for goods, services and capital. The economic changes in Eastern Europe, far from slowing the EC's progress down, seem to have speeded it up. If Japan and East Asian economies find more of their goods shut out of Europe and America, an Asia-Pacific block may emerge by default.

(Source: adapted from: 'A Survey of World Trade' in
The Economist, 22 September 1990)

(a) (i) Calculate and set out clearly the current account position in 1989 for each of:

the European Community;
North America;
Asia/Pacific;
rest of the world.   (4)

(ii) Was international trade in equilibrium in 1989?   (2)

(b) The data show that, for the European Community, the value of its internal trade is greater than that of its exports; the reverse is true for the Asia/Pacific region. How might this be explained?   (6)

(c) The article claims that the world economy is 'moving towards a system partitioned into three blocks' (lines 1–2). Examine the economic implications of this for the European Community and for the world economy.   (8)

(ULEAC, AS-Level, June 1992)

Tutorial note

The data in this question neatly illustrates the modern pattern of world trade. Many students do not realise that during the twentieth century, the pattern of world trade has changed from a 'North/South' to a 'North/North' pattern. Instead of world trade being dominated (as it was in the nineteenth century) by industrialised countries in Europe and North America exporting manufactured goods in exchange for foodstuffs and raw materials produced by tropical countries (which for the most part were their colonies or imperial dependencies), the industrialised economies of the North now trade largely with each other. But at the same time as North/North trade has grown in significance (as illustrated by 'intra trade' data in the question for the EC and North America regions), a large part of world manufacturing, particularly for export, has shifted away from the older industrial areas in western Europe and North America, to the Pacific rim countries of the Asia/Pacific region. These countries include such dynamic 'Newly Industrialising Countries' (NICs) as South Korea, Taiwan and Malaysia, together of course with Japan. The shift of manufacturing industry to the Pacific rim countries and the associated change in the pattern of world trade can both be explained by changes in **comparative advantage**, supplemented by **technology gap** and **product lifecycle** theories. **Technology gap theories** explain the modern pattern of trade in terms of the nature of technical progress. The older, advanced industrial countries have usually been the leaders in developing new technologies and new products and this gives them an advantage, reinforced by economies of scale allowed by long production runs, which the monopoly position of the innovating country creates. However, when the technology 'matures' and becomes available to other countries, comparative advantage may shift to the NICs. Indeed these countries may take the lead in developing later versions of the new technology, and the original leaders may suffer the disadvantage of factories fitted with what has become out-of-date equipment.

Like the technology gap theory, the **product lifecycle theory** explains the pattern of world production, specialisation and trade in manufactured goods in terms of the nature of technical progress. Early in its lifecycle, and immediately following its successful innovation, a product is likely to be strongly differentiated from competing products. Indeed, by creating a highly profitable relative monopoly position for the innovative firm, such product differentiation provides an important motive for technical development. At this stage of the product's lifecycle, manufacture is usually located in the country of origin of the innovative company, where its research and development facilities are concentrated. But at a later stage when the company loses its monopoly over the existing technology, when the product becomes more standardised with agreed international specifications, and when mass production combines economies of scale with the application of routine, relatively unskilled labour, the advanced economies lose their comparative advantage and production shifts to the NICs. Meanwhile, the innovative multinational firms in the advanced industrial countries attempt to maintain their lead by further technical progress and product development, while at the same time owning branch factories or subsidiaries in the NICs in which they manufacture for export back to the developed world the 'older' products well into their lifecycles. As a variant on this theme, North American and European multinationals are increasingly switching out of manufacturing completely by 'contracting out' the manufacture of a finished good or its components to independent producers in the NICs. These goods are then exported back as a 'badge-engineered' products, i.e. marketed under the multinational's brand name, but manufactured by and bought in from an independent supplier in an NIC.

A rather different explanation may throw some light on the North/North pattern of 'intraregional' trade within North America and the EC. The **roles of patterns of income, tastes and consumption, or demand conditions** in the world's most important trading countries, may help to explain why so much of international trade involves the exchange of essentially rather similar manufactured goods between already industrialised economies. It can be argued that a country's comparative advantage often lies in producing goods related to its inhabitants' domestic tastes. Close contact with the needs of the domestic market makes a country's firms efficient at meeting domestic demand and very often the inhabitants of other industrial countries with similar incomes, possess similar demand. Trade therefore takes place between countries with similar tastes and incomes. At the same time, high income consumers value choice and product differentiation. A pattern of trade thus develops between industrialised countries in which a very wide range of differentiated manufactured consumer goods is made available to all – for example, automobiles or fashion goods. A single country could seldom provide its consumers with the desired variety, so international trade extends the range of choice.

Suggested answer

(a) (i) Calculate EC export earnings by adding up $115 bn + $80 bn + $255 bn, which equals $450 bn. In a similar way, imports into the EC can be calculated as $475 bn. In 1989 the EC was thus running a Current Account deficit on its Balance of Payments of $25 bn.

By performing similar calculations, you will find that North America was running a Current Account deficit of $120 bn (since its exports at $315 bn were less than its imports at $440 bn by this amount); whereas the other two world regions both had trade surpluses – $125 bn in the case of the Asia/Pacific region and $20 bn for the 'rest of the world'.

(ii) Since – as yet – the world cannot trade with any other planets in the universe, the Current Account for the world must exactly balance and be in equilibrium. But note that the countries of the 'North' (North America and the EC) were in deficit to the tune of $145 bn – which was, of course, exactly equal to the size of the combined surplus of the Asia/Pacific countries 'rest of the world'.

b) The EC is a customs union which was formed precisely to encourage the development of intra-EC trade. As we have explained in the tutorial notes, much of the growth of world trade in recent years has involved already-developed and rich economies trading essentially similar goods and services with each other. By contrast, the 'Pacific rim' countries of the Asia/Pacific region which have provided the 'engine' of growth for manufacturing in recent decades, have been producing largely for export, as their own markets (with the partial exception of Japan) are too small to absorb the high levels of output that they now produce.

c) As the disputes taking place in 1992 and 1993 over the GATT tariff reduction talks have shown, there is a danger that countries – the EC and North America in particular – will resort to protectionism, both to reduce trade between each other, but also to fend off cheap imports of manufactured goods from the Pacific rim countries and the other countries of the South. Consider whether arguments for such protectionism (based on 'unfair' competition, 'dumping', the use of 'slave labour', etc.) are justified, or whether the protectionist stance adopted by the regional groupings will lead to a failure to organise trade in accordance with the principle of comparative advantage, leading ultimately to output and welfare losses for both the EC and the rest of the world.

Question bank

1 Does the principle of comparative costs convincingly demolish every argument for protection?

(Oxford, June 1990)

2

(a) Explain the difference between a 'free trade area', a 'customs union' and a 'common market'. (10)

(b) To what extent does the European Community match the above theoretical models? (10)

(Cambridge, AS-Level, June 1989)

3 Discuss whether customs unions such as the European Community help or hinder the development of trade in accordance with the principle of comparative advantage.

(AEB, November 1992)

4

(a) Examine the role of comparative advantage in determining what a country produces for international exchange. (70)

(b) How is this concept relevant when analysing the effects of the creation of the single European market in 1992? (30)

(ULEAC, June 1992)

5

(a) With examples, explain what you understand by a 'commodity agreement'. (10)

(b) Why have such agreements had little effect in world trade? (10)

(O&CSEB, AS-Level, June 1990)

6

(a) Examine the benefits that countries derive from international trade. (60)

(b) If there are such benefits from free trade, why is GATT (the General Agreement on Tariffs and Trade) necessary to prevent countries erecting barriers to trade? (40)

(ULEAC, January 1993)

7 Explain what is meant by the 'single European market'. Discuss how the standard of living in Europe in general, and that of Britain in particular, is likely to be affected by the single European market.

(NEAB, June 1991)

8

(a) 'If the government of a country decides to protect certain domestic industries from foreign competition, then although some individuals may gain, there is on balance a net loss for society as a whole.' Consider this argument. (20)

(b) Consider the argument that if a government does decide to assist domestic industries, then direct subsidies are less harmful than tariffs imposed on imports. (5)

(WJEC, June 1991)

9 'Protection of domestic industries will always be in certain producers' interests , but never in the wider public interest.' Consider this view.

(WJEC, June 1992)

THE BALANCE OF PAYMENTS

Chapter objectives

In Chapter 25 we noted how the existence of barriers to trade such as **import controls** can prevent two countries from trading together even though they might both benefit from the exchange. We now go on in Chapters 26 and 27 to examine how **payment difficulties and uncertainties** can cause further barriers to trade, and how they can also affect the domestic economy and the government's economic management thereof. This chapter concentrates on a country's balance of payments, while Chapter 27 looks at the interrelated question of the **exchange rate**. We also introduce important aspects of the **international monetary system,** including the role of reserve currencies and other means of payment, and of international institutions such as the International Monetary Fund (IMF).

26.1 UNDERLYING CONCEPTS

THE BALANCE OF PAYMENTS AS PART OF THE SYSTEM OF NATIONAL ACCOUNTS

Whenever trade takes place between nations, payment must eventually be made in a currency or means of payment acceptable to the country from whom goods or services have been purchased. The Balance of Payments is the part of the National Accounts which records payments to, and receipts from, the rest of the world. Although these payments and receipts are part of a continuous flow of currencies between countries, it is conventional to measure the Balance of Payments over a time-period of either a single month, quarter, or year.

Since the **Balance of Payments** is an official record collected by the government, the presentation of the statistics depends upon how the government decides to group and classify the different items of payment. In 1987 major changes were introduced in the way the UK government presents the Balance of Payments statistics. However, the most important part of the Balance of Payments, the **Current Account**, has remained unaffected by the new changes. We shall therefore explain the Current Account and the nature of the other flows which are measured in the Balance of Payments before we describe the purely presentational changes introduced in 1987.

THE BALANCE OF PAYMENTS ON CURRENT ACCOUNT

This measures the flow of expenditure on goods and services and broadly indicates the **income gained and lost from trade**. The Current Balance is the most important part of the Balance of Payments because it reflects the **international competitiveness** of the UK economy and the extent to which the UK is living within its means. If receipts from exports exceed payments for imports, there is of course a Current Account **surplus**. The Current Balance is obtained by simply adding the **Balance of Visible Trade** to the **Balance of Invisible Trade**.

The Balance of Visible Trade

Although **visible trade** is the most important single item in the Balance of Payments, it is perhaps the most simple to define. The Visible Balance measures the value in pounds sterling of goods exported, minus the value of goods imported. The Visible Trade Balance is often known simply as the **Balance of Trade**, a rather misleading term since it implies (falsely) that all trade, including **invisibles** (or **services**) are included, when in fact the Balance of Trade measures only trade in goods or visibles.

The Balance of Invisible Trade

In general terms this measures the sterling value of services exported minus the value of services imported. However, the Invisible Balance includes a number of rather disparate items. For example, **invisible exports** include:

a large part of the earnings of the City of London, insurance and brokerage services, etc.;

the overseas earnings of British shipping and aviation services;

expenditure by overseas governments on embassies and military bases in the UK;

spending by foreign tourists;

gifts of money from overseas residents to British residents;

dividends or profits remitted to British residents owning capital assets overseas – the difference between such profit inflows and outflows is sometimes known as net property income from abroad.

Conversely, any payments from British residents to overseas residents for shipping services, tourism, the upkeep of embassies, etc, are **invisible imports**. In recent years Britain's net contribution to the EEC budget has developed into an important invisible import. Some forms of aid to developing countries are also classified in the invisible account.

THE CHANGING NATURE OF THE UK CURRENT ACCOUNT

For most of the 20th century the British Balance of Payments on Current Account displayed a deficit on the balance of visible trade and a surplus on the invisible balance, both of which could be explained by the **principle of comparative**

advantage. The emergence of other competing industrial countries reduced or eliminated Britain's comparative advantage in many manufacturing industries but, until very recently at least, she still retained her advantage in services. Whether the overall Balance on Current Account was in surplus or deficit in any single year depended on whether the **invisible surplus** was sufficient to offset the **visible deficit**.

From the 1970s onwards significant changes have occurred in the composition of the Current Account:

❶ The **contribution of North Sea oil revenue** moved the visible balance into surplus (for a while), both through import-saving and oil exports. From about 1976 onwards and reaching a peak in the mid-1980s, North Sea oil revenues transformed the Current Account from deficit into surplus.

❷ However, this disguised the **continuing deterioration of the balance of non-oil visible trade**, reflecting the growing propensity to import in the UK and the uncompetitiveness of British manufacturers. Indeed, it is useful nowadays to divide the visible balance into the separate categories of the **oil balance** and the **non-oil balance** of visible trade and also into the **balance of trade in manufactured goods** and non-manufactures. The balance of trade in manufactured goods remained in surplus from the 18th century through to the early 1980s, reflecting the importance of the United Kingdom as a manufacturing economy. In 1982, however, Britain's imports of manufactured goods began to exceed her exports of manufactures, moving the balance of trade in manufactured goods into deficit for the first time since before the Industrial Revolution. In part this reflects the fact that the revenues of North Sea oil have been largely used to finance improved short-term standards of living through the import of consumer goods and foodstuffs, rather than investment. It also reflects the **deindustrialisation process**, or **structural decline** of a significant part of UK manufacturing industry which occurred in the early 1980s. Although in the boom of the 1980s there was a slow recovery of manufacturing output, the balance of trade in manufactured goods has generally continued to display a growing deficit.

❸ The importance of invisible trade and services in the Current Account has continued to grow in recent years. Invisible exports accounted for 38.5% of total credits in 1970, rising to 51.9% in 1984 and 54.0% in 1989. The contribution of invisible exports to Britain's total trade earnings is thus now greater than that of trade in goods. Invisible imports have also grown in relative importance, from 34.3% of total imports in 1970 to 47.2% in 1989. In part, the growth of invisibles, in both absolute and relative importance, reflects the changing pattern of world trade, in which the richest countries of the world increasingly trade services with each other. The spectacular growth of invisible exports reflects also a surge in dividend income, under net property income from abroad. Following the abolition of exchange controls in 1979, UK residents and companies invested large capital funds overseas. These investments are now profitable, remitting sufficient income to offset the falling contribution of North Sea oil to the visible trade account. However, in the early 1990s, the UK's invisible surplus has dwindled, causing the fear that it may disappear completely. Growing international competition in the provision of services (e.g. tourism, financial services), together with the outward interest payments required to service the capital flows that finance the Current Account deficit, have reduced the invisible surplus.

CAPITAL FLOWS

Before 1987 the United Kingdom government divided the Balance of Payments into three sections:

❶ The Current Account;

❷ Investment and Other Capital Flows (sometimes known as the Capital Account);

❸ Official Financing.

In the presentational changes of the accounts introduced in 1987, **Investment and Other Capital Flows** and **Official Financing** have disappeared from the official accounts. They have been merged together into a new **Transactions in External Assets and Liabilities** section which, together with the Current Account, form the new official Balance of Payments tables. However, before we can understand the new system of presenting the Balance of Payments, we must first explain the meaning of **capital flows** and **official financing**.

An outward capital flow takes place when a country's residents purchase assets in another country. Conversely, an inward capital flow describes a movement of capital funds into the country as residents of other countries purchase domestic assets. Net capital flows are, of course, the difference between outward and inward investment. A positive net capital flow over a period of years means that the country's residents – including its companies – are acquiring overseas assets which are greater in total than those of the country's own assets which are being acquired by the rest of the world. Following the **abolition of exchange controls** in 1979, the UK was for a number of years a very large net exporter of long-term capital. In a sense, UK residents have 'spent' North Sea oil revenues earned in the Current Account, on acquiring overseas assets which are likely to continue to pay dividends – received as invisible exports in the Current Account – long after North Sea oil has run dry. The UK became the second-largest owner of external capital assets after Japan. By contrast, the USA has become a net debtor nation in the sense that other countries now own more assets in America than the US owns in the rest of the world.

In order to understand further the importance of capital flows in the Balance of Payments, it is useful to distinguish between long-term and short-term capital flows.

Long-term capital flows

We can explain **long-term capital flows** by invoking the principle of comparative advantage, which explained the nature of visible trade. A long-term capital flow occurs when residents of one country buy up or invest in the productive resources within another country. They will do so if they believe that their financial assets can be more productively and profitably employed in the other country.

A net outflow of long-term capital means that there is more investment by British residents in real assets in other countries than there is foreign investment in Britain. Such an outflow includes both **real** or **direct investment**, when for example a British company buys or creates a foreign subsidiary, and **portfolio investment**, when British residents purchase the shares of overseas companies or the securities of foreign governments.

Short-term capital flows

Since changes in comparative advantage usually take place relatively slowly, the long-term capital flows tend to be stable and predictable. Movements in the Balance of Payments resulting from the changing pattern of either trade or of long-term capital flows are said to be **spontaneous** or **autonomous**. In contrast, short-term capital flows are neither stable nor predictable, and they frequently occur in response to a change in the autonomous part of the Balance of Payments. A growing proportion of the short-term flows is extremely volatile 'hot money' which, by flowing into – and just as quickly out of – countries, can destabilise the

Balance of Payments, the exchange rate, and indeed the international monetary system as a whole. **Hot money** is the name given to the pool of 'footloose' hard currencies owned by governments, banks, businesses and private individuals, usually outside the exchange controls of the currency's country of origin. A major cause of the growth of hot money flows lies in the emergence of the **Eurodollar market** after 1957.

The pool of Eurodollars grew dramatically in the 1960s and 1970s when the USA persuaded other countries to accept payment for the US Balance of Payments deficit in dollars. Some of these dollars were received in payment for American imports, but others arose from capital investment overseas by American firms and the growth of overseas bank deposits owned by American residents. The early growth of the Eurodollar market was prompted by the imposition of restrictions by the American monetary authorities upon the domestic banking system. In the absence of exchange controls, it became more profitable for American residents to keep their dollars in overseas bank accounts, often in the subsidiaries of US banks, rather than in deposits held within the USA. From these origins in the late 1950s and 1960s the Eurodollar market has grown, hugely supplemented by the injection of '**petrodollars**' after the oil crises in the 1970s when the OPEC countries accumulated large balance of payments surpluses matched by deficits in the oil-consuming industrial countries. The oil-producing countries placed a significant proportion of their oil revenues on deposit in the European banking system, thus adding to the pool of footloose hot money. Indeed the market is perhaps better called the **Eurocurrency market**. Although the dollar is still the most important currency deposited, other currencies such as sterling and the Deutschmark are also involved.

The European banks, including those in London, have developed a thriving business in the short-term borrowing and lending of international currencies, outside the exchange controls which may exist in their countries of origin. These Eurocurrency flows are extremely destabilising because as the flow out of the £, which forced its devaluation on 'Black Wednesday' 16th September showed, the sheer size of the hot money pool means that the financial markets and balance of payments of a single country can be overwhelmed by a sudden inward or outward flow which may often occur for essentially speculative reasons. A hot money flow into a country may be triggered by high rates of interest, by the belief that the exchange rate is undervalued, or by an event such as a Middle East war, when currencies are shifted into countries that are regarded as 'safe havens' for funds. The movement of funds into a country on a large scale itself puts upward pressure on the exchange rate since it creates a demand for the local currency on foreign exchanges, when for example government securities are purchased by the overseas owners of hot money. Conversely, a sudden outflow can cause a rapid deterioration in the balance of payments and downward pressure on the exchange rate.

ACCOMMODATING FLOWS

Like all balance-sheets, the Balance of Payments must balance, at least in a strictly accounting sense. This means that all the items in the Balance of Payments must sum to zero. In principle, therefore, if the autonomous Current Account and capital flows are in surplus or deficit, the surplus or deficit must be financed by an equal accommodating flow, to make the balance-sheet sum to zero.

Traditionally, **changes in official reserves** and **official borrowing**, for example from foreign central banks or from the International Monetary Fund, were regarded as the principal accommodating flows. The current and capital flows added together formed the Balance of Payments for Official Financing, which was financed or accommodated by changes in reserves and in official borrowing in the third part of the Balance of Payments: the Official Financing section. For example, if the autonomous or spontaneous current and capital flows showed a deficit of $-£2000$m, this would be financed by a loss of reserves, or by official borrowing of $+£2000$m. (For accounting reasons, the loss of reserves would be represented by a plus sign!) In this way the Balance of Payments is balanced.

THE 1987 CHANGES IN PRESENTATION OF THE BALANCE OF PAYMENTS

We have just explained how, in principle, the Balance of Payments deficit or surplus, obtained by adding together the Current Account and capital flows, is financed or accommodated by changes in official reserves or by official borrowing. This reflects the fact that the Current Account and capital flows have traditionally been regarded as spontaneous or autonomous, i.e. based on the decisions of private economic agents to trade, while the Official Financing section of the Balance of Payments was purely accommodating. However, it is now realised that this separation of autonomous and accommodating flows is rather artificial. In recent years a Current Account deficit or surplus has been financed not so much by official financing involving a change in reserves, as by private sector capital flows. Indeed, such capital flows which finance or accommodate the Current Account have been actively encouraged and used by the authorities as an alternative to official financing. While it is usually difficult for the authorities to influence quickly the largely autonomous long-term capital flows (except through the imposition or removal of exchange controls and tax advantages), this is not true of short-term or 'hot money' flows. In the case of a Current Account deficit, the authorities may raise interest rates in order to engineer a hot money inflow, thereby avoiding the need to draw on official reserves to finance the deficit. Conversely, when North Sea oil revenues moved the Current Account into surplus, the authorities preferred to encourage a capital outflow rather than finance the surplus through an accumulation of reserves.

In large part, this reflected the change of the **exchange rate regime** in the 1970s and 1980s from **fixed exchange rates** to **floating exchange rates**. As we explain further in Chapter 27, when the exchange rate is fixed, the authorities must actively use official reserves to finance a Balance of Payments deficit or surplus, in order to prevent the exchange rate moving from its fixed parity. When exchange rates were floated in the 1970s, this requirement largely disappeared, and the authorities preferred to allow private sector capital flows rather than changes in reserves to finance the Current Account. During the period in the late 1980s and early 1990s when the £ was first preparing to enter, and then actually in, the exchange rate mechanism of the EMS, official financing was once again actively used to support the exchange rate. Nevertheless, it still remained true that high interest rates which attracted private 'hot money' flows into the £, were the main instrument for supporting the exchange rate and financing the current account deficit.

Table 26.1 shows the new presentation of the Balance of Payments which was introduced when the 1986 statistics were first published in 1987.

As we have already noted, there have been no changes in the presentation of the Current Account. However, the distinction between capital flows and official financing has now been dropped, reflecting the fact that in recent years private sector capital flows, rather than changes in reserves, financed any Current Account imbalance. The new **'transactions' section** of the Balance of Payments therefore comprises all private and public sector movements of capital funds. 'Transactions in assets' measure the outward flow of funds, including investment flows, while **'transactions in liabilities'** represent the inward flow − the rest of the world's assets held in the UK being the United Kingdom's liabilities.

We have already explained that these changes reflect the decreased importance of official financing in the 1980s. Yet, by 1987 when the new presentation was introduced, the exchange rate was being managed by 'shadowing' the DM in preparation for full entry into the EMS. Thus, at a time when the exchange rate

Table 26.1 *The New Presentation of the Balance of Payments*

		1991 £m
	Current Account	
	Visibles	–10 290
	Invisibles	+ 3967
A	Current Balance	– 6321
	UK external assets and liabilities	
	Transactions in assets	+20 969
	Transactions in liabilities	+26 653
B	Net transactions	+ 5686
C	Balancing item	+ 636
	A + B + C	≡ 0

was becoming more like a fixed exchange rate, a new presentation of the Balance of Payments was introduced; more appropriate to a freely floating system than a fixed system. However, with a return to floating exchange rates after the debacle of ERM entry from 1990 to 1992, the method of presentation may once again be suited to the actual exchange rate regime in operation.

THE BALANCING ITEM

The official estimates of the Balance of Payments will seldom be accurate, because of the imperfect nature of data collection. For this reason, a '**Balancing Item**' –analogous to the statistical adjustment in the National Accounts – must be added or subtracted as the last item in the Balance of Payments in order to make the balance-sheet sum to zero. In the years following the first publication of the Balance of Payments, statistics for a particular year are constantly revised. A very large Balancing Item means that not much faith should be attached to any interpretation of the first publication. It is usual for the figures for both the Current Account and capital flows to change and for the Balancing Item to become smaller as it is gradually 'allocated' to one or other of the 'real' items in the Balance of Payments. In this way, an apparent Current Account surplus on first publication may become a deficit when the figures are revised, or vice versa.

26.2 ESSENTIAL INFORMATION

BALANCE OF PAYMENTS EQUILIBRIUM AND DISEQUILIBRIUM

Although in an accounting sense the balance of payments always balances, this can obscure the fact that a country's payments may not be in a state of equilibrium. **Balance of Payments equilibrium** (or **external equilibrium**) is usually taken to mean that the desired spontaneous or autonomous trade and capital flows into and out of the country are equal over a number of years. A state of equilibrium in the balance of payments is perfectly compatible with the existence of short-term surpluses and deficits. But a fundamental disequilibrium in the balance of payments will exist if there is a persistent tendency for the autonomous flows out of the country to be greater or less than the corresponding inflows. When, for example, a persistent deficit occurs in the autonomous items in the balance of payments, it must be accommodated by a loss of reserves, by official borrowing or by 'unofficial' borrowing via a hot money inflow in the transactions section of the Balance of Payments.

THE PROBLEM OF A BALANCE OF PAYMENTS DEFICIT

While a short-run deficit or surplus on the Current Account of the Balance of Payments seldom poses a problem, the same is not true when a **persistent imbalance indicates a fundamental disequilibrium**. It is easy to see why a persistent deficit in the autonomous items in the Balance of Payments is a problem, since the resulting loss of reserves and need for borrowing cannot be maintained indefinitely. However, the extent of the problem depends on a number of factors, including the size of the deficit, its cause and the exchange rate regime.

Obviously, the larger the deficit the greater the problem is likely to be, but it also depends upon which items are in deficit. For example, an overall deficit caused by a long-term capital outflow may produce the long-term benefit of an eventual profits inflow in the invisibles section of the Current Account. In contrast, if the cause of the deficit lies in the Current Account, the problem may be more serious. Although a trade deficit allows the country's residents to enjoy a higher standard of living than would be possible from the consumption of the country's output alone, it may also reflect the uncompetitiveness of the country's goods and services.

In the next chapter we shall examine in some detail the effect of different exchange rate regimes upon the balance of payments. In this chapter we can merely note that a payments deficit is usually considered more of a problem under **fixed exchange rates** than when the exchange rate is **freely floating**. In a floating regime the market mechanism may eliminate the cause of export uncompetitiveness and restore an equilibrium in the balance of payments. In contrast, when the exchange rate is fixed, the government usually has to take action through deflation, import controls, devaluation of the exchange rate, or a combination of all three.

In the 1960s and 1970s it was widely believed that the British Balance of Payments posed a problem in the sense that in a fixed exchange rate regime the exchange rate was 'unavailable' as a policy instrument to cure the persistent payments deficit that Britain experienced at that time. This meant that the internal policy objective of full employment and growth had to be sacrificed to the external objective of protecting the balance of payments and supporting the exchange rate, which imposed a serious constraint on the sustained achievement of the domestic policy objectives. Floating the exchange rate was regarded as an 'escape route' from this constraint; a floating exchange rate would 'look after' the Balance of Payments, allowing economic policy to be devoted to the internal objectives.

However, the last twenty years have witnessed at least two reversals of fashion with regard to whether floating exchange rates are preferable to fixed exchange rates or vice versa. The experience of floating exchange rates in the 1970s and early 1980s led to much disenchantment with the view we have just expressed, namely that by floating the exchange rate the government can pursue domestic economic objectives while the exchange rate 'looks after' the Balance of Payments. During the 1980s many British economists and politicians looked longingly at what they regarded as the stability created for most of the other EC countries as members of the **Exchange Rate Mechanism (ERM)** of the **European Monetary System (EMS)**. Pressure grew for the UK to join the ERM (which is a fixed exchange rate system). But the abortive experience of the UK's short membership of the ERM from 1990 to 1992 has led (at the time of writing) to a return to favour of floating exchange rates. It remains to be seen how long this will last and whether the climate of opinion will shortly swing back to a clamour for re-entry into the ERM! These issues are discussed further in Chapter 27.

THE PROBLEM OF A BALANCE OF PAYMENTS SURPLUS

While it is generally accepted that a persistent Balance of Payments deficit is a problem, it is much less obvious that a surplus can also pose problems. Indeed, because a surplus is often regarded as a symbol of national economic success, many people argue that the bigger the surplus, the more successful the country must be. Nevertheless, there are a number of reasons why a persistently large surplus is undesirable, even though a small surplus may be a more justifiable objective of policy:

❶ **One country's surplus is another country's deficit** It is impossible for all countries simultaneously to run surpluses. If countries refuse to reduce their persistently large surpluses, then deficit countries will find it difficult, and even impossible, to reduce their deficits. The danger then arises that deficit countries will resort to import controls and all countries may suffer from a consequent reduction or collapse in world trade. In recent years the danger posed to the development of world trade by excessive surpluses and deficits has been well illustrated by the problem of recycling the surpluses of the oil-producing countries, though these surpluses have now almost disappeared.

❷ **The 'Dutch disease' effect** The growth of Britain's own oil trade surplus in the 1970s and 1980s illustrates another way in which a surplus can create a problem. In 1980 and 1981 the Current Account surplus, reinforced by hot money inflows, caused the exchange rate to rise to a level which decreased the competitiveness of non-oil visible exports in world markets, and increased the competitiveness of imports in the UK economy. This accelerated the **de-industrialisation** of the British economy and caused much of the benefit of North Sea oil revenues to be 'lost' in financing imports and the upkeep of the growing number of unemployed. The effect of the balance of payments surplus upon the exchange rate and the domestic economy is called the '**Dutch disease**' after the experience of the Netherlands following the discovery and development of natural gas in the 1950s and 1960s.

❸ **In Keynesian terms**, a balance of payments surplus represents an injection of demand into the economy, causing demand-pull inflation if output cannot be raised to meet demand.

❹ **The money supply and a balance of payments surplus** In an open economy the domestic money supply is affected by the balance of payments; a surplus tends to increase and a deficit to decrease the money supply unless the exchange rate is freely floating. When the balance of payments is in surplus, the country's currency is in short supply on foreign exchange markets. If the authorities wish to prevent the exchange rate from rising in response to the excess demand, they must buy the foreign currencies being offered in the market, giving their own currency in exchange. The nation's foreign currency reserves expand, but only at the expense of an increase in the money supply. The process of selling the country's own currency and buying reserves in order to prevent the exchange rate from rising is an example of **exchange equalisation**.

The extent to which a balance of payments surplus (or deficit) leads to an increase (or decrease) in the money supply depends upon the exchange rate policy being pursued. A 'clean' or pure float can eliminate the external imbalance with little or no change in either the reserves or the money supply, but if the exchange rate is fixed or managed, quite large changes in both can result. The impact of the balance of payments upon the domestic money supply clearly poses a problem for monetarist economic policy, with its emphasis on the need to control the rate of growth of the money supply.

Indeed, when the Balance of Payments is in deficit, **Domestic Credit Expansion (DCE)** is a better measure of liquidity in the domestic economy than money supply measures such as **M3** and **M4**. Broadly, DCE is the money supply plus (or minus) the Balance of Payments deficit (or surplus). Thus when the current account is in deficit, DCE exceeds the money supply which falls as the authorities use reserves to 'buy back' pounds in order to support the exchange rate.

POLICIES TO CURE A FUNDAMENTAL DISEQUILIBRIUM IN THE BALANCE OF PAYMENTS

We shall now discuss in more detail the various policy measures of **deflation**, the **imposition of import controls**, and **devaluation** (or a managed or 'dirty' downward float), which can be used to correct a persistent balance of payments deficit. (In Chapter 27 we shall discuss how a payments disequilibrium is automatically corrected without the need for government intervention under freely floating and rigidly fixed (gold standard) exchange rates.)

Deflation

Both fiscal policy and monetary policy can be used to deflate the level of demand in an economy in order to correct a payments deficit. **Deflation** is primarily an **expenditure-reducing policy** which cures a deficit by reducing the demand for imports. The increase in unused capacity produced by the deflation may also encourage firms to seek extra export orders, though many economists argue that a sound and expanding home market is necessary for a successful export drive since exports are usually less profitable than domestic sales. A deflation can also have a subsidiary **expenditure-switching** effect upon the Balance of Payments. Successful deflation results in the domestic inflation rate falling relative to that in other countries, thereby increasing the price competitiveness and demand for British exports, while reducing the demand for imports.

However, a deflationary policy usually involves severe costs, since in modern economies output and employment fall rather than the price level. For this reason, governments may use the **expenditure-switching policies** of **import controls** and **devaluation** as alternatives to expenditure-reducing deflation.

Import controls

Import controls have a direct expenditure-switching effect upon the balance of payments. **Quotas** and **embargoes** reduce or prevent expenditure on imports, while **tariffs** or **import duties** discourage expenditure by increasing the relative price of imports. However, import controls do not deal with the underlying cause of imbalance – usually the uncompetitiveness of a country's industries – and they may provoke retaliation with an undesirable decrease in world trade and specialisation. In any case, import controls may be 'unavailable' because of membership of a trading body such as GATT which discourages their use.

Devaluation

The 'unavailability' of import controls as an effective instrument to correct a payments deficit has meant that the real policy choice has usually been between deflation and devaluation. **Devaluation of a fixed exchange rate, or a** managed or 'dirty' downward float, is essentially an **expenditure-switching policy**. By increasing the price of imports relative to the price of exports, a successful devaluation switches demand away from imports and towards domestically produced goods. Similarly, foreign demand for the country's exports increases in response to the fall in price.

However, the effectiveness of a devaluation (and of any expenditure-switching policy) depends in large part upon the **price elasticities of demand** for **exports and imports**. It is easy to see that when the demands for exports and imports are both highly elastic, a devaluation will be likely to improve the Balance of Payments. Overseas residents will spend more on British exports following a fall in their relative price, while British residents will spend less on imports. But it is rather more difficult to see what will happen if the demands are less elastic. Provided, however, that the sum of the export and import elasticities is greater than unity, it can be shown that a devaluation or downward movement of the exchange rate will be likely to reduce a payments deficit (and that a re-valuation will probably reduce a surplus). This is known as the **Marshall-Lerner condition** or criterion for a successful devaluation or revaluation.

EXPENDITURE-REDUCING VERSUS EXPENDITURE-SWITCHING POLICIES

While the **Marshall-Lerner condition** is a **necessary** condition for a successful expenditure-switching devaluation, it is not a **sufficient condition**. A devaluation could fail if there were insufficient spare capacity within the domestic economy. **Spare capacity** is needed in order to increase supply so as to meet the switching of overseas and domestic demand away from foreign goods and towards the home-produced output. Thus it is far better to regard an **expenditure-reducing deflation** and an **expenditure-switching devaluation** as **complementary** rather than as **substitute** policies in curing a payments deficit. Deflation alone may be unnecessarily costly in lost output and employment, yet may still be necessary to create the spare capacity and 'prepare the way' for a later successful devaluation. Indeed, the devaluation of the £ by about 15 to 20% which occurred on and after 'Black Wednesday', 16th September 1992, may have turned out to be a 'perfect devaluation', even though it was forced on the Conservativeggovernment by speculative 'hot money' flows out of sterling and not undertaken though choice. This is because the large amount of spare capacity, existent in the 'recession hit' UK economy at the time, meant that successful 'expenditure-switching' could take place.

THE J-CURVE EFFECT

Even if an expenditure-reducing deflation creates the spare capacity, a country's industries may still be unable immediately to increase supply following a devaluation. It may also be that the Marshall-Lerner condition is not met in the immediate period, since the demand for exports and imports is likely to be much more inelastic in the short run than in the long run. Thus the balance of payments may actually deteriorate before it improves. This is known as the **J-curve effect**. The deterioration in the balance of payments may reduce confidence in the eventual success of the policy, leading to capital outflows which destabilise both the balance of payments and the exchange rate. The existence of the J-curve effect, which can perhaps be minimised by an expenditure-reducing deflation prior to the devaluation, reduces the attractiveness of exchange rate adjustment as a policy to cure a payments deficit. And even when the benefits of the devaluation are realised, they may be relatively short-lived. The advantages of price competitiveness produced by the devaluation may be lost as a result of increased import prices raising the country's inflation rate.

THE ABSORPTION APPROACH TO THE BALANCE OF PAYMENTS

Whereas the Marshall–Lerner condition illustrates the **elasticities approach** to the balance of payments, the need to deflate domestic demand in order to prepare for a later successful devaluation reflects the **absorption approach**. This examines the balance of payments in an essentially Keynesian way in terms of aggregate demand absorbing, or failing to absorb, a country's output. In Chapter 19 we wrote the equilibrium condition for National Income as:

$$Y = C + I + G + X - M$$

Rewriting the equation, we get:

$$X - M = Y - (C + I - G)$$

Thus the balance of payments (X–M)) will be in deficit if the economy consumes or absorbs more goods and services than it produces: if (C + I + G) is greater than Y.

To put it another way, the balance of payments equals national output less national absorption. If unemployed resources exist, an expenditure-switching devaluation can reduce a payments deficit without having to reduce absorption, but if full employment exists, Y cannot increase. The balance of payments can only improve if the economy is deflated and domestic absorption reduced.

Chapter roundup

The Balance of Payments is one part of the National Income Accounts which have been considered in Chapter 18. The major macroeconomic issues and policies considered in Chapters 15–17 and 19–24 all influence, and are often influenced by, the payments position. Similarly, world trade (Chapter 26) and international exchange rates, which we consider in Chapter 27, have a significant impact upon a nation's balance of payments position and performance.

Illustrative questions and answers

1 Essay Question
a) Discuss the view that the main constraint on the pursuit of full employment and economic growth has been the UK's external balance. (70)
b) Is this likely to change in the 1990s? (30)
(ULEAC, AS-Level, June 1991)

Tutorial note

Begin your answer by outlining the Keynesian view that during the 1960s and 1970s – that is before North Sea oil temporarily moved the UK balance of payments on current account into surplus – the balance of payments did indeed provide the main constraint on UK economic performance. Periods of relatively fast economic growth and falling unemployment which were brought about by expansionary Keynesian policies, would be brought to a halt when the higher levels of demand 'sucked' imports into the economy and caused the current account to deteriorate. The resulting sterling crisis would force the government to deflate the economy, causing growth to slow and unemployment to rise.

You can then develop your answer to the first part of the question by debating whether the inflation constraint, represented by the Phillips curve 'trade-off', was a more significant constraint, particularly after North Sea oil revenues had improved the Balance of Payments position.

There are two views on whether the balance of payments will severely constrain UK economic performance in the 1990s. The Keynesian view is pessimistic. In the past the current account has moved into surplus during a recession when a reduced level of demand draws fewer imports into the economy. However, the current account remained in significant deficit throughout the severe recession of the early 1990s – a legacy (in the Keynesian view) of the deindustrialisation process which has destroyed much of Britain's manufacturing capacity since 1979. Keynesian economists believe that the recovery from the recession must inevitably be weak (and probably short lived), because any growth in demand faster than about 1.5 % a year will lead to a massive and unsustainable deterioration in the current account. But as we have indicated in the context of the previous question, free-market orientated economists have been much more optimistic. They have argued that growth and recovery from a recession can be sustained despite a deteriorating current account, providing that overseas owners of capital maintain confidence in the Conservative government's economic policy. Also, as we have explained, the free-marketeers believe that the recent current account deficit, unlike the external deficits run by previous Labour governments, is a 'private sector matter' that will eventually be self-correcting without the need for any specific corrective action by the government.

Suggested answer plan

1   Outline how the current account can constrain economic performance, and describe briefly how the constraint has affected the UK economy in the past.
2   Debate whether inflation or the state of the current account has provided the main constraint, particularly since 1979.
3   Contrast the Keynesian and the free-market 'supply-side' views on whether a deteriorating current account will severely constrain the UK economy in the 1990s. Appeal to recent evidence.
4   Reach an overall conclusion.

2   Data Question

'The prospect of a major Balance of Payments crisis remains the single most important danger for the UK economy in 1988. The re-emergence of the external constraint will be increasingly important in framing monetary policy though the year.

The manufacturing deficit looks set to worsen further due to two critical factors. The first is the UK's competitiveness. The restrained growth in unit labour costs in 1987 owed a great deal to rapid productivity growth on the back of sharply expanding production. In 1988 production will grow less rapidly, productivity gains will be slow, and unit labour costs could expand sharply.

Meanwhile, the exchange rate will not be allowed to come to the rescue on present policies.

The second factor is the strength of the domestic demand in the UK relative to its main trading partners. The OECD forecast real domestic demand growth of 3¾ per cent in the UK, 2½ per cent in the EC as a whole and only 1 per cent in the US. Under these circumstances the trend for the UK trade deficit has only one direction to go.'

(Source: adapted from *The Times*, 15 February 1988)

(a)   What is meant by 'UK competitiveness' (second paragraph)?
(b)   Analyse the reasoning behind the statement that 'The prospect of a major Balance of Payments crisis remains the single most important danger for the UK economy in 1988' (first paragraph).
(c)   How may the 'strength of domestic demand in the UK relative to its trading partners' cause Balance of Payments problems (fourth paragraph)?

(d) Examine one short term and one long term measure likely to reduce the UK's Balance of Payments deficit.

(ULEAC, June 1990)

Tutorial note

(a) Competitiveness can refer to prices of UK-produced goods, compared to the prices of similar goods produced in other countries, and it may also refer to the relative production costs, especially labour costs, of different countries.

(b) A rapidly deteriorating Balance of Payments deficit on current account could trigger a massive outflow on capital account. The resulting large-scale selling of sterling on foreign exchange markets, would cause an extremely rapid fall in the exchange rate. This might then fuel domestic inflation or result in high domestic interest rates if the authorities take action to support the exchange rate.

(c) A high level of domestic demand contributes directly to a deteriorating current account by drawing imports into the economy (via the marginal propensity to import). Less directly, it will cause a high rate of domestic inflation, reducing the competitiveness of UK industries.

(d) Raising interest rates is a short-term measure. A long-term measure could be any 'supply-side' policy to improve the underlying competitiveness of the UK economy.

Question bank

1 During the 1980s, the United Kingdom's balance of trade in manufactured goods moved from surplus into deficit. Explain why and discuss whether it matters.

(AEB, November 1989)

2 Why might a government wish to eliminate a surplus on its current account balance of payments? What measures could it use to achieve this end?

(ULEAC, June 1987)

3
(a) Discuss the view that the main constraint on the pursuit of full employment and economic growth has been the UK's external balance. (70)
(b) Is this likely to change in the 1990s? (30)

(ULEAC AS-Level, June 1991)

4
(a) What is meant by a current account Balance of Payments deficit? (20)
(b) Explain how a Balance of Payments deficit may be:
    (i) financed in the short run; (40)
    (ii) eliminated in the long run. (40)

(ULEAC, January 1992)

5
(a) Contrast the impact of monetary and fiscal policies which a government might use to rectify a worsening Balance of Payments on current account. (60)
(b) How has the UK's membership of the ERM affected the government's freedom of action in the use of these policies? (40)

(ULEAC, January 1993)

6 'Only a continuing fall in the United Kingdom's inflation rate will lead to a marked improvement in the balance of payments on current account.' Discuss.   (Oxford, June 1991)

7 Does a large deficit on the current account of the balance of payments matter in itself?   (Oxford, June 1991)

8
(a) Discuss the view that the major constraint on the pursuit of full employment and economic growth has been the UK's external balance.   (70)
(b) Is this likely to change in the 1990s?   (30)
                                             (ULEAC, AS-Level, June 1991)

9
(a) Explain the causes of the current problem of international debt.   (50)
(b) Discuss the implications of this problem for the stability of the world economy.   (50)
                                             (ULEAC, AS-Level, June 1991)

EXCHANGE RATES

Units in this chapter

Chapter objectives

In Chapter 26 we emphasised how the method of restoration of equilibrium in the Balance of Payments depends in large measure upon the type of **exchange rate** that exists. In this chapter we examine in greater detail the mechanisms through which **freely floating** and completely **fixed exchange rates** operate, before investigating various types of managed exchange rates that have existed in the world economy since 1945. We shall introduce the role of the **International Monetary Fund (IMF)** in providing the institutional framework within which modern exchange rates operate, and we shall comment on the international payments difficulties and the problems of world liquidity which exist today.

27.1 UNDERLYING CONCEPTS

THE SIMPLE THEORY OF A FREELY FLOATING EXCHANGE RATE

Exchange rates and the existence of **a foreign exchange market** are necessary because different countries use different currencies to pay for **internal** trade. An exchange rate is simply the **external price** of a currency expressed in terms of gold, another currency such as the US dollar, or a weighted average of a sample of important trading currencies. For the sake of simplicity, we shall for the most part follow the convention of expressing the exchange rate of the pound sterling in terms of the dollar, but we shall also note when other expressions of the exchange rate are more appropriate.

In a regime of **freely (or cleanly) floating exchange rates**, the currency of a country is regarded as a simple commodity to be traded on foreign exchange markets, its price or exchange rate being determined by the forces of supply and demand. For the time being we shall assume that a currency is demanded on foreign exchanges only for the payment of trade (we are ignoring the **complications caused by capital flows and speculation**), that a country needs another country's currency to purchase imports from that country, and that all countries will immediately sell on the foreign exchange market any holdings of foreign currencies that are surplus to their requirements.

As in any market, the **demand and supply curves for a currency** (in this case the pound sterling) show the amounts of the currency which traders wish to buy and sell at various possible prices or exchange rates. Since we are assuming that people wish to hold foreign currency only for the purpose of financing trade, the slopes of the demand and supply curves for a currency will depend on the levels of exports and imports that are desired at each exchange rate. The lower the exchange rate of the pound, the more competitive are British exports when priced in foreign currencies and the greater the volume of exports. Thus, the lower the exchange rate, the greater the demand for pounds on foreign exchange markets, since foreigners need more pounds to buy a greater volume of British exports at their current sterling price. The result is the downward-sloping demand curve for pounds illustrated in Fig. 58.

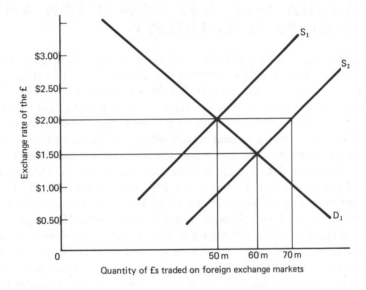

Fig. 59 *Exchange rate adjustment in a system of freely floating exchange rates*

While exports generate a demand for pounds on foreign exchange markets, imports generate the supply of sterling needed to purchase the foreign currencies required to pay for the goods and services demanded. A fall in the exchange rate will reduce the competitiveness of imports when priced in sterling. Provided that the demand for imports is elastic, the quantity of pounds being supplied to pay for imports decreases as the exchange rate falls – and increases as the exchange rate rises – resulting in the upward-sloping supply curve of sterling in Fig. 59.

Fig. 59 illustrates an initial exchange rate of £1 = \$2.00, the demand curve for sterling being D_1 and the supply curve of sterling S_1. Clearly, this is an **equilibrium exchange rate** at which the demand for and the supply of sterling are equal. Since the value of exports (paid for in pounds) equals the value of imports (paid for in foreign currencies), the **balance of payments is also in equilibrium**! This point is well worth stressing: exchange rate equilibrium implies **balance of payments equilibrium** and vice versa. Indeed, the two concepts are merely different sides of the same coin, the one an equilibrium stated in terms of an equilibrium price (the exchange rate), and the other an equilibrium of quantities (currency flows). If the balance of payments is in equilibrium there will be no pressure for a change in the exchange rate.

Suppose now that for some reason, such as an increase in the quality competitiveness of foreign goods, the desire to buy imports increases at all existing prices expressed in sterling. More foreign exchange is demanded in order to purchase imports and the supply curve of sterling in Fig. 59 shifts rightwards to S_2. \$2.00 is no longer an equilibrium exchange rate, since foreigners now

accumulate sterling holdings of £70m, whereas they only require £50m to pay
for their own purchases of British exports at this exchange rate. The market
mechanism now operates to restore simultaneously equilibrium in the balance of
payments and an equilibrium exchange rate. The sale by foreigners of the excess
supply of pounds depresses or depreciates the exchange rate, thereby increasing
the price competitiveness of British exports and reducing that of imports. The
process continues until the new equilibrium exchange rate of $1.50 is reached.
Conversely, if the initial equilibrium is disturbed by an event such as the
production of North Sea oil which moves the balance of payments into surplus,
the exchange rate will rise or appreciate until the excess demand for sterling is
eliminated and a new equilibrium is achieved.

THE MARSHALL-LERNER CONDITION AND EXCHANGE RATE STABILITY

It is important to stress that the result illustrated in Fig. 58 depends critically upon
our assumption that the demand for imports is elastic. If demand is inelastic, more
pounds will be needed as the exchange rate falls in order to pay for imports. The
fall in the quantity of imports at lower exchange rates is insufficient to offset the
effects of the higher sterling price of each unit of imports. In these circumstances,
a downward-sloping (perverse or backward-bending) supply curve for sterling
results. The equilibrium exchange rate is still determined where the demand and
supply curves intersect, but the equilibrium may not always be stable. The
stability condition is provided by the **Marshall–Lerner criterion** which we
introduced and explained in Chapter 26. Provided that the sum of the elasticities
of foreigners' demand for British exports and British demand for imports is
greater than unity, there will be a tendency to move towards a stable equilibrium
exchange rate. Even if the demand for imports is inelastic, provided that the sum
of the export and import elasticities is greater than one and that supply is
sufficiently elastic, then a floating exchange rate system will correct a disequilibrium
in the balance of payments.

THE THEORY OF A FIXED EXCHANGE RATE

In the theory of a **freely floating** exchange rate system, the currency's **external**
value rises or falls to eliminate a Balance of Payments surplus or deficit. In
contrast, in a regime of **fixed** exchange rates, the currency's external value remains
unchanged while the **internal** price level, or possibly the level of domestic
economic activity and output, adjust to eliminate Balance of Payments disequilibrium.
We can approach the adjustment process from either a Keynesian or a monetarist
perspective.

❶The Keynesian approach to Balance of Payments adjustment under
fixed exchange rates The Keynesian approach to the adjustment process
in a system of fixed exchange rates is closely related to the absorption
approach to the Balance of Payments which we described in Chapter 26.
Suppose that initially the level of income is in equilibrium so that:

$$Y = C + I + G + (X - M)$$

and that the Balance of Payments on Current Account is also in equilibrium with X = M. But if exports fall (because for example foreigners
believe the quality of UK goods has deteriorated), the Current Account
will move into deficit with X < M and the equilibrium level of income will
also be disturbed. From a Keynesian perspective, the **Current Account
deficit represents a leakage or withdrawal from the circular flow of
income**. This triggers a negative **multiplier effect**, causing the equilibrium level of income to fall. If we now assume that the level of imports are

partly determined by the level of income, via the **marginal propensity to import**, imports will then also fall, partially or completely eliminating the payments deficit caused by the initial fall in exports.

The Keynesian adjustment process we have just described illustrates how a **Balance of Payments deficit is inherently deflationary**. The leakage of demand represented by the deficit deflates the level of money national income (or nominal national income) within the economy. But nominal income can fall, either because the price level falls, or because the level of real output or income falls. If the domestic price level falls, exports become more price competitive in overseas markets whereas imports become more expensive. Assuming the **Marshall-Lerner condition** holds, the resulting adjustment process which eliminates the payments deficit is essentially **expenditure-switching**. In contrast, if the main effect of the deflation of demand falls not on the domestic price level but on the level of real economic activity within the country, the adjustment process is of a largely **expenditure-reducing** nature. At lower levels of real income, output and employment, fewer imports are demanded.

Conversely, when an increase in exports or a fall in imports moves the Balance of Payments into surplus, the adjustment mechanism is simply the opposite of the process we have just described. Being an **injection of demand** into the flow of income the **surplus has a reflationary or inflationary effect** upon the level of income and output, depending on whether real activity or prices are stimulated. Either way, nominal income rises. If the real level of economic activity is reflated or stimulated, more imports will be 'absorbed' into the economy to meet the increased real demand being exercised by households and firms. But if the main effect is to inflate the price level, payments adjustment occurs as domestic demand switches to the more price competitive imports, while exports lose their competitiveness in world markets.

❷ **The monetarist approach to Balance of Payments adjustment under fixed exchange rates**

The monetarist explanation of the adjustment mechanism which restores equilibrium in a fixed exchange rate system is similar to the Keynesian approach to the extent that a deficit is eliminated by deflation, and a surplus is reduced by reflation or inflation. However, monetarists emphasise the **linkages between the Balance of Payments and the domestic money supply** in the adjustment process. This contrasts with the Keynesian emphasis on the role of the linkages between changes in aggregate demand, the national income multiplier and a resulting increased or decreased absorption of imports. As we explained in Chapter 26, a Balance of Payments surplus leads to a shortage of the country's currency on foreign exchange markets. When the exchange rate is fixed, the country's monetary authorities must then supply more of their own currency onto the foreign exchange market and buy other currencies which accumulate as reserves, in order to keep the currency's market price at the fixed exchange rate. This is called **exchange equalisation**. The country's money supply thus expands as new currency is issued to stabilise the exchange rate. According to monetarists, the increased money supply inflates the domestic price level, improving the price competitiveness of imports while reducing the competitiveness of exports. Conversely, a payments deficit leads to a fall in the domestic money supply because the monetary authorities must sell reserves and buy back their own currency to prevent the exchange rate from falling. The resulting monetary contraction as currency is taken out of circulation depresses or deflates the domestic economy, thereby increasing the relative competitiveness of exports.

27.2 ESSENTIAL INFORMATION

EXCHANGE RATES AND BALANCE OF PAYMENTS ADJUSTMENT

Before we investigate the advantages and disadvantages of freely floating and fixed exchange rates, we shall present a simple summary of the critical difference between the Balance of Payments adjustment mechanism under the two exchange regimes. Under a system of **floating exchange rates**, the **external** price of the currency (the exchange rate) moves up or down to correct a payments imbalance, without requiring an adjustment in domestic output or the internal price level. In contrast, under a system of fixed exchange rates it is the **internal** price level (together with the levels of domestic output and employment) which adjusts to cure the imbalance, the external price of the currency remaining unchanged.

THE ADVANTAGES OF FLOATING EXCHANGE RATES

❶ An important advantage of a freely floating (or flexible) exchange rate stems from the nature of the adjustment mechanism just described. According to the simple theory of a freely floating exchange rate, the exchange rate should never be over- or undervalued for very long. In the event of a 'too-high' exchange rate causing export uncompetitiveness and a payments deficit, market forces should quickly adjust towards an equilibrium exchange rate which also achieves equilibrium in the Balance of Payments – provided of course that the Marshall-Lerner condition holds.

❷ Correctly valued exchange rates are necessary if the world's resources are to be efficiently allocated between competing uses. If efficient resource allocation and use are to be achieved in a constantly changing world, market prices must be free to reflect the shifts in demand and comparative advantage that result from such events as resource discoveries and changes in technology and labour costs. A freely floating exchange rate may automatically adjust to gradual changes in demand and comparative advantage, whereas in a fixed exchange rate system a currency may become gradually over- or undervalued when demand or comparative advantage move either against or in favour of a country's industries.

❸ It has been argued (rather naively, as we shall later see) that when the exchange rate is freely floating, the state of the balance of payments ceases to be both a 'policy problem' and a constraint upon the pursuit of domestic economic objectives. Governments can leave market forces to 'look after' the balance of payments while they concentrate on achieving full employment and growth. If the pursuit of domestic objectives causes the inflation rate to rise out of line with other countries, then, according to the **purchasing power parity theory**, the exchange rate will simply fall to compensate exactly for the higher inflation rate. In this way, the competitiveness of the country's exports is always maintained. In a fixed exchange rate system, the country would 'import' unemployment from the rest of the world as a result of its deteriorating competitiveness and because of the need to deflate the domestic economy in order to correct the payments deficit.

❹ Equally, a 'responsible' country with a lower-than-average inflation rate benefits from a floating exchange rate which insulates it from 'importing' inflation from the rest of the world. There are two ways of explaining this. If the rest of the world is inflating at a faster rate, a fixed exchange rate causes a country to 'import' inflation through the rising prices of goods it purchases abroad. Alternatively, under fixed exchange rates, excess demand in countries with persistent balance of payments deficits causes inflationary pressure to be 'exported' to surplus countries. The deficit countries escape the full inflationary consequences of the excess demand generated by their economies.

❺ When the exchange rate is floating, a country's monetary policy (as well as its fiscal policy) can be completely independent of external influences. This is because the country has no need to keep official reserves to finance a payments deficit or to support the exchange rate. If, for example, the deficit increases, the exchange rate simply corrects the disequilibrium without any loss of reserves. The country's domestic money supply is unaffected by a change in the official reserves, and interest rate policy is not determined by the need to protect the exchange rate.

❻ Because a country has no need to hold large official reserves of foreign currencies, resources which would otherwise be tied up in the reserves can be used more productively elsewhere.

THE DISADVANTAGES OF FLOATING EXCHANGE RATES

❶ It is often argued that floating exchange rates increase business uncertainty and lead to less specialisation, trade, and investment than would otherwise take place. However, uncertainty is probably not the most serious problem that results from a floating exchange rate. Indeed, **hedging**, which usually involves the purchase or sale of currency three months in advance in the **'forward' market**, can considerably reduce the business uncertainties caused by floating exchange rates. It is also the case that fixed and managed exchange rates can, on occasion, be just as uncertain as floating rates, particularly when a currency is obviously overvalued, and a devaluation is expected.

❷ It is also asserted that a floating exchange rate promotes an increase in currency speculation with all its destabilising effects. There are a number of interesting aspects to this question. While it is undoubtedly true that there was a growth in currency speculation in the years of 'dirty' floating, it may have been less related to floating than to the growth of the pool of footloose 'hot-money' – itself a response to the role of the dollar in the Bretton Woods system of managed exchange rates. Secondly, as the events around 'Black Wednesday' in September 1992 illustrate, there is far more scope for speculators to 'win' at the expense of governments in a managed exchange rate system than in a freely floating system. In the former case, a speculator engages in the 'one-way option' of selling currency to the central bank defending the currency, hoping to force a devaluation and to realise a capital gain when the currency is bought back at a lower price. If the pressure fails, the speculator will only make a small loss, since he can buy back the currency at or near the original price. In a freely floating system, however, a speculator wishing to sell must find another wishing to buy – and in the consequent trading the speculator who guesses correctly gains at the expense of the one who guesses wrongly. The successful speculators are those who correctly sell when the exchange rate is too high and buy when it is too low. Their activity speeds the process of adjustment to an exchange rate equilibrium, stabilising rather than destabilising, and smoothing out rather than reinforcing temporary fluctuations.

However, during the regime of 'dirty floating' in the 1970s and 1980s, massive, essentially speculative, short-term capital flows or hot money movements have had seriously destabilising effects upon the exchange rates, balance of payments and, indeed, the structure of the domestic economy of a number of countries. At the beginning of the 1980s, hot money flowed into the UK, forcing the exchange rate up to an uncompetitive level at a time when the British inflation rate was above that of her major trading partners. The overvalued exchange rate was a major cause of deindustrialisation and unemployment.

By contrast, in 1985 the exchange rate fell to nearly $1.00 as hot money flowed out of sterling into the US currency causing the American economy to experience the problems of overvaluation. However, by the late 1980s and early 1990s, the pound was once again overvalued, with a major cause being UK monetary policy. Since the early 1980s, UK monetary policy has relied almost exclusively on the use of interest rates to influence the demand for credit and bank lending. High interest rates, aimed at dampening domestic credit, have attracted capital flows into sterling, forcing up the exchange rate. In the early 1990s, many commentators believed that an overvalued exchange rate, 'locked in' to the rate at which the pound joined the **exchange rate mechanism** of the EMS in 1990, was once again contributing to renewed deindustrialisation and the growth of unemployment.

❸ We have already noted how fixed exchange rates have been blamed for the 'export' of inflation from one country to another. However, other economists believe that floating exchange rates are to blame for inflation and that fixed exchange rates in fact possess a deflationary bias which reduces inflation. In a fixed exchange rate system, such as the ERM, if a country allows its inflation rate to exceed that of its trading competitors, its balance of payments will move into severe deficit. A growing export uncompetitiveness and import penetration will 'discipline' the domestic causesoof cost-push inflation through an increase in the level of unemployment and the number of bankruptcies. At the same time the loss of reserves will put pressure on the deficit country to deflate its domestic economy in order to cure the imbalance, but the system is asymmetrical, since no equivalent pressure is put upon the surplus country to cure its surplus.

In a floating exchange rate system, no such discipline exists to make a country reduce its inflation rate. (Indeed, we argued earlier that the lack of such a discipline is regarded by some as one of the virtues of floating exchange rates, allowing a country to pursue domestic objectives unconstrained by the need to support the balance of payments or the exchange rate.) In fact, however, a policy of pursuing domestic objectives irrespective of their effects on the exchange rate contains two serious dangers. In the first place, through the effects of a falling exchange rate upon import prices and hence upon domestic inflation, such a policy may unleash a **vicious circle or accumulative spiral of ever-faster inflation and exchange rate depreciation** which eventually destabilises large parts of the domestic economy and prevents growth and full employment from being attained. Secondly, a simultaneous expansion of demand in a large number of countries untrammelled by the consequences upon the exchange rate can add to excess demand and fuel inflation on a worldwide scale. In an individual country such inflation may be explained in cost-push terms, since it appears to originate in increased import prices, but the true causes probably lie deeper in an international increase in money demand which far exceeds the short-run ability of industries, and particularly primary producers, to increase world supply.

THE ADVANTAGES AND DISADVANTAGES OF FIXED EXCHANGE RATES

The advantages and disadvantages of fixed exchange rates are closely but oppositely related to the disadvantages and advantages of floating exchange rates which we have already covered in some detail. In summary, we can state that the main advantages usually cited for fixed exchange rates are:

❶ certainty and
❷ the 'discipline' imposed on a country's domestic economic management and upon the behaviour of workers and firms.

In contrast, the main disadvantages are:

❶ in some circumstances uncertainty may actually be increased,
❷ a currency may be over- or undervalued, in which case
❸ severe costs in terms of unemployment and lost output may be imposed on deficit countries, and
❹ in a rigid gold standard system there may not be an adequate adjustment mechanism successfully to cure a payments imbalance.

MANAGED EXCHANGE RATES

During the 1920s, world exchange rates were at times fixed (under a system known as the **Gold Standard**, in which exchange rates were pegged against gold), while, during the 1930s, most exchange rates freely floated. Neither system worked very well. The Gold Standard was too rigid and the floated freely system was too unstable or volatile. Indeed, both systems were blamed for contributing in part to the **Great Depression** of the 1930s. The rigid Gold Standard system forced countries with currencies overvalued against gold into domestic policies of deflation which led to high unemployment. Then, following the collapse of the Gold Standard in 1931, attempts to gain a trading advantage at other countries' expense by floating the exchange rate, together with 'beggar-my-neighbour' protectionism, contributed to the deepening of the Great Depression.

Since the Second World War, exchange rates have never been rigidly fixed and seldom have they freely or 'cleanly' floated. Instead, the exchange rates of the world's principal currencies have to a greater or lesser extent been **managed**. An exchange rate is managed when the country's central bank actively intervenes on foreign exchange markets, buying and selling reserves and its own currency, to influence the movement of the exchange rate in a particular direction. By managing the exchange rate, a country's monetary authorities hope to achieve the stability and certainty associated with fixed exchange rates combined with a floating exchange rate's ability to avoid over- and undervaluation by responding to market forces. But critics of managed exchange rates have argued that, instead of combining the advantages of both fixed and floating exchange rates with the disadvantages of neither, in practice exchange rate management has too often achieved the opposite: the disadvantages of uncertainty and instability combined with the ineffective and wasteful use of official reserves in frequent fruitless attempts by governments to stem speculative 'hot money' flows into or out of currencies.

Since 1945 exchange rates have been managed in a number of different ways, some of which have been closer to a freely floating system, while others have been much more similar to a rigidly fixed regime. The £'s exchange rate has been determined under the following systems:

❶ The **Bretton Woods system** from 1947 to 1972;
❷ '**Managed' floating** (or '**dirty**' **floating**), from 1972 until ERM entry in 1990;
❸ Membership of the **Exchange Rate Mechanism (ERM)** of the **European Monetary System (EMS)**, from 1990 until 1992;
❹ '**Managed**' floating once again since 1992.

THE BRETTON WOODS SYSTEM

Because the **Bretton Woods** exchange rate system, which lasted from 1947 to

1971/72, was a forerunner (on a global scale) of the Exchange Rate Mechanism (ERM) of the European Monetary System (EMS), we shall describe it in some detail. To understand the Bretton Woods System, we must realise that it had much more in common with fixed exchange rates and the Gold Standard, than with freely floating exchange rates. In the early years of the twentieth century, the Gold Standard had failed for two main reasons:

❶ a shortage of gold for the finance of payments deficits; and

❷ the lack of an adequate adjustment mechanism to correct a 'wrongly' valued currency.

To overcome the former problem, the US dollar replaced gold as the central standard or 'pivot currency' when the Bretton Woods system was set up at the end of the Second World War. Supplemented by gold, which still remained (as it does today) a major reserve asset and source of liquidity, the dollar became the **key currency** in the Bretton Woods System. Indeed, because the dollar remained (until 1971) on the Gold Standard, the 'new' system was essentially a **gold exchange standard** in which other currencies' exchange rates were fixed, via the dollar, against gold.

The second problem – the lack of a suitable adjustment mechanism – which had contributed to the abandonment of the Gold Standard, was tackled in the Bretton Woods System through the creation of a **zone of flexibility** around a **fixed peg** exchange rate. Market forces were free to determine the day-to-day exchange rate of a currency between a **ceiling** and **floor** which bounded the zone of flexibility 1 per cent each side of an agreed par value or 'peg'. If the Balance of Payments moved into surplus, the resulting excess demand for the country's currency would cause market forces to bid the exchange rate up above the peg, moving it towards the ceiling. In a similar but opposite way, the exchange rate would be depressed towards the floor in the event of a payments deficit. Each member country of the IMF agreed to intervene in the foreign exchange market to keep its currency's exchange rate within the prescribed zone of flexibility. This was achieved through exchange equalisation. When an exchange rate rose and threatened to move through the ceiling, IMF rules required that the country's central bank should intervene by artificially increasing the supply of its currency on the foreign exchange market. By selling its own currency and purchasing reserves, the exchange rate could be kept below the ceiling and within the zone of flexibility. Conversely, the central bank was required to sell reserves and buy its own currency to prevent market forces from depressing the exchange rate through the floor.

A persistent payments surplus or deficit would, of course, be associated with an equally persistent tendency for the exchange rate to leave the zone of flexibility. This would indicate a **fundamental disequilibrium** in the Balance of Payments and a 'wrongly' valued exchange rate. To deal with this problem, IMF rules allowed a country to adjust the par value of its exchange rate with a formal **revaluation** in the case of a surplus, and a **devaluation** in the case of a deficit.

The Breakdown of the Bretton Woods System of Managed Exchange Rates

In this way, it was hoped that member countries of the IMF would benefit from a **'managed flexibility'** yielded by the Bretton Woods System. But in the 1960s and early 1970s, the fixed peg system increasingly displayed signs of **'managed inflexibility'**. The Bretton Woods System suffered from the same rigidity as the Gold Standard. The IMF interpreted its own rules in such a severe way that devaluation became effectively ruled out, except as a last resort and sign of weakness, for countries suffering from persistent payments deficits. The IMF placed pressure on deficit countries to deflate their domestic economies, but deflation could not be successful without a simultaneous pressure on surplus countries to reflate – and generally this pressure was lacking.

A number of factors eventually caused the Bretton Woods System finally to collapse in 1971/72. We shall mention just one, which has recently been just as significant in putting a similar pressure on the Exchange Rate Mechanism of the EMS. This is the fact that it is always exceedingly difficult to maintain relatively fixed exchange rates if inflation rates differ widely between countries and especially if the inflation rate in deficit countries is markedly higher than in surplus countries. The Bretton Woods System worked best in the 1950s when inflation rates in the developed world were very similar. Strains on the system began to occur in the 1960s when higher inflation rates in deficit countries started to erode their export competitiveness, contributing to the worsening of the payments deficits. As a result, pressures began to mount in deficit countries for a freeing of the exchange rate from the harsh requirement imposed by the IMF, that a deficit should be cured by domestic deflation and not by devaluation.

'DIRTY' FLOATING

Whereas the Bretton Woods System of managed exchange rates (and more recently the ERM of the EMS) resembled fixed exchange rates rather than freely floating exchange rates, the reverse is true of 'dirty' floating. **'Dirty'** or **'managed' floating** occurs when the exchange rate is 'officially' floating in the sense that a country's monetary authorities announce that market forces are determining the exchange rate, though in fact the authorities intervene 'unofficially' behind the scenes to buy or sell their own currency in order to influence the exchange rate. At one extreme, such intervention can be regarded simply as a smoothing operation in a regime of clean or freely floating exchange rates, but when the intervention is designed to secure an **'unofficial' exchange rate target** it is better described as 'dirty' floating. After the breakdown of the Bretton Woods System in 1971/72, the currencies of many of the world's trading countries floated in this way, though there were short-lived periods when governments withdrew their intervention and allowed their currencies to float freely.

After 1985, the UK government adopted an 'unofficial' target for sterling which 'shadowed' the currencies of the European Monetary System, particularly the Deutschmark. This was in preparation for an eventual full entry of the pound into the ERM of the EMS. As we explain in the context of one of the questions at the end of this chapter, in the late 1980s a 'high' exchange rate was also used by the UK government as perhaps the main instrument in its counter-inflation policy. The Conservative government hoped that a high exchange rate would act as a discipline against domestic inflationary pressure.

THE EUROPEAN MONETARY SYSTEM

The **European Monetary System (EMS)**, which began operations in 1979, is both a **revival of the fixed peg exchange rate system** (which we examined earlier in the context of the Bretton Woods System), and a **'joint float'** of the EC currencies against the currencies of the rest of the world. The currencies of the EMS members – or rather those that are members of the system's **Exchange Rate Mechanism (ERM)** – are fixed against each other, but with rather wider zones of flexibility than under the old Bretton Woods System, via a specially created artificial standard or measure, the **European Currency Unit (ECU)**. Inside the 'joint float', currencies can move within the relatively wide and overlapping zones of flexibility. And because the EMS rules supposedly allow for **periodic readjustments or realignments** of the zones of flexibility against the ECU, and require action by both surplus and deficit nations to keep the currencies within the permitted bands, the EMS is (again supposedly) designed to be considerably more flexible or less rigid than the now defunct Bretton Woods System.

THE UK AND THE ERM

Initially, the United Kingdom decided to remain outside the EMS, at least as a full member committed to the Exchange Rate Mechanism, but this decision contradicted the spirit if not the rules of the EC membership. The members of the EC established the EMS so that the Common Market might function better. With erratically floating exchange rates, the EC would find it difficult to implement its **common economic policies**, such as the **Common Agricultural Policy**. For the United Kingdom therefore, the costs and benefits of joining the EMS ought to be closely associated with the costs and benefits of developing the common economic policies of the EC.

We have already noted that in the late 1980s the sterling exchange rate was managed so as to 'shadow' movements of EC currencies, particularly the Deutschmark. Late in 1990, the UK finally made the decision to become a full member of the exchange rate mechanism of the EMS. At the time the Conservative government claimed that a major benefit would be the ability to draw on the help of other members to deter destabilising 'hot money' movements into and out of sterling. The more ardent 'Europhiles' both inside and outside the government also claimed that Britain might benefit if the exchange rate arrangements were eventually to develop into full European Monetary Union (EMU), with the ECU becoming a common EC currency and new source of world liquidity.

However, opponents of both fixed exchange rates and of closer UK integration with the EC opposed entry into the ERM, claiming that the system suffers the disadvantages of any system of relatively fixed exchange rates. They argued that the EMS has tended to become a **'Deutschmark area'** in which the German mark is the key currency. In the 'joint float' of the 1980s (in the period before German reunification), a strong DM tended to pull up the fixed values of the other currencies, leading to their overvaluation against the rest of the world. And although the zones of flexibility had been designed to prevent this happening, great pressure could still be placed on weaker EMS currencies, particularly if member countries experience divergent inflation rates. After 1989, this pressure was exacerbated when the German central bank, the Bundesbank, raised German interest rates in order to dampen domestic inflationary pressures caused by German unification.

We shall explain the effects of ERM membership upon the UK economy in the context of one of the questions at the end of this chapter. Here we shall simply summarise the circumstances which forced the £ out of the ERM on **'Black Wednesday'** September 16 1992. By 1992 high German interest rates were forcing the UK authorities to raise sterling interest rates to prevent capital flows out of the pound and to support the high parity at which the £ had entered the ERM. Perhaps more significantly, the combination of a high ERM parity and high interest rates were causing the UK to suffer severely in terms of lost output and high unemployment. Many economists believed that ERM membership had pushed the UK economy into recession and that the deflationary costs could not be justified. And although, at under 4 per cent, the UK inflation rate had converged to near the EC average, there was a growing consensus – outside the Conservative Government – that the £ was overvalued and that its ERM parity could not be maintained. In the earlier years of the ERM, periodic realignments of currencies had taken place which prevented the system from becoming too inflexible. But by the time the £ joined the ERM in 1990, the ERM had evolved – like the Bretton Woods System almost a generation before – into a system of 'managed inflexibility' in which realignments were strongly discouraged. By September 1992 the £'s exchange rate within the ERM became unsupportable, with devaluation becoming a matter of 'when' and not 'if'. Following a massive speculative 'hot money' flow out of the £, in which the UK authorities used up virtually the whole of the country's foreign exchange reserves in an abortive defence of the ERM parity, the £ was forced to leave the Exchange Rate Mechanism on September 16th. 1992.

Since the devaluation of 1992 and the debacle of exit from the ERM, the £ has once again floated, though as yet it is too early to assess the extent to which this has been a 'free float' or a 'dirty float'. It also remains to be seen whether the UK Government will attempt to re-enter the ERM in the near future, albeit at a significantly lower exchange rate than the parity operating when the £ was originally in the ERM from 1990 to 1992.

THE INTERNATIONAL MONETARY FUND

In earlier chapters we have explained how, in the years following the Second World War, Keynesian economic policies were adopted within countries to pursue the objectives of growth and full employment through an extension of government intervention in the domestic economy. Keynesian economic policies were a response to the Great Depression and to the large-scale unemployment of the interwar years. In part, however, the Great Depression had been caused, and certainly made worse, by the collapse of world trade which followed the breakdown of the Gold Standard system in 1931. Perhaps it is not surprising therefore, that the 1940s were also the decade in which interventionism was extended to the management of exchange rates, through the creation of the **International Money Fund (IMF)**.

Since its inception at the 1944 Bretton Woods Conference, the principal objective of the IMF has been to promote a growing and freer system of world trade and payments. To achieve this general objective, the original Articles of Agreement of the International Monetary Fund specified that the IMF should:

❶ promote international monetary cooperation;
❷ promote stable exchange rates, maintain orderly exchange arrangements and avoid competitive exchange depreciation;
❸ encourage full convertibility between currencies and an ending of exchange controls;
❹ lend its resources to countries to enable them to correct payments imbalances without resorting to harmful restrictions on trade;
❺ shorten periods of disequilibrium in the Balance of Payments of member countries.

Certainly, over the near fifty-year period since the establishment of the IMF, the first two objectives have been achieved, at least among the richer members of the IMF, though not for most developing country members. However, the influence of the IMF upon the stability of exchange rates has diminished rather than increased and it is debatable whether the activities of the IMF have had much effect upon the length of periods of payments imbalance or upon the ease with which payments deficits can be cured.

The three main roles adopted by the IMF have been:

❶ An **advisory role** as a consultant giving expert advice to members.
❷ **'Policing' the Bretton Woods System of exchange rates**, until the system broke down in 1971/72. In recent years the IMF has tried, rather ineffectively, to produce orderly conditions in a world of 'dirty' floating. In recent years the IMF's policing role has been directed less at regulating exchange rates, than at limiting the freedom of deficit countries, who wish to borrow from the Fund, to pursue the domestic economic policies of their choice. Although initially established to reflect Keynesian ideas of economic management, in more recent years the IMF has become generally 'monetarist' in both aim and action. As a result, countries are usually required to adopt 'sound' monetarist policies as a condition for the extension of IMF credit. Developing countries in particular, have been severely hit by the deflationary policies forced on them as a condition of IMF loans.

❸ **A banking role**. In 1944 the Bretton Woods Agreement hoped to promote the orderly development of world trade by ensuring an adequate supply of international liquidity to tide deficit countries over temporary payments difficulties. The dollar provided the main source of primary liquidity, but its own weakening eventually contributed to the downfall of the Bretton Woods exchange rates. To supplement the primary liquidity provided by the dollar, specially created **IMF reserves** were intended to supply a source of secondary liquidity. Initially, when the IMF was first set up, each member paid a **quota** (75% in its own currency and 25% in gold) into an IMF 'basket' or **pool of currency reserves** which were then available for member countries to draw upon when experiencing a payment deficit. In the event of a temporary payments deficit, the first part of a country's drawing entitlement is automatic, but beyond a certain limit the IMF can impose conditions upon a further loan. At regular intervals since 1944, the size of quotas and the IMF's overall reserves have been increased.

Chapter roundup

Exchange rates have a great effect on trade and the balance of payments (Chapters 25 and 26). They also influence macroeconomic policy, affecting the level of demand (Chapters 19 and 20) and inflation (Chapter 22). We also saw in Chapter 24 how Keynesians advocate a managed exchange rate while monetarists favour either a freely floating or a rigidly fixed regime.

Illustrative questions and answers

1   Essay Question
In October 1990 the UK joined the Exchange Rate Mechanism of the European Monetary System. In what ways might entry into the ERM affect the UK economy?
(WJEC, June 1992)

Tutorial note

We have explained in the chapter one of the reasons why the Conservative government decided to take the £ into the ERM in 1990, namely to prove that Britons were 'good Europeans' and to enable the further integration of the UK economy within the EC. However there were other significant ways in which it was hoped that ERM membership would benefit the UK economy, as well as through the greater ease of implementing common EC policies. In the first place, a major benefit for the UK of ERM membership might be the ability to draw on the help of the other members, particularly Germany, to deter destabilising 'hot money' movements into and out of the pound. Britain might eventually also benefit if the EMS, presumably after proceeding much further along the path to EMU, creates a new source of world liquidity which is able to take pressure off the reserve role of the dollar. Supporters of fixed exchange rates also claim that ERM membership will provide a more stable business and exporting environment.

But perhaps the main reason why the Conservatives decided to make the United Kingdom a full member of the ERM in October 1990 relates to the government's **counter-inflation policy**. From about 1985 onwards, the

Conservative government abandoned targeting the domestic money supply (while the exchange rate floated), as the main strategy of its counter-inflation policy. While the then prime minister, Mrs. Thatcher, favoured retaining such a strategy, Nigel Lawson – who was her Chancellor until 1989 – succeeded in switching the thrust of the government's counter-inflation policy towards **maintaining the exchange rate at a high parity**, a policy which became formalised when the £ entered the ERM in 1990.

In theory, a high fixed exchange rate can reduce inflation in two main ways. Firstly, it **reduces the price of imported food and consumer goods** (which directly reduces inflation), and also of imported raw materials and energy which has a more indirect effect, via lower manufacturing costs. Secondly, the exchange rate may act as an '**external source of discipline**' to cost-push pressures within the domestic economy. The theory runs as follows:

1. if workers demand wage rises and firms set prices higher than their overseas competitors, then with a fixed exchange rate, they will lose competitiveness in world markets;

2. the firms are then likely to be punished or disciplined by reduced profits and eventually bankruptcy, while their workers will face the threat of unemployment;

3. but if firms and workers believe that the government 'means business' in maintaining a fixed exchange rate and refusing to devalue, then they will quickly realise that it is in their self-interest to moderate price rises and wage claims.

This was the reasoning that lay behind the decision to fix the £ at a high parity within the ERM and to use the exchange rate rather than 'domestic monetary targetry' as the main source of discipline and credibility in the Conservative Government's counter-inflation policy. But the other side of this argument is that the UK's inflation rate *must* converge to the EC average if the exchange rate is to be maintained at its ERM parity. Without convergence, a higher rate of inflation in the UK would lead to the loss of competitiveness, a deteriorating current account and an unsustainable exchange rate. Eventually devaluation would have to occur.

By 1992 many critics of the ERM – an alliance of right-wing 'floating exchange rate monetarists' such as Professor Sir Alan Walters and left-wing socialists – were arguing that the high ERM exchange rate had unnecessarily condemned the UK economy to deflation, unemployment and depression in what was beginning to look remarkably like a re-run of the 1920s gold standard experience. Monetary policy in general, and interest rates in particular, had to be set so as to support the 'high parity' at which the £ had joined the ERM. This meant that monetary policy was 'unavailable' for the pursuit of domestic economic policy, for example the reduction of interest rates so as to stimulate consumption and investment in order to 'kick-start' the UK economy out of the recession.

Also, before ERM entry, many economists believed that the reserve role of sterling might make it difficult to maintain a fixed parity, as the volume of sterling owned overseas and the attractiveness of London as a centre for 'hot money' operations have in the past caused much greater fluctuations in the exchange rate of the pound than in most other European exchange rates. They argued that the always-present danger of a 'hot money' flow out of the £ would place an even greater pressure on the UK to deflate its economy in order to keep the sterling exchange rate steady against the EMS currencies. The events of 1992 have certainly borne out this fear. During 1992 massive speculative pressure built up as owners of capital sold pounds in the belief that the UK currency was overvalued, and that, however much the Conservative Government declared it would maintain the £'s ERM parity, devaluation within the ERM was inevitable sooner or later.

Suggested answer plan

1 Describe how the ERM of the EMS operates.
2 Outline the advantages of membership to the UK:
   (i) the advantages of fixed exchange rates, including the ERM exchange rate as a source of discipline in the fight against inflation;
   (ii) European co-operation and the implementation of common economic policies;
   (iii) advantages resulting from a new source of world liquidity.
3 Outline the disadvantages:
   (i) the disadvantages of fixed exchange rates;
   (ii) the DM pulling up and overvaluing the other exchange rates;
   (iii) the domestic deflationary costs might be too high.
4 Indicate how ERM exit in September 1992 can be explained by:
   (i) the UK government finally accepting that the disadvantages of ERM membership, particularly in terms of the constraints it imposed on the government's freedom to pursue monetary policy, were exceeding any advantages;
   (ii) more immediately, the UK's inability to resist a massive speculative pressures and a massive 'hot money' flow out of the £.

2 Data Question

The following is an abstract of an article by Professor M. Friedman, published in the Financial Times on December 18 1989.

   Study the passage carefully, then answer each of the questions which follow, explaining your reasoning in each case.

THE CASE FOR FLOATING RATES

1   Discussions of the prospects for a monetary union within the Common Market have generally ignored the difference between two superficially similar but basically very different exchange rate arrangements. One arrangement is a unified currency, the pound sterling in
5   Scotland, England and Wales. Further back in time essentially the same arrangement applied in the late 19th century when pound, dollar, franc, etc., were simply different names for specified fixed amounts of gold. A truly unified European currency would make a great deal of sense.
     An alternative arrangement is a system of exchange rates between
10 national currencies pegged at agreed values to be maintained by the separate national central banks by altering domestic monetary policy appropriately. Many proponents of a common European currency regard such a system of pegged exchange rates (the EMS) as a step towards a unified currency. I believe that is a grave mistake. In my opinion, a system
15 of pegged exchange rates among national currencies is worse than either extreme, a truly unified currency, or national currencies linked by freely floating exchange rates. The reason is that national central banks will not, under modern conditions, be permitted to shape their policies with an eye solely to keeping the exchange rates of their currencies at the agreed level.
20 Pressure to use monetary policy for domestic purposes will from time to time be irresistible. And when that occurs the exchange system becomes unstable. That was certainly the experience under Bretton Woods. Even in its heyday, exchange rate changes were numerous and when they came often massive.
25   Experience since then has strengthened my confidence in a system of freely floating exchange rates, though it has also made me far more sceptical that such a system is politically feasible. Central banks will meddle, always of course with the best of intentions. None the less, even dirty floating exchange rates seem to me preferable to pegged rates,
30 though not necessarily to a unified currency.

(a) Why did the author assert that in effect a unified currency arrangement applied worldwide in the late nineteenth century (lines 4–6)?   (5)

(b) What reasons might justify the author's assertion that a truly unified European currency would 'make a great deal of sense' (lines 7–8)?   (5)

(c) Why does maintenance of pegged exchange rates between national currencies involve separate national central banks 'altering domestic monetary policy appropriately' (lines 11–12)   (5)

(d) What did the author mean when he argued that 'pressure to use monetary policy for domestic purposes will from time to time be irresistible' (line 21)?

(5)

(e) For what reasons could monetary policy used for domestic purposes cause the exchange system to become 'unstable' (line 22)?   (5)

(WJEC, June 1991)

Tutorial note

(a) Milton Friedman was referring to the full Gold Standard exchange rate system in which a country's currency was exchangeable for a gold at a fixed rate both inside and outside a country's frontiers. Since much of the currency was gold coin, gold in effect functioned as the 'unified currency' in all countries which were on the full Gold Standard.

(b) Although as a 'strict' or 'technical' monetarist, Professor Friedman has always been a leading advocate of freely-floating exchange rates, in this article he is arguing that a truly unified currency, which once established would not allow any exchange rate adjustments at all between trading countries or regions, would make sense if countries involved wish to achieve a full economic union. Monetarists often quote the USA as a model: the United States is a political federation but a full economic union; any attempt to introduce separate currencies and exchange rates, say between Texas and Illinois, would harm the development of the continental economy, (though arguably a proliferation of American currencies might benefit some of the poorer American states which have been suffering from a drift of people and businesses to the more prosperous states such as California). If the poorer states could devalue a local currency or allow it to float, they might regain a competitive advantage in the overall US market.

(c) As Britain's experience in the ERM in the early 1990s has shown, maintaining a 'fixed peg' exchange rate requires that monetary policy in general, and interest rate policy in particular, have to be assigned to supporting the exchange rate (for example by deterring speculative capital flows), which means that monetary policy instruments may be not available for the pursuit of domestic policy objectives.

(d) But governments may not be prepared continually to sacrifice domestic policy objectives on the altar of supporting the exchange rate. In the case of an overvalued exchange rate (for example the sterling exchange rate in 1992), the cost in terms of deflation, lost output, and unemployment may be extremely high as the economy suffers both from uncompetitive exports and from the high interest rates which are needed to support the high parity.

(e) This is simply the opposite side of the argument we have just put forward. If interest rates are lowered so as to expand or reflate demand in the domestic economy and encourage economic activity, support of an over-valued exchange rate is immediately undermined. Speculative capital flows out of the currency are likely to put immediate pressure on the exchange rate, with the government then facing the choice of a policy u-turn by deflating the domestic economy so as to support the exchange rate, or abandoning the fixed parity and devaluing (or allowing the currency to float).

Question bank

1
(a) Explain the difference between fixed and floating exchange rates. (8)
b) Suppose the value of the pound moves downwards in the course of a year from $1.90 to $1.60. Discuss the likely effects of this reduction in the value of the pound on the UK economy. (12)
(Cambridge, AS-Level, June 1992)

2 One advantage claimed for a system of flexible exchange rates is that there is a self-regulating mechanism which automatically solves any balance of payments deficits without the need for government intervention.
(a) Explain how this self-regulating mechanism works. (6)
(b) What factors might prevent this mechanism from operating? (14)
(AEB AS-Level, June 1991)

3 Is control of the money supply incompatible with management of the exchange rate?
(Oxford, June 1991)

4
(a) What are the advantages and disadvantages of a stable exchange rate? (12)
(b) How might a stable exchange rate be achieved? (13)
(AEB, June 1990)

5 In October 1990 the UK joined the Exchange Rate Mechanism of the European Monetary System. In what ways might entry into the ERM affect the UK economy? (WJEC, June 1992)

6 'In an increasingly integrated world, the exchange rate is both a key indicator of economic conditions, and a most important part of the transmission mechanism through which monetary policy affects inflation.'
(Nigel Lawson, Mansion House, 19 October 1989)

7 Explain why the exchange rate is an indicator of the state of the economy and how it may be used to control inflation.
(NEAB, June 1990)

8
(a) How do the monetary authorities in the UK intervene in the foreign exchange market? (8)
(b) Explain and comment on the reasons for such intervention. (17)
(Cambridge, June 1991)

10
(a) Distinguish between a country's terms of trade and its balance of trade. (10)
(b) Discuss how both might be affected by a fall in the country's exchange rate. (15)
(AEB, November 1992)

TEST RUN

In this section:

Test Your Knowledge Quiz

Test Your Knowledge Quiz Answers

Progress Analysis

Mock Exam

Mock Exam Suggested Answer Plans

This section should be tackled towards the end of your revision programme, when you have covered all your syllabus topics, and attempted the practice questions at the end of the relevant chapters.

The Test Your Knowledge Quiz contains short-answer questions on a wide range of syllabus topics. You should attempt it without reference to the text.

Check your answers against the Test Your Knowledge Quiz Answers. If you are not sure why you got an answer wrong, go back to the relevant chapter in the text: you will find the reference next to our answer.

Enter your marks in the Progress Analysis chart. The notes below will suggest a further revision strategy, based on your performance in the quiz. Only when you have done the extra work suggested should you go on to the final test.

The Mock Exam is set out like a real exam paper. It contains a wide spread of question styles and topics, drawn from various examination boards. You should attempt this paper under examination conditions. Read the instructions on the front sheet carefully. Attempt the paper in the time allowed, and without reference to the text.

Compare your answers to our Mock Exam Suggested Answer Plans. We have provided tutorial notes to each, showing why we answered the question as we did and indicating where your answer may have differed from ours.

TEST YOUR KNOWLEDGE QUIZ

1   What is the central economic problem?

2   What are the three economic functions of prices in a market economy?

3   Distinguish between the 'goods market' and the 'factor market'.

4   Distinguish between individual demand and market demand.

5   Define planned demand and realised demand.

6   Explain the equilibrium equation: planned demand = planned supply.

7   Why may a demand curve shift?

8   Distinguish between the market period, the short run and the long run.

9   What are the 'conditions of supply'?

10 What is a 'buffer-stock' policy?

11 Distinguish between a 'bad', a 'good' an 'economic good' and a 'free good'.

12 Define 'opportunity cost'. What is the opportunity cost of this exercise you are currently attempting?

13 Who is 'economic man' or 'economic woman'?

14 Define utility.

15 State the consumer's objective in both maximising and minimising terms.

16 What are the constraints facing a consumer in the market?

17 Explain the condition of equi-marginal utility.

18 Distinguish between an income effect and a substitution effect.

19 Distinguish between a normal good, an inferior good and a Giffen good.

20 List reasons why a demand curve may sometimes slope upwards.

21 What is consumer surplus?

22 Explain the shape of the average fixed-cost curve.

23 Explain the principle or 'law' of diminishing returns.

24 What is the relationship between marginal and average returns?

25 How do marginal returns affect marginal costs?

26 Why is a short-run ATC curve u-shaped?

27 Explain the short-run supply curve of a competitive firm.

28 Distinguish between decreasing returns to scale and the 'law' of diminishing returns.

29 Must the long-run ATC curve be u-shaped?

30 Distinguish between technical efficiency and productive efficiency.

31 What are external economies of scale?

32 Write out the formulas for income elasticity of demand and price elasticity of supply.

33 What is meant by elastic demand?

34 What elasticity does a rectangular hyperbola display?

35 What is the most important determinant of price elasticity of demand?

36 Contrast the income elasticity of demand of normal and inferior goods.

37 What can be inferred about the demand relationship between two goods with a cross-elasticity of (+)0.3?

38 Why is perfect competition an unreal market structure?

39 Why is a perfectly competitive firm's average-revenue curve horizontal?

40 Distinguish between normal and abnormal profit.

41 Explain the relationship between average revenue and marginal revenue in monopoly.

42 How does elasticity of demand affect monopoly?

43 Is perfect competition efficient?

44 How do economies of scale affect productive efficiency?

45 In what way is monopolistic competition similar to (a) perfect competition and (b) monopoly?

46 Define an oligopoly.

47 Why is there no general theory of oligopoly?

48 Why may oligopolists collude together and what forms might the collusion take?

49 Define price 'discrimination' and what are the necessary conditions for successful price discrimination?

50 Distinguish between a 'public good' and a 'private good'.

51 Define an externality.

52 How do externalities affect allocative efficiency?

53 What is a merit good?

54 Why may the distribution of income and wealth be regarded as a market failure?

55 How may a mixed economy be defined?

56 What are the three main elements of competition policy?

57 What is a 'natural' monopoly?

58 List alternative possible approaches to the problem of monopoly.

59 What is the theory of 'contestable' markets?

60 Distinguish between collective and non-collective restrictive trading practices.

61 Distinguish between 'privatisation', 'contractualisation', 'marketisation' and 'deregulation'.

62 What is the 'free market' approach to regional policy?

63 Compare Labour and Conservative approaches to the problem of deindustrialisation.

64 Why may a worker's supply curve of labour bend backwards?

65 What is marginal revenue product (MRP)?

66 Distinguish between economic rent and transfer earnings.

67 What is collective bargaining?

68 What are the objectives of macroeconomic policy?

69 Distinguish between a progressive and a regressive tax.

70 Relate the PSBR to the budget deficit and to the National Debt.

71 Define fiscal policy.

72 What is fiscal drag?

73 List the four functions of money.

74 What is the money multiplier?

75 List the three main motives for demanding money.

76 What is liquidity preference?

77 List four ways in which the Bank of England might use monetary policy to reduce bank lending and the money supply.

78 What is meant by 'fully-funding' the PSBR?

79 How may interest rates affect total bank deposits?

80 What are the three ways of measuring national income?

81 Derive a savings function from $C = a + cY$.

82 What is the equilibrium level of national income?

83 What are injections and leakages of demand in a four-sector economy?

84 Distinguish between nominal and real national income.

85 What is a deflationary gap?

86 What is meant by demand management?

87 Explain the national income multiplier and state its formula.

88 What is 'crowding-out'?

89 What is an automatic stabiliser?

90 Explain the role of 'business confidence' and 'expectations' in the marginal efficiency of capital theory.

91 Express the accelerator theory as an equation.

92 List four types or causes of unemployment.

93 State the quantity theory of money.

94 Distinguish between 'demand-pull' and 'cost-push' inflation.

95 What is the Phillips curve relationship?

96 Briefly explain the terms: 'Keynesianism'; 'monetarism'; 'supply-side economics'.

97 Distinguish between absolute advantage and comparative advantage.

98 List the policies that might reduce a Balance of Payments deficit on Current Account.

99 Distinguish between 'flexible', 'fixed' and 'managed' exchange rates.

100 What are the following: IMF; IBRD; EC; EMS; ERM; EMU; CAP; GATT?

TEST YOUR KNOWLEDGE QUIZ ANSWERS

The chapter number in which the answer can be found is given in brackets at the end of the answer.

Award yourself one mark for each correct answer. Do not give yourself a mark if only part of the answer is correct.

1   Resource allocation, involving the allocation of scarce resources between competing uses.   (1)

2   Signalling, the creation of incentives, and the rationing function.   (1)

3   The 'goods market' is the market for 'outputs', i.e. finished goods and services, whereas the 'factor market' is the market for 'inputs' or 'factors of production', such as labour.   (1)

4   'Individual demand' is the planned demand for a good exercised by a single individual, whereas 'market demand' is the sum of the planned demands of all the individuals or prospective buyers in the market.   (1; 2)

5   'Planned demand' is the 'ex ante', 'desired' or 'intended' demand of prospective buyers, whereas 'realised demand' measures the quantities of the good which the buyers actually purchase (also known as 'ex post', 'actual' or 'fulfilled' demand).   (1; 2)

6   Only when 'planned demand = planned supply' can both buyers and sellers fulfil their market plans. When this condition holds, there is no excess demand or excess supply in the market, and hence no reason for the price to change – the market is thus in a state of rest or equilibrium.   (1)

7   A demand curve will shift if any of the 'conditions of demand', such as income and tastes, change.   (1, 2)

8 All the factors of production are fixed and none are variable in the 'market period'; in the 'short run' at least one of the factors of production is fixed and one is variable; in the 'long run' all the factors of production are variable and none are fixed. (4)

9 A supply curve will shift if any of the 'conditions of supply' change. The conditions of supply include costs of production or the prices of the inputs into the production process, the state of technical progress, and any taxes imposed upon (or subsidies given to) firms which vary with the firm's output. (3)

10 A 'buffer stock' is used to stabilise agricultural prices, based on the principle of buying the agricultural product and accumulating a stockpile when there is a glut, and then releasing supply onto the market from the stock in the event of a bad harvest. 'Exchange equalisation' or the use of the country's foreign exchange reserves to stabilise or manage the exchange rate (Chapter 27) works on a similar principle. (5)

11 When consumed, a 'good' yields utility, whereas a 'bad' yields disutility or displeasure. Note that a 'good' becomes a 'bad' if consumed beyond the point of 'satiation'. The supply of an 'economic good' is limited relative to demand, so the problem of scarcity arises, requiring rationing through prices, or some other mechanism. By contrast, a 'free good' is available in unlimited quantities and with no costs of production at zero price. (1, 8)

12 The 'opportunity cost' of any action, choice or decision is the next best alternative foregone. For example, the opportunity cost of attempting this test could be the sacrificed opportunity to watch a football match or play on a computer games machine. (1, 6)

13 'Economic' man or woman always acts rationally in the sense of trying to maximise his or her self-interest or 'private benefit'. He or she never makes a decision which is known in advance to be against his or her self-interest. (1, 2, 6)

14 'Utility' means 'usefulness' and 'fulfilment of need' encompassing 'pleasure' and 'satisfaction'. (2)

15 The consumer's (assumed) objective is to maximise the utility that can be achieved from spending his limited income on the goods or services that are available to buy. This objective can also be defined in terms of the minimisation of the outlay or expenditure needed to purchase a desired bundle of goods. (2)

16 The 'budget constraint' i.e. limited income and a given set of prices at which goods are available; given tastes and preferences; given availability of goods and a time constraint. (2)

17 The 'condition of equi-marginal utility' holds when the ratio of the marginal utility to the price is equal for all goods. When the condition holds, a consumer maximises utility (subject to the constraints faced) and has no incentive to change the bundle of goods purchased. (2)

18 The 'substitution effect' of a price change relates to the fact that following a price change, to maximise utility a consumer must substitute more of the good which has become relatively cheaper in place of other goods previously demanded which are now relatively more expensive. But a price fall also affects the consumer's 'real income' or purchasing power, enabling the consumer to buy more of all goods because he is better off. This is the 'income effect' of the price change. (2)

19 Demand for a 'normal' good increases with income, whereas demand for an 'inferior' good declines as income increases. A 'Giffen' good is so inferior that the perverse income effect following a price fall (causing less to be demanded as the consumer feels better off) outweighs the substitution effect. The result is an upward-sloping demand curve. (2)

20 The 'Giffen good' effect; 'Veblen goods' or 'goods of ostentatious consumption or status'; goods for which 'price is taken as an indicator of quality'; and 'asset demand' or 'speculative demand' for goods. (2)

21 'Consumer surplus' is the utility a consumer gains from the consumption of a good over and above the price paid. (2)

22 The AFC curve falls towards zero as output increases; this is explained by the spreading of overheads. (3)

23 The 'law' of diminishing returns states that as a firm increases output in the short run by adding more of a variable factor of production such as labour to its fixed factors such as capital, eventually an extra worker will add less to total output than the previous worker who joined the labour force, i.e. the marginal product or returns of labour will begin to fall. (3)

24 (i) When marginal returns > average returns, average returns rise;
   (ii) When marginal returns < average returns, average returns fall;
   (iii) When marginal returns = average returns, average returns are constant.

(3)

25 Diminishing marginal returns to the variable factors of production cause the firm's short-run marginal costs to rise. (3)

26 The spreading of fixed costs and increasing marginal returns to the variable factors of production combine to cause ATC to fall as output is increased at low levels of output. But eventually the 'law' of diminishing returns sets in, causing marginal costs to rise. When MC rises above ATC, the ATC curve will be 'pulled up' at higher levels of output. (3)

27 The firm's short-run supply curve is its short-run MC curve, above AVC. (3)

28 Decreasing returns to scale occur in the long run if a change in the scale or ALL the firm's inputs, including capital, leads to a less than proportionate increase in output. By contrast the 'law' of diminishing returns relates to the short run when at least one of the firm's inputs or factors of production is held fixed. (3)

29 No; it will only be u-shaped if 'increasing returns to scale' at low levels of output are followed by 'decreasing returns to scale' at higher levels of output and scales of operation. It would be quite possible, for example, for there to be increasing returns to scale at all possible scales of operation, in which case the LRATC curve would be downward-sloping throughout its range. (3)

30 Production is 'technically efficient' if output is maximised from a given set of inputs or factors of production. This will also be 'productively efficient' if the cost of producing the output is minimised. 'Productive efficiency' can be thought of as the translation into money costs of production of the concept of 'technical efficiency'. The most productively efficient of all the firm's possible levels of output is located at the bottom of the firm's LRATC curve. (6)

31 'External economies of scale' are reductions in a firm's long-run production costs which result from the growth of the whole industry or market of which the firm is a member. (10)

32 Income elasticity of demand $= \dfrac{\text{Proportionate change in quantity demanded}}{\text{Proportionate change in income}}$

   Price elasticity of supply $= \dfrac{\text{Proportionate change in quantity supplied}}{\text{Proportionate change in price}}$

(4)

33 Unless otherwise qualified, 'elastic demand' refers to 'price elasticity of demand'; it means that a change in price results in a more than proportionate change in demand. (4)

34 'Unit elasticity of demand', i.e. neither elastic nor inelastic. (4)

35 The availability of substitutes. (4)

36 The income elasticity of demand is positive for normal goods and negative for inferior goods. (4)

37 The two goods are substitutes and a 10% rise in the price of one good causes a 3% increase in demand for the other good. (4)

38 Because it is impossible in real life for all the 'conditions of perfect competition' to hold at the same time, e.g. a completely uniform good and a very large number of buyers and sellers, each with perfect market information.   (6)

39 Provided the firm sells its output at the ruling market price for the whole industry, it can sell any amount it wishes. Price or average revenue is therefore the same, whatever the level of output the firm chooses to produce and sell.   (6)

40 'Normal' profit is defined as the minimum profit an established firm must make to stay in the market, while being insufficient to attract outside or new firms into the market. Since 'normal' profits are treated as a cost of production which must be covered for a firm to remain in the market, they are included in a firm's cost curves. 'Abnormal' profits (also known as 'above-normal' and 'super-normal' profits) are any profits over and above 'normal' profits.   (6)

41 Since the monopolist faces a downward-sloping AR curve, indicating that to sell more the price must be reduced, the MR curve must be below the AR curve. If the AR curve is linear (a straight line), the MR curve will also be linear and twice as steep as the AR curve.   (6)

42 The profit-maximising level of output will always be located under the elastic section of the monopolist's AR or demand curve.   (6)

43 Provided there are no economies of scale, externalities and that every firm in the economy is perfectly competitive and in long-run equilibrium, it can be shown that each firm would be productively efficient (producing at the lowest point on its ATC curve) and allocatively efficient (P=MC). For the economy as a whole this would mean that all resources would be fully-employed and it would be impossible to increase production of one good without reducing production of at least one other good, or to make one individual better-off without making at least one other individual worse off.   (6)

44 A firm must expand to benefit from full economies of scale if it is to be productively efficient.   (6)

45 'Monopolistic competition' is similar to perfect competition in that there is a large number of firms and there is freedom to enter or leave the market in the long run; it is similar to monopoly in that each firm faces a downward-sloping demand curve for its product (since the products are differentiated and partial substitutes for each other).   (7)

46 'Oligopoly' is best defined as an industry containing a small number of firms, with each firm needing to take account of the likely reactions of the other firms when deciding its own best market strategy.   (7)

47 Because a different theory would be appropriate for each set of assumptions about how the rivals would react to an oligopolists price and output decisions.   (7)

48 To reduce uncertainty and give themselves an easier life. Also, the theory of 'joint-profit maximisation' shows that by acting as a single monopolist, the oligopolists can make larger joint profits than if they act separately and competitively. The oligopolists may enter into restrictive collective trading agreements, or a cartel agreement in which they restrict output, carve up the market and hike up the price.   (7)

49 'Price discrimination' occurs when a firm charges different prices to different customers for the same good with the same costs of supply, the different prices being based on the fact that some customers are prepared to pay a higher price than others. The firm must first identify the different customers with different demands, and then keep the markets separate so as to prevent 'seepage'.   (7)

50 A pure 'public good' is defined by the properties of 'non-excludability' and 'non-diminishability' (or 'non-rivalry'), whereas a pure 'private good' displays the opposite properties of 'excludability' and 'diminishability'.   (8)

51 An 'externality' is a 'spin-off' effect, delivered and received as a benefit or a cost 'outside the market', i.e. a price cannot be charged for it.   (8)

52 Allocative efficiency occurs when P=MSC. A competitive market system may ensure that P= MPC, but if 'negative externalities' or 'external costs' such as

pollution are generated in the course of production (with MSC = MPC + MEC), it follows that P < MSC. In this situation, the price of good is too low since it does not reflect the 'true' marginal cost of production which includes the cost of the negative externality which is being 'dumped' on others. Being too low, the price encourages too much production and too much consumption of the good whose production generates the negative externality. (8)

53 'Merit goods' have two properties. Firstly, the 'social benefits' to the whole community resulting from their consumption are greater than the 'private benefits' to the individual consumers; hence there is a case for the state to encourage their consumption. Secondly, the 'long-term' private benefits to the individual resulting from consuming a merit good such as education or health care may exceed the 'short-term' private benefits. Left to themselves, individuals may be guilty of 'short-termism' by deciding to consume less than is in their long-term interest. This reinforces the case for the state to encourage consumption. (8)

54 A highly unequal distribution of income and wealth is often regarded as a market failure on the grounds of 'inequity' (unfairness) rather than 'ineffi-ciency'. (8)

55 A 'mixed economy' is usually defined as containing a mix of 'private sector' and 'public sector' economic activity, though this definition can be extended to containing a mix of 'market' and 'non-market' economic activity. (9)

56 Policy towards monopolies, mergers and restrictive trading practices. (12)

57 Strictly speaking, a 'natural' monopoly occurs when a particular part of the world has a monopoly over the supply of a mineral or raw material which cannot be produced elsewhere. Usually, however, the term 'natural mo-nopoly' is used rather differently to describe an industry where economies of scale combine with limited market size so that there is only room in the market for one firm benefiting from full-scale economies. The 'utility' industries, such as water supply, provide another example, as there is a case for just one water or gas main, etc. serving each street. (6; 12)

58 (i) Monopoly 'busting' or breaking the monopoly up into smaller firms;
   (ii) allowing the monopoly to exist but exposing it to severe regulation;
   (iii) 'deregulation' and removal of barriers to entry
   (iv) taking a private monopoly into public ownership;
   (v) privatising a nationalised monopoly;
   (vi) taxing excessive monopoly profits. (12)

59 The theory of 'contestable markets' is a part of the 'new' (free-market) industrial economics which argues that it is not necessary to break up or severely regulate an established monopoly if the market can be made potentially 'contestable' by removing barriers to market entry. (12)

60 'Collective' restrictive practices are undertaken jointly by two or more firms via a restrictive agreement such as a cartel agreement. A 'non-collective' restrictive practice is unilaterally undertaken by a firm, e.g. a refusal to supply a particular customer or retail outlet. (12)

61 'Privatisation' involves the transfer, usually through sale, of assets such as nationalised industries from the public sector to the private sector. 'Contractualisation' is a related policy of putting out services to contract supply or tender, e.g. some police services are likely to be contracted out to private security firms. 'Marketisation' (or 'commercialisation') involves shifting the provision of services from the non-market sector (where they are financed by taxation) into the market sector, where the services are commercially provided and sold at a market price. Lastly, 'deregulation' means the abolition of previously imposed regulations, to remove unnecessary 'red tape' and barriers to market entry. (12)

62 This is the 'anti-interventionist' approach to regional policy, which is based on the premise that the regional problem results from 'government failure'

rather than from 'market failure' and that it can be reduced by improving the competitiveness of markets. (12)

63 The Labour Party approach is generally 'interventionist', whereas the Conservative Party approach is 'anti-interventionist' and supportive of the free market. (12)

64 A 'backward-bending' supply curve of labour results when the 'income effect' of a wage-rate change becomes stronger than the 'substitution' effect. (13)

65 A worker's 'marginal revenue product' measures the extent to which a firm's sales revenue rises as a result of employing one more worker. The MRP is calculated by multiplying the worker's 'marginal physical product' (the output produced by an extra worker) by the firm's 'marginal sales revenue': (MRP = MPP x MR). (13)

66 A worker's transfer earnings is the minimum wage he must be paid to prevent him 'transferring out' of the labour market, either by moving to another job or through choosing unemployment in preference to working; by contrast, 'economic rent' is the wage a worker is paid over and above his transfer earnings. (13)

67 'Collective bargaining' occurs when a trade union bargains collectively on behalf of its members with an employer or employers over conditions of work, including pay. (13)

68 Full employment, economic growth, price stability or control of inflation and a satisfactory balance of payments are usually listed as the four main objectives of macroeconomic policy, though not necessarily ranked in the order given here. A satisfactory or fair distribution of income and wealth might be included as another objective, though some might classify this as a microeconomic objective. (17)

69 A tax is 'progressive' if the amount of tax paid rises at a faster rate than income; it is 'regressive' if the tax paid rises at a slower rate than income. (15)

70 When the public sector's finances are in deficit with public spending exceeding revenue, the deficit has to financed by borrowing. The public sector financial deficit and the PSBR are approximately equal. But both are 'flows', whereas the National Debt is a 'stock': the National Debt is the accumulated stock of outstanding central government debt. (16)

71 'Fiscal policy' can be defined quite generally as that part of the government's overall economic policy in which the government tries to achieve its policy objectives using the fiscal instruments of taxation and public spending.
(16; 24)

72 'Fiscal drag' occurs when the government fails to revise income tax thresholds upwards at the same rate as inflation. This means that, in real terms, the tax threshold shifts lower down the 'income pyramid', dragging the low-paid into the tax net. (15)

73 (i)   Medium of exchange or means of payment;
(ii) store of value or wealth;
(iii) unit of account; and
(iv) standard of deferred payment. (14)

74 The 'money multiplier' (also known as the 'credit multiplier', the 'deposit multiplier' and the 'bank multiplier') measures the relationship between a change in the reserve assets (including cash) in the banking system, and the resulting change in total bank deposits. (14)

75 The 'transactions motive', the 'precautionary motive' and the 'speculative motive'. Taken together, the transactions and precautionary motives make up the demand to hold 'active' money balances as a medium of exchange, whereas the speculative motive relates to holding 'passive' or 'idle' money balances as a wealth asset or store of value. (14)

76 'Liquidity preference' relates to the 'speculative motive' for holding or demanding money balances, which Keynes identified. As the rate of interest

falls, people will 'prefer liquidity' in the sense of wishing to hold money as a wealth asset in preference to interest-earning bonds, though expectations of future interest rates and bond prices also influence the decision about which form of wealth asset to hold. (14)

77 (i) Contractionary open market operations;
(ii) 'over-funding' the PSBR or funding the National Debt;
(iii) imposing direct controls on bank lending; and
(iv) raising the Bank of England lending rate. (17)

78 'Fully-funding' the PSBR is generally taken to mean that the government finances the PSBR by borrowing outside the banking system by gilt sales, etc., so that government spending and borrowing have an overall neutral effect on the money supply. However, in the March 1993 budget, the Chancellor slightly relaxed the 'official' definition of full-funding. (16; 17)

79 If interest rates rise on 'non-money' financial assets such as bonds, total bank deposits should fall as people make 'portfolio balance decisions' to hold these assets rather than bank deposits. But these days the banks themselves make interest payments to attract deposits. A rise in the rate of interest offered on 'time deposits' relative to the rate of interest available on 'non-money' financial assets would cause bank deposits to grow – and also cause 'broad' money aggregates such as M4 to grow at the expense of 'narrow' money measures, such as M2. (14; 17)

80 (i) By adding the values added of all the productive industries in the economy;
(ii) by measuring expenditure upon output; and
(iii) by aggregating the incomes received by all the factors of production.
(18)

81 Substituting $(Y - S)$ for C in the equation for the consumption function: $C = a + cY$ and rearranging, we arrive at : $S = -a + (1 - c)Y$
$$\text{or: } S = -a + sY.$$
(19)

82 It is the level of national income at which planned expenditure equals the level of output produced in the economy. (19)

83 The injections of demand into the circular flow of income are investment, government spending and export demand. The leakages from the flow are saving, taxation and imports. (19)

84 'Nominal income' is the money income which people receive, whereas 'real income' is the purchasing power of money or nominal income, i.e its command over goods and services. (19)

85 A 'deflationary gap' is a measure of the extent to which the level of aggregate demand in the economy is insufficient to bring about full employment at the equilibrium level of income, associated with the level of aggregate demand.
(19)

86 'Demand management' is the name given to government fiscal and/or monetary policy which aims to influence and control the level of aggregate demand in the economy, for example to stabilise the business cycle or to 'trade-off' between policy objectives such as reducing unemployment and controlling inflation. (19; 20; 24)

87 The national income multiplier (which is also known as the 'Keynesian multiplier') measures the relationship between a change in any of the components of aggregate demand (such as investment or government spending) and the resulting change in the equilibrium level of national income. The formula for the multiplier is: $\dfrac{1}{s + t + m}$
when the leakages of demand, s, t and m all vary with the level of income.
(20)

88 'Crowding out' is the name given to the neoclassical or anti-Keynesian view that an increase in government spending has little or no effect on the overall

level of output in the long run because it largely or completely displaces private sector spending and output. (20)

89   Progressive taxation and demand-led public spending on unemployment pay and welfare benefits are 'automatic stabilisers', tending to dampen, reduce and stabilise the fluctuations in the business cycle. (20)

90   According to Keynes's 'marginal efficiency of capital' theory, investment is a function of the expected rate of return and profitability of the various capital projects in which businesses are considering investment. The state of business confidence, and businessmen's expectations of the future, colour perceptions of expected future profitability; an increase in business confidence will cause an uprating of each investment project's expected future rate of return, causing the MEC function to shift rightwards. (21)

91   $I_t = v(Y_t - Y_{t-1})$, where 'v' is the accelerator. (21)

92   (i)   'Classical' or 'real wage' unemployment;
     (ii) 'frictional' or 'transitional' unemployment;
     (iii) 'structural' unemployment; and
     (iv) 'Keynesian' or 'demand deficient' unemployment.   (22)

93   The 'quantity theory of money' is a theory of inflation which argues that the underlying cause of inflation or a rising price level is a prior increase in the money supply or stock of money in the economy, created or condoned by the government. (22)

94   In the 'demand-pull' theory of inflation, the price level is pulled up by excess demand for goods and services and/or the wage level is pulled up by an excess demand for labour. In the cost-push theory, increased production costs (wage costs, imported raw material costs, etc.) push up the price level, as monopolistic firms 'mark up' prices in order to maintain profit margins. (22)

95   The 'Phillips curve relationship' is an inverse statistical relationship between the rate of wage inflation and the level of unemployment, which apparently existed – according to the research of A W Phillips – in the UK economy from the 1860s to the 1950s. (22)

96   (i)   'Keynesianism' is the name given to the body of economic theory and policy associated with John Maynard Keynes (1883–1946) and his followers, the 'Keynesians'. Keynesianism is the economics of government interventionism in a market economy and the use of fiscal policy to manage the level of aggregate demand in the economy.
     (ii) In its 'narrow' meaning, 'monetarism' centres on the view that the amount of money in the economy is largely responsible for both the level of money national income and the price level, and that if the money supply increases at a faster rate than real output, it will cause inflation. In its 'broader' meaning, 'monetarism' is associated with anti-Keynesianism, the promotion of the 'free market' and distrust and dislike of government interventionsism.
     (iii) 'Supply-side' economics is another and more recent manifestation of 'free-market' and anti-Keynesian economics. It centres on the proposition that fiscal policy should be used, not to manage demand Keynesian-style, but to create incentives to workers and entrepreneurs to increase the supply of labour, entrepreneurship and output in the economy. (23; 24)

97   'Absolute advantage' is an application of the concept of 'technical efficiency'. A country possesses an absolute advantage over other countries if it can produce a larger absolute output from the same inputs (or produce the same output with fewer inputs). 'Comparative advantage' is measured in terms of 'opportunity cost'. A country possesses a comparative advantage (even though it may still suffer an absolute disadvantage) if, by increasing output of a particular product, compared to other countries it sacrifices less of the alternative products that it might have produced. (25)

98   'Expenditure-reducing' deflation (i.e. contractionary fiscal and/or monetary policy to reduce the level of aggregate demand in the economy) and 'expenditure-switching' devaluation and import controls. (26)

99 (i) 'Flexible' (or 'floating') exchange rates are determined by market forces, or the supply of and demand for currencies.

   (ii) By contrast, an exchange rate is 'fixed' if the country's monetary authorities buy and sell their own currency and reserves of other currencies, to prevent market forces taking the exchange rate away from an officially declared 'par' value or parity.

   (iii) 'Managed' exchange rates, which include 'dirty' floating and 'fixed peg' systems, lie between these extremes.

(27)

100 (i) The International Monetary Fund;

   (ii) the International Bank for Reconstruction and Development (the 'World Bank');

   (iii) the European Community;

   (iv) the European Monetary System;

   (v) the Exchange Rate Mechanism (of the EMS);

   (vi) European Monetary Union;

   (vii) the Common Agricultural Policy (of the EC);

   (viii) the General Agreement on Tariffs and Trade.

(5; 27)

PROGRESS ANALYSIS

Place a tick next to those questions you got right.

Question	Answer	Question	Answer	Question	Answer	Question	Answer
1		26		51		76	
2		27		52		77	
3		28		53		78	
4		29		54		79	
5		30		55		80	
6		31		56		81	
7		32		57		82	
8		33		58		83	
9		34		59		84	
10		35		60		85	
11		36		61		86	
12		37		62		87	
13		38		63		88	
14		39		64		89	
15		40		65		90	
16		41		66		91	
17		42		67		92	
18		43		68		93	
19		44		69		94	
20		45		70		95	
21		46		71		96	
22		47		72		97	
23		48		73		98	
24		49		74		99	
25		50		75		100	

My total mark is: out of 100

ANALYSIS

If you scored 1–25

You need to do some more work. You are not yet ready to take the Mock Exam because you do not have sufficient knowledge or understanding of the syllabus content. Look at the list of chapters at the beginning of this book and revise those chapters on which you scored poorly in the test. When you consider you have completed your revision, get a friend to ask you questions (not necessarily those in the Test) and if you are still weak on some chapters, look at them again. You should then attempt the Test Your Knowledge Quiz again.

If you scored 26–50

You are getting there, but you must do some more work. Go through the list of chapters on the contents page and mark those which you could not answer questions about correctly in the Test. In addition, look through the Practice Questions at the end of each chapter and the notes which accompany them. Go over some of your weak topics with a friend and then attempt the Test Your Knowledge Quiz again.

If you scored 51–75

You are nearly ready to attempt the Mock Exam, but to get the best out of it, brush up on those chapters which the Test shows you have not fully understood. Also look at the Practice Questions at the end of each chapter and check those questions which relate to the subject areas you do not feel confident about. You should then be ready to go on to the Mock Exam.

If you scored 76–100

Well done! You can tackle the Mock Exam with confidence although you will first need to revise some of the chapters which let you down in the Test Your Knowledge Quiz. Reassure yourself that there are no gaps in your knowledge and then set aside a time to do the Mock Exam.

LETTS SCHOOL EXAMINATIONS BOARD
General Certificate of Education Examination

ADVANCED LEVEL
ECONOMICS

Paper 1

Time allowed: 3 hours

THURSDAY 2 JUNE, AFTERNOON

Answer FOUR questions. TWO from Section A and TWO from Section B.
All questions carry equal marks.

Candidates are strongly recommended to read through the paper before attempting
the questions.

Candidates are reminded of the need for good English and orderly presentation.
Credit will be given for the relevant use of diagrams.

SECTION A: DATA QUESTIONS

Answer 2 of the 3 questions

1   The data below was taken from the leader article in the *Daily Telegraph* of 29th March, 1989. It looks at two aspects of the market for petroleum, the change in the number of petroleum outlets and variations in its price in the European Community (EC).

Petroleum Outlets in the UK

	1978		1988	
	Total Supplied	Company Owned	Total Supplied	Company Owned
Esso	5 931	1 094	2 685	1 496
Shell	5 440	1 191	2 886	1 586
BP	5 101	889	2 119	1 257
Others	11 823	n.a.	12 326	n.a.
Total	28 295		20 016	
Visibles	−10 290			

Average Retail Prices of Petroleum per Gallon (£), March 1989

Italy	2.61	Belgium	1.83
Ireland	2.16	Spain	1.81
France	2.14	UK	1.80
Netherlands	2.01	West Germany	1.69
Portugal	2.00		

(Note: n.a. – not available)

(a) (i)   How has the number and distribution of petroleum outlets changed between 1978 and 1988?   (3)

(ii)   Account for the above changes.   (5)

(b) (i)   From the data, what is the most likely market structure of petroleum retailing in the UK? Explain your answer.   (3)

(ii)   What other information would you require in order to make a fuller assessment?   (3)

(c) (i)   Given that the UK and Italy produce competing products, if the retail price of petrol is 31% higher in Italy, can we assume that transport costs for Italy are 31% higher than those for the UK? Explain your reasoning. (6)

(ii)   Over the last 15 years, all EC countries have experienced increased petroleum prices.
Suggest what effects this increase may have had on:
a road freight transport operator;
a chocolate manufacturer.   (5)

(Based on O& CSEB, AS-Level question, June 1990)

2 Study the data and read the passage below and answer the questions which follow.

Table 1 *Sterling Exchange Rates and Official Reserves*

Year	Japanese Yen	United States Dollar	Deutsche Mark	Sterling exchange rate index (1985=100)	United Kingdom Reserves ($ million)
		(Units of currency to the £)			
1980	526	2.33	4.23	118	27 476
1981	445	2.03	4.56	119	23 347
1982	435	1.75	4.24	114	16 997
1983	360	1.52	3.87	105	17 817
1984	317	1.34	3.79	101	15 694
1985	308	1.30	3.78	100	15 543
1986	247	1.47	3.18	92	21 923
1987	237	1.64	2.94	90	44 326
1988	228	1.78	3.12	96	51 685
1989	226	1.64	3.08	93	38 645

Table 2 *Extracts From the United Kingdom Balance of Payments Account*

£ million

Year	Current balance	Net transacations in assets and liabilities	Allocation of SDR's	Balancing item
1980	2 795	–3 930	180	955
1981	6 639	–7 436	158	639
1982	4 606	–2 589	–	–2 017
1983	3 794	–4 552	–	758
1984	1 954	–7 888	–	5 934
1985	3 161	–7 885	–	4 724
1986	–39	–9 868	–	9 907
1987	–3 822	–6 185	–	10 007
1988	–14 672	–4 155	–	10 517
1989	–20 850	–4 341	–	16 509

(Source: *Economic Trends Annual Supplement*, 1990 Edition; *Economic Trends*, March 1990 (Number 437))

ERM...at last

On the 8th of October 1990, the United Kingdom joined the Exchange Rate Mechanism (ERM) of the European Monetary System with a central rate given as DM 2.95 and a band of + 6% or –6% for a transitional period. Exchange rates are now fixed against other ERM currencies, so that exchange rates are no longer available as an *instrument of monetary policy*. The maintenance of central rates has become a *goal of economic policy*, with German commentators suggesting that fiscal policy be tightened to achieve these goals. Strong connections between interest rates and exchange rates will mean that interest rates must be used mainly to keep sterling within its 6% band. Other measures may be necessary to influence domestic demand.

Source: *Bank Information Service Financial Review*, Autumn 1990

(a) Describe the main changes in the value of the pound sterling relative to other major currencies between 1980 and 1989 as shown in Table 1. (4)

(b) (i) With reference to the data, **describe** and **explain** the relationship between the value of the pound sterling and the current account of the

balance of payments in the period 1980 to 1989.   (6)
   (ii) What other factors may have influenced the value of the pound during
      this period?   (5)
(c) In the light of the data and your knowledge of events since 1990, discuss the
   implications of the United Kingdom's membership of the Exchange Rate
   Mechanism for the government's conduct of economic policy.   (10)
                                                (AEB, November 1992)

3

The Achilles heel in GATT

The General Agreement on Tariffs and Trade was founded in 1948
under the auspices of the United Nations as 23 countries began to revive
free trade after World War II. GATT's aims were to liberalise trade in
industrial goods and so improve the prospects for growth in world trade.
5   At the time, direct tariffs on industrial goods averaged some 40%, partly
a legacy of the war, but also a reflection of the 1930s, one of the most
protectionist periods this century. Today, some 96 countries are members
and a further 28 countries apply GATT rules on an informal basis.
GATT's crowning achievement was to bring down industrial tariffs to
10   an average 4.7% since its inception, when rates averaged 40%. In addition
to direct cuts in customs charges in manufactured goods, GATT has also
attempted to reduce the so-called 'non-tariff' barriers to trade. It has also
tried to curb the practice of countries 'dumping' goods below cost in
overseas markets. However, two key trends are emerging. One is the shift
15   in trading patterns towards regional trading blocs such as the EC and the
Caribbean Free Trade Area. The other is the growth in new areas of trade
such as services. Perhaps the most contentious issue in new trading areas
is agriculture. During the 1980s there was increasing recourse to
subsidising farm exports by the EC, which the US countered with
20   measures of its own. As world prices fell, subsidies rose and the struggle
for other markets intensified. This has caused acrimonious discussion in
the current round of GATT negotiations. In practical terms, if the current
round of GATT negotiations fails there is a fear that, in areas such as
agriculture and services, a trade war will ensue and protectionist laws
25   proliferate.
(Source: adapted from P Torday in *The Independent*, 13 November 1990)

(a) What is meant by 'non-tariff' barriers to trade (line 12)?   (2)
(b) Examine the economic reasoning behind GATT's attempt 'to revive free trade
   after World War II' and 'liberalise trade in industrial goods' (lines 2–3).   (6)
(c) Examine the consequences of a trade war and protectionist measures in
   areas such as agriculture and services (lines 23–24).   (6)
(d) Examine the implications of 'the shift in trading patterns towards regional
   trading blocs' (lines 14–15).   (6)
                                                (London, June 1992)

SECTION B: ESSAY QUESTIONS

4   'Prices are the most effective means of allocating resources.' In the light of
   this statement, discuss the case for and against the introduction of meters in
   place of the current system of water rates (flat-rate charges) as a method of
   pricing water.   (AEB, June 1992)

5
(a) Discuss the factors which give rise to a firm being dominant in a market.
   (50%)
(b) Explain how such a firm might be expected to behave if it wishes to preserve
   its market domination.   (50%)
                                                (London, June 1992)

6
(a) Why is it argued that managers of large joint-stock companies do not necessarily pursue policies which maximise the profits of the owners? (20)
(b) What factors might limit the powers of managers in this respect? (5)

(WJEC, June 1990)

7 Explain what you understand by the term 'externalities' and how they might arise in production and consumption. To what extent might 'global warming' be considered an externality and, as such, be solved by economic measures?

(JMB, AS-Level, June 1990)

8 Discuss the main sources of finance available for business finance in
(a) large firms;
(b) small firms.

(O&C, AS Level, June 1990)

9 Are budget deficits necessarily inflationary? (Oxford, June 1991)

10 'There can be no doubt that the transformation of Britain's economic performance in the 1980s ... is above all due to the supply-side policies we have introduced to allow markets of all kinds to work better.' (Nigel Lawson, Chancellor of the Exchequer, July 1988) Discuss.

(London, AS Level, June 1991)

MOCK EXAM SUGGESTED ANSWERS

1 Tutorial note

(a) (i) The total number of petrol stations fell by over a third during the decade. Each of the three big oil companies reduced the outlets they supplied by approximately half, but they actually increased the number they owned as well as supplied.

(ii) Some of the independent outlets previously supplied by the 'majors' probably went out of business over the decade, or they may have been bought up by one of the three big companies, with the remainder being either bought up or supplied by an oil company that would be covered by the label 'others' in the table. If you want to give greater depth to your answer, you could explain the changes in terms of the competitive advantages of larger petrol stations on prime sites which enjoy high daily sales, and the disadvantages suffered by smaller, usually independently owned petrol outlets. However, since only five marks are available, avoid the temptation to overwrite.

(b) (i) You must resist the temptation to stray away from the actual information in the data when answering this part of the question. You can glean from the data that petrol **wholesaling** is ologopolistic, since three firms supply over half the retail outlets. Petrol **retailing** is rather less oligopolistic – in 1988 only a fifth of petrol stations were actually owned by the big three suppliers. However, this figure represents a significant increase on a decade earlier, so there appears to be a trend towards greater concentration of ownership on petrol retailing.

(ii) It is well known that there are seven large oil companies worldwide, nicknamed the 'seven sisters'. These include firms such as Texaco. Indeed in the UK there are 69 recognised petrol suppliers. A greater breakdown of the 'others' category would therefore be useful to ascertain the importance of the other large and medium-sized oil companies and the number of forecourts they own and supply. Petrol sales by supermarket chains such as Sainsbury's and Tesco have also grown rapidly in recent years, but this is not shown by the data. Information about the amount of petrol sold by 'Big-Three owned' petrol stations in comparison to independently owned outlets would also be useful.

(c) (i) The answer is no, if only because fuel costs are only one part of total transport costs. But you can also argue that prices create incentives for people to alter their economic behaviour, and in particular high prices create the incentive to economise. Thus the higher price of petrol probably leads to Italian road transport prices being higher than in the UK, but not necessarily by as much as 31%. Over the years, higher petrol prices have encouraged Italians to drive smaller, more fuel-efficient cars; company cars, which are notorious for encouraging wasteful use of fuel, are less common in Italy; and there may be more miles of motorway which promote more economical use of fuel. Larger, more fuel-efficient lorries may also be more common in Italy, and higher fuel prices may discourage unnecessary journeys. Elasticity of demand is also relevant to your answer: demand would have to be completely inelastic for expenditure on petrol to rise by a full 31%, following a price increase of 31%.

(ii) Assuming that the price of diesel fuel rises by in a similar way to petrol prices, road freight transport operators have seen significant increases in their operating costs. However, we must be careful to distinguish between **nominal** and **real** increases in the price of petroleum. Although nominal prices have risen, petrol's real price is not significantly higher than it was before the first 'oil crisis' in 1973/4. The general price level has risen more or less in line with petrol prices. Thus road freight transport operators have generally raised their own prices to pass on the increased fuel prices they have to pay. As we have already noted, higher fuel prices also encourage operators to search for greater fuel efficiency, e.g. by purchasing larger lorries. And in so far that real fuel prices have risen, they will have contributed to lower profits and possible bankruptcies amongst the less efficient hauliers. Chocolate manufacturers may have experienced similar effects, but probably on a lesser scale because fuel costs are less significant than for transport companies. Chocolate manufacturers may have enjoyed greater scope for switching between alternative energy sources – for manufacturing, if not for transport – though other fuels such as gas and electricity may also have seen similar price changes.

2 Tutorial notes

This question neatly illustrates a feature of many examination papers in economics, and one which is particularly likely to affect data-response questions. Since the questions are set and written several months (and with some examining boards more than a year) before the actual examination, there is always the possibility that real world events will render the question slightly out of date by the time of the examination. With data questions it is also often the case that the most up-to-date data that the Chief Examiner has at hand stops at least a year before he set the paper. Thus this question (answered by candidates in the autumn of 1992 just after the £ had been forced out of the ERM), was set during the winter of 1990/91 and based in part upon data series which end in 1989, nearly a year before the £ had actually entered the ERM! Indeed, at the time the question was set, the £ had only just entered the ERM and lacked a 'track record' within the system. This fact probably influenced the choice of words in part (c), which meant, quite fortuitously as it happens, that the question enabled the candidates to write in a relevant way in their answers about the events leading up to the £'s ignominious withdrawal from the ERM on 'Black Wednesday', 16 September 1992. But the fact that the ERM was so topical at the time the question was answered, did cause some of the candidates who answered the question to waste an opportunity. Instead of explaining that the £ left the ERM precisely because the constraints of membership upon the government's freedom to pursue an independent economic policy meant that the disadvantages of membership were exceeding the benefits, these candidates devoted most of their answers to informing the examiner about something he would have known about anyway: namely the fact that the £ was no longer still in the ERM on the day of the examination. Their answers drifted into irrelevance, with too much space being devoted to lurid and too lengthy 'blow by blow' accounts of the speculative run against the £ in the days and hours before 'Black Wednesday'.

Suggested answer

(a) With a question like this it is vital to avoid copying out the data in full or simply converting numerical data into sentence form. You must 'separate the wood from the trees' by extracting the key changes from the data, and illustrating these with a few chosen statistics. Column 5 tells you that over the ten years covered by the data, the £ depreciated or lost about 21% of its value against the 'basket' of about 16 leading trading currencies from which the 'sterling index' is calculated, though it appreciated marginally at the beginning of the 1980s. Since the Japanese yen, the US dollar and the German DM are all components of this currency 'basket', they all moved broadly in line with the sterling index over the ten-year period, but there were some variations from year to year. The £ depreciated against the yen in every year of the ten-year series, but it appreciated slightly against the DM at the beginning of the period, and rather more significantly against the $ between 1986 and 1988.

(b) (i) Start first with the description, and then move on to the explanation. The description is the easy part: when the £'s exchange rate was high at the beginning of the decade, the current account of the balance of payments was in surplus, but over the decade the current account moved into deficit and the exchange rate fell or depreciated. Start your explanation by noting that the state of the current account can cause changes in the exchange rate. Thus a balance of payments surplus may cause a shortage of the £ on foreign exchange markets, leading to a rising exchange rate. But the current account moving into deficit would have the opposite effect – too much sterling on foreign exchange markets, causing the exchange rate to fall. However, 'reverse causation' is another possibility: namely an overvalued exchange rate (itself probably caused by capital flows into the £) causing the current account to deteriorate.

(ii) We have already mentioned that capital flows into (and out of the £) can be responsible for significant exchange rate changes. During the 1980s, the pound and the US dollar were the main currencies affected by speculative 'hot money' flows or capital movements. For a period at the beginning of the 1980s, sterling was regarded by speculators as a 'petro-currency', made additionally attractive as a haven for 'hot money' by the UK's relative political stability. As speculative funds moved into the pound, the sterling exchange rate was forced up, particularly against the dollar. But around 1984, sentiment changed and the $ replaced sterling as the currency 'flavour of the month'. A massive flow out of the pound and into the dollar caused the £ to fall to $1.30 in 1985 – indeed to as low as $1.00 to the pound for a short period early in 1985. However, this period of 'benign neglect' in the early 1980s (during which the £ for the most part freely floated) gave way during most of the rest of the 1980s to active intervention and 'dirty' floating.

The UK authorities deliberately sought to raise the exchange rate, particularly against EC currencies, by raising interest rates to attract capital flows into the pound. This became known as 'shadowing' the Deutschmark and was responsible for the pound's exchange rate appreciating against the DM in 1988 and 1989, immediately before formal entry into the ERM in 1990.

(c) When the Conservative government finally decided to take the pound into the ERM in 1990, a 'high' parity of around 2.95 DM was chosen in preference to a 'low' parity of, say, 2.40 DM. In Chapter 27 we explained how this was quite deliberate and a part of the government's counter-inflation strategy, since, in theory, a high, fixed exchange rate can reduce inflation by reducing the prices of imported food and consumer goods, and also the prices of imported raw materials and energy which affect manufacturing costs. We then went on to explain how, by causing workers and employers respectively to moderate their wage bargaining and price-setting behaviour, a 'high' exchange rate may act as an 'external source of discipline' to cost-push inflation. But this strategy also imposed severe constraints on the government's freedom to set economic **policy instruments** to achieve **domestic economic goals** or targets. In particular, the need to set interest rates so as to support the pound's high parity within the ERM and to deter capital flows out of the £, meant that monetary policy could not be used to stimulate consumption and investment. In effect, UK interest rates were set by the German Bundesbank while the £ was in the ERM. The 'high' exchange rate at which the £ joined the ERM might not have been the prime cause of the recession which hit the UK economy in 1990, but it certainly made the recession more severe. ERM membership meant that the British authorities were unable to pursue an independent monetary policy to 'reflate' the economy out of the recession which the 'high' pound had exacerbated!

3 Tutorial notes

(a) Non-tariff barriers include quotas and other quantity restrictions, administrative restrictions and 'red tape', and export subsidies.

(b) At the end of the Second World War in 1945, it was generally agreed that the Great Depression had certainly been made worse, even if it had not been caused by, the wave of protectionism that had swept the world in the 1930s. The USA and the UK were the prime movers in the creation of GATT (though the US senate refused to ratify legislation which would have established a much stronger World Trade Organisation) in the belief that the growth of prosperity and the world economy in the postwar era depended on the liberalisation of world trade. Use the principle of comparative advantage to explain how, in theory at least, total world output can increase if countries specialise and trade their surpluses.

(c) This is really the opposite of the previous part of the question: protectionism might mean that the benefits of specialisation in accordance with the principle of comparative advantage will be lost, output and welfare will decline and unemployment grow. On the other hand, countries which might lose out or suffer from a completely liberalised world economy may gain from protectionism, though possibly only in the short term, and at the expense of other countries.

(d) Draw on the section in Chapter 25 on customs unions and free-trade areas. The results will depend on whether regional trading blocks are 'inward' or 'outward' looking, 'trade promoting' or 'trade restricting', and upon whether the really strong and effective trading blocks, such as the EC, end up as 'rich men's clubs', lining their own nests at the expense of the poorer countries in the developing world.

4 Tutorial note

You must avoid the temptation to ignore the statement that provides the lead into the question. Start your answer by explaining briefly the **signalling**, **incentive** and **rationing** functions of prices, and then go on to state that – in the absence of various forms of **market failure** – prices certainly do provide an effective way of allocating resources between competing uses. In competitive markets, prices can succeed in equating supply with demand in an economically efficient way, and ensuring consumer sovereignty and choice.

Another feature of efficient competitive pricing (which promotes **allocative efficiency**), is that the consumer should pay a price which equals the marginal cost of supplying the good or service consumed (P = MC). When water is in plentiful supply and in the absence of drought, the short-run marginal cost of supplying water is very close to zero. Hence the case for paying for water through a flat-rate charge (the water rate) which is independent of the amount of water consumed. In this situation water is a **quasi-free good** which is consumed by households up to the point of satiation where marginal utility is nil. The flat-rate charging system can also be supported on two further grounds: administrative convenience, and because clean drinking and washing water is a form of **merit good**. The argument here is that if water is metered and people are charged according to the amount they consume, there might be a harmful deterioration in public health as the poor react to the new pricing system by washing less and flushing the toilet less often. And under the water-rating system, small (usually better-off) households generally 'cross-subsidise' larger (and usually poorer) families. Some economists justify this on social policy grounds.

What, then, is the case for introducing water metering? Firstly, the abolition of the household rating system when the poll tax was introduced in the late 1980s, means that the basis for administering the water rate no longer exists. A new method of pricing water therefore has to be introduced, though of course it could be a modified flat-rate charge based on property values and the new 'council tax'. The government has instructed the water companies to introduce a new pricing system by the year 2000. More significantly, the greater use of 'water-guzzling' household appliances such as dishwashers and garden sprinklers has shifted the demand curve for water to the right (compared to the 1960s, demand has increased by 70%), while a decline in rainfall (in the South East of England) has moved the supply curve leftwards. With zero prices encouraging people to consume up to the point of satiation, this has led to a shortage of supply and excess demand. Economic theory suggests that the price mechanism should therefore be used to ration demand and to provide a source of finance for increasing long-run supply through reservoir construction or a grid system to transport water from the wetter north west of Britain to the drier south east. Metering is a perfectly acceptable method of pricing for the other 'utilities', gas and electricity, so why not water? Virtually every other country in the world uses a metering system to charge for water, apparently without any significant problems. It can also be argued that any problems affecting the poor which might result from the introduction of metering are better dealt with through the social security system than by requiring some water consumers to cross-subsidise others. The poor could be given special payments or vouchers to help pay their water bills.

But the water companies are **regional monopolies**, and here economic theory suggests that if left to themselves, monopolies will exploit the consumer by charging a price in excess of the marginal cost of supply, in pursuit of monopoly profit (see Chapter 6). Hence, there is a case for strong and effective external regulation of water prices through the **Office of Water Supply (OFWAT)**, whichever system of pricing is eventually introduced. And where household water metering has already been introduced, the flat-rate charge has not been abolished completely. Instead, a two-tier pricing system is used. The metered price reflects the short-run marginal cost of supply, while the flat-rate charge helps to finance long-run supply improvement, including improvements to meet EC environmental regulations.

Suggested answer

1 Explain briefly how prices allocate resources.
2 Explain why economists generally belief that, in the absence of market failure, prices are the most effective way of allocating resources.
3 Outline the case for the flat rate charge, and the case against metering.
4 Then argue the case for metering.
5 Introduce the elements of 'market failure' in the water industry (water as a merit good, and the supply companies as privatised monopolies) and suggest that whichever method of pricing is used, some intervention by the government or by an external regulator such as OFWAT will be necessary to ensure the 'socially optimal' level of consumption.

5 Tutorial note

Having based your answer to the first part of the question on the causes of monopoly, you might organise your answer to the second part around a distinction between 'virtuous' and 'less-virtuous' strategies for maintaining monopoly power and market domination. The 'virtuous' method of market domination is, of course, to produce products or brands which consumers perceive to be the best. New product development, the research and development of more efficient methods of producing existing products, keen pricing, aided and abetted by patenting, market research and advertising and marketing can all be regarded as part of a 'virtuous' market domination strategy. At the other extreme, a 'less-virtuous' strategy might centre on the 'unfair' and even criminal use of barriers to market entry, trading-restrictive practices and the corrupt obtaining of favours from other businesses or government officials. In real life of course, it may sometimes be difficult to draw the line between legitimate and illegitimate business strategies to promote market domination. For example, when a dominant firm sharply reduces prices in the face of increased competition from a new market entrant, does this represent simply the (virtuous) cut and thrust of the market place, or is it something more sinister, such as the temporary reduction of price below cost to see the newcomer off, to be followed by a hike to the old price level once the firm's dominant position has been restored?

Suggested answer

1 Explain briefly that 'dominant in a market' means monopoly or a high degree of monopoly power.
2 List and briefly describe each of the causes of monopoly power, e.g. 'natural' monopoly; legal monopoly; economies of scale, etc.
3 Explain that if market domination has resulted from the firm being more innovative, efficient and competitive than its rivals, with its eventual monopoly position being the result of 'successful competition', it may well try to maintain its position by 'more of the same', i.e. continued R&D, investment, market research and marketing, and keen pricing.
4 However, firms often use anti-competitive methods to maintain market domination, e.g. artificial barriers to market entry and unfair trading restrictive practices. Give examples, and explain that, although these are often illegal, firms may break the law and try to get away with it.
5 Another strategy is to take over or merge with rival firms, though again the law may make this difficult.

6 Tutorial note

In large public limited joint stock companies (PLCs) such as BP and Marks and

Spencer, the entrepreneurial function is split between the shareholders who own the company and the managers they employ to actually run the business. Economic theory conventionally assumes that economic agents always try to act in their own self-interest, but it does not necessarily follow that the self-interest of salaried managers coincides with the interests of shareholders. Partly for this reason, many economists believe that it is unrealistic to model large business corporations as having the sole aim of maximising shareholders' profits. 'Alternative theories of the firm' have therefore been put forward which claim to be more realistic than the traditional profit-maximising theory. These alternative theories of the firm are of two types: **satisficing theories** (also known as **organisational** or **behavioural theories**) and **managerial theories**. Satisficing theories stem from the premise that a large firm is a complicated social organisation, containing many different groupings or vested interests such as different functional departments within the business (marketing, research and development, personnel, etc.) as well as trade unions and shareholders. These different groups may very well have different aims and aspirations which are often mutually incompatible. In order to allow the organisation to function as efficiently as possible, decision-makers within the business therefore try to attain outcomes which are 'satisfactory' for all the groups which make up the 'coalition of the firm': hence the firm as a **profit satisficer** rather than a **profit maximiser**.

The **managerial theories** of the firm are similar to the conventional profit-maximising theory in that they assume that the firm has a maximising objective; their difference lies in the objective which it is assumed that the firm tries to maximise. Three main managerial theories have been put forward: Baumol's theory of **sales maximisation**; Williamson's theory of **managerial utility maximisation**; and Marris's theory of **growth maximisation**. Baumol argues that a manager-controlled firm has sales maximisation as its principal objective, because the salaries and fringe benefits of top managers are related to sales revenue rather than to profits. However, a number of later studies have come to the opposite conclusion and the evidence is generally inconclusive. Williamson's theory is broadly similar to Baumol's and argues that a company's executives seek to maximise other objectives of managerial utility, as well as sales revenue-related perks. In Williamson's theory, increased sales revenue allows managers to spend more on staff levels to enhance managerial status, seniority and promotion prospects. Managers can also spend on 'discretionary' projects which are marginal to the normal operations of the firm, but which add to managerial satisfaction or utility.

Whereas both Baumol and Williamson have suggested a split between shareholders' and managerial objectives, Marris argued that both groups share a common interest in growth maximisation. From the managers' point of view, a firm's growth increases power and status, while shareholders have a vested interest in successful growth because it increases the capital value of their wealth, as distinct from the dividend income generated by profits. Central to Marris's analysis is the **retention ratio**, i.e. company profits 'ploughed back' into the company as a ratio of profits distributed as dividends. If the retention ratio is low, when the company board distributes most of the profits, shareholders' incomes will be high and a resulting high share price may deter takeover bids. But if the managers retain profits in order to maximise company growth, the share price might be low, relative to the true worth of the company's assets, thereby increasing the possibility of an unwelcome takeover bid. Marris therefore concluded that managers therefore aim to maximise growth, subject to generating just sufficient profits to satisfy shareholders, so as to minimise the risk of shareholders selling out to a takeover 'raider' attracted by a low share price.

Following Marris, you should argue that it is unrealistic to assume that managers can maximise their self-interest at the complete expense of shareholders' profits. These days also, financial institutions such as pension funds and insurance companies are the major shareholders in large PLCs, and their professional fund managers keep an active watch for managerial inefficiencies in the companies in which they hold large blocks of shares. You might conclude your answer by suggesting that a firm can possibly reconcile the aims of its shareholders with those of its salaried managers by giving the managers (and indeed the whole of its workforce) a vested interest in the company's profitability. Hence the case for profit-related pay and remuneration, and for share option schemes which allow managers to buy blocks of shares at a greatly reduced price as the reward for loyalty and successful management.

Suggested answer

1   Explain the split in the entrepreneurial function in large PLCs between shareholders and managers.
2   Outline how the self-interest of managers may conflict with the shareholders' aim of profit maximisation.
3   But if shareholders' profits are depressed too far, managers may be dismissed or the firm may become vulnerable to takeover activity. 'Active' shareholders, such as pension fund managers, may also limit the ability of managers to act against the shareholders' interests.
4   Managers may therefore follow a policy of pursuing their own self-interest, subject to making sufficient or 'satisfactory' profits to keep the shareholders happy.
5   Conclude by suggesting that profit-related pay and share option schemes for managers may limit the powers of managers by reconciling the interests of shareholders and managers.

7 Tutorial note

The first part of the question is straightforward and has been explained, with examples, in Chapter 8. Start the second part by arguing that **global warming** can have a natural explanation, relating to periodic changes in the world's climate that take place over thousands of years. If global warming occurs naturally, then it should not be regarded as an externality, i.e. a spin-off or side-effect of mankind's activities discharged and consumed outside the market. However, in so far that current evidence links global warming to the greenhouse effect, caused by mankind's emissions of carbon gases and other pollutants, then the phenomenon is indeed an externality. Explain that most people regard 'global warming' as a **negative externality**, fearing that much of the world's population will eventually suffer from rising sea levels and the spread of desert climates. But indicate that for some peoples and countries, the benefits of global warming may exceed the costs, for example in regions where warmer and longer summers will allow new crops to be grown.

Like any negative externality, global warming might in principle be reduced or eliminated by economic measures such as pollution taxes, regulation and devices such as the sale of 'licences to pollute'. But because global warming is literally an externality dumped on the whole world community by the action of individual economic agents, action on a world scale is needed to slow the process down. Effective action by a single country – even as large as the USA – or by a handful of countries to reduce the pollutants that they emit, will be insufficient to deal with the problem because pollution is likely to grow as Third World nations develop their economies. Arguably, the action on a world scale that will be necessary to reduce global warming will also significantly reduce economic growth and living standards. This will be unacceptable to many governments, particularly in developing countries. They may argue that existing global warming is a 'First World problem' in that it has been caused by pollutants overwhelmingly emitted by already industrialised countries, but that the First World countries are demanding a 'Third World solution', i.e. a slowing down of the growth process necessary to transform the developing countries into modern competitive economies. As the 1992 Rio de Janiero Conference on environmental issues clearly shows, it is almost impossible to get countries to agree to take concrete action which, arguably, is in their long-term interest, if the results of such action are likely to be against their short-term interest. And even if action could be agreed to impose carbon taxes or firmly regulate pollution, there would then be all sorts of problems in effectively enforcing and policing the action on a world scale.

Suggested answer

1   Precisely define an externality as a 'good' or 'bad' generated and received 'outside the market'.
2   Distinguish between 'pure production', 'pure consumption' and 'mixed' externalities, giving examples (see the table in Chapter 8).
3   Briefly indicate why externalities are a 'market failure', i.e. there is no incentive for the 'correct' quantity of an externality to be produced and consumed, where MSB = MSC.
4   If global warming is a natural phenomenon, i.e. not caused by man, then it is not an externality.
5   But if it results from pollution emissions, global warming is a negative externality, perhaps on a cataclysmic scale.
6   However, for some people global warming may produce more external benefits than costs. Give examples.
7   Explain that, in principle, pollution taxes, regulation, etc. might reduce global warming, but there seem to be overwhelming obstacles preventing the effective introduction of such measures on a world scale.

8 Tutorial note

As we have explained in Chapter 11, **self-finance** or **internal finance** is the main source for funding of investment and growth for firms of all sizes and legal status, provided only that the firms are profitable. Likewise, **bank loans** of various types, including overdrafts, are an important source of short- and medium-term finance for firms of all sizes. Large firms may, however, find it easier to borrow from banks on favourable terms, due to factors such as their track records, bargaining power and collateral. Having drawn attention to how both large and small firms have many similar sources of finance, you should then describe the differences. The main points to make are that large firms – which are usually PLCs – generally have access to the **capital market**, whereas small firms may benefit from sources of finance made available both by government agencies and by specialist **venture capital** schemes, whose function is to inject capital in small businesses, usually in return for an ownership stake.

Suggested answer

1   Briefly explain what you understand by 'large' and 'small' firms.
2   Explain how some of the most significant sources of finance are available to firms of all sizes.
3   But generally only large firms have access to the capital market.
4   Describe the various specialist sources of funding for small firms.

9 Tutorial note

There are two possible 'transmission mechanisms' through which a budget deficit can be inflationary. Firstly, in Keynesian analysis the deficit represents an injection of demand into the economy which increases nominal national income via the Keynesian multiplier process. If excess demand and an inflationary gap are created through this process, the price level will therefore be pulled up in a 'demand-pull' inflation. Secondly, monetarists draw attention to the monetary effects resulting from the financing of the budget deficit. They argue that new currency issue or government borrowing from the banking system increase the money supply and thence cause inflation, via the quantity theory of money (see Chapters 17 and 22).

However, Keynesians believe that the deficit will only be inflationary if the economy is already fully employed with little or no spare capacity. By contrast, in conditions of less-than-full employment and spare capacity, deliberate deficit financing can serve to close a deflationary gap without necessarily causing inflation. And if the deficit is financed by selling gilts or National Savings securities to the general public rather than by borrowing from the banking system, the deficit will not cause the money supply to expand. Indeed, since 1990 the Conservative government in the UK has accepted the Keynesian argument that the public sector finances tend to move automatically into deficit during a recession, as tax revenue falls and expenditure on unemployment pay increases. Far from causing inflation, a recessionary budget deficit acts as an automatic or built-in stabiliser, preventing an unnecessary deepening of the recession. But a decade earlier, Mrs Thatcher's government had rejected this Keynesian argument. By cutting public spending and borrowing, when it should have allowed a 'counter-cyclical' increase in the budget deficit, the Conservative government had, through its own policy, deepened the earlier recession at the beginning of the 1980s.

Suggested answer

1 Briefly explain the meaning of a budget deficit.
2 Explain how, in conditions of full employment, a budget deficit can create excess demand and cause 'demand-pull' inflation.
3 Go on to explain the linkages between the deficit, the PSBR, the money supply and inflation.
4 Conclude by describing how Keynesians and 'moderate' monetarists accept that a budget deficit is justified in a recession to stabilise the business cycle and prevent an unnecessarily deep recession.

10 Tutorial note

By the time Nigel Lawson expressed the view quoted in the question in July 1988, the UK economy had benefited from seven years of continuous economic growth, starting from the depths of a severe recession which had lasted from 1979 to 1981. While accepting that growth was to be expected during the 'upswing' of the business cycle, the Conservative government went further and claimed that its 'supply-side' policies were responsible for significantly improving the economy's long-term growth trend. The Government claimed that the abandonment of Keynesian demand management and interventionism had paved the way for a supply-side-led 'British economic miracle'. At the time, the UK had moved close to the top of an EC 'league table', measured in terms of the growth in productivity and employment, the fewest days lost in strikes, etc.

But by 1991, the picture was much less rosy. 1990 saw the collapse of the 'Lawson boom' and the UK economy entered the longest (if not the deepest) recession since the 1930s. Initially, the Conservative government believed that the recession would be a mere blip, interrupting only temporarily the continuation of growth and economic success brought about by its supply-side 'revolution'. However, with the recession fast developing into a more severe 'slump' or 'depression', Keynesian economists have argued that it was the boom years of the mid- and late-1980s that constituted the true 'blip', temporarily disrupting the ongoing and depressing story of low growth, deindustrialisation and declining competitiveness that have afflicted the UK economy since at least the 1970s. The Keynesians further argue that the 1980s boom, far from being the result of successful supply-side policies, was largely caused by a massive and irrespon-sible boost to demand, brought about by tax cuts and the removal of controls on bank lending – policies introduced by the Chancellor of the Exchequer Nigel Lawson himself.

Suggested answer

1 Briefly describe the state of the UK economy in the late 1980s.
2 Explain how, in principle, supply-side policies could have brought about the economic success experienced at the time.
3 Discuss whether the evidence supports the view that supply-side policies were responsible for this success.
4 Introduce the possibility that demand expansion rather than supply-side policies were responsible for the 1980s boom.
5 Draw an overall conclusion and indicate that, whatever the truth, the economic success did not continue into the early 1990s.

INDEX

Note: This index is not comprehensive. Many passing references have been omitted. It is intended only as a guide to the book.